MW01620867

Studies in the History of Art
Published by the National Gallery of Art, Washington

This series includes: Studies in the History of Art, collected papers on objects in the Gallery's collections and other art-historical studies (formerly Report and Studies in the History of Art); Monograph Series I, a catalogue of stained glass in the United States; Monograph Series II, on conservation topics; and Symposium Papers (formerly Symposium Series), the proceedings of symposia sponsored by the Center for Advanced Study in the Visual Arts at the National Gallery of Art.

[1] *Report and Studies in the History of Art*, 1967
[2] *Report and Studies in the History of Art*, 1968
[3] *Report and Studies in the History of Art*, 1969
[In 1970 the National Gallery of Art's annual report became a separate publication.]
[4] *Studies in the History of Art*, 1972
[5] *Studies in the History of Art*, 1973
[The first five volumes are unnumbered.]
6 *Studies in the History of Art*, 1974
7 *Studies in the History of Art*, 1975
8 *Studies in the History of Art*, 1978
9 *Studies in the History of Art*, 1980
10 *Macedonia and Greece in Late Classical and Early Hellenistic Times*, edited by Beryl Barr-Sharrar and Eugene N. Borza. Symposium Series I, 1982
11 *Figures of Thought: El Greco as Interpreter of History, Tradition, and Ideas*, edited by Jonathan Brown, 1982
12 *Studies in the History of Art*, 1982
13 *El Greco: Italy and Spain*, edited by Jonathan Brown and José Manuel Pita Andrade. Symposium Series II, 1984
14 *Claude Lorrain, 1600–1682: A Symposium*, edited by Pamela Askew. Symposium Series III, 1984
15 *Stained Glass before 1700 in American Collections: New England and New York (Corpus Vitrearum Checklist I)*, compiled by Madeline H. Caviness et al. Monograph Series I, 1985
16 *Pictorial Narrative in Antiquity and the Middle Ages*, edited by Herbert L. Kessler and Marianna Shreve Simpson. Symposium Series IV, 1985
17 *Raphael before Rome*, edited by James Beck. Symposium Series V, 1986
18 *Studies in the History of Art*, 1985
19 *James McNeill Whistler: A Reexamination*, edited by Ruth E. Fine. Symposium Papers VI, 1987
20 *Retaining the Original: Multiple Originals, Copies, and Reproductions*. Symposium Papers VII, 1989
21 *Italian Medals*, edited by J. Graham Pollard. Symposium Papers VIII, 1987
22 *Italian Plaquettes*, edited by Alison Luchs. Symposium Papers IX, 1989
23 *Stained Glass before 1700 in American Collections: Mid-Atlantic and Southeastern Seaboard States (Corpus Vitrearum Checklist II)*, compiled by Madeline H. Caviness et al. Monograph Series I, 1987
24 *Studies in the History of Art*, 1990
25 *The Fashioning and Functioning of the British Country House*, edited by Gervase Jackson-Stops et al. Symposium Papers X, 1989
26 *Winslow Homer*, edited by Nicolai Cikovsky, Jr. Symposium Papers XI, 1990
27 *Cultural Differentiation and Cultural Identity in the Visual Arts*, edited by Susan J. Barnes and Walter S. Melion. Symposium Papers XII, 1989
28 *Stained Glass before 1700 in American Collections: Midwestern and Western States (Corpus Vitrearum Checklist III)*, compiled by Madeline H. Caviness et al. Monograph Series I, 1989
29 *Nationalism in the Visual Arts*, edited by Richard A. Etlin. Symposium Papers XIII, 1991
30 *The Mall in Washington, 1791–1991*, edited by Richard Longstreth. Symposium Papers XIV, 1991
31 *Urban Form and Meaning in South Asia: The Shaping of Cities from Prehistoric to Precolonial Times*, edited by Howard Spodek and Doris Meth Srinivasan. Symposium Papers XV, 1993
32 *New Perspectives in Early Greek Art*, edited by Diana Buitron-Oliver. Symposium Papers XVI, 1991
33 *Michelangelo Drawings*, edited by Craig Hugh Smyth. Symposium Papers XVII, 1992
34 *Art and Power in Seventeenth-Century Sweden*, edited by Michael Conforti and Michael Metcalf. Symposium Papers XVIII (withdrawn)
35 *The Architectural Historian in America*, edited by Elisabeth Blair MacDougall. Symposium Papers XIX, 1990
36 *The Pastoral Landscape*, edited by John Dixon Hunt. Symposium Papers XX, 1992
37 *American Art around 1900*, edited by Doreen Bolger and Nicolai Cikovsky, Jr. Symposium Papers XXI, 1990
38 *The Artist's Workshop*, edited by Peter M. Lukehart. Symposium Papers XXII, 1993
39 *Stained Glass before 1700 in American Collections: Silver-Stained Roundels and Unipartite Panels (Corpus Vitrearum Checklist IV)*, compiled by Timothy B. Husband. Monograph Series I, 1991
40 The Feast of the Gods: *Conservation, Examination, and Interpretation*, by David Bull and Joyce Plesters. Monograph Series II, 1990
41 *Conservation Research*. Monograph Series II, 1993
42 *Conservation Research: Studies of Fifteenth- to Nineteenth-Century Tapestry*, edited by Lotus Stack. Monograph Series II, 1993
43 Eius Virtutis Studiosi: *Classical and Postclassical Studies in Memory of Frank Edward Brown*, edited by Russell T. Scott and Ann Reynolds Scott. Symposium Papers XXIII, 1993
44 *Intellectual Life at the Court of Frederick II Hohenstaufen*, edited by William Tronzo, Symposium Papers XXIV, 1994
45 *Titian 500*, edited by Joseph Manca. Symposium Papers XXV, 1994
46 *Van Dyck 350*, edited by Susan J. Barnes and Arthur K. Wheelock, Jr. Symposium Papers XXVI*
47 *The Formation of National Collections of Art and Archaeology*, edited by Gwendolyn Wright. Symposium Papers XXVII*
48 *Monarca della Pittura: Piero and His Legacy*, edited by Marilyn Aronberg Lavin. Symposium Papers XXVIII*
49 *Architectural Sculpture in Fifth-Century Greece*, edited by Diana Buitron-Oliver. Symposium Papers XXIX*

*Forthcoming

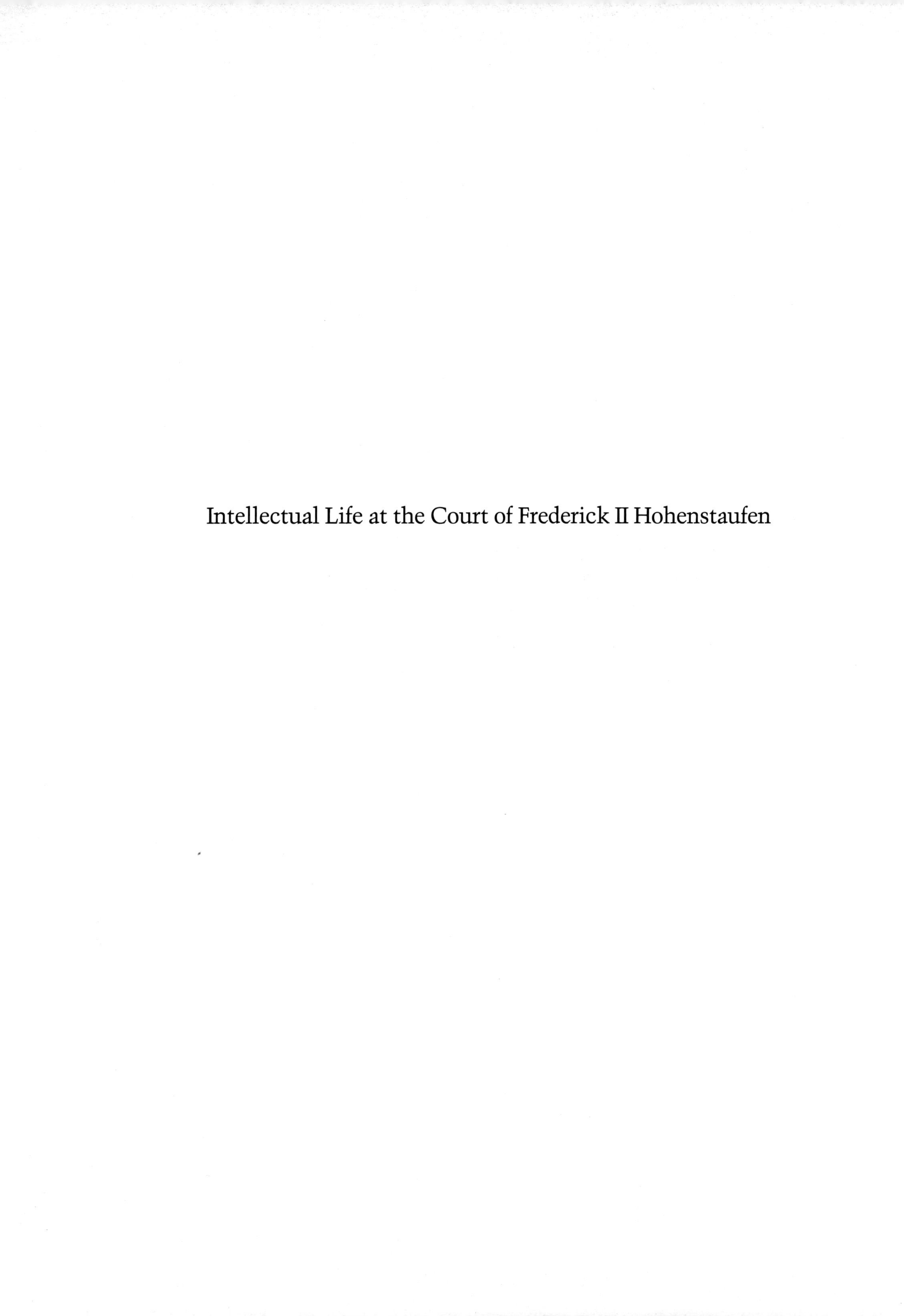

Intellectual Life at the Court of Frederick II Hohenstaufen

STUDIES IN THE HISTORY OF ART · 44 ·

Center for Advanced Study in the Visual Arts
Symposium Papers XXIV

Intellectual Life at the Court of Frederick II Hohenstaufen

Edited by William Tronzo

National Gallery of Art, Washington
Distributed by the University Press of New England
Hanover and London

This publication was produced by the Editors Office, National Gallery of Art, Washington
Editor-in-Chief, Frances P. Smyth

The type is Trump Medieval, set by BG Composition, Baltimore, Maryland

The text paper is 80 pound LOE Dull

Printed by Schneidereith & Sons, Baltimore, Maryland

Distributed by the University Press of New England, 23 South Main Street, Hanover, New Hampshire 03755

Abstracted by RILA (International Repertory of the Literature of Art), Williamstown, Massachusetts 01267

Proceedings of the symposium "Intellectual Life at the Court of Frederick II Hohenstaufen," sponsored by the Center for Advanced Study in the Visual Arts, Washington, D.C., 18–20 January 1990

ISSN 0091-7338
ISBN 089468-200-8

Contents

HENRY A. MILLON
Dean, Center for Advanced Study in the Visual Arts

Preface

The Center for Advanced Study in the Visual Arts was founded in 1979 as part of the National Gallery of Art to promote study of the history, theory, and criticism of art, architecture, and urbanism through the formation of a community of scholars. The activities of the Center include a fellowship program, meetings, research, and publication.

The symposium, "Intellectual Life at the Court of Frederick II Hohenstaufen," held in Washington in January 1990, was the first major gathering on an aspect of medieval culture held under the auspices of the Center. The program included eighteen papers on scientific, historical, and art-historical themes during the reign of Frederick II and encompassing developments in both the northern and southern realms of the Hohenstaufen empire. It was planned in consultation with Alberto A. Weissmüller, who also greatly assisted the Center for Advanced Study in the symposium preparations.

The Center is grateful to the Banca Commerciale Italiana, the Samuel H. Kress Foundation, and Alitalia for making the symposium possible. The combination of support from diverse and generous sources has been essential to the program of scholarly meetings at the Center over the years. The initial and substantive contribution from the Banca Commerciale was particularly important for the Frederick II program and the resulting proceedings.

William Tronzo generously agreed to edit the papers for publication and to write the introduction. The collected papers unfortunately do not include those presented by Hermann Fillitz, Alessandro Tomei, and Rainer Kahsnitz; these speakers were unable to prepare their contributions for publication. It is regrettable that Wolfgang Krönig died while this volume was in production and that he was unable to see it completed.

This publication is the twenty-fourth in the symposium series, Studies in the History of Art, which is intended to document such gatherings and to stimulate further research. Future volumes will chronicle additional symposia held under the sponsorship of the Center for Advanced Study and other departments of the National Gallery of Art. A listing of published and forthcoming titles may be found on the opening leaf of the volume.

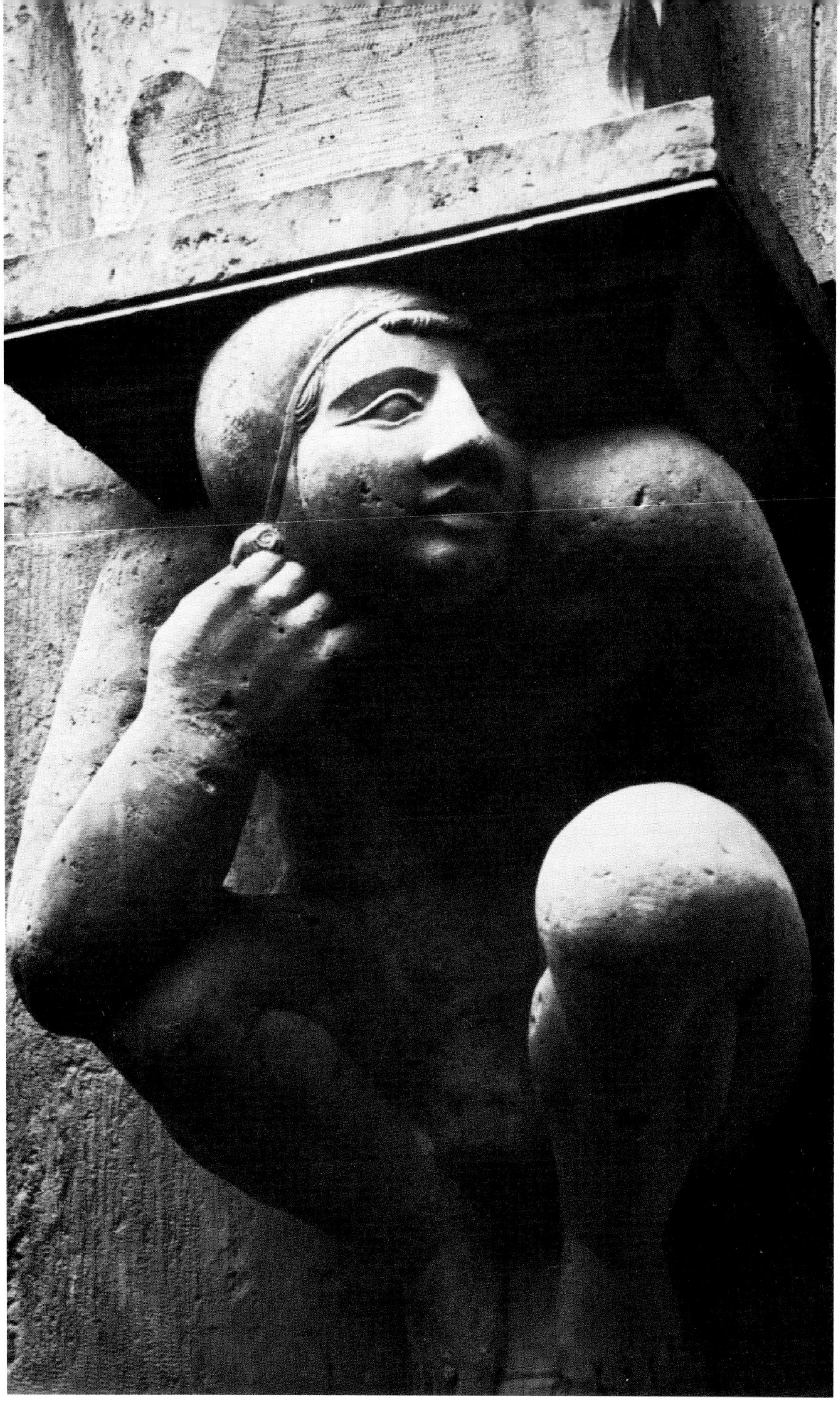

WILLIAM TRONZO
Duke University

Introduction

By any account, Frederick II (1194–1250) was a remarkable man, one of the most energetic rulers the Middle Ages produced: statesman and crusader, founder of the University of Naples and author of a treatise on hunting, *De arte venandi cum avibus*, patron of poetry, architecture, and art. He was born into the combined worlds of German emperor and Sicilian king—his father was Emperor Henry VI from the house of Hohenstaufen, and his mother, Constance, the daughter of Roger II, the first Norman king of Sicily—and to a large extent his life was played out on the stages of North and South. These were difficult territories and contentious times, however, and even though he was crowned at Aachen in 1215 with the support of the German nobles, and in Rome in 1220 by Pope Honorius III, Frederick spent most of his life attempting to consolidate his position. He found strong opposition both without and within, from the treachery of blood relations and close friends to the enmity of the popes, by whom he was excommunicated in 1227 and again in 1239. Nonetheless, he numbered among his successes a treaty with Sultan al-Malik al-Kamil of Egypt for the return of Jerusalem (1229), the promulgation of the *Liber Augustalis* (Constitutions of Melfi, 1231), and numerous victorious military campaigns. He also managed to gather around him a group of philosophers, scientists, poets, and artists who were among the most active of their time.

These papers[1] take the intellectual life of Frederick's reign as their point of departure, a point rather broadly defined to embrace not only philosophy, science, and the *Ars dictaminis* (Morpurgo; Oldoni, Orofino, Thiery; Herde), but also manuscript production (Corrie), architecture and sculpture (Ghisalberti, Radke, Meredith, Krönig; Pace, Kaufmann, Sauerländer), and even social attitudes and economic affairs (Abulafia; Powell). Thus what tends to emerge is not so much the nature of the debate that has taken place in the scholarly literature over specific issues (although some of these questions at times become very clear), but a picture of the culture as a whole. As such this study follows earlier scholars, among them Hans Niese and Charles Homer Haskins, who also attempted to formulate a historical view of the intellectual life of Frederick's court on a large scale.[2]

In dealing with any aspect of the emperor or his reign, one must contend with mythology and the strength of Frederick's reputation, from the *Kyffhäusersage* to the fresh roses today's visitor to the Cathedral of Palermo still often finds on the emperor's great porphyry tomb (which was taken by Frederick from the Cathedral of Cefalù, where it was intended to have been used by his grandfather, Roger II). Surprisingly enough, only two of the contributors make reference to this problem outright (Herde; Sauerländer), although it forms an undercurrent in most of the other papers in the following sense. What stands behind the modern view of Frederick is the work of historians of the nineteenth and early twentieth centuries—Jakob Burckhardt, Eduard Winkelmann, Karl Hampe, and above all, Ernst Kantorowicz—at whose hands the emperor has suffered a kind of crisis of overevaluation. He has often been spoken of as if he were larger than his role. Burckhardt characterized him as the first Renaissance tyrant ("der erste moderne Mensch auf dem Throne"), and Kantorowicz as a leader of heroic proportions, a caesar, a messiah-emperor, and a visionary beyond almost all imagining.[3] To a great extent these views privileged Frederick's achievements over those of his contemporaries and his immediate (Norman) predecessors. Implicitly or explicitly, much of recent scholarship has set out to adjust this perception of his role.

In the context of this volume, the process of reassessment has taken place on several fronts. In discussing the *Ars dictaminis,* for instance, Peter Herde sets out not only to describe the conditions of epistolary production at the time of Frederick's court, but also to call into question the value of many of the surviving letters as historical documents. These letters served as the basis of the work of Kantorowicz (among others) on Frederick II, but one would now have to say that Kantorowicz' use of them was ideological. As Herde points out, in many cases it is not clear whether these letters were official documents that were actually sent or simply private exercises for perfecting one's style and bearing no reflection whatsoever of a public reality. Similarly, Willibald Sauerländer takes a hard look at the works of art in both Germany and Italy from the first half of the thirteenth century that have been associated with the emperor and finds them wanting on two scores. In Germany, the direct involvement of Frederick II is ascertainable without the shadow of a doubt in only one case, namely, the figure of the emperor on the shrine of Charlemagne in Aachen; as for the others, including the famous Bamberg and Magdeburg Riders, Sauerländer is skeptical or at least advises extreme caution. The salient feature of thirteenth-century German art, stylistically speaking, is its diversity, and this characteristic, as Sauerländer indicates, does not speak very strongly for the controlling voice of a single individual. In Italy, imperial patronage is better known, but even here monuments like the Capua bridgehead and Castel del Monte can no longer be thought of as extraordinary singularities in isolation. Sauerländer sketches a context and tradition for both. He finds what one might call his "contractionist" approach to Frederick's patronage supported by Valentino Pace, who wants to strip of Frederick's name many monuments in southern Italy that had only the merest circumstances to connect them to the emperor. Pace also argues for the strength of local traditions and for the availability of local antique sources in the making of Frederician sculpture.

Complementary, too, are the contributions of David Abulafia and James Powell. Abulafia takes as his subject Frederick's relations with Muslims and Jews, and argues that they were not as atypical of those of his contemporaries as has often been assumed. Frederick was guided more by an understanding of practical realities, as witness the settlement of Muslims at Lucera, where, in Abulafia's view, Frederick probably expected Islam to wither and die, and the settlement of Jews near Palermo for purely economic reasons. Frederick's aim was never to revive the multicultural court of his grandfather, Roger II. Powell also questions a widely held view of Frederick as an economic innovator. The picture that he presents is one of a ruler who was as concerned with rights and privileges, and as capable of exploiting the situation to *his* advantage (and not that of his subjects), as any medieval emperor or king.

It is noteworthy that, from a time and place from which so many names are known, only one individual is the subject of a paper: Michael Scot, renowned as Frederick's astrologer and translator, and celebrated as well as an occupant of Dante's *Inferno.* Piero Morpurgo investigates Michael's sources, particularly those of the *Liber Introductorius,* and argues that they are more varied than traditionally seen, with a stronger debt to Augustine and Avicenna. The text of the *Liber* has a direct bearing on Frederick II because it, as well as the *Liber Particularis,* was written in response to questions from the emperor; thus both can be used, as Morpurgo suggests, to reconstruct the emperor's thinking as well as that of the author.

Nor is Frederick's *De arte venandi cum avibus* the subject of an individual presentation, although questions of naturalism and manuscript illustration are treated by Giulia Orofino. Her survey makes concrete the degree to which the pictorial imagination was driven by an innovative force that expressed itself in a new naturalism and a new interest in the realities of daily life. Frederick's desire that his court become a "fonte di scienze e seminario di dottrine" also made itself concrete in the foundation of the University of Naples, which is examined by Massimo Oldoni. He finds the roots of the institution in the Cassinese culture of southern Italy, mediated and reinforced by the School of Salerno. Antonio Thiery, on the other hand, attempts to place Frederick's scientific interests in the broader framework, ranging from the Cappella Palatina in Palermo to the Foligno of Francis of Assisi.

Problems of political iconography are considered by Jill Meredith in her paper on the Capua bridgehead. She analyzes the sources and meaning of the sculptural program of the bridgehead, and, in contrast to Sauerländer, who considers it a "would-be Roman monument executed with the craftsmanship of the Dark Ages," sees it as "the culmination of a tradition in medieval Italy" in its use of *spolia*, its antique style, and its classicizing message. Virginia Roehrig Kaufmann also grapples with a serious iconographic problem in the identity of the Magdeburg Rider. This sculpture, identified as Frederick II by some, is here argued to represent Otto I and to have been set up in Magdeburg as a reaffirmation of the granting of privileges by the emperor to the original archbishop. Kaufmann delineates a context for this enigmatic work in the interests and patronage of Frederick in the South. Wolfgang Krönig considers the best-known castle associated with Frederick II, Castel del Monte, with a view to the symbolism of the building. Krönig characterizes the structure as an "Idealbau," for which he sees a tradition that reaches back to the architecture of the Roman Empire and forward to the Renaissance in Italy, and that also includes the early medieval Islamic world.

There are inevitably questions in any area of medieval research for which the evidence is still insufficient to provide answers, although these too may be of great interest. One concerns the production of manuscripts in thirteenth-century Italy, which Rebecca Corrie discusses within the framework of the Conradin Bible. The problem here is not only one of chronology; given the distinctive use of Byzantine and French sources by a number of the illuminators of the Bible and related works, it is also one of models (model books?) and patronage, which raises in a most pointed way the issue of the nature of scriptoria as centers of manuscript production at this time. With regard to the question of models, Corrie adduces the art of Norman Sicily, and particularly Monreale, as potentially holding the key. The study of Frederick's building activities, and especially his palaces, is also hampered by a lack of sources, both visual and verbal, as Gary Radke points out. The few structures or parts of structures that survive, however, demand some explanation in terms of a larger context. Here again the Norman tradition of twelfth-century Sicily may provide a key—after all, Frederick himself grew up in the Norman palace in Palermo. And finally there is the question of connections between North and South with regard to artistic ideas and styles (a question also taken up by Sauerländer and Pace), which is treated by Carla Ghisalberti within the frame of reference of Cistercian architecture and sculpture. Ghisalberti focuses on a few selected examples, such as Santa Maria di Sambucina and Santa Maria di Ripalta, to trace the nature of relationships that in certain cases, the author observes, were extraordinarily close.

Bearing in mind the diversity of subjects and approaches, and the many relevant areas left unexplored, one may still come away from the present volume with two predominant impressions. On the one hand, there is the sense that the evidence—from the letters and other documents to the treatises and works of art—that must serve as the building blocks of our historical picture of the emperor and his reign has only now come to receive the kind of scrutiny it deserves—and in many cases in the most preliminary way, with regard to date, place of origin, original form and purpose. It is this process that has served and continues to serve to refine our views. But one cannot help feeling that larger forces are at work in our reassessment of Frederick and the quality of the intellectual life of his time, forces relating to our changing ideas about the role of the individual in history and the very nature of the creative process itself, with which we can begin to contend only from a different and much broader perspective.

NOTES

1. This volume publishes the papers of a symposium held at the National Gallery of Art in January 1990 on the theme of "Intellectual Life at the Court of Frederick II Hohenstaufen." The symposium followed hard on the heels of the first of a three-part series of week-long *Convegni* sponsored by the Italian government at Erice, Sicily, on aspects of the emperor and his reign, not to mention a volume of collected studies on Frederick II published by the Centro di Studi sulla Civiltà del Tardo Medioevo, San Miniato (Pisa), and a new biography of the emperor by one of the symposium participants, David Abulafia. It is also the case that the eight hundredth anniversary of Frederick's birth occurs in 1994, with which this volume coincides.

The Sicilian conference, the "International Seminar on Frederick II," was held at the Ettore Majorana Centre for Scientific Culture in Erice beginning in 1989 and was divided into three parts: (1) "Theory and Practice of Government"; (2) "Culture and Knowledge at the Time of Frederick II"; (3) "Frederick II and the Italian Cities." The first volume of the *Collana di studi e ricerche* of the Centro di Studi sulla Civiltà del Tardo Medioevo, San Miniato, was devoted to *Politica e cultura nell'Italia di Federico II*, ed. Sergio Gensini (Pisa, 1986). David Abulafia's biography, *Frederick II: A Medieval Emperor*, was first published in London in 1988. See also W. Stürner, *Friedrich II.*, vol. 1 (Darmstadt, 1992).

2. Hans Niese, "Zur Geschichte des geistigen Lebens am Hofe Kaiser Friedrichs II.," *Historische Zeitschrift* 108 (1912), 473–540; Charles Homer Haskins, *Studies in the History of Medieval Science* (Cambridge, Mass., 1924).

3. Jakob Burckhardt, *Die Cultur der Renaissance in Italien, ein Versuch* (Basel, 1860), 3 (trans. into English by Samuel G. C. Middlemore and published in many editions beginning in 1878); Ernst H. Kantorowicz, *Kaiser Friedrich der Zweite* (Berlin, 1928) (trans. Emily O. Lorimer, London, 1931; repr. 1957). Kantorowicz' work, essentially an unannotated narrative, was followed four years later by his volume on the sources. With regard to Kantorowicz' biography, see also *Stupor mundi: Zur Geschichte Friedrichs II. von Hohenstaufen*, ed. Gunther Wolf (Darmstadt, 1966) and David Abulafia, "Kantorowicz and Frederick II," *History* 62 (1977), 193–210.

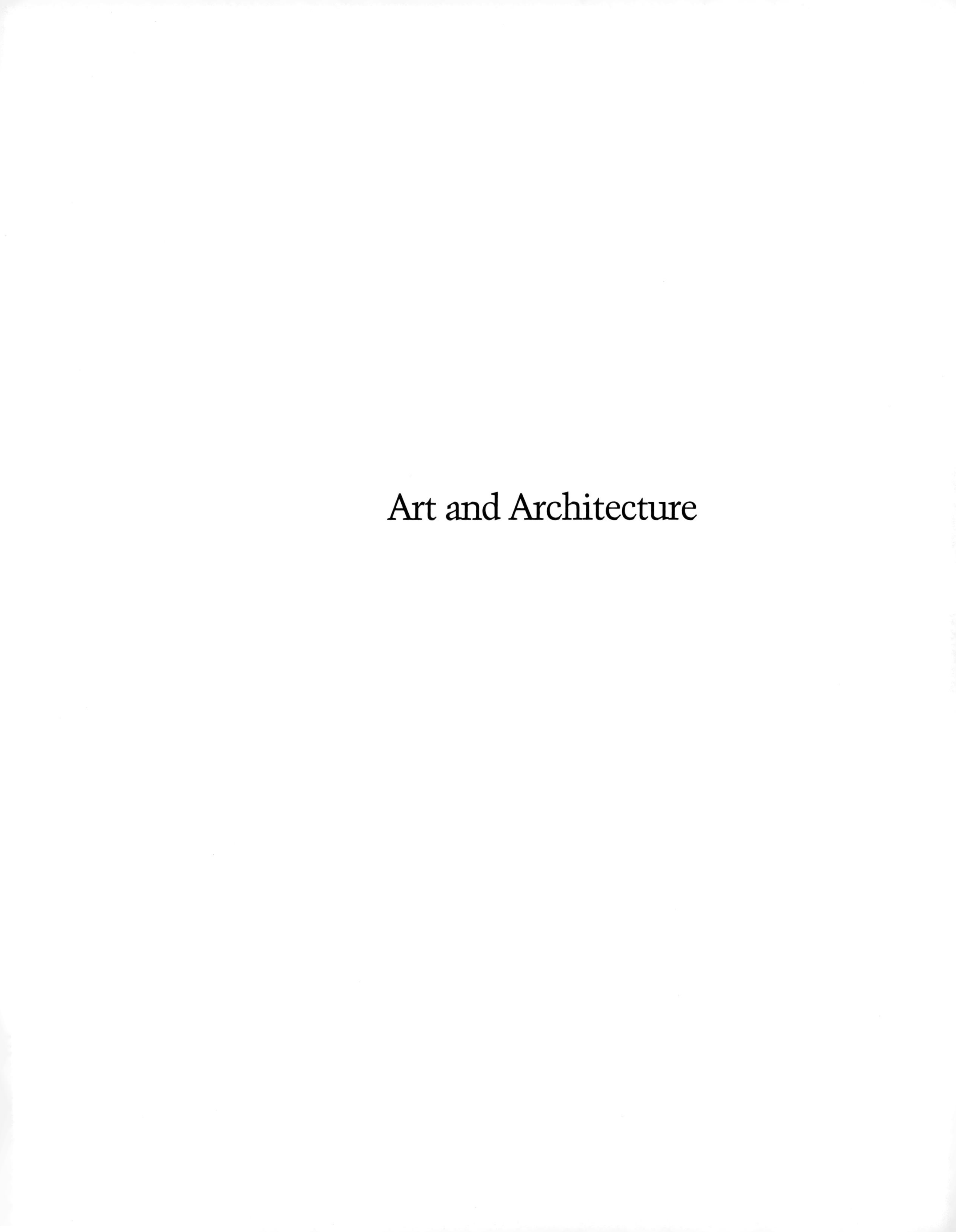

Art and Architecture

si explicui. Penulam quam reliqui troade apud carpum, ueniens affer tecum et libros: maxime autem membranas. Alexander erarius multa mala mihi ostendit. Reddet illi dominus secundum opera eius. Quem et tu deuita. Valde enim restitit uerbis nostris. In prima mea defensione nemo mihi affuit, sed omnes me dereliquerunt. Non illis imputetur. Dominus autem mihi astitit et confortauit me. ut per me predicatio impleretur. et audiant omnes gentes. et liberatus sum de ore leonis. Liberauit me dominus ab omni opere malo. et saluum faciet in regnum suum celeste. cui gloria in secula seculorum. amen. Saluta priscam et aquilam. et onesifori domum. Erastus remansit corinthi. Trophimum autem reliqui infirmum mileti. Festina ante hiemem uenire. Salutat te eubulus. et pudens et linus et claudia. et fratres omnes. Dominus noster ihesus christus cum spiritu tuo. Gratia uobiscum. amen.

Titum autem commonefacit et instruit de constitutione presbiterii, et de spirituali conuersatione et hereticis uitandis, qui in scripturis iudaicis credunt. Scribens ei a nicopoli.

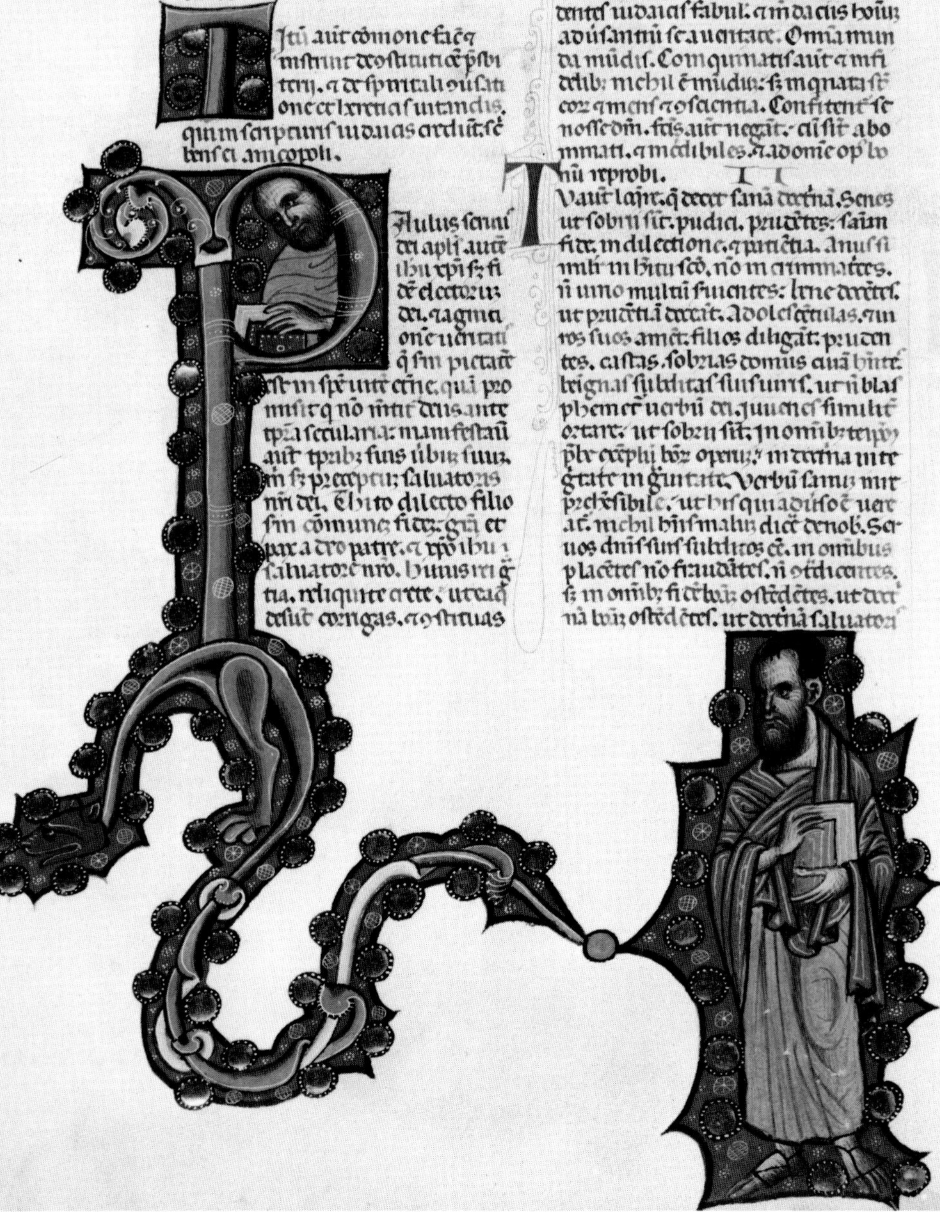

Paulus seruus dei apostolus autem ihesu christi secundum fidem electorum dei, et agnitionem ueritatis que secundum pietatem est in spem uite eterne, quam promisit qui non mentitur deus ante tempora secularia: manifestauit autem temporibus suis uerbum suum in [predicatione que credita est mihi] secundum preceptum saluatoris nostri dei. Tito dilecto filio secundum communem fidem. gratia et pax a deo patre. et christo ihesu saluatore nostro. Huius rei gratia reliqui te crete, ut ea que desunt corrigas, et constituas presbiteros sicut et ego tibi disposui. Si quis sine crimine est unius uxoris uir, filios habens fideles, non in accusatione luxurie aut non subditos. Oportet enim episcopum sine crimine esse sicut dei dispensatorem. non superbum, non iracundum, non uinolentum, non percussorem, non turpis lucri cupidum: sed hospitalem, benignum, sobrium, iustum, sanctum, continentem: amplectentem eum qui secundum doctrinam est fidelem sermonem: ut potens sit exhortari in doctrina sana, et eos qui contradicunt arguere. Sunt enim multi inobedientes, et uaniloqui, et seductores, maxime autem qui de circumcisione sunt. quos oportet redargui: qui uniuersas domos subuertunt, docentes que non oportet, turpis lucri gratia. Dixit quidam ex illis proprius eorum propheta. Cretenses semper mendaces, male bestie, uentris pigri. Testimonium hoc uerum est. Quam ob rem increpa illos dure: ut sani sint in fide, non intendentes iudaicis fabulis, et mandatis hominum, auersantium se a ueritate. Omnia munda mundis. Coinquinatis autem et infidelibus nichil est mundum: sed inquinata sunt eorum et mens et conscientia. Confitentur se nosse deum. factis autem negant. cum sint abhominati, et incredibiles, et ad omne opus bonum reprobi.

II

Tu autem loquere que decet sanam doctrinam. Senes ut sobrii sint, pudici, prudentes: sani in fide, in dilectione, in patientia. Anus similiter in habitu sancto, non criminatrices, non uino multo seruientes: bene docentes. ut prudentiam doceant. Adolescentulas, ut uiros suos ament, filios diligant, prudentes, castas, sobrias, domus curam habentes, benignas, subditas suis uiris, ut non blasphemetur uerbum dei. Iuuenes similiter hortare, ut sobrii sint. In omnibus te ipsum prebe exemplum bonorum operum, in doctrina, in integritate, in grauitate. Verbum sanum irreprehensibile, ut is qui aduersus est uereatur, nichil habens malum dicere de nobis. Seruos dominis suis subditos esse, in omnibus placentes, non fraudantes, non contradicentes, sed in omnibus fidem bonam ostendentes, ut doctrinam saluatoris

REBECCA W. CORRIE
Bates College

The Conradin Bible and the Problem of Court Ateliers in Southern Italy in the Thirteenth Century

We know very little about manuscript production in the time of Frederick II, as Florentine Mütherich observed more than a decade ago.[1] From the few court commissions that survive, it is difficult to isolate a characteristic style or to understand how manuscript illumination fit into court life and culture.[2] A similar problem obtains for southern Italy in the period following the Hohenstaufen era during the rule of the Angevins in the last quarter of the thirteenth century. Many manuscripts have been associated with southern Italy in the Angevin period, but the variation in quality and style among them is tremendous. Some are distinctly French.[3] Others—clearly court commissions—are such simple copies of Hohenstaufen works that we are inclined to believe that no sophisticated court ateliers existed in Naples in the late thirteenth century.[4] Indeed, documents dated between 1278 and 1282 regarding a manuscript project for Charles of Anjou show that artists as well as scribes had to be recruited.[5] Only from the period between the death of Frederick and the arrival of the Angevins is there extensive and consistent evidence of manuscript production that illuminates the organization of the production of luxury manuscripts close to the Hohenstaufen court in thirteenth-century Italy. For the most part, these manuscripts appear to date from the reign of Frederick's son, Manfred, prince of Taranto from 1250 to 1258 and king of Sicily between 1258 and his death in 1266.[6] Dates after Manfred's death have been suggested for some of the manuscripts, which would place them in the era of the struggle between the Angevin house and the last adherents to the Hohenstaufen cause.

Among the South Italian manuscripts of the third quarter of the thirteenth century, two distinct groups have been isolated. The first is associated with the so-called Manfred Bible (Vat. lat. 36).[7] This group includes the *Baths of Pozzuoli* (Biblioteca Angelica MS. 1474) and a large number of one-volume Bibles, as well as Manfred's copy of the *Art of Hunting with Birds* (Vat. pal. lat. 1071), written by Frederick.[8] To the second group belong the manuscripts associated with the so-called Conradin Bible (Walters Art Gallery, MS. 152), which tradition claims was sent as a gift from Sicily to King Conradin, grandson of Frederick II, nephew of Manfred, and the last Hohenstaufen claimant to the throne of Sicily, shortly before his execution at Naples in 1268.[9] The two manuscript groups share inconographic motifs, figure types, and ornamental details based on French models, but there are many differences too. The manuscripts of the Conradin Bible atelier use Byzantine models much more extensively, and the ornamental repertoire is simpler. For example, elements such as strap-work and diapered backgrounds are much rarer. Moreover, as we shall see, while both ateliers illuminated one-volume Bibles, the other texts they worked on were quite different. The two manuscript groups share one other characteristic that should be noted. Studied less thoroughly than thirteenth-century manuscripts from centers such as Bologna and Paris, they have often been overlooked by scholars. In the last two decades this has changed, and the lists for both manuscript groups are expanding rapidly.

This paper focuses on the manuscripts of the Conradin Bible atelier, adding a new Bible to that group and discussing the less well known antiphonaries. My comments have two goals: to assist in the ongoing process of localizing and dating the activity of this often brilliant atelier, and to see whether the study of this atelier can lend some insight into the organization of manuscript production in southern Italy in the thirteenth century in general. While we often speak of court ateliers, these manuscripts suggest an arrangement closer to the situation in Paris and Bologna, where independent masters and shops worked side by side on commissions and occasionally carried out royal projects.[10]

Localization and Chronology

The Conradin Bible first came to the attention of the scholarly world in the second quarter of the nineteenth century, and for some time thereafter it remained an isolated manuscript with its association with the tragic Conradin unquestioned. By the middle of the twentieth century, however, scholars began to doubt the Conradin connection and the attribution to southern Italy or Sicily, in part because that attribution rested entirely on the report of a now lost modern inscription, presumably based on a previously lost medieval colophon.[11] Over the years, primarily on the basis of general comparisons with faces and figures in panel painting and frescoes, several historians including Roberto Longhi, Ilaria Toesca, and Antonio Caleca reattributed the Conradin Bible to the *maniera greca* of Tuscany and Umbria.[12]

In addition to new suggestions regarding the localization of the atelier of the Conradin Bible, new attributions have also been made. In 1964 Angela Daneu Lattanzi observed that the Bassetti Bible (Trento, Biblioteca Comunale, MS. 2868) was the work of the master of the Conradin Bible or his atelier, an attribution that has been universally accepted.[13] In 1979 Hélène Toubert added three more Bibles to the oeuvre of the master of the Conradin Bible: one is in the Bibliothèque Ste-Geneviève, Paris (MS. 14), one in the Bodleian Library (MS. Canon. Bibl. lat. 59), and one in the Biblioteca Centrale della Regione Siciliana in Palermo (MS. I.C.13), a manuscript originally attributed by Daneu Lattanzi to the Manfred manuscript group. All of these manuscripts include elements of the characteristic ornamental style of the manuscript group, such as foliate finials or tails, as well as the distinctive faces and bodies.[14]

In addition to the Bibles, another group of manuscripts has surfaced—antiphonaries. In 1978 Antonio Caleca accurately identified a large fragment of an Augustinian antiphonary in Pisa as the work of the master of the Conradin Bible. It seems quite likely that fragments identified earlier by Ilaria Toesca came from the same antiphonary, for the format of the illuminations, the codicological characteristics, and the condition are the same.[15] In 1982 I published a Franciscan antiphonary, now in the collection of the Colchester Castle Museum in Colchester, England, which I will discuss more extensively below (fig. 16).[16] A two-volume antiphonary now in Volterra, mentioned by Antonio Caleca, does not belong to the atelier or to the Conradin Bible master.[17]

A few other manuscripts can be associated with the Conradin Bible manuscript group, although they differ somewhat from the others. They are a copy of the *Liber Annayde* of Boniface of Verona composed for Cardinal Ottaviano degli Ubaldini, first published by Toubert, and two copies of the Medical Encyclopedia or al-Hāwī made for Charles of Anjou, associated with the Conradin Bible by Daneu Lattanzi.[18]

As the group of manuscripts produced by this artist and his assistants grew, many scholars working in the field returned to the original attribution to southern Italy. Hélène Toubert and I in particular have argued for the South Italian attribution, while Florentine Mütherich and Angela Daneu Lattanzi never abandoned that localization and recent writers have echoed variations of this theme.[19] Indeed, the consensus has returned to a localization in southern Italy.

Daneu Lattanzi attributed the Conradin

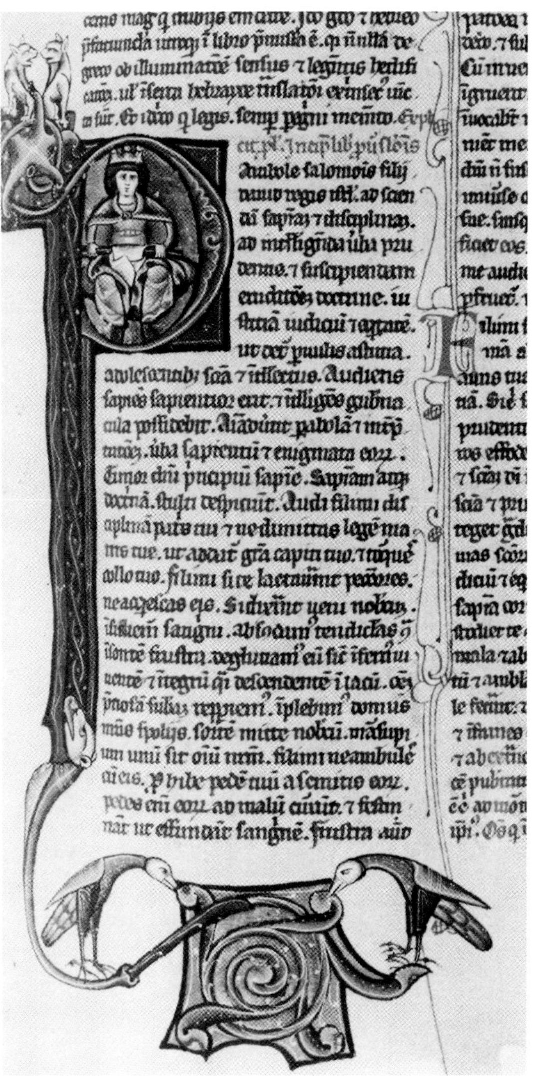

1. Solomon, Proverbs, Bible, c. 1260, folio 214r, detail
Biblioteca Centrale della Regione Siciliana, Palermo (MS. I.C. 13)

Bible to the South on the basis of nineteenth-century opinion and her accurate observation that many of the Bible's figures are remarkably close to the mosaics at Monreale,[20] but we have more evidence today. As I have argued in the past, the Palermo Bible, while undoubtedly the work of the master of the Conradin Bible, ties the group directly to works associated with Manfred's court whose attribution to southern Italy has never been questioned. Folios from the Palermo Bible are decorated with motifs such as complicated vine scrolls inhabited by nude figures, as well as paired birds and dogs, also found in the Manfred Bible but not in the rest of the Conradin Bible group (fig. 1).[21] The manuscript also has long-haired male figures dressed in knee-length, long-sleeved tunics fitted at the waist, typical of the Manfred group but rarely found elsewhere in the Conradin Bible group (figs. 1, 2).[22] Other evidence can be found in the Bodleian Bible, which has a heraldic crest indicating that it was in southern Italy in 1600.[23] Finally, as we shall see, the two copies of the al-Ḥāwī Medical Encyclopedia were produced in Naples between 1278 and 1282.

I would like to add another manuscript to this group: a one-volume Bible in the Vatican Library, Vat. lat. 4195, that further anchors the Conradin Bible group in southern Italy.[24] The Vatican Bible shares elements with nearly every manuscript in the group. Like the other Bibles, its decoration is a more modest version of the historiated initials with dragons found in the Conradin Bible, with floral finials substituting for the figures found in its margins (figs. 4–5, 7, 11–13, 15).

The Vatican manuscript shares many idiosyncratic foliate motifs with the other Bibles from the Conradin Bible group. A striking comparison can be made between the illumination from the Epistle to the Romans in the Vatican Bible and the book of Luke in the Palermo Bible (figs. 3, 4), particularly in the position of the dragon and the floral form in the dragon's tail. Perhaps even closer is another example from the Vatican Bible's Epistle to the Colossians, where the position of the dragon has changed, but the foliate motif is now identical (figs. 3, 5). The dragon from Romans finds other close parallels in the decoration of 4 Kings in the Palermo Bible and of the Epistle to the Colossians in the Conradin Bible (figs. 2, 4, 6).

Another motif in the Palermo and the Trento Bibles, a floral form that has been transformed into a starfish shape, also occurs in the Vatican Bible. It appears in the upper corner of the letter *P* in the Epistle to the Colossians (fig. 5). An excellent example from the Palermo Bible's Book of Proverbs has its dot connecting it to the vine off-center (fig. 1). Another variation of this form can be found in the pinwheel of the Vatican Bible's Book of Proverbs (fig. 7). This same dragon and pinwheel combination can also be found in the Paris Bible (figs. 7, 8).

This folio in the Vatican manuscript brings us to another parallel, for the two-legged,

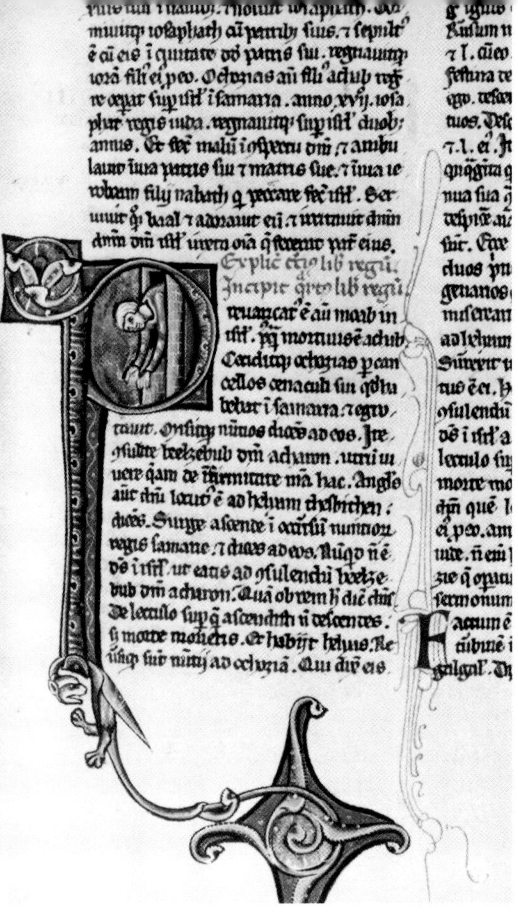

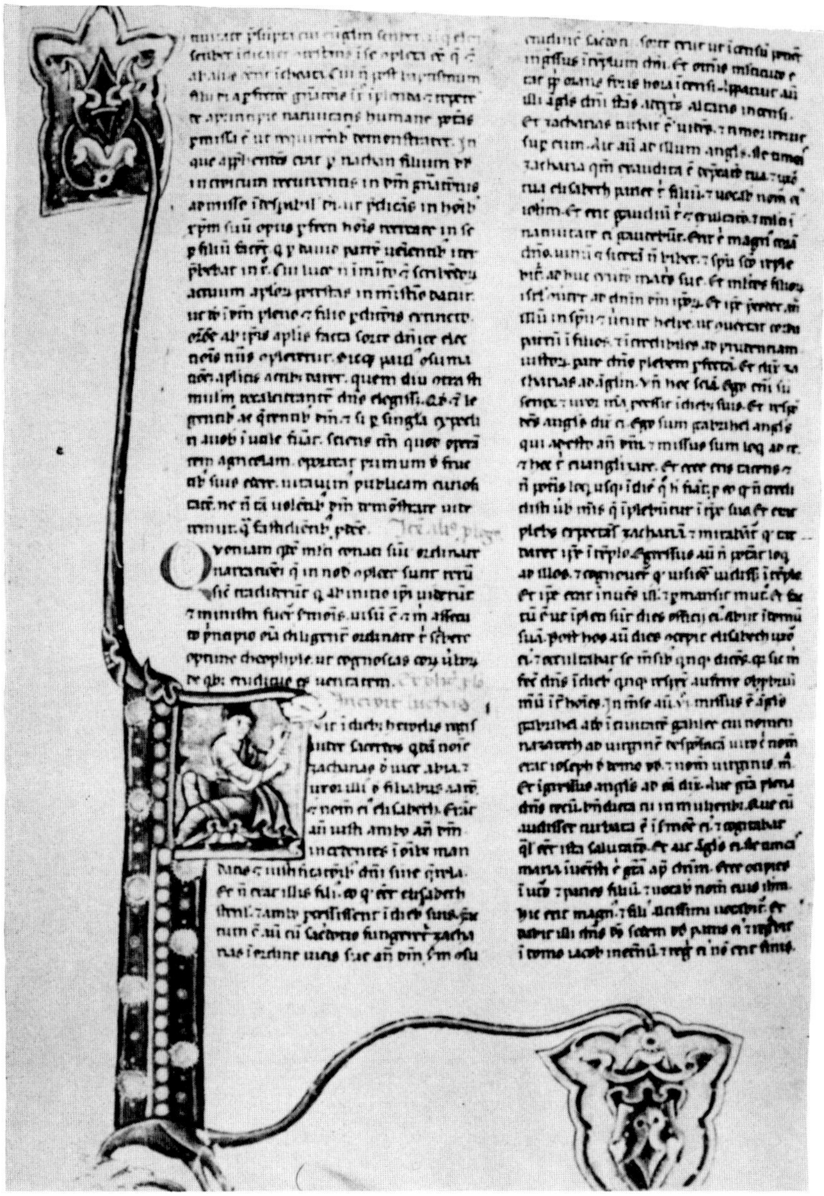

2. Fall of Ahaziah, 4 Kings, Bible, c. 1260, folio 126r, detail
Biblioteca Centrale della Regione Siciliana, Palermo (MS. I.C. 13)

3. Saint Luke, Gospel of Luke, Bible, c. 1260, folio 367v
Biblioteca Centrale della Regione Siciliana, Palermo (MS. I.C. 13)

blunt-nosed dragon who turns back to bite the stem of the letter *P* resembles many dragons in the Conradin Bible, including the one from Colossians (figs. 6, 7). Yet another motif occurs on the opening folio from Proverbs in the Vatican Bible. In the upper left corner is a trilobed flower curled around a vine scroll. This motif occurs prominently in the Trento Bible and the Paris Bible, and can be seen here in Chronicles of the Paris manuscript (figs. 7, 10). It can also be found in the Manfred Bible.[25]

The variety of ornamental motifs in the Vatican Bible is paralleled by the inclusion of both figure types found in the manuscripts produced by the Conradin Bible atelier. Some have the long hair and the knee-length tunics of many figures in the Palermo Bible (figs. 1, 2, 7, 11). But others are entirely based on the bullet-headed, short-haired Byzantine types found in the Conradin Bible (figs. 4–6, 9, 12–14).[26] This striking resemblance to the figures in the Conradin Bible extends to the rendering and arrangement of drapery folds. All seven examples just cited use a form of fine-line highlighting that corresponds to chrysography in Byzantine mosaics. Furthermore, the configuration of the drapery in two of our pairs matches very closely: Paul from the Epistle to the Galatians in the Vatican Bible with Paul from the Epistle to Titus in the Conradin Bible (figs. 13, 14), and Paul from the Epistle to the Ephesians in the Vatican Bible with Paul from 2 Corinthians in the Conradin Bible (figs. 12, 9).

Because of its extensive ensemble of decorative and figure motifs, the Vatican Bible, like the Palermo Bible, provides evidence of a

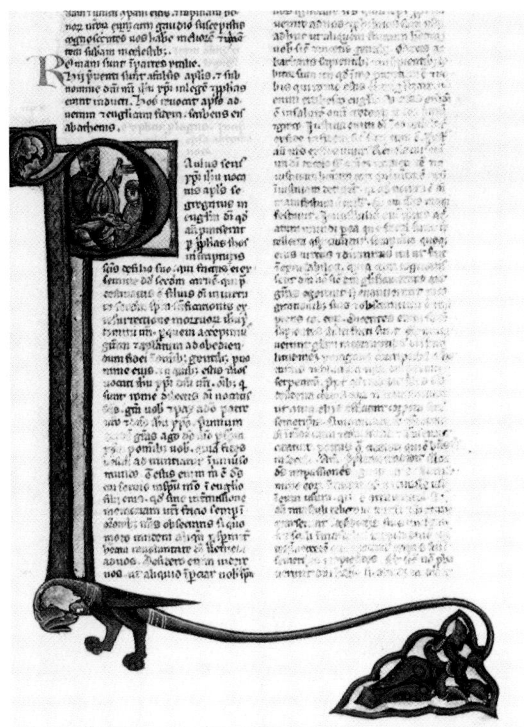

4. Saint Paul Preaching, Romans, Bible, third quarter of the thirteenth century, folio 347r
Biblioteca Apostolica Vaticana (MS. Vat. lat. 4195)

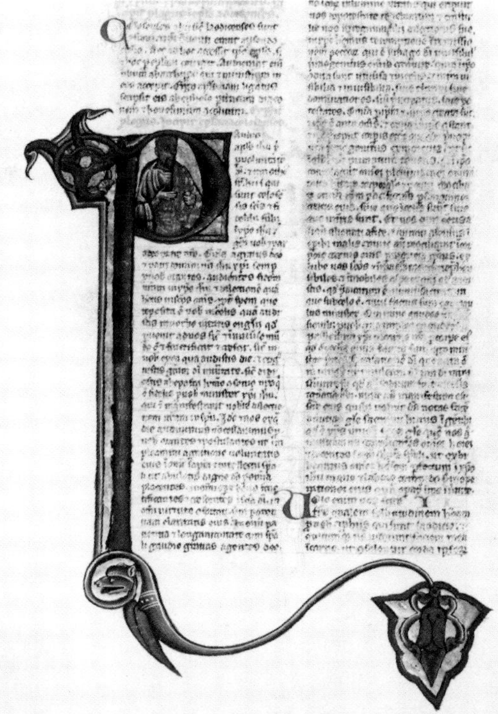

5. Saint Paul, Colossians, Bible, third quarter of the thirteenth century, folio 365v
Biblioteca Apostolica Vaticana (MS. Vat. lat. 4195)

link between the Conradin Bible manuscript group and the Manfred Bible manuscript group. The Vatican Bible shares with the Palermo Bible motifs that do not occur in other manuscripts in the rest of the Conradin Bible manuscript group, but do occur in the Manfred group. The male figures with long hair and knee-length skirts, such as Cyrus from 1 Ezra, are among these (fig. 11). A telling example is a pair of facing dragons with long tails from 1 Kings (fig. 15). While the spiky flower between them is typical of the Conradin Bible manuscript group, the dragon pair is not (figs. 10, 15). Instead it resembles paired birds with long, waving tails found in the Manfred Bible.[27] Indeed, owing to its similarity to both the Palermo and Conradin, the Vatican Bible affirms Hélène Toubert's decision to move the Palermo Bible from the atelier of the Manfred Bible to the Conradin Bible manuscript group.

The Vatican manuscript ties the Conradin Bible group to southern Italy in another way, for like the Bodleian Bible it possesses a colophon that indicates a connection to the South around 1600. On folio 1r is an inscription that describes the Bible as the gift of the Neapolitan scholar Giovanni Domenico Traiano. A notation at the end of the manuscript on folio 438v in the same hand suggests that Traiano gave the manuscript to the Vatican on 26 July 1600. The catalogue number of the manuscript substantiates that date, since it places the manuscript among gifts presented to the Vatican Library around 1600.[28] Traiano, who worked for the church primarily in southern Italy, visited Rome frequently beginning in 1572 and worked for the Vatican Library after 1611.[29] Although Traiano's connection with the Vatican Bible does not guarantee that the manuscript came from the South, the fact that he came from Naples, coupled with his professional concern for South Italian culture, suggests that the manuscript originally came from the South.

Two other manuscripts merit closer attention, namely, the Augustinian antiphonary now in the Museo Nazionale e Civico di S. Matteo in Pisa, which probably once included the fragments published by Ilaria Toesca, and the Franciscan antiphonary now MS. 222.32 in the Colchester and Essex Museum in Colchester, England.[30] Of these, the Colchester Antiphonary probably tells us more about the atelier.[31] On the basis of figure types alone, there can be little doubt that the Colchester Antiphonary came from the Conradin Bible atelier. That the resemblances are so striking argues that the Bible and the antiphonary belong to the same period of the atelier's activity.[32] The face of John the Baptist from the Office for the Feast of the Nativity of that saint is a close match for all three images of Saint Paul illustrated here (figs. 6, 9, 14, 16).

The Colchester Antiphonary, a nearly complete sanctorale, has no useful provenance, but it helps date the activity of the atelier since its text has numerous characteristics making likely a date no earlier than 1260 and probably not much later than 1270. The text and its rubrics conform to liturgical corrections, clarifications, and simplifications made by Haymo of Faversham in the 1240s and 1250s, and incorporated more fully into the Franciscan Breviary under Bonaventura at the Chapter of Narbonne in 1260.[33] In addition, the rhythmical office for Saint Francis composed by Julian of Speyer around 1231 includes a textual change instituted at the same chapter by Saint Bonaventura.[34] These details and others require a date after 1260 and suggest that the antiphonary was written under the scrutiny of the Franciscans who used it, if not by them.

But if this manuscript was made after 1260, it was clearly not much later than that date. It omits entirely two of Haymo's major rubrics on feasts of the Virgin, the sort of omission that Stephen van Dijk has argued indicates uncertainty about their permanence immediately following the rubrics' introduction in 1260.[35] Moreover, while the manuscript is written in square notation, it belongs to the period of transition from Beneventan style, for the clef system used is almost entirely the red and yellow lining of Beneventan notation. Standard clefs are rarely used. Furthermore, unlike the standard notation form required by the Franciscans by the 1260s, this notation uses staffs with black lines, not red. Such irregularities can also be found in Franciscan breviaries from the 1260s.[36]

The Pisa Antiphonary, which has no collection number, is quite different. It has a fully developed square notation, is red-lined, and is written in a much finer Bolognese rotunda. Above all, it follows an Augustinian usage that persisted into the sixteenth century, a combination of an established office for Saint Augustine and texts and rubrics reformed by the Franciscans between 1255 and 1260 but abandoned by them in 1260.[37] In fact it seems likely that the commissions for the antiphonaries were not related, for not

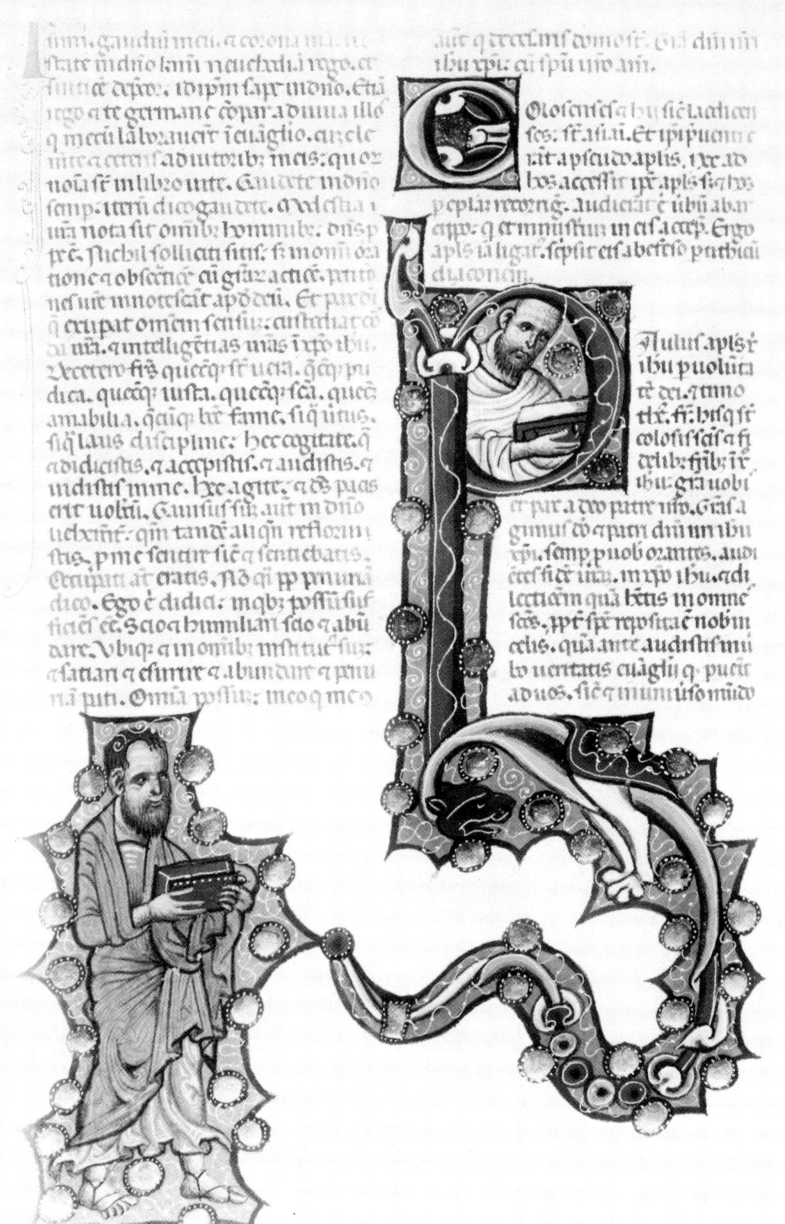

6. Saint Paul, Colossians, Conradin Bible, third quarter of the thirteenth century, folio 119r, detail
Walters Art Gallery, Baltimore (MS. 152)

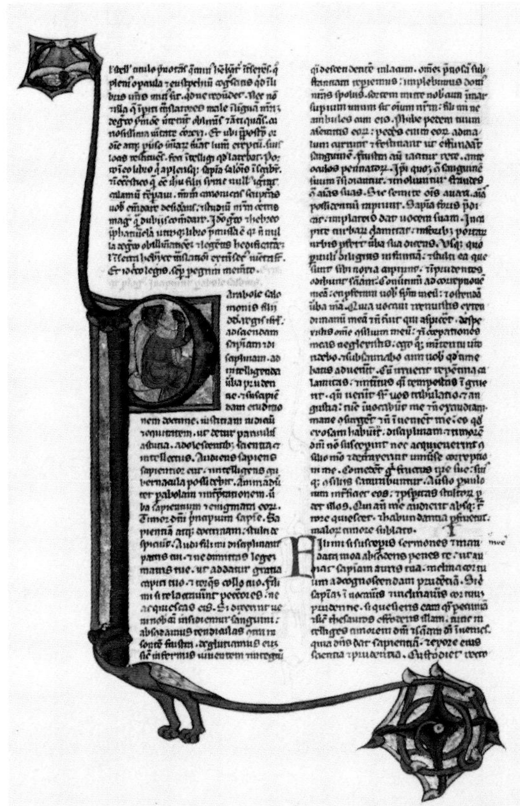

7. Solomon, Proverbs, Bible, third quarter of the thirteenth century, folio 145v
Biblioteca Apostolica Vaticana (MS. Vat. lat. 4195)

8. "Post," Judges, Bible, third quarter of the thirteenth century, folio 94r
Bibliothèque Ste-Geneviève, Paris (MS. 14); photograph: Jean-Loup Charmet

only are the texts and codicology different, but the Pisa Antiphonary was a more expensive project. Both manuscripts have historiated initials at most double feasts, but where the Pisa Antiphonary has painted foliate initials on others, the Colchester Antiphonary uses pen-sketch initials. Thus we have no reason to argue for a single patron commissioning these works as gifts for local orders. Instead, we have a scenario in which the houses themselves had the manuscripts made when the orders issued rules requiring new antiphonaries. According to Van Dijk, although the history of the antiphonary is quite elusive, there is evidence that antiphonaries for both orders or at least instructions for their correction were issued after 1254 and 1256.[38]

The date not much later than the 1260s provided by the Colchester Antiphonary is supported by information from another manuscript. This is an illuminated copy of the *Liber Annayde*, written by Boniface of Verona for the powerful Ghibelline cardinal Ottaviano degli Ubaldini, now MS. lat. 8114 in the Bibliothèque Nationale in Paris.[39] When Hélène Toubert first published this manuscript as the product of the Conradin Bible atelier, I had already seen it and concluded that it was not the work of our illuminators. However, a second look has convinced me that she is correct and that the illuminations in this volume are the work of the Conradin Bible atelier, although the painting of the faces and the foliate initial on the dedication page is not of the same quality as most of the work of the atelier's leading master. On the other hand, a lively figure of the Virgin on folio 6r is remarkably like the painting in the Paris Bible. Toubert rightly observed that the association of this manuscript with Ottaviano degli Ubaldini offers an opportunity to date the activity of this artist and his assistants. She suggested an approximate date for this manuscript, obtaining a date for an early stage in the career of our master. I would argue, however, that the *Liber* appears to offer only one secure date, and that is a *terminus ante quem* for the manuscript itself. Toubert argued appropriately that the depiction of the presentation of the manuscript to the cardinal on folio 1r suggests that this was the presentation copy of the text. However, on the basis of the cardinal's appearance in

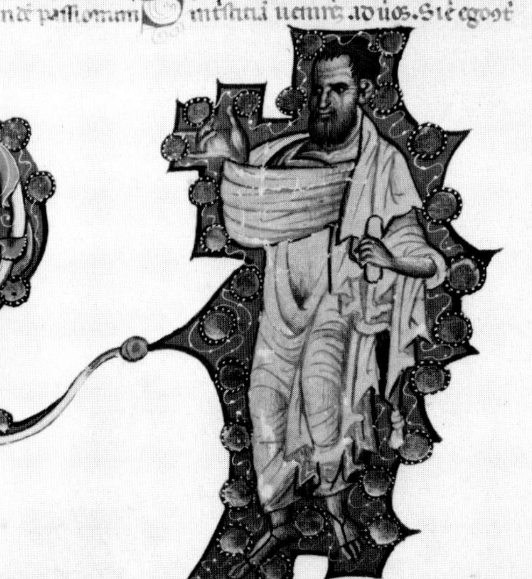

9. Saint Paul, 2 Corinthians, Conradin Bible, third quarter of the thirteenth century, folio IIIv
Walters Art Gallery, Baltimore (MS. 152)

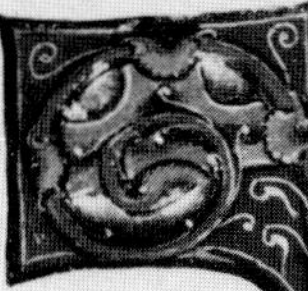

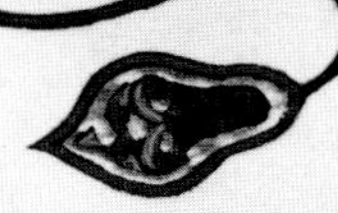

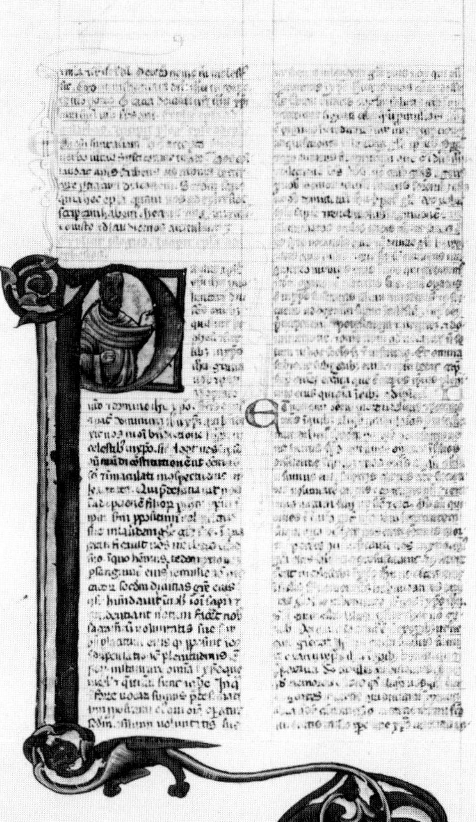

10. Scribe, I Chronicles, Bible, third quarter of the thirteenth century, folio 157v, detail
Bibliothèque Ste-Geneviève, Paris (Ms. 14); photograph: Jean-Loup Charmet

11. Cyrus, I Ezra, Bible, third quarter of the thirteenth century, folio 104r, detail
Biblioteca Apostolica Vaticana (MS. Vat. lat. 4195)

12. Saint Paul, Ephesians, Bible, third quarter of the thirteenth century, folio 362v, detail
Biblioteca Apostolica Vaticana (MS. Vat. lat. 4195)

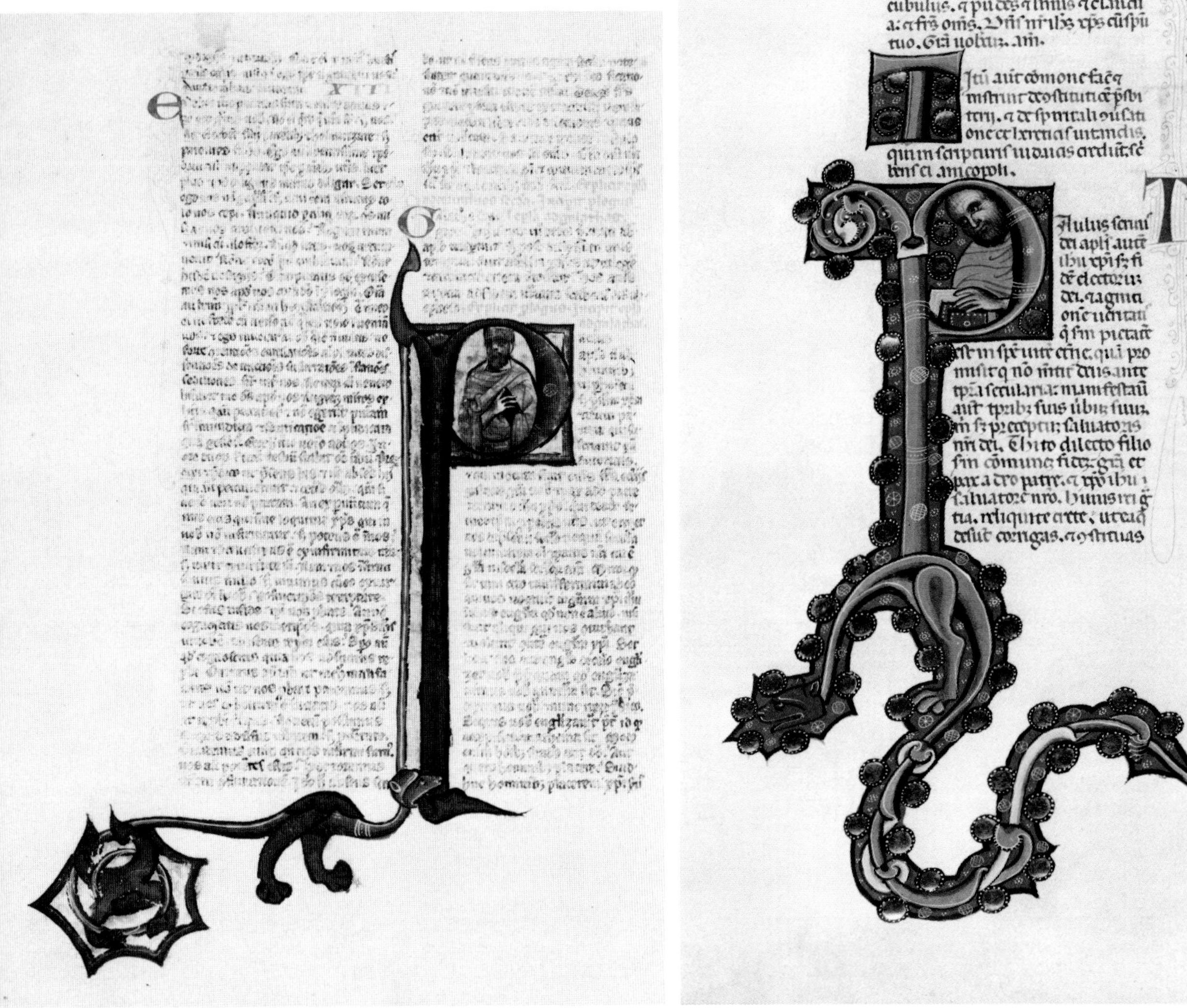

the dedication miniature and her assumption that the *Liber* was written for the elevation of Ottaviano to cardinal in 1245, she concluded that the *Liber Annayde* in Paris was decorated within several years of that event. But Clelia Maria Piastra, who has worked on Boniface of Verona, maintains only that the poem must have been written between 1245 and Ottaviano's death in 1272.[40] Thus it seems judicious to conclude only that this luxury copy of an ode to the Virgin written specifically for Ottaviano, whether as the dedication copy or as a later gift to him, must have been decorated in his lifetime. This gives us a date before 1272 for the manuscript. In sum, the Colchester Antiphonary, which must be after 1260, and the *Liber* from before 1272, may provide rough dates for the activity of the atelier, beginning not much later than 1260, certainly active before 1272.

The only manuscripts related to the Conradin Bible with demonstrably later dates are the two extensively documented copies of the Medical Encyclopedia or al-Hāwī, one in the Vatican Library (MS. Vat. lat. 2398–2399) and the other in the Bibliothèque Nationale in Paris (MS. lat. 6912). It was Daneu Lattanzi who noticed that these manuscripts were related to the Conradin Bible, and Toubert has accepted her observations.[41] Daneu Lattanzi noted that the treatment of the vine scrolls and the blue fields behind them is

13. Saint Paul, Galatians, Bible, third quarter of the thirteenth century, folio 360v
Biblioteca Apostolica Vaticana (MS. Vat. lat. 4195)

14. Saint Paul, Titus, Conradin Bible, third quarter of the thirteenth century, folio 124v, detail
Walters Art Gallery, Baltimore (MS. 152)

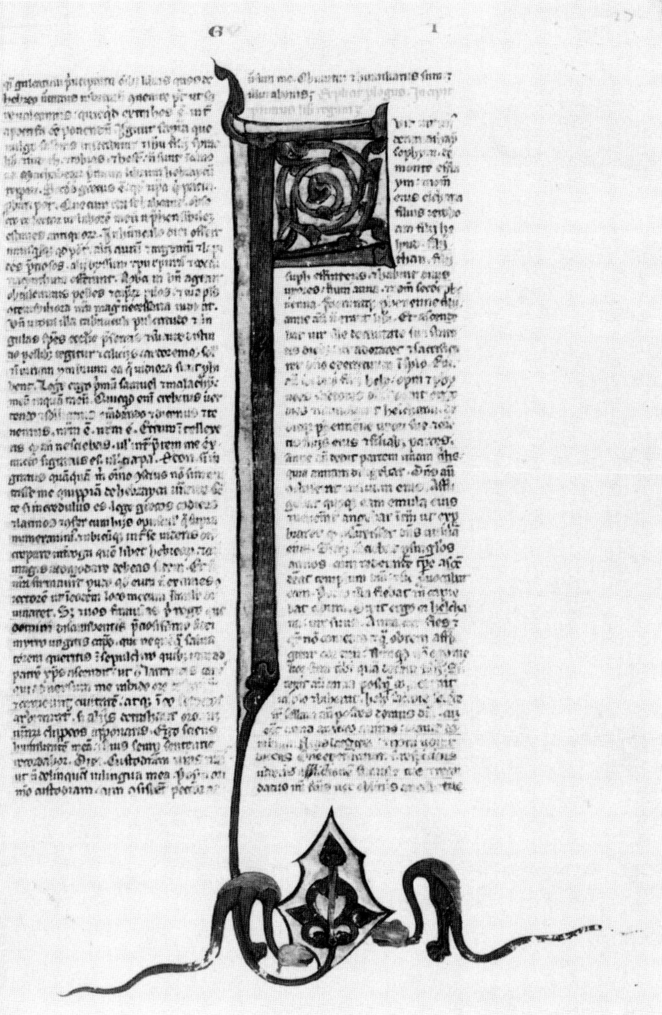

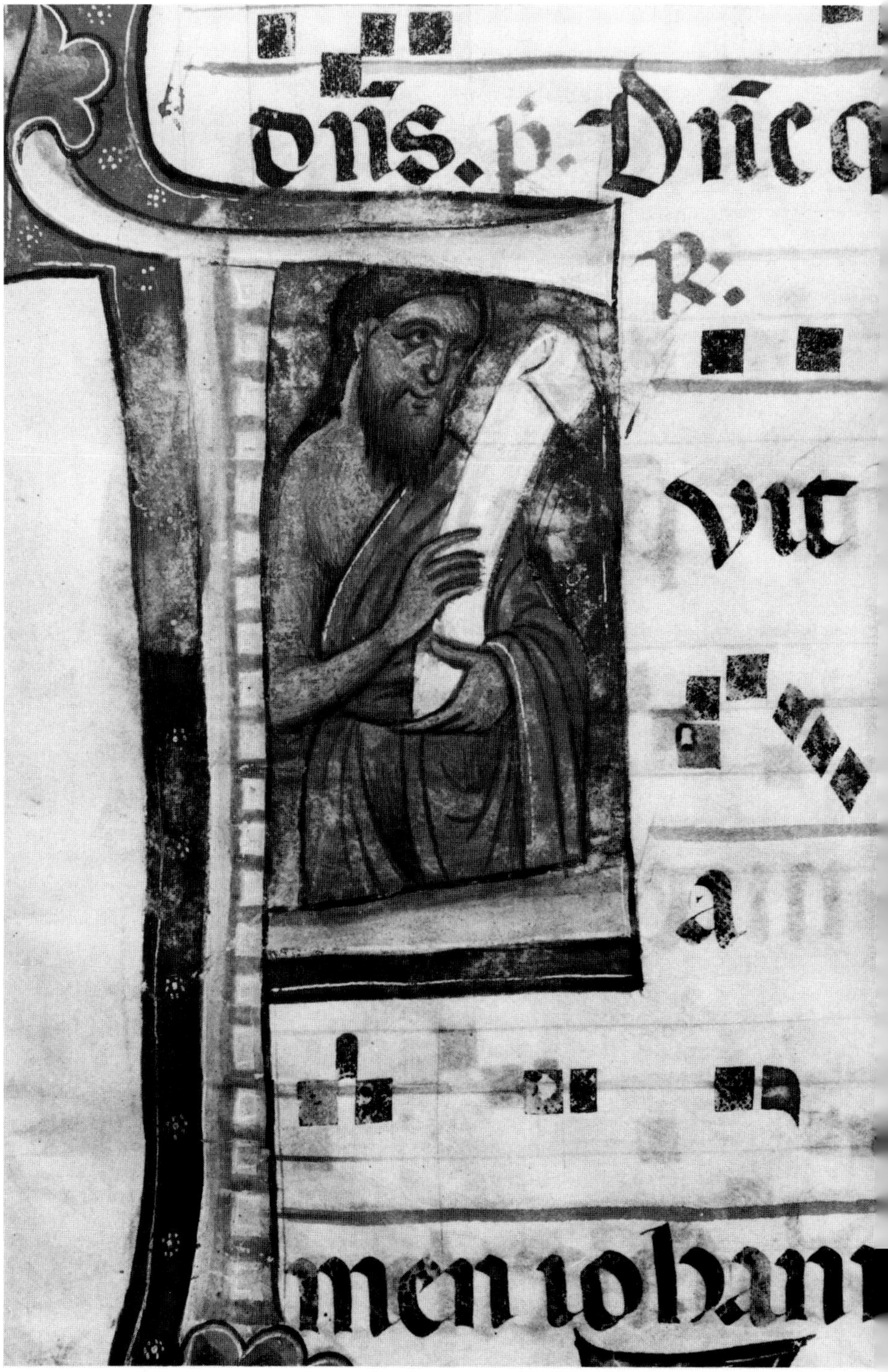

15. "Fuit," I Kings, Bible, third quarter of the thirteenth century, folio 27r
Biblioteca Apostolica Vaticana (MS. Vat. lat. 4195)

16. Saint John the Baptist, First Response for the Office of the Feast of the Nativity of John the Baptist, Antiphonary, third quarter of the thirteenth century, folio 70r, detail
Colchester and Essex Museum, Colchester, England (MS. 222.32)

very close to that of the Trento Bible. A good comparison can be made between folio 285v of the Vatican copy and the opening folio of the Book of Judith from the Trento Bible (figs. 17, 18). The ornamentation of these manuscripts also includes the gold dots found throughout the works produced by the Conradin Bible atelier (figs. 14, 17, 18). Many of the foliate finials in the al-Hāwī manuscripts compare easily to examples in the Paris Bible (figs. 17, 19). Even the dots that appear as anchors between vines and foliate finials through the manuscript group occur in the ornamentation of these works (figs. 1, 3, 4, 6, 9, 14, 17). But the al-Hāwī manuscripts are not the products of this atelier at its height. The ornamental forms are broader and looser than those in the rest of the group. Moreover, the figures resemble only the smallest from the Trento Bible. Surviving documentation suggests that the artist who executed the decoration of these manuscripts was the monk Giovanni da Montecassino, described as living with the archbishop of Naples in 1281. In him we may well have the last painter of our atelier.[42]

Conclusions and Questions for Further Study

What can we conclude about the atelier that produced this group of manuscripts and by extension about manuscript production in southern Italy in the thirteenth century? To begin, it is clear that its style is related to or even rooted in the art of the Manfred Bible manuscript atelier and that this style was formulated by a very self-conscious combination of French ornamental elements and Byzantine models. But does that mean that all of the products of the Conradin Bible atelier are later than all of the products of the Manfred Bible atelier? Our evidence suggests otherwise. Although the Manfred Bible is usually dated around 1258, Silvana Pettinati, Toubert, and others have argued that the Manfred Bible style persisted after Manfred's death in 1266.[43] We have seen that the Conradin Bible atelier was active in this same period. Thus, while the two ateliers might have been connected at the outset in some manner, for the most part they seem to have been contemporary, independent organizations.

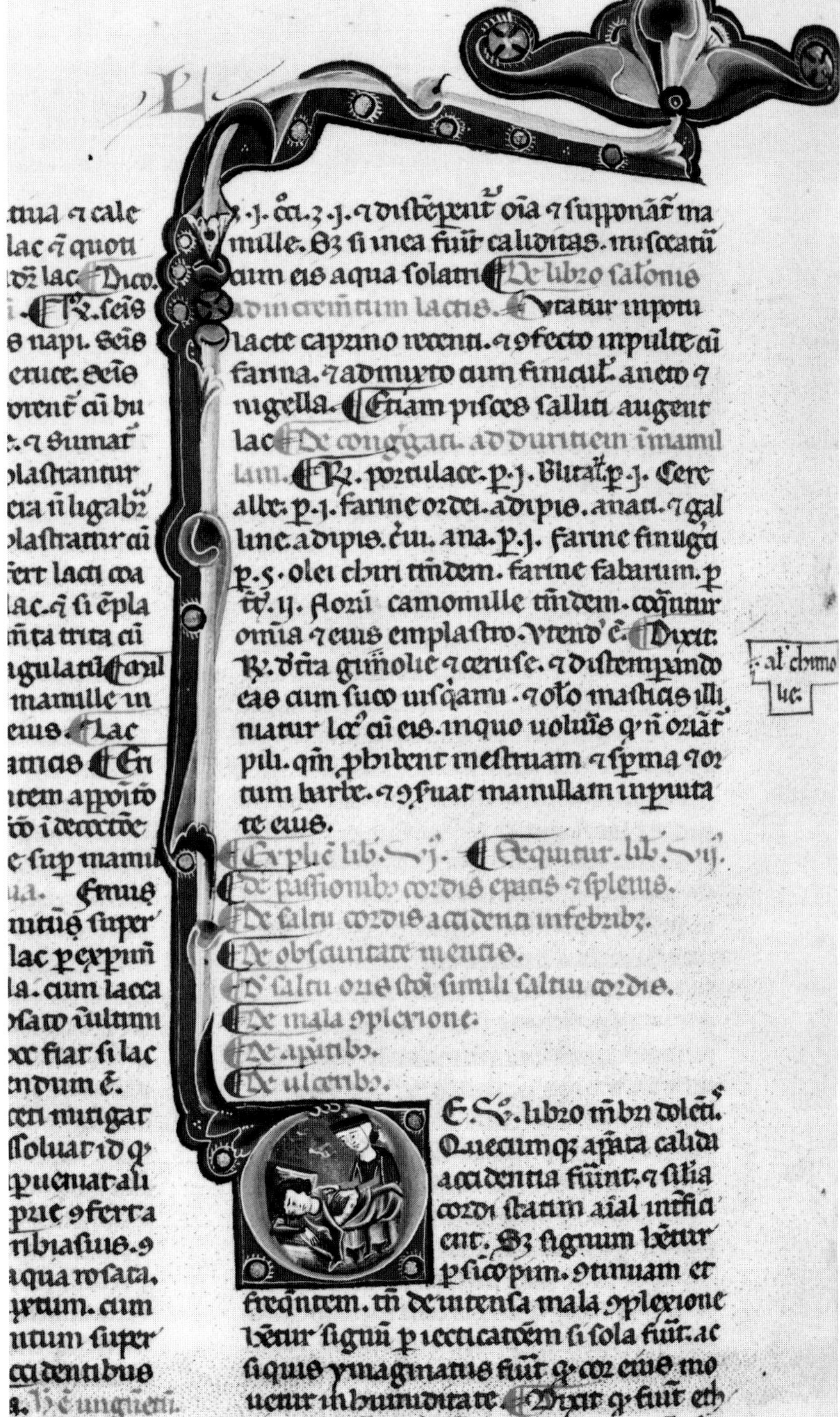

17. Physician and Patient, Medical Encyclopedia or al-Hāwī, 1281–1282, folio 285v, detail
Biblioteca Apostolica Vaticana (MS. Vat. lat. 2398)

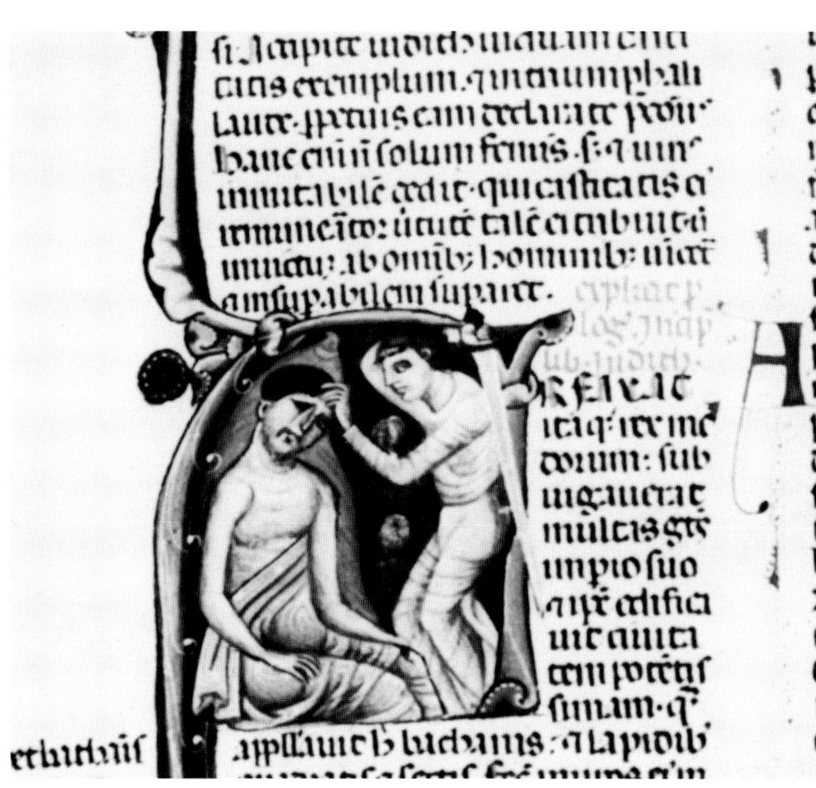

18. Judith Slays Holofernes, Judith, Bassetti Bible, third quarter of the thirteenth century, folio 474, detail
Biblioteca Comunale, Trento (MS. 2868)

In fact, beyond the most general perimeters, the diversity in the decoration of the Bibles of the Conradin Bible atelier calls into question our ability to arrange the production of this atelier chronologically as I, for one, have done in the past.[44] We should recall that the Vatican Bible has figures that resemble both the fully developed Byzantinizing types of the Conradin Bible and the long-haired types found in the Palermo Bible and the manuscripts of the Manfred Bible atelier. Indeed, each Bible seems to have a distinctive character based in part on choices made from a general repertoire. In some cases, such as the Paris Bible, the repertoire includes distinctly French motifs such as diapered grounds; in others, such as the Conradin and the Bodleian Bibles, it includes cusping around the decorative areas (figs. 6, 9, 14, 19). Rather than reflecting the general evolution of a single master's style, these variations, at least in part, may have been due to the wishes of the patrons, who may have chosen a style becausc of its regional affiliation, either French or Byzantine, for example.[45]

Such observations regarding the relationship between the Vatican Bible and the other manuscripts produced in the same atelier lead us to consider another aspect of shop organization: the use of model books or motif books as a means of preserving consistent motifs within the shop itself, and especially as a means of maintaining an elaborate repertoire of figures and decorative motifs.[46] We have already seen very specific similarities between the ornamentation of the Vatican and the Palermo Bibles. Particularly striking is the reuse in the Vatican Bible in half-length form of figures found in full-length in the Conradin Bible, although not in the same locations (figs. 9, 12–14). Similar repetitions occur in the Paris and the Trento Bibles.[47] Such repetitions argue for the use of what we have called, for lack of a better term, *motif books,* most likely loose sheets of individual figure and ornamental motifs. Indeed, there is good evidence throughout the Conradin Bible itself of a practice of taking individual figures from one context—for instance, Byzantine—and using them in a different setting. This suggests that the artists of the Conradin Bible atelier were not thinking in terms of full Byzantine iconographic models

dimittas iniquitatem hanc. Quibus auditis:
flevit ioseph. Veneruntque ad eum fratres
sui; et proni in terram adoraverunt et dixerunt.
Servi tui sumus. Quibus ille respondit. No
lite timere. Num dei possumus resistere
voluntati? Vos cogitastis de me malum.
et deus vertit illud in bonum: ut exal
taret me sicut in presentiarum cernitis:
et salvos faceret multos populos. Noli
te metuere. Ego pascam vos et par
vulos vestros. Consolatusque est eos: et
blande ac leniter est locutus. Et habitavit in e
gipto cum omni domo patris sui. vi
xitque centum decem annis: quibus vidit ef
fraim filios usque ad tertiam generationem.
Filii quoque machir filii manasse na
ti sunt in genibus ioseph. Quibus transac
tis: locutus est fratribus suis. Post mortem
meam deus visitabit vos. et ascendere fa
ciet de terra ista ad terram quam iuravit
abraham ysaac et iacob. Cumque ad
iurasset eos atque dixisset. deus visitabit
vos. asportate vobiscum ossa mea de
loco isto. Mortuus est expletis centum
decem vite sue annis: et conditus aro
matibus repositus est in loculo in egipto.

Explicit liber genesis. Incipit liber exodus

ellesmoth: id est

A.

HEC SVNT
nomina
filiorum
israel qui
ingressi
sunt in e
gyptum
cum ia
cob singuli cum
domibus
suis in
troierunt. Ruben symeon. levi. iudas
ysachar. zabulon. beniamin. dan. et
neptalim: gad. et aser. Erant igitur
omnes anime eorum. qui egressi sunt
de femore iacob: lxx. Ioseph autem erat
in egipto. Quo mortuo. et universis fra
tribus eius omnique cognatione illa: fi
lii israel creverunt. et quasi germinantes mul
tiplicati sunt. ac roborati nimis impleverunt
terram. Surrexit interea rex novus super

B.

egiptum qui ignorabat ioseph: et
ait ad populum suum. Ecce populus filiorum
israel. multus et fortior nobis est. Veni
te sapienter opprimamus eum: ne for
te multiplicetur. Et si ingruerit con
tra nos bellum. addatur inimicis nostris. et
expugnatisque nobis. egrediatur de ter
ra. Preposuit itaque eis magistros ope
rum. ut affligerent eos oneribus. Edifi
caveruntque urbes tabernaculorum pha
raoni: phytom et ramesses. Quantoque
opprimebant eos: tanto magis multi
plicabantur et crescebant. Oderantque
filios israel egiptii: et affligebant illuden
tes eis: atque ad amaritudinem perdu
cebant vitam eorum operibus duris lu
ti et lateris. omnique famulatu. quo in
terre operibus premebantur. Dixit autem rex
egipti obstetricibus hebreorum. quarum
una vocabatur sephora. altera phua.
precipiens eis. Quando obstetricabitis
hebreas. et partus tempus advenerit: si
masculus fuerit interficite illum: si fe
mina reservate. Timuerunt autem obstetri
ces deum: et non fecerunt iuxta preceptum regis
egipti: sed conservabant mares. Quibus ad
se accersitis: rex ait. Quid nam est hoc
quod facere voluistis: ut pueros servare
tis? Que responderunt. Non sunt hebree.
sicut egiptie mulieres. Ipse enim obste
tricandi habent scientiam: et priusquam ve
niamus ad eas pariunt. Bene ergo fecit
deus obstetricibus: Et crevit populus. et confor
tatusque est nimis. Et quia timuerunt ob
stetrices deum: edificavit illis domos.
Precepit ergo pharao omni populo suo:
dicens. Quicquid masculini sexus na
tum fuerit. in flumen proicite: quicquid
feminini. reservate.

II

Egressus est post hec vir de domo levi.
et accepit uxorem stirpis sue. que conce
pit et peperit filium. Et videns eum ele
gantem: abscondit tribus mensibus. Cumque
iam celare non posset: sumpsit fiscel
lam scirpeam. et linivit eam bitumi
ne. ac pice: posuitque intus infantulum:
et exposuit eum in carecto ripe flumi
nis: stante procul sorore eius. et conside
rante eventum rei. Ecce autem descendebat fi

19. Moses Naming the Children of Israel, Exodus, Bible, third quarter of the thirteenth century, folio 24v Bibliothèque Ste-Geneviève, Paris (Ms. 14); photograph: Jean-Loup Charmet

but in terms of motifs, isolated figures in some cases, which could be moved from one context to another. And this in turn implies that the artists had collected and had available an assortment of images from a variety of sources in a motif repertoire. Certainly it is difficult for us to imagine artists leafing through numerous Byzantine manuscripts to copy out different figures in preparation for each of the projects that they worked on. Moreover, the detailed repetition of individual lines and drapery folds rather than general types argues against the proposal that artists worked from memorized figures alone.

One further aspect of this problem merits mention here. The figures we have been looking at are among an array of Byzantine types that find their closest parallels in the Monreale mosaics. Indeed, as Daneu Lattanzi observed long ago, there is a stylistic correspondence between these mosaics and the Conradin Bible figures.[48] Of particular interest is the fact that the figures in the Conradin Bible find their closest parallels not in the single figures of the apse mosaics but in individual figures in the narrative scenes at Monreale.[49] This and other factors argue strongly that the artists of the Conradin Bible atelier were familiar, not necessarily with the mosaics themselves, but with works related to them, most specifically, the motif repertoire that Ernst Kitzinger proposed in his reconstruction of the working method of the Monreale mosaicists.[50] Also meriting further study is the relationship between the mosaics, the Conradin Bible atelier, and the so-called Freiburg Leaf, associated by some scholars with the Hohenstaufen court.[51]

With some remarks regarding the working methods of the artists of this atelier and their sources in place, what can we say about the localization of this atelier? The Conradin Bible atelier seems different in a significant way from the atelier that produced the Manfred Bible and the *Baths of Pozzuoli*. Both shops produced luxury one-volume Bibles, but the personal royal commissions such as the *Baths of Pozzuoli* are missing from the known list of manuscripts from the Conradin Bible atelier, and liturgical manuscripts have been added. Yet some of the commissions received by the Conradin Bible atelier were important ones. The Boniface of Verona manuscript was intended for one of the most powerful men in the Church. We can only speculate as to why the atelier was given this commission. Toubert has suggested that the master of the Conradin Bible atelier spent time in Rome, and while it is possible, it may not have been necessary for this master to have been in Rome to receive such a commission.[52] Ottaviano had been in Naples in the 1250s, when the cardinals met to elect the new pope following the death of Innocent IV there in 1254.[53] While our atelier does not appear to go back that far, Ottaviano might have encountered some of the artists at that time. But the manuscript could have been given to Ottaviano as a gift at a later date, and both Hohenstaufen and Angevin rulers are likely donors. Ottaviano came from a famous Tuscan family that had traditionally supported the imperial cause. His personal Ghibelline connections have been the source of controversy since his own lifetime, when he was accused, among other things, of being too friendly with Manfred during the failed siege of Lucera in 1255.[54] At the same time, during the 1260s, the Angevin rulers of Naples found it necessary to cultivate the cardinal whom many historians have considered the shadow pope of this period. Finally, it is entirely possible that this manuscript was a gift from another South Italian cleric, such as the archbishop of Naples.

The story of the al-Hāwī medical manuscripts also argues that this was a prominent atelier, for, according to the extant documentation, the artist who carried out this project for Charles of Anjou was considered one of the two most appropriate masters in Naples for a royal commission.[55]

Finally, the so-called Conradin Bible itself was certainly an expensive manuscript, for the documents describing the commission of the al-Hāwī manuscripts show that patrons paid for each ornamental motif according to its size and that the use of gold added to the cost. We can only imagine the price of a manuscript with scenes and figures replacing foliated tails and the extravagant use of gold dots seen in the Conradin Bible. Moreover, the Byzantinizing figures in the Conradin Bible, which include a representation of Paul for the Epistle to the Hebrews copied from the image of Luke in the eleventh-century Byzantine Gospel (Vat. gr. 756), are evidence that the painters had access to a fine collection of Greek manuscripts.[56] We should also consider the suggestion that the artists of the Conradin Bible atelier were working with motif books originally devised for the execution of the Monreale mosaics. If such model books had survived to the second half of the thirteenth century, they would most likely have been in royal hands. One conclusion of such speculation would be that the commission for the Conradin Bible, at least, was made close to the Hohenstaufen court.[57]

Where was this atelier and how did it function? Scholars have noted that most thirteenth-century manuscript ateliers were located in urban settings, close to universities. The similarities between the Manfred Bible manuscript group and the Conradin Bible manuscript group indicate that these two ateliers may have been in the same center, and Toubert, Mario Rotili, and Claus M. Kauffmann have all suggested that the Manfred Bible group was executed by an atelier in Naples.[58] There are good reasons to argue that the Conradin Bible manuscript atelier was also based in Naples: the presence of at least one member of the atelier in Naples in 1282, the Franciscan and the Augustinian antiphonaries (Naples had both orders before 1260), and the association of both the Bodleian and the Vatican Bibles with Naples by 1600.[59] Still it is possible that both groups of artists worked earlier at Foggia or another South Italian center such as Messina and moved on to Naples after Manfred's defeat and death in 1266.[60]

Wherever they were based, it would be a considerable stretch to call the Conradin Bible master and his assistants a court atelier. While we do not need to characterize the leading master of the atelier as an itinerant artist, it seems most prudent to suggest that this was an independent atelier in an urban setting, working at times for members of the court or other wealthy clients. We should also keep open the possibility that the atelier was connected formally or informally to the archbishop of Naples, a theory suggested by the documents associated with the al-Hāwī commission. Since there is every indication that this master and his atelier continued to work after Manfred's death, they may have worked for members of the Angevin court as well. This would describe a situation akin to the arrangement that had evolved in Paris and Bologna, where independent professional ateliers worked side by side taking commissions.[61] Certainly by 1282, the phrase "court atelier" seems a misnomer, for Charles of Anjou had to recruit both artists and scribes for the al-Hāwī project. Not only was the painter of the al-Hāwī manuscripts not a member of a court atelier, but there seems to have been no court atelier at work for Charles at all. We are thus left with questions. Was it unusual for an artist such as the master of the Conradin Bible to work independently, or is this an indication of the way commissions were handled in southern Italy in the thirteenth century? Should we infer from our information on the Conradin Bible atelier that other South Italian ateliers, such as the one that produced the Manfred Bible, worked in the same manner? Indeed, has the case for court ateliers been overdrawn and inflated by scholars?[62]

NOTES

1. Florentine Mütherich, "Handschriften im Umkreis Friedrichs II.," in *Probleme um Friedrich II.*, Studien und Quellen zur Welt Kaiser Friedrichs II., 4, ed. J. Fleckenstein (Sigmaringen, 1974), 9–21. This paper is based on my dissertation and subsequent research carried out in preparation for a book on the Conradin Bible. (I am grateful for the recent support of the Roger Schmutz Faculty Grant program of Bates College, which provided me with time in England to work on the Colchester Antiphonary, and a fellowship from the National Endowment for the Humanities that provided an essential year in Italy in 1987–1988.) Rebecca W. Corrie, "The Conradin Bible, MS. 152, the Walters Art Gallery: Manuscript Illumination in a Thirteenth-Century Italian Atelier," doctoral dissertation, Harvard University, 1986 (hereafter Corrie diss.). Brief portions of this material have been published in Rebecca W. Corrie, "The Conradin Bible: Since 'Since de Ricci,'" *Journal of the Walters Art Gallery* 40 (1982), 13–24, and in a paper I delivered in 1981: "The Conradin Bible: East Meets West at Messina," in Vladimir P. Goss and Christine V. Bornstein, eds., *The Meeting of Two Worlds: Cultural Exchange between East and West during the Period of the Crusades* (Kalamazoo, Mich., 1986), 295–307, figs. 41–47. I wish to acknowledge my particular indebtedness to Michael Norris and to Jonathan Alexander who, respectively, generously brought the Bible, Vat. lat. 4195, and the Colchester Antiphonary to my attention; to Ernst Kitzinger and Paul Meyvaert for their patient guidance on my dissertation.

2. Helpful insights regarding these problems are provided by Giulia Orofino, "Il rapporto con l'antico e l'osservazione della natura nell'illustrazione scientifica di età sveva in Italia meridionale," in this volume. See also "Handschriften aus dem Umkreis Friedrichs II.," in *Die Zeit der Staufer: Geschichte—Kunst—Kultur* [exh. cat., Württembergisches Landesmuseum], ed. Reiner Haussherr, 6 vols. (Stuttgart, 1977–1979), 1:645–663.

3. For examples see N. Bux, *I codici liturgici miniati dell'archivio di S. Nicola* (Bari, 1983).

4. Bernhard Degenhart and Annegrit Schmitt, "Frühe angiovinische Buchkunst in Neapel: Die Illustrierung französischer Unterhaltungsprosa in neapolitanischen Scriptorien zwischen 1290–1320," in *Festschrift Wolfgang Braunfels* (Tübingen, 1977), 71–92.

5. A fascinating discussion of this text can be found in Cornelia C. Coulter, "The Library of the Angevin Kings at Naples," *Transactions and Proceedings of the American Philological Association* 75 (1944), 141–155.

6. Steven Runciman, *The Sicilian Vespers* (Cambridge, 1958), offers a brief history of the period, as does Denis Mack Smith, *A History of Sicily: Medieval Sicily 800–1713* (New York, 1968.) A more recent review can be found in David Abulafia, *Frederick II: A Medieval Emperor* (London, 1988), 408–422. There are numerous sources on Manfred, including Helene Arndt, *Studien zur inneren Regierungsgeschichte Manfreds* (Heidelberg, 1911), and Raffaello Morghen, "L'età degli Svevi in Italia," in Pier Fausto Palumbo, *Contributi alla storia dell'età di Manfredi* (Rome, 1959). For a thorough recent bibliography on Manfred's policies, see Kenneth M. Setton, *The Papacy and the Levant (1204–1571)* (Philadelphia, 1976), 1:81–84.

7. On the Manfred Bible see Adalbert, Graf zu Erbach-Furstenau, *Die Manfredbibel* (Leipzig, 1910); Hélène Toubert, "Trois nouvelles Bibles du maître de la Bible de Manfred et son atelier," *Mélanges de l'École Française de Rome* 89 (1977), 777–810; and Hélène Toubert, "Influences gothiques sur l'art frédéricien: Le maître de la Bible de Manfred et son atelier," in *Federico II e l'arte del Duecento italiano*, ed. Angiola M. Romanini, 2 vols. (Galatina, 1980), 2:59–83.

8. In addition to the sources cited above, see Angela Daneu Lattanzi, "Ancora sulla scuola miniaturistica dell'Italia meridionale sveva," *La bibliofilia* 66 (1964), 105–162, and *Lineamenti di storia della miniatura in Sicilia* (Florence, 1966), 53–58; Carl Willemsen and others, "Handschriften aus dem Umkreis Friedrichs II.," in *Die Zeit der Staufer*, 1:645–663; Silvana Pettinati, "Un altra 'Bibbia di Manfredi,'" *Prospettiva* 4 (1976), 7–15; Claus Michael Kauffmann, *The Baths of Pozzuoli: A Study of the Medieval Illuminations of Peter of Eboli's Poem* (Oxford, 1959); Angela Daneu Lattanzi, *Petrus de Ebulo. Nomina et Virtutes Balneorum seu de Balneis Puteolorum et Baiarum, Codice Angelico 1474*, facsimile (Rome, 1962); Carl Willemsen, *Fredericus II, De arte venandi cum avibus*, facsimile (Graz, 1969).

9. The provenance of the Conradin Bible recounted in Seymour de Ricci, *Census of Medieval and Renaissance Manuscripts in the United States and Canada* (New York, 1935), 1:764. The literature on the Conradin Bible is vast. Important nineteenth-century publications include Auguste, comte de Bastard d'Estang, *Peintures et ornaments des manuscrits, classés dans un ordre chronologique, pour servir à l'histoire des arts du dessin, depuis le quatrième siècle de l'ère chrétienne jusqu'à la fin du seizième* (Paris, 1837–1846); Léopold V. Delisle, *Les collections de Bastard d'Estang à la Bibliothèque Nationale, catalogue analytique* (Nogent-le-Rotrou, 1885), 263 and 276; Auguste, Émile Louis Marie Molinier, and Léopold Delisle, *La collection Spitzer* (Paris, 1892), 5:124–126, 141–143. Recent important publications include Daneu Lattanzi 1964 and 1966, 58–61; Hélène Toubert, "Autour de la Bible de Conradin: Trois nouveaux manuscrits enluminés," *Mélanges de l'École Française de Rome* 91 (1979), 729–784. Further sources are cited in notes below. The story of Conradin has never ceased to fascinate scholars and the public alike. Among the many sources on Conradin are Ferdinand Geldner, *Konradin: Das Opfer eines grossen Traumes: Grösse, Schuld, und Tragik der Hohenstaufen* (Bamberg, 1970); Raouel Manselli, "Corradino di Svevia e Roma," *Studi romani* 15.3 (1968), 280–285; R. M. Kloos, "Petrus de Prece und Konradin," *Quellen und Forschungen aus italienischen Archiven und Bibliotheken* 34 (1954),

88–108; Karl Hampe, *Geschichte Konradins von Hohenstaufen* (Leipzig, 1940); E. Müller, *Peter von Prezza, ein Publizist der Zeit des Interregnums* (Heidelberg, 1913). On the historiography of Conradin see Klaus Schreiner, "Die Staufer in Sage, Legende und Prophetie"; Aarno Borst, "Die Staufer in der Geschichtsschreibung"; Walter Migge, "Die Staufer in der deutschen Literatur seit dem 18. Jahrhundert"; Kurt Löcher, "Die Staufer in der bildenden Kunst," all in *Die Zeit der Staufer,* 3:249–262, 263–274, 275–286, 291–309, among other essays.

10. Robert Branner, *Manuscript Painting in Paris during the Reign of Saint Louis: A Study of Styles* (Berkeley, Calif., 1977) and Christopher de Hamel, *A History of Illuminated Manuscripts* (Oxford, 1986), 107–135.

11. That such a colophon might have existed and been subsequently lost would be no surprise, for the manuscript today is not complete. Instead it is the large, mutilated, remaining portion of a one-volume Bible. For descriptions of the Bible see Corrie 1982 and Corrie diss. Both describe the fragments sold at auction at Sotheby's in 1981 and the history of the Bible's mutilation. Through the efforts of Michael Ward of New York and Lilian Randall of the Walters Art Gallery and the generosity of J. Paul Getty II, most of these fragments have been reunited with the Bible in the Walters collection. Because the fragments had just come on the market and were rapidly changing hands when I wrote about them, descriptions of a few of the fragments in "Since 'Since de Ricci'" and my dissertation are not accurate. The illumination for Psalm 80 (Corrie 1982, fig. 2; Corrie diss., fig. 30) did not go to Michael Ward or the Walters, but is instead in private hands in Europe. Corrie 1982, fig. 3 is an illumination from Psalm 38 now in the Walters, while a similar illumination identified as Psalm 38 but actually 1 Kings and given to the Walters Art Gallery in Corrie diss., fig. 27, is also in a private collection in Europe. See Sotheby, Parke Bernet & Co., *Catalogue of Illuminated Manuscripts and Single Leaves from the Ninth to the Sixteenth Century,* 14 July 1981, 10–14.

12. The attributions vary. See Roberto Longhi, "Apertura sui Trecentisti Umbri," *Paragone* 191 (1966), 3–7, and "Postilla all'apertura sugli umbri," *Paragone* 195 (1966), 3–8, to Umbria; Ilaria Toesca, "Qualche foglio del Maestro 'di Corradino,'" *Paragone* 235 (1969), 68–72, to Pisa; Antonio Caleca, "Un codice pisano di fine Duecento," in *La miniatura italiana in età romanica e gotica,* Atti del I congresso di storia della miniatura italiana, Cortona, 26–28 maggio 1978 (Florence, 1979), 207–221, to Pisa; and Dorothy Miner, *Illuminated Books of the Middle Ages and Renaissance* (Baltimore, 1949), 16, to the Veneto. By and large such comparisons have been unsuccessful, for they are based on very general comparisons between the Conradin Bible and many works similarly based on Byzantine models. Dependent for the most part on facial types, these comparisons do not take into account body types, nor do they consider the ornamental repertoire of the atelier as a whole. Most importantly these localizations have been overturned by the provenances of newly identified manuscripts discussed below.

13. Daneu Lattanzi 1964. The Bassetti Bible has an ample bibliography. The most recent publication on the Bible provides a thorough bibliography and review of the literature; see Marina Bernasconi and Lorena dal Poz, *Codici miniati della Biblioteca Comunale di Trento* (Florence, 1985), 69–120.

14. Toubert 1979. Charles Köhler, *Catalogue des manuscrits de la Bibliothèque Sainte-Geneviève* (Paris, 1893), 1:15–17. The Bodleian Bible was first published with an illustration in Otto Pächt and Jonathan Alexander, *Illuminated Manuscripts in the Bodleian Library, Oxford* (Oxford, 1970), 2:10. On the Palermo Bible see Angela Daneu Lattanzi, *Una bibbia prossima alla bibbia di Manfredi* (Palermo, 1957), and *I manoscritti ed incunaboli miniati della Sicilia: I Biblioteca Nazionale,* I manoscritti miniati delle biblioteche italiane 2 (Rome, 1965), 49–58.

15. Caleca 1979. The fragments are now dispersed among a private collection, the Musée Marmottan in Paris, the Fondazione Cini in Venice, and the Saint Louis City Museum. Most were first published by Ilaria Toesca (Toesca 1969). See also Pietro Toesca, *Miniature di una collezione veneziana* (Venice, 1958), no. LXXVII, and Dorothy Miner, "Since de Ricci—Western Illuminated Manuscripts Acquired since 1934," *Journal of the Walters Art Gallery* 32 (1969), 87–92. The Pisa Antiphonary is a fragment, missing sections that would be filled by the texts associated with the known fragments. Similarly a number of the fragments and many of the illuminations in the Pisa Antiphonary are extensively rubbed. These factors suggest that the fragments came from the Antiphonary now in Pisa.

16. Corrie 1982. This antiphonary was first published in Neil R. Ker, *Medieval Manuscripts in British Libraries* (Oxford, 1977), 2:408. Ker's notation does not identify the manuscript as part of the Conradin Bible group. I am grateful to Jonathan Alexander for bringing the manuscript to my attention.

17. This antiphonary in two volumes merits study on its own. It is decorated in a Tuscan variation of the Bolognese style of around 1300. Additional information can be found in Paolo Ferrini, *Volterra* (Volterra, 1978), 31. I am indebted to Franco Lessi for assistance during my visit to Volterra. Caleca 1979, 208 and *Momenti dell'arte a Volterra,* Volterra, Palazzo Minucci Solaini, agosto-settembre 1981 (Pisa, 1981), 20–21. The attribution to the Conradin Bible atelier was originally made by Carlo Ragghianti in Mellini, *L'arte in Italia* (Milan, 1969), 2:872 and 875–876.

18. Toubert 1979, 780–783; Angela Daneu Lattanzi, "Una 'Bella Copia' di al-Hāwī tradotto dall'arabo da faraq Moyse per Carlo I d'Angio (MS. Vat. lat. 2398–2399)," *Miscellanea di studi in memoria di Anna Saitta Revignas,* Biblioteca di bibliografia italiana 86 (Florence, 1978), 149–169.

19. Toubert 1979, 784. I must apologize here to Hélène Toubert, for in a previous paper (1982) I misstated her position on the localization of the production of the

Conradin Bible as Rome. In her 1979 article Toubert localized a stage of the career of the Master of the Conradin Bible in Rome. In fact she clearly stated that on the basis of the Bodleian Bible's colophon we can place the bulk of his career in the South. It is important to underline our agreement on this major issue, although on smaller points such as her attribution of a fresco in the church of the Quattro Coronati in Rome to our master, which I question, we have some small differences. For Mütherich see *Die Zeit der Staufer*, 1:662–663. For recent opinions see Pierluigi Leone de Castris, *Arte di Corte nella Napoli Angioina* (Florence, 1986), 104–105, 110, who attributes the manuscript to Sicily around 1260, and Bernasconi and dal Poz 1985, 75–76, who accept the South Italian origins of the Conradin Bible style but suggest that we may be looking at an itinerant painter. Among the recent scholars writing about the Conradin Bible, one has repeated the Umbrian association. See Luiz C. Marques, *La peinture du Duecento en italie centrale* (Paris, 1987), 140, 169, 247–248. Undoubtedly there are general similarities in the facial types used in the Conradin Bible and in many Umbrian and Tuscan panel paintings. However, these can be attributed to the pervasive imitation of Byzantine art in thirteenth-century Italy.

20. Daneu Lattanzi 1966, 58–61.

21. Daneu Lattanzi 1957, pls. 1 and 3, and Pettinati 1976, figs. 2, 5–8.

22. Examples of this type from the Manfred Bible group are illustrated in Daneu Lattanzi 1957, pl. 3 and Pettinati 1976, fig. 12. Convincing comparisons include the depiction of King David with the Amalekite from 2 Kings in the Palermo Bible, fol. 104r, which is a simpler version of a depiction of the same scene in Paris, Bib. Nat., MS. lat. 10428, produced in the Manfred Bible atelier and illustrated in Toubert 1980, fig. 13.

23. Toubert 1979, 776. See also Otto Pächt and J. J. G. Alexander, *Illuminated Manuscripts in the Bodleian Library at Oxford, Italian School* (Oxford, 1970), 10. Although Pächt and Alexander mention the Auria of Lucera crest and suggest a South Italian origin for the manuscript, they do not associate it with the Conradin Bible. This is probably because the manuscript has only one figured initial. Nevertheless, Toubert's attribution is utterly convincing.

24. MS. Vat. lat. 4195 is included in *Inventorium Librorum Latinorum MSS. Bib. Vat. Tomus Quintus. Inventorio Florio*, 1613. This is a medium-sized, one-volume Bible, which begins with chap. 23 of Deuteronomy on fol. 1r and finishes on fol. 439v with the Interpretation of Hebrew names. Folios measure 9 x 6¹/₄ inches. The manuscript is divided into quires of twelve folios or six bifolios, each closing with a catch word at the bottom of the final side. Each book of the Bible opens with a foliate or an historiated initial. Although the manuscript is generally in good condition, the illuminations are uniformly darkened and discolored, which suggests that they may have been varnished at some point and accounts for the darkness of the photographs reproduced here. For a full codicological description of the other manuscripts in the Conradin Bible group, see Corrie diss., 536–544.

25. Erbach-Fürstenau 1910, 1 Kings and the Epistle of James, fols. 61r and 466v, pl. XII.

26. The best example of the long-haired, short-skirted type in the Palermo Bible is illustrated in Daneu Lattanzi 1957, pl. 3.

27. Erbach-Fürstenau 1910, pl. X and Daneu Lattanzi 1964, fig. 4 illustrate the Gospel of John, which has at the base of its ornamentation paired birds with similar long, waving tails.

28. Jeanne Bignami Odier, *La Bibliothèque vaticane de Sixte IV à Pie XI: Recherches sur l'histoire des collections de manuscrits, avec la collaboration de José Ruysschaert*, Studi e testi 272 (Vatican City, 1973), 82, 97, note 105.

29. Willibrordo van Heteren, "Breve discorso sopra l'aiuto spirituale e ridottione grecia (dal P.J.D. Trajani S.J.)," *Bessarione* 7 (1902), 174–187. According to Van Heteren, Traiano entered the Jesuit order at Naples in 1555 at the age of fourteen and was educated in Naples as a humanist. He spent his career in southern Italy and Rome, working for the Church toward the union of the Greek and Latin churches. Apparently he was also at work for the Vatican Library by 1595; see Vittorio Peri, "Due protagonisti dell'editio romana dei concili ecumenici: Pietro Morin ed Antonio d'Aquino," *Mélanges Eugène Tisserant: Vol. VII, Bibliothèque Vaticane*, Studi e testi 237 (Vatican City, 1964), 146, 230, and Odier 1973, 117, note 12.

30. These manuscripts are the subject of a much more extensive article, which I am completing at this time for the *Journal of the Walters Art Gallery* (1993).

31. I am indebted to Jonathan Alexander for bringing this manuscript to my attention, and to D. T.-D. Clarke, curator of the Colchester and Essex Museum, for his generous help on my visits to Colchester. The provenance of the Colchester Antiphonary can be traced to the collection of Baron Alexander Peckover of Wisbech in the late nineteenth and early twentieth century. A description of it has recently been identified in an inventory of the collection. I am particularly grateful to Antony Penrose, Michael Sweeney, and Frances Thackway for their assistance in tracing this information. The manuscript consists of 255 fols.: 1r–204v form a sanctorale that begins in the office for the Feast of the Purification and ends with Saint Clement; 205r–255v is the common of saints. The notation is written on black lines with filigree initials for the major feasts of the year and painted historiated initials for the responses of only eight double feasts.

32. Faces are reproduced with comparisons in Corrie 1982, figs. 6 and 16, and Corrie 1986, figs. 42 and 43. The ornamental style of both antiphonaries is less flamboyant than that of the Bibles. Missing are nude figures, dragons, animal and foliate forms, other than the simplest leaves. This may well reflect rulings from the Franciscans, such as that at Narbonne forbidding "curiosities" in ornamentation. See Maria

Grazie Ciardi Duprè dal Poggetto, "La nascita dei cicli corali umbri," *Francesco d'Assisi: Documenti e archivi codici e biblioteche miniature* (Milan, 1982), 331.

33. Stephen J. P. van Dijk and Joan Hazelden Walker, *The Origins of the Modern Roman Liturgy: The Liturgy of the Papal Court and the Franciscan Order in the Thirteenth Century* (London, 1960), 280–320. The basic source on Haymo's rubrics is Stephen J. P. van Dijk, *Sources of the Modern Roman Liturgy: The Ordinals of Haymo of Faversham and Related Documents* (1243–1307), 2 vols. (Leiden, 1963). The details of the rubrics of the Colchester Antiphonary indicate that this may well be the earliest post-Haymo antiphonary extant. Dal Poggetto 1982, 338, argues that five codices in Cortona were the first official choral manuscripts produced after the reformations of Narbonne in 1260. But our manuscript does not seem to be dependent on a particular official Umbrian model for the antiphonary. Instead, the oddities we see indicate that our antiphonary may have been assembled from earlier antiphonaries such as S. Rufino MS. 5 in Assisi and breviaries produced after 1260.

34. Saint Bonaventura apparently altered the text of the antiphon "Hic vir in vanitatibus" because he found it offensive. See *Analecta Franciscana sive chronica aliaque varia documenta ad historiam fratrum minorum spectantia edita a patribus collegii S. Bonaventurae adiuvantibus aliis eruditis viris* (Florence, 1926–1941), 10:379.

35. Missing from the codex are the rubrics that normally precede the feasts of the Annunciation and the Nativity. Van Dijk and Walker 1960, 373–375. Van Dijk notes that Haymo's rubric on the octave of the Nativity was not included in the ordinal of the papal court until the reign of Clement IV, 1265–1268. We cannot be sure that the omission of this rubric from the Colchester Antiphonary is related to the same omission from the papal ordinal. However, if it was, then we have rough dates for the Colchester Antiphonary between 1260 and 1268.

36. Two noted breviaries with similar dislocations can be found in the Vatican Library. See MS. Vat. lat. 12992, fols. 13r and 24v, for example, and MS. Reg. lat. 2050–2051, fols. 149v and 175v. A discussion of the development of notation can be found in Carl Parrish, *The Notation of Medieval Music* (New York, 1957), 109–141. See also Van Dijk and Walker 1960, 329–331.

37. Van Dijk and Walker 1960, 399–401, point out that the Augustinians were given permission to use the Franciscan liturgy in 1254. We have very little information on the Augustinian liturgy, as Van Dijk notes. To my knowledge, the feast of Saint Augustine that appears here at the feast for the Translation of Saint Augustine (fol. 9r) has never been fully edited by modern scholars. Indeed, it perplexed Van Dijk when he encountered it in a Tuscan breviary, and he described it as local and unusual (1963, 2:158–159). In fact, it is a standard text that appears for several centuries in liturgical manuscripts intended for use by the Augustinians in centers across Italy, and may have been taken over from the Dominicans, for it occurs in two earlier thirteenth-century Dominican manuscripts. On the combination of Dominican and Franciscan usage, see P. C. L., "De liturgische Verorderingen OESA van de 13e Eeuw," *Nederlandse Analecta* 3 (1960), 71–75. Older sources such as Esteban, "De festis et ritibus sacris ordinis Eremitarum S.P. Augustini," *Analecta Augustiniana* 8 (1919), 111–136, are little help. Indeed, the best way to get a sense of the Augustinian liturgy is still to survey Augustinian breviaries. Careful reading of manuscripts such as Vatican MSS. Rossiana 112 (attributed to fourteenth-century Padua), Chigi D.V.68 (dated c. 1300 from southern Italy), and Ottobon. lat. 544 (from the fifteenth century) makes it clear that the Pisa Antiphonary conforms to Augustinian usage. These manuscripts are remarkably consistent in their use of rubrics made obsolete by Haymo's corrections, the same rubrics found in the Pisa Antiphonary. It seems likely then that the liturgy taken on by the Augustinians was a Franciscan pre-Haymo form. A more extensive report of my research on the liturgical sources of the Pisa Antiphonary is in preparation.

38. Van Dijk and Walker 1960, 339–340, 399–401. The decoration of both antiphonaries is restrained in comparison to the one-volume Bibles. Because they are liturgical manuscripts, neither contains the characteristically elaborate ornamental repertoire of dragons, birds, and gold.

39. The career of the powerful cardinal Ottaviano degli Ubaldini, a member of one of the most powerful Ghibelline families of Florence, is fascinating, for he maintained a careful balance between the needs of his family and his expected allegiance to the papal, Guelf side of the dispute between the Hohenstaufen family and the popes of his era. His loyalty to the papacy has been called into question many times. See Albert Hauss, *Kardinal Ottavian Ubaldini, ein Staatsmann des 13. Jahrhunderts*, Heidelberger Abhandlungen zur mittleren und neueren Geschichte, Heft 35 (Heidelberg, 1913); Pietro Santoni, *Il Cardinale Ottaviano degli Ubaldini: La pieve di Fagna e Dante* (Florence, 1960); Raffaello Morghen, *Il Tramonto della potenza sveva in Italia 1250–1266* (Rome and Milan, 1936); and Guido Levi, "Il cardinale Ottaviano degli Ubaldini secondo il suo carteggio ed altri documenti," *Archivio della R. Società Romana di Storia Patria* 14 (1891), 42. A number of sources are available on Boniface of Verona. See G. Arnaldi, "Bonifacio Veronese," *Dizionario biografico degli italiani* (Rome, 1970), 12:191–192; Clelia Maria Piastra, "Nota sull' 'Annayde' di Bonifacio Veronese," *Aevum* 28 (1954), 505–521 and "Nota sulla 'Veronica' di Bonifacio Veronese," *Aevum* 33 (1959), 356–381; and Conradum Eubel, *Hierarchia Catholica medii aevi sive summorum pontificum, s.r.e. cardinalium, ecclesiarum antistitum series ad anno 1198 usque ad annum 1431 perduta e documentis tabularii praesortium vaticani collecta, digesta, edita* (Regensburg, 1913), 7–8. On the manuscript itself and for illustrations, see Toubert 1979, 781–784, fig. 58; Elisabeth Pellegrin, *La Bibliothèque des Visconti et des Sforza, ducs de Milan au XV siècle, Supplément* (Florence,

1969), fig. 52; and François Avril and Marie-Thérèse Gouset, *Manuscrits enluminés d'origine italienne, 2, XIIIe siècle* (Paris, 1984).

40. Piastra 1954, 506–507.

41. Daneu Lattanzi, 1978 and Toubert 1979, 774. The fascinating tale of the commissioning of these manuscripts is recounted in Coulter 1944, 144–149. See also Paul Durrieu, "Un portrait de Charles Ier d'Anjou, roi de Sicile, frère de Saint Louis, peint à Naples en 1282 par le miniaturiste Jean moine du Mont-Cassin dans un manuscrit aujourd'hui à la Bibliothèque Nationale de Paris," *Gazette archéologique* 11 (1886), 192–201.

42. Daneu Lattanzi may well have identified the master of the Conradin Bible in her article on the al-Hāwī manuscripts. Despite the differences in scale of the ornamentation, the flat painting and the basic rhythm of the ornamentation are so much like that found not only in the Trento Bible, but also the Conradin Bible and even the Colchester Antiphonary, that we must consider the possibility that this individual, Giovanni da Montecassino, was the leading figure usually called the Master of the Conradin Bible. The difference in scale and figure style can easily be explained by the nearly ten years that appear to have elapsed between this project and the others that are extant, and by the influence of the French style that must have been imported by the Angevins. Moreover, we may be looking at the work of an older artist. Daneu Lattanzi equivocates in her published writings about this. But in conversation with me in 1978 she said that she believed she had found the name of the Master of the Conradin Bible, and there is a chance that she was right.

43. Pettinati 1976 and Toubert 1980.

44. One problem that I cannot discuss here has been addressed by most scholars, namely, the division of hands within the atelier and within individual manuscripts. To my mind, no fully successful breakdown of hands has been offered even for the Conradin Bible itself, which most writers agree is the work of several painters who can be distinguished at least in part by palette. Certainly it seems likely that we are looking at a leading master and his assistants, for as one goes through the manuscripts, changes in color, drapery painting, and the treatment of faces indicate a group of painters rather than a single artist. Yet the distinct facial types and the persistence of a somewhat eccentric and lively handling of ornamentation argue for a leading master. In terms of chronology such Morellian characteristics can be useful. The Conradin Bible, the Bodleian Bible, and the Colchester Antiphonary appear to come from the same period. However, the Vatican Bible brings together elements from all of these. The Trento Bible seems to be later than the other Bibles; the *Liber Annayde* is also problematic, but probably belongs to the period of the Paris Bible. The Palermo Bible appears to belong to the period of the Manfred Bible group around 1260 or slightly earlier, and the al-Hāwī manuscripts date from around 1281 to 1282. Although I am no longer entirely convinced of my conclusions, I do discuss these issues in my dissertation, 55–137, and provide reference to other scholars' observations.

45. I have broached the issue of the significance of national or regional styles in the eyes of thirteenth-century patrons in two papers. See "Shop Procedures and the Formulation of the *Maniera Greca*," Fourteenth Annual Byzantine Studies Conference, Houston, Texas, 10–13 Nov. 1988, and "The Atelier of the Conradin Bible and the Use of Byzantine Style in Thirteenth Century Italy," the Robert Branner Forum for Medieval Art, Ninth Annual Symposium, *Byzantine Art and the West*, Columbia University, 1 Apr. 1990.

46. Hélène Toubert has also suggested the use of motif repertoires in her articles on the Manfred Bible and Conradin Bible ateliers; see Toubert 1977 and 1979. The literature on the problem of motif and model books is large and growing. For discussions of motif repertoires see Ernst Kitzinger, "The Role of Miniature Painting in Mural Decoration," in *The Place of Book Illumination in Byzantine Art* (Princeton, 1975), 99–142, esp. 100–109; Larry Ayres, "Problems of Sources for the Iconography of the Lyre Drawings," *Speculum* 49 (1974), 61–68, and his doctoral dissertation, "Studies in the Winchester Bible," Harvard University, 1970; R. W. Scheller, *A Survey of Medieval Model Books* (Haarlem, 1963); Hugo Buchthal, *The "Musterbuch" of Wolfenbüttel and Its Position in the Art of the Thirteenth Century* (Vienna, 1979). For a more extensive treatment of the problem, see Corrie diss., 141–163. This will be one focus of my much longer study of the Conradin Bible.

47. Of particular interest is a figure discussed in Corrie 1986, figs. 46 and 47, which appears as Paul in the Epistle to the Hebrews in the Conradin Bible, fol. 125v. This figure, drawn directly from a Byzantine manuscript, Vat. gr. 756, fol. 11v, is repeated as a half-length figure in the Trento Bible as Paul in the Epistle to the Thessalonians, fol. 1106, and as Peter in the Paris Bible, fol. 526r.

48. Daneu Lattanzi 1966, 58–61. We should acknowledge, of course, that the influence of Monreale was pervasive in Italy especially in Rome and to the south in the thirteenth century. See, for example, John Mitchell, "St. Silvester and Constantine at the SS. Quattro Coronati," in *Federico II e l'arte del Duecento italiano*, 2:15–32. But close study of the Conradin Bible reveals an extensive repetition of Monreale motifs that surpasses any of the other examples.

49. Corrie diss., 138–162, 279–369, esp. 340–343.

50. Ernst Kitzinger, *The Mosaics of Monreale* (Palermo, 1960), 58–63.

51. I have discussed the use of Byzantine sources in the Conradin Bible atelier at greater length in my papers delivered in Washington in 1986 and in Houston in 1988. This issue will be a major focus in my forthcoming book on the Conradin Bible. On the Freiburg Leaf see Otto Homburger, "Das Freiburger Einzelblatt—Der Rest eines Musterbuches der Stauferzeit?" in Ingeborg Schroth, *Studien zur Kunst des Oberrheins: Festschrift für Werner Noack* (Freiburg and Constance, 1958), 17–23.

52. Toubert 1979, 782.

53. Hauss, 1913, 52–53.

54. Laura Magna, "Gli Ubaldini del Mugello: Una signoria feudale nel contado fiorentino," in Comitato di studi sulla storia dei ceti dirigenti in Toscana, *I ceti dirigenti dell'età comunale nei secoli XII e XIII*, Atti del II Convegno: Firenze, 14–15 decembre 1979 (Pisa, 1982), 41, note 117, 44–46. Magna recalls that Dante condemned Ottaviano as a heretic. About his relationship with Manfred in 1255, see in particular Morghen 1936, 175–176.

55. Durrieu 1886, Coulter 1944, and Daneu Lattanzi, 1978.

56. Corrie 1986, figs. 46 and 47. A colophon in this manuscript indicates that it was in the library of the monastery of San Salvatore in Lingua Phari in Messina, by 1294. See Robert Devreesse, ed., *Codices Vaticani Graeci* (Vatican City, 1950), 3:274. The Gospel may have been in Jerusalem in the twelfth century. See Hugo Buchthal, *Miniature Painting in the Latin Kingdom of Jerusalem* (Oxford, 1957), 26. There is also considerable evidence that the atelier or its leading master had access to a collection of northern European manuscripts or a related motif book. See, for example, Corrie 1986, figs. 44 and 45.

57. At this stage in the research on the Conradin Bible and the manuscripts associated with it, we should entertain the possibility that there once was a colophon in the manuscript that described the Bible as a gift to Conradin. This tradition is based on a note described by Léopold Delisle in two publications (Delisle 1885, 263, 276 and Molinier and Delisle 1892, 142). According to Delisle, the note claimed that the Bible had been made in Sicily for Conradin and sent to him in the North shortly before his execution in 1268. The addition of the Bodleian and Vatican Bibles and the Colchester Antiphonary and al-Ḥāwī Medical Encyclopedia to the manuscript group localizes the production of the manuscript to southern Italy in the third quarter of the thirteenth century. This means that the nineteenth-century localization was accurate. It is difficult to imagine that nineteenth-century scholars or collectors, on the basis of prestige or sentiment, were able to guess the origin of the Bible so accurately, since in the nineteenth century scholarship tended to date Italian manuscripts, including the Bassetti Bible, about a century late. While it is judicious to avoid "over-concluding" on the basis of the evidence we have, it would also be remiss to deny the possibility that so eminent a scholar as Delisle was correct, for the sake of skepticism alone.

58. Toubert 1977, 808–810; Mario Rotili, *La miniatura gotica in Italia* (Naples, 1968), 1; and Kauffmann 1959, 31. Toubert's description of the Manfred Bible atelier here is very much like the one that I am proposing for the atelier of the Conradin Bible.

59. On the presence of the Franciscans in Naples, see P. Gioacchino D'Andrea, *I Frati minori napoletani nel loro sviluppo storico* (Naples, 1967), 68, 69, 72, 73; Jürgen Krüger, *S. Lorenzo Maggiore in Neapel: Eine Franziskanerkirche zwischen Ordensideal und Herrschaftsarchitektur. Studien und Materialien zur Baukunst der ersten Anjou-Zeit*, Franziskanerische Forschungen 31 (Werl/Westphalia, 1985), 34, 36. On the Augustinians see S. Lopez, "De conventu S. Augustini neapolitano documenta et notitiae," *Analecta Augustiniana* 12 (1927–1928), 128–146.

60. Despite the problems between the Church and the Hohenstaufen house, the Franciscans and Augustinians were established at Foggia and Messina early in the thirteenth century. See Emilio Benevenuto, "Chiese e conventi francescani a Foggia," *Miscellanea Francescana* 64 (1964), 150–152. For a number of reasons, I originally attributed the Conradin Bible to Messina in a paper delivered in 1981 and published in 1986; see Corrie 1986 and Corrie diss., 465–470. As I noted in my dissertation (chap. 6), good arguments can also be made for Foggia and Naples, however, and caution in localizing this atelier to a particular city seems wise. Still, it is interesting to note that Leone de Castris (1986, 105) localizes the group in "Sicily," citing cities such as Messina.

61. See de Hamel 1986, 107–135; Branner 1977.

62. The assumption that South Italian rulers maintained scriptoria and manuscript ateliers whose activities were determined by court taste colors the work of both historians and art historians. It appears in the most general texts and in detailed studies. In his survey of medieval art, James Snyder wrote of Frederick II that he "gathered poets, philosophers, scientists, and artists about him to generate his Roman empire." See *Medieval Art: Painting, Sculpture, Architecture, 4th—14th Century* (New York, 1989), 445; also Thomas Curtis Van Cleve, *The Emperor Frederick II of Hohenstaufen: Immutator Mundi* (Oxford, 1972), 333, 346. Van Cleve even suggests that Frederick himself was an artist, referring to his "artistic skill" evident in the *Art of Hunting with Birds* (333).

But scrutiny of artistic production in the thirteenth-century South is not sufficient to substantiate this assumption and suggests that this impression arises in part from comparison with later and more northerly examples. In the case of northern Europe, art historians suggest that court interest in regularly patronizing luxury book production emerged in the middle of the thirteenth century. Nigel Morgan proposed that artists were patronized by the English court, possibly in imitation of the French court, in the second half of the thirteenth century. See *Early Gothic Manuscripts [1] 1190–1250* (London, 1982), 13. He argues that there may have been a Court School producing Apocalypses in London. See *Early Gothic Manuscripts [2] 1250–1285* (London, 1988), 23. But so far as we know, artists did not achieve positions in the entourages of rulers until later. Our uncertainty disappears with the early fourteenth century, when artists were included in the household rolls of Angevin Naples. See Andrew Martindale, *The Rise of the Artist in the Middle Ages and the Early Renaissance* (New York, 1972), 35–63. Our perception of the shop organization of artists in the thirteenth century is probably influenced by descriptions of fourteenth-century art patronage such as those in *Transformations of the Court Style: Gothic Art in Europe 1270 to*

1330 (Providence, R.I., 1977) and Lucy Freeman Sandler, *Gothic Manuscripts 1285–1385* (London, 1986), 24–25.

Although only a few scholars have addressed the issue directly, an assumption of similar court involvement in southern Italy pervades the discussion of manuscripts associated with Manfred, in part because of their elaborate decoration and the association of the so-called Manfred Bible and the *Art of Hunting with Birds* with Manfred. Although most scholars are inclined to caution, court involvement is often implied. In his book on the copy of the *Baths of Pozzuoli* in Rome, Claus M. Kauffmann carefully suggests that the manuscript group can be associated with Naples, but in speaking of the name of the scribe who wrote both the *Baths of Pozzuoli* and the Manfred Bible, he writes: "But, granted that the form existed, it is possible that Johensis was the scribe's nickname at Manfred's court or in a Neapolitan scriptorium." See Kauffmann 1959, 29–30. Ferdinando Bologna describes the artist who painted this manuscript as one who participated intimately in the realistic climate of the "cerchie fridericiano-manfrediane." See *I pittori alla corte angioina di Napoli 1266–1414 e un riesame dell'arte nell'età fridericiana* (Rome, 1969), I-25. In his monograph on the Manfred Bible, Erbach-Fürstenau (1910, 53) speculated that the manuscript was produced originally by Manfred as a gift for one of his half-brothers, and placed its production close to Manfred's court. More recent scholarship has followed the same pattern. Daneu Lattanzi wrote of the manuscripts of the Manfred Bible group and of the Conradin Bible as Hohenstaufen manuscripts and the products of scriptoria connected to the Hohenstaufen court with the imprint of the mentality of both Frederick II and Manfred; see Daneu Lattanzi 1964, 143, 159. Florentine Mütherich, too, connects the manuscripts associated with the Manfred Bible and the Conradin Bible itself with a scriptorium in the Hohenstaufen court; see Mütherich 1974, 17. And Silvana Pettinati (1976, 7) proposes that the Manfred Bible group was produced in a Hohenstaufen sciptorium.

Other art historians writing on the subject have been more circumspect. Indeed, Carl Willemsen argues strongly from the other side that we have no proof that the scriptorium that produced the *Baths of Pozzuoli* or the Bibles associated with Manfred had any actual contact with him. See "Handschriften aus dem Umkreis Friedrichs II.," in *Die Zeit der Staufer*, 1:647. My own dissertation skirted the issue of South Italian court ateliers, although I argued that a prominent atelier had to be close to the court. See Corrie diss., 462–474. Hélène Toubert takes what is probably the most judicious and convincing position, describing the Manfred Bible atelier as a bit more independent of the orbit of the court than the name "Manfred Master" might suggest. She characterizes it as an atelier simultaneously in the service of the court and the city, a suggestion similar to the one I make here for the Conradin Bible atelier; see Toubert 1977, 779, 808.

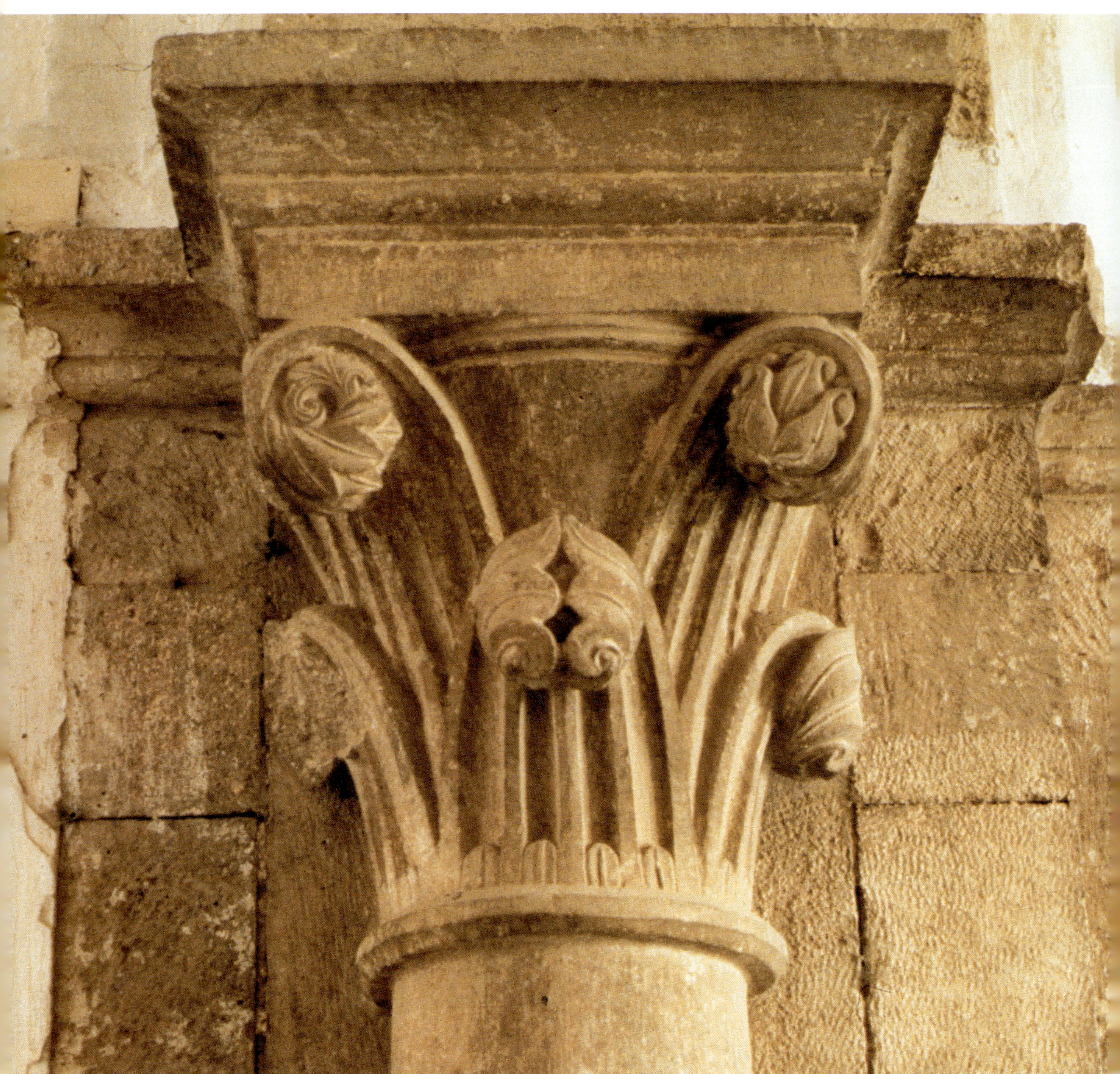

CARLA GHISALBERTI
Università degli Studi di Roma "La Sapienza"

I legami culturali e stilistici tra la scultura architettonica federiciana dell'Italia meridionale e il mondo cistercense

Nel poliedrico e complesso panorama delle componenti artistiche e di pensiero con cui l'arte federiciana entrò in contatto e che influirono sulla sua formazione a diversi livelli, il mondo cistercense ha ricoperto un ruolo di primaria importanza.[1] Come già più volte è stato ribadito, i due ambiti culturali hanno avuto più di un punto di contatto e sostanzialmente devono considerarsi legati tra loro da una complessa rete di rapporti che spesso si sono rivelati, in particolare in Italia meridionale, di scambio reciproco.

Una breve premessa di carattere più generale riguardante la decorazione architettonica delle chiese e degli edifici monastici cistercensi può essere di qualche utilità per ricordare che essa, in ambito critico, ha costituito spesso un complesso nodo di problemi. La nuda essenzialità dal punto di vista decorativo che contraddistingue oggi[2] le chiese e i complessi abbaziali in tutte le loro parti, soprattutto quelli appartenenti alla fase "bernardina," ha accreditato un'ipotesi, sostenuta da molti studiosi, secondo cui non sarebbe lecito parlare di una vera e propria decorazione architettonica cistercense;[3] andrebbe considerata piuttosto come elemento fuorviante all'interno di un contesto che, sia dal punto di vista del pensiero, sia da quello più strettamente oggettuale sembra in un certo senso volerne negare la stessa esistenza. Limitata effettivamente—quanto meno negli edifici appartenenti alla sua fase precoce—a semplici e schematici esempi di chiavi di volta, capitelli o mensole a sostegno dei costoloni delle volte, la decorazione architettonica delle abbazie cistercensi veniva a trovarsi altresì in contraddizione con il pensiero dello stesso Bernardo che considerava ogni forma di abbellimento quale elemento di distrazione dalla preghiera e dalla meditazione del monaco e, in ragione di ciò, da abolire.[4]

Per lungo tempo lo studio della decorazione scultorea che compariva all'interno delle abbazie non ha dunque goduto di nessuna fortuna critica, in ragione appunto di questo vizio di fondo che ha voluto considerarla come estranea al pensiero bernardino e, in un certo modo, risultato di contaminazioni locali.[5] Da alcuni anni a questa parte, invece, gli studi hanno dimostrato una rinnovata attenzione al problema che ha finalmente permesso una più reale chiave di interpretazione del fenomeno.[6] Gli studi sulla prima architettura cistercense, cui hanno dato l'avvio le ricerche della Romanini,[7] hanno avuto il merito di chiarirne e ribadirne la peculiarità rispetto al più generale fenomeno del Gotico: l'architettura cistercense ha smesso di venir considerata una sorta di emanazione regionale delle più alte espressioni del Gotico di Francia e i monaci cistercensi, fossero essi architetti, scultori o lapicidi, non sono stati più considerati esclusivamente quali "passivi" diffusori per l'Europa, di modelli e tipologie costruttive elaborate nella loro terra d'origine, la Borgogna.[8] Secondo questa nuova prospettiva sono state colte inoltre alcune costanti che, tanto dal punto di vista architettonico, quanto da quello decorativo, si ripropongono grossomodo invariate nella stragrande maggioranza degli esempi di edilizia cistercense. Questo fenomeno ha fatto supporre che, all'interno dell'Ordine, fosse stato elaborato un preciso programma con il fine di regolare le scelte tematiche e strutturali da adottare di volta in volta durante la costruzione dei singoli edifici.[9]

Ispirato ad un ideale di povertà e di estremo rigore, questo programma sembra attingere a una nuova concezione astratta dello spazio—le cui basi poggiano direttamente sul pensiero riformatore di Bernardo—fondata essenzialmente su precisi rapporti matematici e geometrici. Gli esiti che tale novità raggiunse in campo architettonico sono ben noti e comunque, esulando dal discorso legato più direttamente alla scultura architettonica, non troveranno qui che brevi cenni. Nell'espressione decorativa tali scelte programmatiche si tradussero di fatto nell'uso di pochi elementi: quasi sempre temi a carattere vegetale, ripetuti in forma sintetica, individuabili in alcuni casi come vere e proprie sigle.[10]

Salvo rare eccezioni, quasi sempre tarde, questo scarno repertorio iconografico appare limitato principalmente alla ripetizione di motivi vegetali, per lo più legati ad una matrice classica, comune con il primo Gotico, in particolare quello borgognone. Accanto ai più diffusi motivi a foglia d'acqua o lanceolata che si ripetono più di altri, tuttavia, occorre segnalare anche la presenza di un ulteriore tema decorativo, finora quasi del tutto ignorato dalla critica: la figura umana. Il suo manifestarsi anche nelle architetture cistercensi precoci, ha costretto, ovviamente, ad una rilettura che ne tenesse conto come di un elemento altrettanto importante all'interno del complesso panorama artistico cistercense.

Secondo la logica ispiratrice del pensiero bernardino, l'immagine dell'uomo, la figura umana in tutte le sue espressioni, non avrebbe dovuto far parte del repertorio iconografico cui attingevano gli scultori e i lapicidi dei cantieri cistercensi. Bernardo nella *Apologia ad Guillelmum abbatem* si scaglia nella sua polemica contro le sculture che si trovano nelle chiese romaniche, dove la figura dell'uomo appare, il più delle volte, in espressioni contorte e deformi, che egli stesso definisce come *ridicula monstruositas.*[11] Ciò nonostante la presenza dell'immagine umana è ravvisabile, con una sua particolare valenza, anche in costruzioni cistercensi abbastanza precoci.[12]

Conclusa tale premessa di ordine più generale riguardo alla decorazione architettonica cistercense, rimane ora da accentrare l'attenzione su quello che costituisce l'argomento di questa analisi, cioè i rapporti tra la plastica architettonica di alcuni edifici federiciani e quella realizzata all'interno dei cantieri cistercensi in Italia meridionale. Quali possono considerarsi come reali punti di tangenza e nel contempo quali sono le differenze che temi iconografici, come il mondo vegetale o la figura umana, hanno assunto all'interno di questi due ambiti culturali, quello federiciano e quello cistercense?

Il caso dell'abbazia di Ripalta in Puglia viene considerato come uno dei monumenti maggiormente legati all'esperienza federiciana in Italia meridionale e nel contempo una delle testimonianze più significative dell'arte cistercense.[13] L'analisi di alcune soluzioni decorative che nel caso di Ripalta si propongono in un'espressione che può considerarsi—anche dal punto di vista cronologico—già matura prende tuttavia le mosse da un episodio che precede quello pugliese e che da questo è anche molto distante: l'abbazia di Valle Crucis nel Galles. L'aver preso in esame due monumenti-chiave tra loro così lontani nel tempo e nello spazio non è dettato da una scelta casuale. Il confronto, al contrario, è utile per dimostrare ancora una volta come, nel mondo cistercense, le affinità riguardanti le scelte costruttive e decorative adottate nei singoli cantieri fossero tra loro intimamente legate dall'evolversi di un'unica imprescindibile logica interiore.

La data di fondazione dell'abbazia di Valle Crucis, nel Galles del Nord, viene concordemente fatta risalire al 28 gennaio dell'anno 1201.[14] Madoc ap Gruffyd Maelor, discendente dalla stirpe dei principi di Powys, volle che tredici monaci provenienti dalla vicina abbazia cistercense di Strata Marcella (1170) si

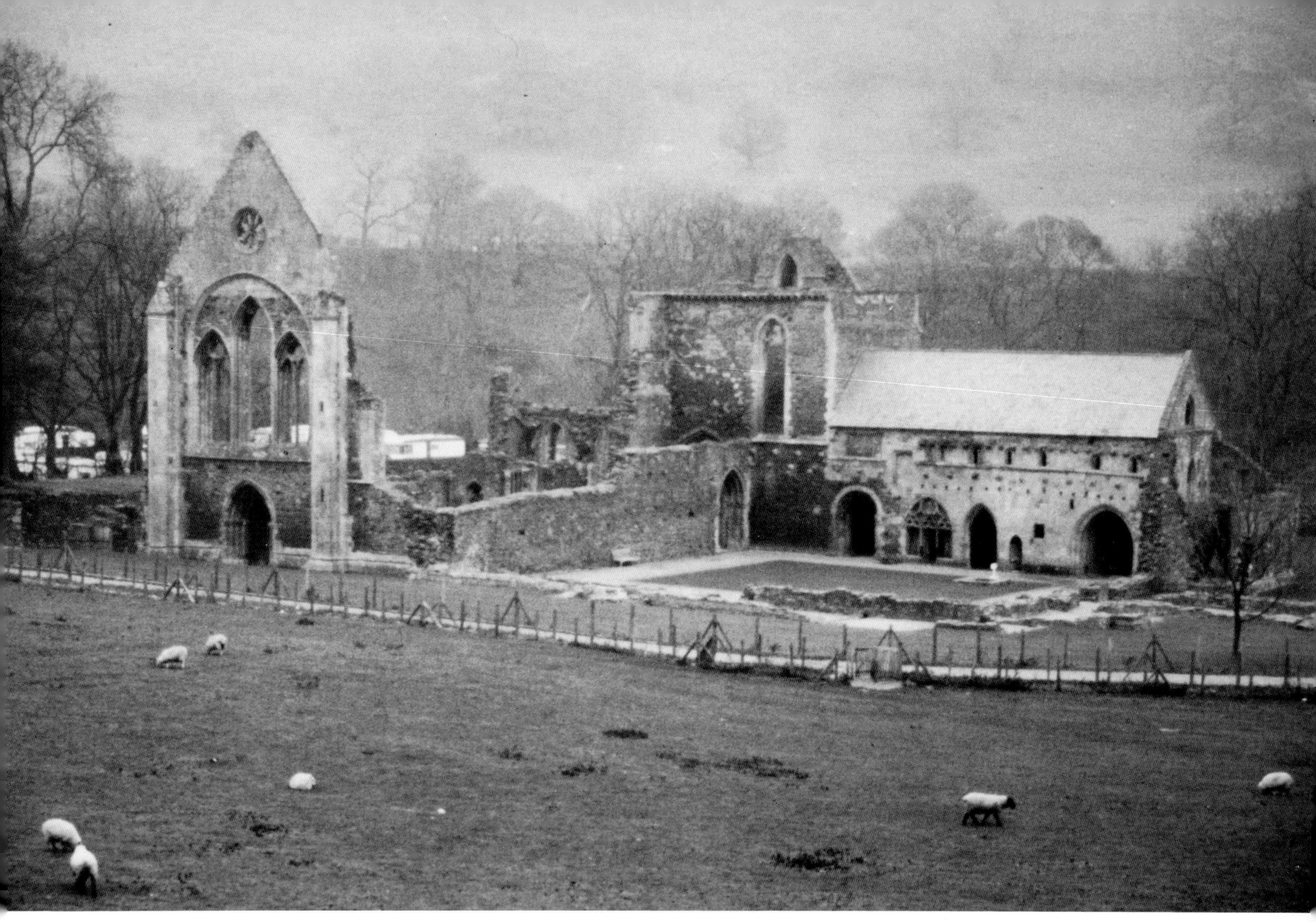

1. Valle Crucis, Galles del Nord, complesso abbaziale, del Duecento

insediassero nei pressi della cosiddetta "Pillar of Eliseg," una croce risalente al IX secolo, da cui il nome della località Valle Crucis, per costruire un nuovo monastero.[15] I lavori presero immediatamente l'avvio e già nel primo quarto del Duecento, dovevano essere completati gran parte della chiesa e degli edifici monastici attigui. Intorno agli anni quaranta, probabilmente in seguito ai numerosi conflitti di cui il Galles fu teatro, l'abbazia venne colpita da un tremendo incendio che ne distrusse gran parte delle strutture. Ma già alla metà del secolo, i lavori di riedificazione delle zone più colpite erano ricominciati. In questa seconda fase, tuttavia, vennero apportate rispetto al progetto originario alcune sostanziali modifiche a livello strutturale che ancora oggi sono facilmente individuabili nel tessuto murario. Un'ulteriore fase di intervento si ebbe nel corso del Trecento e riguardò soprattutto gli ambienti monastici e solo in minima parte le strutture della chiesa.

La costruzione del complesso abbaziale (fig. 1) può essere suddivisa sostanzialmente in tre distinti momenti: una fase iniziale che prese l'avvio nei primi anni del Duecento e si spinse grossomodo fino al 1225; un secondo momento, intorno alla metà dello stesso secolo, in cui i lavori si incentrarono quasi esclusivamente sugli interventi di ricostruzione—anche attraverso la ricomposizione di frammenti superstiti[16]—delle parti crollate dopo l'incendio; quindi una terza fase, palesemente più tarda, nel Trecento avanzato, che riguardò in gran parte la zona orientale degli ambienti comuni (sala capitolare, latrine e dormitori al primo piano). La pianta, secondo uno schema consueto in moltissime altre fondazioni cistercensi,[17] è a croce, il coro a terminazione rettilinea è fiancheggiato da due cappelle laterali quadrate.

L'analisi delle strutture architettoniche è stata oggetto di studio di archeologi inglesi che hanno inoltre curato lo scavo di alcune zone nella parte del chiostro, delle cucine e di alcuni ambienti comuni nel lato occidentale e orientale del complesso.[18]

La decorazione architettonica, testimoniata solo da pochi frammenti ancora *in situ*, ha goduto di minor fortuna, nonostante presenti alcuni momenti di altissima qualità cronologicamente appartenenti per massima parte alla prima campagna di lavori, al principio del Duecento. Dal punto di vista decorativo, sono essenzialmente due le caratteristiche che accomunano Valle Crucis al resto della produzione, quanto meno a quella precoce, di marca cistercense:[19] da un lato, il ripetersi di un repertorio iconografico comune, tutto sommato scarno e schematizzato nelle forme; dall'altro il rifarsi ad una logica, per così dire matematica, secondo cui il motivo decorativo si concretizza esclusivamente laddove si trovi in diretto dialogo con la forma architettonica, come a volerne sottolineare il valore strutturale. In questo senso vanno letti, infatti, i semplici capitelli a fascio che si ripetono, a partire dagli esempi più rovinati sui pilastri della controfacciata, nella zona del transetto e dell'incrocio (fig. 2) e nei due portali che collegano il chiostro rispettivamente alla chiesa e alla sacrestia.[20]

Il motivo vegetale della foglia lanceolata, sostanzialmente liscia, caratterizzata solo dalla costola centrale, così come è ripetuto più volte nei capitelli dell'incrocio, è comune, nella sua caratteristica astrazione formale, al gusto che ha segnato, fin dalla fase più precoce, la decorazione architettonica di ambito cistercense.[21] Che l'origine di questo tema iconografico non sia maturata all'interno dell'Ordine, è fatto scontato, come per altro verso sembrano altrettanto innegabili la diversa logica astrattiva che da parte cistercense viene conferita alla forma medesima e il nuovo valore che essa quasi improvvisamente si trova ad assumere e che, per il suo continuo ripetersi in esempi tra loro anche molto distanti, può definirsi peculiare di un preciso ambito, quello cistercense appunto.[22] Ugualmente i capitelli delle colonnine a fascio che in origine dovevano

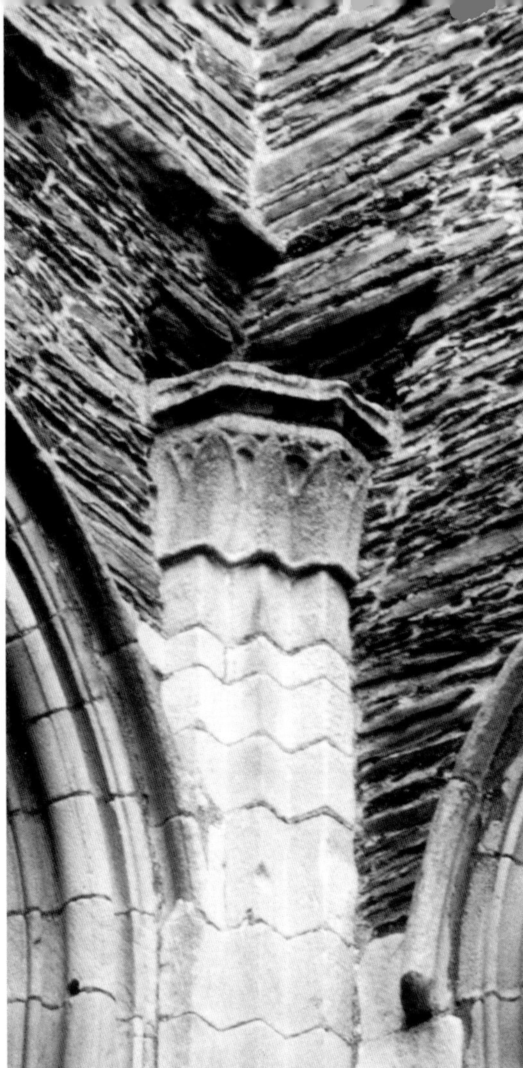

2. Valle Crucis, Galles del Nord, capitello del transetto, principio del Duecento

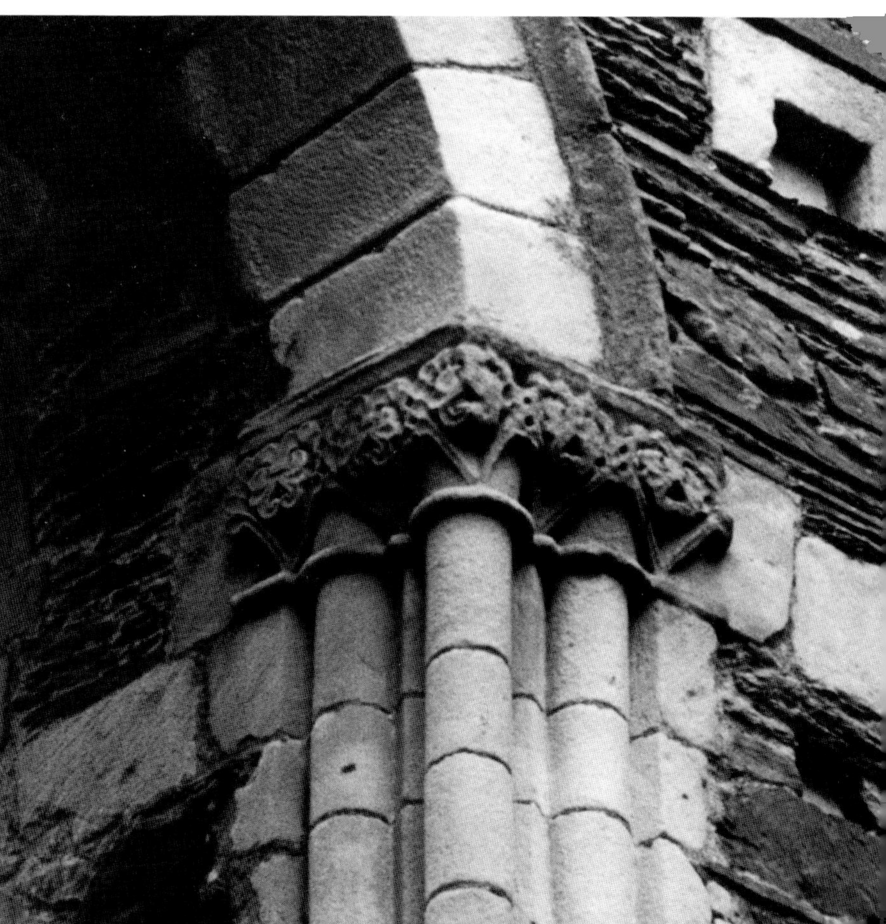

3. Valle Crucis, Galles del Nord, capitello del finestrone absidale, principio del Duecento

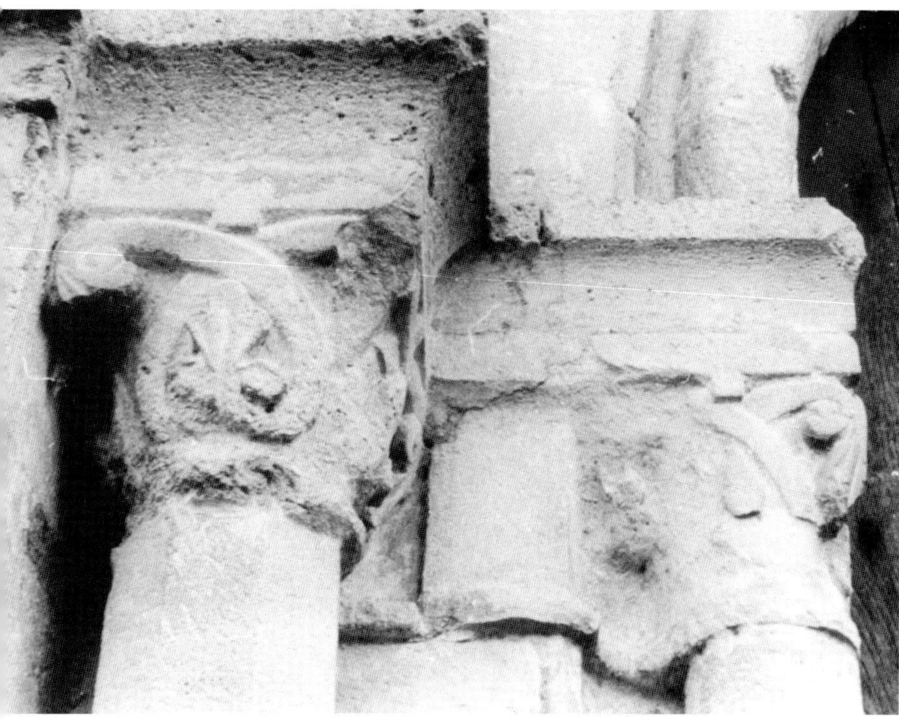

4. Santa Maria di Sambucina, Calabria, capitello del portale, principio del Duecento
Fotografia: Ugliano 1978, fig. 52

5. Valle Crucis, Galles del Nord, capitello del portale dell'ambiente di passaggio, principio del Duecento

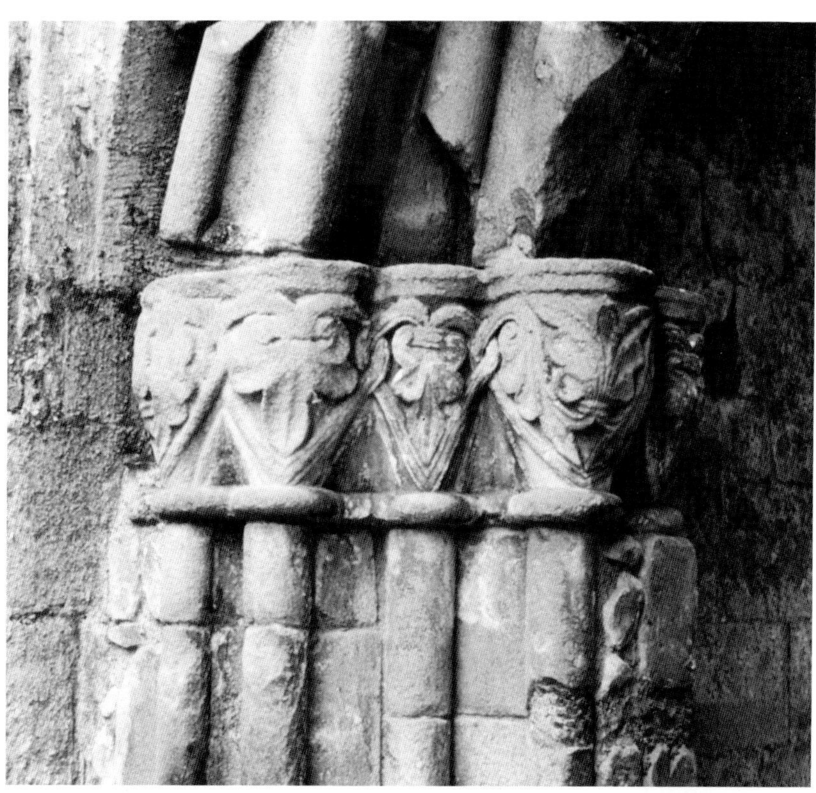

sostenere la volta del coro, così come quelli dei tre finestroni che si aprono sulla parete di fondo (fig. 3), rappresentano un ulteriore esempio della rielaborazione di temi iconografici di carattere vegetale, quali sono la palmetta e l'acanto—entrambi di matrice classica, in una chiave che ne sintetizza la forma nelle sue linee essenziali. L'elemento naturale che ha costituito il modello per questo tipo di soluzione decorativa assume così un valore nuovo, diverso: diventa "il segno" (la sigla, l'essenza) di se stesso. Per trovare una ulteriore conferma del fatto che il repertorio iconografico cui i monaci cistercensi si ispirarono per decorare le loro abbazie è tutto sommato sempre il medesimo e ugualmente contrassegnato da uno stesso gusto per l'essenzialità delle forme, si può fare un breve riferimento a un altro termine di confronto rappresentato dall'abbazia di Sambucina, nei pressi di Crotone, in Calabria, dove si ritrovano essenzialmente identiche le soluzioni decorative adottate a Valle Crucis. Nel portale, uno dei pochissimi frammenti superstiti dell'intero complesso (solo di recente oggetto di uno studio più approfondito teso alla puntualizzazione della sua cronologia[23]), che può essere datato anch'esso al principio del Duecento, si ripropongono i medesimi capitelli a fascio (fig. 4), visti nel portale dell'ambiente di passaggio a sud nel complesso gallese (fig. 5), contraddistinti da un motivo vegetale estremamente stilizzato che, senza soluzione di continuità, avvolge e racchiude in sè l'insieme delle colonnine sottostanti. Tale confronto non pretende assolutamente di dimostrare dal punto di vista stilistico un diretto rapporto tra le due abbazie, quanto piuttosto di sottolineare quanto già prima accennato: il rifarsi da parte delle maestranze cistercensi ad un medesimo patrimonio iconografico che si ripete senza significative varianti anche in edifici tra loro distanti geograficamente e inseriti in ambiti culturali tutto sommato abbastanza diversi.[24] D'altronde il medesimo rigore formale che si ritrova nei precoci esempi di Valle Crucis e della Sambucina, contraddistingue anche esperienze cistercensi più tarde.

Basti ricordare per esempio il caso di alcuni capitelli all'interno della chiesa di Santa Maria d'Arabona in Abruzzo,[25] dove la decorazione diventa più complessa e articolata dal punto di vista formale, pur rimanendo ancorata a medesimi temi e principi compositivi. L'elemento vegetale è, anche in questo caso, espresso in forma rigorosa, essenziale, tuttavia qualcosa sembra essere mutato: per esempio nel confronto tra i capitelli a fascio (fig. 6) del portale che mette in comunicazione la chiesa di Valle Crucis con il chiostro con uno dei capitelli della navata centrale della chiesa di Arabona (fig. 7), dove si ritrova lo stesso motivo a ciuffi di foglie, si nota come l'elemento astrattivo nell'esempio inglese risulti dominante rispetto a quello naturalistico, in un certo senso "classico," mentre nel secondo esempio viene ridimensionato, pur rimanendo presente, quasi a voler cifrare l'intera composizione. Nel capitello di Arabona si trova accentuato, invece, il gusto per la rappresentazione realistica del modello. Le foglie si caratterizzano nei loro particolari e soprattutto si movimentano rispetto al contesto architettonico in cui sono inserite. Evidentemente l'esperienza maturata all'interno dei cantieri delle grandi cattedrali gotiche rispetto al modello classico del capitello corinzio—matrice comune al caso di Valle Crucis e di Arabona—ritrova, anche in ambito cistercense, una sua eco particolare.[26] Ma negli esempi dei capitelli delle due chiese cistercensi ancora una volta si è di fronte ad una soluzione originale rispetto a quella più genericamente definibile gotica *tout court.*[27] La decorazione architettonica presente nelle abbazie cistercensi di epoca anche matura mantiene, nei confronti del più vasto panorama gotico, una sua propria costante peculiarità: essa non è mai il frutto di una scelta puramente decorativa, al contrario essa si presenta sempre e invariabilmente legata al principio che la vuole, nella sua espressione formale, rigorosa ed essenziale.

Da Arabona il passo verso uno dei più pregevoli esempi di architettura cistercense italiana, rappresentato dall'abbazia di Ripalta in Puglia, è molto breve. La pregevolissima qualità della decorazione architettonica ha fatto sì che essa sia stata sempre considerata una delle più alte espressioni raggiunte dall'arte gotica in Puglia e in questo senso, sia stata sempre confrontata con la grande esperienza artistica di ambito federiciano. Ormai può considerarsi storia documentata la presenza presso la corte imperiale di maestranze uscite dall'ambiente cistercense,

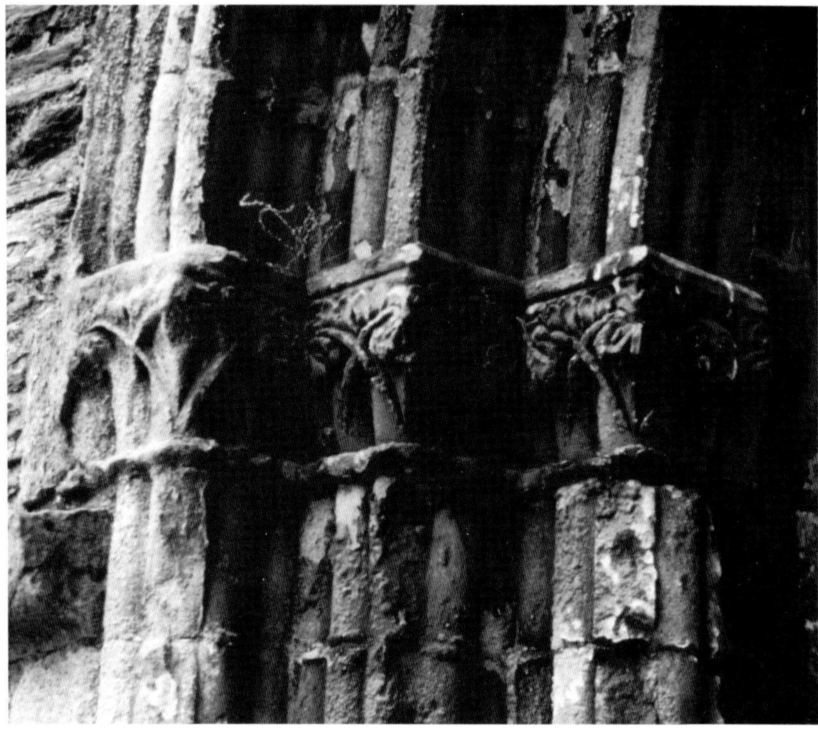

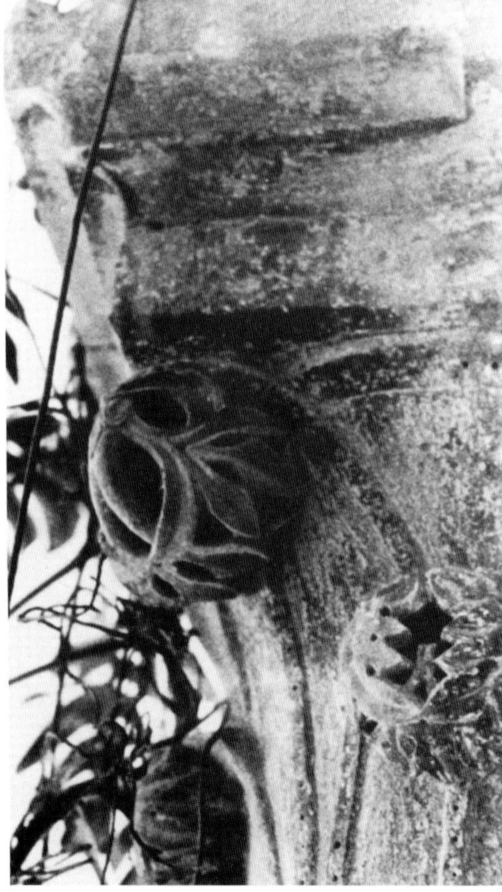

6. Valle Crucis, Galles del Nord, capitello del portale del chiostro, prima metà del Duecento

7. Santa Maria di Arabona, Abruzzo, capitello della navata, prima metà del Duecento
Fotografia: Righetti Tosti-Croce

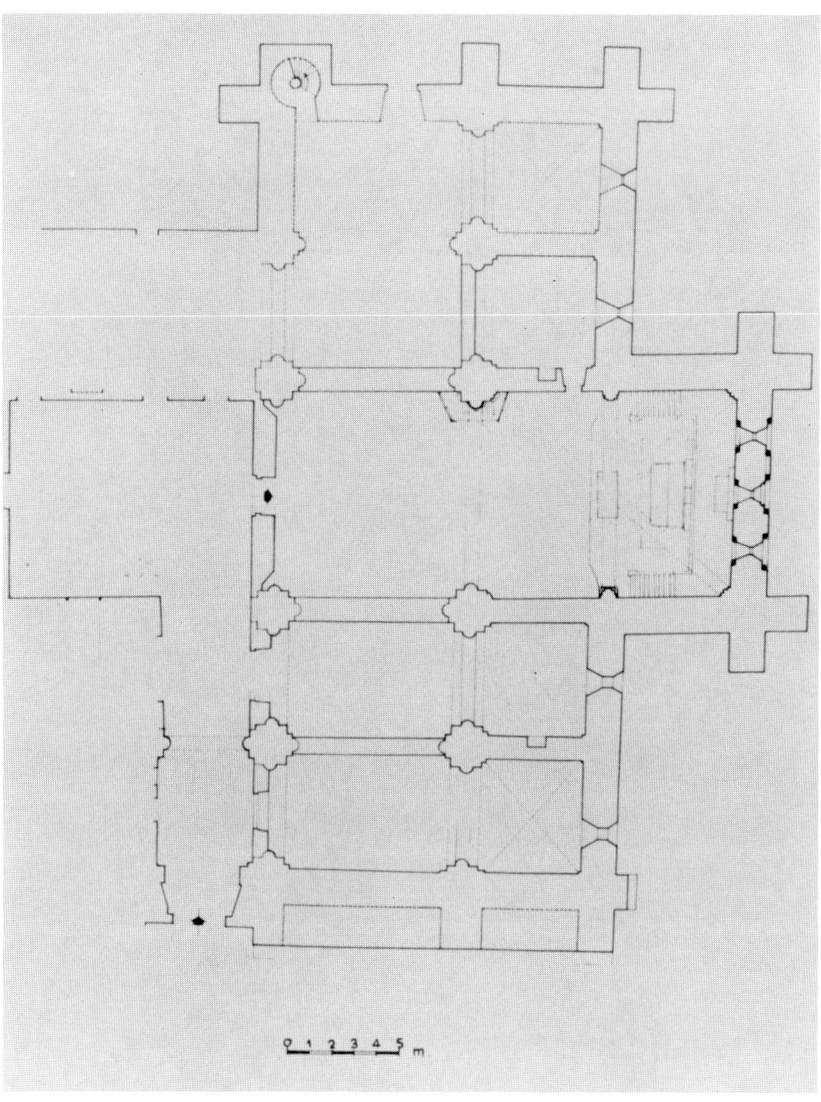

8. Santa Maria di Ripalta sul Fortore, Puglia, pianta della chiesa

come testimonia la *Ignoti monaci cisterciensis Sanctae Mariae de Ferraria Chronica*,[28] secondo cui l'imperatore aveva avuto il permesso di far lavorare presso di sè conversi di tutte le abbazie cistercensi della Sicilia, della Puglia e della Terra di Lavoro. Ancora nel 1234 è testimoniato nel cantiere della porta di Capua il cistercense *Donnus Bisancius*, sono inoltre documentate le numerose soste dell'imperatore a Casamari, l'attività presso la cancelleria di corte dell'abate Giovanni, i numerosi benefici di Federico a monasteri dell'Ordine, e, secondo quanto riporta Mattheus Paris, l'episodio secondo cui l'imperatore in punto di morte volle essere sepolto con l'abito cistercense. Una serie di confronti stilistici possono aggiungersi come altrettanto valida testimonianza documentaria dell'avvenuto contatto tra questi due universi culturali, cistercense e federiciano.[29]

L'insediamento cistercense a Ripalta, costituito da monaci provenienti dall'abbazia abruzzese di Casanova, si stabilì intorno al 1201 su una preesistente struttura benedettina.[30] Essa doveva presentarsi a quel momento in condizioni piuttosto fatiscenti e con strutture ormai inutilizzabili, considerato il fatto che il complesso ancora oggi appare, nonostante le successive superfetazioni, frutto di un progetto omogeneo (fig. 8) eccezione fatta per l'ambiente a sud attualmente utilizzato come ingresso al cortile della casa colonica oggi insediata sopre le strutture originarie. Questo corridoio di passaggio, per il suo anomalo orientamento rispetto al resto delle strutture, denuncia una modifica sopravvenuta durante la costruzione o piuttosto, un riutilizzo di un ambiente già esistente, appartenuto credibilmente al complesso benedettino.

Già nei primi decenni del Trecento, l'abbazia doveva essere molto fiorente, se addirittura il pontefice Onorio III affida all'abate insieme al vescovo di Civitate, l'incarico di visitatori apostolici al monastero di Pulsano, o ancora nel 1237 Gregorio IX incarica l'abate di svolgere un'inchiesta sul vescovo di Salpi e di occuparsi della riforma spirituale e temporale del monastero femminile di S. Bartolomeo di Carbonara.[31] Dunque sembra assai probabile che nel primo trentennio del secolo l'abbazia fosse, quanto meno nelle sue strutture principali, ultimata.

Le parti del complesso cistercense ancora leggibili si limitano alla zona orientale della chiesa, al transetto e alla prima campata. Il coro è a terminazione rettilinea coperto da una volta esapartita e fiancheggiato da due cappelle per lato, anch'esse piatte, oggi riutilizzate come magazzini (la prima cappella del lato settentrionale del transetto ospita la sacrestia). Dell'attacco del corpo longitudinale della chiesa non rimane che la prima campata, in corrispondenza della quale sembra essersi fermata la costruzione. Sono ancora in vista, tuttavia, murati nelle pareti degli edifici che in seguito si sono aggiunti alla costruzione originaria, gli archi della seconda e terza campata della navata centrale.[32] Se dal punto di vista architettonico l'abbazia di Ripalta offre una lettura piuttosto difficoltosa, riguardo alla sua decorazione scolpita la situazione appare ben diversa. Essa sembra il frutto di un progetto unitario, seppure estremamente ricco di varianti.

La tipologia dei capitelli della sacrestia (fig. 9) risulta ancora fortemente legata alla tradizione formale più rigorosa ed essenziale, vista più volte in esempi anche anteriori fino a quelli di Fontenay, o nella stessa Valle Crucis, ripetuti più volte. Rispetto ai loro prototipi le foglie d'acqua stilizzate, piuttosto affusolate e scanalate con rigore geometrico al centro in corrispondenza della costola, sono tuttavia già consapevoli dei risultati raggiunti in quegli stessi anni nelle cattedrali gotiche; lo si nota principalmente per la loro più complessa articolazione in tre ordini tra loro sfalsati sul supporto che le accoglie e per la loro maturità compositiva espressa solo nel tratto lineare che ne riassume il volume e ne definisce contemporaneamente i particolari. Quel medesimo gusto che si è notato nel caso dei capitelli dell'abbazia di Arabona, si ripropone qui a Ripalta in modo ancora più convincente: l'inserto vegetale all'interno di una precisa struttura architettonica quale è il capitello prende vita, raggiunge una sua autonomia formale e di significato che fino ad ora era rimasta solo latente. Già negli esempi dei caulicoli dei capitelli della seconda cappella del transetto settentrionale, così caratterizzati nell'elemento naturalistico, o in quelli dei due esemplari affrontati che si trovano nell'ambiente di passaggio (fig. 10) o, ancora, in quello inserito in un pilastro della chiesa, si può agevolmente seguire lo svolgersi di tale percorso. Si assiste a un vero e proprio liberarsi della forma che prende vita come se realmente esistesse. Già nel Gotico transalpino legato alle fabbriche delle grandi cattedrali francesi aveva avuto luogo un fenomeno analogo dove le rappresentazioni di elementi fitomorfi si erano caricate di nuove valenze che le avevano caratterizzate fino al punto di dare vita a un vero e proprio "atlante botanico,"[33] come testimoniano per esempio i capitelli del piano superiore della Sainte-Chapelle o quelli del triforio di Reims.[34] Ancora di più questa novità

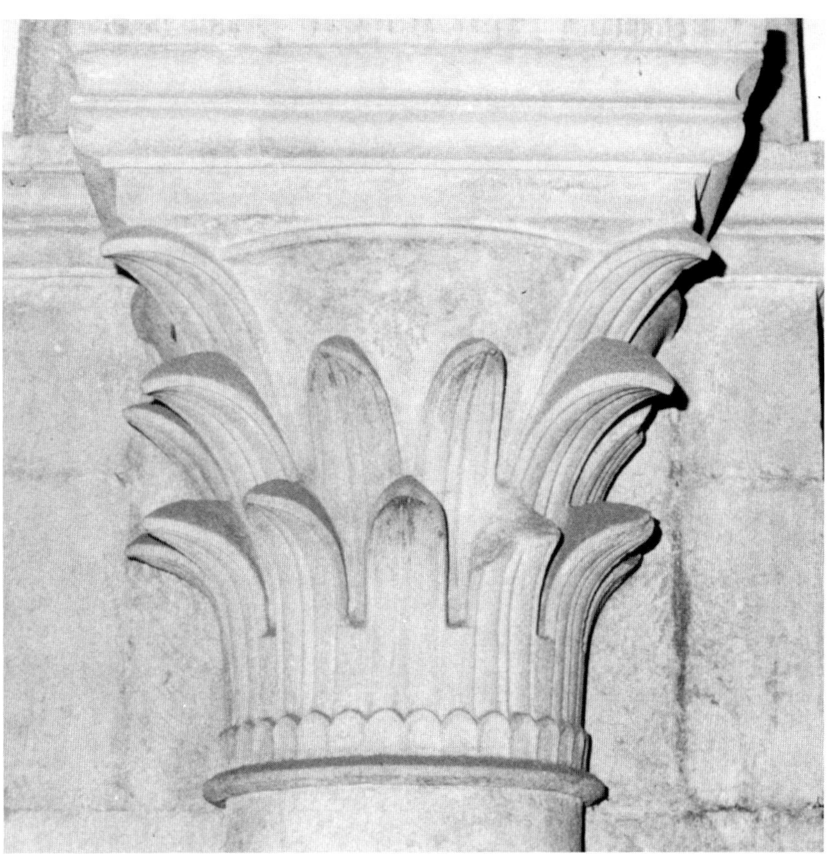

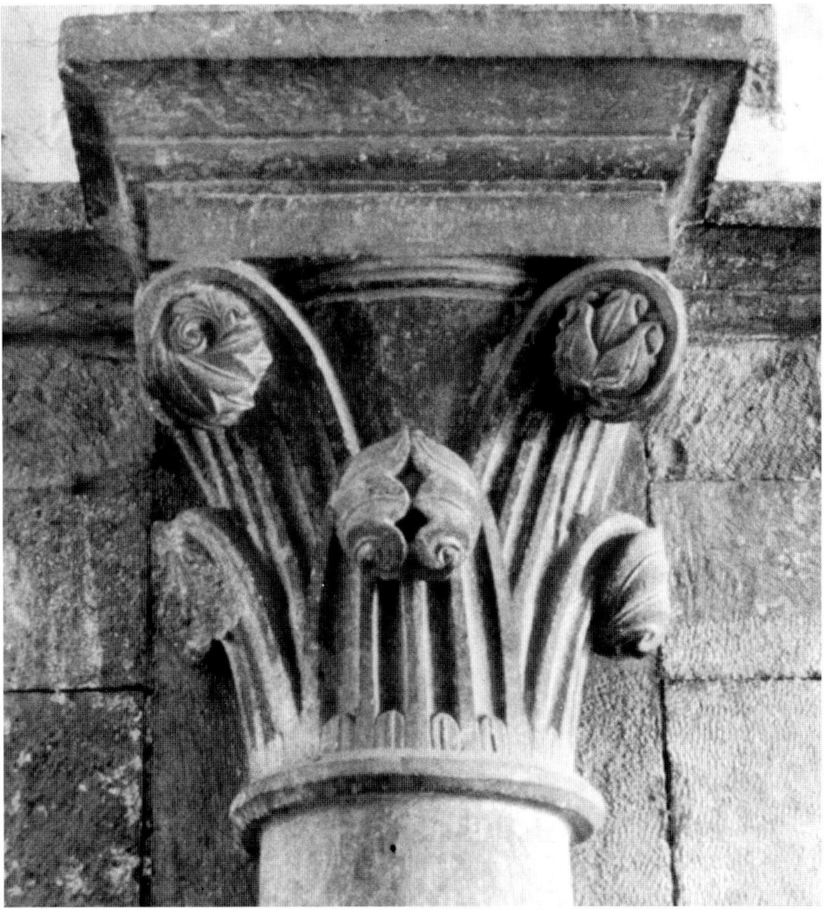

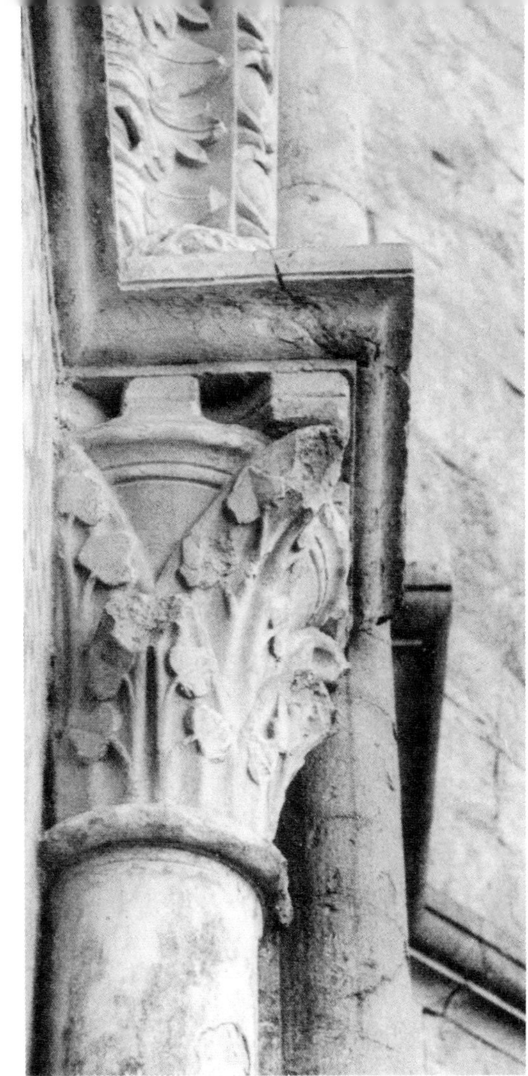

9. Santa Maria di Ripalta sul Fortore, Puglia, capitello della sacrestia, terzo decennio del Duecento

10. Santa Maria di Ripalta sul Fortore, Puglia, capitello dell'ambiente di passaggio, terzo decennio del Duecento

11. Castel del Monte, Puglia, capitello di una finestra del primo piano, quarto decennio del Duecento

12. Lagopesole, Puglia, castello, mensola, quarto decennio del Duecento
Fotografia: Pistilli

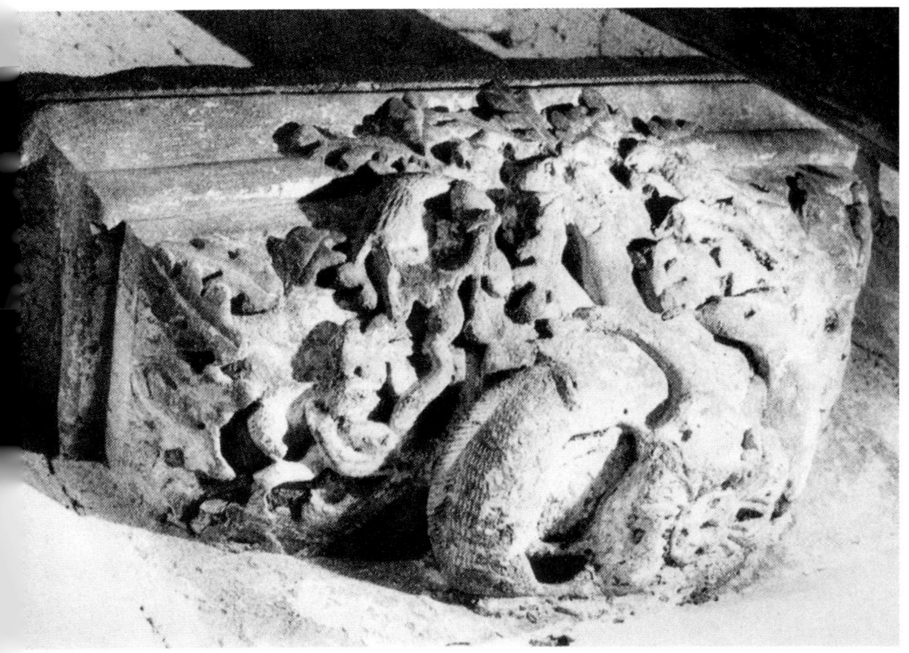

di scelte tematiche si coglie nell'ambito dei cantieri tedeschi (Gelnhausen, Naumburg) dove, accanto all'elemento vegetale si trova l'inserto di piccoli animali e dove il realismo si accentua con ancora maggiore evidenza rispetto al prototipo francese.[35] Ed è proprio rispetto a questo ultimo punto che si individua uno dei più profondi punti di contatto tra il mondo federiciano, quello del Gotico transalpino e quello cistercense.

Nel repertorio dei temi decorativi presi a prestito dalla *Bauplastik* che decora i castelli dell'imperatore il motivo di carattere vegetale è certamente preponderante e legato da una costante che ne accomuna le singole scelte decorative. Anche qui—come nel mondo del Gotico d'Oltralpe—molto spesso ci si trova di fronte a un attento quanto puntuale riferirsi a un modello preso dal vero, a una conoscenza diretta che, in alcuni casi indulge verso l'attenzione scientifica; una ricerca che, dal punto di vista della resa, ha come fine ultimo il riproporre l'elemento reale; per usare un'espressione coniata dallo stesso Federico II: "Manifestare ea quae sunt sicut sunt." Secondo questa chiave dunque si possono interpretare alcuni capitelli delle finestre del primo piano di Castel del Monte (fig. 11), o le altrettanto note mensole di Castel Lagopesole,[36] dove addirittura la nozione della struttura architettonica si perde nel complesso intreccio degli elementi vegetali; essi prendono vita nel loro articolarsi rispetto al supporto e rispetto allo spazio che li avvolge ma anche in una sorta di racconto che si snoda, per esempio, tra le foglie su cui si colgono piccoli uccelli seminascosti nell'atto di beccare, o cinghiali che si protendono verso le ghiande tra le foglie di quercia (fig. 12).

Palesi assonanze in questa direzione si possono cogliere nel confronto tra alcuni capitelli di Castel del Monte con altri esempi di Ripalta, dove l'attenzione al vero di natura si trova espressa in soluzioni piuttosto accentuate—da considerarsi forse un *unicum* per l'ambiente cistercense. Ciò testimonia da un lato una evidente comunanza rispetto alle scelte formali che si attuarono all'interno dei due ambiti, dall'altro tuttavia, altrettanto chiare divergenze di carattere più sostanziale. Il capitello a foglie di sedano, inserito in un pilastro all'interno della chiesa di Ripalta (fig. 13), può essere confrontato con un analogo esemplare che si trova in una sala del primo piano di Castel del Monte (fig. 14). Il motivo decorativo si presenta sostanzialmente invariato. In entrambi gli esempi si tratta di rielaborazioni di un modello classico,[37] in cui grande attenzione viene conferita all'aspetto naturalistico della foglia, ma in quello cistercense sussiste un maggiore rigore espresso attraverso una più sintetica resa formale: la foglia risulta come riassunta nei suoi elementi caratterizzanti. Nell'esempio federiciano, al contrario, traspare una maggiore attenzione nei confronti dell'aspetto esteriore del modello reale cui ci si è voluti ispirare. Allo stesso modo le foglie di fico che si trovano scolpite su una mensola all'interno della chiesa di Ripalta risultano, ad un'analisi attenta di particolari quali le nervature o, più generalmente, relativa all'aspetto compostivo, ben diverse da quelle scolpite su una mensola di Lagopesole, caratterizzate fin nel più sottile dettaglio e collocate in una composizione spaziale di ben più complessa articolazione. Il rigore geometrico sotteso ad ogni immagine scolpita che compone la decorazione dei capitelli di Ripalta—quella medesima figura geometrica che Villard d'Honnecourt traccia nel suo *Livre de portraiture*[38] come punto di partenza per ogni raffigurazione—non si coglie più nelle mensole di Lagopesole dove l'indagine "scientifica" ha decisamente il sopravvento.[39]

Il discorso relativo alle assonanze e alle divergenze che esistono tra la *Bauplastik* delle chiese cistercensi e quella dei castelli di Federico II si presenta comunque molto più complesso. Vanno tenuti presenti numerosi fattori quali non ultimo l'ambiente culturale in cui si inseriscono, nel caso specifico la Puglia, territorio estremamente ricco di testimonianze classiche. Rispetto a questo comune denominatore entrambi gli ambiti si dimostrano particolarmente ricettivi. La grande sensibilità dimostrata dall'imperatore per il mondo classico, non solo a livello culturale o politico, ma anche sul piano più direttamente artistico si esplica di continuo e si può dire che pervada ogni espressione dell'arte di corte.[40] Possono considerarsi infatti precise citazioni alcuni capitelli di Castel del Monte, o—nel campo della scultura a tuttotondo—le statue di Barletta, di Lucera o della porta di Capua.[41] Il tramite con il mondo antico fu spesso diretto, ma

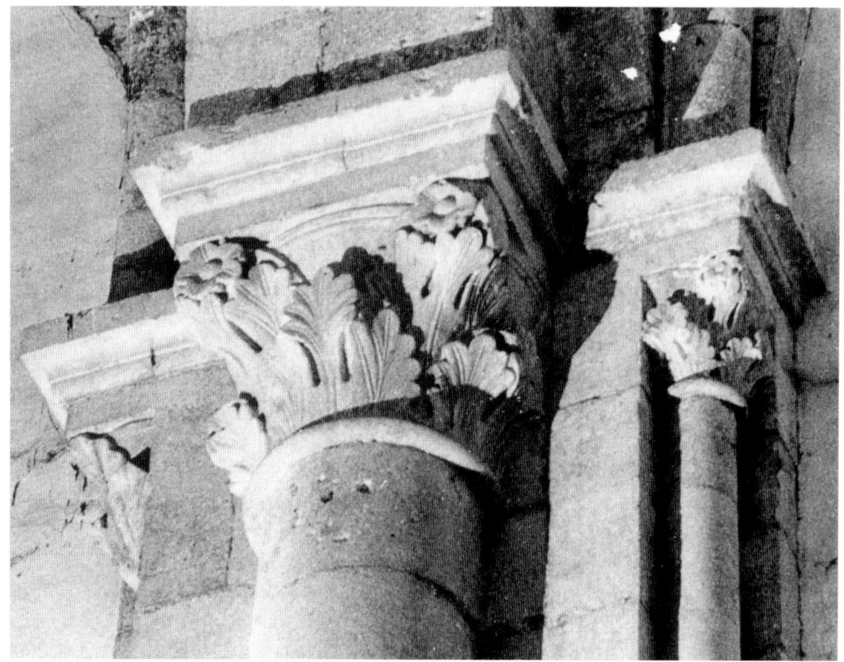

13. Santa Maria di Ripalta sul Fortore, Puglia, capitello della navata, terzo decennio del Duecento

14. Castel del Monte, Puglia, capitello di una sala al primo piano, quarto decennio del Duecento

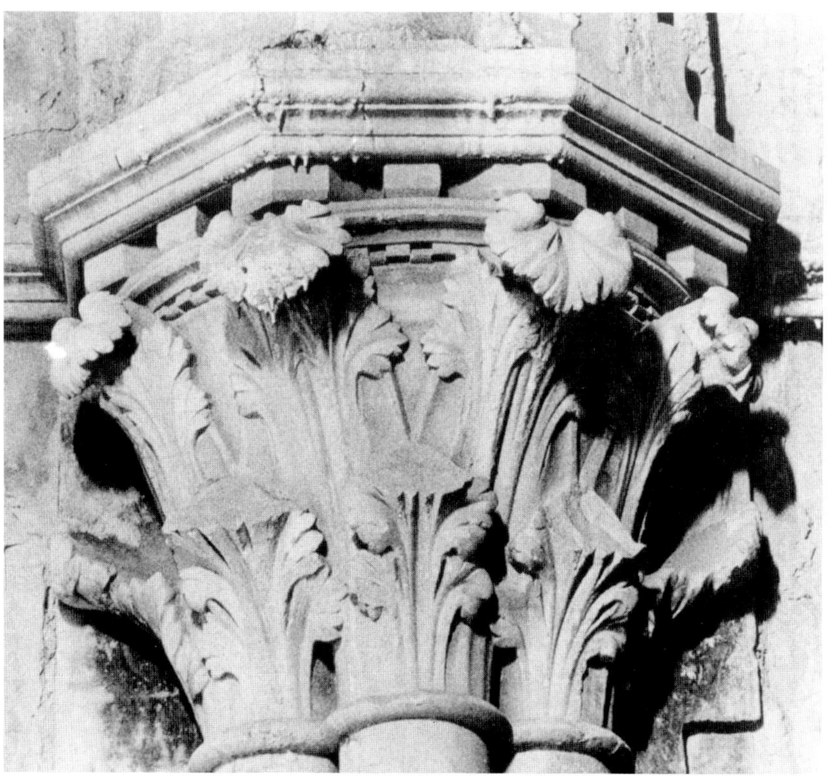

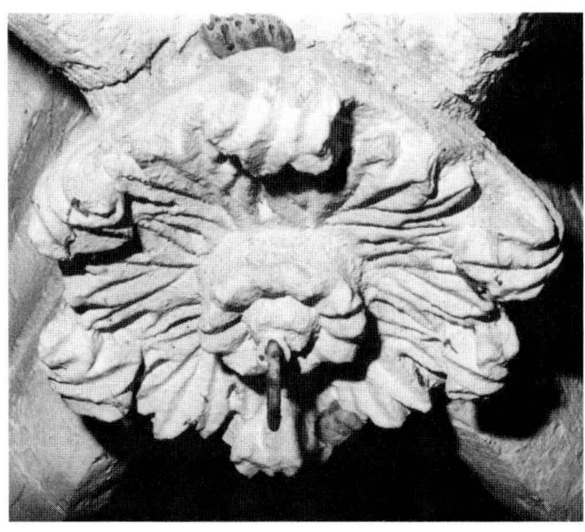

15. Santa Maria di Ripalta sul Fortore, Puglia, chiave di volta del transetto meridionale, terzo decennio del Duecento

anche filtrato, in alcuni casi, attraverso l'esperienza del Gotico françese e tedesco che certamente Federico II doveva ben conoscere, o, ancora più direttamente, attraverso l'esperienza della scultura romanica locale, pugliese.[42] I rapporti che poterono intercorrere con quest'ultima in particolare sono stati già più volte indagati e fornirebbero da soli argomento di altrettanto complesse indagini. Basti ricordare solo a titolo di esempio i due leoni su cui si imposta l'arco del portale di ingresso di Castel del Monte o molti dei capitelli del piano terreno nello stesso castello, o ancora il fregio superstite del portale del palazzo imperiale di Foggia,[43] tutti esempi di richiami diretti a modelli della plastica dell'epoca normanna, a sua volta legata a prototipi di matrice classica o tardoantica. Le stesse componenti fortemente classicistiche che contraddistinguono la produzione federiciana nell'Italia meridionale, sono state individuate anche a Ripalta.[44] Nell'abbazia cistercense si assiste alla ripresa di temi classici filtrati attraverso l'esperienza romanica pugliese, come testimoniano per esempio alcune delle formelle del finestrone del transetto settentrionale, legate al repertorio diffuso tra i secoli dodicesimo e tredicesimo soprattutto in Abruzzo e in Capitanata[45] a cui però si intercalano altre formelle, tra cui quella a racemi di vite, di estrazione diversa molto più legata all'esperienza cistercense (si pensi ai motivi dei portali o delle stesse lastre d'altare di Casamari[46] o a quelli di San Martino al Cimino).[47] Anche il leone su cui poggiava una colonnetta della cornice dello stesso finestrone, o l'inedito frammento di un arredo della chiesa (probabilmente la base di un cero pasquale) costituito da una colonnetta su cui si avvolgono spirali di tralci d'uva con piccoli uccelli che ne beccano i frutti, o ancora di più una chiave di volta nel transetto meridionale (fig. 15),[48] finora inedita perché visibile solo dal sottotetto, realizzata con un tipo di foglie che si ispirano evidentemente a un modello classico,[49] costituiscono una concreta testimonianza dell'avvenuto contatto con maestranze locali, legate a scelte la cui matrice è ancora quella classica. In ragione di questo riferimento al mondo romanico pugliese e, più o meno direttamente, al mondo classico—peculiare della cultura della corte di Federico II in Italia meridionale—l'abbazia di Ripalta è sempre stata considerata la più federiciana tra le abbazie cistercensi. Il suo carattere particolare, talvolta inteso come *extravagans* rispetto al panorama in qualche modo omogeneo rappresentato dalle altre abbazie dell'Italia centro meridionale, è stato interpretato come il frutto di una diretta influenza a livello stilistico esercitata dall'ambiente culturale legato all'imperatore.[50] A ben vedere i termini della questione si prospettano in un'ottica leggermente diversa. A prescindere dal fattore meramente cronologico, che vedrebbe la costruzione dell'abbazia non superare la soglia del terzo decennio del Duecento (quindi contemporanea alla maggior parte dei castelli federiciani, se non addirittura di poco precedente), si coglie nelle scelte decorative elaborate a Ripalta una coerente continuità rispetto a quel "programma" di cui si parlava al principio, a cui si rimase fedeli evidentemente anche in esempi di architetture più tarde come quella pugliese. L'aver sottolineato certe costanti in esempi quali Valle Crucis, Arabona o Ripalta induce a pensare che i legami e le assonanze con il mondo gotico transalpino e quello classico provengano da una direzione diversa, non necessariamente ed esclusivamente federiciana. Dunque non fu tanto—o quanto meno non solo—l'ambiente di corte che, venuto in contatto con quello dei Cistercensi di Ripalta, trasmise e diffuse il gusto per un accentuato naturalismo (filtrato sempre attraverso l'esperienza del mondo classico); quanto piuttosto i due esiti espressivi tra loro affini sono la risultante di evoluzioni di pensiero e percorsi maturati, tuttavia, in molti dei loro aspetti autonomamente.

In entrambe le esperienze, federiciana e cistercense, hanno di certo contato alcuni fattori comuni, quali il mondo classico, sperimentato per via diretta o filtrato attraverso l'arte romanica pugliese, oppure gli ultimi esiti del Gotico francese del "*domaine royale*," fattori che evidentemente le hanno, per certi versi, rese affini ma che hanno potuto nel contempo anche raggiungere talvolta esiti diversissimi tra loro.

Ciò nonostante, accanto a queste esperienze affini, dagli esiti spesso lontani, vanno tenuti presenti anche rapporti di duplice scambio, talvolta di osmosi, che innegabilmente esistettero tra il mondo cistercense e quello federiciano in Italia meridionale. D'altronde anche in Germania, come dimostrano per esempio le affinità tra le soluzioni decorative e strutturali adottate nei cantieri della cattedrale di Bamberga e della vicina abbazia di Ebrach, i rapporti tra la committenza laica imperiale e le maestranze cistercensi furono diretti.[51]

Volendo tuttavia ritornare all'ambiente dell'Italia meridionale, il frutto di questo tipo di legame è stato colto per esempio nel rigore geometrico di chiara marca cistercense di alcuni capitelli o di alcuni peducci di volta nella settima torre di Castel del Monte (fig. 16), dove le tre foglie d'acqua lisce, caratterizzate esclusivamente da un motivo ad anello che le separa si ritrova in molti esempi di capitelli di abbazie cistercensi, fino a giungere ai prototipi borgognoni di Fontenay.[52] O ancora nella chiave di volta con il motivo a foglie a spirale in una delle sale di Castel del Monte che si ripete sostanzialmente identica nella chiesa di San Galgano. Per contro l'accentuato sapore naturalistico che ha ispirato lo scultore di un capitello della finestra del coro di Ripalta, dove le foglie si avvolgono con le loro punte al bordo superiore del capitello, entrando in un dialogo diretto con l'architettura, è evidentemente connesso con le esperienze maturate alla corte di Federico II. Ancora di più lo è forse il capitello a foglie di vite della seconda cappella del braccio settentrionale del transetto, oggi in un ambiente adibito a magazzino, da considerarsi in assoluto uno dei più alti esempi raggiunti dall'arte cistercense (fig. 17). Un vero

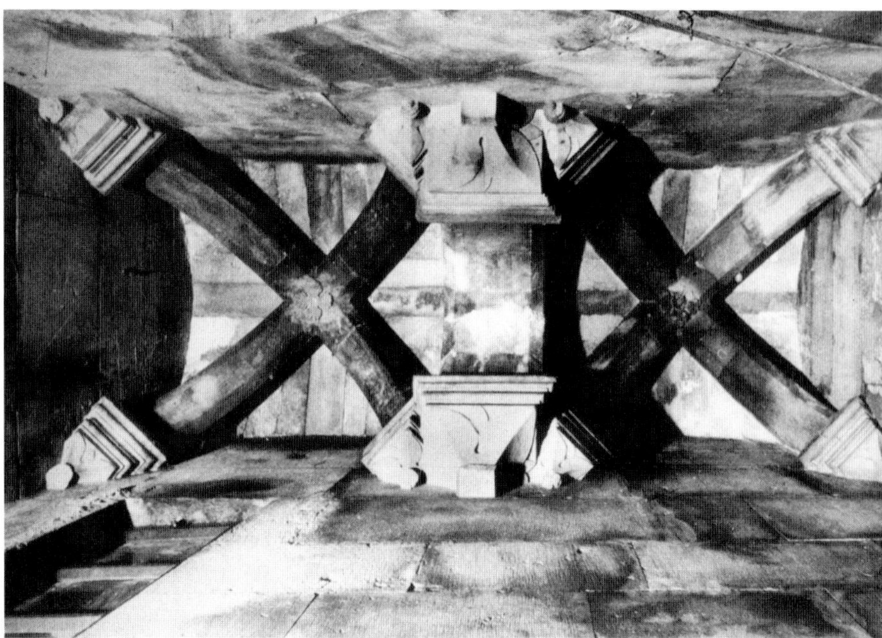

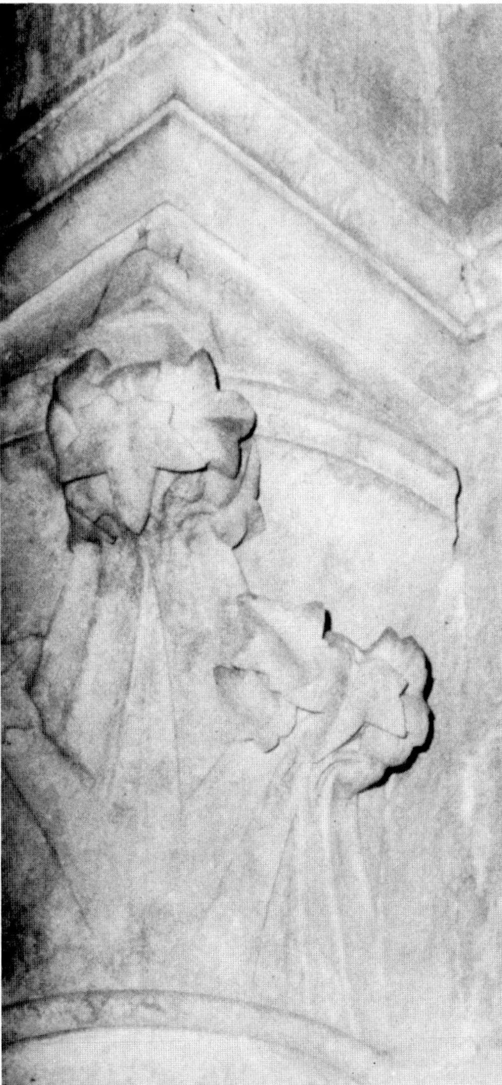

16. Castel del Monte, Puglia, volte della settima torre, quarto decennio del Duecento

17. Santa Maria di Ripalta sul Fortore, Puglia, capitello del transetto settentrionale, terzo decennio del Duecento

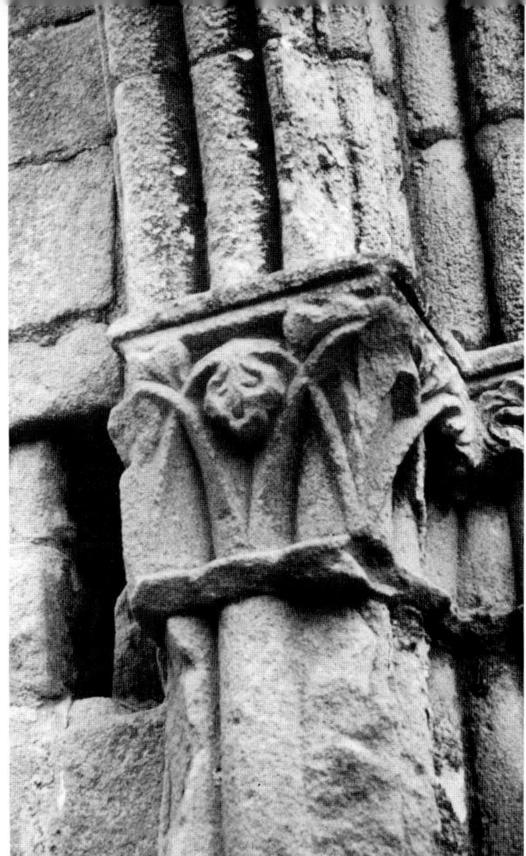

18. Valle Crucis, Galles del Nord, capitello del portale del chiostro, principio del Duecento

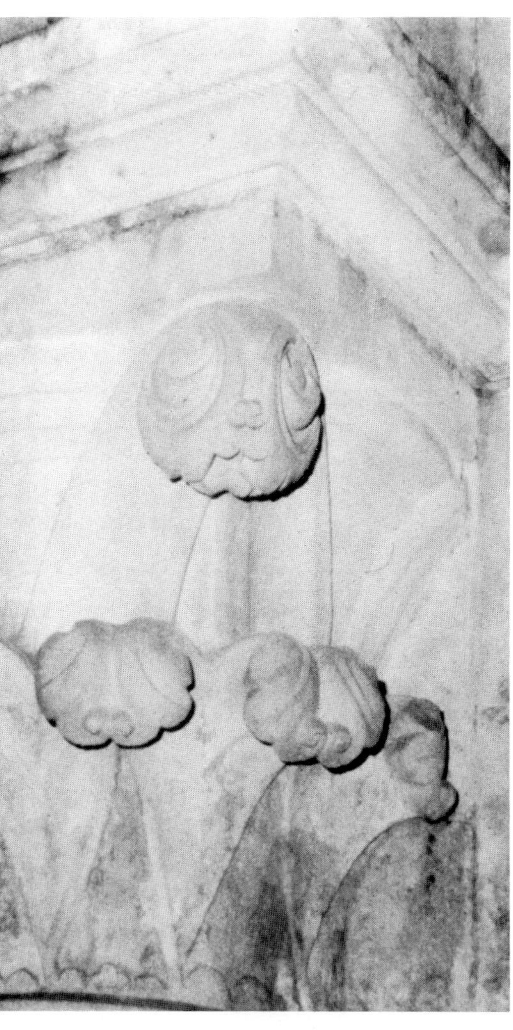

19. Santa Maria di Ripalta sul Fortore, Puglia, capitello del transetto settentrionale, terzo decennio del Duecento

capolavoro dal punto di vista formale, nella resa così puntuale delle venature dalle foglie e, dal punto di vista compositivo, nell'estrema armonia tra le foglie che danno vita ai *crochets* aggettanti e quelle piatte e stilizzate che fasciano la campana del capitello.

Il secondo aspetto di questa analisi che vede a confronto alcuni momenti della scultura architettonica nei castelli federiciani italiani con il mondo cistercense si incentra su un ulteriore punto di grande interesse per la comprensione di quelli che furono i rapporti tra queste due sfere: si tratta del ruolo assunto nei due ambiti da parte dell'elemento umano inteso come motivo decorativo.

Una delle caratteristiche che contraddistingue il panorama iconografico proprio del mondo cistercense è la quasi assoluta mancanza dell'immagine umana. Come si era accennato all'inizio ciò dipese soprattutto dalla posizione rigorista di Bernardo rispetto a qualsiasi forma di decorazione iconica: l'intera struttura architettonica fin nel più piccolo dettaglio doveva ispirarsi ad un ideale di estrema spiritualità che anche dal punto di vista formale escludeva qualsiasi tipo di deroga. Ma se la regola dettata da Bernardo ebbe un seguito nelle prime fondazioni cistercensi, in un certo senso già molto presto venne disattesa, o, per meglio dire, venne reinterpretata secondo una diversa accezione. È possibile, difatti, individuare esempi relativamente precoci di capitelli in cui la figura umana fa la sua comparsa all'interno dell'apparato decorativo delle abbazie cistercensi.[53] Non si può certo intendere il suo ruolo come di protagonista all'interno dell'elemento architettonico in cui si trova inserita; essa appare spesso ancora celata sotto una diversa apparenza formale. Una testimonianza tangibile di quanto detto potrebbe essere rappresentata da un particolare di un capitello a fascio del portale del chiostro di Valle Crucis, dove, nascosta in un elemento vegetale, si configura, sebbene in modo ancora molto schematico, una testina umana (fig. 18).

In un certo senso ancora fedeli ai dettami di Bernardo, i monaci che decorarono l'abbazia di Valle Crucis, con un sensibile gusto ironico nei riguardi della forma, preferirono non rappresentare palesemente il tema iconografico in questione ma "mascherarlo" onde renderlo in certa misura meno riconoscibile. Il medesimo gusto per lo scherzo con le forme iconiche, celate all'interno della struttura architettonica, sembra ripetersi anche in esempi più tardi, laddove ormai non era più dettato da alcuna necessità di coerenza assoluta al pensiero bernardino. Per esempio, in un capitello che si trova nella seconda cappella del transetto settentrionale di Ripalta (fig. 19), il *crochet*, realizzato da elementi vegetali, pare nascondere dentro di sè—solo se guardato frontalmente—l'immagine di una protome animale.[54]

Tuttavia, va sottolineato che, accanto a scelte di questo tipo, già molto presto in ambito cistercense si trovano a convivere anche episodi in cui l'elemento antropomorfo come tema iconografico raggiunge una sua più preponderante autonomia rispetto al contesto architettonico in cui si inserisce e viene rappresentato in tutta la sua realtà figurale. La stessa Valle Crucis può fornire un modello dell'evoluzione che tale tema iconografico ebbe più su larga scala in ambito cistercense. In un primo momento esso appare in qualche modo ancora celato, come una breve citazione *extravagans* all'interno della struttura architettonica: la testina sopra citata nel capitello. In una fase cronologicamente di poco posteriore esso si configura già isolato e assume un ruolo protagonista, come testimonia per esempio la testa di moro, oggi conservata a Cardiff (fig. 20), che costituiva in origine il lettorino del pulpito della chiesa. Più avanti ancora, in un momento individuabile a cavallo del Trecento, la figura umana viene collocata—al fine di sottolineare il ruolo portante di singoli elementi architettonici—nei punti nodali della struttura stessa, come dimostrano per esempio le due teste-mensola che sostengono la volta che copre l'ambiente di passaggio dal chiostro alla zona delle latrine (fig. 21).

Nelle cattedrali francesi sorte nei primi trent'anni del Duecento spesso ci si imbatte in tipologie decorative simili, inserite anch'esse singolarmente nel tessuto architettonico con una preciso intento strutturale, siano esse peducci, chiavi di volta o mensole. Ma come sottolineava Sauerländer,[55] a proposito dei cantieri di Reims e Amiens, l'intento di rappresentare la figura umana

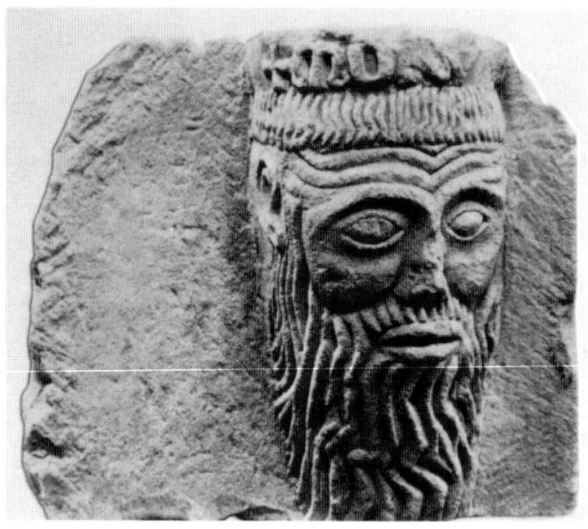
20. Museo di Cardiff, frammento scolpito proveniente dall'abbazia di Valle Crucis, prima metà del Duecento

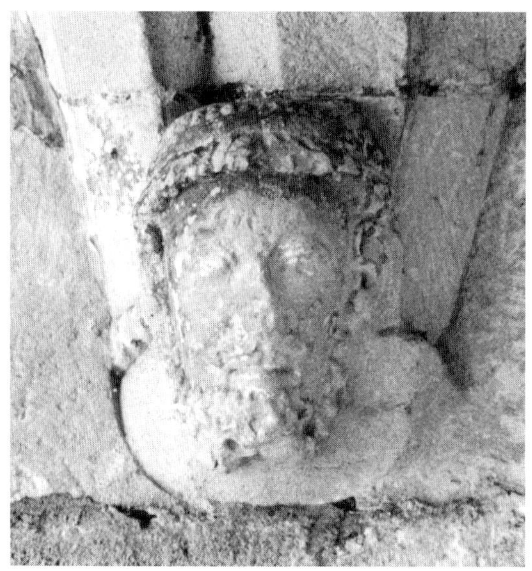
21. Valle Crucis, Galles del Nord, testa scolpita nell'ambiente di passaggio, principio del Trecento

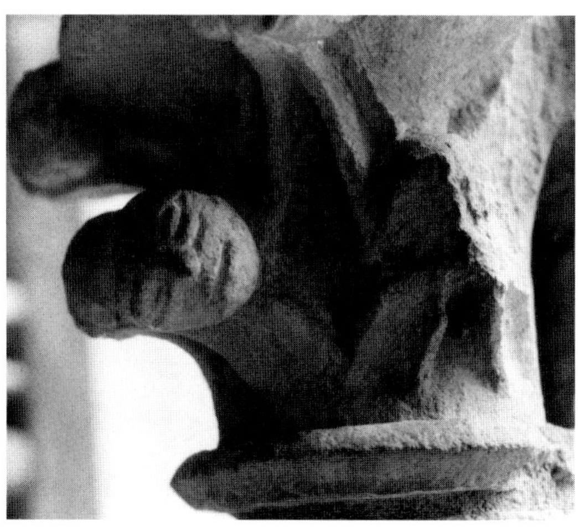
22. Noirlac, Cher, capitello del chiostro, 1270 circa

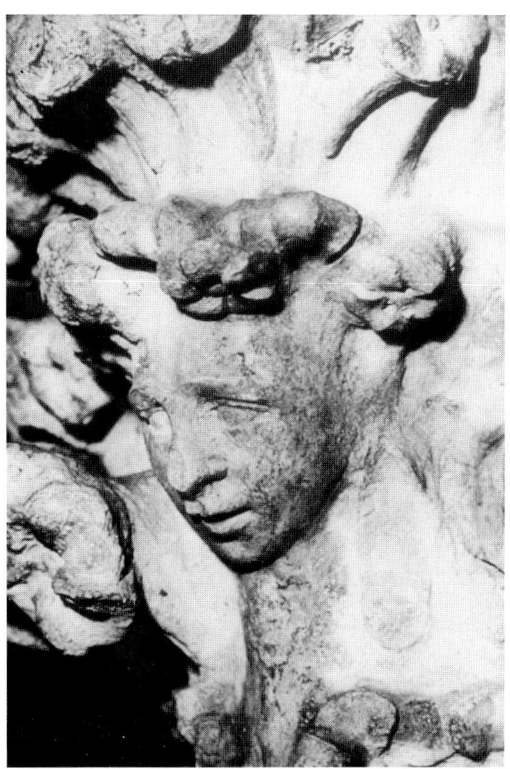

23. Fossanova, Lazio, capitello del chiostro, del Trecento

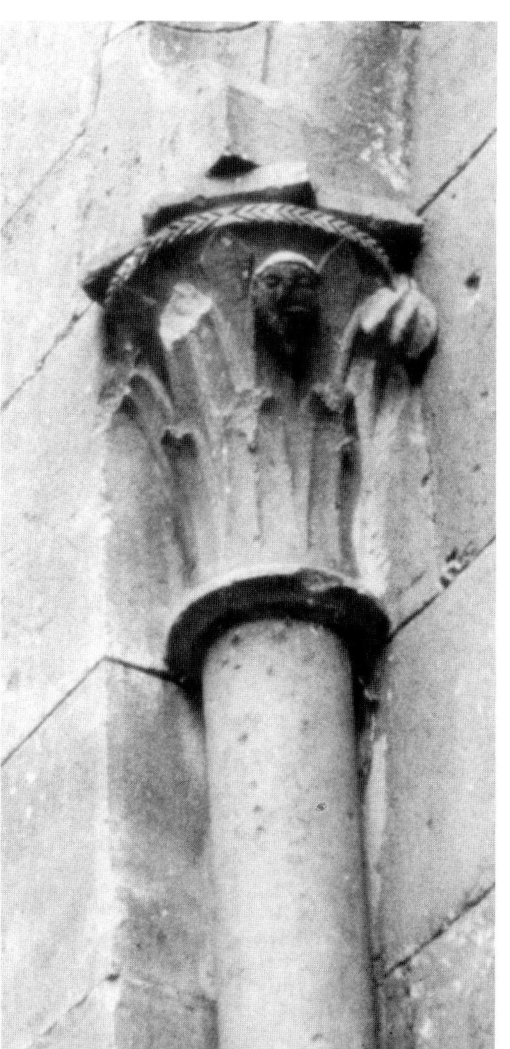

24. Santa Maria di Ripalta sul Fortore, Puglia, capitello della finestra del coro, terzo decennio del Duecento

poteva essere dettato probabilmente da un'esigenza di "realismo sociale," in esse era del tutto assente quel gusto ironico, peculiare della decorazione cistercense che poneva il soggetto in dialogo diretto con la struttura architettonica. La sostanziale diversità tra gli esempi delle cattedrali transalpine rispetto alla esperienza cistercense consiste appunto nella assoluta mancanza, nel primo caso, di una giocosa commistione tra l'elemento strutturale e quello decorativo. È pur vero che l'esperienza romanica ha conosciuto questo tipo di interpolazione tra diversi elementi, come testimoniano molteplici esempi di capitelli in cui le testine umane si affacciano tra le foglie dei capitelli, ciò nonostante la loro caratteristica fantastica e mostruosa, spesso deformante, permette di distinguerla da quella maturata in ambito cistercense dove la *ridicula monstruositas* era del tutto assente. Secondo questa chiave di lettura sono stati interpretati alcuni esempi di capitelli in cui la testina umana si sostituisce al caulicolo del capitello a *crochets*, tipologia diffusa soprattutto nell'ambito del Gotico borgognone. Solo per citare alcuni esempi basterà ricordare un capitello del chiostro di Noirlac (fig. 22), dove al posto dei caulicoli si trovano testine tonsurate di monaci, oppure ancora i ben conosciuti esempi di Casamari, con le cosiddette teste dell'imperatore, di Pier delle Vigne e di un monaco, probabilmente l'abate stesso, o ancora il volto nascosto tra le foglie in un capitello nel chiostro di Fossanova (fig. 23) o la testa di vecchio in un esempio nella chiesa di San Galgano;[56] fuori d'Italia in un capitello a Royaumont, oggi reimpiegato come acquasantiera e in una chiave di volta a Sulejow in Polonia.[57] Nella stessa Ripalta si trovano ripetute, in uno dei capitellini delle finestre del coro (fig. 24), una piccola protome umana che si confonde tra i caulicoli e una seconda leggermente sorridente in corrispondenza della chiave dell'arco del finestrone centrale. Rispetto alla presenza più o meno diffusa del tema della figura umana, Ripalta rappresenta comunque, nel panorama della produzione decorativa cistercense, quasi un "*unicum*."[58]

Si contano difatti un insolito numero di figurazioni che si distinguono dal punto di vista formale per la loro eccezionale vivacità. Otre alla testa-mensola posta all'interno della chiesa, caratterizzata dalla corona di foglie di fico, vanno menzionate le quattro mensole su cui si imposta la volta del transetto settentrionale. La loro particolarità consiste nella citazione quasi abbreviata della forma. Accanto a figure di telamoni, si trova una mensola in cui è scolpita semplicemente una mano, a voler sottolineare—ancora secondo quella chiave ironica—il valore di sostegno strutturale rivestito dall'elemento architettonico. Di carattere moraleggiante sembra essere la mensola angolare dove è ritratto un monaco a mezzo busto circondato da tre mani, di cui la prima nell'atto di tirargli il cappuccio, la seconda che tiene la barba e la terza chiusa a pugno nel gesto di colpire (fig. 25).

Ritornano anche in questi esempi certe costanti individuate come precipue della decorazione cistercense: in primo luogo la figura umana risulta inserita in un dialogo diretto, per alcuni aspetti quasi di gioco, con l'architettura, in seconda istanza, ci si trova di fronte a una resa formale piuttosto concisa o piu semplicemente solo accennata. Laddove tuttavia la forma non indugi più nel tratto riassuntivo si possono cogliere straordinari esempi di naturalismo: è il caso di una testa di uomo scolpita in una mensola del medesimo lato settentrionale del transetto (fig. 26); i tratti del volto scavato dalle rughe ne fanno quasi un ritratto. Questa volontà di realismo è comunque, nel panorama della scultura di Ripalta, da considerarsi ancora sporadico. La costante che lega le mensole del transetto e gli altri inserti iconici prima citati è data dalla loro essenzialità spesso risultante in una forma quasi abbreviata.

Si confrontino a tale proposito i ben noti telamoni che sostengono la volta di una delle torri di Castel del Monte con le mensole figurate appena illustrate che sorreggono la volta del transetto settentrionale a Ripalta (fig. 27). Lasciando da parte le dovute e innegabili differenze esistenti dal punto di vista stilistico tra gli esempi di Ripalta e quelli di Castel del Monte, si nota immediatamente che nel caso dell'edificio federiciano si è di fronte ad una diversa valenza conferita al soggetto raffigurato: esso diviene soprattutto misura dello spazio. Come ha più volte ricordato la Romanini,[59] le singole direttrici spaziali vengono segnate attraverso la posizione di gambe e braccia, nel caso dei telamoni (fig. 28),

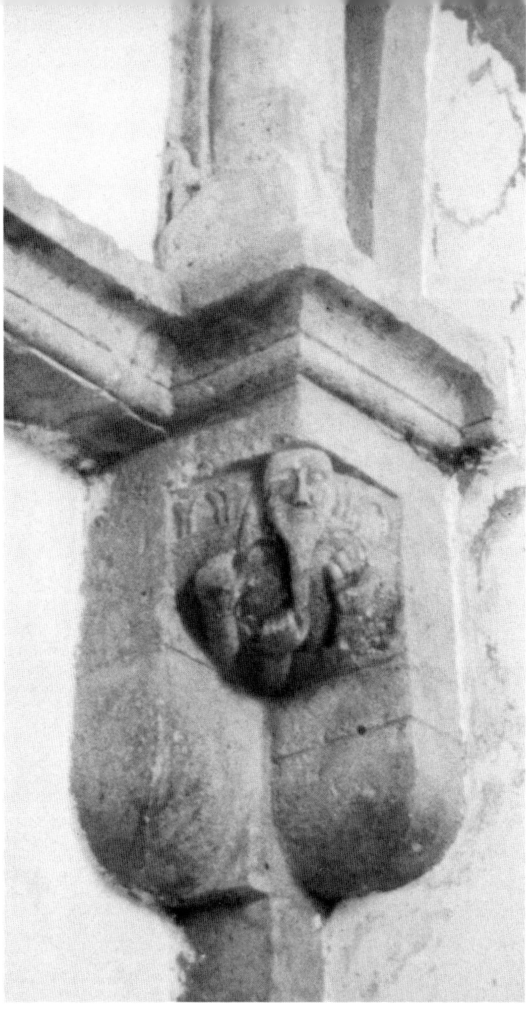

25. Santa Maria di Ripalta sul Fortore, Puglia, mensola del transetto settentrionale, terzo decennio del Duecento

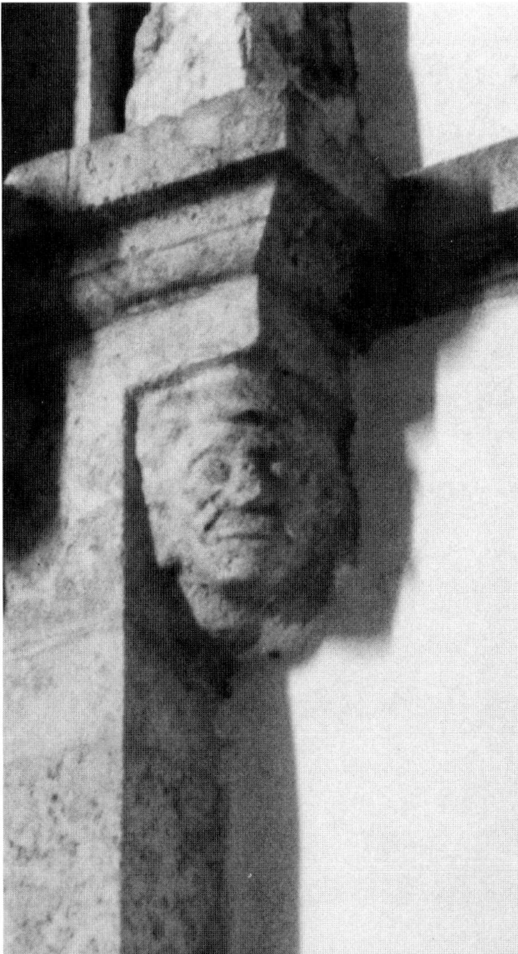

26. Santa Maria di Ripalta sul Fortore, Puglia, mensola del transetto settentrionale, terzo decennio del Duecento

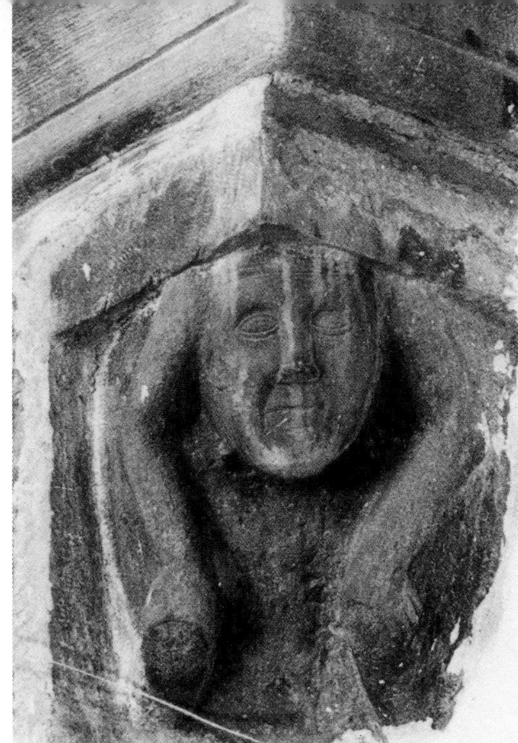

27. Santa Maria di Ripalta sul Fortore, Puglia, mensola del transetto settentrionale, terzo decennio del Duecento

28. Castel del Monte, Puglia, telamone, quarto decennio del Duecento

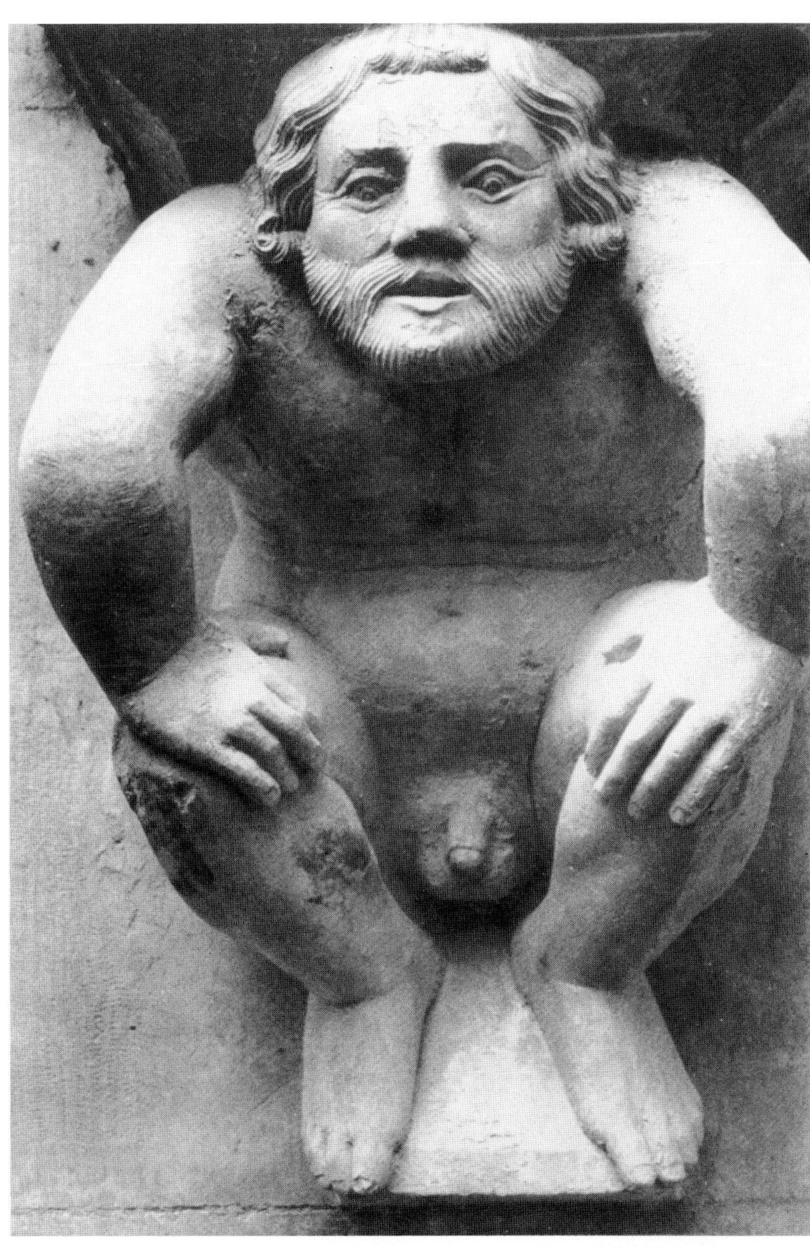

oppure dal protendersi in avanti del collo e delle teste, negli esempi dei capitelli erratici di Troia e del Metropolitan Museum di New York, o nelle teste-mensola del *donjon* di Lagopesole. In tutti questi esempi si ripropone un'impostazione formale che molti studiosi giustamente hanno visto in connessione con il mondo gotico d'Oltralpe.[60] Le teste-mensola di Lagopesole sono state assimilate più in particolare alla cultura francese, dove all'accentuato realismo si oppone un gusto più carico di valori spirituali, intimistici che si esprime in forme più aggraziate, come quelle di certe sculture della cattedrale di Strasburgo, ma ancora di più nelle teste mutile appartenute alla Galerie des Rois de Juda nella chiesa di Notre-Dame a Parigi.[61] Ancora all'esperienza francese sono stati avvicinati i due capitelli di Troia e New York, in particolare alla compagine di quegli "artisti più naturalisti," definiti così da Gnudi,[62] attivi a Chartres nel portale di Salomone o in quello dei Confessori.

Nonostante i confronti appena accennati testimonino che gli esiti raggiunti nelle cattedrali transalpine, pur tenute presenti le diverse varianti esistenti tra il panorama tedesco e quello francese, abbiano influenzato la scultura architettonica sveva in Italia, tuttavia è possibile individuare almeno due fattori che permettono di distinguere quest'ultima da quella gotica francese prima e tedesca poi.

Anzitutto anche riguardo alla scultura di soggetto antropomorfo ritorna una più netta e precisa attenzione naturalistica, derivante certamente anche dal diretto contatto che l'ambiente di corte ebbe con la cultura araba, già notata a proposito dei motivi fitomorfi, individuabile anche nei confronti dello studio diretto del patrimonio classico che viene così a essere rimodellato in una accezione moderna, a tutti gli effetti gotica. Il secondo fattore di distinzione, invece, riconduce ancora una volta al mondo cistercense. All'interno di edifici come Castel del Monte o Lagopesole ma in realtà anche altrove, la decorazione architettonica, in particolare quella di soggetto antropomorfo, appare regolata al suo interno e nel suo rapporto con la struttura architettonica da un rigore fino ad allora sconosciuto. Quel medesimo rigore geometrico che ha sempre contraddistinto la produzione cistercense, dalla scansione dei volumi in campo architettonico, fino nei più piccoli dettagli della decorazione. Spetta infatti ai monaci bianchi l'elaborazione di una regola secondo cui la figura umana come motivo decorativo si proponga laddove essa trovi una precisa rispondenza architettonica, cioè a dire nei punti-chiave della struttura volumetrica. In quest'ottica si devono collocare i telamoni di Castel del Monte, le numerose teste-mensola o le chiavi di volta. A Castel del Monte, a Capua, a Lagopesole—solo per citare alcuni esempi—l'elemento antropomorfo è ripreso con gusto realistico, pur rimanendo chiuso in un suo rigore interiore che non lascia spazio a deroghe di tipo ornamentale finalizzate a sè stesse.

Non solo: negli ignudi di Castel del Monte—dove l'elemento umano, pur restando fedele al modello reale, riesce quasi a trasfigurarsi in sigla geometrica che ne riassume l'interezza—la maggior sintesi formale trae la sua origine dalle concezioni spaziali che, affondando le radici nel lontano "iconoclasmo" voluto da Bernardo, distinguono le opere medievali di marca cistercense.

Il gusto per la breve citazione di motivi iconici, frutto di una vena ironica da parte dei lapicidi che è stata notata in alcuni esempi della decorazione di abbazie cistercensi, a prima vista, sembra entrare in contraddizione con quanto appena detto: esso costituisce al contrario un ulteriore aspetto che si aggiunge al complesso quadro rappresentato dall'arte cistercense e non nega altresì l'esigenza di un'espressione di pura essenza geometrica che non lasci possibilità allo sviluppo del puro e semplice decorativismo.

Concludendo brevemente si può riassumere affermando che i rapporti e le influenze reciproche che esistettero tra la decorazione architettonica federiciana e quella cistercense in Italia si presentano nella loro estrema complessità. L'aver notato la presenza di evidenti assonanze tematiche, talvolta di sostanziali diversità di intenti, di analogie d'impostazione, non fa altro che accreditare ancora una volta ciò che già Prandi aveva lucidamente individuato in proposito:[63] l'arte federiciana è il frutto di quella *plenitudo temporum* che contraddistinse i primi decenni del Duecento e in cui giocarono ruoli determinanti componenti diverse: il mondo gotico transalpino, francese prima, tedesco poi, il mondo classico, sia in linea diretta, sia filtrato attraverso l'arte pugliese, la cultura araba e, *last but not least*, il mondo cistercense.

NOTE

All photographs are by the author unless otherwise indicated.

1. Il mio ringraziamento particolare va all' Angiola M. Romanini, la quale, ancora una volta, mi ha dimostrato la sua fiducia e il suo affetto di maestra nel guidarmi e consigliarmi in questa ricerca. Un sentito grazie va anche a Enrico Zanini, attento e affettuoso mio interlocutore.

2. Esistono tuttavia testimonianze, seppure molto frammentarie, di pavimenti decorati e vetrate che dovevano trovarsi in uso nelle chiese come negli edifici monastici. Le caratteristiche relative al tipo di decorazione, anche in questo caso, si uniformano a quelle della scultura architettonica, ci si trova di fronte, cioè, a un panorama piuttosto omogeneo di forme geometriche più o meno complesse che non lasciano spazio a soluzioni coloristiche e che anzi, nel caso delle vetrate, si presentano rigorosamente monocrome. Wolfgang Bickel, "Die Kunst der Cistercienser," in *Die Cistercienser. Geschichte. Geist. Kunst*, a cura di Ambrosius Schneider, Adam Wienland, Wolfgang Bickel, e Ernst Coester (Köln, 1974), 193–340, pp. 308–334; Helen Jackson Zakin, *French Cistercian Grisaille Glass* (New York, 1979); Michael Cothren, "Cistercian Tile Mosaic Pavements in Yorkshire: Contexts and Sources," in *Studies in Cistercian Art and Architecture (= Studies)* (Kalamazoo, Mich., 1982), 1:112–129; Catherine Brisac, "Romanesque Grisailles from the Former Abbey Churches of Obazine and Bonlieu," in *Studies*, 1:130–139; Helen Jackson Zakin, "Cistercian Glass at La Chalade (Meuse)," in *Studies*, 1:140–151; Richard Marks, "Cistercian Window Glass in England and Wales," in *Cistercian Art and Architecture in the British Isles*, a cura di David Park e Christopher Norton (Cambridge-New York, 1986); Christopher Norton, "Early Cistercian Tile Pavements," in Park e Norton 1986, 228–255.

3. Fino agli anni Cinquanta rimase invalsa la tendenza sviluppatasi tra la fine dell'Ottocento e il principio del Novecento, a partire dagli studi di Dehio e di Enlart che considerava il fenomeno dell'architettura cistercense come marginale rispetto al panorama del Gotico. Si veda al proposito Antonio Cadei, "Immagini e segni nella scultura architettonica cistercense," in *Presenza benedettina nel Piacentino 480/1980*. Atti delle giornate di studio, Bobbio-Chiaravalle della Colomba, 27–28 giugno 1981 (Bobbio, 1982), 145–158, p. 147, nota 1; G. Dehio, "Zwei Cisterzienserkirchen. Ein Beitrag zur Geschichte der Anfänge des gotischen Stils," *Jahrbuch der Königlichen Preussischen Kunstsammlungen* 12 (1891) 91–103; Camille Enlart, *Origines françaises de l'architecture gothique en Italie* (Paris, 1894).

4. H. B. Dewarren, "Bernard et les premiers Cisterciens face au problème de l'art," in *Bernard de Clairvaux* (Paris, 1953), 487–534; Adriano Prandi, "S. Bernardo e l'arte cistercense," in *I Cistercensi e il Lazio*. Atti delle giornate di studio dell'Istituto di Storia dell'arte dell'Università di Roma, 17–21 maggio 1977 (Roma, 1978), 213–231, con bibliografia precedente.

5. Cadei 1982, 147, nota 1.

6. K. H. Esser, "Über den Kirchenbau des Hl. Bernard von Clairvaux. Eine kunstwissenschaftliche Untersuchung aufgrund der Ausgrabung der romanischen Abteikirche Himmerod," *Archiv für mittelrheinische Geschichte* 5 (1953), 195–222; Renate Wagner-Rieger, *Die italienische Baukunst zur Beginn der Gotik*, 2 voll. (Graz e Köln, 1956–1957); François Bucher, *Notre-Dame de Bonmont und die ersten Zisterzienserabteien der Schweiz* (Bern, 1957); Hanno Hahn, *Die frühe Kirchenbaukunst der Zisterzienser. Untersuchungen zur Baugeschichte von Kloster Eberbach im Rheingau und ihren Europäischen Analogien im 12. Jahrhundert* (Berlin, 1957); Anselme Dimier, *Recueil de plans d'églises cisterciennes* (Paris, 1948) e Supplément, 2 voll. (Paris, 1967).

7. Angiola M. Romanini: *L'architettura gotica in Lombardia* (Milano, 1964); "Povertà e razionalità nell'architettura cistercense del XII secolo," in *Atti dell'VIII Congresso internazionale dell'Accademia Tudertina* (Todi, 1967), 189–225; "Le abbazie fondate da San Bernardo in Italia e l'architettura cistercense 'primitiva,'" in *Studi su S. Bernardo di Chiaravalle nell'ottavo centenario della canonizzazione*. Convegno internazionale Certosa di Firenze, 6–9 novembre 1974 (Roma, 1975), 281–303; "La storia architettonica dell'abbazia delle Tre Fontane a Roma. La fondazione cistercense," in *Mélanges Anselme Dimier* (Arbois, 1982), 3, 6:653–695.

8. La ricerca si è concentrata principalmente intorno agli anni accademici 1973–1974, 1974–1975, e 1976–1977 e quindi nell'organizzazione delle due settimane di studio presso l'Istituto di Storia dell'arte dell'Università di Roma i cui atti sono pubblicati rispettivamente in *I Cistercensi*, in *Storia della città* 15–16 (1980) e in *Federico II e l'arte del Duecento italiano*. Atti della III settimana di studi di storia dell'arte medievale dell'Università di Roma, 15–20 maggio 1978, 2 voll., a cura di Angiola M. Romanini (Galatina, 1980).

9. Angiola M. Romanini, "Appendice a 'I Cistercensi e la città,'" in *I Cistercensi*, 289–292, e "I cistercensi e la formazione di Arnolfo di Cambio," in *Studi di storia dell'arte in memoria di Mario Rotili*, 2 voll. (Napoli, 1984) 1:235–259.

10. Romanini 1984, 1:237: "La scultura gioca in questa storia una sua parte di altissima portata. Rientra nel 'progetto' di Bernardo—alla stregua di ogni altra forma artistica—come forza espressiva da imbrigliare nelle maglie di un ferreo sistema di produzione pianificato di tipo modulare; e quindi rappresenta con rara evidenza le vicende secolari di questo 'progetto' dal cui rigore rinacque con rinnovata energia una forma ad un tempo astratta e corposamente incarnata nell' *hic et nunc* del fenomeno vivo."

11. *Apologia ad Guillelmun Sancti Theodorici abbatem*, in Patrologia Latina, a cura di J.-P. Migne, vol. 182, coll. 914–916.

12. Riguardo al contenuto simbolico di alcuni esempi piuttosto tardi di scultura figurativa presente in edifici cistercensi, si veda Adam Weinland, "Heils-Symbole und Dämonen-Symbole im Leben der Cis-

terzienser-Mönche," in Schneider et al. 1974, 509–552.

13. Maria S. Calò Mariani, *L'arte del Duecento in Puglia* (Torino, 1984), 65–84, con bibliografia precedente.

14. D. H. Williams, *The Welsh Cistercians*, 2 voll. (Caldey Island, Tenby, 1984), con bibliografia precedente.

15. D. H. Evans, *Valle Crucis Abbey* (Cardiff, 1987).

16. In particolare fu rimontata gran parte della zona del coro e il portale che mette in comunicazione con l'esterno verso l'ovest il complesso degli edifici monastici.

17. Hahn 1957.

18. Lawrence S. Butler, "Valle Crucis Abbey: An Excavation in 1970," in *Archaeologia Cambrensis* 125 (1976), 80–126, con bibliografia precedente.

19. Illuminanti a questo proposito sono alcuni confronti tra le mensole a foglie d'acqua nella zona del transetto di Valle Crucis con quelle delle abbazie inglesi di Fountains e Jervaulx o con alcuni capitelli a fascio della sala capitolare di Fontenay. Il motivo geometrico a quattro fogliette che danno vita a una piccola bugna, visibile nell'attacco superstite della scala che conduceva al pulpito del refettorio a Valle Crucis si trova analogo a Jervaulx e a Byland. Peter Fergusson, *Architecture of Solitude: Cistercian Abbeys in Twelfth-Century England* (Princeton, 1984), figg. 34, 36, 87, 105.

20. Motivi analoghi si ritrovano assai di frequente nell'architettura romanica locale come testimoniano per esempio alcune lastre tombali ancora oggi visibili nel dormitorio del primo piano sopra la sacrestia nell'abbazia di Valle Crucis, o in ambito cistercense in un capitello dell'abbazia irlandese di Boyle o in alcuni nel refettorio di Rievaulx. Roger Stalley, "The Architecture of the Cistercian Churches in Ireland, 1142–1272," in Park e Norton 1986, 117–138, fig. 43; Peter Fergusson, "The Twelfth-Century Refectories at Rievaulx and Byland Abbeys," in Park e Norton 1986, 160–180, figg. 58, 60.

21. Oltre agli esempi citati in precedenza si può ricordare anche il caso di un capitello dell'abbazia di Santes Creus (seconda metà del XII secolo) in Catalogna, dove le foglie sono disposte in doppio ordine sfalsato e segnate solo nella costola centrale. Anselme Dimier e J. Porcher, *L'art cistercien (hors de France)* (St. Marie de la Pierre-qui-Vire, 1971), 2:fig. 109.

22. Cadei 1982, 157.

23. F. R. Ugliano, *L'abbazia di Santa Maria di Sambucina e l'architettura cistercense in Italia*, tesi di laurea dattiloscritto presso la cattedra di Storia dell'arte medievale, Università degli Studi di Roma, anno accademico 1975–1976, e "L'abbazia di S. Maria di Sambucina," in *I Cistercensi*, 83–89.

24. Il motivo iconografico e in particolare la sua resa formale che si può definire quasi lineare riconduce per certi aspetti alla produzione inglese di epoca normanna, lasciando aperta l'ipotesi di un tramite seppure indiretto tra la cultura maturata nell'isola e quella testimoniata nell'abbazia calabrese.

25. La chiesa è stata oggetto recentemente di uno studio più sistematico nell'ambito di una tesi di laurea presso la prima cattedra di storia dell'arte medievale dell'Università delgi Studi di Roma La Sapienza. Per l'aspetto architettonico si veda Wagner-Rieger 1956–1957, 2:52–54.

26. Antonio Cadei, "Scultura architettonica cistercense e cantieri monastici," in *I Cistercensi*, 157–164.

27. Lottlisa Behling, *Die Pflanzenwelt der mittelalterlichen Kathedralen* (Köln-Graz, 1964); Denise Jalabert, *La flore sculptée des monuments du moyen Age en France* (Paris, 1965); Willibald Sauerländer, *Gotische Skulptur in Frankreich, 1140–1270* (München, 1970).

28. A cura di Augusto Gaudenzi, in *Monumenti storici della Società Napoletana di Storia* (Napoli, 1988), 88.

29. Calò Mariani 1984, 125, con bibliografia precedente.

30. Calò Mariani 1984, 65.

31. Calò Mariani 1984, 65–66, con bibliografia precedente.

32. Wagner-Rieger 1956–1957, 2:55–58.

33. Marina Righetti Tosti-Croce, "La scultura del castello di Lagopesole," in Romanini 1980, 237–252, p. 240.

34. Joachim Poeschke, "Zum Einfluss der Gotik in Süditalien," *Jahrbuch der Berliner Museen* (1980), 91–120.

35. Nel *lettner* della chiesa di Santa Maria a Gelnhausen (1230–1240) alcuni capitelli sono decorati da motivi vegetali estremamente realistici, in uno addirittura si affacciano tra le foglie uccelli colti nell'atto di beccare dai grappoli d'uva. Poco posteriori sono i capitelli del coro della cattedrale di Naumburg (1250 ca.) dove l'elemento vegetale raggiunge livelli di raffinato virtuosismo. Righetti Tosti-Croce 1980, 242, figg. 8–10.

36. Righetti Tosti-Croce 1980, 241.

37. Antonio Cadei, "Fossanova e Castel del Monte," in Romanini 1980, 191–215, p. 213, fig. 26; Helmut Buschhausen, *Die süditalienische Bauplastik im Königreich Jerusalem* (Wien, 1978). Il motivo trova altri riferimenti in particolare in epoca tardoantica in area pugliese. Solo per citare qualche esempio il capitello conservato presso il Museo Archeologico di Brindisi o quello erratico trovato nell'area sacra di San Leucio a Canosa; Maria S. Calò Mariani, "Aspetti della scultura sveva in Puglia e in Lucania, *Archivio Storico Pugliese* 26 (1973), 440–474; Calò Mariani 1984, 113–145.

38. A cura di Hans Robert Hahnloser (Wien, 1935); Romanini 1967, 189–225.

39. Righetti Tosti-Croce 1980, 241.

40. Hans Wentzel, "Antiken-Imitationen des 12. und 13. Jahrhunderts in Italien," *Zeitschrift für Kunstwissenschaft* 9 (1955), 29–72; Ferdinando Bologna, *I*

pittori alla corte angioina di Napoli, 1266–1414, e un riesame dell'arte nell'età fridericiana (Roma, 1969); Helmut Buschhausen, "Die Rezeption der Antike und der Einbruch der französischen Gotik in der Unteritalienischen Plastik des 13. Jahrhunderts," in *Studi di Storia dell'arte in memoria di Mario Rotili* (Napoli, 1984), 1:201–209.

41. Bologna 1969, con bibliografia precedente; Cesare Gnudi, "Considerazioni sul Gotico francese, l'arte imperiale e la formazione di Nicola Pisano," in Romanini 1980, 1–17; Willibald Sauerländer, "Intentio vera nostra est manifestare . . . ea quae sunt sicut sunt. Bildtradition und Wirklichkeitserfahrung im Spannungsfeld der Stauferzeit," in *Stauferzeit. Geschichte, Literatur, Kunst* (Stuttgart, 1978), 220–243; Maria S. Calò Mariani, "La scultura in Puglia durante l'età sveva e proto-angioina," in *La Puglia tra Bisanzio e l'Occidente* (Milano, 1980) 254–316, con bibliografia precedente.

42. Pina Belli d'Elia, "Scultura pugliese di epoca sveva," in Romanini 1980, 265–287, con bibliografia precedente; Mariani 1984, 113–145, con bibliografia precedente.

43. A tale proposito si può ricordare il confronto fatto tra questo fregio e un analogo motivo presente nel portale del fianco meridionale della chiesa di Santa Maria Maggiore a Lanciano; Marina Righetti Tosti-Croce, "La chiesa di S. Maria Maggiore a Lanciano: un problema dell'architettura italiana del Duecento," in *I Cistercensi*, 187–211.

44. Belli d'Elia 1980, 265–287; Calò Mariani 1984, 65–84, con bibliografia precedente.

45. Calò Mariani 1984, 74.

46. Cadei 1982, 154.

47. Joselita Raspi Serra, "Problems of Non-Decoration in the Architecture of Cistercian Buildings," in *Studies in Cistercian Art and Architecture* (Kalamazoo, Mich., 1982), 1:45–48.

48. Un ringraziamento particolare alla gentile proprietaria della tenuta di Ripalta, la signora Galante, la cui ospitalità e cordialità mi ha permesso di conoscere direttamente e nel dettaglio l'intero complesso abbaziale.

49. La chiave di volta in questione richiama molto da vicino un esempio nella torre di sud-ovest della cattedrale di Bamberga, a sua volta presa a confronto con altre chiavi di Santa Maria Maggiore a Lanciano e San Galgano; Righetti Tosti-Croce 1978, 202, figg. 147a, 147c.

50. Calò Mariani 1984, 65–84.

51. Angiola M. Romanini, "Federico II e l'arte italiana del Duecento: introduzione," in Romanini 1980, v–ix, p. vii.

52. Il motivo si ripete anche a Fossanova dove è proposto in alcune varianti tra loro leggermente diversificate; Cadei 1982. Anche a Pontigny in un pilastro proveniente dagli edifici conventuali oggi a sud della chiesa abbaziale si ripete il motivo analogo. C. Wilson, "The Cistercians, 'Missionaries of Gothic' in Northern England," in Park e Norton 1986, 86–116, fig. 25.

53. D'altronde nel campo della decorazione dei manoscritti il fenomeno aveva raggiunto già una considerevole maturità, al proposito si confronti Angiola M. Romanini, "Il Maestro dei 'Moralia' e le origini di Citeaux," *Storia dell'arte* 34 (1978), 221–245.

54. Il fenomeno risulta comunque molto diffuso e si trovano esempi anche nell'abbazia di Fossanova in un capitello del chiostro. Cadei 1980, 191–215, fig. 22.

55. Cadei 1982, 152.

56. Paola Puglisi, "Componenti federiciane in S. Galgano," in Romanini 1980, 379–389.

57. Cadei 1982; Romanini 1984, figg. 2, 4, 11.

58. In ambito pugliese sono molteplici gli esempi di capitelli con teste figurate, ma la sostanziale differenza che permette di distinguerli dagli esempi cistercensi consiste nella diversità di impostazione: la testa umana è il più delle volte al centro del capitello a scopo decorativo e non a sottolineare le direttrici spaziali e, laddove essa sia in corrispondenza dello spigolo, non si sostituisce affatto all'elemento architettonico. Al proposito si veda un capitello nel matroneo nella cattedrale di Altamura o in quello del portale principale nel duomo di Bisceglie: Horst Schäfer Schuchardt, *Die figürliche Steinplastik des 11.–13. Jahrhunderts in Apulien* (Bari, 1986), 1:tavv. 17 a–b, 194 a–b.

59. Angiola M. Romanini, *Federico II e l'arte del Duecento in Italia. Appunti dalle lezioni di storia dell'arte medievale, Università degli Studi di Roma* (Roma, 1978).

60. Calò Mariani 1984, 134, con bibliografia precedente.

61. Righetti Tosti-Croce 1980, 237–252.

62. Gnudi 1980, 3.

63. Adriano Prandi, "Il ritratto medievale fino a Federico II," in Romanini 1980, xi–xv, p. xv.

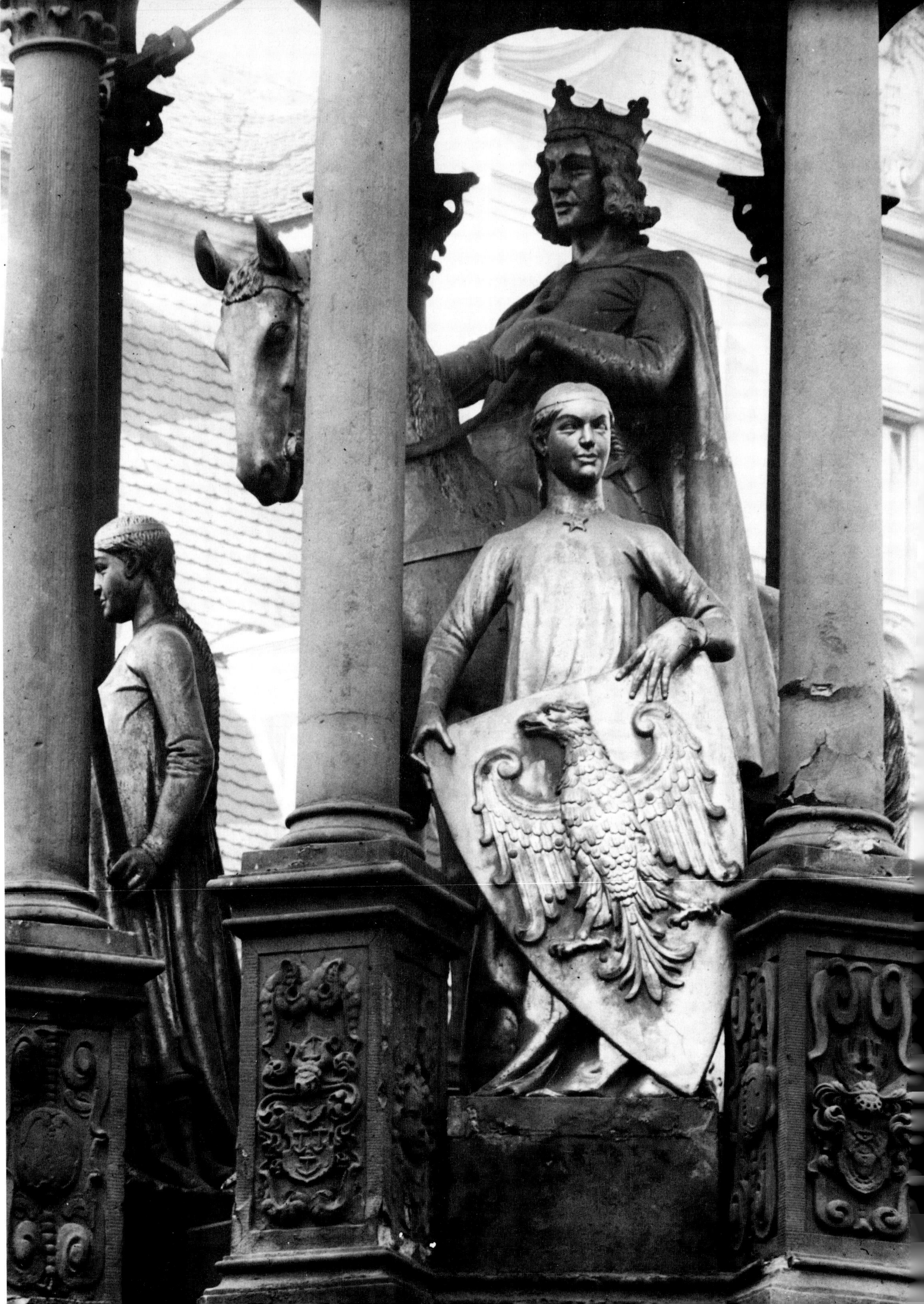

VIRGINIA ROEHRIG KAUFMANN
Princeton, New Jersey

The Magdeburg Rider: An Aspect of the Reception of Frederick II's Roman Revival North of the Alps

The Magdeburg Rider has been connected with, and even occasionally identified as, Frederick II by scholars interested in the emperor's northern sphere, but has been overlooked by those concerned primarily with his Italian activities.[1] The Rider is the first postclassical, freestanding, life-size equestrian sculpture in Europe. It currently stands in the Cultural History Museum in Magdeburg, where it was placed after the Second World War, being judged too fragile to return to its pedestal beneath a baldachin in Magdeburg's Old Market Square.[2] During restoration in the 1960s a bronze cast of the Rider and its accompanying figures was made and placed on the reassembled monument (fig. 1). The monument is composed of the mounted ruler and two female figures bearing, respectively, a shield and a spear or lance.[3] Even in the earliest depictions of the monument a banner was attached to the spear, and insofar as can be documented, it remained there until the restoration, when it was removed and not replaced. The female was thus a "standard bearer" (figs. 3–5).[4] The bronze cast differs from the stone figure in that the left arm of the standard bearer was restored to the original form: with raised arm she holds a spear (fig. 2).[5]

The present baldachin dates to 1651. It appears to have replaced one that was presumably ruined in 1631, during the Thirty Years War, when Magdeburg was almost completely destroyed. The medieval baldachin is known from a late sixteenth-century drawing from Pomarius' *Chronika der Sachsen und Niedersachsen* (Wittenberg, 1588) (fig. 6). It was composed of eight towerlike gables, four of which had female figures leaning from windows. It was crowned by a pointed metal roof, on the top of which a sculpted image of Saint Maurice was placed at some time. Maurice was the patron saint not only of Otto I, who founded Magdeburg, but also of the archbishop and of Magdeburg cathedral.

Although thought by some to be a later addition,[6] the baldachin depicted in Pomarius' chronicle probably belonged to the original medieval monument. Comparison of the towerlike gables with similar features also sculpted in stone on waterspouts of Bamberg and Naumburg cathedrals (fig. 7) provides evidence to support the conclusion that from the beginning the baldachin belonged to the monument. The delightful figures leaning from windows of the Naumburg spouts have their counterparts in the Magdeburg gables. The Naumburg and Bamberg forms have always been dated roughly to the same period as the Magdeburg monument, in the second quarter of the thirteenth century. Furthermore, recent evidence suggests that the Naumburg workshop can be directly associated with sculpture in Magdeburg.[7]

One can easily understand why the Mag-

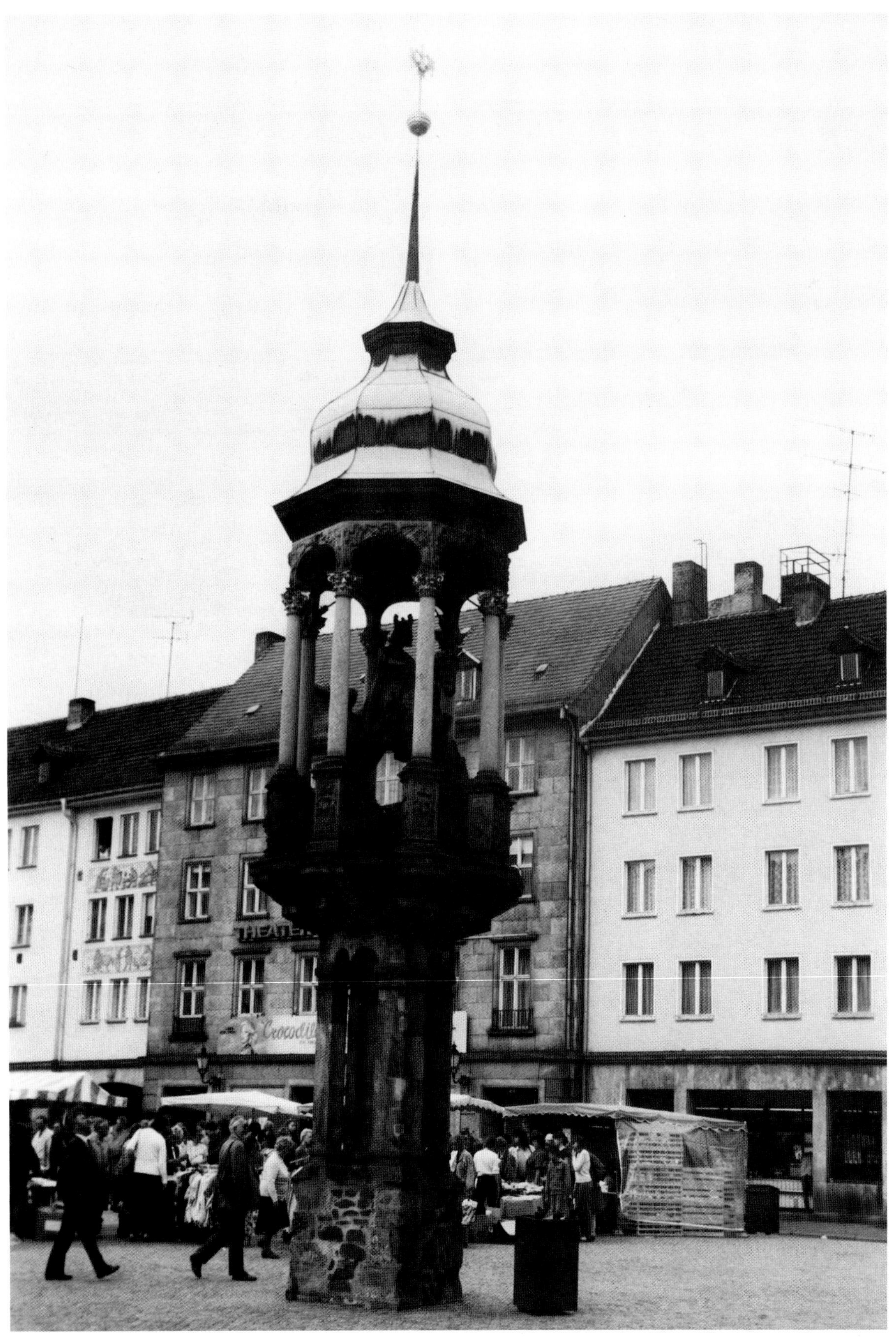

1. Magdeburg Rider, Old Market Square, Magdeburg, present monument with postwar bronze-cast figures, second quarter of the thirteenth century

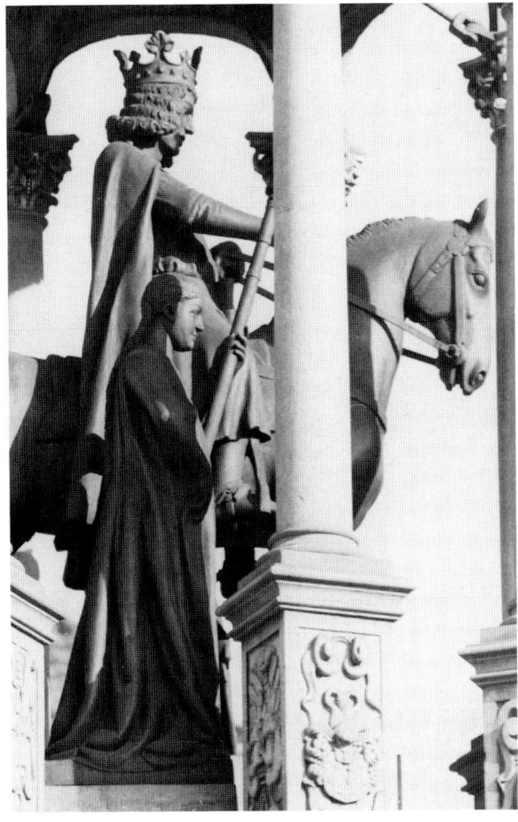

2. Magdeburg Rider, Old Market Square, Magdeburg, present monument with postwar bronze-cast figures; detail: Standard Bearer, second quarter of the thirteenth century
Photograph: Helga and Willi Kühne, Magdeburg

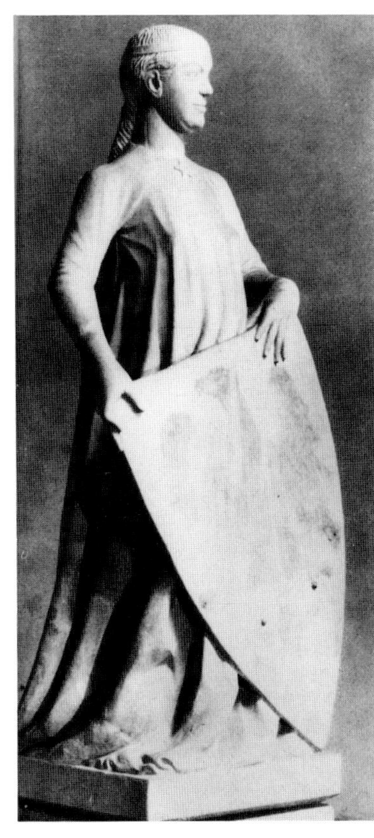

4. Shield Bearer from the Magdeburg Rider monument, sandstone, second quarter of the thirteenth century
Kulturhistorisches Museum, Magdeburg; photograph: Paulmann-Jungeblut, Berlin

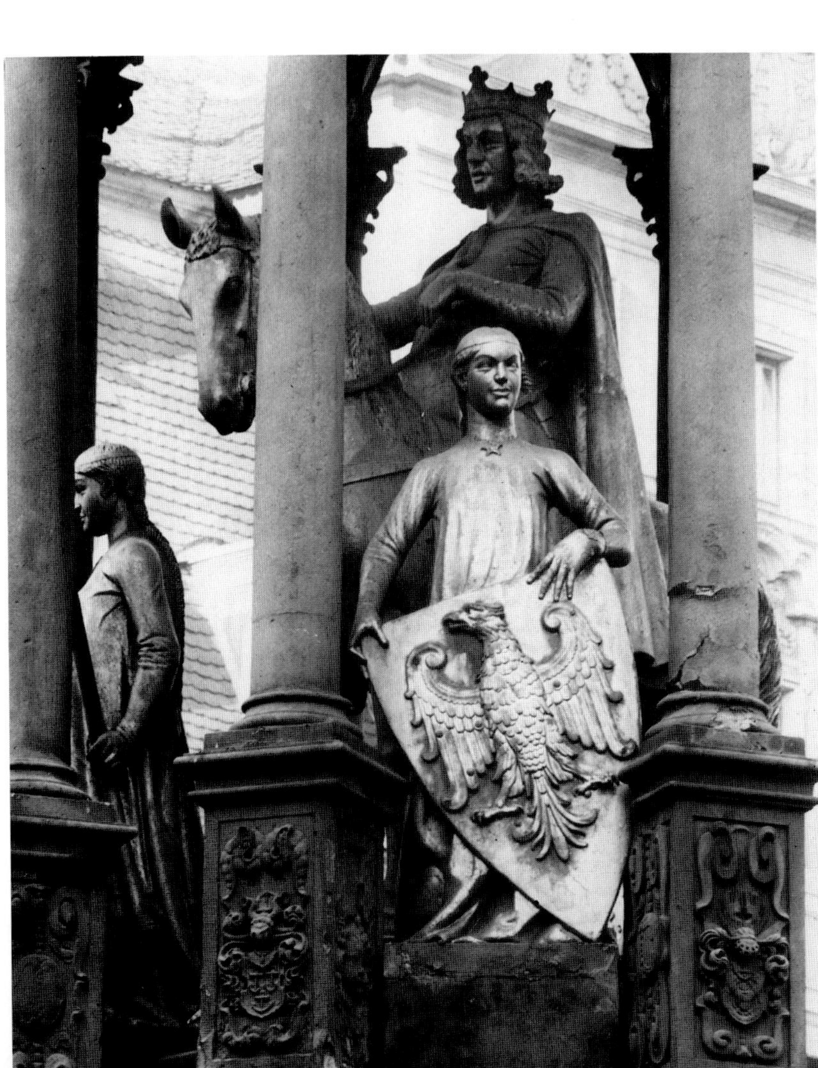

3. Magdeburg Rider, Old Market Square, Magdeburg, monument as it appeared in 1920s with original sandstone figures, second quarter of the thirteenth century
Bildarchiv Foto Marburg

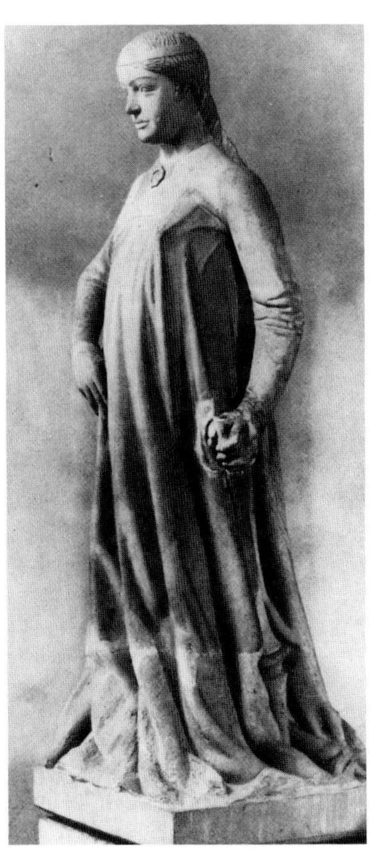

5. Standard Bearer from the Magdeburg Rider monument, sandstone, second quarter of the thirteenth century
Kulturhistorisches Museum, Magdeburg; photograph: Paulmann-Jungeblut, Berlin

deburg Rider has been overlooked by those interested in the art of Frederick II. Unlike the Italian art associated with Frederick, this monument is in a northern Gothic style. The columns and the tracery of the arches above them, and the towerlike gables of the baldachin, are reminiscent of Gothic cathedral sculpture throughout northern Europe at the time. The figures of the Rider and accompanying females are also thoroughly northern in dress and demeanor. All wear clothing typical of the mid-thirteenth century. The standard and shield are well known as imperial arms as depicted in generations of earlier northern imperial art, and even at Magdeburg in images of Saint Maurice.[8] All of these features differentiate the Magdeburg Rider monument distinctly from the South Italian sculpture associated with Frederick II in which features of ancient Roman art, including dress and hairstyle, often dominate the overall appearance.

Before turning to those aspects of the monument that link it with Frederick II and Italy, it will be instructive to set it further in its northern medieval context. Their life-size and naturalistically carved features give the Magdeburg figures a real-life appearance. The Rider's open mouth suggests, moreover, that he was in the process of speaking.[9] Both Herbert von Einem and Berent Schwineköper have suggested that the monument depicts an imperial entry, an *adventus regis*, of a medieval emperor into Magdeburg.[10] During such events, which occurred throughout the Middle Ages, the privileges of the archbishop of Magdeburg, in whom all legal authority over the city resided, would have been granted and reconfirmed. Another sculpture probably depicting the *adventus regis* ceremony is found in Magdeburg cathedral, where figures of Otto I and his wife Edith appear beneath a baldachin, holding gifts given to them by their subjects.[11] Otto and Edith were sculpted by the same artists, and at the same time as the Magdeburg Rider, suggesting that all of these works belonged to the same program celebrating the ceremonial entry of a medieval emperor. The fact that baldachins are intimately connected with such entries, and that Otto and Edith also appear beneath one, is further evidence for the association of the baldachin of the Magdeburg Rider with the original monument.

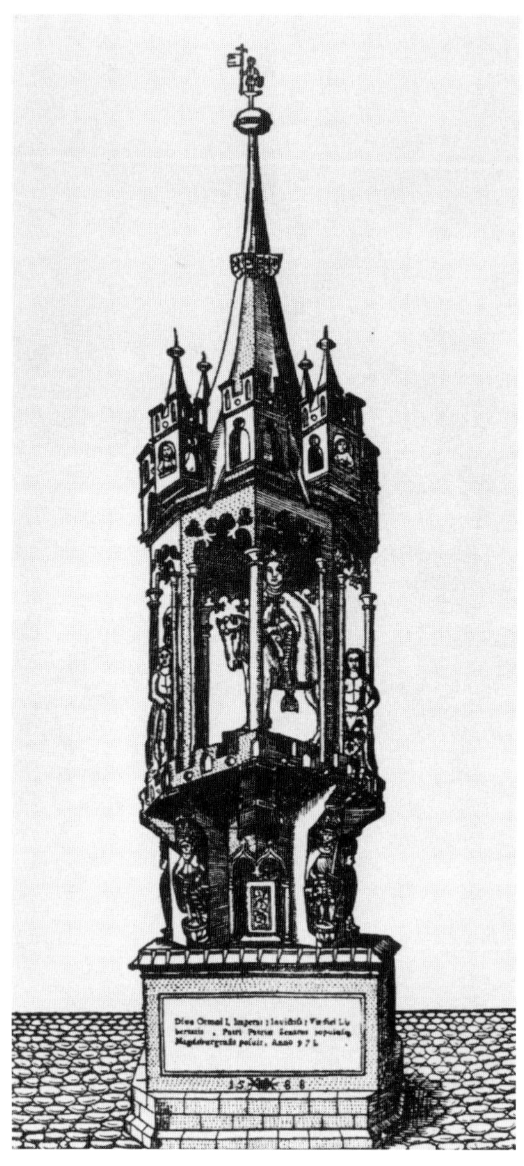

6. Magdeburg Rider monument from woodcut print in Johann Pomarius' *Chronika der Sachsen und Niedersachsen* (Wittenberg, 1588)

There is no systematic study of early and high medieval *adventus regis* ceremonies, and few preserved descriptions of them are published. However, we know that they frequently occurred when a ruler visited a city for the first time. Published descriptions suggest that the tradition was strongest in the North, where medieval emperors generally lived and ruled. Thus this aspect of the iconography of the Magdeburg monument also can be considered northern.

The historical reasons for the erection of the Magdeburg Rider monument appear to be

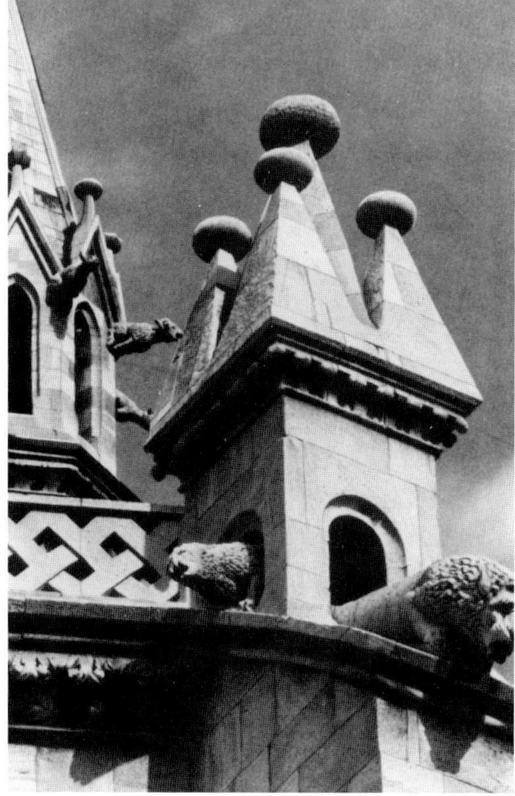

7. Waterspouts on Naumburg cathedral, stone, second quarter of the thirteenth century
After Ernst Schubert, *Der Naumburger Dom* (Berlin, 1968), fig. 27

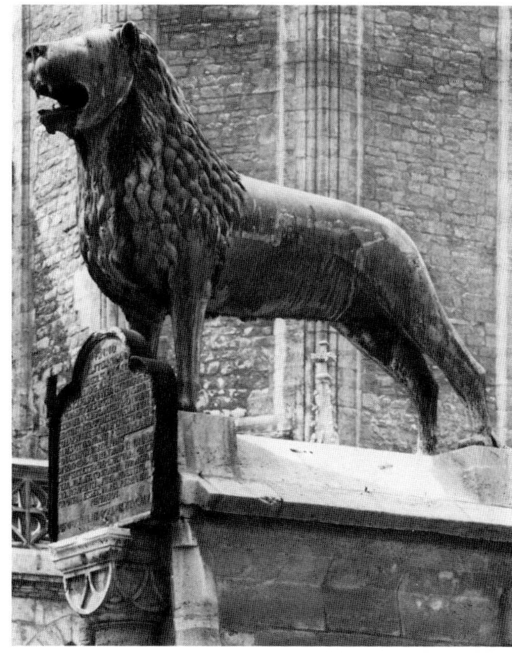

8. Braunschweig Lion monument, in the Burgplatz before the cathedral, Braunschweig, bronze, 1166 (photographed before 1980 when the original monument was removed from the square, replaced by a copy, and eventually installed in the Burgmuseum Dankwarderobe)
Photograph: Jutta Brüdern

largely the result of local tension between the archbishop and the citizens of the town, who wanted a greater share in legal and political matters and seem to have grown restive in the first half of the thirteenth century. By 1230 the *universitas civium* was an acknowledged voice in the community.[12] The archbishop would have had good reason to want to demonstrate his authority in the major public space of Magdeburg, the Old Market Square. The depiction of an imperial entry with the emperor uttering the grant of confirmation of privileges to the archbishop would have been a most effective way of demonstrating to Magdeburg's citizens his ultimate authority over them, and the source of that power. Schwineköper has demonstrated convincingly that the Rider monument served this function in Magdeburg, where it was situated before the archiepiscopal court of justice. There the archbishop himself, or his representative, sat facing the gesturing and "speaking" equestrian emperor, seemingly in the process of granting or reconfirming the archbishop's powers.[13]

Such a monument demonstrating the source of the legal authority of a ruler (*Rechtszeichen*) belonged to a type already known in northern Germany in the thirteenth century. One need go no further than Braunschweig to see the most famous medieval German *Rechtszeichen* of them all, the twelfth-century bronze lion that stood in a public space before the residence of the Guelphs, and symbolized their legal power through an image associated with their name (Guelph = small lion) (fig. 8).[14] It is tempting to see the erection of the Magdeburg monument as a Hohenstaufen response to the Guelph monument in Braunschweig. Still closer to home, in a political sense, is a statue erected about the same time as the Magdeburg Rider in the main square in Halle. This over-life-size stone sculpture depicts the Magdeburg archbishop's representative (Burggraf), Burchard VI of Querfurt, who administered his legal authority in that city.[15]

Thus the Magdeburg Rider not only looks thoroughly northern, and is a legal monument for which a local Saxon precedent existed, it was also made to serve the local political needs of the Magdeburg archbishop. But that is not all. When we examine the Magdeburg Rider further, it becomes apparent that it is a much more complex work of art, having a historical link with the reigning emperor, who was born, raised, and at that time mainly resided in southern Italy. The various threads linking the Magdeburg Rider to Frederick II are the main subject of this article.

Let us first return to the monument itself. Some scholars have accepted the findings of the nineteenth-century restoration, which concluded that the medieval baldachin depicted in Pomarius' chronicle was not part of the original monument which, the report suggests, looked much like figure 9.[16] Whether or not the baldachin belonged to the original version of the monument, this sketch, which accompanied the restoration report of the state conservator, Friedrich von Quast, who was responsible for the restoration, allows us to see what a remarkable work the equestrian figure is.

The Magdeburg Rider revives an ancient Roman art form, like many other forms that had been revived by a whole series of medieval Roman emperors.[17] But neither the politics of the Roman revival, nor the revival of ancient imperial forms that helped to show the succession of the ancient Roman rulers by the medieval emperors, can be attributed exclusively to Frederick II. The idea dates at least as early as Charlemagne, and almost every Roman art form cultivated by Frederick II can be shown to imitate a practice already established in the North. For example, the imitation of ancient coins, cameos, portrait busts, and even bridge towers bearing imperial images can be found in northern art associated with Frederick's grandfather, Frederick Barbarossa. Thus it will not be sufficient to show that the Magdeburg Rider is an intentional revival of an ancient Roman form; it must be demonstrated that its revival can be directly associated with Frederick II and Italy. Frederick's interest in the revival of Roman law and the ideal of justice is a key factor, because the imperial equestrian figure itself had legal implications, especially in connection with the equestrian sculpture of Constantine (now known to be Marcus Aurelius), which stood during the Middle Ages in front of the papal palace of the Lateran, where it served to demonstrate the source of the pope's legal power, which came from the Donation of Constantine. Like the Magdeburg Rider, there is evidence that it also stood near the papal court of justice.[18]

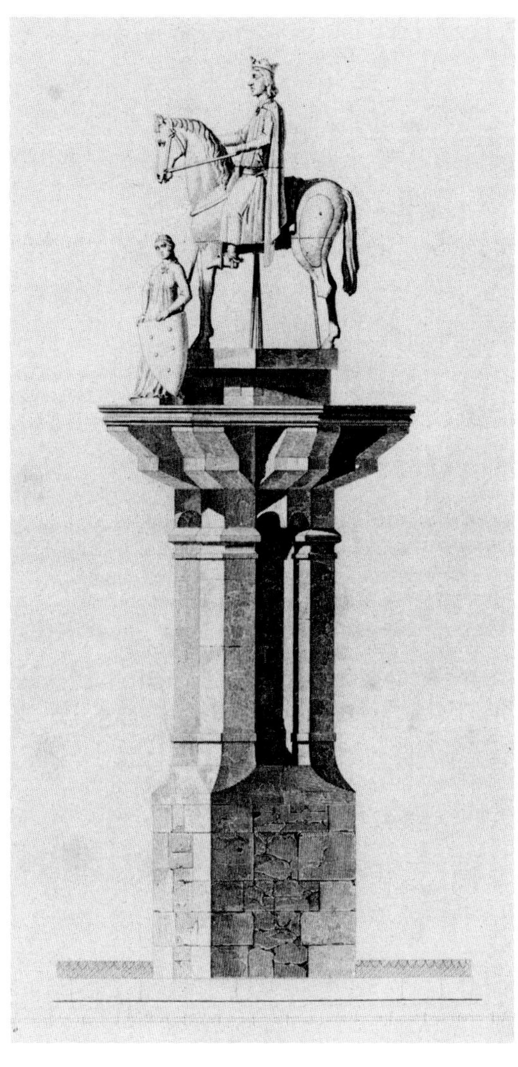

9. Magdeburg Rider monument, drawing published by Friedrich von Quast
After von Quast 1856, pl. 7

Further analysis of the Magdeburg Rider reveals that the mounted emperor can be compared best not with imperial equestrians from northern Europe but with ancient Roman works and particularly the Marcus Aurelius in Rome (fig. 10). Like that work, the Magdeburg Rider is depicted in the everyday dress of his time, holding the bridle in his left hand and gesturing with his right. This type of image differed considerably from earlier stone equestrian sculpture in Germany, as for example the figure of a Roman emperor found at Breitfurt.[19] It also contrasts remarkably with the late antique and early medieval images in which emperors held some attribute of imperial power, as for example the sixth-century image identified as Justinian which once stood in Constantinople,[20] or the ninth-century miniature

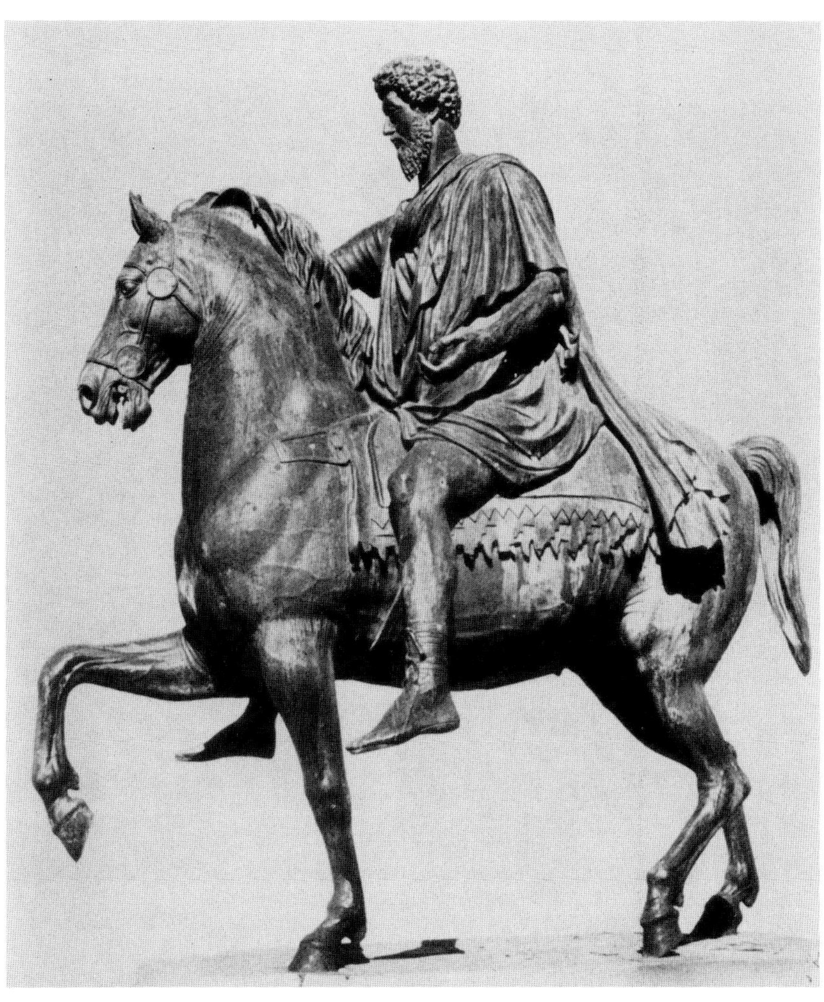

10. Marcus Aurelius, Capitoline, Rome, second century A.D. (photographed before removal of sculpture to Capitoline Museum)

equestrian bronze image of Charlemagne.[21] There are also Roman imperial equestrian images made of stone like the Magdeburg Rider. Because they share the same weakness of material—as stone, they can more easily fracture, and so need special support—they also have struts beneath the bellies of the horses. Some of the horses also stand on all four hooves. Images such as those reconstructed at Castel Gandolfo[22] or in Naples[23] might have inspired confidence in a medieval sculptor that he could erect a statue in stone before the capability of casting one in bronze had been reacquired. It is not likely that any of the monuments just referred to were known in the thirteenth century, but others may have been.

By the mid-thirteenth century, equestrian images appear to have almost completely lost their association as imperial images. From his study of the archaeological and textual evidence, Peter Seiler has found that virtually all monumental Roman equestrians known in the Middle Ages had been reidentified by the mid-thirteenth century as mythical personages or local heroes. For example, the Justinian in Constantinople, just mentioned, had become Hercules, the Theodoric in Pavia, the "Regisole," and even the Marcus Aurelius in Rome was no longer considered Constantine by most but rather a local mythical hero called Marcus or Quintus Quirinus.[24] On the strength of the forged "Donation of Constantine" which granted him imperial rights, the pope also claimed the right to appear officially on horseback and to have himself depicted on horseback as had earlier emperors: witness the murals in the thirteenth-century chapel of Saint Silvester in the Quattro Coronati in Rome.[25] Increasingly in the high Middle Ages the lesser nobility appears to have seized on the equestrian image as a means of enhancing its members' individual status. Hence those in a position to have seals made often portrayed themselves on horseback.[26]

Although earlier medieval emperors had revived other Roman forms, not even Frederick Barbarossa appears to have successfully revived the imperial equestrian. There is much evidence to suggest, however, that Frederick II consciously sought to reintroduce the equestrian as an imperial image—and that the Magdeburg Rider was the most remarkable accomplishment in this effort. Three thirteenth-century equestrian images, and possibly a fourth in Apulia, can be directly connected with Frederick's patronage, and each has been argued to represent him. Above the portal on the north aisle of Foggia cathedral is an equestrian image, now partially destroyed, but whose rider with swept-back mantle has been convincingly identified as an imperial image (fig. 11). The identification of the rider as an emperor can hardly be disputed, since the cathedral is the only one in Apulia known from documents to have been financed by the emperor.[27] In the mid-1220s when the sculpture is dated, Frederick II was often in Foggia, one of his favorite residences, so he is likely to have played a role in planning the sculptural program.[28] The rider is accepted by some as Constantine because of Frederick's special relation to this emperor,[29] as well as its similarities to other images of the first Christian ruler with swept-back mantle (as for example those on the façades of churches in western France). But others have identified it as Frederick himself, depicted as protector of the church and Constantine's follower.[30] A lost equestrian relief is also recorded for another of Frederick II's castles, at Lagopesole.[31]

Another partially destroyed but still recognizable equestrian appears in the interior court, above an entry, at Castel del Monte (fig. 12).[32] Because it appears within a building built and used by Frederick II, its identification as an image of an emperor is beyond question. Indeed, it has always been identified as Frederick II.[33] This figure is believed to be by the artist of the console figures at Castel del Monte,[34] who has been associated with sculpture at Reims and Bamberg (and thus directly associated with the Magdeburg Rider workshop).[35] Another work believed by many to be Frederick II is the bust now in the Museo Civico in Barletta (fig. 13). The identification of this work as a fragment of a life-size, freestanding equestrian figure that might be compared with the Bamberg and Magdeburg Riders has been accepted by many.[36] It has also been suggested that it was attached to a wall in a manner similar to the Bamberg Rider.[37]

The tradition of equestrian emperors that seems to have been revived by Frederick II lived on in the North throughout the thirteenth century. Besides the Bamberg and Magdeburg Riders, several other monumental, virtually freestanding imperial equestrian images appeared in the late thirteenth century on the façade of Strassburg cathedral. None of the originals still exist (they were destroyed in 1793), although we know three of them from drawings (fig. 14). Viollet-le-Duc restored the façade figures and expanded the gallery to the lateral façades in the nineteenth century.[38]

A stone equestrian sculpture erected in Augsburg cathedral to celebrate the Hapsburg emperor Maximilian I, while made three centuries after the Magdeburg Rider, is particularly relevant in this context. The sculpture itself is not preserved, but we know what it

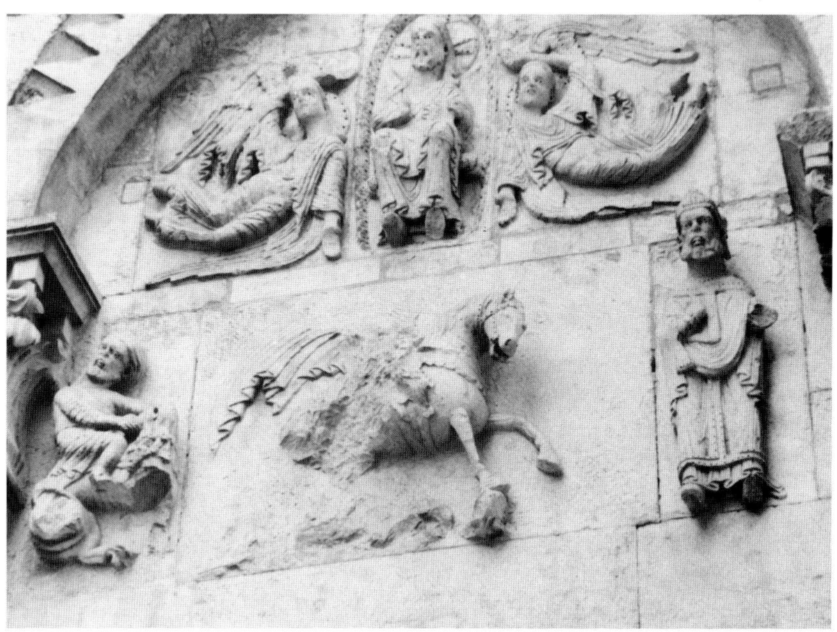

11. Equestrian emperor (Frederick II?), stone relief on the north portal of Foggia cathedral, 1220s
Author photograph

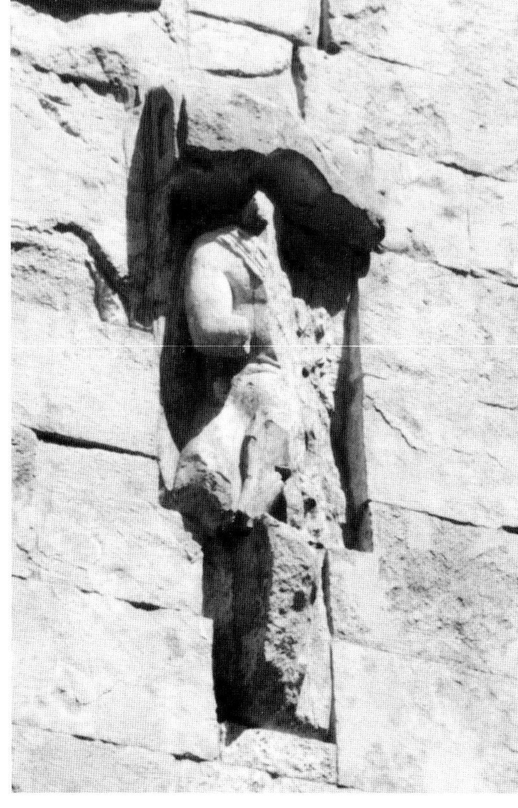

12. Equestrian relief of Frederick II, Castel del Monte, stone, after 1240
Author photograph

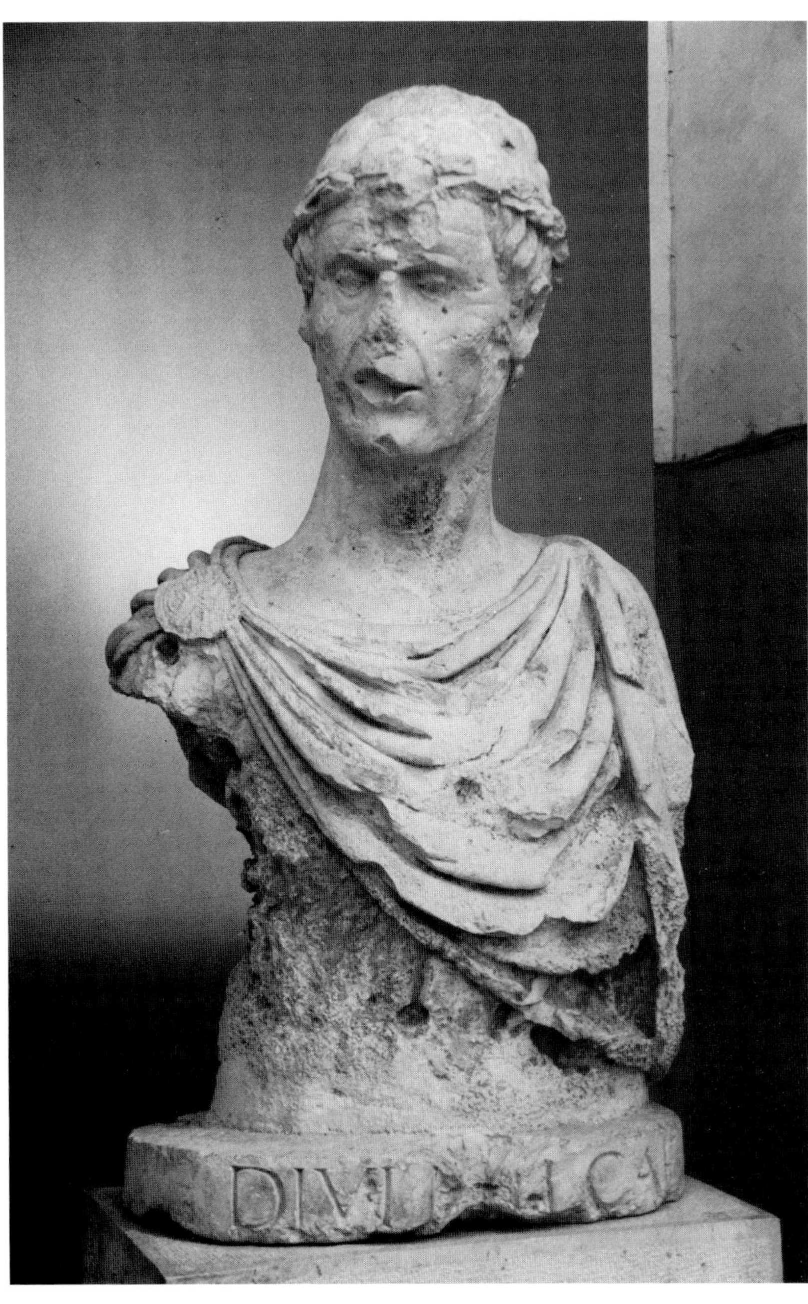

13. Bust of an emperor (Frederick II?), limestone and stucco, second quarter of the thirteenth century
Museo Civico, Barletta

looked like from an early seventeenth-century drawing by Hans Burgkmair (fig. 15).[39] A conscious choice seems to have been made to represent this life-size monumental image of the Holy Roman emperor in stone since it was created at a time when bronze casting was again more common for such monumental work. It has been suggested that the Magdeburg Rider served as a model for the Augsburg equestrian monument, and the idea is intriguing. In so doing, was an intentional reference being made to an earlier imperial monument with which the Hapsburgs wished to associate themselves? The Hapsburgs were an Austrian family who were establishing themselves as Holy Roman emperors. Just as Frederick II had shown his legitimacy through association with ancient Roman emperors, earlier Saxon and Salian families, and of course Charlemagne, an aim that he achieved partially by imitating their art, so the Hapsburgs needed to show themselves as the legitimate heirs of the Hohenstaufen, a goal aided by making reference to the Magdeburg Rider.

The presence of ancient Roman stone equestrians in Italy may explain, at least partially, why early medieval freestanding monumental equestrians prior to the Magdeburg Rider are found almost exclusively in Italy. Elsewhere the type seems to have disappeared. Indeed, the bronze figure of Charlemagne on horseback from the late ninth century, mentioned above, is virtually the only known earlier medieval freestanding equestrian image of an emperor—and it is only 22 centimeters high and thus decidedly not monumental. In Italy, however, at least as early as the twelfth century, works that prefigure the Magdeburg Rider began to appear. The figures of Antelami related to his series of labors of the months at Ferrara and Parma cathedrals are quite small, but the figure of Oldrado da Tresseno on the exterior of the Broletto in Milan, which has also been associated with Antelami, is almost life-size.[40] It is attached to the wall and appears beneath an arch, so that it was never intended to be seen from more than one side; nevertheless it is almost completely freestanding. This type of figure (which is still attached to the wall) and its frame can be related to works outside Italy like the earlier French equestrians, as for example at Melle, where the figure also appears under an arch,[41] and the Bassenheim Rider, contemporary with Oldrado, by the workshop of the Naumburg Master.[42] The most remarkable medieval stone equestrian antedating the Magdeburg Rider is undoubtedly the second version of Saint Martin and the Beggar, which was on the façade of Lucca cathedral.

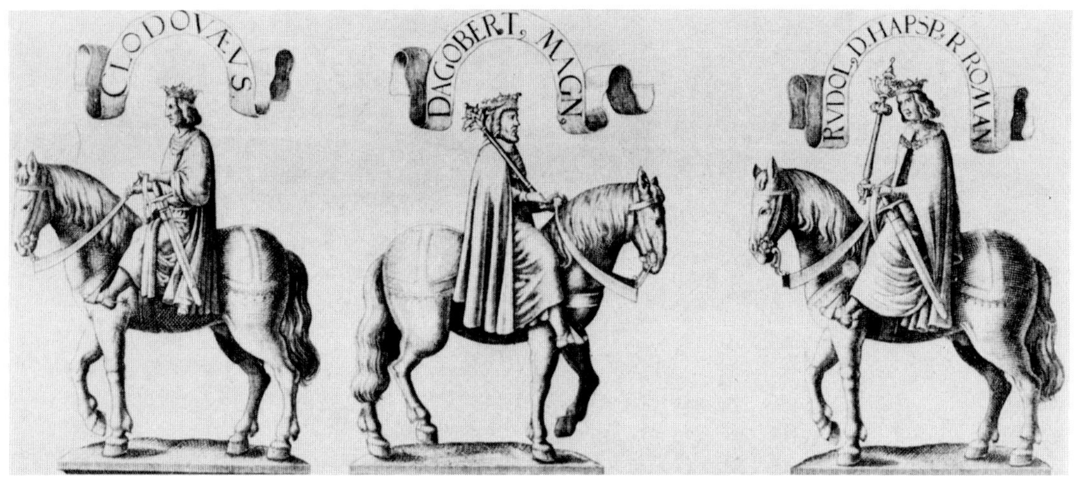

14. Equestrian emperors from the façade of Strassburg cathedral, eighteenth-century engraving by J. Brunn of three original late thirteenth-century stone figures destroyed in 1793
After Otto Schmidt, *Gotische Sculpturen des Strassburger Münsters* (Frankfurt, 1924), 1: fig. 27

The figures were intended for a wall setting and not to be seen in the round, but they are life-size and sculpted with much more complexity than the Milan figure and its relatives, all of which betray the limitation of the shape of the stone blocks from which they were carved.[43] The Lucca figures are made up of several pieces, and in this way the limitation imposed by the medium has been substantially overcome.[44] The technique of constructing monumental sculpture from more than one piece of stone can also be associated with the Magdeburg Rider.

The achievement in Magdeburg of a freestanding, slightly over-life-size equestrian monument may have been possible for the first time in the North because of certain techniques that have been detected in sculpture in Bamberg and Magdeburg. Many blocks of stone are used, and smaller forms that extend beyond the block are attached, enabling the creation of larger and more complex forms.[45] In Magdeburg, where the *Anstückelung* technique was most fully developed, it would appear to have been possible for the first time to bring together the desire for a freestanding equestrian and the means of achieving it. After a freestanding stone equestrian was created in Magdeburg in the first half of the thirteenth century, it was copied elsewhere. The two accompanying females on either side of the freestanding equestrian figure of Bernabò Visconti on his

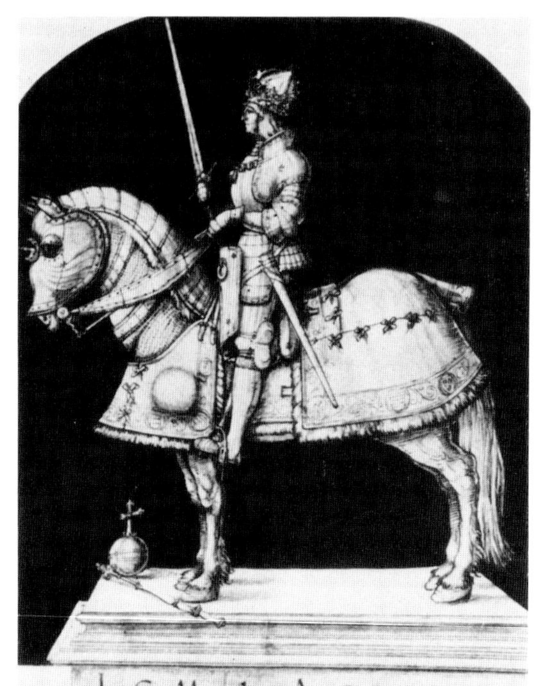

15. Equestrian monument of Maximilian I for Augsburg cathedral, drawing to serve as design for the monument, by Hans Burgkmair, 1608–1609
After Falk 1968, fig. 45

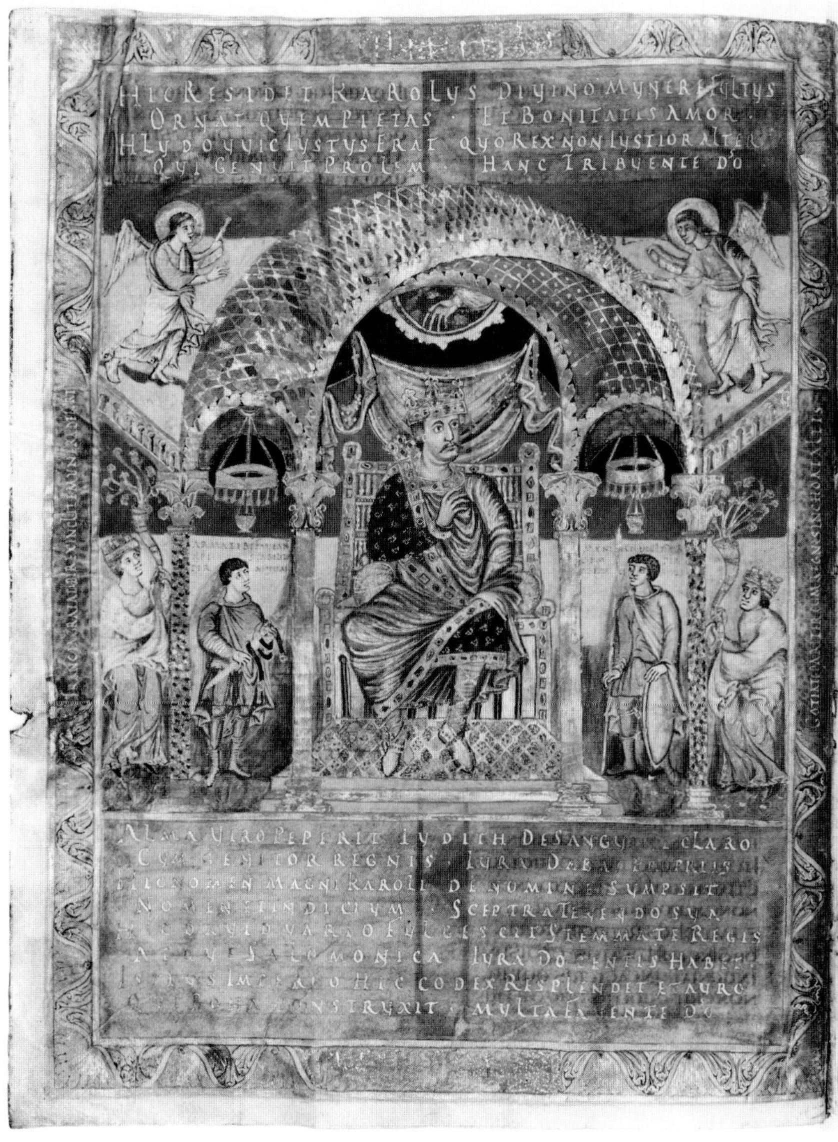

17. Charles the Bald Enthroned, Codex Aureus of St. Emmeram, Munich, Bayerische Staatsbibliothek, MS Clm 14000, fol. 5v, Court School of Charles the Bald, vellum, 870
Bayerische Staatsbibliothek

undoubtedly saw the Regisole, which is thought by some also to have been used in this way.[66] The Marcus Aurelius, the Regisole, and the Magdeburg Rider were also all located near courts of justice and bore some relation to them. Albrecht's travels with Eckbert in Italy in the early 1230s might very well have been the occasion when both the Bamberg and Magdeburg Riders were conceived as monuments reflecting the emperor's predilection for equestrian imperial images in the service of imperial legal thinking and politics. It is possible that such a Roman imperial image can be associated with Frederick II's interest in establishing a legal system based on Roman law. In this context one is even tempted to speculate that the two imperial judges from Pavia, mentioned above, who were put at Albrecht's disposal when in north Italy, might have played a role in the creation of such an image, and that their legal thought might well be reflected in the Magdeburg monument.

A closer look at the two female figures accompanying the Magdeburg Rider also suggests a renewed contact with ancient Roman images, occurring perhaps during Albrecht's Italian travels, or indirectly through contact with Frederick II and his court. The relationship has been overlooked by scholars such as Hans Jantzen and Herbert von Einem who, in seeking iconographic precedents, searched only as far back as late antiquity. They concluded that no specific identification could be made (von Einem) or that the figures were unidentifiable (Jantzen), an argument hard to square with the standard and shield they carry.[67] Both Jantzen and von Einem seem to have neglected to look for precedents earlier than the late antique because they relied on Percy Schramm's work on earlier medieval ruler imagery. Schramm's 1922 study of such Carolingian and Ottonian images as the miniatures in the Codex Aureus of Saint Emmeram[68] (fig. 17) and the Gospels of Otto III[69] traced their sources to Byzantine and late antique art.[70] In these and other early medieval images, female figures in single or double pairs appear near the emperor paying homage to him. They personify his realms and are depicted in such a way as to demonstrate a medieval feudal relationship to him. Although related to ancient personifications, the female personifications of Carolingian and Ottonian manuscripts have been transformed: these medieval women bear gifts and bend down before the emperor as a symbolic gesture of fealty. But the Magdeburg maidens are indeed very different from the Ottonian and Byzantine examples. The Magdeburg maidens no longer stoop before the emperor, or bear gifts, or in any way demonstrate a feudal (that is, medieval) relationship to him. They are, on the contrary, proud—we might even say triumphant—as they bear the emperor's arms. We shall have to look further for comparative material.

The most important comparisons with the

Magdeburg females are found on the Byzantine silk of the ninth to eleventh century called the "Günther cloth," now in the Bamberg Cathedral Treasury (fig. 18).[71] Since the silk was found buried with a Bamberg bishop who died in 1065, there has been some question as to whether it could have been known in the thirteenth century, and so it has not been studied as carefully as it might be as a possible source for the Magdeburg monument. But the striking parallels with the Magdeburg Rider suggest strongly that the Günther cloth—or some reflection of it—was known.[72] It is important first of all because equestrian images of an emperor are rare in the East as well as in the West, and this is perhaps the only one earlier than the Magdeburg Rider with accompanying female personifications. Not only are the females identically dressed, but they also have long braids, similar to the Magdeburg maidens. They have been identified variously as Constantinople and Athens (Grabar), or Rome and Constantinople (Schramm).[73] The event depicted is the triumphal entry of the emperor, the *adventus*, at which event he is proffered a crown and a helmet by the two personifications.[74]

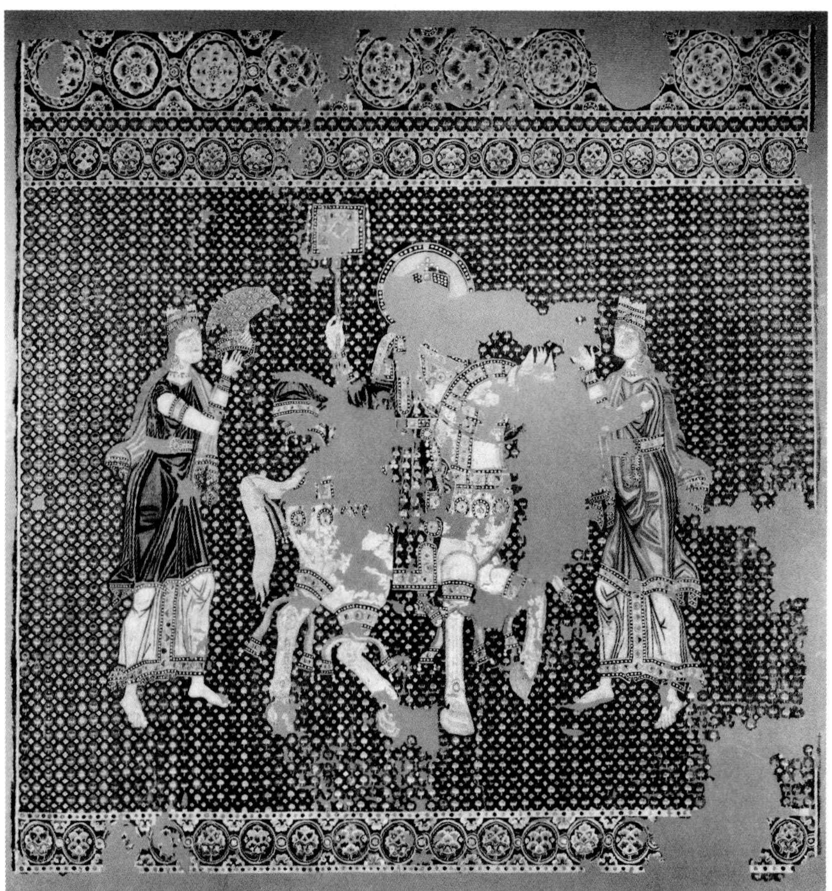

Besides cities and provinces, the two Byzantine women with braids might also represent imperial spouses. Many Byzantine empresses had braids, and two of them—Zoe and Theodora—are represented on either side of the emperor in Byzantine images.[75] Ancient Roman empresses also had braids, although they were usually wrapped around their heads in official depictions. If the Magdeburg Rider was intended to represent Otto I, it is possible that his two wives, Edith and Adelheid, were also represented by the Magdeburg females. They appear with him elsewhere in Magdeburg, in etched images on the north wall of the cathedral cloister (fig. 19), which is roughly contemporary with the Magdeburg Rider.[76] As imperial wives, the bands in their hair might be compared to the fillets worn by the Frederick II in Berlin[77] or the Frederick Barbarossa in Cappenburg.[78] The identification of both sets of females associated with the Byzantine and Magdeburg works as imperial wives would not preclude their being depicted with the attributes of other personifications. It would have been most appropriate to depict Otto I

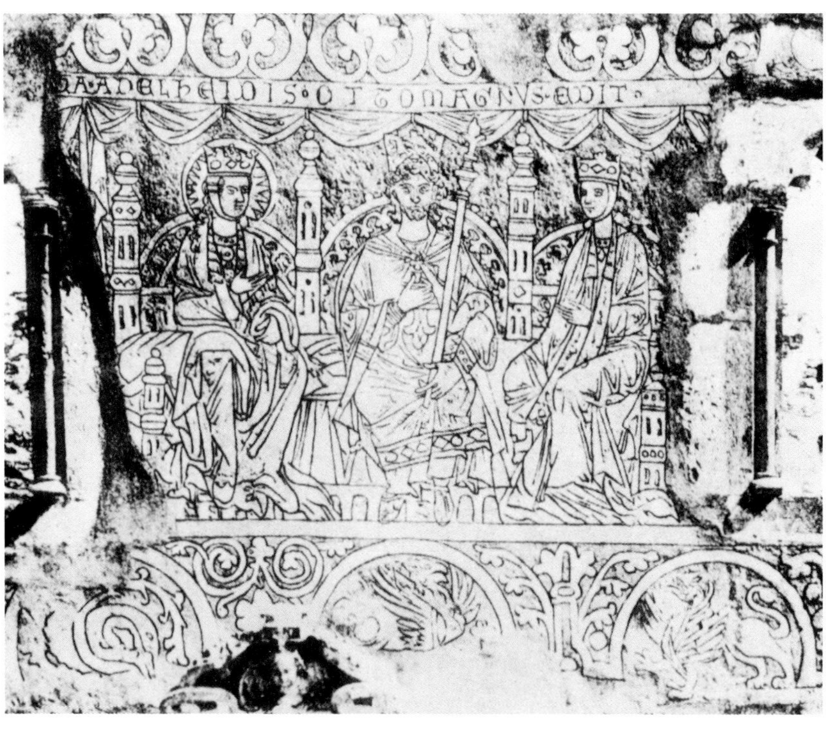

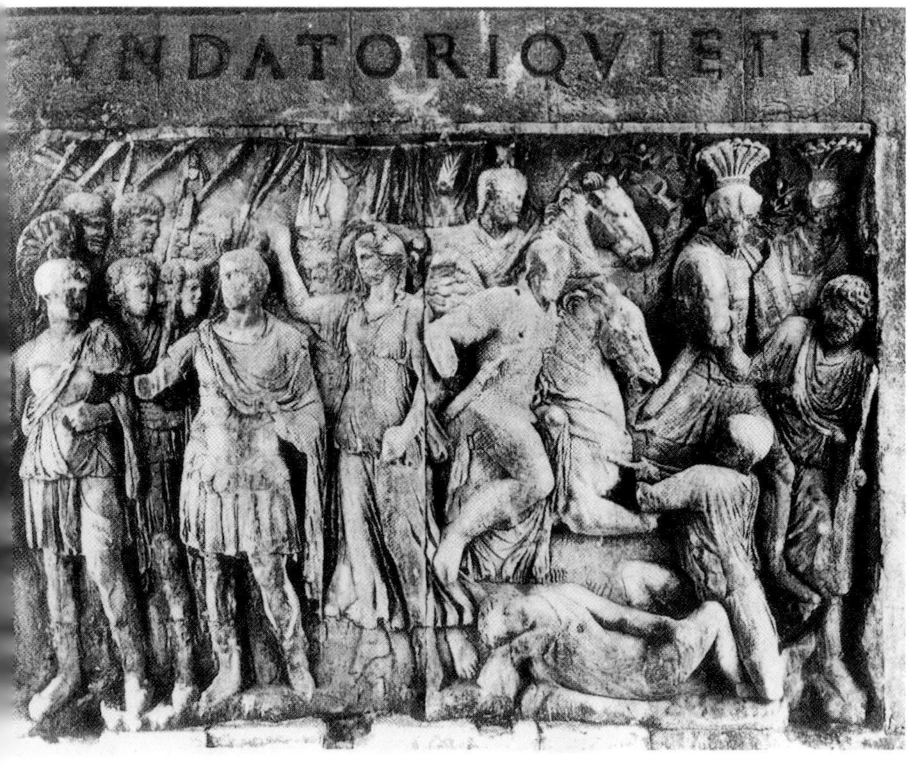

18. Günther Cloth with equestrian Byzantine emperor and two accompanying females, Bamberg cathedral Treasury, Byzantine, ninth to eleventh century
Photograph: Ingeborg Limmer

19. Otto I with his wives Edith and Adelheid, interior wall of courtyard of Magdeburg cathedral, drawing in stucco, second quarter of the thirteenth century
After *Der Magdeburger Dom* (Leipzig, 1989), fig. 68

ABOVE:
20. Triumphal Entry of Trajan accompanied by Roma and Victory, Trajanic frieze reused on the Arch of Constantine, Rome, stone relief, early second century A.D.
After Peirce 1989, fig. 4

accompanied by his wives in Magdeburg, since his first wife, Edith, brought the city into his possession as part of her dowry, and his second wife, Adelheid, helped provide for its development. Thus both wives were remembered in the thirteenth century for their importance in the city's early history.

In presenting the emperor with crown and helmet, the two Byzantine female personifications have taken over the role of victories in ancient Roman images of the *adventus*. Victories appear in *adventus* reliefs on many Roman triumphal arches including the Arch of Constantine (fig. 20).[79] Victories often appear with the emperor on horseback, as for example in the medallion depicting Constantine's triumphal entry. In both of these representations, and in many other Roman images, the victories appear with other females accompanying the emperor. One female can be identified by her helmet and the arms she bears as "Roma" (fig. 20). The spear and shield appear clearly on Roman coins and on the famous Gemma Augustea. Thus ancient Roman images of the *adventus regis* can be suggested as a possible source for the Magdeburg Rider. In these ancient images, two female personifications accompanied the emperor, who usually appeared on horseback. Medieval imperial entries were not associated with military triumph in the way that Roman and even Byzantine ceremonies signaled victories. So accompanying females in medieval images would not have had to assume the role of victories. But at Magdeburg, female figures accompanied the Rider, bearing his arms, in the manner of Roma.

Thus the Magdeburg females might be compared to images of Roma in the same way that the female figures of the Günther cloth might be compared to victories. They might at the same time personify parts of the emperor's realm, and the emperor's wives like the Byzantine images, but here depicted with the attributes of Roma. Roma had long been associated with the western medieval empire. She appears on the reverse of Ottonian seals (fig. 21), of which at least one is known to have been preserved at Magdeburg.[80] In these images she holds a shield and a spear which, like that of the Magdeburg maidens, had a banner attached, making it a standard. The banner in the medieval image provides further evidence for the conclusion that one of the Magdeburg maidens originally bore a standard. In other medieval images, such as that in the thirteenth-century north German *Historiae Romanorum*, Roma does not wear a helmet.[81] In relation to such images of Roma accompanying, if not leading, the emperor to Germany, we should observe that in a letter of 1238 Frederick II referred to himself as having been led by Roma. Thus, just about the time the Bamberg and Magdeburg Riders were conceived, Frederick was asserting that "Roma herself, like a mother her son, had sent him out to Germany, in order to reach the summit of his empire."[82]

Jantzen associated the towerlike gables of the baldachin over the Magdeburg Rider with cityscapes of Rome, and especially with those found on Hohenstaufen seals with the inscription: ROMA CAPUT MUNDI REGIT ORBIS FRENA ROTUNDI.[83] The best comparison—on a seal of Frederick I—is rather close, with towers attached to what is clearly a circular city wall, from which figures lean out of windows in a manner similar to figures

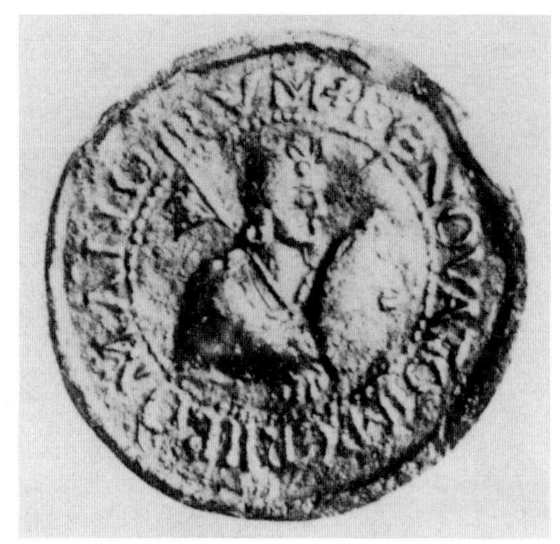

21. Roma on reverse of a seal of Otto III with inscription "Renovatio Imperii Romanorum," eleventh century
Reichsarchiv, Munich; after Posse 1909, pl. 10, no. 3

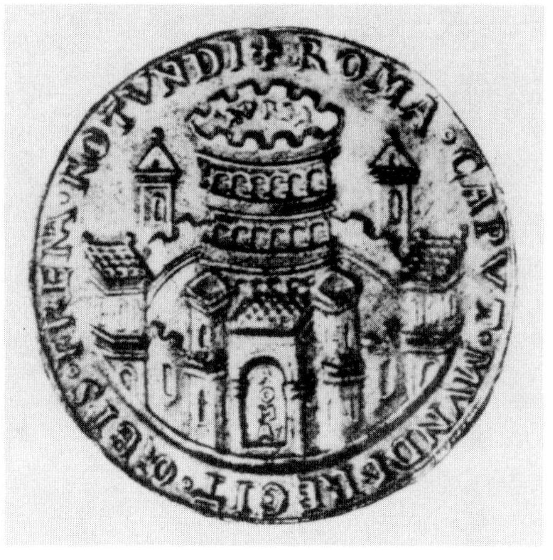

22. Cityscape of Rome on reverse of seal of Frederick I with inscription "Roma caput mundi regit orbis frena rotundi," 1154
Wolfenbüttel, Niedersächsisches Landeshauptarchiv; after Posse 1909, pl. 21, no. 4

on the Magdeburg baldachin (fig. 22). Frederick II's seals are similar and clearly modeled on the earlier Hohenstaufen seals, but much of the detail is missing, including the figures in the towers.[84] These images of Rome appear on the reverse of seals whose obverses depict the emperor seated and holding his regalia. So the Magdeburg Rider image resonates with the images on both sides of the seals. On the other hand, the cityscape of the Magdeburg baldachin probably represents Magdeburg, not Rome, and the females leaning out of windows of the gables probably depict citizens of Magdeburg greeting the emperor. As such the Magdeburg cityscape provides a particularly good example of the type of imperial entry described by Ernst Kantorowicz, which reflects the biblical imagery of Christ's entry into Jerusalem. In both the biblical and imperial images, citizens lean out of the city gate to greet the entering king, who is mounted and accompanied by companions.[85]

While performing a function with respect to the emperor which is comparable to that of their Carolingian and Ottonian sisters, the Gothic maidens of the Magdeburg monument belong to a different chapter in medieval imperial history. The concept of empire that emerged after the investiture conflict, and that can be identified with the Hohenstaufen dynasty, presupposed a very different relationship between the medieval state and ancient Rome. As described by Hans Martin Schaller, the Hohenstaufens rebuilt the secular empire distanced from the Church, on the basis of Roman law. They saw their empire as a revival of ancient Rome, including Rome itself and the church lands, and their process of rebuilding might be called "Romanization."[86] In this context a reference to the goddess Roma in the Magdeburg monument could be understood as intentional.

The standard held by the Magdeburg maiden and medieval images of Roma (fig. 21) is an example of the medievalization of the Roman spear.[87] The spear had always been an imperial weapon, but in the Middle Ages it acquired a banner. The bands around the hair of both female figures may be another such reference. They may reflect ancient Roman laurel wreaths worn by emperors and their wives,[88] which would have seemed out of place in the North during the thirteenth century.

The relation of the Magdeburg *adventus* image to the development of western imperial entries would be a fitting subject for another article.[89] Here it will suffice to note that the Magdeburg image appears to follow ancient Roman depictions of entries insofar as two female personifications accompany the emperor bearing shield and spear, and further that these personifications seem more closely associated with Roma. It is fitting that Roma should be personified by figures

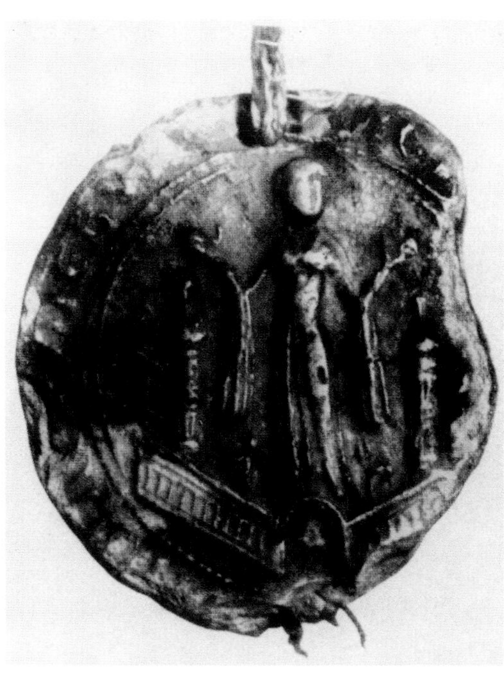

23. The Maid of Magdeburg on the city seal of Magdeburg, 1244
After von Einem 1953, fig. 5

accompanying the medieval Roman emperor as he enters a city in his realm. In later imperial images of entries, as for example of Maximilian I, the Hapsburg emperor is accompanied by crowned female family members also carrying his arms, in this case shields and scepters.[90] Perhaps they should also be seen as personifying Roma.

The Magdeburg females thus appear to have many layers of identification and symbolic meaning. These include references to earlier imagery of the two parts of the medieval empire, Italy and Germany, and what appears to be a novel western reference to imperial wives accompanying their husbands and bearing their arms, taken from Byzantine imagery and perhaps specifically from the Günther cloth. On the other hand, it seems unlikely that the females were intended as symbolic representations of Magdeburg, for they are distinctly shown accompanying the emperor rather than greeting him.[91] In earlier and later images of imperial entries, personifications of the cities visited by the emperor greeted rather than accompanied him. But most likely after it was erected, the image of the woman who brought Magdeburg to the empire as her dowry (Edith), and who may well be the Magd (maiden) after whom Magdeburg was named, does seem to have been taken over in the seal of the city (fig. 23). On this seal of 1244, a single female figure is depicted in a manner similar to the maidens of the monument. She is dressed similarly and also appears surrounded by the walls of the city.

As we have seen, the political function of the Magdeburg Rider as a symbol of the source of the legal power of the archbishop—a *Rechtszeichen*—suggests that what is represented is an *adventus* or ceremonial entry of the emperor who granted or reconfirmed rights. It is difficult to determine which grant or reconfirmation of power was considered by the archbishop to be the most significant in the thirteenth century. Otto I made the original grant, and Otto II reconfirmed these privileges and added others. Philip of Swabia had been most recently received ceremonially in Magdeburg. The numerous other sculpted figures appearing throughout Europe in the thirteenth century to "document" grants of privileges are of "founders."[92] The existence of these other sculpted founders, and the similar political use to which they were put, would suggest that the Magdeburg Rider, too, represents Magdeburg's founder, Otto I. The suggestion made above, that the two accompanying females can be associated with Otto I's two wives and a tradition of imperial images of emperors with two female members of their family holding imperial regalia, provides additional support for the identification.

The identification of the Rider as Frederick II was introduced into the discussion of the monument by just those scholars who first correctly assessed the importance of the historical links between the Magdeburg and Bamberg archbishops. Hans Fiedler suggested such an identification but concluded that it would be impossible to prove, for lack of evidence of the actual appearance of the emperor.[93] W. R. Valentiner went further, using literary sources which he admitted were still vague (fig. 24). On the basis of the historical relationship of the ecclesiastics and Frederick II and the similarity of the Bamberg Rider's profile and the emperor's profile on one of his coins (Augustales) (fig. 25), he nevertheless concluded that both the Bamberg and Magdeburg Riders represented

Frederick II.[94] Gerhart Ladner suggested that both Riders represented other personages with traits of Frederick II. In addition to the Augustales, he mentioned several other works depicting Frederick that he claimed were similar to the Riders, including the relief on the chancel at Bitonto cathedral.[95] But these comparisons, like others, have remained problematic.[96]

The Bamberg and Magdeburg Riders do not closely resemble even the best portraits of Frederick II. Even the sculpted image of Philip Augustus at Reims cathedral (fig. 26) is closer to the German riders than the Augustales portrait of Frederick. What all the Italian images have in common would appear to have nothing to do with how the emperor appeared in real life but rather to be idealized traits that are meant to define a ruler in general. Some of these characterizations go back to the Roman images of Caesar, including those found on the ancient coins imitated by Frederick's Augustales.[97] An almost contemporary witness of the Capua gateway, Andrew of Hungary, confirms this intention of the imperial image: "construxit ibique suam ymaginem in eternam et immortalem memoriam sculpi fecit."[98] Thus it was not meant to be a true-to-life portrait of the emperor but to show him in the way he wanted to be remembered for eternity.

I would like to suggest that the notion of the idealized imperial portrait, developed for images of Frederick II in Italy, seems also to be reflected in the northern imperial and royal images, including the Bamberg and Magdeburg Riders. Like the German Riders, some of the Italian imperial portraits of the first half of the thirteenth century are near life-size and sculpted in the round.[99] They appear superficially different from the northern images, mainly because the emperor is always dressed according to Roman custom, in ancient Roman dress, whereas the northern images appear in thirteenth-century dress. So the Bamberg and Magdeburg Riders seem more lifelike.[100]

The near life-size bust now preserved in the Museo Civico in Barletta, mentioned earlier for stylistic reasons, serves as a focal point of comparison (fig. 13). It certainly represents an emperor *all'antica,* and most likely it was intended to depict Frederick II. As we have seen, the Barletta bust has been

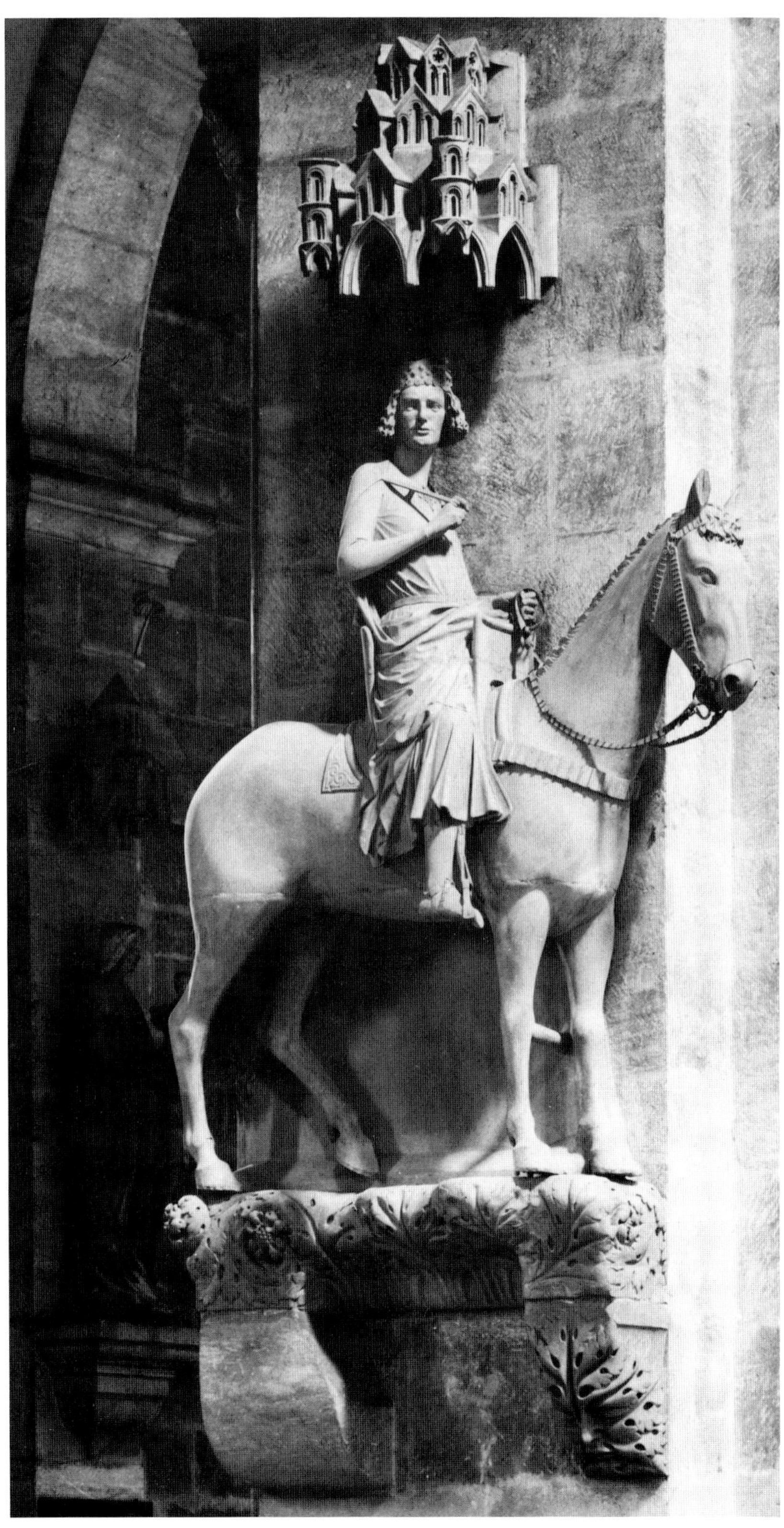

24. Bamberg Rider, stone relief on wall before west choir of Bamberg cathedral, 1230s
Bildarchiv Foto Marburg

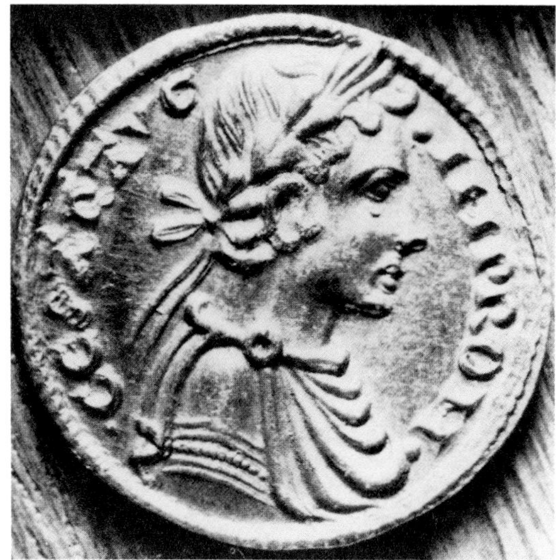

25. Frederick II on Augustalis coin, c. 1230
After Valentiner 1956, fig. 39

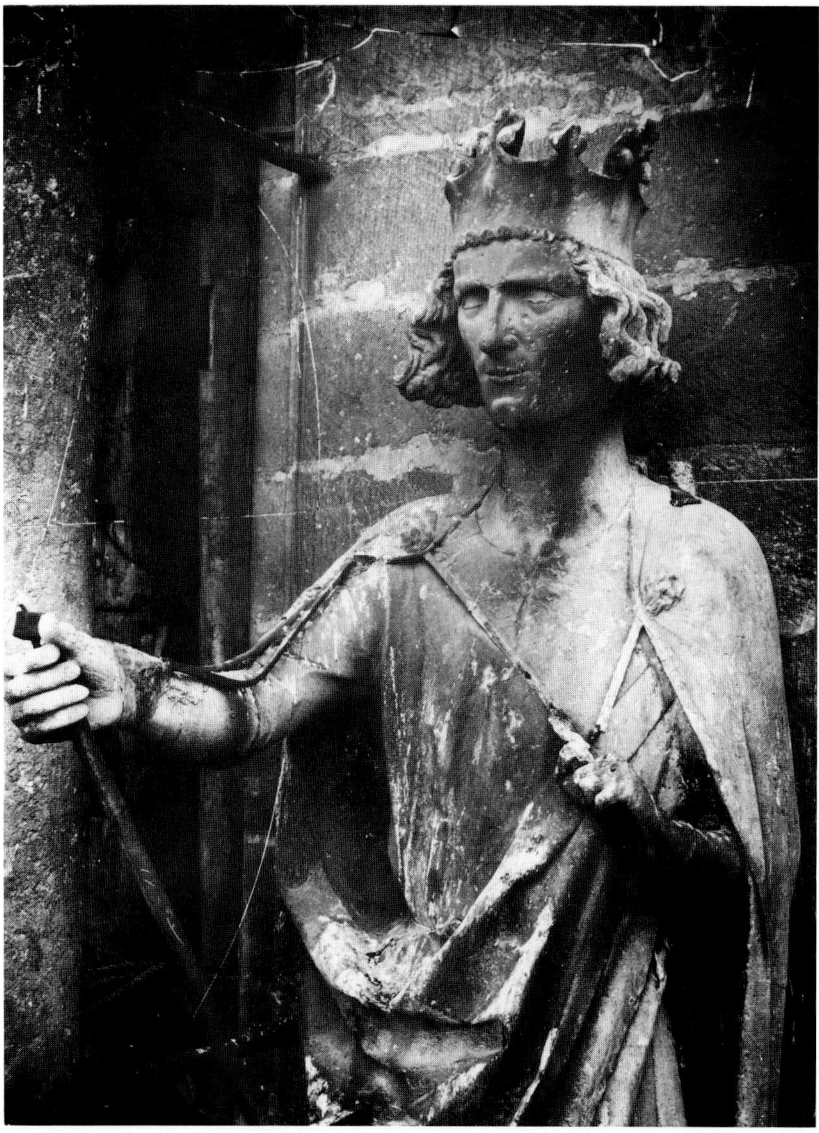

26. Philip Augustus from the façade of Reims cathedral, stone relief, second quarter of the thirteenth century
Bildarchiv Foto Marburg

compared to the Bamberg and Magdeburg Riders, and to other naturalistic sculpture in Germany (Meissen, Naumburg, and Mainz) since Guido Kaschnitz-Weinberg and Walter Schumacher first published it extensively in 1955.[101] According to Schumacher, it is a portrait with a very significant kernel of individualization, distinguishing it from other contemporary imperial images made in Italy.[102] I would suggest that such a task seems to imitate that of ancient Roman portrait busts, in which individualizing characteristics help create the effect of "lifelikeness" in a manner similar to the German equestrians. The exaggeration of such features—the wrinkled forehead, the deep-set eyes, and the large mouth—can be found in ancient Roman portrait busts, the Barletta bust, and the Magdeburg Rider (and related works in Magdeburg cathedral).

Schumacher already related the sculptor of the Barletta bust to the workshop that did the consoles at Castel del Monte, which also have northern stylistic and iconographic counterparts.[103] Joachim Poeschke and others have elaborated on the association of the Castel del Monte sculpture, including the riding figure, with the North, especially Reims. Indeed, much of the present literature on Apulian sculpture relates numerous sculptural works associated with Frederick II to the Gothic North, especially Reims, since sculpture on that cathedral has generally been considered the source for the German sculpture at Bamberg and Magdeburg.[104] An analysis of local traditions will probably demonstrate that most of the sculptors were South Italian rather than northern. But northern influence in these works will still need to be taken into account. The case of the Barletta figure may provide helpful clues for determining how the influence came south, for there is some technical evidence that the sculptor himself was from the North. Furthermore, Schumacher suggested that the Barletta bust was the remains of an equestrian sculpture and thus even closer in form to the Magdeburg Rider. This suggestion has been accepted by many, although it would be impossible to prove conclusively.

The preceding analysis of the close personal connection between Frederick II and Eckbert, bishop of Bamberg, and Albrecht, archbishop of Magdeburg, has suggested a context for the creation of the Bamberg and Magdeburg Riders. If we can accept these conclusions, then we might consider the possibility that Italy, as well as France, was a major source of influence on sculpture in Bamberg and Magdeburg. We have found evidence for the presence of a German artist associated with Bamberg and Magdeburg working in Apulia on sculpture in Roman form and in Roman dress. His experience in Apulia might help us understand the presence in the related Bamberg works (including the Visitation pair) of Roman dress. Sculptures at Bamberg, including these works and the Bamberg Rider, were made when Eckbert, Albrecht, and Frederick were in close association, when Eckbert is known to have visited Apulia, and when there is every reason to assume that they might have shared artistic contacts. Northern Gothic influence on Frederician art in Apulia might be best understood from the historical association of German ecclesiastics with Frederick much more easily than from vague stylistic comparisons made with Reims.

The Bamberg workshop that created the Visitation group and the Bamberg Rider is generally thought to have been trained at Reims cathedral, and it is believed that the German works were derivative. But this direction of influence has already been challenged by recent studies, which date relevant parts of the building campaign earlier, and thus before Reims.[105] The documentation we now have for Magdeburg shows convincingly that the related works there, including the Rider, must also have been made earlier than formerly accepted, since after Albrecht's death in 1232 there was no money to continue the building. Already in 1975 the suggestion was made that consideration should be given to revising our idea of the direction of influence.[106]

NOTES

The author wishes to thank William Jordan, John Pinto, and Linda Seidel for their interest in and support of her work on the Magdeburg Rider. For help on specific points the author is grateful to Johannes Bergemann, Chiara Frugoni, Hugo Meyer, and Peter Seiler. Special thanks to William Tronzo for many stimulating discussions that helped focus the research and argument.

1. The text for this manuscript was completed in 1991. Some of the material was collected for a book I am preparing on the Rider. Chapters of this work are devoted to many themes touched on here, including the function of the monument as a symbol of the source of legal power; the relation of the Rider to many other thirteenth-century images of "founders" throughout Europe, which seem to have been made to "document" the original grant of power to a ruler or ruling body; and the remarkable difference between the original function of the monument as an archiepiscopal symbol and its reception by the citizens of Magdeburg.

2. Herbert Brüning, "Das Nachkriegsschicksal des Magdeburger Reiters," *Neues Archiv für Niedersachsen* 10(15) (1961), 151–154.

3. The present metal crown is a new creation and not the first to replace the original, whose shape is now impossible to determine. The sculptor-restorer Heinrich Apel, who made the present crown, informed me that his examination determined that the Rider had always been crowned, thus reconfirming the conclusion of the nineteenth-century restoration of Friedrich von Quast ("Die Statue Kaiser Ottos des Grossen," *Zeitschrift für christliche Archäologie und Kunst* [Leipzig] (1856), 108–124. Von Quast's diagram of the original monument, with crown, is illustrated in my figure 9.

4. During this restoration an attempt was made to bring some aspects of the monument back to their original condition. So, for example, the eagle in relief seen in figure 3 was removed because it was said to date only from the nineteenth century. This theory of restoration has also been given as the reason for the removal of the later medieval figures of knights from the base of the pediment.

5. Heinrich Apel was able to determine from the raised left breast of the standard bearer that she had once held her arm up. But whereas the bronze-cast figure on the monument in the Old Market Square has been corrected, the original in the museum has not.

6. Von Quast 1856, 118–119; Berent Schwineköper, "Motivationen und Vorbilder für die Errichtung der Magdeburger Reitersäule: Ein Beitrag zur Geschichte des Reiterbildes im hohen Mittelalter," in *Institutionen, Kultur und Gesellschaft im Mittelalter: Festschrift für Josef Fleckenstein zu seinem 65. Geburtstag*, ed. Lutz Fenske, Werner Rösener, and Thomas Zotz (Sigmaringen, 1984), 377–379.

7. Hans-Henning Grote, "Magdeburg and Naum-

burg," in *Der Magdeburger Dom: Ottonische Gründung und staufischer Neubau*, Bericht über ein wissenschaftliches Symposion in Magdeburg vom 7. 10. bis 11. 10. 1986, Schriftreihe der Kommission für Niedersächsische Bau- und Kunstgeschichte bei der Braunschweigischen Wissenschaftlichen Gesellschaft 5 (Leipzig, 1989), 187–193.

8. Wolfgang Götz, "Der Magdeburger Domchor: Zur Bedeutung seiner monumentalen Ausstattung," *Zeitschrift des deutschen Vereins für Kunstwissenschaft* 19 (1965), 10–13, 16; Percy Ernst Schramm, *Herrschaftszeichen und Staatssymbolik: Beiträge zu ihrer Geschichte vom dritten bis zum sechzehnten Jahrhundert*, Schriften der Monumenta Germaniae Historica 13.2 (Stuttgart, 1955), 509–517; A. J. Herzberg, "Der heilige Mauritius: Forschungen," *Volkskunde Heft* 25–26 (Düsseldorf, 1936), 73–74.

9. The use of life-size, naturalistically rendered northern Gothic sculpture to help document historical events promoting the legal needs of their patrons was the subject of a lecture I gave at the annual conference of the International Congress of Medieval Studies, Kalamazoo, Michigan, 1989. This material will appear in my book on the Magdeburg Rider.

10. Herbert von Einem, "Zur Deutung des Magdeburger Reiters," *Zeitschrift für Kunstgeschichte* 16.1 (1953), 54; Berent Schwineköper, "Zur Deutung der Magdeburger Reitersäule," in *Festschrift Percy Ernst Schramm zu seinem siebzigsten Geburtstag von Schülern und Freunden zugeeignet*, 2 vols. (Wiesbaden, 1964), 1:136–139; Virginia Roehrig Kaufmann, "Magdeburg Rider Group: State of Research and Preliminary Suggestions for Further Work," in *Der Magdeburger Dom*, 208.

11. Schwineköper 1964, 138; *Die Zeit der Staufer: Geschichte—Kunst—Kultur* [exh. cat., Württembergisches Landesmuseum], 6 vols. (Stuttgart, 1977–1979), 1:340, no. 460, ill. 262.

12. Schwineköper 1964, 126.

13. Schwineköper 1964, 139–141; Schwineköper 1984, 347–348, 379.

14. Although Johannes Fried has criticized the older theory of Herbert Meyer that the Braunschweig Lion was always intended as a *Gerichtszeichen*, he acknowledges the documentary evidence that it functioned in this way by 1270 when judicial activity was carried out in front of it ("Königsgedanken Heinrichs des Löwen," *Archiv für Kulturgeschichte* 55 [1973], 316). See also Schwineköper 1964, 139–141. This function has also been suggested for a twelfth-century equestrian figure in relief that was once attached to the side of the Zurich Grossmünster: Adolf Reinle, "Der Reiter am Zürcher Grossmünster," *Zeitschrift für Schweizerische Archäologie und Kunstgeschichte* 26 (1969), 21–46, esp. 37–44. For discussion of the relation of the monument to the name "Guelph," see Dieter von der Nahmer, "Heinrich der Löwe: Die Inschrift auf dem Löwenstein und die geschichtliche Überlieferung der Welfenfamilie im 12. Jahrhundert," in *Der Braunschweiger Burglöwe* (Göttingen, 1985), 201–219; Karl Schmid, "Weltisches Selbstverständnis," in *Gebetsgedanken und adliges Selbstverständnis im Mittelalter* (Sigmaringen, 1983), 423–453.

15. Antonius David Gathen, *Rolande als Rechtssymbole: Der archäologische Bestand und seine rechtshistorische Deutung* (Berlin, 1960), 104–105; T. Goerlitz, *Der Ursprung und die Bedeutung der Rolandsbilder* (Weimar, 1934), 154–155; Rita Lejeune and Jacques Stiennon, *La légende de Roland dans l'art du moyen age*, 2 vols. (Brussels, 1966), 1:354, no. 1; 2:fig. 438.

16. Von Quast 1856. Von Quast showed that the sandstone sheathing the base of the monument, which supported the baldachin, was from a different quarry than that of the rest of the monument—a fact which supports his conjecture that the supports, and the medieval baldachin, were added after the construction of the original monument.

17. This idea has been accepted by various scholars including, most recently, Ernst Badstübner, "Justinianssäule und Magdeburger Reiter," in *Skulptur des Mittelalters: Funktion und Gestalt*, ed. Friedrich Möbius and Ernst Schubert (Weimar, 1987), 184–210. Badstübner compared in general terms the Magdeburg Rider and the sixth-century equestrian of Justinian described by Procopius which stood in Constantinople until 1453. He also associated the Magdeburg Rider with the Hohenstaufen revival of the ancient Roman Empire, but did not mention Frederick II specifically. The familiarity of the Magdeburg archbishops with north Italy, and specifically Pavia, suggested to Schwineköper that the antique figure called the "Regisole" in Pavia was most likely to have been the model for the Magdeburg Rider: Schwineköper 1984, 364–374.

18. For discussion of the placement of the Marcus Aurelius at the Lateran, see Antonio Giuliano, "La statua di Marco Aurelio prima del suo trasferimento in Campidoglio," *Xenia* 7 (1984), 67–76; Lucilla de Lachenal, "Il gruppo equestre di Marco Aurelio e il Laterano: Ricerche per una storia della fortuna del monumento dall'età medievale fino al 1538," *Bollettino d'arte* 75 (1990), 1–52, esp. 1–7, 19–22; Norberto Gramaccini, "Die Umwertung der Antike—Zur Rezeption des Marc Aurel in Mittelalter und Renaissance," in *Natur und Antike in der Renaissance* [exh. cat., Liebighaus and Museum Alter Plastik] (Frankfurt, 1985), 51–83. For discussion of the role of the Marcus Aurelius in respect to the papal court of justice at the Lateran, see Ingo Herklotz, "Der Campus Lateranensis im Mittelalter," *Römisches Jahrbuch für Kunstgeschichte* 22 (1985), 3–43, esp. 17–28; Gramaccini 1985, 55–57 and note 23. The placement of the Magdeburg Rider near the archiepiscopal court of justice is discussed by Schwineköper 1964, 129–131. The medieval tradition for using equestrians as legal symbols is discussed by Schwineköper 1984, 348–351.

19. Harald von Roques de Maumont, *Antike Reiterstandbilder* (Berlin, 1958), 65–66, fig. 35.

20. Badstübner 1987, figs. 5–8, with further bibliography in note 33.

21. Gramaccini 1985, 54–55, fig. 35; de Lachenal 1990, fig. 2; Florentine Mütherich, "Die Reiterstatuette aus

der Metzer Kathedrale," in *Festschrift Theodor Müller* (Munich, 1965), 9–16; Florentine Mütherich and Percy Ernst Schramm, *Die Denkmäle der deutschen Könige und Kaiser* (Munich, 1981), no. 58, 137, pl. 58; Percy Ernst Schramm, *Die zeitgenössischen Bildnisse Karls des Grossen*, Beiträge zur Kulturgeschichte des Mittelalters und der Renaissance 29 (Leipzig, 1928), 29–41; Percy Ernst Schramm, *Sphaira, Globus, Reichsapfel* (Stuttgart, 1958), 58.

22. Von Roques de Maumont 1958, 54–55, fig. 28a; Johannes Bergemann, *Römische Reiterstatuen: Ehren Denkmäler im öffentlichen Bereich* (Mainz, 1990), 63–64, pls. 20–23c, with extensive bibliography. The marble sculpture was reconstructed after its rediscovery in 1933. The rider is almost entirely modern, except for the neck and head, which may not have belonged to the original monument.

23. Von Roques de Maumont 1958, 79–82, figs. 41a–b; Bergemann 1990, 86–90, pls. 59–66. Bergemann has catalogued the remains of at least twenty Roman marble equestrian monuments.

24. Peter Seiler, "Mittelalterliche Reitermonumente in Italien: Studien zu personalen Monumentsetzungen in den italienischen Kommunen und Signorien des 13ten und 14ten Jahrhunderts," doctoral dissertation, Heidelberg, 1989. I want to thank Peter Seiler especially for his generosity in sharing his knowledge of medieval equestrian monuments at many stages of my work, and in making available to me many of the insights of his finished dissertation. See also the lengthy discussion of three identifications and interpretations of the Marcus Aurelius monument in the twelfth-century *Mirabilia Urbis Romae* and *Graphia Aureae Urbis* and the thirteenth-century *Guide to Antique Monuments* of Master Gregorius, in Gramaccini 1985, 57–61.

25. Jörg Traeger, *Der reitende Papst: Ein Beitrag zur Ikonographie des Papsttums*, Münchner Kunsthistorische Abhandlungen 1 (Munich, 1970). See also the review by Elisabeth Garmes-Cornides, *Art Bulletin* 55 (1973), 451–456.

26. Brigitte Bedos Rezak has discussed the seals and the social and political origin of the equestrian image depicted on them in a series of articles of which I cite only the most relevant: "The Social Implications of the Art of Chivalry: The Sigillographic Evidence (France 1050–1250)," in *The Medieval Court in Europe*, ed. Edward R. Haymes, Houston German Studies 6 (1986), 142–175; Bedos Rezak, "Medieval Seals and the Structure of Chivalric Society," in *The Study of Chivalry: Resources and Approaches*, ed. Howell Chickering and Thomas H. Seiler (Kalamazoo, Mich., 1988), 313–372; Bedos Rezak, "Idéologie royale, ambitions princières, et rivalités politiques d'après le témoignage des sceaux (France, 1380–1461)," in *La "France anglaise" au moyen age*, Actes du IIIe Congrès National des Sociétés Savantes (Paris, 1988), 483–511.

27. Carl A. Willemsen and Dagmar Odenthal, *Apulien, Land der Normannen—Land der Staufer* (Cologne, 1958), 37.

28. Fritz Jacobs, *Die Kathedrale S. Maria Icona Vetere in Foggia: Studien zur Architektur und Plastik des 11.–13. Jh. in Süditalien*, dissertation, Hamburg, 1968, 209. Frederick II also wanted to have his heart buried in Foggia cathedral during this same period in the 1220s (Jacobs 1968, 200).

29. Frederick II's mother had wanted to give him the name Constantine at his baptism. See further in Hans Martin Schaller, "Die Kaiseridee Friedrichs II.," in *Probleme um Friedrich II.*, Studien und Quellen zur Welt Kaiser Friedrichs II., 4, ed. Josef Fleckenstein (Sigmaringen, 1974), 114; Ernst H. Kantorowicz, *Friedrich der Zweite*, Ergänzungsband (Berlin, 1963), 295.

30. Jacobs 1968, 200–212, identifies the rider as Frederick. See earlier discussion in Wilhelm R. Valentiner, *The Bamberg Rider* (Los Angeles, 1956), 120 and fig. 35. For a discussion of the imperial refutation of the Donation of Constantine and the effect of the political struggle on the propagandistic uses to which the Marcus Aurelius was subjected, see Gramaccini 1985, 57–61. The use of the type of Constantine image familiar from France required further explanation. One possible explanation for its use by Frederick II in Foggia would be to reclaim the type of equestrian image for imperial purposes, with the implied refutation of papal claims. The subject requires more study.

31. Walter N. Schumacher, "Rekonstruktionsvorschlag zur Büste," in Guido Kaschnitz-Weinberg, "Bildnisse Friedrichs II. von Hohenstaufen," *Mitteilungen des Deutschen Archäologischen Instituts, Römische Abteilung* 62 (1955), 23 and note 52.

32. Maria Stella Calò Mariani, *L'arte del Duecento in Puglia* (Torino, 1984), 138–142; discussed within the context of Frederick's interest in equestrian imagery and related to the Bamberg Rider by Chiara Frugoni, "L'antichità: Dai Mirabilia alla propaganda politica," in *Memoria dell'antico dell'arte italiana*, I, *L'uso dei classici*, ed. Salvatore Settis, Biblioteca di storia dell'arte, n.s. 1 (Rome, 1984), 32. A relief fragment at Castel del Monte with equestrian accompanied by at least two females, which may be of ancient Roman origin, has recently been published by Lucilla de Lachenal (1990, fig. 17). Her article appeared after this text was finished, so the importance of this relief for the study of the Magdeburg Rider could not properly be assessed. The arch in the background and the two females suggest an imperial *adventus*, which could be significant for the origin of the Magdeburg Rider, since it can be associated with Frederick II.

33. Frugoni 1984, 32 and note 3.

34. Joachim Poeschke, "Zum Einfluss der Gotik in Süditalien," *Jahrbuch der Berliner Museen* 22 (1980), 115–116.

35. Schumacher, in Kaschnitz-Weinberg 1955, 22–23.

36. Schumacher, in Kaschnitz-Weinberg 1955, 1–52. Although some of the evidence adduced by Schumacher could not be reconfirmed by the examination made and reported on by Peter Eichhorn, "Zur Büste von Barletta," in *Die Zeit der Staufer*, 5:419–430, the equestrian suggestion does explain the unusual situation of such a long torso, the base of which appears to have been cut down at some time after its creation.

Of those accepting Schumacher's thesis, see Helmut Buschhausen, "Das Altersbildnis Kaiser Friedrichs II.," *Jahrbuch der Kunsthistorischen Sammlungen in Wien*, N.F. 70 (1974), 28–29; Otto von Simson, "Nuovi temi della scultura monumentale tedesca nell'età di Federico II di Hohenstaufen," in *Federico II e l'arte del Duecento italiano*, ed. Angiola M. Romanini (Galatina, 1980), 1:399; and recently Heinz Götze, *Castel del Monte: Gestalt und Symbol der Architektur Friedrichs II.* (Munich, 1984), 13. Carl Willemsen accepts the work as part of an equestrian but rejects the identification with Frederick II, in *Die Bildnisse der Staufer: Versuch einer Bestandsaufnahme*, Schriften zur staufischen Geschichte und Kunst, Gesellschaft der Freunde staufischer Geschichte in Göppingen (Göppingen, 1977), 36–37.

37. Traeger 1970, 4. The original placement of the Rider has often been argued, although the evidence seems conclusive that it is now situated where it has always been, just before the east choir. See also Johan J. Morper, "Zur Technik des Reiterstandbildes im Dom zu Bamberg," *Belvedere* 6 (1924), 19.

38. Otto Schmitt, *Gotische Skulpturen des Strassburger Münsters*, 2 vols. (Frankfurt, 1924), 1:31.

39. Tilman Falk, *Hans Burgkmair: Studien zu Leben und Werk des Augsburger Malers* (Munich, 1968), 72–73.

40. De Lachenal 1990, 30–31, fig. 20; Géza de Francovich, *Benedetto Antelami: Architetto e scultore e l'arte del suo tempo* (Milan and Florence, 1952), pl. 292, no. 484, text 439–441, with further bibliography; related images of "March" at Ferrara cathedral, pl. 316, no. 519 and at Parma, pl. 186, no. 307.

41. Gramaccini 1985, 61–62, fig. 36; de Lachenal, 31–32, fig. 22.

42. René Crozet, "Nouvelles remarques sur les cavaliers sculptés ou peints dans les églises romanes," *Cahiers de civilisation médiévale X^e–XIIe siècles* 1 (1958), 27–36; Hubert Le Roux, "Figures équestres et personnages du nom de Constantin aux XIe et XIIe siècles," *Bulletin de la Société des Antiquaires de l'Ouest et des Musées de Poitiers* (1974), 379–394, with illustration; Linda V. Seidel, "Holy Warriors: The Romanesque Rider and the Fight against Islam," in *The Holy War*, ed. Thomas Patrick Murphy (Columbus, Ohio, 1976), 33–54, with further bibliography. For the Bassenheim Rider, see *Die Zeit der Staufer*, 1:331–332, no. 451, with additional bibliography, and 2:fig. 252.

43. De Lachenal 1990, 30–31, fig. 21; Gabriele Kopp, *Die Skulpturen der Fassade von San Martino in Lucca* (Worms, 1981), 113–117, fig. 183.

44. Piero Sanpaolesi, "Restauro del gruppo di S. Martino a Lucca," *Bollettino d'arte* 40 (1955), 167–172.

45. These techniques are described in detail by Robert Suckale, "Die Bamberger Domskulpturen: Technik, Blockbehandlung, Ansichtigkeit und die Einbeziehung des Betrachters," *Münchner Jahrbuch der bildenden Kunst* 38 (1987), 27–82. The relation of the recovery of certain techniques which may be associated with antique sculpture and the development of freestanding monumental work in the thirteenth century cannot be discussed in detail here, although its importance for further study can be best assessed with respect to the Bamberg and Magdeburg Riders.

46. Kurt Bauch, *Das mittelalterliche Grabbild* (Berlin, 1976), 192–193; Judith Hurtig, *The Armored Gisant before 1400* (New York, 1979), 183–184.

47. Many of these works will be the subject of Peter Seiler's forthcoming book on Italian equestrian tomb monuments, based on his dissertation, "Mittelalterliche Reitermonumente in Italien" (see above, note 24).

48. Schumacher, in Kaschnitz-Weinberg 1955, 18–44; Maria Stella Calò Mariani, "Aspetti della scultura sveva in Puglia e in Lucania," *Archivio storico pugliese* 26 (1973), 463–474; Poeschke 1980, 110–120; Francesco Aceto, " 'Magistri' e cantieri nel 'Regnum Siciliae': L'Abruzzo e la cerchia federiciana," *Bollettino d'arte* 75 (1990), 63– 67, 80–83, with further bibliography.

49. Hans Martin Schaller, "Albrecht II.: Erzbischof von Magdeburg," *Neue Deutsche Biographie* (Berlin, 1953), 1:165 ff; H. Silberborth, "Erzbischof Albrecht II. von Magdeburg," *Geschichtsblätter für Stadt- und Land Magdeburg* (1910), 110–175, 177–232; J. Schäfer, "Personal- und Amtsdaten der Magdeburger Erzbischöfe," dissertation, Greifswald, 1908, 36–42. For discussions of Albrecht of Käfernberg's family and its relation to Eckbert and Frederick II, see also Hans Fiedler, *Dome und Politik: Der staufische Reichsgedanke in Bamberg und Magdeburg* (Berlin, 1937), 154–163; Valentiner 1956, 105–115; Schwineköper 1984, 351–354 and 368–374.

50. E. Frh. Oefele, *Geschichte der Grafen von Andechs* (Innsbruck, 1877); Schwineköper 1984, 352–354.

51. R. Klauser, *Der Heinrichs- und Kunigundenkult im mittelalterlichen Bamberg* (Bamberg, 1957), 67 ff; Otto von Simson, "Gedanken zur Adamspforte des Bamberger Domes," in *Festschrift für Ingeborg Schröbler zum 65. Geburtstag* (Tübingen, 1973), 429–431.

52. A. von Reitzenstein, "Die Baugeschichte des Bamberger Domes," *Münchner Jahrbuch der bildenden Kunst*, N.F. 11 (1934), 148; von Simson 1973, 430 and note 18 (where he estimates that this amount would have paid for the entire church).

53. Fiedler 1937, 159.

54. Gottfried Wentz and Berent Schwineköper, *Das Erzbistum Magdeburg*, Germania Sacra I, 1–2 (Berlin, 1972), 1:218; Schwineköper 1984, 254, 352; Valentiner 1956, 109.

55. Johann F. Böhmer, *Regesta Imperii*, 5, vol. 1, *Die Regesten des Kaiserreichs unter Philipp, Otto IV., Friedrich II., Heinrich VII., Conrad IV., Heinrich Raspe, Wilhelm und Richard, 1198–1272,* revised edition by Johannes Ficker (Innsbruck, 1881), 209 (no. 858); *Regesta Archiepiscopatus Magdeburgensis*, vol. 2, *Dom 1192 bis 1269* (Magdeburg, 1881), 226–227 (no. 503, 1 May 1216); Schwineköper 1984, 353.

56. The first record of Frederick II's payment to Al-

brecht for his journeys to Italy on his behalf is recorded: *Regesta Archiepiscopatus Magdeburgensis*, 2:291, no. 639 (17 September 1221) and 2:293, no. 641 (20 September 1221); Schwineköper 1984, 370.

57. Jacobs 1968, 211; Jörg Traeger, "Der Bamberger Reiter in neuer Sicht," *Zeitschrift für Kunstgeschichte* (1979), 9–10.

58. *Regesta Imperii*, 5, 1:269 (no. 1396), 313 (nos. 1522 and 1523), 315 (no. 1541): itinerary of Archbishop Albrecht as imperial legate in Italy 1222–1232; A. Ruppel, "Zur Reichslegation des Erzbischofs Albrecht von Magdeburg (1222–1224)," *Quellen und Forschungen aus italienischen Archiven und Bibliotheken* 13 (Rome, 1910), 103–134; Schwineköper 1984, 370.

59. *Regesta Imperii*, 5, 1:313 (nos. 1522 and 1523), 315 (no. 1541); Schwineköper 1984, 370, 372, and note 186.

60. *Regesta Imperii*, 5, 1:no. 1644; compare to Eduard Winkelmann, ed., *Acta Imperii inedita*, 2 vols. (Innsbruck, 1880–1885; repr. Aalen, 1964), 1:257, no. 283; Schwineköper 1984, 370–371.

61. Ruppel 1910, 107, note 2 and 122: Albricus de Rovereto Papiensis civis.; Schwineköper 1984, 370–371.

62. *Regesta Imperii*, 5, 1:no. 1597, 1598, 1601; Schwineköper 1984, 370.

63. Schwineköper 1984, 371–373.

64. Schwineköper 1984, 348–351.

65. Herklotz 1985.

66. Schwineköper 1984, 365; Harald Keller, "Der Gerichtsort in oberitalienischen und toskanischen Städten," *Quellen und Forschungen aus italienischen Archiven und Bibliotheken* 49 (1969), 1–72; C. Brühl, "Die Stätten der Herrschaftsausübung in der frühmittelalterlichen Stadt," *Settimana di studio del Centro italiano di studi sull'alto medioevo, 21, Topografia urbana e vita cittadina nell'alto medioevo in occidente* (Spoleto, 1974), 2:621–640.

67. Hans Jantzen, "Zur Deutung des Kaiser-Otto-Denkmals in Magdeburg," *Repertorium für Kunstwissenschaft* 46 (1925), 128–130; von Einem 1953, 54–55.

68. Munich, Bayerische Staatsbibliothek, Clm 14000, fol. 5v: G. Leidinger, *Der Codex Aureus der Bayerischen Staatsbibliothek in München*, 6 vols. (Munich, 1921–1925), 1:pl. 10. W. Koehler and Florentine Mütherich, *Die karolingischen Miniaturen*, 5, *Die Hofschule Karls des Kahlen* (Berlin, 1982), 175–198.

69. Munich, Bayerische Staatsbibliothek, Clm 4453, fols. 23v and 24r: *Das Evangeliar Ottos III. Clm 4453 der Bayerischen Staatsbibliothek München*, facsimile and commentary volume with contributions by F. Dressler, Florentine Mütherich, and H. Beumann, 2 vols. (Frankfurt, 1977–1978).

70. Percy Ernst Schramm, "Das Herrscherbild in der Kunst des frühen Mittelalters," *Vorträge der Bibliothek Warburg* 2 (1922), 145–224.

71. Schramm 1922, 159–166; André Grabar, "La soie byzantine de l'évêque Gunther à la cathédrale de Bamberg," *Münchner Jahrbuch der bildenden Kunst* 7 (1956), 7–26; S. Müller-Christensen, *Das Günthertuch im Bamberger Domschatz* (Bamberg, 1983). The Roman equestrian figures from Cartoceto may also prove to be important as models for the Magdeburg monument. Two similarly dressed standing females associated with the equestrians have been identified by some as imperial wives. One of the equestrians has also been identified as depicting an imperial entry. See Bergmann 1990, 50–54, pls. 6a, 8–11, with further bibliography.

72. It is possible that Günther's tomb was opened during the first half of the thirteenth century when the new cathedral was being built on a new axis which required the disturbance of many tombs, and when several of them are known to have been opened.

73. Grabar 1956, 25; Schramm 1922, 161.

74. The helmet is said to be the "tupha" represented in other Byzantine imperial images including the equestrian statue of Justinian once in Constantinople (Schramm 1922, 161, note 55). Here it is offered by the personification identified as Roma, suggesting that it may be related to the helmet she wore in ancient representations, and used here as a symbol of the pretension of imperial authority over Rome.

75. Middle Byzantine miniature from Mount Sinai: André Grabar, *L'empereur dans l'art byzantin* (Paris, 1936), pl. XIX, 2; Grabar 1956, 13, note 3.

76. Johann-Christian Klamt, "Zur Datierung der Putzritzungen im Magdeburger Domkreuzgang," in *Der Magdeburger Dom: Ottonische Gründung und Staufischer Neubau* (Leipzig, 1989), 124–131.

77. *Die Zeit der Staufer*, 1:668, no. 845, fig. 624.

78. *Die Zeit der Staufer*, 1:393–394, no. 535, fig. 324.

79. Philip Peirce, "The Arch of Constantine: Propaganda and Ideology in Late Roman Art," *Art History* 12.4 (1989), 387–417. The equestrian frieze at Castel del Monte recently published by Lucilla de Lachenal (see notes 18 and 32) has two females accompanying the equestrian figure on foot, a scene which may be ancient Roman and depict an emperor and an imperial entry: thus it may provide an important model for the females of the Magdeburg Rider monument.

80. Otto Posse, *Das Siegelwesen der deutschen Kaiser und Könige von 751 bis 1913*, 3 vols. (Dresden, 1909–1913), 3:115–116.

81. Hamburg, Staats- und Universitätsbibliothek, Codex 151 in Scrin., fol. 97v: *Historiae Romanorum*, facsimile, with remarks by Tilo Brandis and Otto Pächt (Frankfurt am Main, 1974), 138–140, 197–202, with comparative material illustrated; J. M. C. Toynbee, "Roma and Constantinopolis in Late-Antique Art from 312 to 365," *Journal of Roman Studies* 37 (1947), 135–144, pls. I–XIII; Anthony Cutler, " 'Roma' and 'Constantinopolis' in Vienna," in *Byzanz und der Westen: Studien zur Kunst des europäischen Mittelalters*, ed. Irmgard Hutter (Vienna, 1984), 43–64, pls. I–IX. Scattered references also in Wilhelm Erben, *Rombilder auf kaiserlichen und päpstlichen Siegeln des Mittelalters* (Leipzig, 1931).

82. Schaller 1974, 116; Jean L. A. Huillard-Bréholles, ed., *Historia Diplomatica Friderici Secundi . . .*, 6 vols. (Paris, 1852–1861), 5.1:162; *Regesta Imperii*, 5:no. 2311.

83. Jantzen 1925, 125–133.

84. Posse 1909–1913, 1:17–19, pls. 21 no. 4, and 23 no. 6; Willemsen 1977, figs. 13, 15, 34, 48, 56, 58, 60. Josef Deér's work on early Hohenstaufen seals revealed that top-quality artists associated with Wibald of Stavelot and many of the most skillfully executed Mosan works of the late twelfth century were employed to make Frederick I's and Henry I's seals, whereas Frederick II seems to have been unable to call upon metalworkers with a high degree of skill. See Josef Deér, "Die Siegel Kaiser Friedrichs I. Barbarossa und Heinrichs VI. in der Kunst und Politik ihrer Zeit," in *Festschrift Hans R. Hahnloser zum 60. Geburtstag 1959* (Stuttgart, 1961), 47–102, esp. 88–89. Thus we need not determine from the evidence of the existing seals that Frederick II's seal intentionally removed the variety of tower types and women leaning out of windows, but only that his artists were not skilled enough to depict such detail clearly. See also Erben 1931, 87.

85. Ernst H. Kantorowicz, "The 'King's Advent' and the Enigmatic Panels in the Doors of Santa Sabina," *Art Bulletin* 26 (1944), 207–231.

86. Schaller 1974, 109–134.

87. Schramm 1955, 651–652.

88. See, for example, the sculpted image of Faustina of A.D. 138: Theodor Kraus, *Das Römische Weltreich*, Propyläen Kunstgeschichte 2 (Berlin, 1967), no. 303, p. 257.

89. The contribution of art associated with the Hohenstaufen and especially Frederick II to the development of Renaissance triumphal imagery would not only include the Magdeburg image. The female personification on the Capua gateway, which is identified variously as Capua, Justizia, or Concordia, may also be considered an important step in this development, for many personifications in later triumphal imagery appear to greet the emperor rather than accompany him. Such a figure could be compared with the personification of the city of Paris, which was also identified as Fama, which greeted Henry VI upon his entry into the city in 1431. Like the Capua image, her presence was intended to remind those greeting her of the importance of ruling her well, as we learn from a poem she recited to him (Bernard Guenée and Françoise Lehoux, *Les entrées royales françaises de 1328 à 1515* [Paris, 1968], 64–65). Such female images greeted visitors on gateways elsewhere, including triumphal arches designed for imperial entries. Austria bearing a spear and shield (and thus with the arms of Roma, whose qualities she assumes) appears on a triumphal arch erected for Rudolph II (Vienna, Niederösterreichisches Landesarchiv, Ständerarchiv A 9/26 fol. 19v: see Thomas DaCosta Kaufmann, "Astronomy, Technology, Humanism and Art at the Entry of Rudolph II into Vienna 1517," *Jahrbuch der Kunsthistorischen Sammlungen in Wien* [forthcoming]).

90. Illustrated in color: Peter Strieder, *Albrecht Dürer: Paintings, Prints, Drawings* (New York, 1982), 72–73, fig. 76.

91. Although they are sculpted in the round to enable viewing from all sides, it is inconceivable that they were ever reversed in the positions to be seen welcoming. If they had been, their backs would have been turned to viewers and their shields and standards would have been impossible to see!

92. See, for example, Dorothy Gillerman, "The Portal of St. Thibault-en-Auxois: A Problem of Thirteenth-Century Burgundian Patronage and Founder Imagery," *Art Bulletin* 68 (1986), 567–580; Willibald Sauerländer, "Die Naumburger Stifterfiguren, Rückblick und Fragen," in *Die Zeit der Staufer*, 5:169–245.

93. Fiedler, 1937, 244.

94. Valentiner 1956, 100–105, 115, 124–126.

95. Hans Martin Schaller, "Das Relief an der Kanzel der Kathedrale von Bitonto: Ein Denkmal der Kaiseridee Friedrichs II.," *Archiv für Kulturgeschichte* 45 (1963), 295–312.

96. Gerhart Ladner, "Die Anfänge des Kryptoporträts," in *Von Angesicht zu Angesicht: Michael Stettler zum 70. Geburtstag* (Bern, 1983), 84–88. Identification of both Riders as "crypto-portraits" of Frederick II was accepted by Adolf Reinle, *Das stellvertretende Bildnis: Plastik und Gemälde von der Antike bis ins 19. Jahrhundert* (Munich, 1984), 260—261.

97. Most of those writing on the images associated with Frederick reject any possibility that they resemble the emperor as he appeared in life. For lengthy discussion with extensive bibliography, see Helmut Buschhausen, "Probleme der Bildniskunst am Hof Kaiser Friedrichs II.," in *Stauferzeit: Geschichte, Literatur, Kunst*, ed. Rüdiger Krohn, Bernd Thum, and Peter Wapnewski (Stuttgart, 1978), 220–243, esp. 237–238.

98. Kaschnitz-Weinberg 1955, 1–3; Buschhausen 1978, 238.

99. For discussion of the progression to sculpting the images more fully in the round, see Buschhausen 1978, 226–236. For lengthier discussion of busts of Frederick, see Buschhausen 1974, 7–38; Kaschnitz-Weinberg 1955, 1–52; Willemsen 1977; Peter Cornelius Claussen, "Die Statue Friedrichs II. vom Brückentor in Capua (1234–1239): Der Befund, die Quellen und eine Zeichnung aus dem Nachlass von Seroux d'Agincourt," in *Festschrift für Hartmut Biermann* (Weinheim, 1990), 19–39, 291–304.

100. The Bamberg and Magdeburg Riders appear in thirteenth-century dress rather than that of the tenth or eleventh century (when Otto I lived) because the thirteenth-century images needed to be politically effective in convincing their viewers of the reality of the image before them. So they were made to seem familiar, and thus more convincing as "living memories." The "Founders" at Naumburg cathedral were similarly portrayed in thirteenth-century dress, although they represent people who had lived two hundred years earlier (see Sauerländer 1979).

101. Schumacher, in Kaschnitz-Weinberg 1955, 30–44.

102. He related this characteristic to a Frederician origin in Italy, which dictated the task of directly experiencing the presence (but not the likeness) of a significant person (Schumacher 1955, 24–25, 38–40).

103. Schumacher 1955, 42.

104. Poeschke 1980, 110–120.

105. Dethard von Winterfeld, *Der Dom in Bamberg, I, Die Baugeschichte bis zur Vollendung im 13. Jahrhundert: Der Befund, Bauform und Bautechnik* (Berlin, 1979); Robert Suckale, "Nach Dethard von Winterfelds Monographie über den Bamberger Dom," *Bericht des Historischen Vereins Bamberg* 123 (1978), 161–169.

106. "Der Bamberger Dom und seine plastische Ausstattung bis zur Mitte des 13. Jahrhunderts: Fortsetzung des Berichts über das Kolloquium in Bamberg vom 8. und 9. April 1975," *Kunstchronik* 28.12 (December 1975), 436–437.

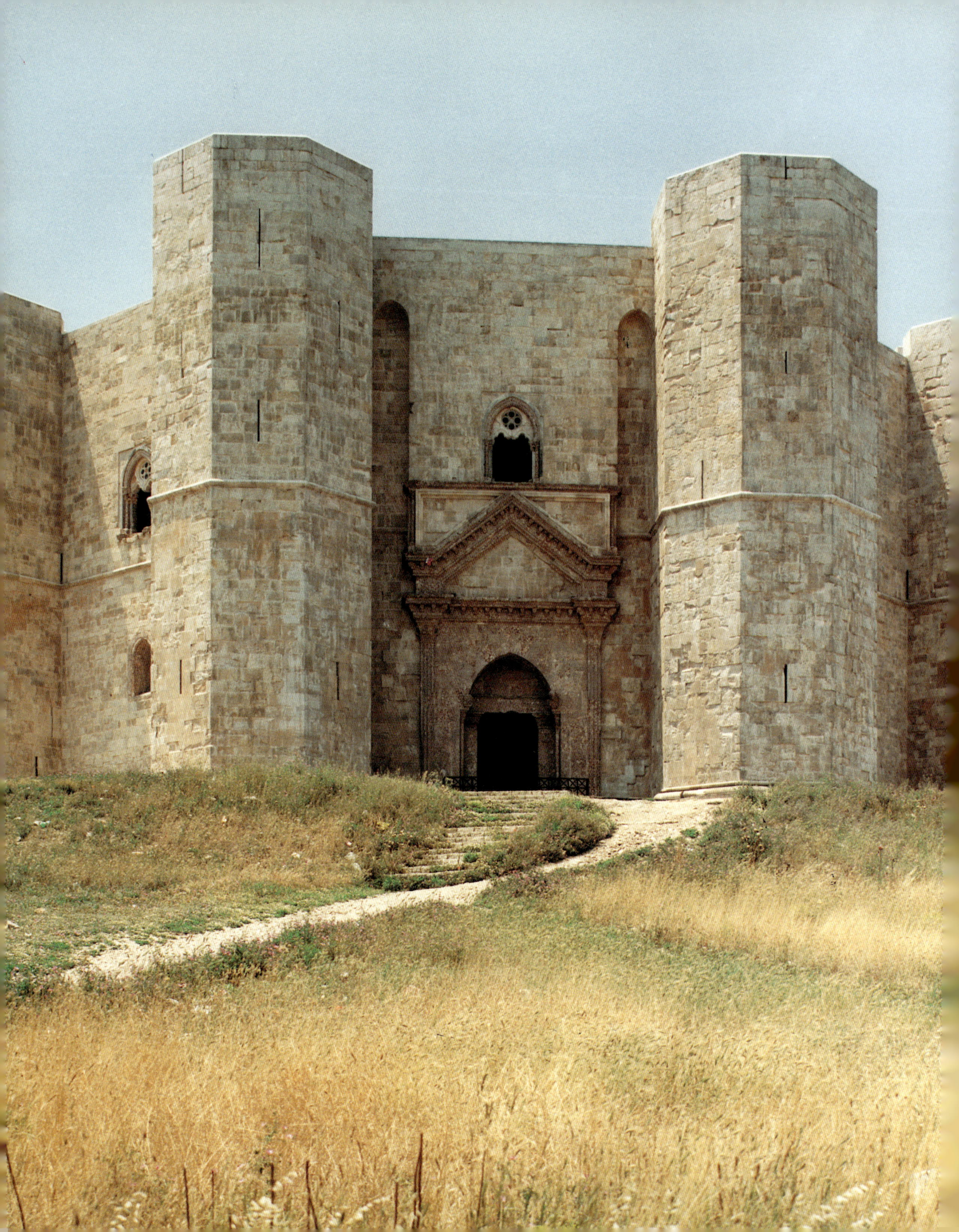

WOLFGANG KRÖNIG

Castel del Monte. Der Bau Friedrichs II.

Form und Lage von Castel del Monte entsprechen, ja bedingen sich; sie steigern sich wechselseitig zu einer zwingenden Wirkung (Abb. 1). Der Bau hat die Form eines sich allseitig gleichmäßig entfaltenden gleichseitigen Achtecks, dem an jeder Ecke ein wiederum achteckiger Turm vorgelegt ist, mit zwei seiner acht Seiten in das große Oktogon eingebunden (Abb. 2, 3). Die einzigartige Geschlossenheit und regelmäßige Klarheit in Grundriß und Aufbau dieser Anlage scheint keinerlei Abweichung von der idealen, der geometrischen Form zuzulassen. Wie die Gesamtform, so sind auch die acht Türme aus dem Achteck entwickelt und ebenso der konzentrisch angelegte Hof in der Mitte. Ganz folgerichtig ergibt sich auch die Achtzahl der unter sich völlig gleichen trapezförmigen Räume durch die acht radialen Innenmauern, welche die Ecken des inneren Hof-Oktogons mit denen des äußeren verbinden. In dem zweigeschossigen Aufbau des Ganzen ist die hiermit knapp beschriebene Grundriß-Disposition in beiden Geschossen vollkommen gleichartig durchgeführt.

Es erweist sich aber, daß innerhalb einer so zwingenden Gesetzmäßigkeit, die alles einer gleichsam vorher festgelegten geometrischen Form unterwirft, dennoch eine Differenzierung im Einzelnen, ein lebensvoller Reichtum unterschiedlicher praktischer Zwecke und künstlerischer Formen verwirklicht ist. Die verschiedene Gestaltung aller Aufrißformen in Wänden und Gewölben der beiden Geschosse ist dafür das wichtigste Anzeichen.

Das alleinige große Portal gibt der allseitig-gleichmäßigen Gesamtform des Bauwerks dennoch eine eindeutige Ausrichtung (Abb. 4); es ist zugleich die genaue Ost-West-Achse des Ganzen, und zwar dergestalt, daß mit ihm der Eingang im Osten ist und daß in der Disposition des Inneren alles auf den Osten zurückweist, deutlich zumal in der Tatsache eines kleinen zweiten, schlichten Portals im gegenüber liegenden Raum V, also an der "Rückseite" des Baus, womit zugleich einer praktischen Notwendigkeit Rechnung getragen ist. Das Hauptportal ist Stirn und Fassade des ganzen Baus durch seine reiche architektonische Gliederung: die doppelläufige symmetrische Treppe führt hinauf zur Plattform und zum spitzbogigen Portal, flankiert von ursprünglich je zwei schlanken Säulchen hintereinander im Gewände, über deren Kapitellen Löwen-Figuren ruhen, das alte Hoheits- und Rechts-Symbol an Portalen. Hinter dem ersten Säulchen-Paar befindet sich ein schmaler, schachtartiger Zwischenraum, in welchem das Fallgitter vom darüber befindlichen "Hauptraum" aus herabgelassen werden kann. Gerahmt wird das zweifach sich verengende eigentliche Portal beiderseits durch zwei schlanke kannelierte Pilaster mit Konsolen-Gesims, Attika-Zone und Dreiecks-Giebel; das Ganze

1. Castel del Monte in Apulien, Unteritalien
Photograph: Heinz Götze, Heidelberg

eine wenn auch freie, so doch bewußte Rezeption römisch-antiker Formen als Träger imperialer *majestas romana.* Zugleich muß schon an dieser Stelle der Baubeschreibung erwähnt und sozusagen vorweggenommen werden, daß in die Betonung der Eingangsseite und ihre Ausrichtung nach Osten der sich über dem Portal im Obergeschoß befindende, besonders ausgezeichnete "Hauptraum I," der soganannte Thronsaal, entscheidend einbezogen ist.

Betritt man durch das Hauptportal den Raum I, so gelangt man von ihm aus nicht sogleich in den Hof, sondern zunächst nach Durchschreiten des Durchgangs in der Mitte (was allein hier der Fall ist) der rechten Seitenwand in den benachbarten Raum II, und erst von diesem aus in den Hof. Beide Räume aber sind durch türlose Mauern von der Folge der übrigen sechs Räume abgeschlossen; sie sind damit als Durchgangs- oder Vestibül-Räume gekennzeichnet. Diese Brechung des Zugangswegs zum Hofe ist durchaus verständlich; sie entspricht dem im Mittelalter geübten Brauch. Folgerichtig ist es nun, daß von den drei den Räumen I und II benachbarten Türmen 8, 1 und 2 sozusagen nur die unumgängliche Mindestzahl zugeordnet wurde, da zusätzlicher räumlicher Komfort hier unangebracht erscheinen mußte. Das geschah in der alleinigen Zuordnung von Turm 1 zu Raum I; und dieser Turm ist ein solcher ohne weiterführende Treppe mit einfachem achteckigen Innenraum ohne jedes Nebengelaß. Raum II aber hat überhaupt keine Verbindung zu einem Turm. Hier sieht sich daher der Eintretende sogleich eindeutig hingewiesen auf die reich gegliederte Fassade eines spitzbogigen Portals, das ihn einlädt, in den Hof einzutreten. Diese in das Innere des Raumes gewendete Schauwand bestätigt dadurch die beiden Räume I und II in ihrem Charakter als alleinige Eingangs- und Durchgangsräume. Durch dieses Tor in den Hof gelangt, sieht man vor sich die beiden weiteren Portale mit ihren Schmuckfronten. Sie laden ein zum Eintritt in die Räume, ebenso wie das nach innen gewandte Portal in Raum II zum Eintritt in den Hof einlädt. Die Anordnung dieser drei Durchgänge in den acht Seiten des Hofes stellt eine auffällige Durchbrechung der strengen Symmetrie-Achse des Bauwerks dar, die durch das Hauptportal (I) und das

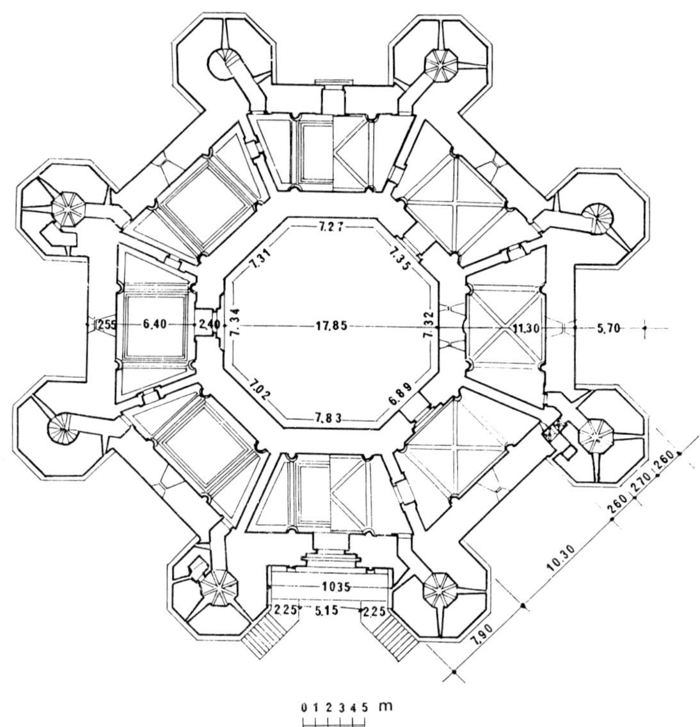

2. Castel del Monte, Architekturplan des Erdgeschosses
Aus Wolfgang Krönig, *L'Art dans l'Italie méridionale . . .* (Rom, 1978)

3. Castel del Monte, Architekturplan des oberen Stockwerks
Aus Krönig 1978

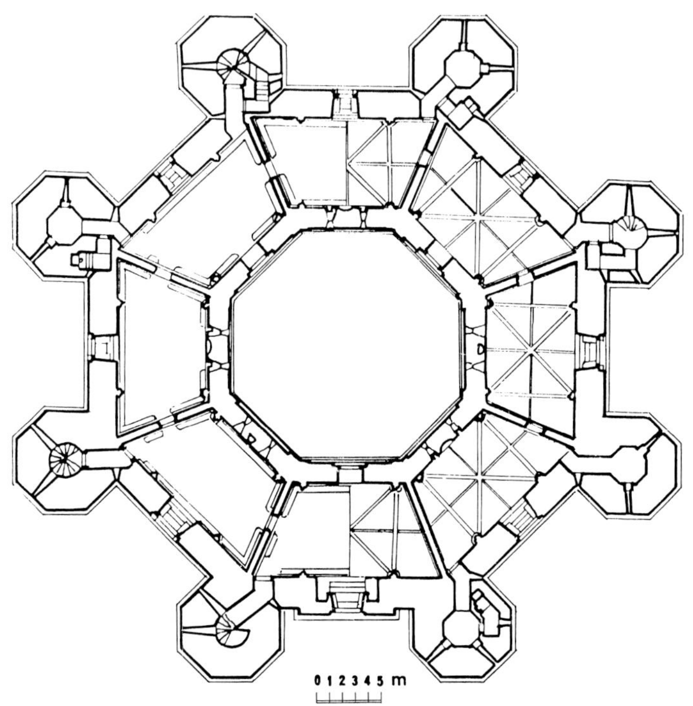

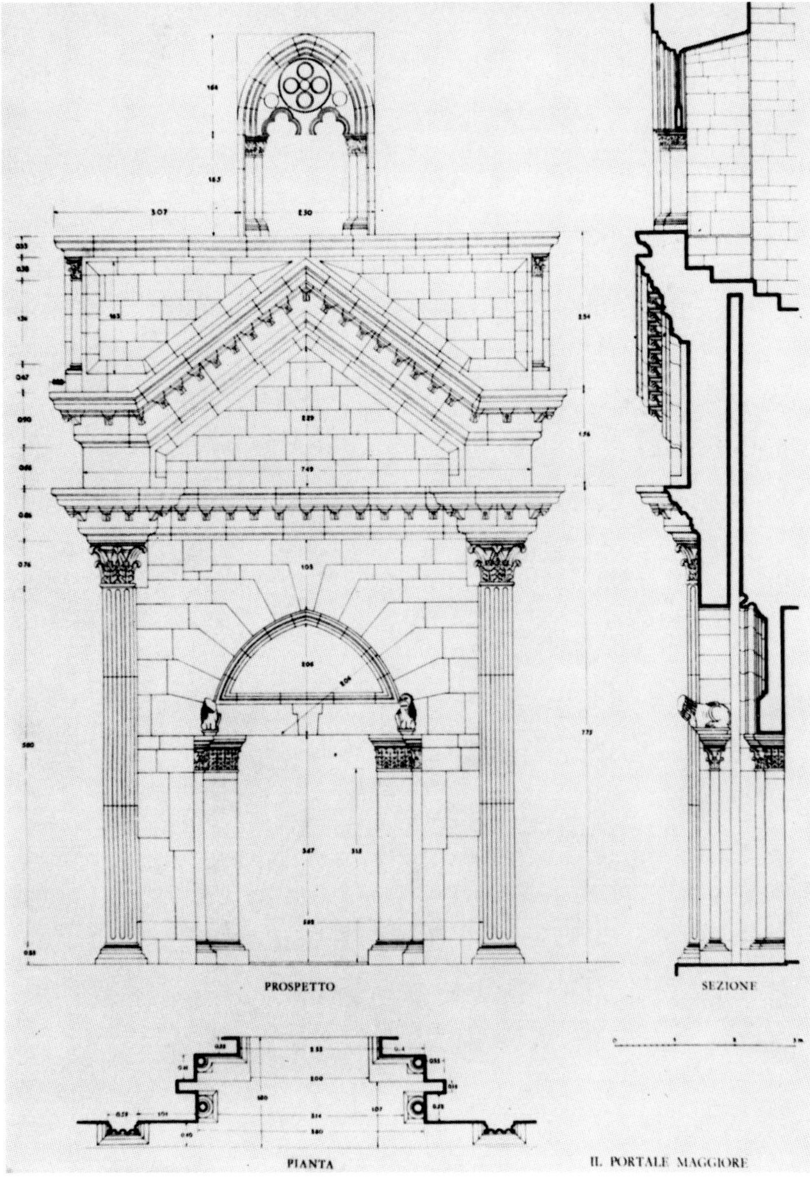

4. Castel del Monte, Architekturplan des Hauptportals
Aus Krönig 1978

Nebenportal (Raum V) gebildet wird; die beiden eigentlichen Eingangsportale des Hofes sind aber ebenso wenig achsial-symmetrisch bezogen auf die in Raum II durch das Hofportal gegebene seitlich versetzte Achse. Es zeigt sich vielmehr, daß die beiden Hofportale als Zugänge zu den Räumen bezogen sind auf die Raumfolge selbst, und das heißt auf die Mittelachse der beiden "Durchgangs-Räume" I und II und der übrigen "Wohn-Räume" (III bis VIII), welche durch die Mittelwand zwischen den beiden Durchgangs-Räumen gegeben ist, und diese Achse ist zugleich identisch mit der einzigen Trennungswand der Räume im Obergeschoß. So erweist sich die Anordnung der beiden Portale als höchst sinnvoll; sie führen jeweils in den mittleren Raum einer Folge von je drei Räumen: das linke Portal in Raum VII (zwischen VI und VIII) ist das reichere. Seine zusätzliche Rahmung mit Dreiecksgiebel erinnert an das gleiche Motiv des Hauptportals. Es weist damit den Weg zu dem in der Tat auf dieser Seite zugänglichen "Hauptraum" I ("Thronsaal") im Obergeschoß. Das rechte Portal in Raum IV (zwischen III und V) ist einfacher. Es weist den Weg zu dem mit besonderer "Wohnqualität" ausgestatteten Raum II im Obergeschoß. Im Erdgeschoß sind durch die Anordnung der beiden Portale alle sechs Räume auf das bequemste zugänglich, ohne daß jemals mehr als eine Innentür durchschritten werden müßte. Auch die Anordnung der drei Treppentürme erweist sich in gleicher Weise wie die der beiden Hofportale als bezogen auf die schräge Mittelachse der Raumfolge. Diese Achse trifft auf Turm 5, von dem die beiden anderen, 3 und 7, gleich weit entfernt sind.

Durch Kamine an der Hofwand ausgezeichnet sind im Erdgeschoß allein die Räume III und VIII. Sie erscheinen dazu als besonders geeignet, weil sie die einzigen sind, die als Endglieder der Raumfolge je eine türlose Schmal- oder Seitenwand haben und dadurch besonders zum Verweilen einladen, zugleich auch nach dem Hofe zu geschlossen bleibend, mit dem sie gleichwohl durch den ihnen jeweils benachbarten Raum (IV und VII) verbunden sind. Vollends zwingend erscheint diese Anordnung, wenn die Gesamtplanung auch des Obergeschosses einbezogen wird. Dort nämlich befinden sich drei Kamine, und zwar in den Räumen II, V und VII; es sind in allen Fällen solche, die sich nicht über den Kaminräumen des Untergeschosses befinden. Deren Kamine gehen in der Mitte der jeweiligen Wandabschnitte durch beide Geschosse hindurch, in der Dachhöhe der Hofinnenseite endigend. Man hat also in jedem Falle vermieden, die Kamine der beiden Geschosse in einen gemeinsamen Rauchfang münden zu lassen; eine Maßnahme von grosser praktischer Sorgfalt.

Das Obergeschoß, absolut identisch mit

dem Erdgeschoß in der Achtzahl seiner trapezförmigen Räume, hat statt der zwei Trennmauern, welche unten die zwei "Durchgangsräume" von den übrigen sechs abtrennen, nur eine. Sie liegt in der gleichen Achse, die sich im Erdgeschoß als bestimmend erwies. Den sechs vom "Vestibül" und Durchgang abgetrennten Wohnräumen im Erdgeschoß entspricht also die volle Achtzahl der Wohnräume im Obergeschoß. Die hier als besonders wohnlich sich heraushebenden Endglieder der Raumfolge sind Raum I und II. Sie sind in der Tat auch sonst besonders ausgezeichnet vor den anderen Räumen: Raum I hat unmittelbar über dem Hauptportal eine nur hier anzutreffende breite und festliche Wandnische, innerhalb derer sich die allen Räumen des Obergeschosses gemeinsame Fensternische mit den seitlichen Sitzbänken befindet, zu denen man auf vier Stufen hinaufgelangt, und er besitzt weiterhin nach dem Hofe zu eine Türöffnung auf den ursprünglich ringsum laufenden Balkon (Abb. 5). Hinzu kommt schließlich in dem einzigen von hier aus zugänglichen Turm 8 eine Wendeltreppe, die im Gegensatz zu allen drei anderen Treppentürmen (3, 5, 7) erst hier beginnt und allein dem Zugang des Daches dient. Alle genannten Sonderformen dieses Raumes kennzeichnen ihn als einen solchen der Repräsentation des Herrschers; und gerade auch das Fehlen der eigentlich wohnlichen Elemente, wie Kamine und Nebenräume in zugeordneten Türmen, bestätigt diesen Charakter. Hier also wird die in dem Hauptportal einsetzende und nach außen sich bekundende machtvoll-repräsentative Geste und zugleich achsiale Ausrichtung des ganzen Bauwerks folgerichtig fortgesetzt und vollendet. Die Ausrichtung auf die sinngebende Mitte dieses "Thronsaals" (Raum I) wird vollends deutlich dadurch, daß nicht nur diese Achse der doppelten Öffnungen nach Frontseite und Hofseite zugleich durch diesen Raum geht, sondern auch die beiden anderen Balkon-Portale in Raum IV und VI des Obergeschosses "achsial-symmetrisch" auf diese Achse bezogen sind. Vom "Thronsaal" aus ist alles überschaubar: das Gelände vor dem Hauptportal ebenso wie auf der Hofseite die drei Portale des Erdgeschosses und die zwei Balkon-Portale des Obergeschosses.

Auch wenn das Hofportal in Raum VII allein teilhat an dem Rahmenmotiv des Hauptportals und damit zugleich hinweisen soll auf den grösseren Formen-Reichtum und den höheren Rang des Obergeschosses und seine der Repräsentation dienenden Raumteile auf dieser Seite, so bleibt es doch ganz ohne antikisierende Formen. Um so auffallender ist es, daß die drei Fenster-Portale des Obergeschosses, die ursprünglich auf den umlaufenden Balkon führten, mit ihrem horizontalen Tür-Sturz über seitlichen Konsolen, und mit ihrem halbrunden Bogen über

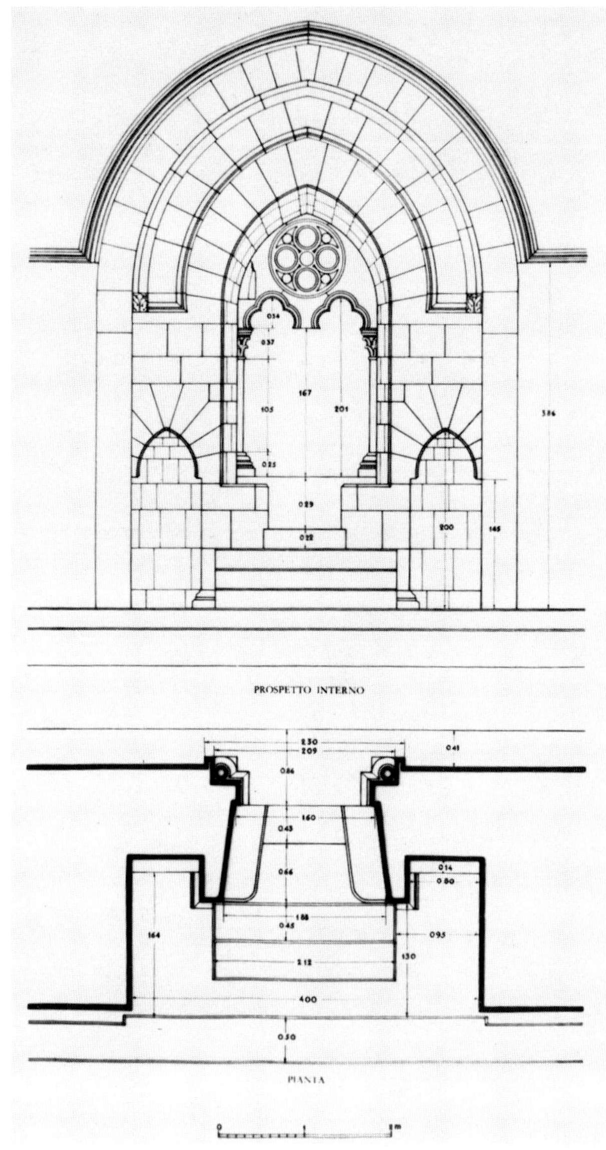

5. Castel del Monte, Architekturplan einer Fensternische mit seitlichen Sitzbänken
Aus Krönig 1978

seitlichen Säulchen ausgesprochen antikisierende Formen zeigen. Alle drei Portal-Öffnungen haben als äußere Rahmenform über der inneren Blattwelle ihrer halbrunden Bögen dreifach verschiedene Formen antikisierenden Ornaments: das Portal in Raum I einen Eierstab, das in Raum IV einen Kranz von Lorbeerblättern, das in Raum VI eine Perlschnur. In allen drei Fällen verbinden sich diese Elemente mit dem inneren Bogen der geschwungenen Blattwelle.

Die Säulchen mit ihren Knollenblätter-Kapitellen sind das wichtigste gemeinsame Element aller Portale in Erd- und Obergeschoß. Es ist der Bereich der von burgundisch-zisterziensischen Formen bestimmten Architektur, der hier entgegentritt. Auch die antikisierenden Elemente sind hier beheimatet. Doch bleibt wichtiger als der Nachweis der Herkunft einzelner Motive die Feststellung der bewußt differenzierenden Verwendung eines reichen Formenschatzes an den verschiedenen Teilen von Castel del Monte. Die Konzentration der spezifisch antikisierenden Motive auf Hauptportal und Obergeschoß muß daher als eine wohl bedachte und höchst sinnvolle Auszeichnung gewertet werden, die allein dem "Thronsaal," Raum I, vorbehalten bleibt.

Dem "Thronsaal" von Raum I ist in Raum II das andere Endglied der Raumfolge unmittelbar benachbart, wenn auch durch eine türlose Wand getrennt. Im Gegensatz zum Thronsaal ist dieser Raum durch eine Reihe von Einzelheiten als besonders wohnlich, als "Wohnsaal" gekennzeichnet. Abgeschlossen gegen den Hof besitzt er einen Kamin und den weiteren Komfort zweier ihm zugeordneter Türme mit ihren Nebenräumen, Turm 1 mit Abtritt. So befinden sich "Thronsaal" und "Wohnsaal" entsprechend ihren gegensätzlichen Zwecken an den entgegengesetzten Enden der Raumfolge; doch haben sie dies gemeinsam, daß sie als Endglieder der Raumfolge bestimmt sind zum Verweilen, nicht zum Durchschreiten. Unmittelbar unter ihnen befinden sich aber die beiden einzigen "Durchgangsräume" des Erdgeschosses, die also den beiden einzigen "Verweilräumen" des Obergeschosses entsprechen. Man muß daher sagen, daß die Einzigartigkeit von "Thronsaal" und "Wohnsaal" des Obergeschosses folgerichtig bereits im Erdgeschoß vorbereitet ist.

Die architektonische Gliederung der trapezförmigen Räume beider Geschosse erfolgt durch je vier Wandpfeiler, die sich an den verschieden grossen Seiten des Trapezes paarweise gegenüberstehen, ein mittleres Quadrat aussondernd, das mit einem Kreuzrippengewölbe versehen ist, während die seitlichen verbleibenden Raumteile mit spitzbogigen Tonnengewölben überwölbt sind. Für Proportion und Wirkung der architektonischen Gliederung aller Räume ist die Tatsache entscheidend, daß die Gewölbe etwa in halber Höhe ansetzen und daß die Kämpferhöhe des Raumes durch ein umlaufendes Gesims als wichtiges Gelenk betont ist.

Bereits die Außenansicht wie auch die Hofansicht machen deutlich, daß das Obergeschoß mit der grösseren Pracht seiner architektonischen Formen, seinen grösseren und reicher ausgebildeten Fenstern als das eigentliche Wohngeschoß vor dem Erdgeschoß ausgezeichnet ist. Grundriß und Aufriß lassen zugleich erkennen, daß alle Räume in beiden Geschossen völlig gleichwertig in Grösse und Gestalt sind. In der Tat sind aber die Raumfolgen beider Geschosse nur durch die Mittel künstlerischer Charakterisierung unterschieden. Damit ist in einer Konsequenz, welche bereits die Theorie und Praxis der Renaissance-Architektur vorwegnimmt, der "piano nobile," die "belle étage" verwirklicht. Im Erdgeschoß gliedern stämmige, unverjüngte Halbsäulen mit attischen Basen und schlichten zweireihigen Blätterkapitellen die Wände über polygonalen Sockeln und mit ebensolchen reich profilierten Deckplatten. Im Obergeschoß sind es aus drei Dienstsäulchen gebündelte Wandpfeiler, die sich auf ringsum geführten Sitzbänken erheben, eine wohnliche Einzelheit, die nur das Obergeschoß auszeichnet. Und die zusätzliche Feinheit, ja Eleganz gegenüber dem Erdgeschoß wird auch darin sichtbar, daß die Wandpfeiler nicht nur in den Deckplatten, sondern auch in ihren fein profilierten Sockeln einbezogen sind in ein ringsum laufendes Horizontalgesims. Das Obergeschoß ist bei geringerer Mauerdicke seiner zugleich auch etwas höheren Räume zumal durch reichlichere Lichtzufuhr ausgezeichnet, vor allem aber durch die tiefen und breiten Nischen der Aussenfenster. Besondere Aufmerksamkeit verdient auch die Tatsache, daß in den Räumen des Obergeschosses das Rautenmuster des sogenannten *opus reticulatum*, also die römische Mauertechnik der Antike, verwendet ist, hier als ein Element sichtbaren Schmucks der Wand; und dies geschieht ganz offenbar im Zusammenhang mit den römisch-antiken Schmuckformen, die als Ausdruck kaiserlicher Hoheit an dem Bau allein das Hauptportal und das Obergeschoß besonders auszeichnen. Ein gezielter bauplastischer Schmuck ist überall mit Bedacht eingesetzt. Ein System der Wasserversorgung mit Hilfe von Zisternen und Sanitärräumen kann noch einmal die Verbindung von rationaler Zweckmäßigkeit und hoher gestalterischer Vollendung des ganzen Bauwerks beweisen.

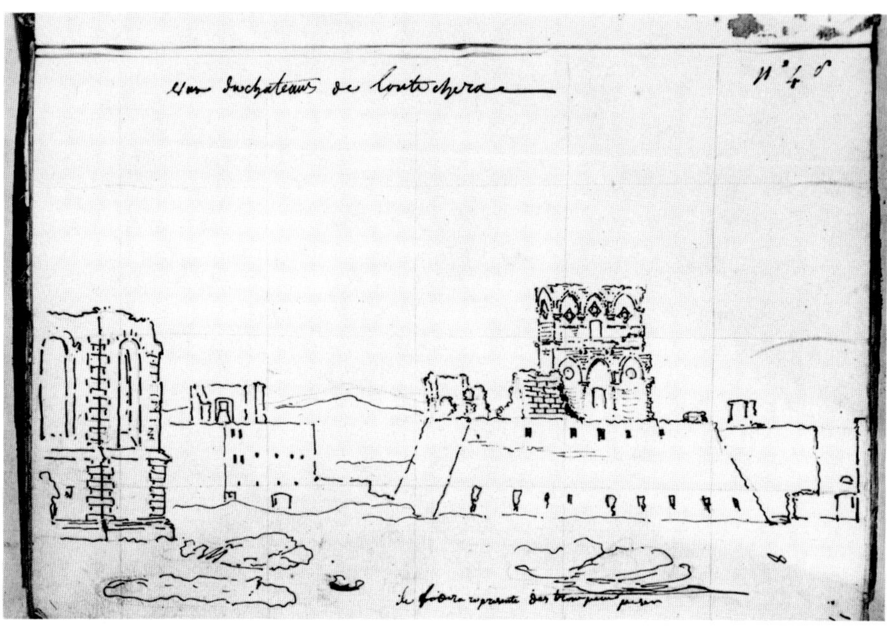

6. Jean Louis Desprez, *Lucera*, 1778
Nationalmuseum Stockholm

II

Die schriftlichen Quellen geben uns keine Auskunft über Zweck und Bedeutung von Castel del Monte. Auch für die vier anderen, eng verwandten Bauten ist die Quellenlage nur wenig günstiger. Wir müssen daher fragen, was die besondere architektonische Form dieser Bauten selbst über Zweck und Bedeutung aussagen kann, und das vor allem im Hinblick auf Castel del Monte. Alle vier im Jahrzehnt 1230–1240 errichteten Bauten, das Kastell von Lucera in Apulien und die drei an der Ostküste Siziliens, Syrakus, Catania und Augusta, werden in den Urkunden abwechselnd *palatium* und *castellum* genannt. Die volle Berechtigung dieser doppelten Bezeichnung kann man in der Sorgfalt und Schönheit der architektonisch-künstlerischen Ausgestaltung erblicken: die Bauten konnten also nach Bedarf Verteidigungs-Anlagen oder kaiserliche Wohnstätten sein. Allen vier Bauten gemeinsam ist die absolut regelmäßige, aus dem Quadrat des Grundrisses entwickelte Planung, verbunden mit der konsequenten Anwendung des gotischen Wölbungssystems, wobei beides sich gegenseitig bedingt. Erstaunlich ist aber, daß innerhalb dieser strengen Bindung doch in keinem Falle eine Wiederholung der einmal gefundenen architektonischen Lösung gegeben wird, daß vielmehr in einem angespannten Willen zur Gestaltung die Planung von einem Bau zum anderen weiter entwickelt wird.

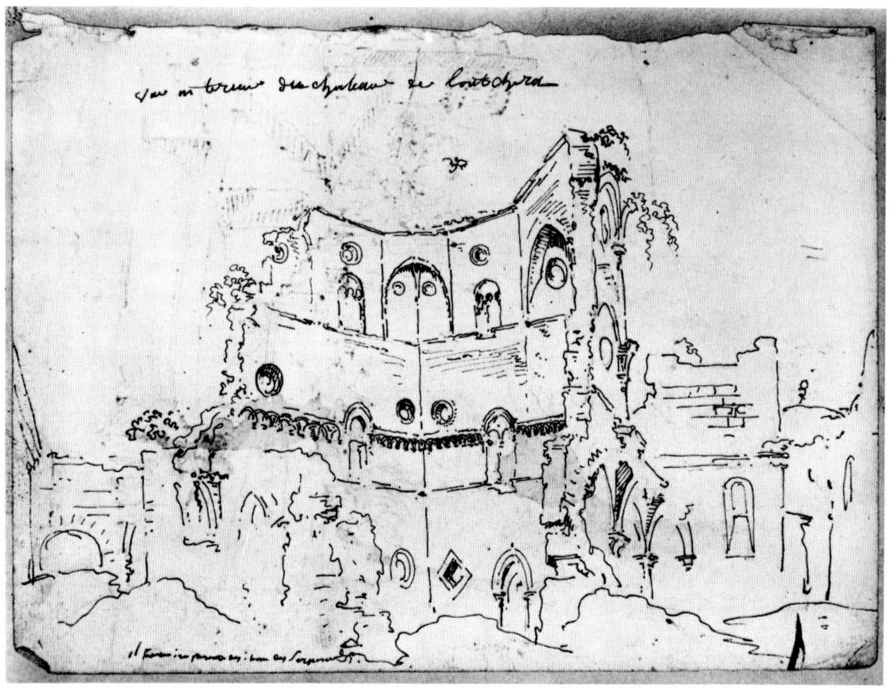

7. Jean Louis Desprez, *Lucera*, 1778
Nationalmuseum Stockholm

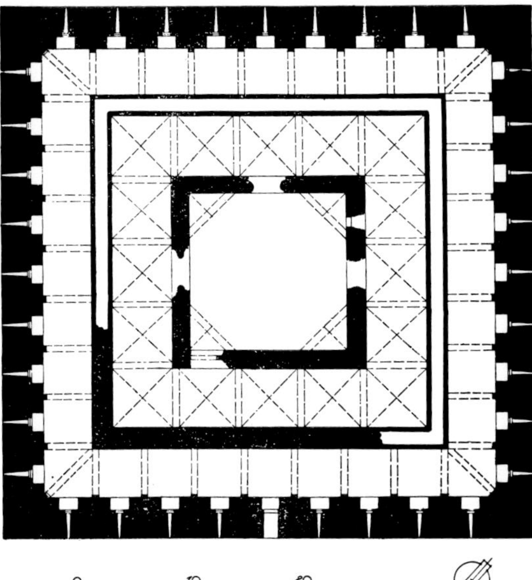

8. Kastell von Lucera, Grundriss. Versuch einer teilweisen Rekonstruktion mit Angabe der unvollständig erhaltenen Mauern
Aus Krönig 1978

Die Ruine von Lucera kann in unserer Anschauung durch zwei Zeichnungen des Malers Jean Louis Desprez von 1778 kurz vor der endgültigen Zerstörung weitgehend rekonstruiert werden (Abb. 6, 7). Der quadratische Baukörper hatte die ungewöhnliche Höhe von drei Geschossen gewölbter Räume (Abb. 8, 9). Der quadratische Hof wird im obersten, dritten Geschoß durch übereckgestellte spitzbogige Gurten mit kleinen Dreiecks-Gewölben in ein regelmäßiges Achteck überführt. Dadurch ergab sich für die Dachterrasse auf der Innenseite eine Achteckform, die derjenigen von Castel del Monte überraschend entspricht. Nach Aussage der Zeichnung besaß der Hof einen außerordentlichen Reichtum architektonischer Gliederung. Der Außenbau bleibt in seinem ursprünglichen Aussehen weitgehend ungewiß, zumal die ihn jetzt auf allen vier Seiten umgebende, mit einer Halbtonne überwölbte sogenannte Schützengalerie vielleicht erst eine Zufügung anjouinischer Zeit ist und die Annahme von vier Ecktürmen zwar ungewiß, aber wahrscheinlich da notwendig bleibt. Die ziemlich allein dastehende Höhenentfaltung des Baus bedeutete demnach offenbar auch eine wohnliche Entfaltung, was in bemerkenswertem Einklang steht mit den schriftlichen Quellen. Übrigens führte der Hauptzugang zum Inneren des Kastells in zweimal rechtwinklig gebrochener Linie in den Hof; es ist die gleiche Anlage des Zugangs wie in Castel del Monte.

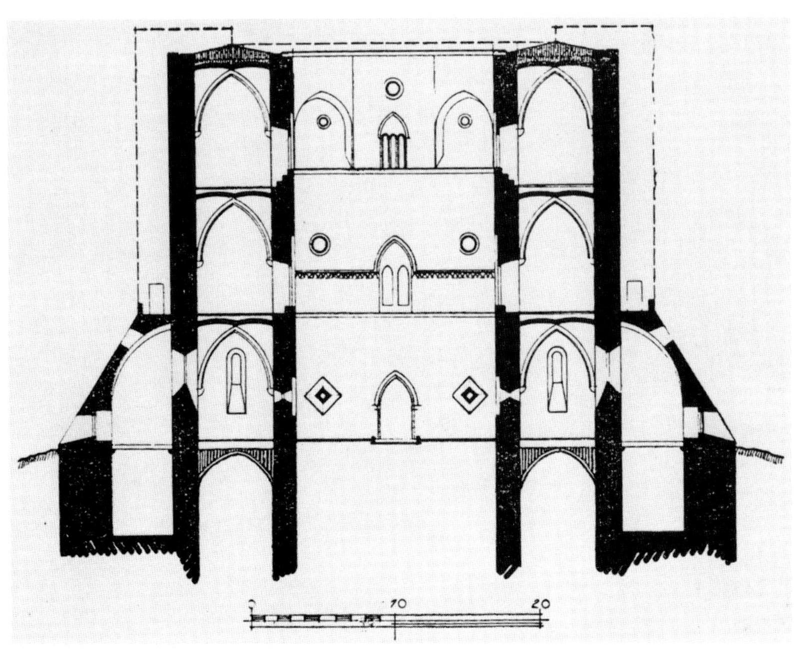

9. Kastell von Lucera, Schnitt. Versuch einer Rekonstruktion
Aus Krönig 1978

Während in Lucera schon die Wahl des Ortes als in einer a priori nicht feindlichen Umgebung die doppelte Bestimmung des Baus verständlich erscheinen läßt, müssen die drei an der Ostküste Siziliens errichteten Kastelle von Syrakus, Catania und Augusta als in entscheidender Hinsicht von strategischen Erwägungen bestimmt erscheinen. Gleichwohl widerspricht dem entschieden das ungewöhnlich sorgfältig und schön, bis in alle architektonisch-plastischen Einzelheiten ausgeführte Kastell von Syrakus (Abb. 10). Auf der Spitze der Halbinsel Ortygia gelegen, bildet der in seinem ursprünglichen Grundriß rekonstruierte, als Ruine vor uns stehende quadratische Bau mit seinen vier runden Ecktürmen das Innere als eine einzige große Halle: fünf mal fünf, also fünfundzwanzig, quadratische, mit Kreuzrippengewölben über Säulen gedeckte Raumteile, von denen nur der mittlere geöffnet war—weniger "Hof" zu nennen als eine Art von *impluvium*. Die letzte, in den 1980er Jahren erfolgte Restaurierung hat einen Teilaufbau der Säulenhalle ergeben, verbunden mit der wichtigen Erkenntnis, daß allein das kleine mittlere Raum-Quadrat nicht Säulen hatte, sondern durch vier aus drei Halbsäulen zusammengesetzte Pfeiler ausgezeichnet war. Ein oberes Geschoß ist nur noch zu erschliessen. Treppen finden sich in den Türmen, ihnen benachbart in den Ecken des Erdgeschosses große Kamine. Sowohl in diesen Dispositionen als auch in der Durchführung der Einzelformen zeigt sich nahe Verwandtschaft mit Castel del Monte, das in vielfacher Hinsicht im Castel Maniace von Syrakus vorbereitet erscheint. Das manifestiert sich nicht nur in der allein in diesem sizilischen Bau vorhandenen Sorgfalt der vorzüglichen Quadertechnik, sondern in dem achsial angelegten großartigen Hauptportal mit seinen Formen zisterziensischer Gotik, mit seinen skulptierten Löwen über den eingestellten Säulchen der Gewände; vor allem aber in dem großartigen, aufs Meer hinausgehenden Prachtfenster der Südostseite, das in dem allein durch ein dreiteiliges Prachtfenster ausgezeichneten Raum II in Castel del Monte seine auffallende Parallele hat; ferner an den figürlichen Konsolen der Rippengewölbe in einem der kleinen Nebenräume in der Mauerdicke. Besonders hervorzuheben ist schließlich die Tatsache der zu beiden Seiten des großen Portals befindlichen Postamente für die antiken Bronzewidder, die dort bis zum Jahre 1448 standen und deren einer im Museum zu Palermo erhalten ist—erstaunliches Beispiel für die auch sonst zu belegende bewußte Hochschätzung und Wiederverwertung der antiken Kunst im Kreise Friedrichs II. Sie hat in den Nachrichten über den Transport antiker Skulpturen zur Ausstattung des *palatium* von Lucera wie in den in Castel del Monte vorgefundenen Resten von Skulpturen ihre weiteren Parallelen.

Vor einer abschliessenden Betrachtung des Castel Maniace seien die Kastelle von Catania und Augusta (der Stadtgründung des "Augustus" Friedrich) kurz gewürdigt. Beide bestätigen, mit ihren Türmen auch in den Seitenmitten, also der Achtzahl ihrer Türme, daß die Lösung von Syrakus einmalig blieb. Das Kastell von Augusta (Abb. 11), das größte und nicht zufällig auch das differenzierteste der Gruppe, ist das einzige, das einen Hof mit offenen Hallen besaß; es stellt eine Antithese dar zur "idealen" Grundrißform von Syrakus.

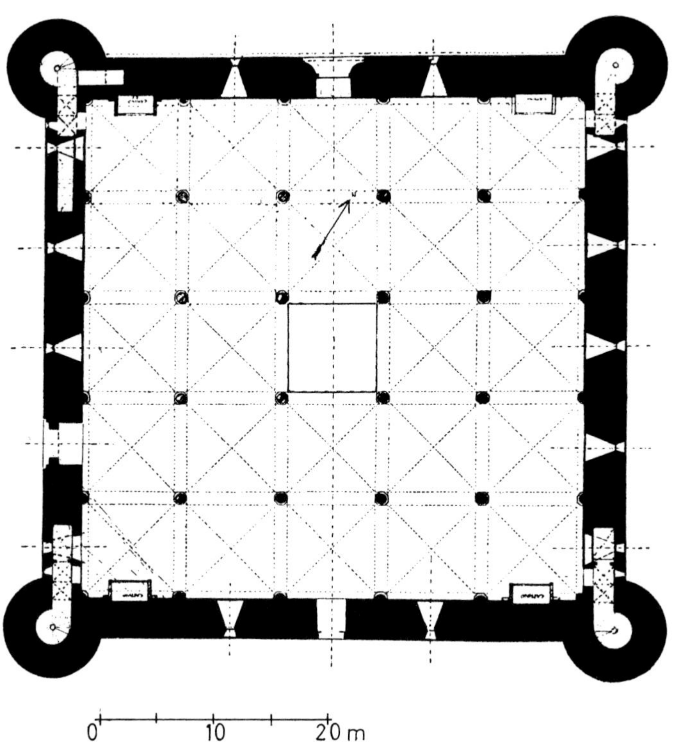

10. Kastell von Syrakus, Sizilien; Grundriss
Aus Krönig 1978

Das Kastell von Catania (Abb. 12) kann in seiner besonderen Lösung nur ganz verstanden werden durch einen Vergleich mit den beiden anderen Bauten. Es ist gleichsam eine Synthese beider Bauten: der "idealen" Grundrißform von Syrakus und der stärker differenzierten von Augusta.

Noch einmal zurückkehrend zum Bau von Syrakus ergibt sich als Fazit, daß alle zuvor genannten Elemente seiner architektonisch-künstlerischen Erscheinung den Wehrzweck einer *architectura militare* weitgehend zurücktreten lassen zu Gunsten des Charakters eines fürstlichen Wohnsitzes. Das Fehlen der "flankierenden" Türme in den Seitenmitten ist dafür ein wichtiges Kennzeichen. Es ist zugleich der "ideale" Charakter des Baus, womit ein Wesenszug ge-

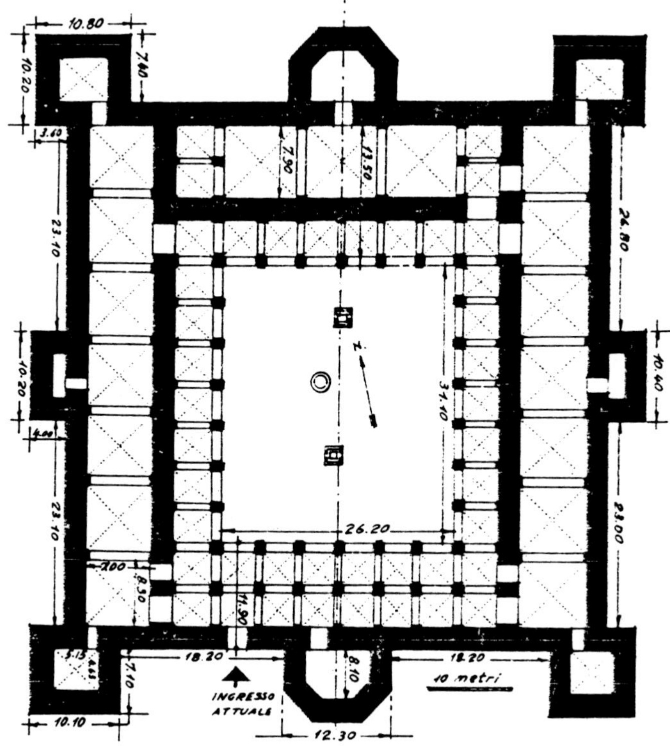

11. Kastell von Augusta, Sizilien; Grundriss
Aus Krönig 1978

12. Kastell von Catania, Sizilien; Grundriss
Aus Krönig 1978

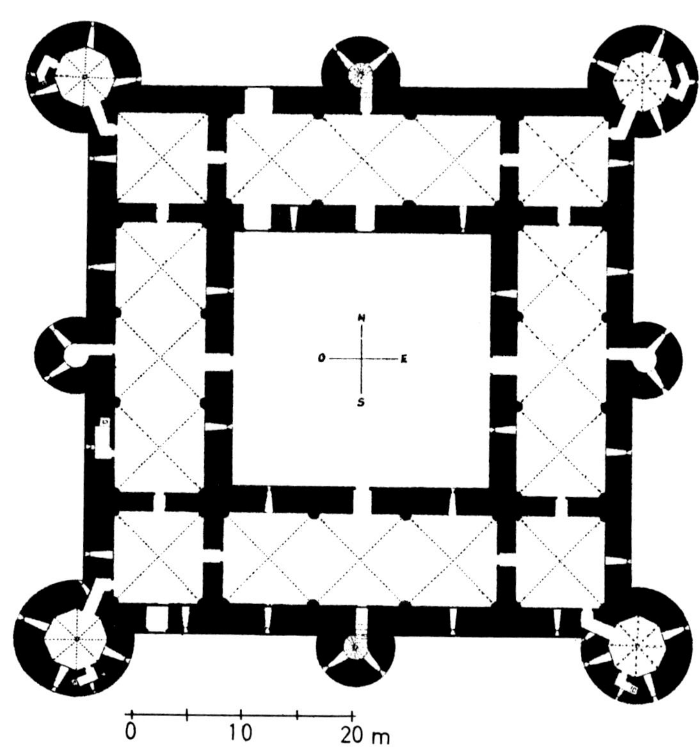

meint ist, der über die Kategorien von Zweck und Bestimmung hinausgehend ein Element von erstrebtem Ausdruck sichtbar macht. Und dieser bekundet sich in der bevorzugten Wahl zentralisierender Planung, in Grundriß und Baukörper verbunden mit der Wahl eines isolierten Bauplatzes, auf drei Seiten unmittelbar vom Meer umgeben, der keine Beeinträchtigung durch andere Bauten zuläßt. Zugleich ist aber dies von Syrakus ausgesagte zutreffend und gültig auch für Castel del Monte, womit der engere Zusammenhang gerade dieser beiden Bauten zum Ausdruck kommt. Mit dieser Aussage ist selbstverständlich nicht aufgehoben die umfassendere Feststellung, daß Castel del Monte das Endergebnis der architektonischen Gedanken ist, die in allen vier genannten Bauten Gestalt gewonnen haben. Der größere Reichtum seiner Achteckgestalt geht doch zugleich Hand in Hand mit der größten überhaupt möglichen "Vereinfachung," oder zutreffender gesagt "Reduktion," des Grundrisses und der gesamten Disposition des Inneren auf *eine* gemeinsame Norm: die Achtzahl. Jede Unterscheidung von Anzahl der Seiten und Anzahl der Türme, ja auch von Form und Seitenzahl der Türme ist aufgehoben, wie sie alle anderen Bauten noch aufweisen. Allein Syrakus präludiert der Gestalt von Castel del Monte in seiner Strenge in folgenden "Eigenschaften": Vierzahl der Seiten (seines Quadrats) und Vierzahl der (freilich runden) Türme; Reichtum seiner architektonischen Außenglieder (Portal); Einsamkeit (Isoliertheit) seiner Lage als Voraussetzung und Motivierung der beiden vorgenannten Tatbestände. Erst in Castel del Monte ist alles aus *einer* idealen Norm entwickelt, der Achtzahl; erst in Castel del Monte ist die strengste und höchste Form des "Idealbaus" verwirklicht.

III

Die historische Bestimmung der architektonischen Formensprache von Castel del Monte als französischer Gotik hat danach eine Zusammenfassung gefunden in dem grossen Buch von Émile Bertaux.[1] Danach hat die wichtige Darstellung der entscheidenden Bedeutung der Zisterzienser und ihrer burgundisch geprägten architek-

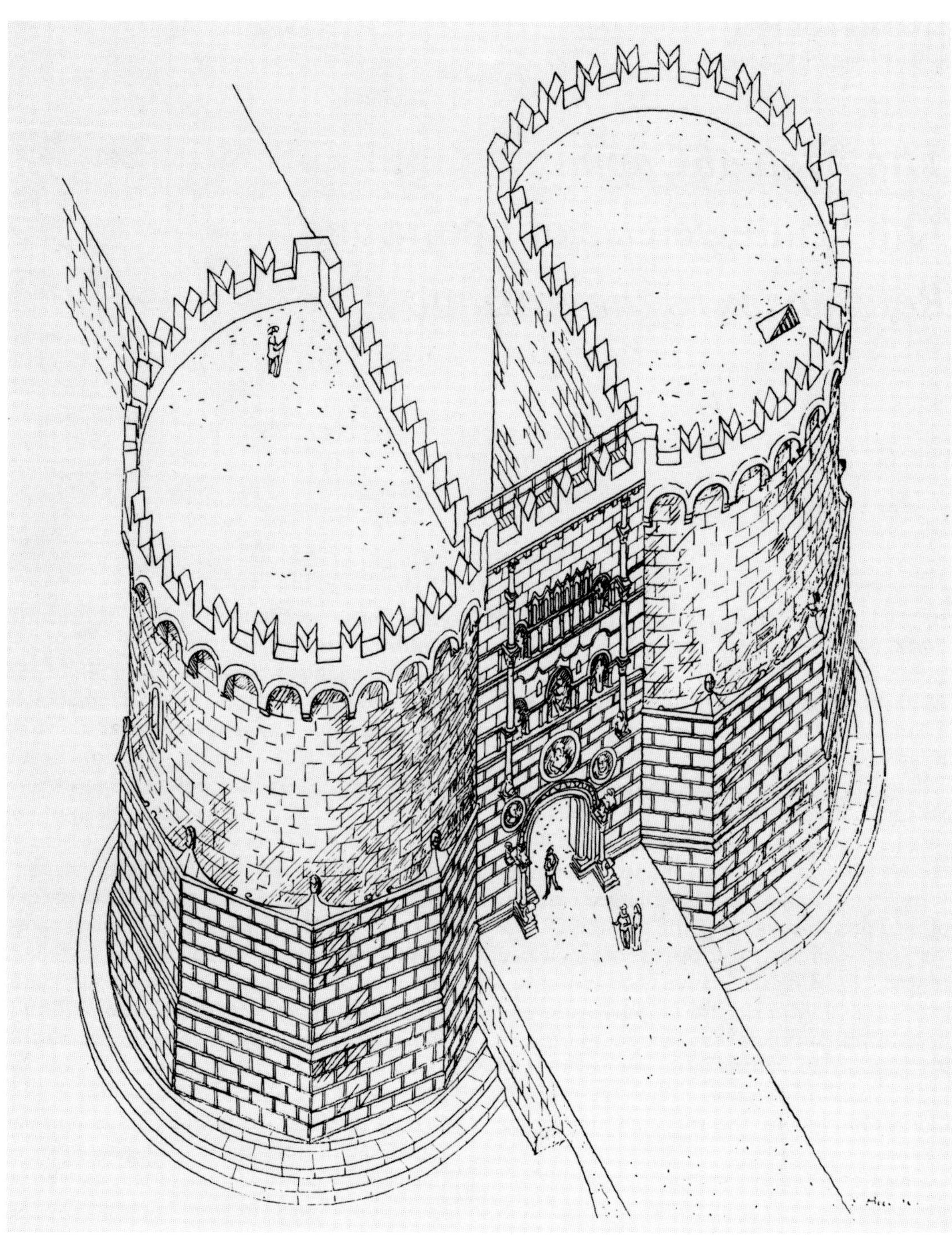

1. Arch at Capua, 1234–1240, reconstruction drawing
After Willemsen 1953

tions of the 1230s—the gold coin issue known as the *Augustalis* and an imperial portrait from Barletta (fig. 3)—rely on Roman prototypes, as did features of Frederick's public ceremonies, law code, speeches, edicts, and letters.[8] The Capua Gate has been regarded by Ernst Kantorowicz, Carl Willemsen, and others as the most ambitious and effective expression of Frederick's position as Caesar Augustus, reviver of the Roman Empire.[9]

The gateway epitomized his Sicilian kingdom and, by extension, his soon-to-be consolidated world empire. It proclaimed the emperor's supreme authority as promoter of justice and the concomitant benefits of order, peace, and prosperity. As a triumphal arch, it

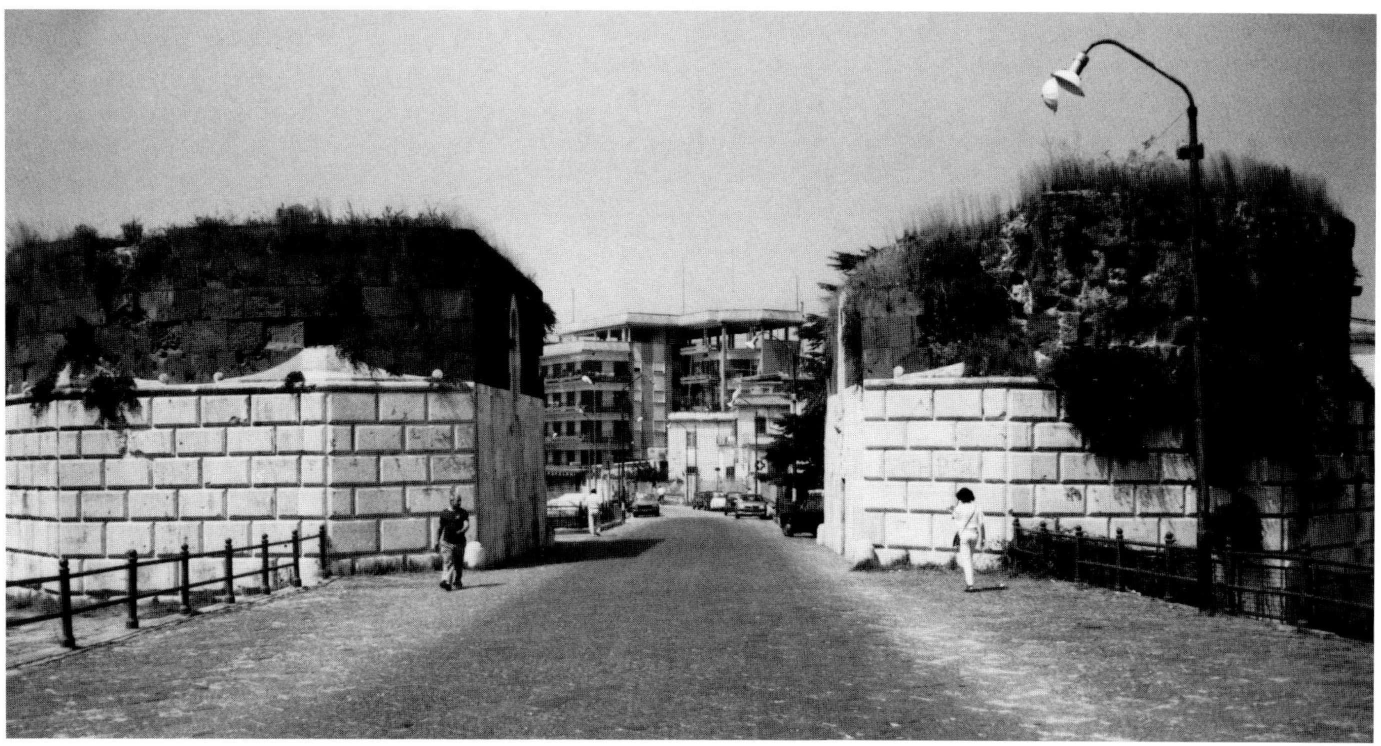

2. Arch at Capua tower bases
Photograph: Sam Gruber

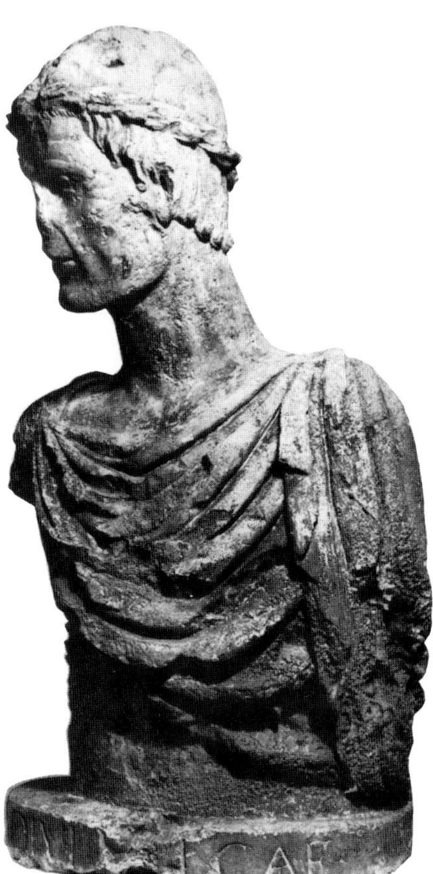

3. Imperial portrait bust, c. 1230
Museo Civico, Barletta; after *Die Zeit der Staufer*

can be seen as celebrating his 1236 victory against the Lombard League at Cortenuova and the imminent fulfillment of his personal destiny as world ruler. The intended audience included his own subjects, his adversary Pope Gregory IX, and the patrician families of Rome who sided with Frederick. The advertisement of this political agenda was enhanced by the calculated, programmatic use of Roman architectural design, actual *spolia*, and newly synthesized medieval "antiquities."

A medieval traveler from Rome would have been confronted with a stunning visual effect on the approach to Capua: a towered archway of seemingly impenetrable mass that was also opulently decorated—an architectural wonder that recalled Roman imperial monuments, especially the massive towered gateways in the ancient city walls of Rome, the most important of which were faced in marble and decorated with statuary. The Porta Appia and the Porta Ostiensis (fig. 4) exemplify the genre that Frederick's monument follows: a recessed multistory archway flanked by projecting towers.[10] The Capua Gate would appear to have been intended as a counterpart to such city gates

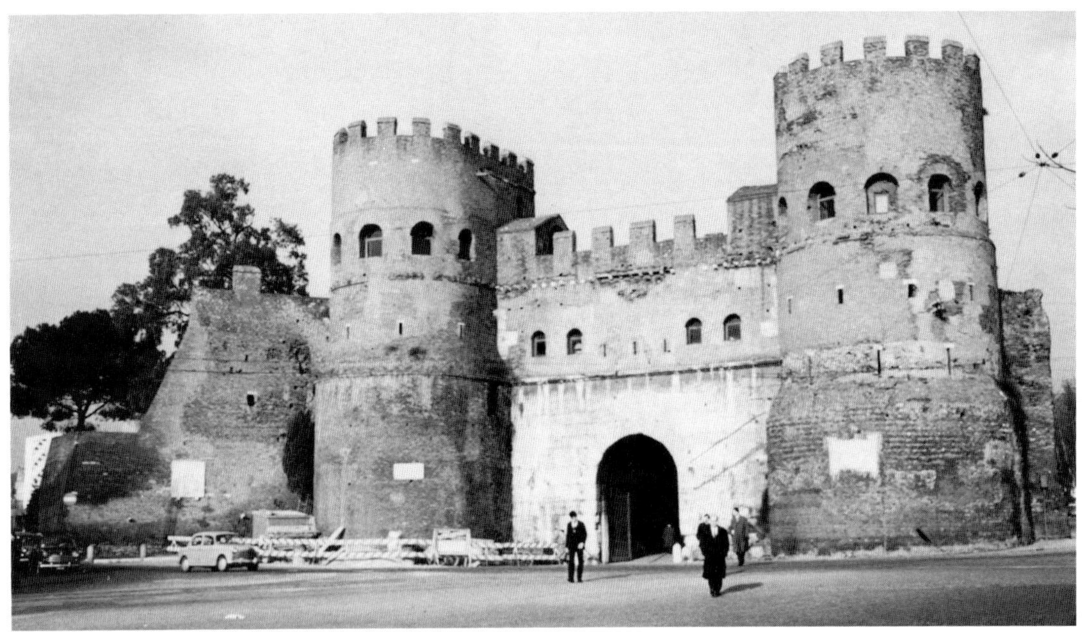

4. Rome, Porta Ostiensis, c. A.D. 161–180

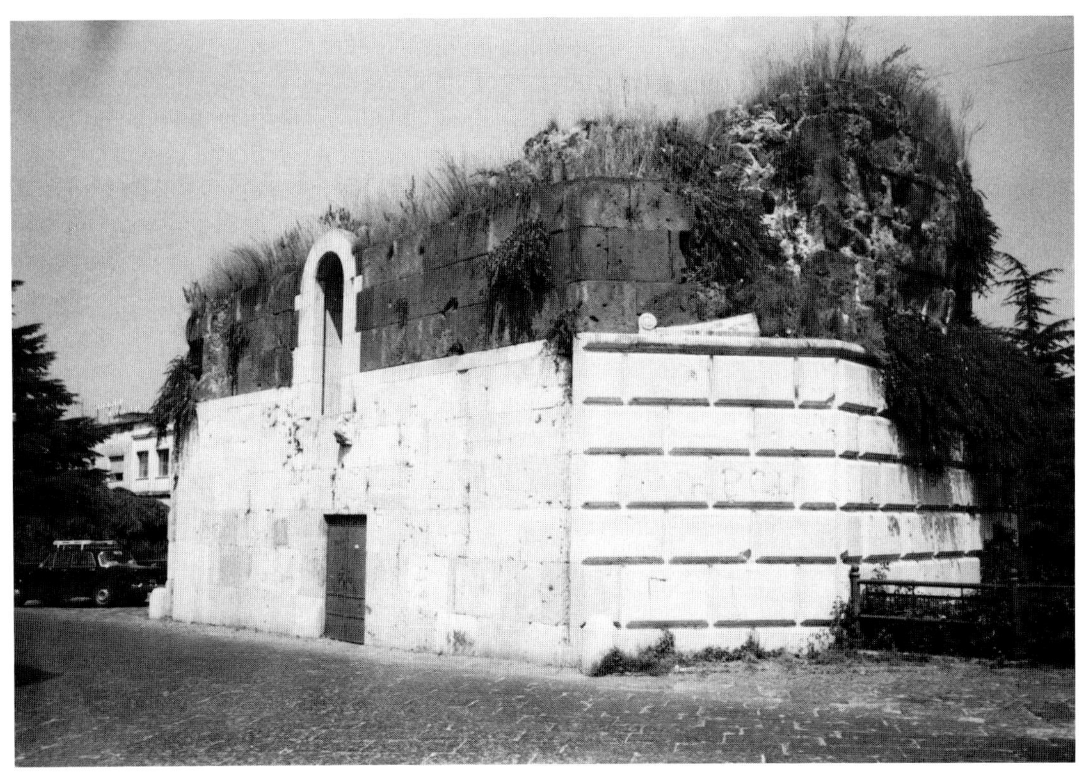

5. Arch at Capua tower base
Photograph: Sam Gruber

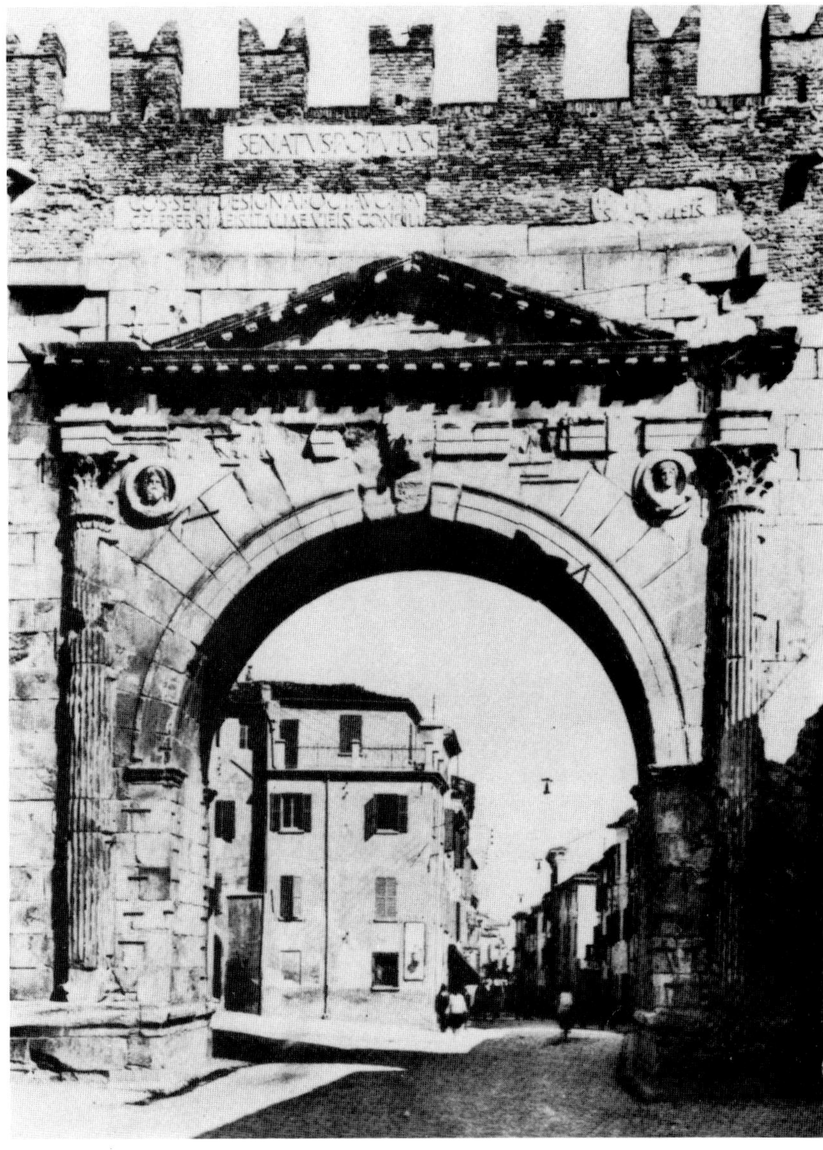

6. Arch at Rimini, c. 27 B.C.
After MacDonald 1986

in Rome whose design was meant to impress the viewer as it expressed the empire's strength and prosperity. Frederick's masons exaggerated this effect by installing massive rusticated white travertine blocks on the Capua tower bases (fig. 5) "quarried" from the Roman amphitheater at Capua Vetere.[11] The distinctive architectural design of the gate and its masonry spoils thus provided Capua with a "new" Roman imperial monument, one that also functioned honorifically.

To underscore his association with Augustus, Frederick may have drawn upon an unusual monument that was also both a city gate and a triumphal arch and that also preceded a bridge—the arch at Rimini, a town that Frederick visited in 1235. This city gate (fig. 6) commemorated Octavian's designation as Augustus in 27 B.C. and is one of a pair erected at opposite ends of the Via Flaminia when he undertook the repair of Italy's main roads leading to Rome.[12] Like Frederick's arch at Capua, the Rimini arch was flanked by projecting towers and faced with stone to match *its* nearby amphitheater. The façade treatment of each side of the Rimini arch includes engaged Corinthian columns supporting a ressaut surmounted by a pediment. This distinctive design was also utilized on the Capua arch according to an incomplete Renaissance drawing of its town façade.[13] The similarity between the Rimini arch and Frederick's arch at Capua also extends to the sculptural decoration. The Rimini arch likewise originally displayed a group of monumental statues, although their arrangement is unknown. Even its distinctive arch spandrel medallions bearing the busts of Roman divinities have been adapted on the Capuan arch, as seen in the façade reconstruction (fig. 7).[14] As the Rimini arch was the counterpart to the arch at the Milvian Bridge in Rome, each marking a key point along the major artery, the Via Flaminia, so also Frederick's arch on the Via Appia at Capua became the pendant to the late antique Porta Appia, a magnificent towered and marble-faced structure, at the beginning of the Via Appia in Rome.

Some of the features of the exterior arch façade at Capua can be reconstituted from medieval and Renaissance descriptions as well as from two Renaissance drawings.[15] The literary accounts convey the salient features and offer transcriptions (often contradictory) of the inscriptions; two even refer to the appearance of ancient sculpture.[16] The fifteenth-century bishop of Teramo, Giovanni Antonio Campano, provides a description of the gateway in his biography of Braccio da Montone and mentions marble statues and ancient figures installed in the story above the arch.[17] Scipione Sannelli's chronicle of the city of Capua up to the year 1571 offers a more complete account of the sculpture, including the suggestion of *spolia* when he refers to the upper part of the arch

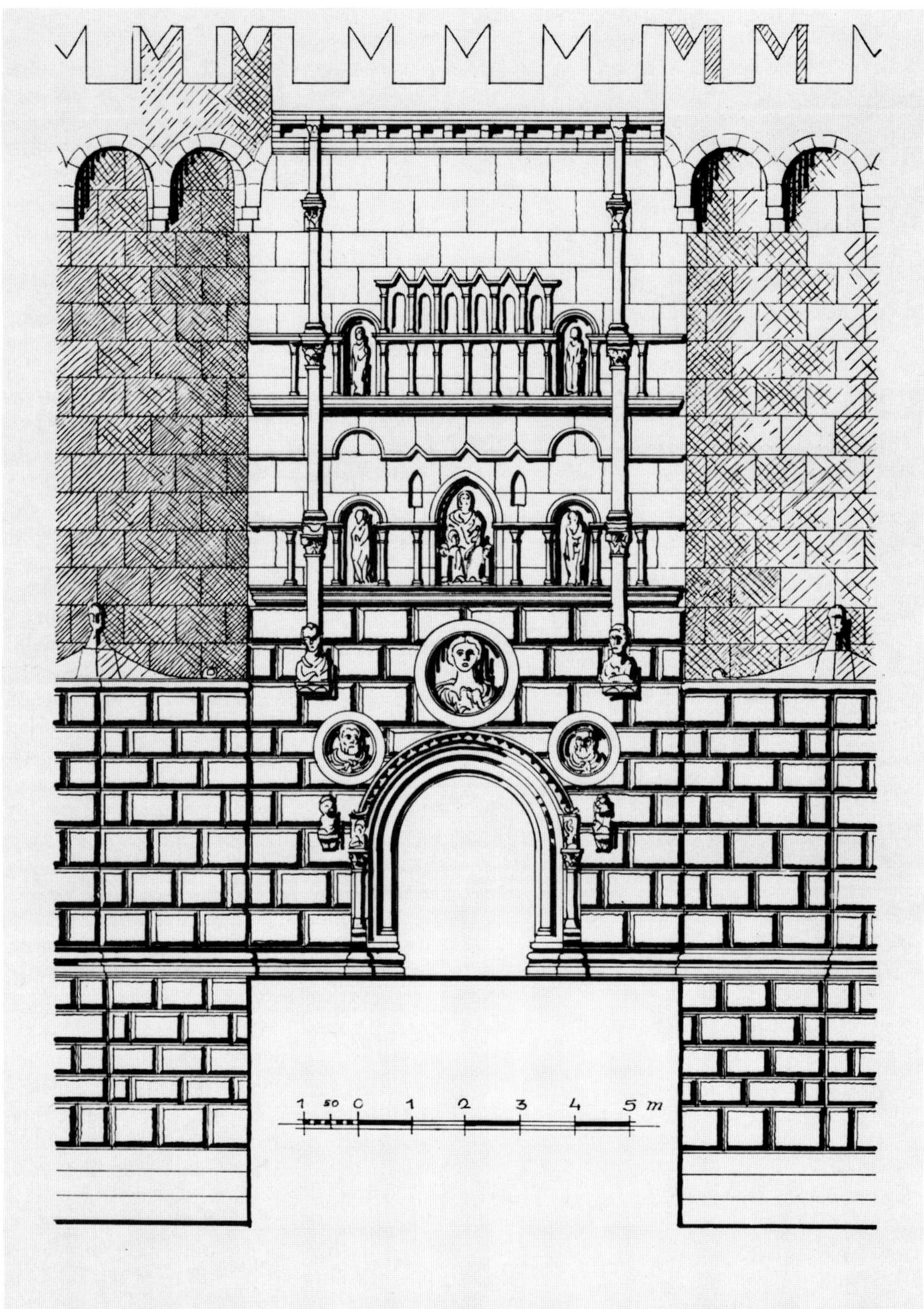

7. Arch at Capua, façade reconstruction drawing
After Shearer 1935

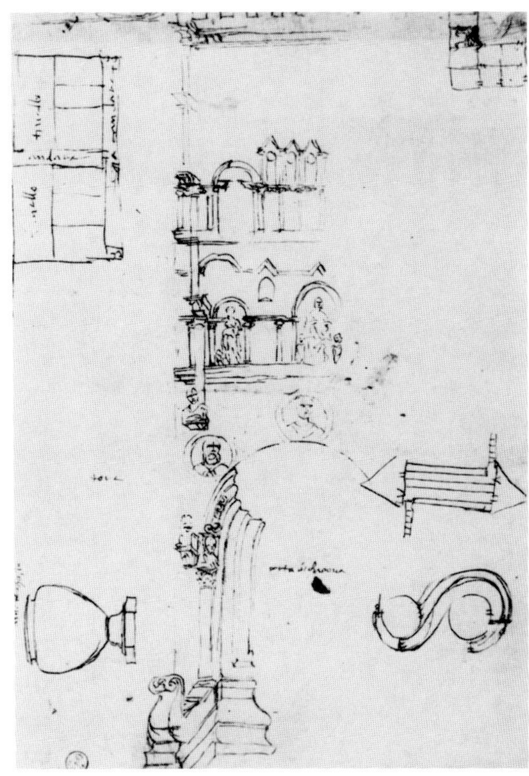

8. Francesco di Giorgio Martini, arch at Capua façade drawing, 1480s
Uffizi, Florence, MS. 333A; Scala/Art Resource, New York

9. Capua Vetere, Roman amphitheater, c. A.D. 117–138, arcade detail
Photograph: David Castriota

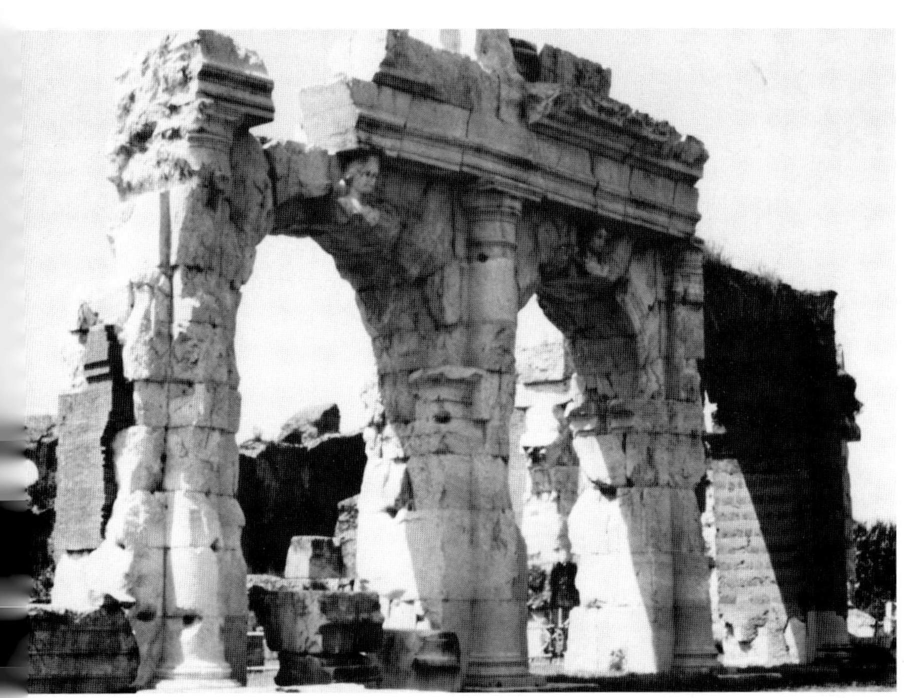

façade with its statues taken from the ruins of ancient Roman Capua and, below, the victories and trophies of the emperor carved in white marble.[18] Although the Renaissance drawings are incomplete, Francesco di Giorgio Martini's façade sketch of the 1480s (fig. 8) is considered fairly reliable due to his accurate rendering of the extant sculpture. These drawings, literary accounts, and the surviving decorative elements together reveal a complex sculptural program and help to distinguish actual Roman spoils from the thirteenth-century classicizing elements.

A distinctive feature of the Capuan sculpture program is the frequent use of figural busts: three were installed in roundels, others surmount corbels, and a large group terminated the white travertine courses of the tower bases. Although the Rimini arch undoubtedly provided a tectonic model for the roundels or monumental *clipei* with busts at Capua, another source, even closer at hand, was equally significant. The Roman amphitheater at Capua Vetere, a veritable medieval quarry for building materials, abounded in figural busts of Roman divinities.[19] Numerous examples still in situ, as well as fragments immured throughout the new town of Capua built during the Middle Ages, indicate that the exterior arches of the amphitheater displayed busts of divinities in their apices (fig. 9), comprising a decorative scheme that is rather complex and opulent as Roman amphitheaters go. As in the reuse of the amphitheater's travertine masonry on the tower bases, the extravagant use of figural busts on Frederick's Capuan arch should be seen as an intentional reference to Roman Capua. To similar effect, the builders of the ninth-century campanile and the eleventh-century castle already had incorporated busts of divinities despoiled from the amphitheater. Yet instead, and for programmatic reasons, the thirteenth-century masons carved *new* figural busts in a classicizing manner.

Among the best preserved of these thirteenth-century busts are the two identical male figures from the arch spandrel medallions (figs. 10, 11). Local Capua tradition and later chronicles identify them as leading members of Frederick's court circle, Piero della Vigna of Capua and Taddeo da Suessa.[20] However, instead of portrait likenesses in the ancient Roman manner, these are idealized

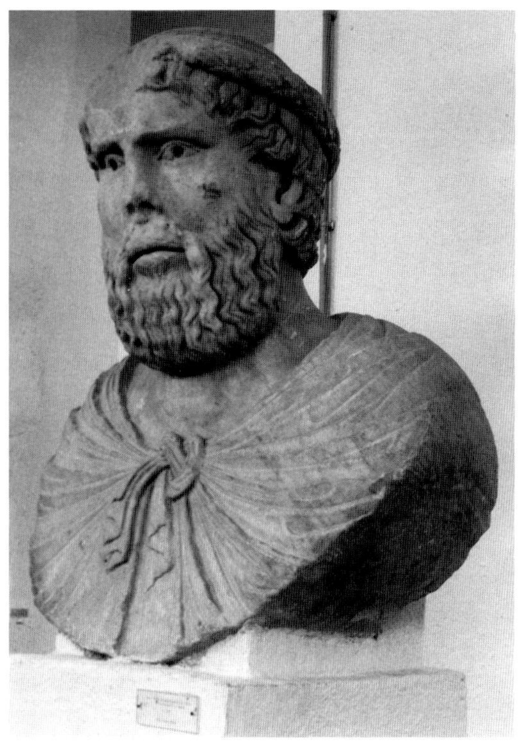

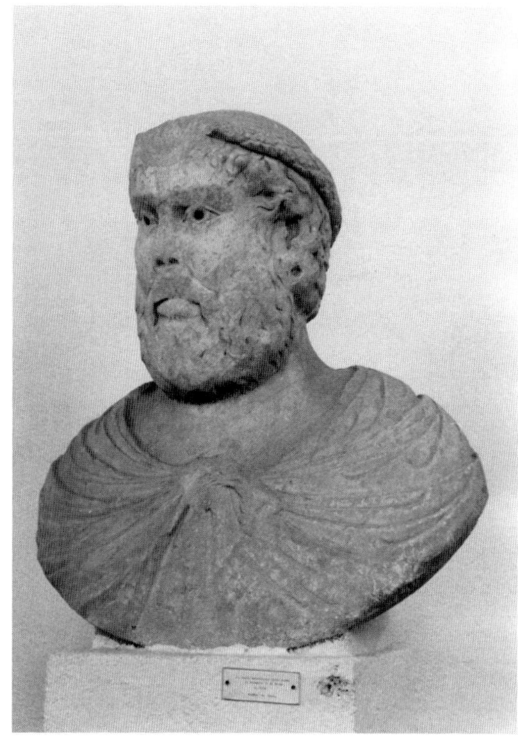

10. Piero della Vigna bust from Capua arch, 1234–1240
Museo Provinciale Campano, Capua; photograph: David Castriota

11. Taddeo da Suessa bust from Capua arch, 1234–1240
Museo Provinciale Campano, Capua; photograph: David Castriota

images that recall the bearded Greco-Roman philosopher type—a flattering prototype since both men were lawyers, rhetoricians, and high court judges. The distinctive facial type marked by squared proportions, strong brows, deep-set drilled eyes, broad rounded cheeks, and pressed lips is unmatched elsewhere in the Capua Gate sculpture but closely resembles the so-called Jupiter bust on the Capua amphitheater (fig. 12).[21] Was such a visual allusion in a "portrait" of Capua native son Piero della Vigna intended as a sculptural counterpart to his own classical allusions in the rhetoric of the court chancery?

The circular borders around the Vigna and Suessa busts contained inscriptions that emphasized their roles as executors of imperial justice and, above all, the recently completed law code of Frederick, the *Liber Augustalis* or Constitutions of Melfi, which Piero della Vigna helped formulate.[22] Their inclusion on the Capua Gate, as well as their association with the statue of Frederick just above, recalls the two statues that flank Emperor Constantine on the oration frieze on

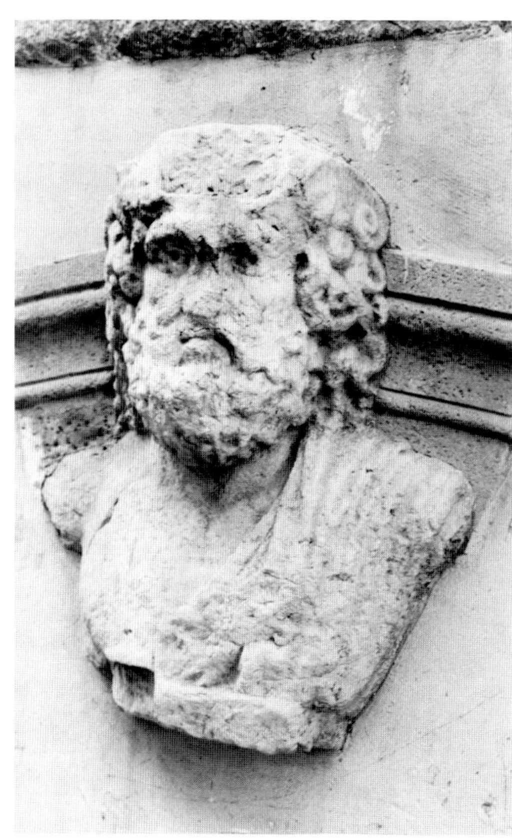

12. Capua Vetere, bust of Jupiter from Roman amphitheater, c. A.D. 117–138, façade of Palazzo Municipio
Photograph: David Castriota

the Arch of Constantine.[23] This relief detail shows the rostra in the Roman Forum with a seated statue of the judicial reformer, Emperor Hadrian, at left and his legal counselor, the great jurist Salvius Julianus, depicted at right, with a now headless figure of Constantine standing in the middle.[24] By such a reference Frederick and *his* legal counselors would consider themselves to be their successors. Like Constantine, Frederick can be seen here as addressing contemporary Romans as well as his Sicilian subjects in familiar visual terms.

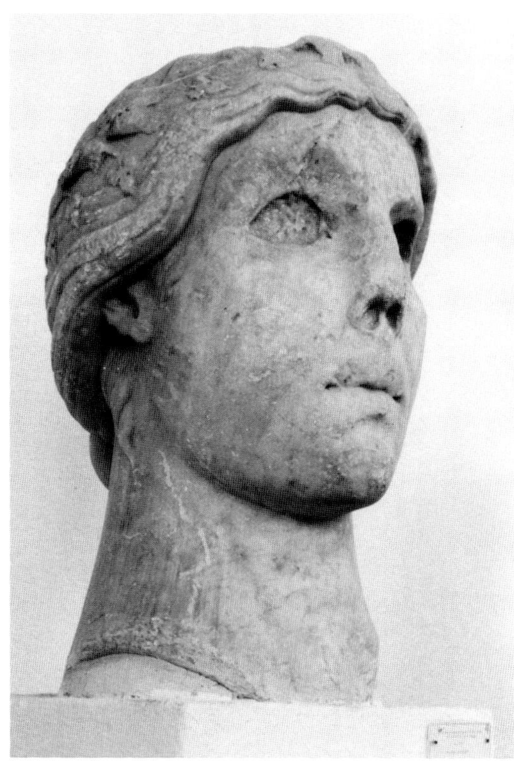

13. Female head of Custodia/Capua, 1234–1240
Museo Provinciale Campano, Capua; photograph: David Castriota

The Capua Gate's central roundel was occupied by a female bust whose parted drapery revealed the imperial eagle.[25] Only the damaged head of this thirteenth-century work survives (fig. 13). Displaying the formal details and attributes of a Roman deity, she recalls the bust of a female divinity in the arch spandrel at Rimini (fig. 6). Equally compelling typological and formal prototypes can also be found among the female busts from the Roman amphitheater at Capua such as the bust identified as Diana (fig. 14), a local patron deity.[26] Perhaps these and other busts of locally venerated divinities from Capua Vetere provided the inspiration for the more novel conception of this protective female divinity on Frederick's arch, which has been considered the tutelary deity of the Sicilian state, the embodiment of Frederician justice, even Capua personified.[27]

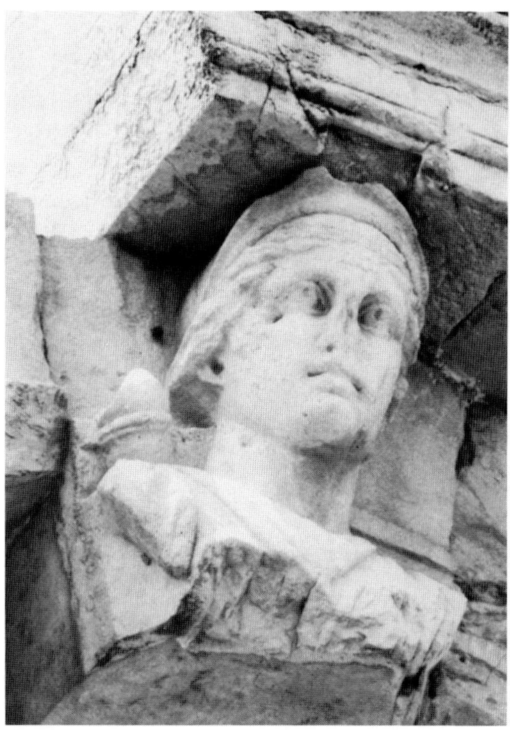

14. Capua Vetere, bust of Diana, Roman amphitheater, c. A.D. 117–138
Photograph: David Castriota

The enthroned statue of Frederick occupied the so-called *regium cubiculum* at the center of the first arcaded story.[28] For the first time since antiquity, as far as we know, a living secular ruler now presented himself as a three-dimensional enthroned figure to monumentalize his imperial authority. Surviving torso fragments (fig. 15) suggest its original appearance and convey the extent of its classicism.[29] Statues of emperors were frequently installed on Roman triumphal arches and city gates. Some of these may have been known to Frederick and his masons, either from firsthand knowledge or from literary descriptions by ancient authors. The Augustan arch at Rimini, already cited as an analogous bridgehead arch and city gate with spandrel roundels and busts, once displayed a statue of Augustus.[30] The Arch of Hadrian in Athens contained a seated statue of the emperor installed in an upper niche.

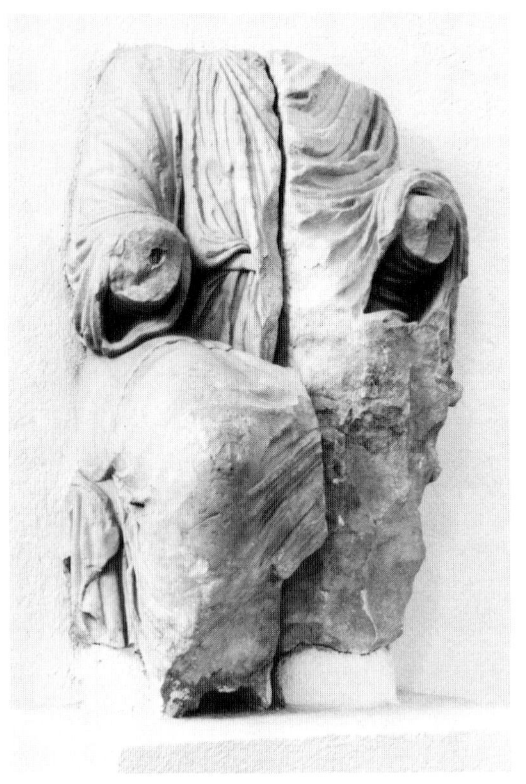

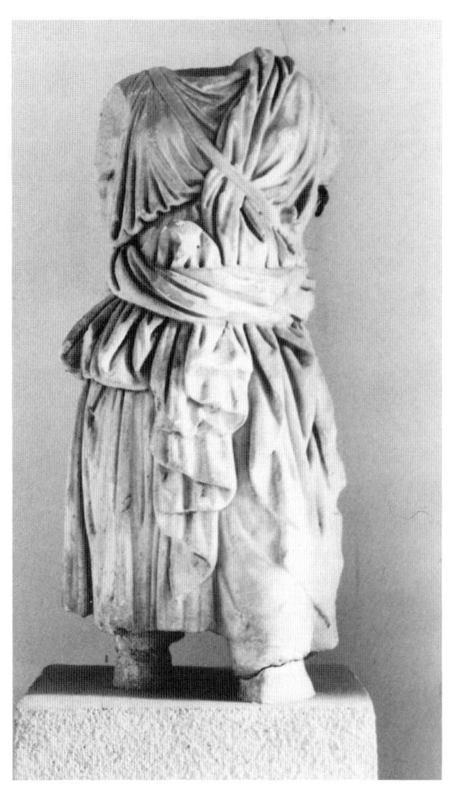

15. Statue of Emperor Frederick II from Capua arch, 1234–1240
Museo Provinciale Campano, Capua; photograph: David Castriota

16. Torso fragment of Diana, second century A.D.
Museo Provinciale Campano, Capua; photograph: David Castriota

17. Rome, Arch of Constantine, southeast façade, right tondo, A.D. 117–138
After L'Orange and von Gerkan 1939

Another seated emperor portrait, a bronze effigy of Julius Caesar, once enriched the Porta Aurea in Ravenna, a monument Frederick is known to have despoiled for its marbles which he then had shipped to Palermo.[31] Although the exact programmatic significance of these ancient examples of seated emperor statues can only be surmised, they undoubtedly demonstrated aspects of imperial magnificence. A small-scale relief version of this arrangement, the enthroned figure of Constantine distributing largesse on the northwest frieze of the Arch of Constantine in Rome, may also have informed Frederick's version specifically since the largesse is one of the many Roman imperial institutions that he used to win the favor of the Roman aristocracy and to demonstrate his renewal of the ancient empire.[32]

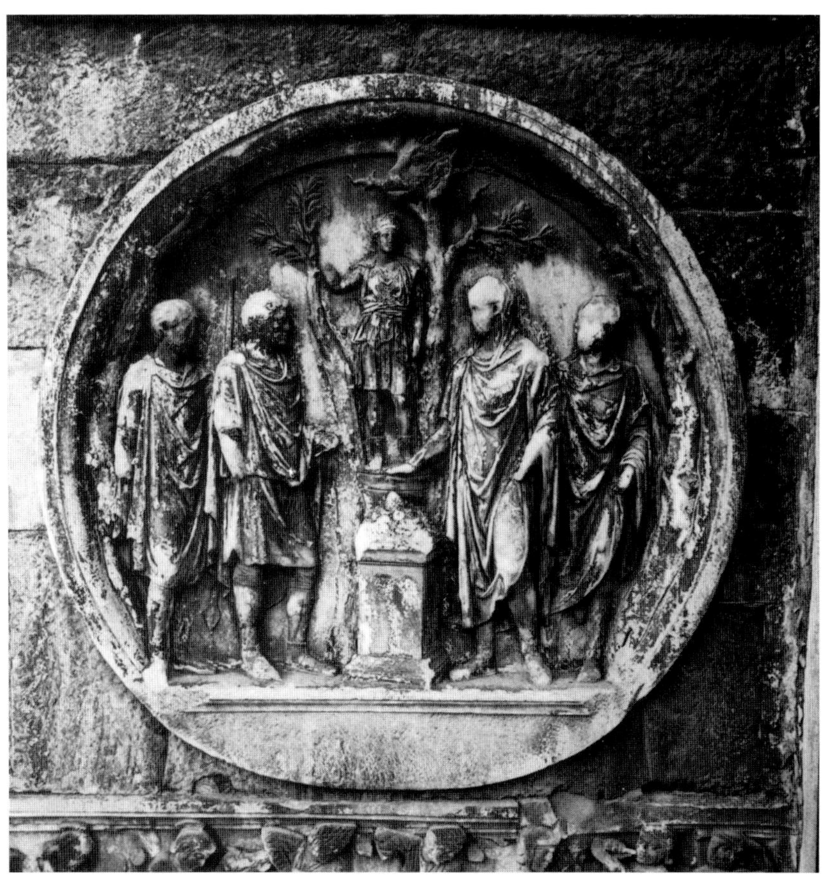

Originally Frederick's statue was flanked by two standing statues. The Martini drawing (fig. 8) provides sufficient detail of the left figure to discern a classically garbed female with a seated dog. Gustina Scaglia has identified the figure in the drawing as a torso fragment in the Museo Campano in Capua (fig.

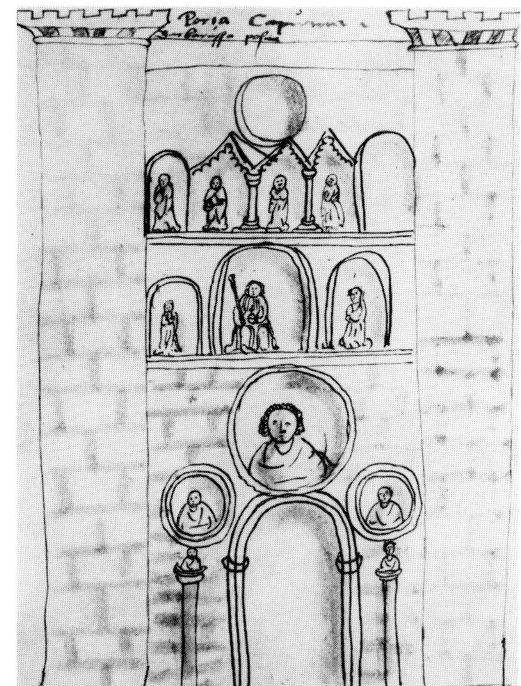

18. Arch at Capua façade drawing, c. 1500
Vienna, Österreichische Nationalbibliothek, MS. 3528, fol. 51v; after Willemsen 1953

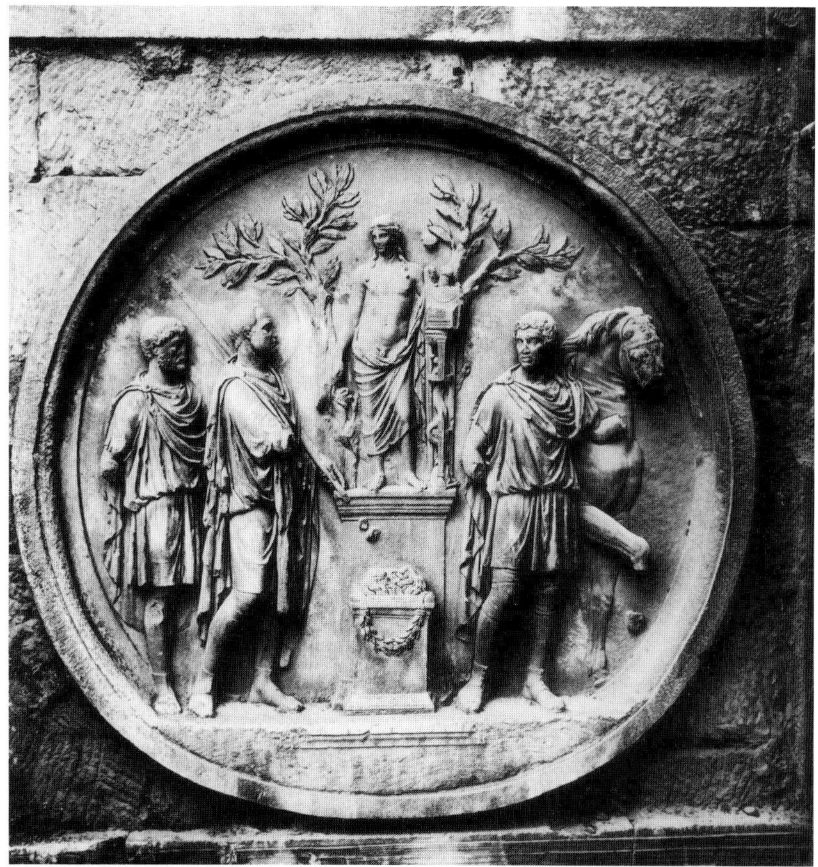

19. Rome, Arch of Constantine, northeast façade, right tondo, A.D. 117–138
After L'Orange and von Gerkan 1939

16) which depicts the locally venerated goddess Diana Tifatina.[33] This attribution lends credibility to the sixteenth-century chronicler Sannelli's comment that ancient figures on the arch had been taken from the ruins of Roman Capua. But the use of local *spolia* is far from haphazard. Rather, the deliberate choice of a Diana statue may stem from Frederick's interest in hunting as a courtly activity, as illustrated by his detailed treatise, *De arte venandi cum avibus*, and his numerous hunting lodges.[34] The incorporation of an actual Roman statue of Diana on the Capua Gate may have been inspired as well by the distinctive hunting imagery of the Arch of Constantine: the right tondo on the southeast arch façade (fig. 17) contains the emperor before a statue of Diana that is virtually identical to the Capua torso.[35]

A rather free early sixteenth-century drawing, now in Vienna (fig. 18), indicates a statue to the right of Frederick. Although generally assumed to have been another female statue, it was probably a reused statue of Diana's brother Apollo, again following the format of the Arch of Constantine (fig. 19).[36] Among the Roman antiquities in the Museo Campano at Capua is a torso fragment of a seminude Apollo or Dionysos type (fig. 20). Although its original height is uncertain, in scale the extant portion is only slightly larger than the Capua Diana torso. Perhaps this was another of the sculptures retrieved from Capua Vetere by Frederick's builders to be installed along with the Diana statue beside the emperor's image. Such a pairing of Diana and Apollo on the Capuan arch façade would have emulated not only the Arch of Constantine but also, more locally, the Capua amphitheater where both deities had already appeared jointly in bust format.[37] This iconography would have been especially appropriate to Frederick since they were the patrons of his chief courtly pursuits, hunting and intellectual activities.

The Capua Gate has long been seen as Frederick's triumphal arch, an interpretation enhanced by the multiple artistic references to the Arch of Constantine. Apparently this function was made explicit by other sculpture since, according to Sannelli's account, directly above the arch (its interior or vault?) were victories and trophies sculpted in white marble.[38] Since the Renaissance drawings only depict façade details, this description is difficult to corroborate. Nevertheless, a little-known Roman relief fragment, also in the Museo Campano in Capua (fig. 21), depicts the spoils of military victory. The heap of trophies includes weapons, standards, shields, ship prows, and other paraphernalia and symbols, plus a victory torch—the standard format for such displays. This distinctive genre of sculpture is reminiscent of Frederick's victory parades at which he revived the Roman imperial triumphal displays of military spoils. Following his 1236 victory against the Lombards at Cortenuova, for instance, he paraded his booty, trophies, and prisoners through Cremona and subsequently Rome.[39] A comparable triumphal display in sculpture would be consistent with Roman traditions as exemplified by the Arch of Titus in Rome, the Tiberian arch at Orange in Provence (also a city gate), and the arch of Augustus at Rimini.[40] The abrupt breaks along its outer edges indicate that this relief was part of a larger composition. Its original format is unknown, but two rect-

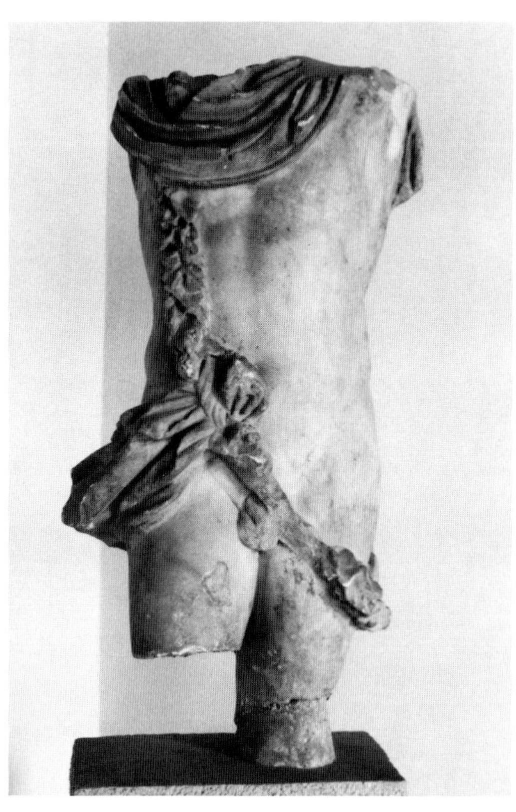

20. Torso fragment of Apollo or Dionysos, second century A.D.
Museo Provinciale Campano, Capua; photograph: David Castriota

21. Trophy relief fragment, second century A.D.
Museo Provinciale Campano, Capua; photograph: David Castriota

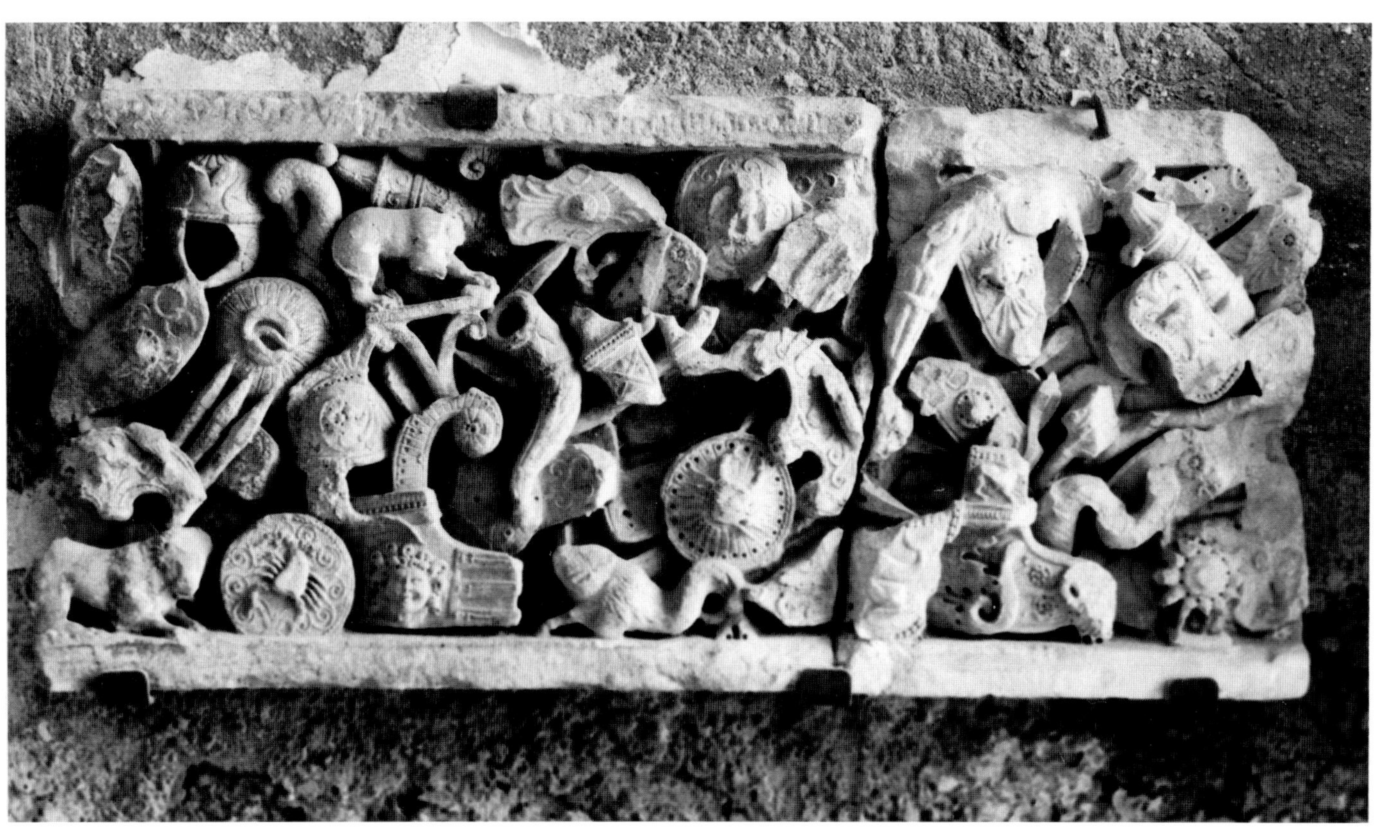

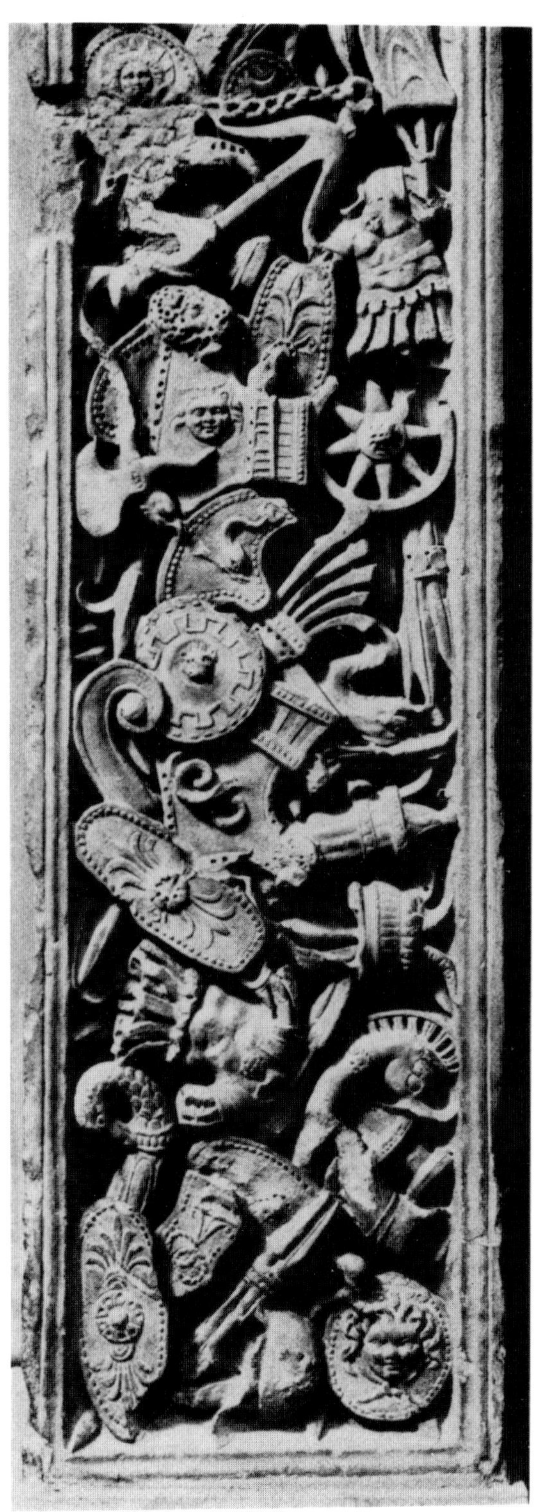

22. Trophy relief, second century A.D.
Uffizi, Florence; after Crous 1933

angular piers, now in the Uffizi (fig. 22), are carved with similar motifs on four sides, and these offer a close formal and stylistic parallel although they are approximately half the size.[41] Other comparative works would include relief friezes from honorific arches, such as a less crowded Augustan example in Turin.

Might the Capua trophy relief be a surviving fragment of what Sannelli described as displayed on Frederick's arch? According to another local historian, Granata, when the Capuan arch was dismantled in 1557 its sculptural decoration was pulled off and piled up near the base of the new bastions and "many marble statues and numerous sculptured reliefs" were carried off.[42] Although there has been considerable discussion about the "marble sculptures," the identity and present whereabouts of the "sculptured reliefs" have been neglected. Apparently there were two long trophy reliefs, according to a photograph of an early twentieth-century installation of the Capuan arch sculpture at the Museo Campano.[43] It shows two relief fragments set within the pilasters of a Renaissance trabeated architectural arrangement that includes the inscribed tablet commemorating the later restoration and reinstallation of the sculpture within one of the tower bastions by the Senate of Capua in 1583. This sculpture—the female bust, the male judge busts, the emperor statue, and the two trophy reliefs—would seem to correspond to Granata's description. Although the two longer trophy reliefs illustrated in the photograph cannot be located at present, the smaller piece discussed above evidently belongs to the pair that it closely resembles typologically and stylistically.

The extant Capua trophy relief (as well as its missing companions) has no earlier provenance. Like the Uffizi trophy piers that were brought to Florence from Rome, the Capua trophy relief might have come to Capua from elsewhere, much as marble spoils from Ravenna were taken to Palermo by Frederick. However, if this trophy relief was looted from Capua Vetere, then it probably did not decorate the amphitheater, whose decoration consists mostly of mythological subjects. The more appropriate context for trophy reliefs would be an honorific arch such as the Arch of Hadrian at Capua Vetere, near the amphitheater. This arch (fig. 23), astride the Via Appia, today remains in sadly mutilated condition, having been stripped of most of its original marble revetment and statues in niches. How it appeared in the thirteenth century is unknown, but perhaps it provided Frederick and his builders with design features for the Capua Gate, such as the prominent niches, and even actual spoils.

The Capua Gate marked the beginning of Frederick's domain, the kingdom of Sicily, along the Via Appia from Rome. In a sense, then, the gate mediated between Rome and the papal territories to the north, and Frederick's kingdom. Its appearance also alluded to Rome and Capua simultaneously. The gate's design and sculptural decoration appropriated and emulated the antique. Significantly, these visual references recall both the ancient capital of the empire and Roman Capua, in its heyday second only to Rome in size and monuments. For Capuans like Frederick's adviser Piero della Vigna, the overall splendor and antique elements of the Capua Gate would have reinstituted the past glory of Roman Capua in the appropriate manner: a combination triumphal arch, city gate, and bridgehead monument that celebrated the policies and triumphs of the restorer-emperor. The reuse of Capuan antiquities such as the travertine of the amphitheater and various statues and reliefs, as well as the imitation of other Capuan antiquities, notably the amphitheater divinity busts, underscored this *renovatio* of Capua in the local artistic idiom. The inclusion of Diana, who had an important temple nearby (reused in the Middle Ages as the site of Sant'Angelo in Formis), and a thirteenth-century classicizing city goddess, "Capua," had obvious local appeal. The Capua Gate in a sense became another Capuan "antiquity," a counterpart to the amphitheater and a pendant to the Hadrianic arch farther along the Via Appia. It reflected the former prestige of Capua in antiquity and, by extension, Rome itself.

While the complex programmatic use of antique elements was a distinctive feature of Frederick's Capua Gate, it was not without precedent in the city. The despoliation of Capua Vetere, particularly the amphitheater, for building materials and decorative sculpture such as the divinity busts had been a tradition in medieval Capua since its foundation under Longobard rule in the mid-ninth century.[44] Ecclesiastical foundations like Sant'Angelo in Formis and the cathedral also contain Roman architectural remains; and civic constructions, such as the eleventh-century Palazzo dei Principi Normanni and private towers, prominently displayed Roman spoils as well. Nor are the political overtones of such *spolia* unique to Frederick's Capua Gate. The descriptions of local chroniclers imply that these earlier medieval displays of Capuan antiquities were also politically motivated and were intended to underscore the continuity of new Capua with old Roman Capua. If, then, Frederick's Capua Gate program functions within this medieval Capuan tradition, then the monument possessed considerable resonance.

The Capua Gate's Roman-derived function and design, as well as its programmatic display of antique *spolia* and contemporary imitations, can also be seen as the culmination of a tradition in medieval Italy. As Michael Greenhalgh has enumerated at length, the principal cities of Pisa, Verona, Genoa, Brescia, and Lucca, to name a few, incorporated Roman material remains into their civic and ecclesiastical structures to attest to the town's ancient origins.[45] Even monumental remains like triumphal arches were saved and symbolically transformed in this way. The Arch of Augustus at Fano became a city gate in the medieval walls as well as an emblem of civic pride when depicted on the thirteenth-century city seal.[46] And even nearer to Capua, farther along the Via Appia at Benevento, the Arch of Trajan also served as a medieval city gate.[47] The revival of architectural sculpture occurs early and richly throughout the Italian peninsula in the eleventh century. This so-called Romanesque phase of monumental sculpture was aptly termed since it was inspired by antique survivals. Perhaps one of the best known early examples of the use of Roman *spolia* alongside "modern" imitations is the sculpture associated with Wiligelmo and his workshop at Modena cathedral circa 1100.[48] The use of *spolia* in Rome itself occurs at this time for similar reasons of prestige and political purpose, closely connected with the rise of the commune and papal power in the twelfth century. As Richard Krautheimer has noted, in twelfth-century Rome a number of

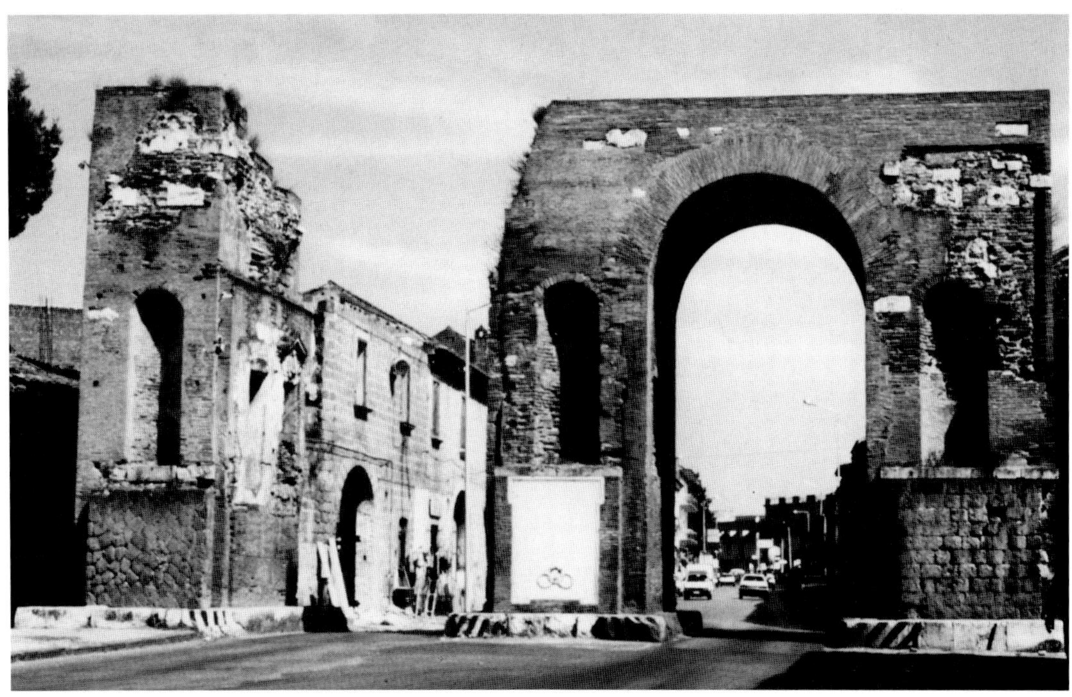

23. Capua, Arch of Hadrian, c. A.D. 117–138
Photograph: David Castriota

churches were built or refurbished using Roman imperial architectural spoils together with twelfth-century imitations, including San Clemente, Santi Quattro Coronati, and San Giovanni a Porta Latina.[49] More recently Dale Kinney has commented on the programmatic use of *spolia* from the Baths of Caracalla in the nave of Santa Maria in Trastevere.[50] The fascinating medieval eyewitness accounts in the form of tourist or pilgrim guides attest to the availability of antique monuments and convey a concern for historical context and interpretation.[51] Krautheimer has discussed, in particular, the implications of Rome's abundant antiquities and the architectural revival for the mid-twelfth-century Roman Republic and the expression of this new-found civic pride in domestic architecture and fortifications.[52] As it faced the medieval viewer arriving from Rome, the Capua Gate symbolically addressed medieval Rome itself. It declared Frederick's *imperium* and policies in a visual language highly meaningful to the nationalistic Romans of the day. In this regard the antique *spolia* and replicas were crucial components of the arch, as were the numerous references to monuments associated with the great ancient Roman emperors. Generically the Capua Gate most closely recalls the Augustan arch at Rimini. This is especially significant since Frederick emulated Augustus, the emperor of peace, in other artworks and activities. The formal analogies and borrowings from Roman Capua serve to associate him also with Emperor Hadrian who restored the Capuan amphitheater and built an arch across the Via Appia. And, by its many references to that well-known and prestigious marvel of medieval Rome, the Arch of Constantine, the Capua Gate neatly linked Frederick with Constantine, the first Christian Roman emperor.

Frederick and his colleagues extrapolated and condensed significant details of the Constantinian arch to emphasize the military, judicial, ceremonial, and even hunting activities of ancient Roman emperors. Moreover, there can be little doubt that Frederick knew this arch intimately. He was, after all, a collector of antiquities himself, both the small-scale and the monumental.[53] In fact, as Kantorowicz has noted, he owned the Arch of Constantine.[54] It was one of several Roman landmarks (including the Arch of Titus and the Mausoleum of Augustus) that Frederick began to purchase from the Roman patrician families in 1236. He then gave them back as fiefs, literally, in order to secure for himself the Rome of the Caesars and its powerful nobles as vassals. These families, in turn, were invited into the imperial bureaucracy so that his empire would be ruled from Rome by descendants of the ancient senatorial class. The intent of the Capua Gate's allusions to the Arch of Constantine seems to have been to address his supporters among the Roman aristocracy. The gate demonstrated his fulfillment of promise to the Romans. Although other features of Frederick's sculptural program directly addressed his Sicilian nobles and the papacy, much of its form and iconography, its antiquarian elements, and the use of actual *spolia* were meant specifically to impress and arouse contemporary Romans in a way that would flatter them as well as their emperor.

Clearly Frederick intended the Capua Gate as a triumphal arch in the manner of the ancient Roman Caesars to celebrate his military, diplomatic, and political accomplishments. The use of ancient Roman *spolia* together with classicizing medieval versions contributed to an effective presentation. The Capua Gate thus became, among other things, an essential facet of Frederick's policy of reviving the ancient state life of Rome through art, public display and ceremony, court literature, and coinage.

NOTES

1. For the glowing description by the court panegyrist Andrew of Hungary, writing in the service of Manfred's adversary, Charles of Anjou, in 1265, see Andrei Ungari, *Descriptio Victoriae per Carolum Regem Siciliae contra Manfred in Siciliae Regem*, Monumenta Germaniae Historica, *Scriptores*, 26 (Leipzig, 1925), 571. See also Cresswell Shearer, *The Renaissance of Architecture in Southern Italy: A Study of Frederick II of Hohenstaufen and the Capua Triumphator Archway and Towers* (Cambridge, 1935), 16–17 and notes for the Latin text and English translation of Andrew's comments.

2. In addition to Shearer 1935, see especially Carl A. Willemsen, *Kaiser Friedrichs II. Triumphtor zu Capua* (Wiesbaden, 1953). Recent articles include Michele Cordaro, "La porta di Capua," *Annali dell'Istituto di Storia dell'Arte, 1974–1976* (Rome, 1977), 41–63; Carl A. Willemsen, "Die Bauten Kaiser Friedrichs II. in Süditalien," in *Die Zeit der Staufer: Geschichte—Kunst—Kultur* [exh. cat., Württembergisches Landesmuseum], 5 vols. (Stuttgart, 1977–1979), 3:143–164; Gustina Scaglia, "La 'Porta delle Torri' di Federico II a Capua in un disegno di Francesco di Giorgio," *Napoli Nobilissima* 20 (1981), 203–222 and 21 (1982), 123–134; Jill Meredith, "The Revival of the Augustan Age in the Court Art of Emperor Frederick II," in *Artistic Strategy and the Rhetoric of Power: Political Uses of Art from Antiquity to the Present*, ed. David Castriota (Carbondale, Ill., 1986), 39–56; Peter Cornelius Claussen, "Die Statue Friedrichs II. vom Brückentor in Capua (1234–1239)," in *Festschrift für Hartmut Biermann*, ed. Christoph Andreas, Maraike Bückling, and Roland Dorn (Weinheim, 1990), 19–39.

3. Shearer 1935, 24–29.

4. See Willemsen 1953, 7–10 and Shearer 1935, 11–16, for discussions of the foundation and construction of the Capua Arch according to the primary sources. One of the emperor's secretaries, Richard, provides a contemporary account: *Ryccardi de Sancto Germano, Chronica Priora*, ed. Augusto Gaudenzi (Naples, c. 1888), 145–146. His entry for February 1234 includes the statement, "Imperator de Apulia venit in terram Laboris, et tunc ab ista parta Capue fieri super pontem castellum iubet, quod ipse manu propria consignavit," which has been interpreted as referring to Frederick's personal involvement with the architectural design.

5. Hans Wentzel, "Antiken-Imitationen des 12. und 13. Jahrhunderts in Italien," *Zeitschrift für Kunstwissenschaft* 9 (1955), 29–72, esp. 29–31 and 69–70; Cesare Gnudi, "Considerazioni su gotico francese, l'arte imperiale e la formazione di Nicola Pisano," in *Federico II e l'arte del Duecento italiana*, ed. Angiola M. Romanini, 2 vols. (Galatina, 1980), 1–17; Charles Seymour, Jr., "Invention and Revival in Nicola Pisano's 'Heroic Style,'" in *Acts of the Twentieth International Congress of the History of Art, Studies in Western Art* (Princeton, 1963), 1:207–226, esp. 213; Eloise M. Angiola, "Nicola Pisano, Federigo Visconti,

and the Classical Style in Pisa," *Art Bulletin* 59.1 (1977), 1–27, esp. 21.

6. Angiola M. Romanini, *Arnolfo di Cambio e lo "stil novo" del gotico italiano* (Florence, 1980), 159, pl. 162; Martin Weinberger, "Arnolfo und die Ehrenstatue Karls von Anjou," in *Studien zur Geschichte der Europäischen Plastik* (Munich, 1965), 63–72.

7. George L. Hersey, *The Aragonese Arch at Naples, 1443–1475* (New Haven and London, 1973), 17, 23, 31.

8. This coin type and its ancient Roman prototypes are discussed in Heinrich Kowalski, *Die Augustalen Kaiser Friedrichs II. von Hohenstaufen* (Geneva, 1976). Regarding the Barletta portrait bust, see Hermann Fillitz in *Die Zeit der Staufer*, 1:669–670, fig. 627, and Adriano Prandi, "Un documento d'arte Federiciana—Divi Friderici Caesaris Imago," *Rivista dell'Istituto Nazionale d'Archeologia e Storia dell'Arte* 2 (1953), 263–302.

9. Ernst Kantorowicz, *Kaiser Friedrich der Zweite* (Berlin, 1928), English trans., Emily O. Lorimer, *Frederick the Second, 1194–1250* (London, 1931), 530–534; Willemsen 1953, 43; Meredith 1986, 40–48, 55.

10. See Ian A. Richmond, *The City Wall of Imperial Rome* (Oxford, 1930), 257–262, for a discussion of the fifth-century restoration of the wall under Honorius, and also 109–144 for the Porta Ostiensis (East) and the Porta Appia, which were faced in white travertine and white marble respectively. See Michael Greenhalgh, *The Survival of Roman Antiquities in the Middle Ages* (London, 1989), 49–51, regarding Roman city walls and the prestige of its marble city gates in the Middle Ages.

11. Shearer 1935, 49–51. See Greenhalgh 1989, 54, on Frederick's castle at Naples, which was built from materials taken from Roman aqueducts, temples, and theaters.

12. William MacDonald, *The Architecture of the Roman Empire* (New Haven and London, 1986), 2:92–93; Ian A. Richmond, "Commemorative Arches and City Gates in the Augustan Age," *Journal of Roman Studies* 23 (1933), 149–174; Sandro de Maria, "La porta augustea di Rimini," in *Studi sull'arco onorario romano*, ed. Guido A. Mansuelli (Rome, 1979), 73–91.

13. Shearer 1935, 117, fig. 57; Willemsen 1953, 31–32, who see this as a precedent for the pedimented portal designs of Frederick's Castel del Monte and Prato castle.

14. On the prototypes of the Rimini arch's design and sculptural decoration, see Richmond 1933, 161–162, for a discussion of the Republican period city gates of Perugia: the Porta di Augusto and the Porta Marzio. The latter incorporates arch spandrel busts and divinity statues in a loggia into its arch design. A peripatetic emperor, Frederick undoubtedly knew these two famous city gates firsthand as well.

15. The drawings are reproduced and discussed in Willemsen 1953, 26–32, figs. 98, 99. See also Scaglia 1981 and 1982; Shearer 1935, 22–23; and Pietro Toesca, "L'architettura della porta Capua," in *Mélanges Bertaux: Recueil de travaux dédié à la mémoire d'Émile Bertaux* (Paris, 1924), 292–299.

16. See Shearer 1935, 11–31, for the literary documentation and relevant passages reproduced in Latin, many of which have been summarized here. The reliability of these descriptions has been debated, especially concerning the reuse of ancient Roman sculpture, even as recently as David Abulafia, *Frederick II: A Medieval Emperor* (London, 1988), 284. Nevertheless, these local historians seem aware of the distinction between the Roman spoils and Frederick's sculpture, either due to personal familiarity with the abundant Roman ruins around them or as a reflection of local tradition. I reject the assumption that either in the Middle Ages or the Renaissance the Capuan arch sculptures would have appeared historically (or stylistically) indistinguishable from one another. Rather, given the availability of Roman statuary and decorative sculpture at Capua Vetere, and the frequency of its reuse all over modern Capua since its foundation in the ninth century, local historians might well have expected purloined Roman sculpture to have appeared!

17. Joannis Antonii Campani, *De Rebus Gestis Andreae Brachii Perusini*, in Ludovicus Muratori, ed., Rerum Italicarum Scriptores, 19 (Milan, 1731), 597, and also reproduced in Shearer 1935, 19–20: "Qua iter erat supra caput altissima prominet testudine, marmoreis statuis vetustisque imaginibus distinctum, atque ornatum."

18. Scipione Sannelli, *Annali della Città di Capua*, manuscript, Museo Campano, Capua, as transcribed and translated by Shearer 1935, 20–22.

19. Gennaro Pesce, *I rilievi dell'anfiteatro campano, Studi e materiali del Museo dell'Impero Romano* (Rome, 1941), 11–16.

20. Willemsen 1953, 49–55.

21. Pesce 1941, 12–13.

22. Meredith 1986, 51–53.

23. Donald Strong, *Roman Art*, 2d ed. (Harmondsworth, 1988), fig. 199.

24. Hans Peter L'Orange and Armin von Gerkan, *Der spätantike Bildschmuck des Konstantinbogens* (Berlin, 1939), 82–83; Lawrence Richardson, Jr., "The Tribunals of the Praetors of Rome," *Mitteilungen des Deutschen Archäologischen Instituts, Römische Abteilung* (hereafter *Römische Mitteilungen*) 80 (1973), 219–233, esp. 219.

25. This description is based on the sixteenth-century account of Scipione Sannelli's *Annali della Città di Capua* as cited in Shearer 1935, 22.

26. Pesce 1941, 11–12.

27. Claussen 1990, note 17; Meredith 1986, 50–51; Shearer 1935, 22, 74; Willemsen 1953, 48; Kantorowicz 1931, 532.

28. Shearer 1935, 19–20, citing Campano's description of this register.

29. The antique features nevertheless relate also to classicizing trends in Mosan metalwork and thirteenth-century Gothic sculpture at Reims, Chartres, and Strasbourg. See Claussen 1990, 22–29, for an excellent recent discussion of the enthroned emperor

torso, based on the surviving fragments and the Séroux d'Agincourt drawings, which considers the stylistic problems with regard to Gothic sculpture.

30. Cassius Dio Cocceianus, *Dio's Roman History*, trans. Earnest Cary (Cambridge, 1960), 6:251 (LIII.22).

31. Greenhalgh 1989, 210, citing *Spicilegium Ravennatis Historiae*, in Rerum Italicarum Scriptores, 1.2:575.

32. L'Orange and von Gerkan 1939, pls. 5b, 16, 17; Kantorowicz 1931, 109.

33. Scaglia 1981, 208. See also Alfonso de Franciscis, "Templum Dianae Tifatinae," *Archivio storico di Terra del Lavoro* 1 (1956), 301–358, regarding her cult shrine and its reuse in the Middle Ages as Sant'Angelo in Formis.

34. Carl A. Willemsen, *De arte venandi cum avibus* (Leipzig, 1942) and Willemsen, "Die Bauten Kaiser Friedrichs II.," in *Die Zeit der Staufer*, 3:145. Frederick's artistic patronage has also been linked to a cameo of 1220–1240 from southern Italy which depicts a Gothic-style mistress of the hunt accompanied by a dog and a falcon; see *Die Zeit der Staufer*, 1:696, 2:fig.663.

35. L'Orange and von Gerkan 1939, 168.

36. Vienna, Österreichische Nationalbibliothek, MS. 3528, fol. 51v; Toesca 1924, 295–296; Shearer 1935, 123. An allegorical description of this portion of the Capua Arch in Tale 54 of the *Gesta Romanorum* identifies the figure of Frederick as Christ, flanked by his mother the Virgin and Saint John the Evangelist. For further discussion of this text and the pairing of Diana and Apollo in Roman art and literature, see Meredith 1986, 49–50.

37. See Pesce 1941, 13, pl. VIIa, for the amphitheater bust of Apollo which is now immured in the ground-story façade of the Palazzo dei Giudici, now the Palazzo Municipio.

38. Shearer 1935, 22.

39. Kantorowicz 1931, 437; Ferdinand Gregorovius, *History of the City of Rome in the Middle Ages* (London, 1906), 5:185–186.

40. For an illustration of the arch at Orange, see John Bryan Ward-Perkins, *Roman Imperial Architecture*, 2d ed. (Harmondsworth, 1981), fig. 147.

41. Jan Willem Crous, "Florentiner Waffenpfeiler und Armilustrium," *Römische Mitteilungen* 48 (1933), 1–119, pls. 1–18; Phyllis P. Bober and Ruth Rubenstein, *Renaissance Artists and Antique Sculpture* (London, 1986), 206, no. 175, figs. 175i, 175ii.

42. F. Granata, *Storia civile di Capua* (Naples, 1756), 2:34, as cited by Shearer 1935, 24–26.

43. Willemsen 1953, pl. 30.

44. Greenhalgh 1989, 24, 29, 242; P. Delogu, "Proposte per lo studio delle città campane nell'alto medioevo," *Bolletino di storia dell'arte del Centro studi per i nuclei antichi e documenti artistici della Campania meridionale*, Università degli studi di Salerno (hereafter *Bolletino*), 2 (1979), 53–59; N. Cilento, "Origine e struttura della città in Campania," *Bolletino* 2 (1979), 15.

45. Greenhalgh 1989, 45, 55, 74–76.

46. Greenhalgh 1989, 116.

47. Greenhalgh 1989, 117; Mario Rotili, "L'eredità del antico a Benevento dal VI all'VIII secolo," *Napoli Nobilissima* 14 (1975), 121–128.

48. Fernando Rebecchi, "Il reimpiego di materiale antico nel Duomo di Modena," *Lanfranco e Wiligelmo: Il Duomo di Modena* (Modena, 1984), 319–353.

49. Richard Krautheimer, *Rome: Profile of a City, 312–1308* (Princeton, 1980), 161–176; see also 182–187 regarding the twelfth-century mosaic campaigns *all'antica* in these churches.

50. Dale Kinney, "*Spolia* from the Baths of Caracalla in Sta. Maria in Trastevere," *Art Bulletin* 68 (1986), 379–397.

51. Krautheimer 1980, 187–197; James B. Ross, "A Study of the Twelfth-Century Interest in the Antiquities of Rome," in *Medieval and Historical Essays in Honour of James Westfall Thompson*, ed. James Lea Cate and Eugene N. Anderson (Chicago, 1938), 302–321; Herbert Bloch, "The New Fascination with Ancient Rome," in *Renaissance and Renewal in the Twelfth Century*, ed. Robert L. Benson and Giles Constable (Cambridge, Mass., 1982), 615–636. For recent annotated translations of the twelfth-century travel accounts, see John Osborne, ed., *Master Gregorius: The Marvels of Rome* (Toronto, 1987) and F. Morgan Nicols, ed., *The Marvels of Rome: Mirabilia Urbis Romae*, 2d ed. (New York, 1986). For a discussion of the medieval attitude toward the pagan past, based on contemporary texts, illuminated manuscripts, and sculpture, see Michael Camille, *The Gothic Idol: Ideology and Image-Making in the Middle Ages* (Cambridge, 1989), 73–128.

52. Krautheimer 1980, 197–199.

53. See Greenhalgh 1989, 240, regarding the antique bronze rams that Frederick installed outside of Castel Maniace at Siracusa.

54. Kantorowicz 1931, 452. As he and others have pointed out, these Roman triumphal arches had become private fortifications of the Roman aristocracy during the Middle Ages. Therefore the Arch of Constantine was, indeed, a significant prototype for Frederick's Capuan arch, that is, a *fortified* triumphal arch, during the thirteenth century.

coprehendant. Sit agilis et
promptus in suis motibus ut cito
succurrat avi sue quotiens expe
dierit. Sit audax in tantum q
n timeat ptransire loca aspera
qn convenerit. Sciat natare ut si
avis sua transvolaverit aquam
invadibilem ipam aquā natādo
transeat. et avem sequatur. et ipsi
ubi oportuerit succurrere succur
rat. Non sit minoris nimium
iuvenilis. ne puericia inducat
ipm aliquid facere qd avem. Illi
pueri consueverunt esse gulosi. et
delectantur videre plimu amenos
volatus et plures. nec tamē pu
eros ex toto repellimus cū possint
esse prudentiores. non eni pueri
sufficiunt mansuefacere aut alit
docere aves. aut cū eis venari
cū non constet eos esse prudentes
in his. s. discant a doctis q usq

cogatur p gulositatem sua redire
domu citius. Aut etiam si in do
mo fuerit non obliviscatur avis sue
habendo intentione ad gulosi
tatem suā. Non sit ebriosus
qm ebrietas quam insania est
p quam avem suā facillime de
vastabit. Quamvis etiam credat
eam bene tractare. et ab ebrio et
fatuo custodienda est avis. Non
sit iracundus. neque facilis ad iram
accendit eū p sepe. q avis fiat ea
p que ille qui custodit eā ad ira
cundiam provocatur. et nisi illā ira
cundiam dimittat malo motu
moveri poterit qd avem ex q
malo illato avi p iram avis ipa
cū sit res debilis citissime deva
statur. Non sit piger aut ne
gligens. quoniam ars ista multoru
laboru est et magni studii. Nō
sit girovagus ne p suos mot

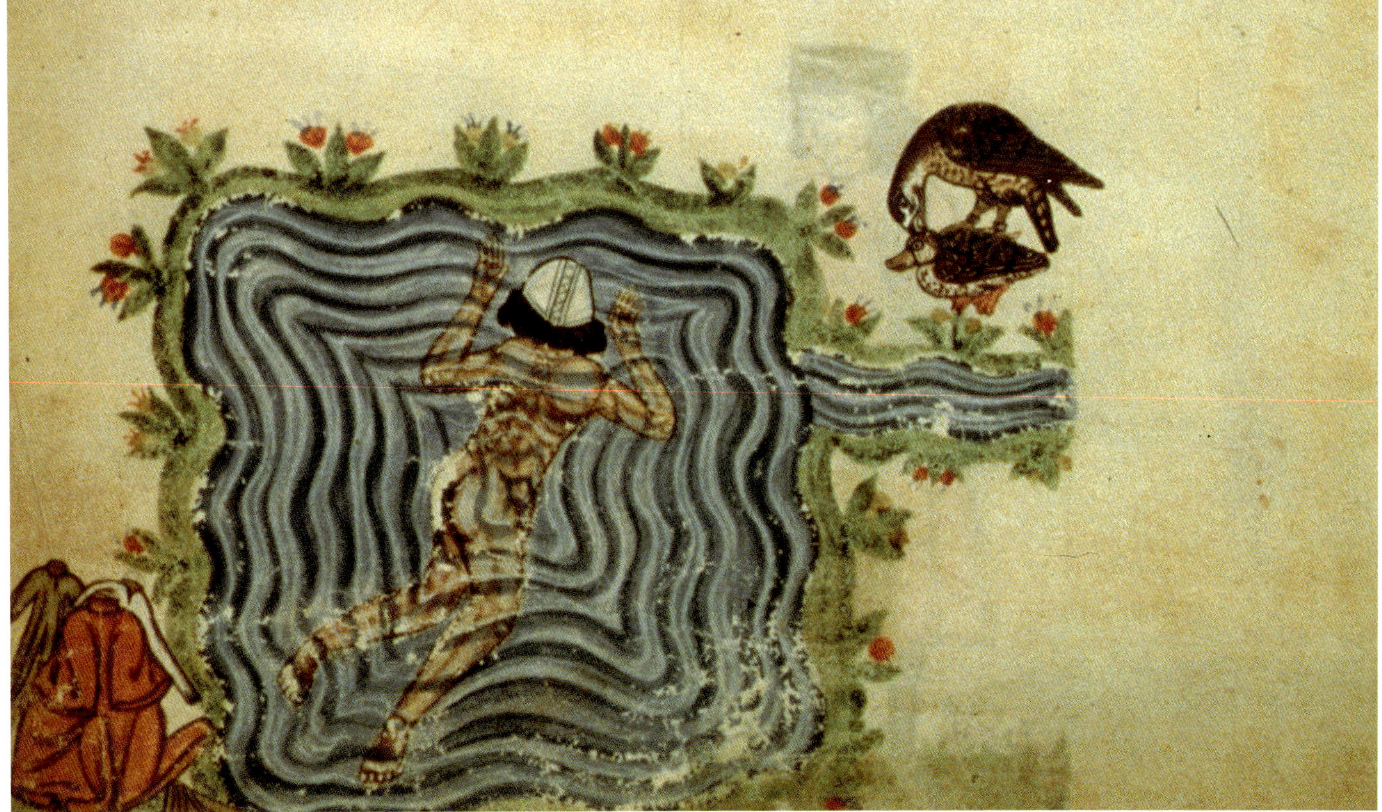

GIULIA OROFINO
Università degli Studi di Cassino

Il rapporto con l'antico e l'osservazione della natura nell'illustrazione scientifica di età sveva in Italia meridionale

Fin dalla nostra giovinezza, prima di assumere l'onere del regnare, abbiamo sempre cercato i sapori della scienza, e amato la bellezza, respirando instancabilmente il profumo dei suoi unguenti. Dopo aver assunto il peso del regno, benché l'incessante quantità di negozi ci distragga continuamente . . . , quel poco tempo che riusciamo a strappare alle nostre occupazioni abituali, non sopportiamo di trascorrerlo nell'ozio; preferiamo invece dedicarlo all'esercizio della lettura, affinché si rafforzi la disposizione dell'animo nell'acquisire il sapere, senza il quale la vita dei mortali non è condotta in modo degno di uomini liberi.[1]

La lettera che accompagna le opere aristoteliche inviate da Federico agli studenti e ai professori bolognesi, tramanda un vivo autoritratto intellettuale dell'imperatore, la cui ansia di sapere e il cui desiderio di bellezza si oggettivano nel diletto, anche tattile, per i libri: "voltiamo le pagine dei volumi . . . che arricchiscono i nostri armadi, in cui conserviamo le cose più preziose." Ma Federico non è solo un appassionato bibliofilo, non si limita a raccogliere i codici "scritti in varie lingue e con caratteri diversi." Promuove egli stesso una importante editoria scientifica di lusso, della quale sopravvivono numerose testimonianze, quasi tutte molto note. Proprio per questo se ne può tentare oggi uno studio comparato, che ricostruisca le direttrici del progetto culturale di cui sono espressione.

Valutata nel suo complesso infatti, questa produzione si rivela una straordinaria cartina al tornasole dell'atteggiamento federiciano nei confronti dell'arte e della scienza, oltre che uno specchio fedele dei suoi poliedrici interessi.

All'autore del più importante trattato di storia naturale del Medioevo, il *De arte venandi cum avibus*, è legato il celebre esemplare Vaticanus Palatinus latinus (Vat. Pal. lat.) 1071, approntato da Manfredi ricalcando l'originale, saccheggiato nella tenda dell'imperatore il 18 febbraio 1248, dopo la rotta di Vittoria.[2]

Nell'ambiente della Magna Curia, dove si studiano le virtù delle erbe e dove maestro Teodoro, medico e speziale oltre che filosofo, è rinomato per i suoi sciroppi e per un costosissimo zucchero di violette, capace di guarire Pier delle Vigne,[3] vanno inquadrati i due erbari gemelli della Österreichische Nationalbibliothek di Vienna, MS. 93, e della Biblioteca Medicea Laurenziana di Firenze, Pluteus (Plut.) 73.16.[4]

Al "metges Frederic," immortalato dal poeta provenzale Aimeric de Pegulhan come medico salernitano generoso e sapiente, mandato da Dio agli uomini perché li sollevi dalle infermità,[5] non deve stato essere estraneo il *De Chirurgia Liber* di Rolando da Parma, tramandato dal MS. 1382 della Biblioteca Casanatense di Roma.[6] Il manoscritto, finora genericamente attribuito, seguendo un'indicazione di Pietro Toesca,[7] all'Italia meridionale e alla fine del Duecento, può a buon diritto inserirsi in quel filone della miniatura sveva segnato da una forte impronta bizantina e islamica, che ha il suo primo rappresentante nel *Liber ad Honorem Augusti* della Bürgerbibliothek di Berna, MS. 120—eseguito probabilmente a Palermo tra il 1195 e il 1196[8]—e che, partendo dalla Sicilia, raggiunse verso la metà del Duecento la Campania costiera.

Del resto, è proprio con Federico II che la chirurgia entra ufficialmente a far parte del *cursus studiorum* della Scuola Medica Salernitana. La *civitas hippocratica* è al centro dell'illuminata riforma sanitaria emanata dall'imperatore per proteggere i suoi sudditi dal dispendio e dall'irrecuperabile danno derivati "ex imperitia medicorum"; le severe norme legislative obbligano l'aspirante medico a studiare per un anno chirurgia e anatomia, "sine qua nec incisiones salubriter fieri potuerunt, nec factae curari."[9]

All'ambiente campano rimanda anche la copia manfrediana del *De Balneis Puteolanis*, conservata alla Biblioteca Angelica di Roma, MS. 1474.[10] Federico, al quale Pietro da Eboli dedica il suo poema sulle virtù idroterapiche delle terme flegree, aveva avuto modo di sperimentare personalmente la qualità dei bagni tra l'ottobre e il novembre del 1227, in seguito a una malattia che lo aveva colto a Brindisi, mentre si accingeva a salpare per la Crociata in Terra Santa.[11] Probabilmente fu proprio la singolare attività fumarolica e idrominerale di quella terra "infuocata" a dare lo spunto per la formulazione dei celebri quesiti cosmologici che Federico indirizzò a Michele Scoto nello stesso anno e che questi poi personalmente redasse.[12]

Il formidabile stimolo intellettuale che veniva dal "vir inquisitor et sapientiae amator," capace di riempire il mondo di interrogativi e di meraviglia, agì da catalizzatore non solo per le sottili esegesi degli scienziati, ma anche per la fantasia dei miniatori.

Ancora all'imperatore curioso delle stelle che, "auditu mirabile," come racconta l'astioso Saba Malaspina, "dum subtili indagatione naturalia vestigabat, astrologos et nigromaticos adeo venerabatur,"[13] si possono ricondurre altri due manoscritti splendidamente illustrati: l'esemplare palatino del *Liber Astrologiae* di Georgius Zothorus

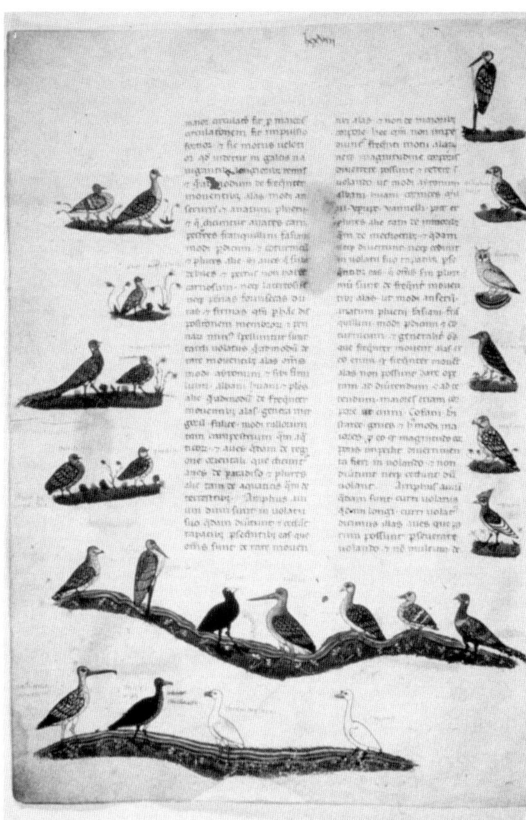

1. Federico II, *De arte venandi cum avibus*, prima metà del Duecento, fol. 39v
Biblioteca Apostolica Vaticana (MS. Palatinus latinus 1071)

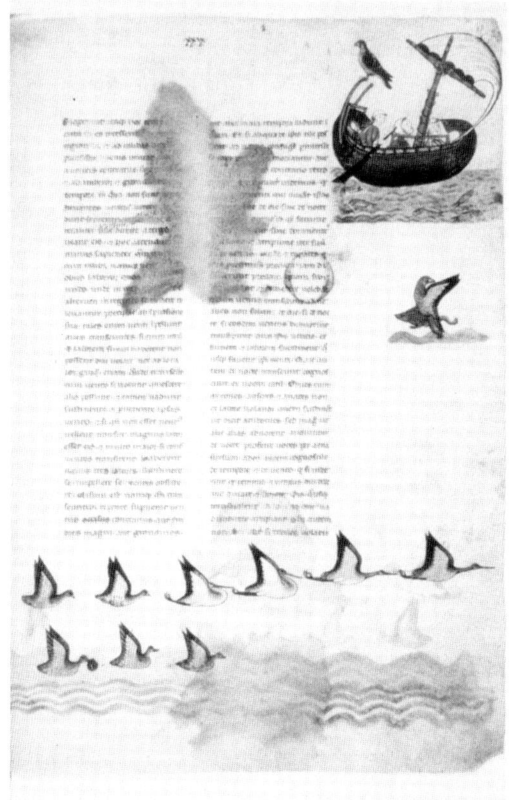

2. Federico II, *De arte venandi cum avibus*, prima metà del Duecento, fol. 15r
Biblioteca Apostolica Vaticana (MS. Pal. lat. 1071)

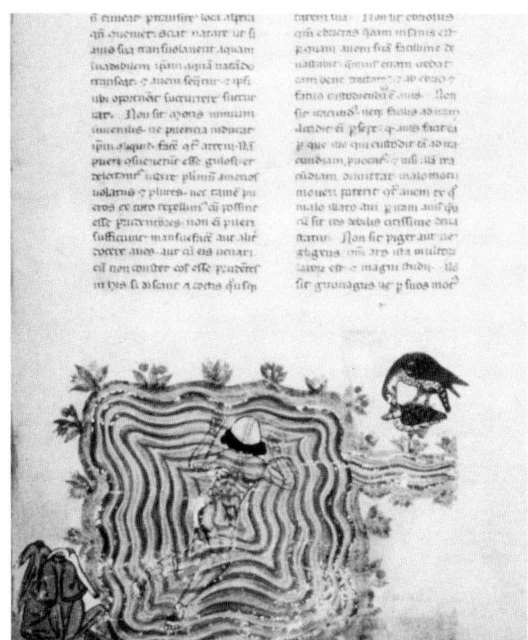

3. Federico II, *De arte venandi cum avibus*, prima metà del Duecento, fol. 69r
Biblioteca Apostolica Vaticana (MS. Pal. lat. 1071)

Zaparus Fendulus, Parigi, Bibliothèque Nationale (Paris. lat.) 7330—eseguito nel secondo quarto del Duecento, forse nello stesso *atelier* del vindobonense 93[14]—e il *Liber Introductorius*, nella copia padovana di Monaco, Bayerische Staatsbibliothek Clm 10268,[15] la più antica che sia sopravvissuta—databile a metà Trecento—grazie alla quale è possibile ricostruire il corredo iconografico dell'originale consegnato a Federico da Michele Scoto nel 1228.

Che anche l'*exemplar* fosse illustrato, lo dimostrano le dettagliate indicazioni contenute nel testo: evidentemente consapevole della loro importanza, Scoto fa espliciti riferimenti alle immagini. All'inizio della seconda "distinctio" aggiunge per esempio, accanto alle caratteristiche di ciascuna costellazione, "sic in pictura figuratur."[16] Tutti i manoscritti citati, attribuibili direttamente o per provata discendenza all'Italia meridionale sveva e a una raffinata committenza di corte, sono accompagnati da centinaia di miniature.

Possediamo una preziosa testimonianza di come lo stesso Federico concepisse un libro illustrato. Nel 1264–1265 il milanese Guglielmo Bottatius decide di offrire a Carlo d'Angiò un manoscritto così splendido che per rendere la sua meravigliosa bellezza "non vi sarebbero parole sufficienti," come egli ammette nella lettera di accompagnamento. Conscio dell'eccezionale valore del dono, Guglielmo si cimenta comunque, per nostra fortuna, in una breve e compiaciuta descrizione: adorna di fregi d'oro e d'argento e impreziosita dal ritratto dell'imperiale maestà, l'opera insegna tutto quanto c'è da sapere sui falchi, gli astori, i girifalchi e i cani "et quomodo versari venator se debeat ad perfectionem artis venatorie demonstratur."[17] Quasi sicuramente grazie al generoso milanese la biblioteca angioina si arricchiva dell'esemplare personale del *De arte venandi* posseduto da Federico II e depredato a Vittoria proprio mentre, ironia della sorte, l'imperatore era a caccia nell'acquitrinosa valle del Taro.

Questa *édition de luxe* in due volumi, che segue Federico persino in circostanze così tragiche e tumultuose, presentava nei margini immagini di cani e di uccelli "ingeniosissime depicti," con l'indicazione delle loro malattie, dei modi di curarle e delle varie fasi dell'addestramento. È molto probabile che l'apparato illustrativo del codice, di cui il Vat. Pal. lat. 1071 restituisce un'eco fedele, sia stato dettato o almeno supervisionato dallo stesso Federico. Le miniature "universa sicut per litteram denotantur," seguono con piena aderenza i passi corrispondenti del trattato. Di questo condividono dunque il carattere spregiudicatamente empirico, basato sull'indagine di prima mano, nell'intento dichiarato di "manifestare ea quae sunt sicut sunt."

Sono raffigurazioni scientifiche, esemplificative, concepite "ad decus et utilitatem operis." Il limite didascalico, evidente soprattutto nelle tavole "classificatorie" delle varie specie ornitologiche (fig. 1), non annulla però il valore di arricchimento e integrazione del testo: quel "decus" lascia evidentemente ampio spazio all'autonomia immaginativa dell'artista se questi, almeno nell'esemplare manfrediano, si permette di trasformare le tinte sobrie e mimetiche delle vesti prescritte dall'autore ai falconieri, nei più sgargianti abiti della moda del tempo, o se coglie prontamente ogni occasione narrativa, dalla piccola gita in barca in attesa dei migratori (fig. 2),[18] al cacciatore che, lanciato all'inseguimento della preda, non esita a tuffarsi nelle verdi acque di un piccolo lago e a concedersi il gusto di una vigorosa nuotata (fig. 3).[19] I miniatori svevi affiancano sempre alla più rigorosa esigenza didattica quella di divertire, nel senso etimologico del termine, il lettore. Accogliendo e sviluppando gli spunti digressivi del testo, coniugano lo scopo pratico al piacere dell'occhio e alla divagazione fantastica.

Approfittano dei riferimenti mitologici di cui è ricco l'erbario dello Pseudo Apuleio per dar vita ad epici duelli, di classico pathos (fig. 4),[20] mentre l'improbabile farmaco a base di urina di fanciullo consigliato da Sesto Placito (fig. 5)[21] offre l'occasione per una gustosa scena di genere, con la vergine che si ritrae come una scandalizzata Annunciata.

Assecondano il senso del meraviglioso che pervade il poema di Pietro Ebolitano e visualizzano le leggende che avevano identificato, nell'immaginario popolare, il "Sudatorium" di San Germano con l'ingresso del Purgatorio (fig. 6)[22] e il "Balneum Tripergula," nei pressi del Lago Averno, con il luogo dove Cristo infranse le porte dell'Inferno (fig. 7).[23]

Persino l'astrusa, ermetica iconografia dei decani, nel Paris. lat. 7330,[24] viene sottoposta a un vigoroso processo di traduzione al contemporaneo. Nemmeno gli arcani simboli dell'iconografia greca, egizia, mesopotamica, sfuggono alla volontà affabulatoria dell'artista federiciano. Dalle *membra disiecta* delle costellazioni, inquietanti panoplie di gambe, teste, mani, piedi, gocciola il sangue. Le remote "figure" delle tre sfere diventano il pretesto per mettere in scena uno dei più ricchi commenti illustrati che il mondo medievale ci abbia trasmesso, pari forse solo al *De Universo* di Rabano Mauro, Casinensis 132, miniato a Montecassino sotto l'abate Teobaldo (1022–1035).[25] Nel "thesaurus" svevo sfilano cavalieri e contadini, pastori e fabbri, negri ed etiopi, donne vanitose intente a pettinarsi, donne ambiziose che pretendono indumenti per i loro figli, donne pie consumate dal desiderio di pregare, e poi cani, elefanti, cammelli, cervi, cinghiali, e i "monstra"—cinocefali, minotauri, l'uomo nero e l'uomo pantera—e tutto un inventario di oggetti, dagli strumenti musicali agli aratri, dai carri ai fusi, dalle navi ai letti, dai *vasa lignea* ai *vasa pecuniae*, dagli specchi alle armi.

Registrando insieme i linguaggi del mito e

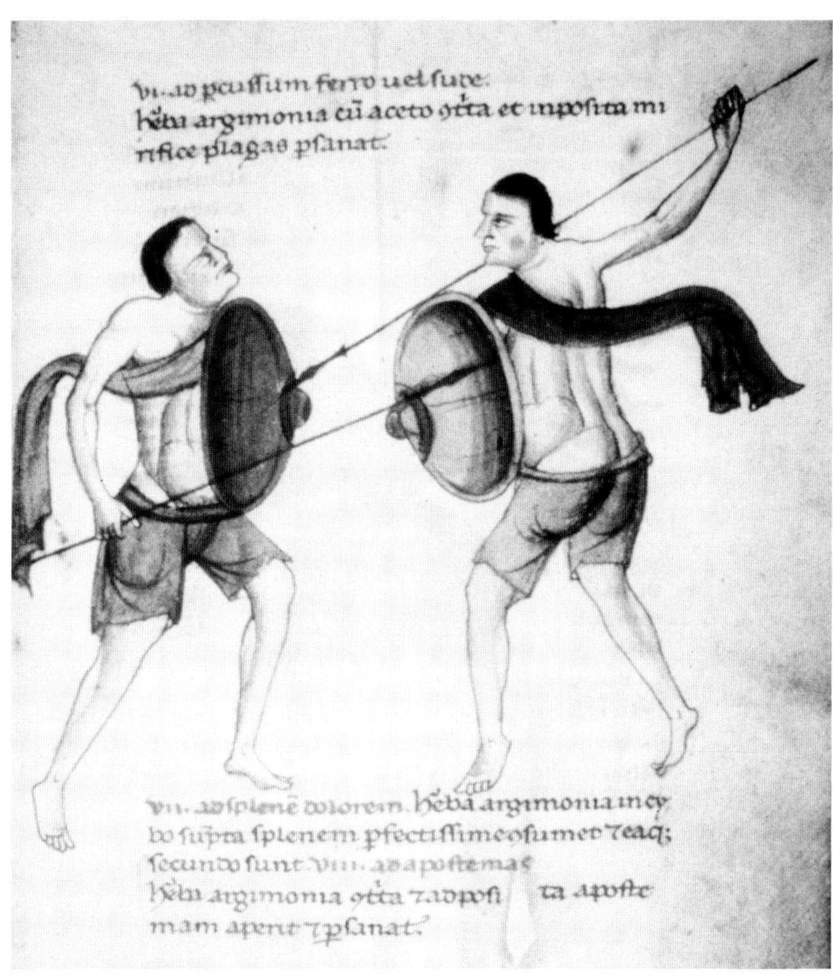

4. *Varia Medica*, prima metà del Duecento, fol. 65r
Biblioteca Medicea Laurenziana, Firenze (MS. Pluteus 73.16)

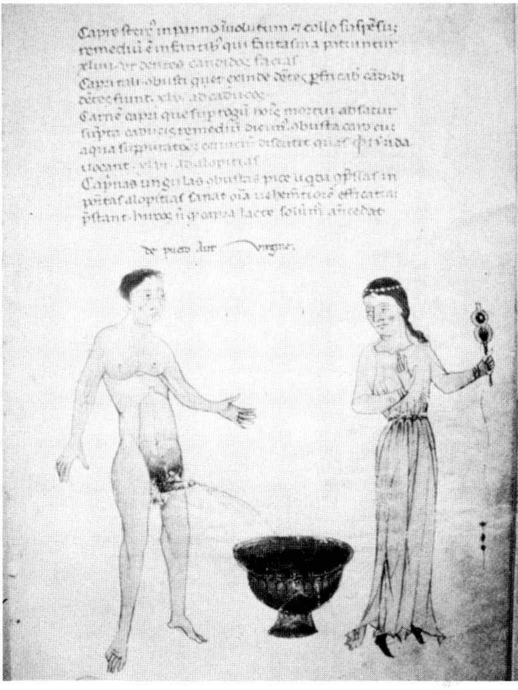

5. *Varia Medica*, prima metà del Duecento, fol. 169r
Biblioteca Medicea Laurenziana, Firenze (MS. Plut. 73.16)

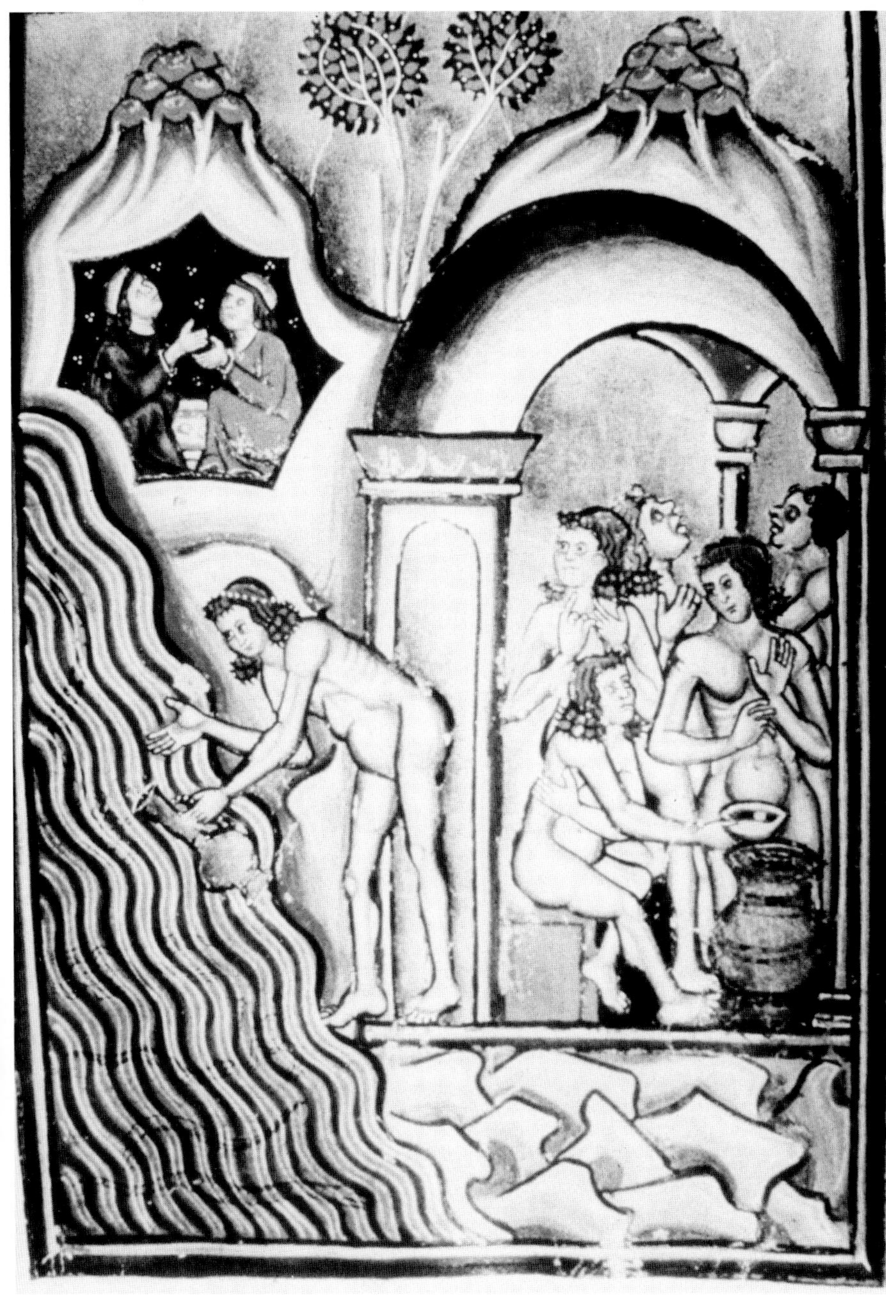

6. Pietro da Eboli, *De Balneis Puteolanis*, prima metà del Duecento, fol. 2r
Biblioteca Angelica, Roma (MS. 1474)

della scienza, della leggenda e dell'esperienza quotidiana, gli apparati illustrativi fanno dei volumi scientifici svevi non dei libri tecnici, ma piuttosto delle sontuose edizioni di intrattenimento e di divulgazione, nello spirito del mecenatismo federiciano, che piega agli svaghi della corona gli slanci della scienza, e che potrebbe avere come motto quel "leviter" imposto dall'imperatore a Michele Scoto nella composizione del suo trattato di astronomia.[26]

Ma soprattutto queste illustrazioni, anche per la loro attenzione all'"accidente"—sia lo spogliatoio, con la "natura morta" dei panni appesi, dove un bagnante viene colto mentre si sfila la veste (fig. 7),[27] sia un agguato di ladroni nel bosco (fig. 8);[28] siano i serpenti e le rane di cui è "plenus" il Lago Averno presso cui sorge il "Balneum Sudatorium" (fig. 6) o le differenze morfologiche che distinguono i volatili nel *De arte venandi*—testimoniano il ruolo pilota assegnato alla miniatura in quel globale progetto di indagine sulla natura e sulla varietà del mondo che costituisce il momento culminante della civiltà sveva.

I miniatori sono sollecitati a soddisfare le esigenze emergenti di un pubblico laico in trasformazione, interessato al sapere del mondo antico, ma straordinariamente aperto alle culture "diverse"—quelle orientali in primo luogo—e capace di imporre nuove formule di conoscenza, e quindi di rappresentazione, della realtà. Alla base dei programmi illustrativi sta infatti la volontà di recuperare la tradizione classica, aggiornandola ai metodi di naturalismo sperimentale cari a Federico. La maniera gotica, moderna, non contrasta con i dati più anticheggianti: nei due casi si tratta di rinnovare un linguaggio figurativo ormai esaurito, per piegarlo a una diversa funzione, a una diversa "curiosità" del mondo e del vero. Solo in questa prospettiva si spiega come l'autorità di vetusti cicli miniati continui ad esercitare una profonda influenza negli spregiudicati *ateliers* legati alla corte staufica.

L'archetipo tardo antico è chiaramente riconoscibile nei due erbari: da esso derivano sicuramente gli indici premessi ai singoli trattati della silloge, incorniciati entro arcate affiancate da coppie di uccelli, simili alle Tavole Canoniche dei Vangeli (fig. 9);[29] uno schema con i *pondera medicinalia* (i pesi e le misure cui si fa riferimento nelle ricette),[30] e i quattro ritratti d'autore affrontati all'*incipit* delle rispettive opere, insieme alle loro città.[31] Il primo di questi ritratti (fig. 10), dove i tre maestri della medicina antica, "Plato [Sesto Placito Papiriense], Ypocras, Dioscurus," appaiono seduti con i volumi delle loro opere e sono accompagnati da due rizotomisti che discutono su un'erba, discende dai due ritratti collettivi di medici e erboristi, guidati da Chirone e da Galeno, premessi al celebre Dioscoride di Vienna eseguito a Costantinopoli nel 512 per la principessa Giuliana Anicia.[32]

I segni zodiacali del *Liber Astrologiae* di Fendulo, benché illustrino un testo che è la traduzione dall'arabo dell'opera di Albumasar, seguono sostanzialmente, con poche isolate eccezioni,[33] l'iconografia classica canonica, mediata probabilmente da un manoscritto di Arato attraverso un modello del XII secolo, che Saxl ipotizza italomeridionale, se non addirittura cassinese.[34]

Nelle due grandi miniature a piena pagina (figg. 11, 12) illustranti i vari tipi di cauteri e le loro applicazioni, che precedono il testo di Rolando nel MS. 1382 della Casanatense, i piani della rappresentazione sono distribuiti sulla superficie pergamenacea in senso verticale; le singole figure allineate in file sovrapposte sono riunite con una serie di arcate. Solo nella prima scena il medico è accanto al paziente. In tutte le altre appare solo la sua mano, come se il medico stesso fosse nascosto dietro le quinte delle colonne, che assumono dunque valore di indicazione spaziale oltre che decorativo. Il testo è ridotto a brevi didascalie. L'organizzazione della pagina riflette un sistema illustrativo tipico del momento di passaggio dal rotulo al codice, quando le immagini intercalate alle colonne di scrittura del papiro vengono estrapolate e trasferite nel nuovo *medium*, condensando composizioni originariamente più ricche e collegando le sintetiche unità narrative così ottenute grazie a cornici architettoniche.[35] L'isolamento e il raggruppamento delle miniature è un fenomeno che interessa soprattutto i manoscritti medici, per evidenti scopi pratici, e in particolare i disegni dimostrativi relativi alla cauterizzazione.

Nell'XI secolo sedici tavole del termocauterio furono legate in appendice a un manoscritto eseguito in ambito cassinese tra la fine del IX e l'inizio del X secolo, il laurenziano Plut. 73.41, foll. 122r–129v. Le tavole presentano il medico che opera malati distesi su materassi sospesi nel vuoto, mentre in primo piano arde il fornello su cui si arroventano i ferri.[36] Lo stesso ciclo di illustrazioni viene replicato in un prodotto campano dei primi decenni del Trecento, il MS. Rowlinson 328 della Bodleian Library di Oxford,[37] che mostra singolari analogie anche con la Rolandina, a conferma di modelli comuni, circolanti per secoli nello stesso ambiente. Il nucleo principale del MS. laurenziano Plut. 73.41 contiene l'erbario dello Pseudo Apuleio nella recensione *beta*, la stessa dei due esemplari svevi, ed è possibile stabilire significative concordanze iconografiche tra i tre codici.[38]

L'Italia del Sud vantava una lunga tradizione in fatto di trasmissione dei testi scientifici classici. I miniatori federiciani

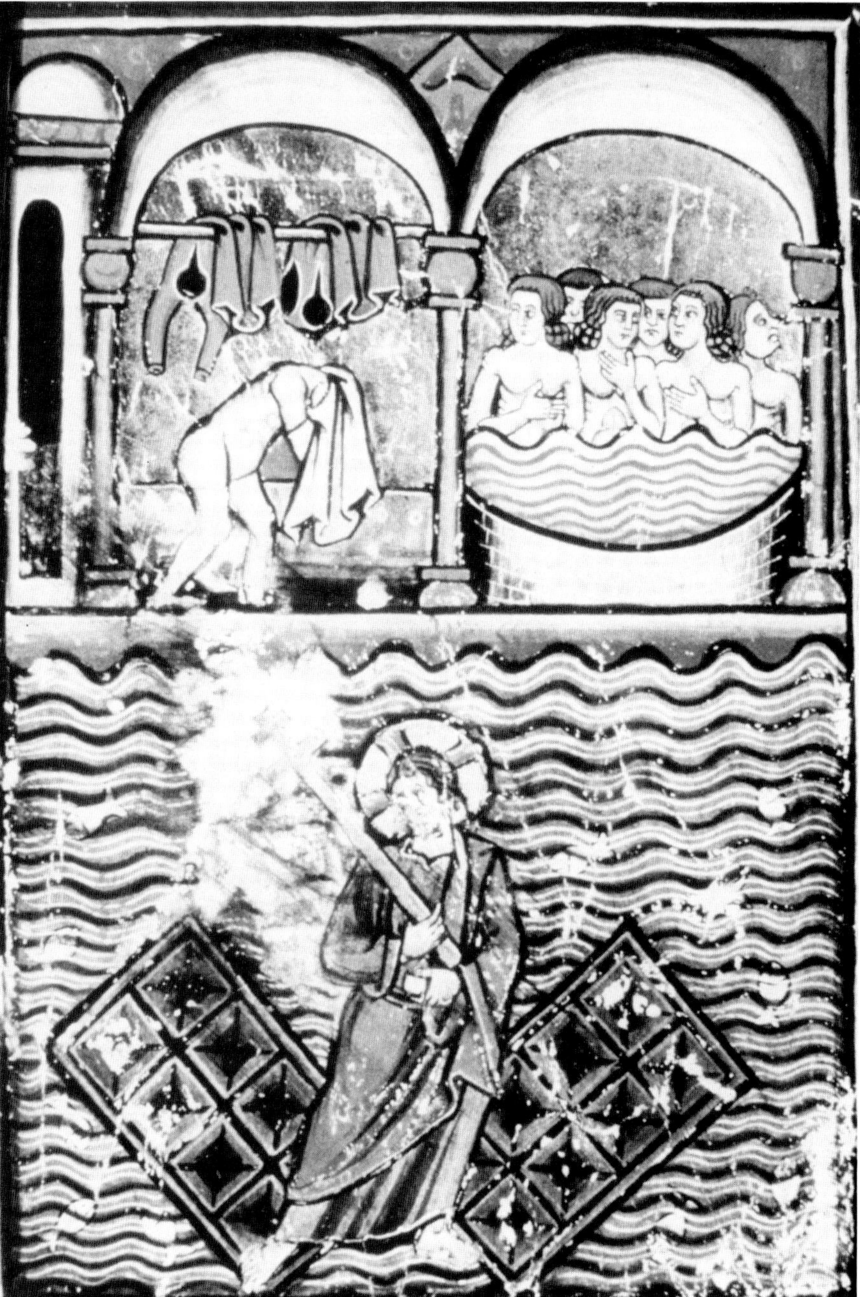

7. Pietro da Eboli, *De Balneis Puteolanis*, prima metà del Duecento, fol. 101r
Biblioteca Angelica, Roma (MS. 1474)

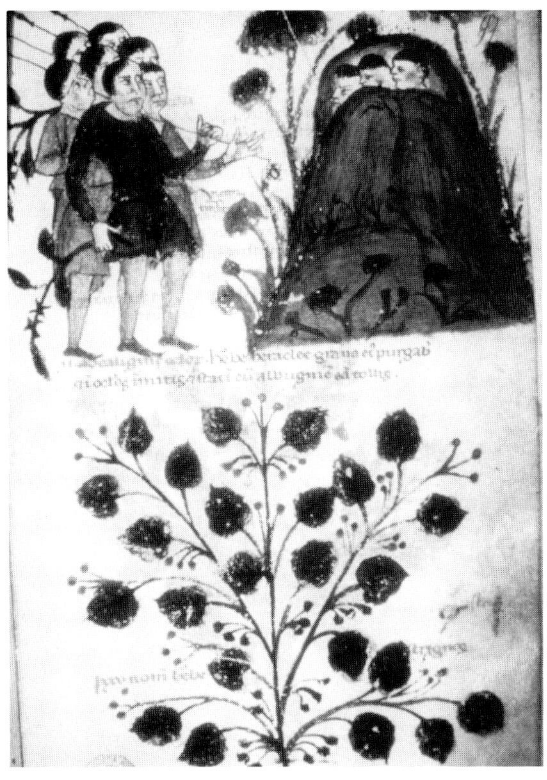

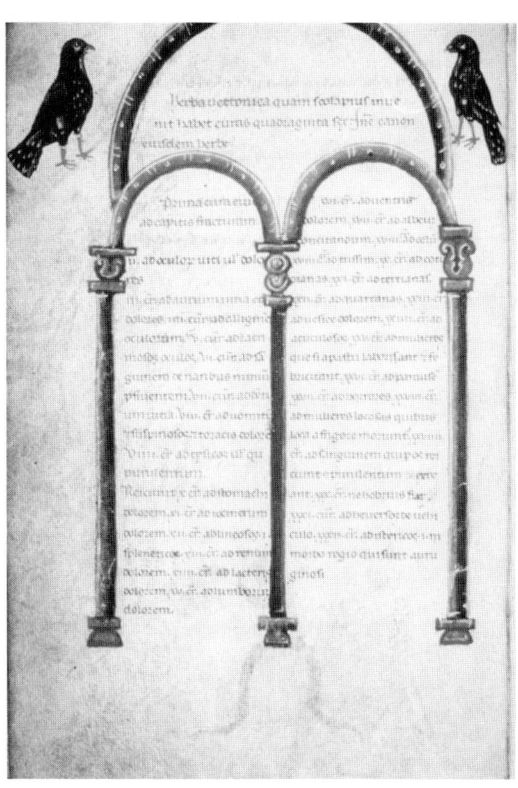

8. *Varia Medica*, prima metà del Duecento, fol. 99r
Biblioteca Medicea Laurenziana, Firenze (MS. Plut. 73.16)

9. *Varia Medica*, prima metà del Duecento, fol. 3v
Biblioteca Medicea Laurenziana, Firenze (MS. Plut. 73.16)

10. *Varia Medica*, prima metà del Duecento, fol. 2v
Biblioteca Medicea Laurenziana, Firenze (MS. Plut. 73.16)

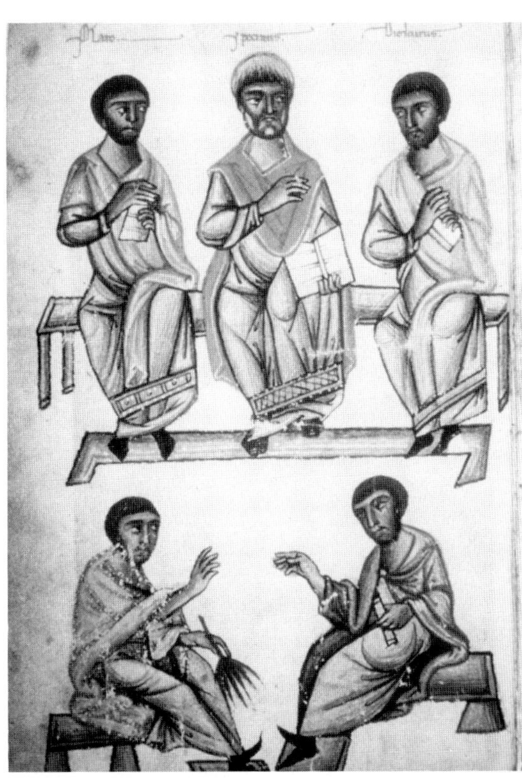

non dovettero incontrare molte difficoltà né cercare lontano nel reperimento dei loro modelli. La biblioteca dell'abbazia di Montecassino conservava per esempio, oltre alle tavole del termocauterio e a vari codici miniati di argomento botanico e zoologico,[39] anche edizioni illustrate di *Aratea*, come il Casinensis 3, eseguito nella seconda metà del IX secolo.[40] I quaranta disegni di costellazioni che accompagnano il *Libellus de signis coeli* migrarono nell'opera dello Pseudo Beda da un ciclo illustrato degli *Scholia Sangermanensia*, e derivano da un prototipo dell'VIII secolo, probabilmente transalpino.[41] Da un archetipo diverso, anch'esso verosimilmente dell'VIII secolo ma assegnabile all'Italia del Sud, discende il MS. 19 della Biblioteca Nacional di Madrid[42] che fu, come è ormai assodato, una delle fonti figurative utilizzate da Michele Scoto.[43] Il rapporto con il *background* locale, postulabile in via ipotetica per gli altri codici scientifici svevi italo-meridionali, diventa così un dato certo per il *Liber Introductorius*. Il manoscritto madrileno, datato al XII secolo, presenta ai foll. 57r–74v gli *Aratea* di Claudio Germanico, illustrati da quarantatre miniature incorniciate tra le righe del testo. Variamente assegnato all'Italia meridionale o alla Catalogna,[44] il codice è comunque legato a Montecassino: esso contiene un carme di Paolo Diacono per Adelperga e fu copiato, almeno in parte, da un esemplare in beneventana.[45] Poiché il carme di Paolo Diacono (del 763 circa) è presente anche nel manoscritto laurenziano Strozzi 46, che appartiene a un ramo separato dello stesso stemma,[46] è probabile che *Aratea* e carme fossero insieme già nell'archetipo, quasi sicuramente localizzabile a Montecassino *ante* 800.

Da questo stesso archetipo deriva—lo si ricostruisce da venticinque apografi quasi tutti del Quattrocento—il *Liber Siciliensis*, ossia il frammento dell'*Aratea* di Germanico scoperto da Poggio Bracciolini in Italia meridionale nel 1429:[47] non è escluso che il Siciliense sia stato esemplato appunto in Sicilia nel Duecento, e possa quindi essere in qualche modo collegato all'attività di Michele Scoto. Uno studio comparato delle illustrazioni dei discendenti del *Liber Siciliensis* potrebbe stabilire eventuali rimaneggiamenti di età federiciana.

È comunque indubbio che Scoto riesumò attivamente quanto si era conservato dell'archetipo dell'VIII secolo per il suo *Liber Introductorius*. La fonte immediata, sia per il testo che per le illustrazioni, fu il manoscritto madrileno, o un suo gemello, di cui il *Liber Introductorius* ripete anche le rarità iconografiche e i fraintendimenti:[48] le corna del Sagittario per esempio, raffigurato come centauro e non come satiro, nascono probabilmente dalla libera interpretazione delle due stelle che brillano sulla testa della costellazione.[49] L'immagine di Eridano (fig. 13)[50] combina il tipo astrologico del dio fluviale sdraiato, appoggiato a un vaso da cui sgorga l'acqua,[51] e l'identificazione mitologica dell'astro con Fetonte precipitato nel fiume da Giove, identificazione assente in Arato, ma accolta in Germanico[52] e nell'iconografia della classe del Siciliense, dove addirittura vengono rappresentate le due fasi dell'azione: Fetonte bruciato dalle fiamme del sole e Fetonte che precipita in acqua.[53] Anche Scoto fa esplicito riferimento nel suo testo al mito di Fetonte,[54] ma la traduzione visiva

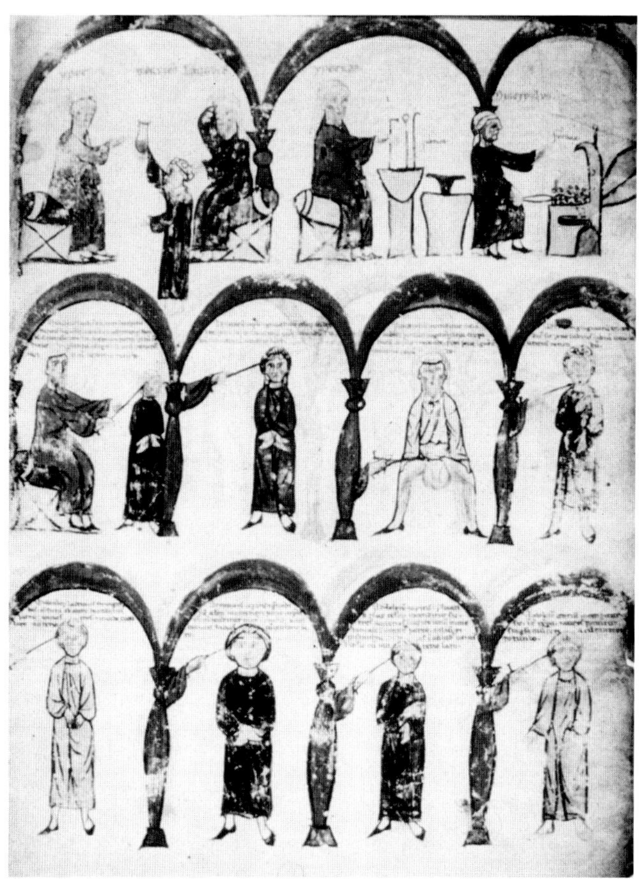

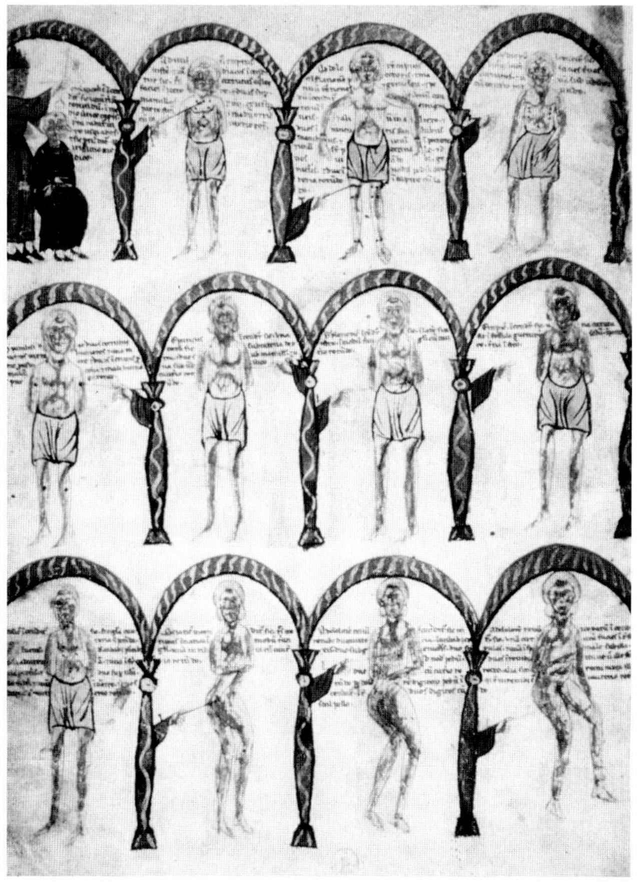

11. Rolando da Parma, *De Chirurgia Liber*, prima metà del Duecento, fol. 2v
Biblioteca Casanatense, Roma (MS. 1382)

12. Rolando da Parma, *De Chirurgia Liber*, prima metà del Duecento, fol. 1r
Biblioteca Casanatense, Roma (MS. 1382)

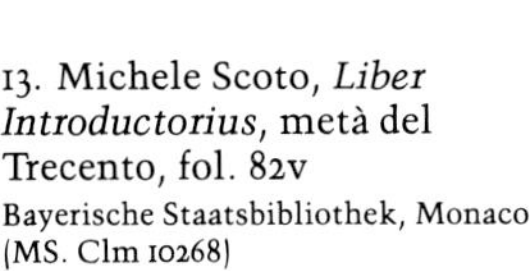

13. Michele Scoto, *Liber Introductorius*, metà del Trecento, fol. 82v
Bayerische Staatsbibliothek, Monaco (MS. Clm 10268)

14. Michele Scoto, *Liber Introductorius*, metà del Trecento, fol. 81r
Bayerische Staatsbibliothek, Monaco (MS. Clm 10268)

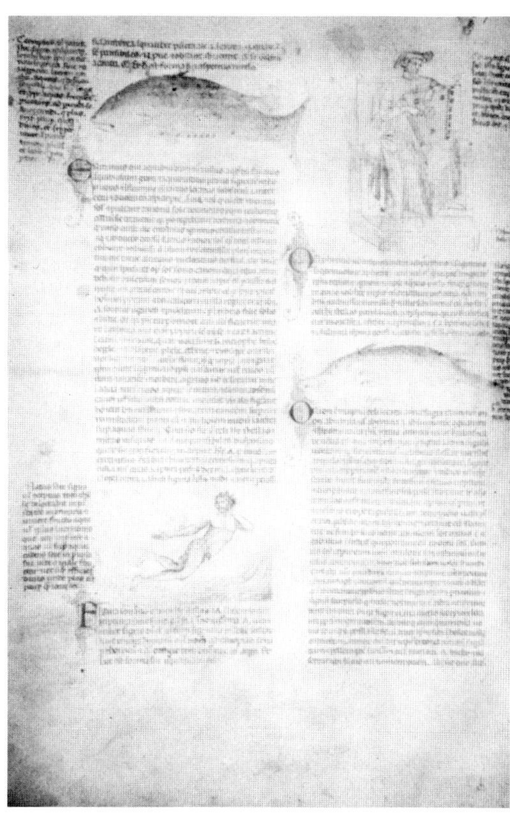

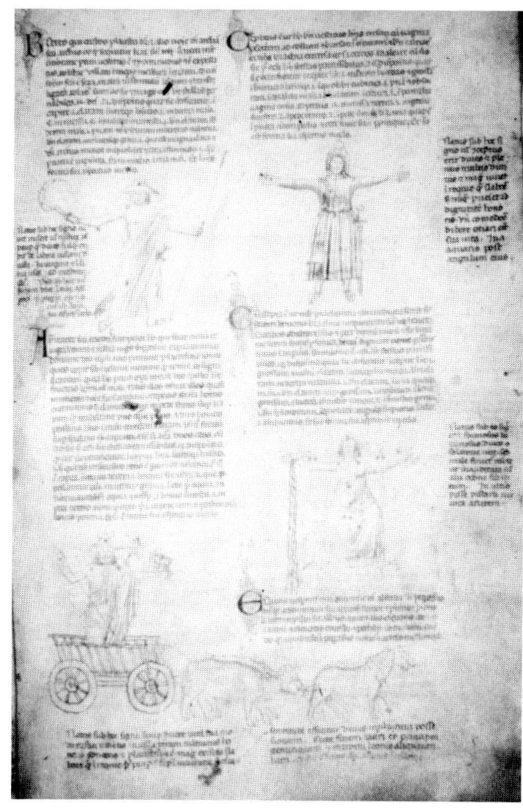

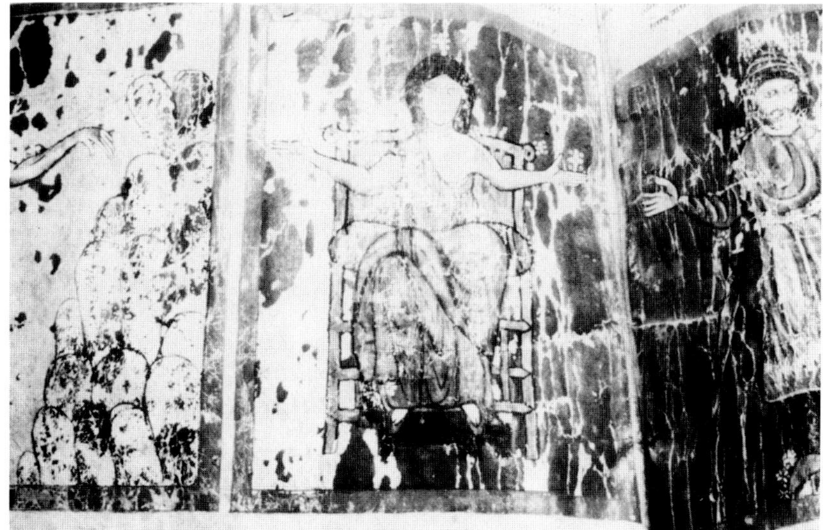

15. *Aratea*, XII secolo, fol. 60r
Biblioteca Nacional, Madrid (MS. 19)

mostra, come nel manoscritto madrileno, un ibrido, contorto nuotatore il quale ricorda, più che il figlio di Elios, un altro celebre nuotatore della miniatura federiciana, quello del Vat. Pal. lat. 1071, fol. 69r (fig. 3).

"Cassepia est ut mulier pulcherrima et bene inducta sedens super sedem honoris brachijs nudis extensis ut tenet sacerdos ad altare[m] habens et pectus dextrum nudum et sit in manu dextra fortiter perforata de cuius stigmate currit grandis rivus sanguinis."[55] Il brano di Scoto con la sua traduzione visiva—Monacensis Clm 10268, fol. 81r (fig. 14)—sembra una descrizione puntuale della miniatura del modello, Matritensis 19, fol. 60r (fig. 15): il seno destro nudo, le braccia drammaticamente stese, quasi che la bella regina si disperi per la sorte della figlia innocente, il trono, e soprattutto il flusso di sangue che zampilla dal polso destro di Cassiopea e che farebbe pensare a influssi islamici, già accolti nel manoscritto più antico, poiché per gli arabi la superba madre di Andromeda è appunto la donna dalla mano ferita.[56]

I testi dell'astronomia orientale circolavano nell'Italia del Sud fin dall'età normanna: la traduzione latina del *Liber de locis stellarum* di Al-Sûfi (903–986) fu eseguita a Palermo per volere di Guglielmo II (1166–1189)—"Willelmus rex Sicilie felicis memorie in civitate Palermi"[57]—che si avvaleva di un astrologo arabo, raffigurato al suo capezzale nel *Liber ad honorem Augusti* di Berna, fol. 97r. Il più antico esemplare della traduzione di Al-Sûfi, il MS. 1036 della Bibliothèque de l'Arsenal di Parigi, da sempre ritenuto italo-meridionale, è stato recentemente attribuito ad un *atelier* bolognese e al terzo quarto del Duecento.[58] Che si condivida o no l'ipotesi, basata su confronti stilistici non del tutto convincenti, è certo che l'Arsenal 1036 fu redatto sulla base di un prototipo siciliano.

La circolazione del *Liber de locis stellarum* nell'Italia del Sud è estremamente importante, perché insieme al testo l'opera trasmetteva anche l'iconografia araba delle costellazioni: il più antico testimone dell'originale di Al-Sûfi, l'oxoniense Marsh 144, degli inizi dell'XI secolo, è illustrato.[59] Le stravaganti figure arabe, se popolavano il cielo di personaggi da Mille e una notte, versione "turchesca" degli dei e degli eroi greci che avevano prestato i loro nomi ai corpi celesti, ristabilivano comunque l'attendibilità scientifica dell'*imagérie* astronomica: turbanti e scimitarre non inficiano la possibilità di localizzare esattamente i raggruppamenti di stelle.[60] Federico coltiva l'interesse per l'astronomia araba, anche come mediatrice di un'antichità non inquinata dalle degenerazioni dell'Alto Medioevo occidentale.

Tra le cose più care—addirittura quanto l'erede Corradino—che custodisce nel Tesoro di Venosa c'è il meraviglioso orologio donatogli dal sultano di Damasco Al-Ashraf nel 1232, dove le figure del Sole, della Luna e degli altri pianeti "riprodotti con la migliore abilità," azionati da un sistema di pesi e di ruote, segnano le ore, mentre i dodici segni dello Zodiaco, "con certe caratteristiche appropriate" si muovono nel firmamento.[61] L'arrivo di nuovi manoscritti e oggetti suntuari, preziosi veicoli di schemi figurativi, stimolò certo Michele Scoto—che dal canto suo a Toledo, tra il 1217 e il 1220, aveva lavorato alla traduzione dell'astronomo Al-Bitrugi[62] e che cita il *Liber Novem ludi-*

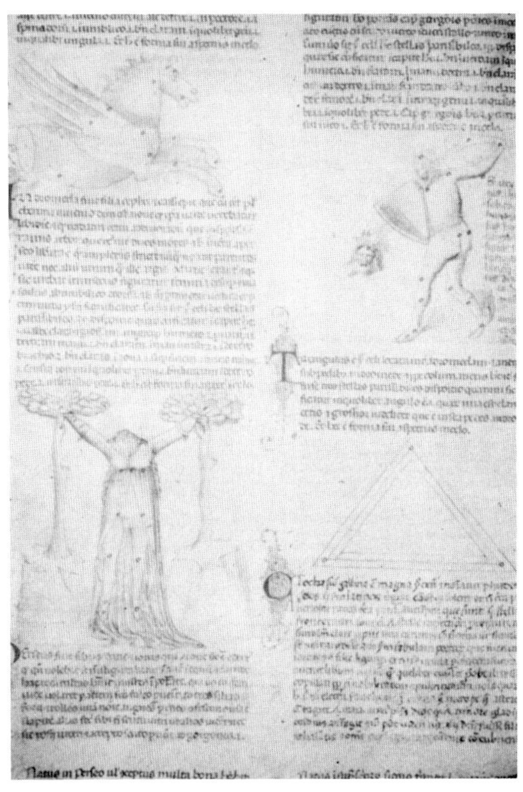

16. Michele Scoto, *Liber Introductorius*, metà del Trecento, fol. 81v
Bayerische Staatsbibliothek, Monaco (MS. Clm 10268)

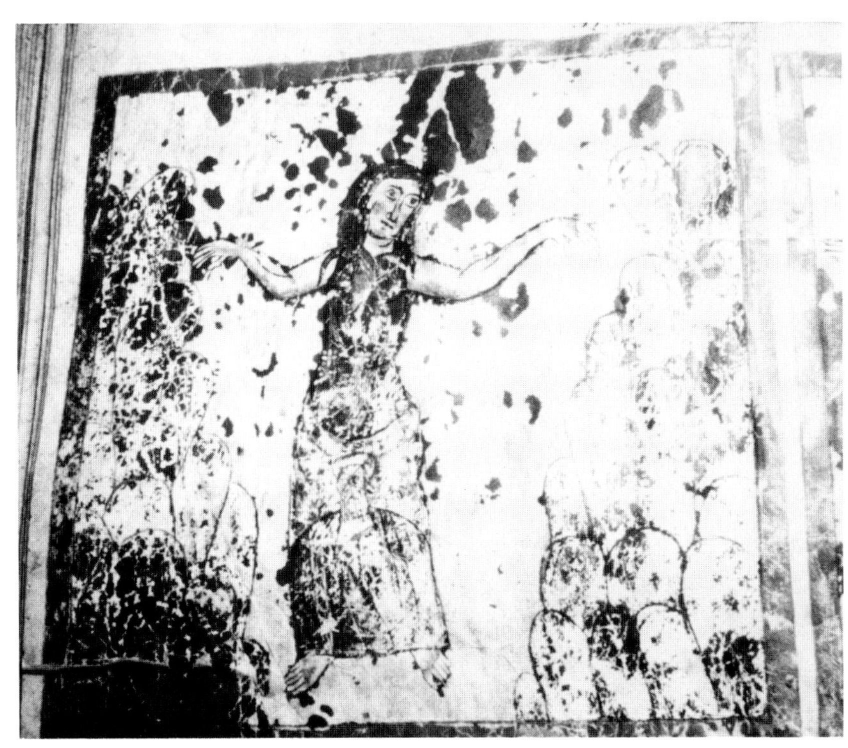

17. *Aratea*, XII secolo, fol. 60r
Biblioteca Nacional, Madrid (MS. 19)

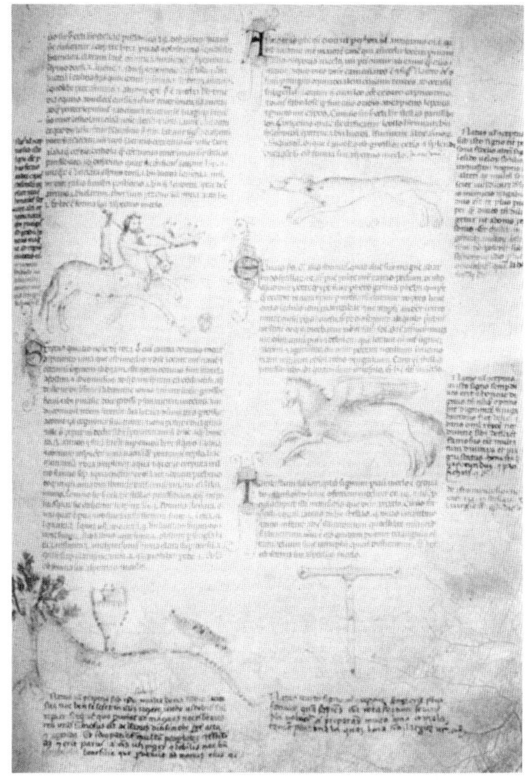

18. Michele Scoto, *Liber Introductorius*, metà del Trecento, fol. 84r
Bayerische Staatsbibliothek, Monaco (MS. Clm 10268)

cum, donato all'imperatore dal Sultano d'Egitto[63]—ad ampliare il riferimento alle fonti islamiche. Da queste prende in prestito intere costellazioni, come il "Tarabellum" (fig. 18) e il "Vexillum,"[64] che proiettano sulla volta celeste oggetti di vita quotidiana, sull'esempio di Albumasar,[65] e dettagli iconografici che rivelano la specifica conoscenza di cicli arabi illustrati: la testa barbuta della Medusa (fig. 16)[66] non è altro che il demone Algol, il quale a sua volta aveva mutuato la barba dal sangue grondante dalla gola recisa del mostro greco.[67] Il parallelo tra la Gorgone e Algol è sottolineato nello stesso *Liber Introductorius*: "Perseus trahens per capillos caput hominis truncatum cuius nomen erat Gurgenus; hoc enim est, quod a multis dicitur caput Algol."[68]

L'immagine di Perseo mostra però come Scoto non si sia accontentato di rinnovare l'ormai sclerotizzato sistema figurativo degli *Aratea* occidentali con l'innesto islamico,[69] ma l'abbia arricchito di nuovi elementi tratti dalla più pura tradizione classica: lo "scuto vitreo seu cristallo" brandito dall'eroe, non ha precedenti nelle illustrazioni astronomiche e rimanda direttamente ad Ovidio, *Metamorfosi* IV, 782–783: "Se tamen horrendae clipei, quod laeva gerebat, aere repercusso formam adspexisse Medusae." La singolare androginia di Andromeda legata tra i pali, "femina desuper et masculus ab umbilico deorsum" (fig. 16),[70] più che come un fraintendimento dei lembi del mantello annodati sul davanti nel manoscritto madrileno (fig. 17),[71] o della catena che pende tra le gambe della giovane vittima di Al-Kazwini,[72] sembra spiegarsi con la conoscenza delle *Thesmophoriazusae* di Aristofane, dove il ruolo di Andromeda è parodisticamente interpretato da un personaggio maschile, Mnesilochus, salvato da Perseo-Euripide.[73] Può essere interessante ricordare a questo proposito che un esemplare delle *Commedie* di Aristofane era conservato proprio nell'Italia meridionale sveva, nella ricca biblioteca del monastero greco di Casole, il cui abate Nicola d'Otranto-Nettario fu per più versi legato a Federico II.[74]

Scoto deve essersi servito anche del *Poeticon astronomicon* di Igino, che gli ha suggerito, per esempio, l'aggiunta dell'albero di fichi nella figura del Serpente con l'idra e il corvo (fig. 18),[75] un particolare molto raro negli *Aratea*—manca nel manoscritto di Madrid, fol. 66r—e giustificato appunto dalla favola iginiana del corvo di Apollo, al quale il troppo amore per i fichi costò la sete eterna.[76] L'astrologo di Federico ricorse anche ad altre fonti per integrare la sua opera: l' "uter vini aceti" che il Centauro regge con la destra (fig. 18) è tipico dell'iconografia degli *Scholia Sangermanensia* e non della recensione madrilena.[77] La strana testa antropomorfa del leone Nemeo, attributo di Eracle (fig. 19),[78] potrebbe invece giustificarsi con l'associazione Medusa/Algol già accolta per Perseo; Scoto spiega infatti: "Hercules . . . habens in manu dextram corium leonis involutum . . . cui nomen erat viroplus secundum quosdam et secundum ceteros Algol et est verius";[79] negli *Scholia Basileensia* si dice appunto che la pelle del leone eracleo "arreptam pro scuto usum . . . media pelle Gorgoneum capud habere."[80]

In alcuni casi Scoto non rinuncia ad intervenire personalmente: ispirato dalla leggenda che lega la costellazione del "Sacrarium"[81] (fig. 20) al mito dei Titani—secondo Igino e gli scoliasti di Arato è l'altare sul quale Zeus e i Ciclopi giurarono la loro vendetta su Crono[82]—e assecondando le sue vocazioni alchemiche, trasforma l'ara classica in un terribile "putheus," "locus secretus" dove si danno convegno i negromanti e dal quale escono "lampades et sagitte tonitruales opere spirituum inferiorum," con quattro demonietti spaventati che schizzano via. Altre volte fa invece prevalere motivi squisitamente estetici: attratto da una superba immagine antiquaria, l'apoteosi di Zeus sull'aquila che nel madrileno (fig. 21) segna l'*incipit* del testo di Arato—"Da Zeus tutto comincia"[83]—egli non esita ad appropriarsene (fig. 22) per illustrare il corpo celeste chiamato "Vultur Cadens," da lui stesso creato estrapolando una delle dieci stelle che nell'astrologia araba formano la Lira.[84]

Questa singolare "manipolazione" è sintomatica di un atteggiamento nuovo nei confronti delle *auctoritates*. Autentico uomo federiciano, Scoto usa modelli diversi con assoluta libertà, li fonde e li adatta alle sue esigenze con spregiudicata disinvoltura, come quando si inventa un'iconografia planetaria che non ha precedenti e che resterà in vigore fino al Rinascimento, passando attraverso i cicli affrescati e scolpiti del Trecento, dal Cappellone degli Spagnoli al Campanile di Giotto. Stravolgendo l'amorfa tradizione classica, tramandata dal Matritensis 19, fol. 68r, e quella islamica di radice babilonese, Scoto fa vestire agli olimpici Giove, Mercurio, Saturno, Marte e Venere e agli esotici Marduk, Nebo, Nergal, Ninib e Ishtar, gli abiti di un giudice, di un vescovo, di un guerriero e di una dama, ancorandoli alla realtà contemporanea e ai destini degli uomini.[85] Porta così a compimento un processo innovativo timidamente accennato all'inizio dell'XI secolo, quando il miniatore cassinese dell'enciclopedia di Rabano Mauro aveva messo in mano a Saturno non la comune e classica falce corta, ma la più moderna falce fienaia.[86]

In tutto questo fervore inventivo, Scoto dimentica l'intento più puramente scientifico. Difficilmente potremmo attribuirgli il rigore programmatico di Al-Sûfi: "Noi tracceremo le figure che danno il loro nome alle costellazioni sulla base delle somiglianze ri-

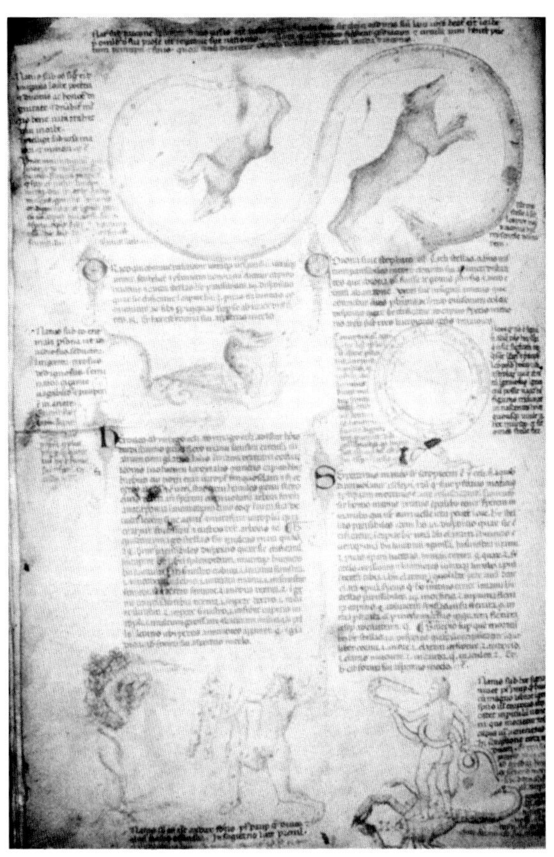

19. Michele Scoto, *Liber Introductorius*, metà del Trecento, fol. 80v
Bayerische Staatsbibliothek, Monaco (MS. Clm 10268)

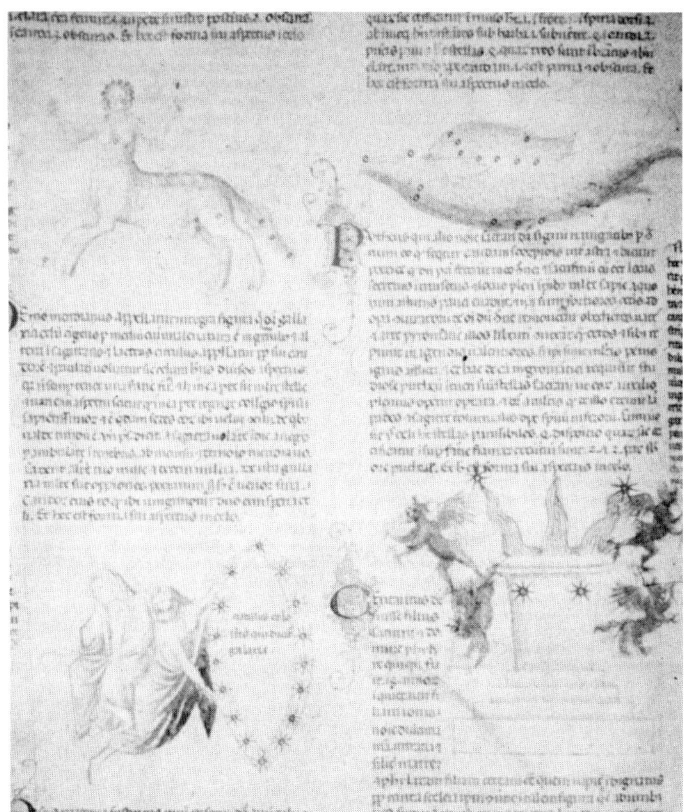

20. Michele Scoto, *Liber Introductorius*, metà del Trecento, fol. 83v
Bayerische Staatsbibliothek, Monaco (MS. Clm 10268)

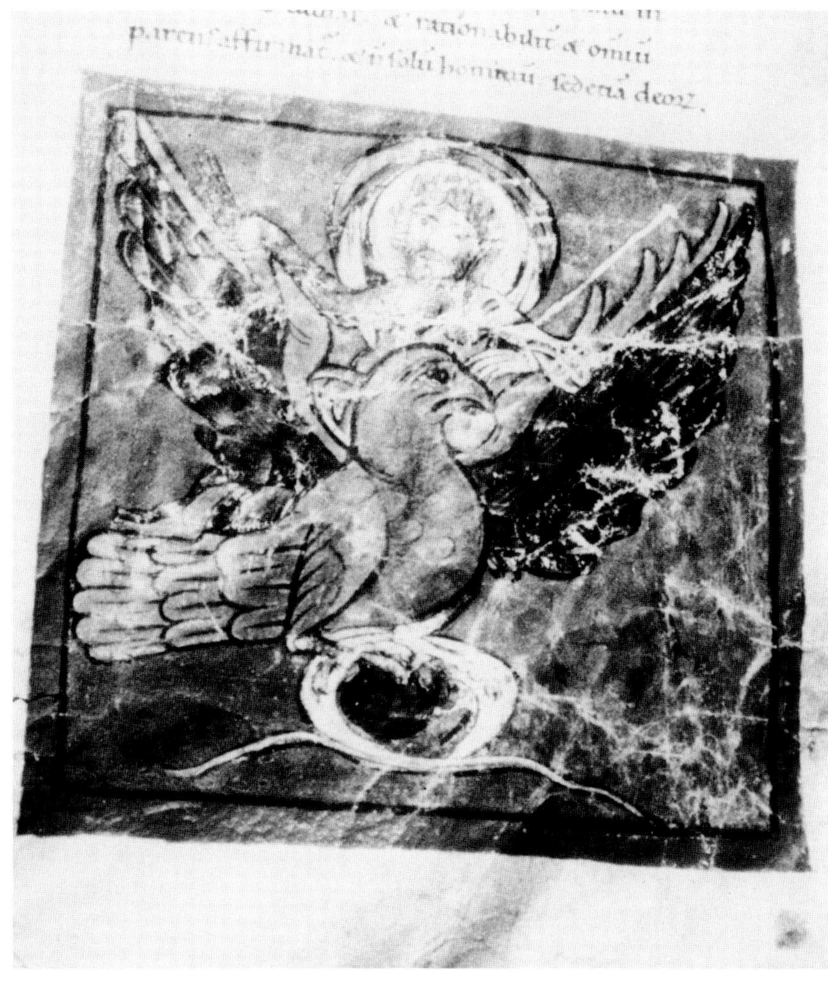

21. *Aratea*, XII secolo, fol. 55r
Biblioteca Nacional, Madrid (MS. 19)

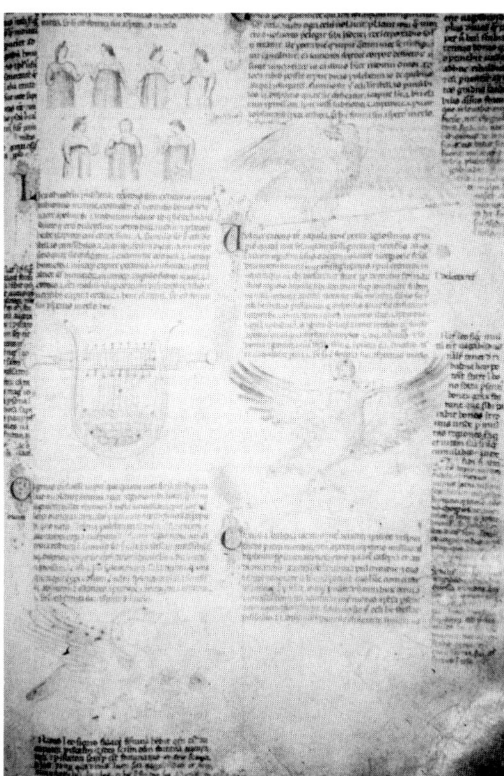

22. Michele Scoto, *Liber Introductorius*, metà del Trecento, fol. 82r
Bayerische Staatsbibliothek, Monaco (MS. Clm 10268)

scontrate e assegneremo alle stelle la loro posizione corretta all'interno di queste figure, al fine di rappresentare ciò che si vede nel cielo."[87] Gli astri del *Liber Introductorius* hanno un'esistenza puramente "libraria," brillano nell'universo letterario e dell'arte, non certo nel firmamento: belle immagini capaci di appagare il gusto "umanistico" di un colto pubblico di non specialisti, piuttosto che le esigenze degli astronomi.

Molto più importanti per la storia dell'illustrazione scientifica, botanica e zoologica, dai *Secreta Salernitana* fino ai *Tacuina Sanitatis*, sono le miniature degli erbari e del *De arte venandi*: qui il ricorso a uno stile classico, rinnegando le copie altomedievali corrotte, esprime la volontà di ritrovare strumenti efficaci per "manifestare ea quae sunt sicut sunt," un aiuto al recupero della verità di natura, spesso supportato e verificato dall'osservazione diretta.[88] Certe verosimiglianti figure di leoni, leopardi, lupi, cinghiali, che accompagnano il Sesto Placito nel laurenziano Plut. 73.16 e nel vindobonense 93, ambientate tra alberi e arbusti (fig. 23), rispecchiano il profondo interesse nutrito da Federico per gli animali, che allevò, studiò e collezionò in grande stile. L'elefante per esempio[89] (fig. 24) non è più la creatura fantastica, assolutamente stravolta nel suo aspetto oggettivo, dei bestiari altomedievali. Dietro la miniatura federiciana si intuisce una nuova esperienza del reale. L'ipotesi acquista credibilità se si pensa alle straordinarie occasioni di verifica offerte dai famosi serragli che seguivano l'imperatore ovunque, in Italia e persino in Germania, all'elefante che i monaci di San Zeno dovettero ospitare a Verona nel 1245 insieme a cinque leopardi e a quarantaquattro cammelli, o a quello che Federico donò ai cittadini di Cremona e che Matteo Paris immortalò in un celeberrimo ritratto nella sua *Cronaca*.[90] Così i rapaci e i volatili da cui ricavare le sostanze terapeutiche trovano i paralleli più puntuali nelle illustrazioni ornitologiche che popolano i margini del MS. Vat. Pal. lat. 1071 (figg. 25, 26). Un confronto con gli animali del Casinensis 97, manoscritto cassinese di tre secoli anteriore (fig. 27),[91] è illuminante per capire la portata rivoluzionaria dell'atteggiamento di Federico II nei confronti dei testi dell'antica scienza, che egli rimise in circolazione per offrirli a coloro che sanno

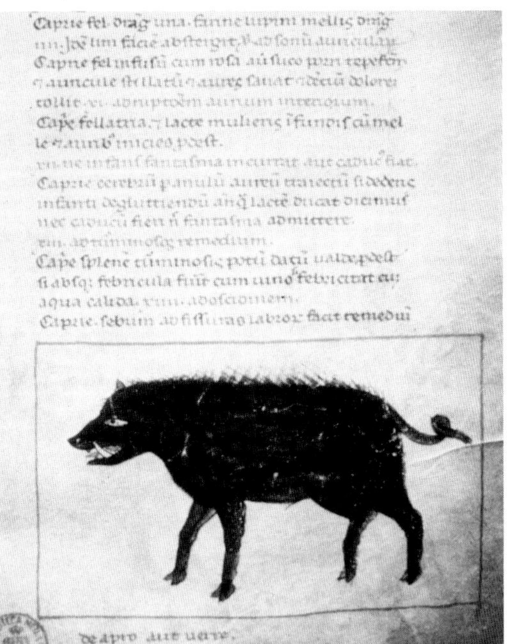

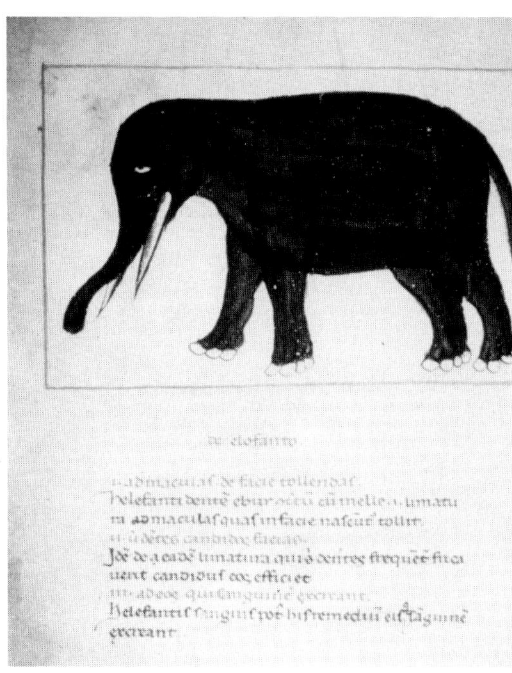

23. *Varia Medica*, prima metà del Duecento, fol. 161r
Biblioteca Medicea Laurenziana, Firenze (MS. Plut. 73.16)

24. *Varia Medica*, prima metà del Duecento, fol. 164v
Biblioteca Medicea Laurenziana, Firenze (MS. Plut. 73.16)

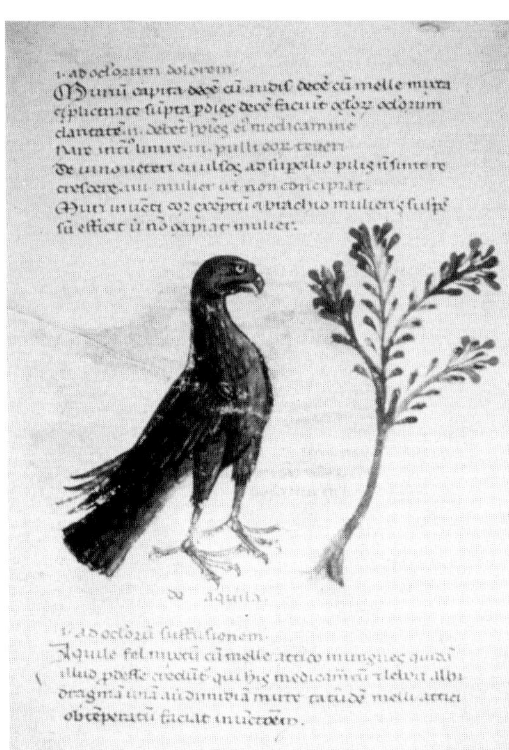

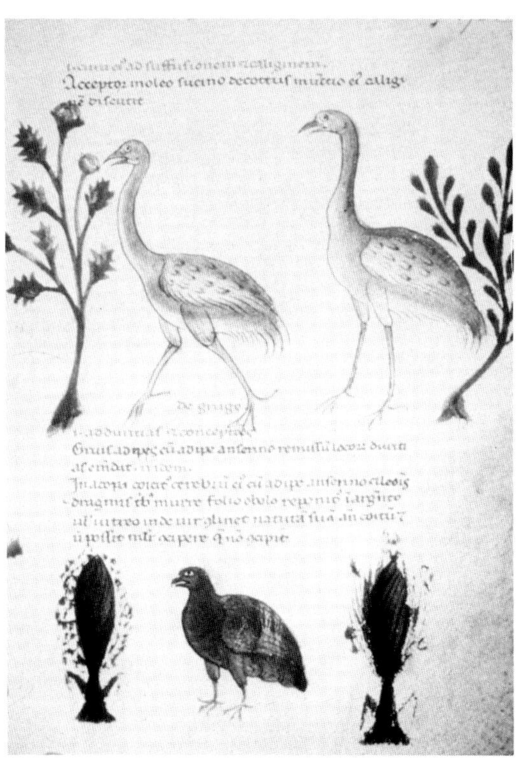

25. *Varia Medica*, prima metà del Duecento, fol. 171v
Biblioteca Medicea Laurenziana, Firenze (MS. Plut. 73.16)

26. *Varia Medica*, prima metà del Duecento, fol. 173r
Biblioteca Medicea Laurenziana, Firenze (MS. Plut. 73.16)

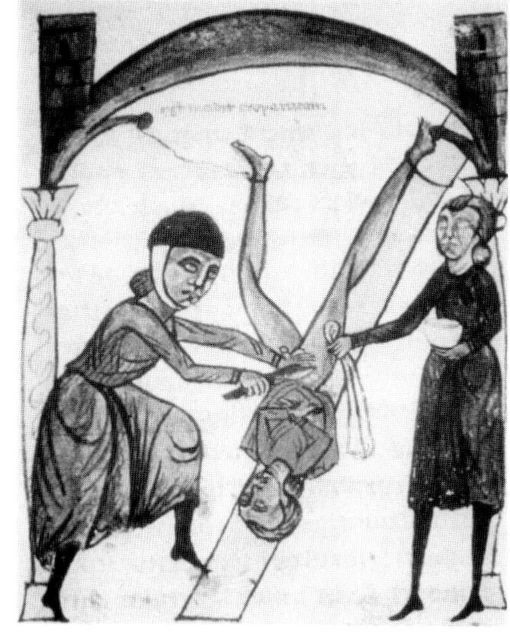

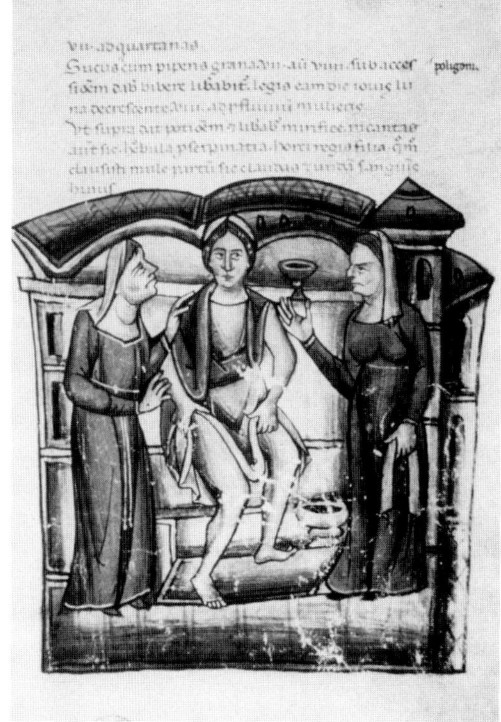

27. *Varia Medica*, inizio del secolo nono, pag. 537
Archivio dell'Abbazia, Montecassino (Casinensis 97)

28. Rolando da Parma, *De Chirurgia Liber*, prima metà del Duecento, fol. 25r
Biblioteca Casanatense, Roma (MS. 1382)

29. *Varia Medica*, prima metà del Duecento, fol. 52r
Biblioteca Medicea Laurenziana, Firenze (MS. Plut. 73.16)

attingere "de cisternis veteribus aquas novas."[92]

Nella Rolandina della Casanatense i medici smettono i panni all'antica e il gusto antiquario fa posto alla veridica documentazione dello strumentario e delle tecniche chirurgiche più aggiornate: la miniatura che illustra l'intervento di ernia inguinale (fig. 28) registra accuratamente la posizione rovesciata del paziente, adottata per la prima volta da Rolando.[93] Anche la massiccia presenza delle donne impegnate nei due erbari in ruoli medici e paramedici (fig. 29) sembra rispecchiare una pratica reale, tipica della Scuola Medica Salernitana, da Abella a Mercuriade, da Guarna a Costanza Calenda, fino a Trocta.[94] E nelle burrascose miniature del *Liber ad Honorem Augusti* di Berna, altre donne figurano come infermiere e dottoresse, pronte a soccorrere i loro uomini feriti. Questo aggancio al contemporaneo tocca il suo punto più alto nel manoscritto angelicano.

La concezione iconografica complessiva del ciclo del *De Balneis*, unico in tutta la miniatura medievale, perché nessun altro trattato idrologico del Duecento e Trecento è illustrato, deriva dalle *ymagines* stuccate e dipinte nei bagni della dorata aristocrazia imperiale a Baia e a Pozzuoli.[95] Le *ymagines*, di cui i visitatori medievali, da Corrado di Querfurt a Francesco Petrarca, conservano il ricordo,[96] raffiguravano personaggi indicanti i loro organi malati, come tramanda la miniatura di una copia angioina del poema di Pietro Ebolitano, il Vaticanus Rossianus 379, fol. 37r, col *titulo*: "Ymagines trituli, ostendentes infirmitates."[97] La memoria delle didascaliche decorazioni tardo romane, evidente per esempio nella miniatura del "Balneum Petrolei" (fig. 30),[98] non è però che uno spunto per raccontare, in presa diretta, il brulicante mondo che gravita intorno alle terme napoletane, tornate a nuovo splendore proprio con Federico. All'interno degli stabilimenti o nel paesaggio vulcanico di smagliante bellezza (fig. 31), uomini e donne mangiano e dormono,[99] si lavano la testa e il viso,[100] parlano animatamente, si rincuorano e si salutano,[101] scavano per far scaturire l'acqua,[102] alimentano con i mantici le fiamme per provocare i fumi di zolfo, saggiano la temperatura delle vasche,[103] partono o arrivano a piedi e sugli asini, col fardello attaccato al bastone (fig. 32).[104] È un'umanità nuova, che si muove e agisce con ritrovato naturalismo di gesti, di forme, di sentimenti, protagonista della più vivace cronaca di vita quotidiana illustrata del Medioevo. Un ulteriore contributo dell'età sveva alla riscoperta e allo straordinario allargamento dell'iconografia profana.

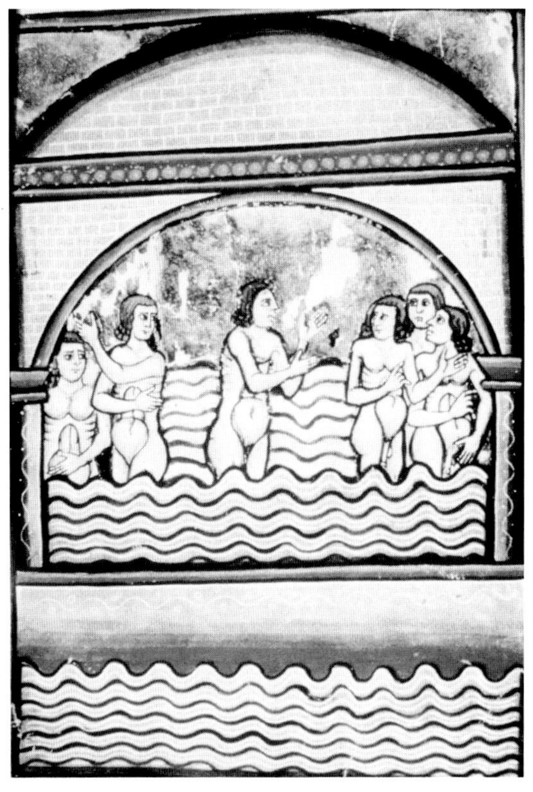

30. Pietro da Eboli, *De Balneis Puteolanis*, prima metà del Duecento, fol. 16r
Biblioteca Angelica, Roma (MS. 1474)

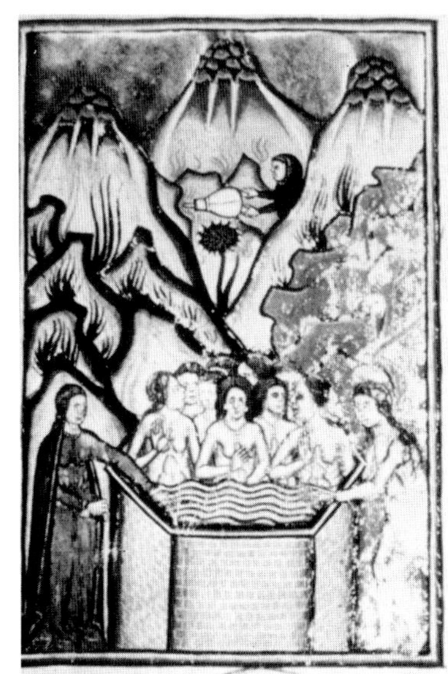

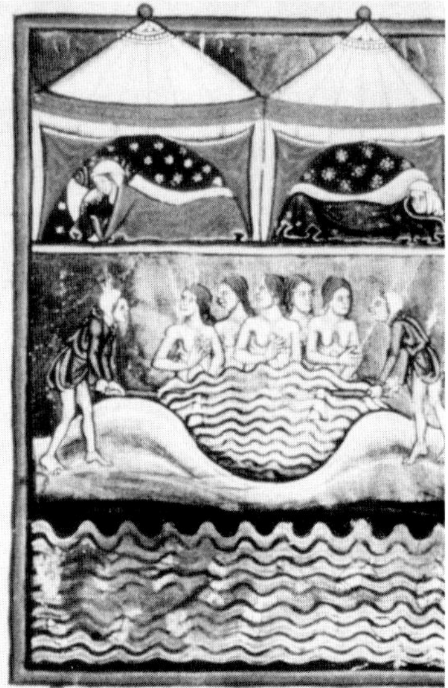

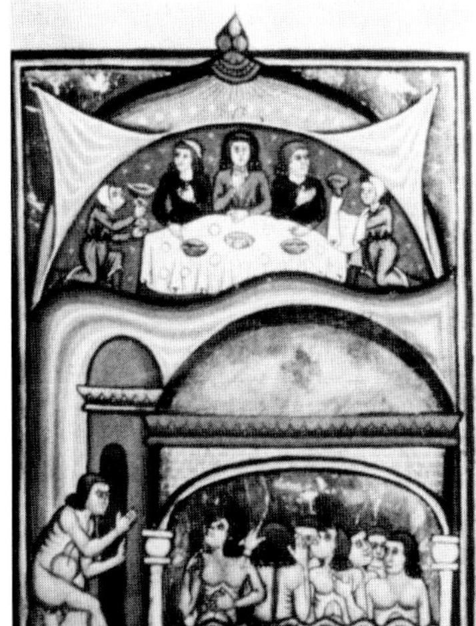

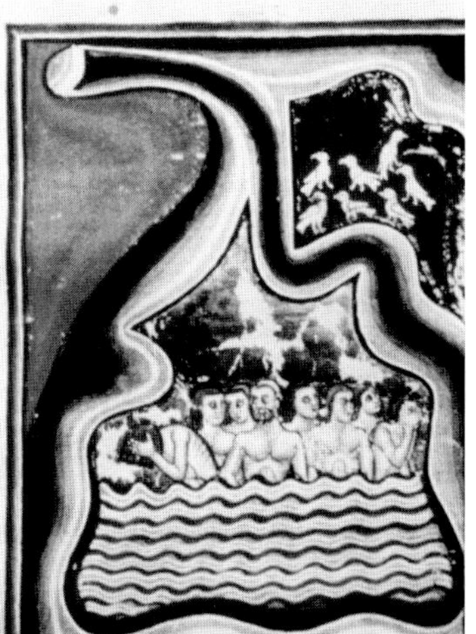

31. Pietro da Eboli, *De Balneis Puteolanis*, prima metà del Duecento, foll. 4r, 8r, 7r, 14r (dall'alto in basso, da destra a sinistra)
Biblioteca Angelica, Roma (MS. 1474)

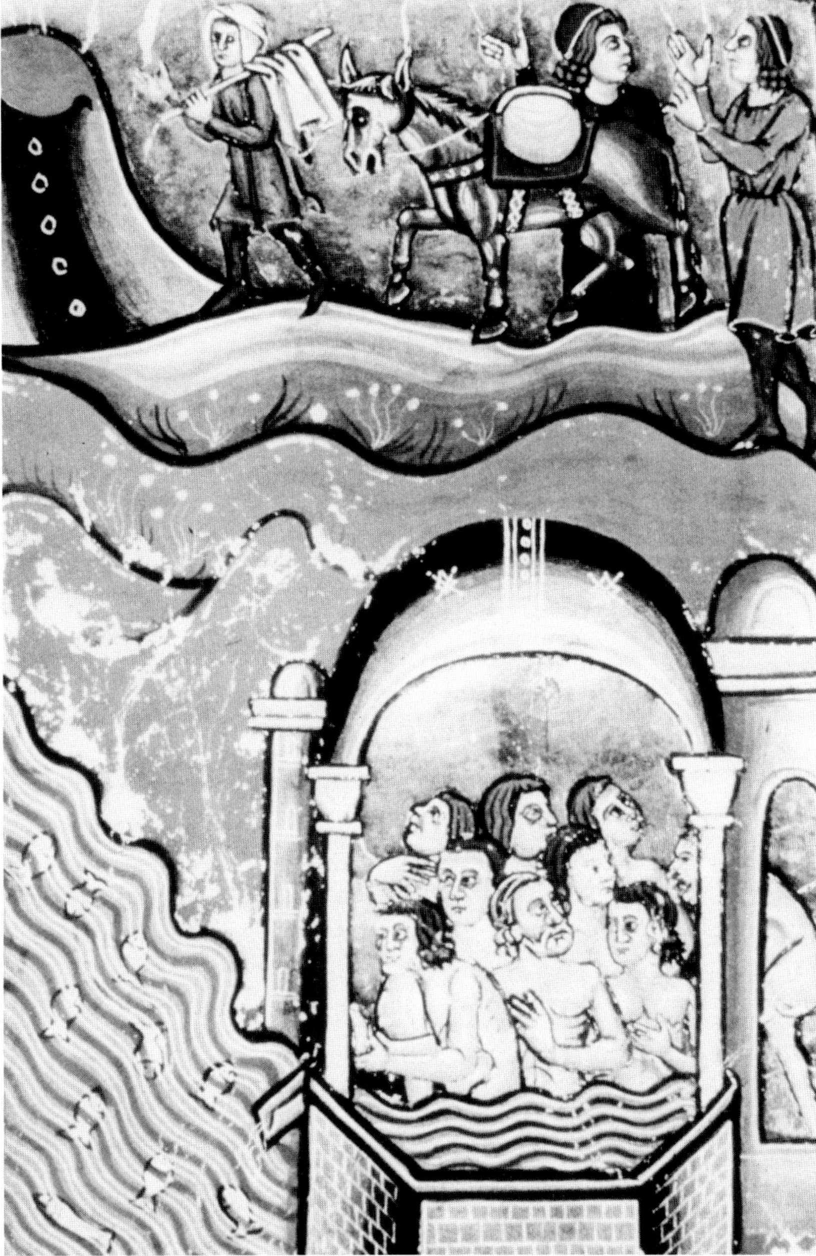

32. Pietro da Eboli, *De Balneis Puteolanis*, prima metà del Duecento, fol. 3r
Biblioteca Angelica, Roma (MS. 1474)

NOTE

1. "... Semper a iuventute nostra [eam] quesivimus, formam eius indesinenter amavimus, et in odore unguentorum suorum semper aspiravimus indefesse. Post regni vero nostri curas assumptas, quamquam operosa frequenter negociorum turba nos distrahat, ... quidquid tamen temporis de rerum familiarium occupatione decerpimus, transire non patimur ociosum; sed totum in lectionis exercitatione gratuite libenter expendimus, ut anime clarius vigeat instrumentum in acquisitione scientie, sine qua mortalium vita non regitur liberaliter. Dum librorum ergo volumina, quorum multifarie multisque modis distincta chirographa nostrarum armaria divitiarum locupletant, sedula meditatione revolvimus." Jean L. A. Huillard-Bréholles, *Historia Diplomatica Friderici Secundi*, 6 voll. (Paris, 1852–1861), 4.1:384 [*Encyclica Friderici Romanorum imperatoris qua magistris in philosophia docentibus libros quosdam sermoniales et mathematicos, ab Aristotele aliisque philosophis sub graecis et arabicis vocabulis conscriptos, nunc in latinum ipso curante translatos, mittit*].

2. Carl A. Willemsen, *Fredericus II, De arte venandi cum avibus, Ms. Pal. lat. 1071, Biblioteca Apostolica Vaticana. Faksimile-Ausgabe, Kommentar* (Graz, 1969); Florentine Mütherich, "Kaiser Friedrich II., Das Falkenbuch. De arte venandi cum avibus," in *Die Zeit der Staufer: Geschichte—Kunst—Kultur* [cat. mostra, Württembergisches Landesmuseum], ed. Reiner Haussherr, 6 voll. (Stuttgart, 1977–1979), 1:n. 824, 658–659, con bibliografia precedente.

3. Huillard-Bréholles, 5.2:750; Jean L. A. Huillard-Bréholles, *Vie et Correspondance de Pierre de la Vigne, ministre de l'empereur Frédéric II* (Paris, 1865; Aalen, 1966), 348; Antonino De Stefano, *La cultura alla corte di Federico II Imperatore* (Bologna, 1950), 42.

4. Lo studio più completo sui due erbari, databili tra il secondo e il terzo quarto del Duecento, con una lieve anticipazione del laurenziano sul viennese, si deve a Heide Grape-Albers, *Spätantike Bilder aus der Welt des Arztes. Medizinische Bilderhandschriften der Spätantike und ihre mittelalterliche Überlieferung* (Wiesbaden, 1977). Si veda anche Giulia Orofino, "Gli erbari di età sveva," in *Gli Erbari tra scienza, simbolo, magia*, Atti del VII Colloquio Medievale, Palermo 5–6 maggio 1988, in *Schede medievali* 19 (1990), 325–346. Dell'esemplare di Vienna è stato pubblicato il facsimile, *Medicina Antiqua. Libri quattuor medicinae. Codex Vindobonensis 93* (Graz, 1972), con volume di commento a cura di Charles H. Talbot e Franz Unterkircher. I due manoscritti contengono l'*Herbarium* dello Pseudo Apuleio, nella recensione *beta*, e altri trattati medici minori, tra cui il *De Herba Vettonica liber* e il *Liber de animalibus* di Sesto Placito Papiriense. Per la tradizione testuale si rimanda a *Antonii Musae de Herba Vettonica Liber, Pseudo Apulei Herbarius, Anonimi de Taxone liber, Sexti Placiti liber medicinae ex animalibus, ed. Ernst Howald et Henry Sigerist, Corpus Medicorum Latinorum IV* (Leipzig e Berlin, 1927).

5. Sulla *Metgia* di Aimeric de Pegulhan si veda De Stefano 1950, 69; Antonio Viscardi, *Le letterature d'Oc e d'Oil* (Firenze, 1967), 365.

6. Anna Maria Torroncelli, "Flos Medicinae," *Kos* 19 (1986), 17–26; Emilia Alfinito, "La Chirurgia," in *La Scuola Medica Salernitana. Storia, immagini, manoscritti dall'XI al XIII secolo* [cat. mostra], a cura di Maria Pasca (Napoli, 1988), 130.

7. Pietro Toesca, *Storia dell'arte italiana, 2, Il Medioevo* (Torino, 1927), 1133.

8. Florentine Mütherich e Hans Martin Schaller, "Petrus de Ebulo, Liber ad Honorem Augusti," in *Die Zeit der Staufer*, n. 810, 647–648, con bibliografia precedente; Helga Georgen, "Der Ebulo-Codex als Ausdruck des Konflikts zwischen Städten und Staufischem Hof," in *Bauwerk und Bildwerk im Hochmittelalter. Anschauliche Beiträge zur Kultur- und Sozialgeschichte*, a cura di Karl Clausberg et al. (Giessen, 1981), 145–167. Giulia Orofino, "La decorazione del libro di storia tra età normanna ed età sveva: epos, cronaca, manifesto," in *Civiltà del mezzogiorno d'Italia. Libro, scrittura, documento in età normanno-sveva*, Atti del Convegno Nazionale dell'Associazione Italiana dei Paleografi e Diplomatisti, Napoli, 14–18 ottobre 1991, in corso di stampa.

9. Sulla legislazione medica di Federico II, raccolta nelle Costituzioni di Melfi del 1231, si veda Paolo Picca, *Federico II e la sua legislazione sanitaria* (Roma, 1939); De Stefano 1950, 297–301; Paul O. Kristeller, "The School of Salerno," in *Studies in Renaissance Thought and Letters* (Roma, 1969), 528–532.

10. Angela Daneu Lattanzi, *Petrus de Ebulo. Nomina et Virtutes Balneorum seu de Balneis Puteolorum et Baiarum, Codice Angelico 1474*, facsimile (Roma, 1962); Florentine Mütherich e Hans Martin Schaller, "Petrus de Ebulo, De Balneis Puteolanis," in *Die Zeit der Staufer*, n. 822, 656–657, con bibliografia precedente; Giulia Orofino, "Nel nome del bagno," *Kos* 3 (1984), 36–53.

11. Ryccardi de Sancto Germano, *Chronicon*, a cura di Carlo A. Garufi, in Ludovico Antonio Muratori, Rerum Italicarum Scriptores, VII (Bologna, 1725), 1003.

12. Charles H. Haskins, *Studies in the History of Medieval Science*, 3° ed. (New York, 1960), 292–297.

13. Saba Malaspina, *Rerum Sicularum libri IV*, citato in Ernesto Pontieri, *Federico II d'Hohenstaufen e i suoi tempi* (Napoli, 1957), 88.

14. Marie-Thérèse Gousset e Jean-Pierre Verdet, *Georgius Zothorus Zaparus Fendulus. Liber Astrologiae* (Paris, 1989); sul manoscritto si veda anche V. Armstrong Clark, *The Illustrated "Abridged Astrological Treatises of Albumasar": Medieval Astrological Imagery in the West* (Ann Arbor, Mich., 1979).

15. Ulrike Bauer, *Der Liber Introductorius des Michele Scotus in der Abschrift Clm 10268 der Bayerischen Staatsbibliothek München* (München, 1983).

16. Monac. Clm 10268, fol. 55v.

17. Il testo della lettera di Guglielmo è riportato in Haskins 1960, 308–310.

18. Vat. Pal. lat. 1071, fol. 15r.

19. Vat. Pal. lat. 1071, fol. 69r.

20. Laur. Plut. 73.16, fol. 65r.

21. Laur. Plut. 73.16, fol. 169r.

22. Nella miniatura dell'Ang. 1474, fol. 2r, in alto Germano, vescovo di Capua, prega per l'anima dell'eretico Pascasio, costretto a "purgare" la sua colpa sulla terra, come garzone dei bagni. Il testo di Pietro dice "Germano, vescovo di Capua, avendoti qui trovato, ti rinviò, o Pascasio, ai sacri pascoli, grazie all'incenso": Daneu Lattanzi 1962, 77. È Gregorio Magno, *Dialogi* IV, 42 a raccontare la storia del diacono Pascasio, vissuto santamente alla fine del V secolo, ma colpevole di aver parteggiato per l'antipapa Lorenzo contro il papa Simmaco. Molti anni dopo la sua morte, il vescovo di Capua, Germano (516–541) recatosi alle terme di Agnano "pro corpore salutis," vi trova appunto Pascasio che sconta "in hoc poenali loco" l'errore scismatico. Le preghiere di Germano valsero al dissidente diacono la salvezza. Sulla connessione tra terme e Purgatorio per cui, con una sorta di legge del trapasso, gli antichi luoghi di lussuria e perdizione della civiltà pagana vengono riconvertiti in senso cristiano come luoghi di pena, si veda Jacques Le Goff, *La nascita del Purgatorio* (Torino, 1982), 100–105.

23. L'episodio occupa la metà inferiore della fol. 10r dell'Angelicano (Ang.) 1474, unica miniatura di soggetto religioso nel ciclo del *De Balneis*: Claus M. Kauffmann, *The Baths of Pozzuoli. A Study of the Medieval Illustrations of Peter of Eboli's Poem* (Oxford, 1959), 51–52.

24. Paris. lat. 7330, foll. 6v, 7, 7v, 9, 9v, 10, 11v, 12, 12v, 14, 14v, 15, 16v, 17, 17v, 19, 19v, 20, 21v, 22, 22v, 24, 24v, 25, 26v, 27, 27v, 29, 29v, 30, 31v, 32, 32v, 34, 34v, 35. Per la riproduzione dei trentasei disegni dei decani si rimanda a Gousset e Verdet 1989.

25. Un rapporto tra il Casinensis 132 e il Paris. lat. 7330 era stato già ipotizzato da Fritz Saxl: Fritz Saxl e Hans Meier, *Verzeichnis astrologischer und mythologischer illustrierter Handschriften des lateinischen Mittelalters, Bd. III: Handschriften in englischen Bibliotheken*, 2 voll., a cura di Harry Bober (London, 1953), lxviii. Nonostante l'eccezionale importanza del Casin. 132, l'unica edizione cui fare riferimento per una riproduzione, almeno parziale, delle sue trecento miniature, resta quella di Ambrogio Amelli, *Miniature sacre e profane dell'anno 1023 illustranti l'Enciclopedia medioevale di Rabano Mauro* (Montecassino, 1896)! La recente monografia di Marianne Reuter, *Text und Bild im Codex 132 der Bibliothek von Montecassino, "Liber Rabani de originibus rerum"* (München, 1984) è purtroppo corredata da un apparato fotografico di qualità asssai scadente.

26. Monac. Clm. 10268, fol. 1r: "Incipit prohemium libri introductorii, quem edidit Michael Scottus, astrologus Frederici imperatoris Romanorum et semper Augusti, quem ad eius preces leviter in astro-

nomia composuit . . . scholares novitios et pauperes intellectu."

27. Ang. 1474, fol. 10r.

28. Laur. Plut. 73.16, fol. 99r. La miniatura illustra gli effetti dell'erba eraclea: se il viandante porterà con sé un rametto della pianta, non avrà da temere i ladroni: "Fugat eos, quia pro unius viatoris persona multae videntur." I tre malviventi, nascosti tra gli anfratti di un monte, colpiti dal potere allucinogeno dell'eraclea, invece di un solo viandante indifeso ne vedono sette, tutti armati di lance oltre che dell'antifurto vegetale.

29. Laur. Plut. 73.16: foll. 3v; 4r–13r; 152v–156v; 179r–182r. Vindobonensis (Vindob.) 93: foll. 4v; 5r–8v; 120v–122r; 134r–135v.

30. Laur. Plut. 73.16: fol. 3r; Vindob. 93: fol. 4r.

31. "Plato, Ypocras, Dioscurus": Laur. Plut. 73.16: fol. 2v, Vindob. 93: fol. 3v; "Ypocrates": Laur. Plut. 73.16, fol. 17v, Vindob. 93, fol. 10r; "Plato": Laur. Plut. 73.16, fol. 150v, Vindob. 93, fol. 119r; "Dioscorius": Laur. Plut. 73.16, fol. 178r, Vindob. 93, fol. 133r. Le città, raffigurate come un insieme di variopinti edifici racchiusi entro mura, sono: "Urbs Platonis Medicis et Ipocra[ti]s et Diascoris Medicis" (Laur. Plut. 73.16, fol. 1r; Vindob. 93, fol. 2r); "Urbs Coa Ypocratis" (Laur. Plut. 73.16, fol. 2r; nel Vindob. 93 la raffigurazione è stata aggiunta a penna, a fol. 3r); "Urbs Apolia Platonis" (Laur. Plut. 73.16, fol. 26v; Vindob. 93, fol. 18r); "Urbs Placiti Papirion" (Laur. Plut. 73.16, fol. 151r; Vindob. 93, fol. 119v).

32. Vienna, Österreichische Nationalbibliothek, Medicus graecus 1, foll. 2v–3v: Hans Gerstinger, *Dioskurides. Codex Vindobonensis Med. Gr. 1 der Österreichischen Nationalbibliothek. Kommentarband zu der Faksimileausgabe* (Graz, 1970).

33. Armstrong Clark 1979, 114–127. Una deviazione dalla tradizione rappresentativa classica va riconosciuta nel segno dei Gemelli, fol. 11r, raffigurati come siamesi, con un solo corpo e due teste. La variante, di origine orientale, è accolta in Occidente anche nella raccolta astronomica di Alfonso X di Castiglia (1252–1284), MS. Vaticanus Reginensis latinus 1283, fol. 4v: Gousset e Verdet 1989, 93, fol. 22.

34. Saxl e Meier 1953, lxiii.

35. Kurt Weitzmann, *Illustrations in Roll and Codex: A Study of the Origin and Method of Text Illustration*, 2° ed. (Princeton, 1970), 103.

36. Hans Belting, *Studien zur beneventanischen Malerei* (Wiesbaden, 1968), 130–132, fig. 162; Carlo Bertelli, "L'illustrazione dei testi classici nell'area beneventana dal IX all'XI secolo," in *La cultura antica nell'Occidente latino dal VII all'XI secolo*, Settimane di Studio del Centro Italiano di Studi sull'Alto Medioevo 22 (Spoleto, 1975), 899–926, a pp. 99–911.

37. Otto Pächt e Jonathan J. Alexander, *Illuminated Manuscripts in the Bodleian Library Oxford* (Oxford, 1970), 2:n. 167, 17; Bertelli 1975, 910.

38. Bertelli 1975, 909.

39. Sabina Adacher, "La trasmissione della cultura medica a Montecassino tra la fine del IX sec. e l'inizio del X sec.," in *Montecassino. Dalla prima alla seconda distruzione. Momenti e aspetti di storia cassinese (secc. VI–IX)*, Atti del II Convegno di Studi sul Medioevo Meridionale, 1984 (Montecassino, 1987), 385–400.

40. Giulia Orofino, "Considerazioni sulla produzione miniaturistica altomedievale a Montecassino," *Monastica* 3 (Montecassino, 1983), 131–185.

41. Giulia Orofino, "Il ciclo illustrativo del 'Libellus de signis coeli' dello Pseudo Beda, cod. Cass. 3: interessi scientifici e cultura figurativa a Montecassino durante l'abbaziato di Bertario," in *Montecassino. Dalla prima alla seconda distruzione*, 571–595.

42. Jésus Domínguez Bordona, *Manuscritos con pinturas* (Madrid, 1933), 1:n. 411, 234–235, fig. 219; Alfred Cordoliani, "Un manuscrit de comput ecclésiastique mal connu de la Bibliothèque Nationale de Madrid," *Revista de archivos, bibliotecas y museos* 57 (1951), 5–35; Alfred Cordoliani, "Les manuscrits de comput ecclésiastique des Bibliothèques de Madrid," *Hispania Sacra* 8 (1955), 177–208; Juan Ainaud, "Beda, Isidoro, Aratos: Obras científicas, códice," in *El Arte Románico* [cat. mostra, Museo del Palacio Nacional, Barcelona] (Barcelona, 1961), n. 36, 21; Alfred Cordoliani, "Le comput ecclésiastique à l'Abbaye du Mont-Cassin au XIe siècle," *Anuario de estudios medievales* 3 (1966), 65–89; Patrick McGurk, *Catalogue of Astrological and Mythological Illuminated Manuscripts of the Latin Middle Ages*, IV, *Astrological Manuscripts in Italian Libraries other than Rome* (London, 1966), XVI, XXIV; Michael Reeve, "Some Astronomical Manuscripts," *Classical Quarterly* 30 (1980), 508–522, a p. 513.

43. Franz Boll, *Sphaera. Neue griechische Texte und Untersuchungen zur Geschichte der Sternbilder* (Leipzig, 1903; Hildesheim, 1967), 445; Saxl e Meier 1953; XXXV–XLIII; per una collazione puntuale tra le illustrazioni del Matrit. 19 e quelle del Monac. Clm 10268 si rimanda allo studio di Ulrike Bauer 1983.

44. Per un'attribuzione a Montecassino si era espresso Paul von Winterfeld, "De Germanici codicibus," in *Festschrift Johannes Vahlen* (Berlin, 1900), 392–407, seguito da Domínguez Bordona 1933, da McGurk 1966 e da Reeve 1980. José Millás Vallicrosa, *Assaig d'història de les idees físiques i matemàtiques a la Catalunya medieval* (Barcelona, 1931), 1:237–240, Cordoliani 1951 e Ainaud 1961, 21, assegnano invece il manoscritto al monastero di Santa María de Ripoll, ipotesi che sembrerebbe avallata da ragioni stilistiche.

45. Cordoliani 1966, 66–67; Reeve 1980, 513; Francesco Lomonaco, "Per una storia delle relazioni culturali cassinesi tra i secoli VIII e IX," in *Montecassino. Dalla prima alla seconda distruzione*, 552. Altre prove testuali legano il Matrit. 19 all'Italia meridionale: esso contiene infatti un'antologia di brevi poemi astronomici che precedono gli *Aratea*, gli stessi che compaiono anche nel ms. 3 dell'Archivio della Badia della Santissima Trinità di Cava dei Tirreni, scritto in beneventana nel tardo XI secolo (Cordoliani 1966, 74–

76) nonché, parzialmente, nel *Liber Introductorius* di Scoto (Reeve, 1980, 517). Il manoscritto di Cava—sul quale si veda Mario Rotili, *La miniatura nella Badia di Cava* (Cava dei Tirreni, 1976), 1:21–26, 101—contiene inoltre, come il madrileno, il *De Temporum Ratione* di Beda. Entrambi poi presentano (il Matrit. 19 ai foll. 2v–4v e il Cav. 3 al fol. 3v) analoghe illustrazioni per la "loquela digitorum," dimostrata da figure virili che indicano i numeri con le dita.

46. Il manoscritto laurenziano, che appartenne a Coluccio Salutati, è datato dal Reeve 1980, 511, al Quattrocento. Si veda anche Lomonaco 1987, 552.

47. Reeve 1980, 511.

48. Il Matrit. 19 appartiene alla stressa famiglia iconografica del MS. AN IV 18 dell'Universitätsbibliothek di Basilea, da Fulda, del IX secolo. I due esemplari furono riuniti in un'unica classe da Georg Thiele, *Antike Himmelsbilder* (Berlin, 1898), 143. A questa famiglia appartiene anche il MS. 735c di Aberystwyth, National Gallery of Wales, dell'inizio dell'XI secolo, da Limoges(?): Patrick McGurk, "Germanici Caesaris Aratea cum Schoolis: A New Illustrated Witness from Wales," *National Gallery of Wales Journal* 18 (1973–1974), 197–216.

49. Monac. Clm 10268, fol. 80r; Matrit. 19, fol. 63v. Bauer 1983, 39–40.

50. Monac. Clm 10268, fol. 82v; Matrit. 19, fol. 67r.

51. Valga per tutti l'esempio del MS. Voss. Lat. Q. 79 della Bibliotheek der Rijksuniversiteit di Leida, fol. 68v (Thiele 1898, fig. 50), splendido codice carolingio dell'inizio del IX secolo, esemplato da un prototipo tardo antico: Jeffrey C. Anderson, "Aratea," in *Age of Spirituality: Late Antique and Early Christian Art, Third to Seventh Century* [cat. mostra, Metropolitan Museum of Art], a cura di Kurt Weitzmann (New York, 1979), n. 190, 214.

52. Germanicus, *Phaenomena*, V, 363–369, a cura di D. B. Gain, *The Aratus Ascribed to Germanicus Caesar* (London, 1976), 32: ". . . Amnem qui Phaethonta suas defleuit ad undas, postquam patris equos non aequo pondere rexit."

53. Si veda per esempio il MS. XIV D 37 della Biblioteca Nazionale di Napoli, del terzo quarto del Quattrocento (McGurk 1966, 62–64), fol. 33r.

54. Monac. Clm 10268, fol. 82v: ". . . ille Eridanus ignitus cecidit in flumine aque et adducens deorsum flamas radiorum solis quasi totam tellurem combuxit et combussisset nisi in flumen totus cecidisset": Bauer 1983, 136 nota 402.

55. Montac. Clm 10268, fol. 81r: Bauer 1983, 129 nota 308.

56. Saxl e Meier 1953, 1:xl; Bauer 1983, 52.

57. Così si ricava dal testo stesso: Saxl e Meier 1953, xxxii nota 41.

58. Marie Thérèse Gousset, "Le *Liber de locis stellarum fixarum* d'Al-Sûfi, ms. 1036 de la Bibliothèque de l'Arsenal à Paris: une réattribution," *Arte medievale* 2 (1985), 93–106.

59. Emmy Wellesz, *An Islamic Book of Constellations* (Oxford, 1965).

60. Sull'iconografia araba delle costellazioni e la sua influenza in Occidente, si rimanda soprattutto a Erwin Panofsky e Fritz Saxl, "Classical Mythology in Mediaeval Art," *Metropolitan Museum Studies* 4 (1932–1933), 228–280; Jean Seznec, *The Survival of the Pagan Gods* (New York, 1953), 149–183; Fritz Saxl, "The Revival of Late Antique Astrology," in Fritz Saxl, *Lectures* (London, 1957), 1:73–84.

61. Alessandro Bausani, "Il contributo scientifico," in *Gli Arabi in Italia*, a cura di Francesco Gabrieli e Ugo Scerrato (Milano, 1979), 629–660.

62. Francesco Gabrieli, *Gli Arabi in Italia*, 203–204.

63. Il colophon di una copia napoletana del *Liber Novem Iudicum*, MS. Royal 12 G VIII della British Library, riporta: "Liber novem iudicum quem misit soldanus Babilonie imperatori Federico tempore quo et magnus Khalif misit magistrum Theodorum eidem imperatori Federico": Florentine Mütherich e Hans Martin Schaller, "Liber Novem Iudicum," in *Die Zeit der Staufer*, 1:n. 820, 655.

64. Monac. Clm 10268, foll. 84r, 84v.

65. Saxl e Meier 1953, 1:lxvii.

66. Monac. Clm 10268, fol. 81v.

67. Saxl 1957, 75.

68. Monac. Clm 10268, fol. 77v: Bauer 1983, 133 nota 355.

69. Altri debiti di Scoto nei confronti dell'astronomia araba sono per esempio la "Figura sonantis canonis" (Monac. Clm 10268, fol. 82v: Bauer 1983, 63–64), l' "Equus secundus" (Montac. Clm 10268, fol. 84r: Bauer 1983, 77–78), lo scudo di Orione (Monac. Clm 10268, fol. 83r: Bauer 1983, 65–66).

70. Monac. Clm 10268, fol. 81v.

71. Matrit. 19, fol. 60r. Questa è l'interpretazione di Frit Saxl: Saxl e Meier 1953, 1:xl.

72. Bauer 1983, 54.

73. Kyle M. Phillips Jr., "Perseus and Andromeda," *American Journal of Archaeology* 72 (1968), 1–23.

74. I rapporti tra la scuola di Otranto e la corte sveva erano stretti; l'abate Nettario guidò, tra l'altro, un'ambasceria di Federico presso l'imperatore greco a Nicea. Sull'Aristofane di Casole si veda Walter Berschin, *Medioevo greco-latino* (Napoli, 1989), 306.

75. Monac. Clm 10268, fol. 84r.

76. Igino, *Poeticon astronomicon*, II, 9, a cura di Franco Serra, *Hyginus astronomus* (Pisa, 1976), 72–74. Altre derivazioni da Igino sono Boote raffigurato come contadino (Monac. Clm 10268, fol. 81r: Bauer 1983, 48–49); l'iconografia della Via Lattea (Monac. Clm 10268, fol. 83v: Bauer 1983, 69–71); l'interpretazione mitologica di Pegaso come Melanippa (Monac. Clm 10268, fol. 81v: Bauer 1983, 53).

77. Monac. Clm 10268, fol. 84r, Matrit. 19, fol. 66r: Bauer, 1983, 74–76. L' "uter vini aceti" è presente per esempio nel Casinensis 3, p. 192: Orofino 1987, 594, fig. 14.

78. Monac. Clm 10268, fol. 80v.

79. Monac. Clm 10268, fol. 80v: Bauer, 1983, 126 nota 265.

80. *Scholia Basileensis*, a cura di Alfred Breysig, *Aratus, Germanici Caesaris Aratea cum Scholiis* (Berlin, 1867; Hildesheim, 1967), 73. Nel Matrit. 19, fol. 56r, la testa del leone non si vede. Nel manoscritto spagnolo del XII secolo, Vat. lat. 643, fol. 83v, Eracle regge solo una testa barbuta e la pelle è scomparsa, per un chiaro fraintendimento con Perseo.

81. Monac. Clm 10268, fol. 83v.

82. Igino, *Poet. astron.* II, 39, edizione Serra 1976, 72; *Scholia Basileensis*, edizione Breysig 1867, 99; *Scholia Strozziana e Sangermanensia*, edizione Breysig 1867, 177. Bauer 1983, 75–76.

83. Matrit. 19, fol. 55r.

84. Monac. Clm 10268, fol. 82r: Bauer 1983, 59–61.

85. Monac. Clm 10268, fol. 85r. Sulla portata rivoluzionaria dell'iconografia scotiana dei pianeti, si rimanda a Panofsky e Saxl 1932–1933, 242–246; Seznec 1953, 156–163; Saxl 1957, 76–79; Erwin Panofsky, *Il significato nelle arti visive* (Torino, 1962), 53; Erwin Panofsky, *Rinascimento e rinascenze nell'arte occidentale* (Milano, 1971), 126–127. Per un esame specifico delle singole iconografie, si veda Bauer 1983, 79–90.

86. Casin. 132, p. 382: Raymond Klibansky, Erwin Panofsky e Fritz Saxl, *Saturno e la melancolia* (Torino, 1983), 186–187.

87. Citato in Armstrong Clark 1979, 131.

88. Otto Pächt, "Early Italian Nature Studies and the Early Calendar Landscape," *Journal of the Warburg and Courtauld Institutes* 13 (1950), 13–47, a pp. 24–25.

89. Laur. Plut. 73.16, fol. 164v.

90. Haskins 1960, 254–256. William Heckscher, "Bernini's Elephant and Obelisk," *Art Bulletin* 29 (1947), 155–182.

91. Adacher 1987, 396–399. Il manoscritto contiene la stessa silloge botanico-zoologica dei due erbari svevi, ma nella recensione *alfa*.

92. La volontà federiciana si esplicita nella stessa lettera di accompagnamento delle opere aristoteliche destinate a Bologna, da cui è tratta appunto la citazione: Huillard-Bréholles, 4.1:385.

93. Mario Tabanelli, *La chirurgia italiana nell'Alto Medioevo, 1. Ruggero, Rolando, Teodoro* (Firenze, 1965), 111–191.

94. Pina Cavallo Boggi, "Il corpo, la donna, la malattia," in *Trotula de Ruggiero, Sulle malattie delle donne* (Torino, 1979), v–xxxiv; Massimo Oldoni, "Un Medioevo senza santi: la Scuola medica di Salerno dalle origini al XIII secolo," in *La Scuola Medica Salernitana* (Napoli, 1988), 18–22.

95. Kauffmann 1959, 59–65.

96. Kauffmann 1959, 59–60.

97. Kauffmann 1959, 62, fig. 101.

98. Ang. 1474, fol. 16r.

99. Ang. 1474, fol. 7r, "Balneum Calatura"; fol. 8r, "Balneum S. Anastasiae."

100. Ang. 1474, fol. 5r, "Balneum Bullae"; fol. 6r, "Balneum Petrae"; fol. 7r, "Balneum Calatura."

101. Ang. 1474, fol. 15r, "Balneum Culma"; fol. 16r, "Balneum Petrolei."

102. Ang. 1474, fol. 8r, "Balneum S. Anastasiae."

103. Ang. 1474, fol. 4r, "Balneum Sulphatara."

104. Ang. 1474, fol. 3r, "Balneum Balneolum"; fol. 12r, "Balneum Raynerii."

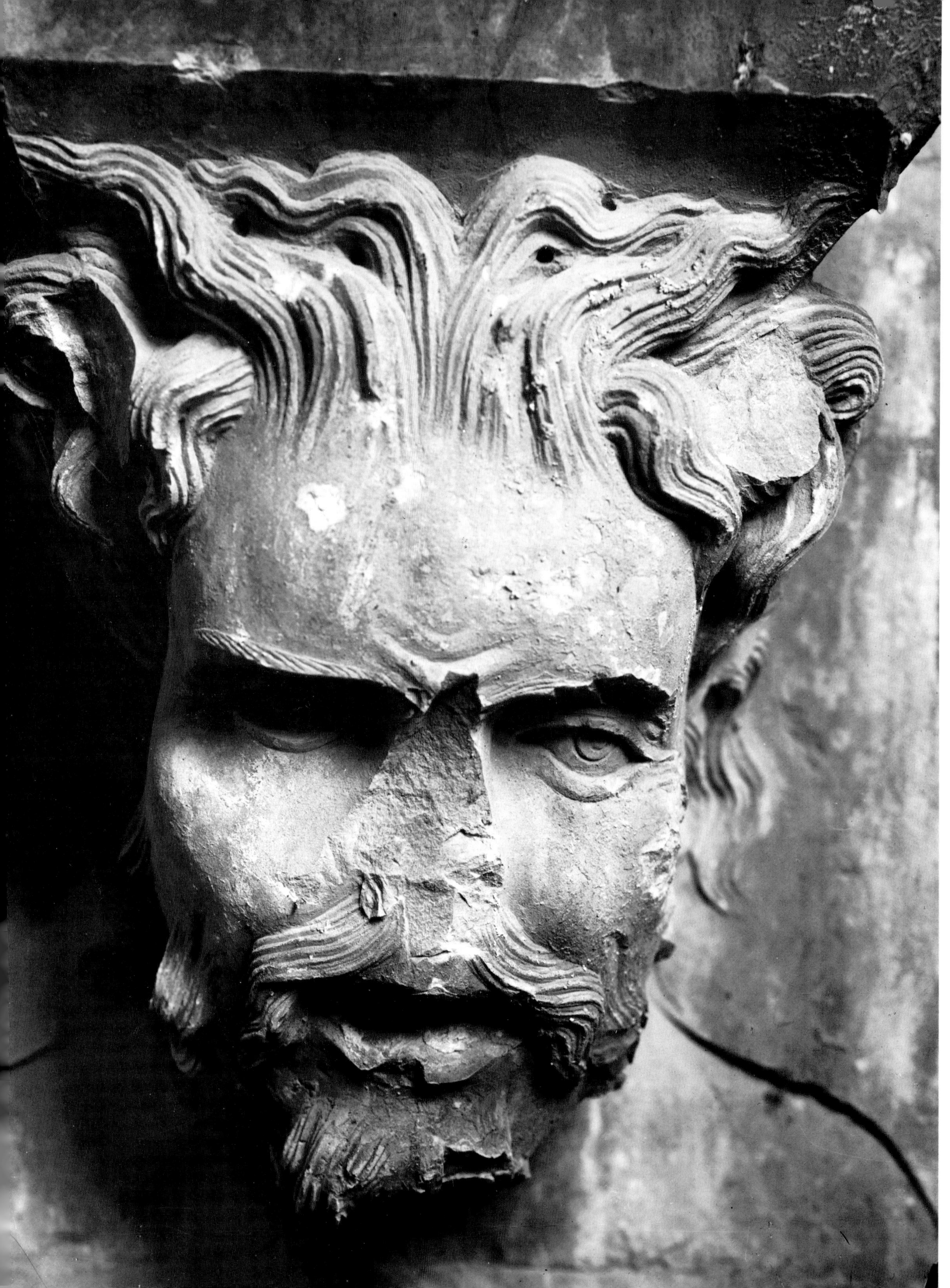

VALENTINO PACE
Università degli Studi di Roma "La Sapienza"

Scultura "federiciana" in Italia meridionale e scultura dell'Italia meridionale di età federiciana

Testimonianza primaria della grandezza intellettuale di Federico II sono i monumenti e le opere di cui fu committente. Significato ideologico e valenze estetiche vi si combinano in espressioni formali di grande fascino, i cui referenti furono sia l'Antico che il Moderno (cioè la tradizione classica d'un lato, le innovazioni della moderna civiltà "gotica" di Francia e di Germania dall'altro), sia la cultura occidentale che quella bizantina e quella islamica.

Per questa fitta maglia di conoscenze e di esperienze, per questa situazione di estrema circolarità delle più diverse culture, per la loro importanza, le opere di committenza federiciana—le opere "d'arte" per lo specifico di questo saggio, ma non solo queste—sono state sottoposte a ripetuti scrutini. Con impegno la storiografia artistica federiciana ha affrontato i temi cruciali delle motivazioni ideologiche e dei rapporti con l'arte europea, del bacino mediterraneo.[1]

Benché possa sembrare superfluo il ritornare su questi argomenti, tanto dibattuti, ciò tuttavia non lo è nella misura in cui sui temi e sui quesiti più controversi—quale, per esempio, quello delle scelte formali—può in taluni casi offrirsi il contributo di nuovi dati oppure può esperirsi una verifica di carattere metodologico delle risposte finora offerte, mentre su altri temi—quale il concetto stesso di "arte federiciana"—può formularsi qualche precisazione. Sarà privilegiato il fenomeno della scultura e, in particolare, della scultura "figurativa," perché è essa su cui il dibattito si articola con maggiore diversità di opinioni.

Monumento paradigmatico della committenza federiciana è la porta di Capua.[2] Che in essa la scelta del linguaggio artistico sia stata effettuata con la precisa consapevolezza di usarne le valenze ideologiche, è stato da tempo assai bene compreso.[3] Resta in ogni modo controverso su quali specifici canali si siano attivate le forme artistiche ivi espresse, ovvero a quali modelli concreti i suoi scultori si siano rivolti e quale educazione essi stessi abbiano ricevuto. Che la statuaria classica sia servita come modello di base per la formulazione delle sue emblematiche immagini (da quella della statua stessa di Federico II o della cosiddetta *Iustitia imperialis* ai due busti o alla protome leonina) non è messo in dubbio da nessuno. Discusso è invece il referente culturale e figurativo che nella Campania "federiciana" ha condotto a reinterpretare l'Antico: la Provenza romanica, la Francia gotica o altri ancora.[4]

Alla luce di questa situazione storiografica—ricca di intelligenti aperture critiche e pur conflittuale nelle sue soluzioni—non sarà dunque infondata l'esigenza di un rinnovato vaglio critico delle opere stesse. Al proposito dovrà preliminarmente tenersi soprattutto conto di due importanti—quasi ovvii—fattori di giudizio: le sculture capuane fecero parte di uno stesso complesso plastico e il programma da esse visualizzato fu, come sempre riconosciuto, di rigoroso impianto ideologico; in secondo luogo, che l'opera capuana si colloca in una fase dell'"età federiciana" piuttosto avanzata (tra il 1234 e il 1239), anche se per la nostra esperienza essa vale come monumento iniziale della scultura—ovvero, della scultura figurativa e monumentale—federiciana. Ne scaturiscono due conseguenze: che a Capua lo "stile" è, per usare un'espressione altrove corrente, "eterodiretto," cioè in stretta funzione delle ragioni ideologiche della committenza;[5] che, al di là della testimonianza della monetazione e delle poche sculture frammentarie (per giunta mai o ben di rado databili con sufficiente approssimazione) la scultura capuana ha assunto un'innaturale valenza di "opera prima" (della produzione figurativa federiciana) che ovviamente rende ancor più difficile precisarne la genesi formale.

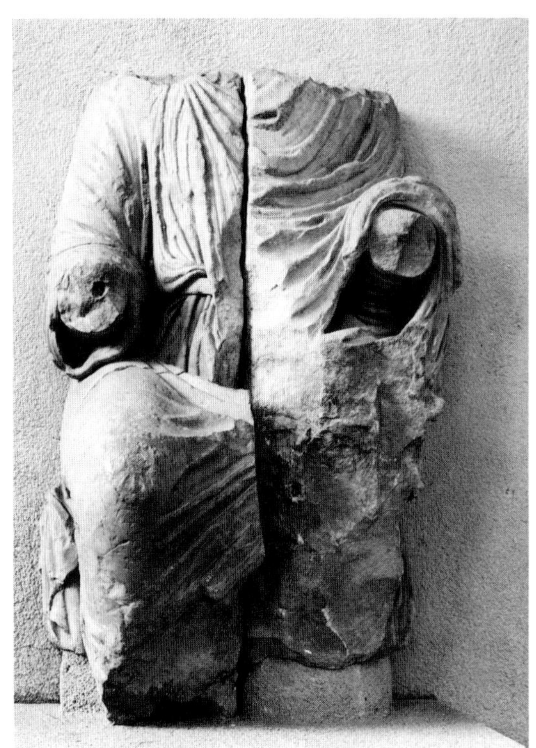

1. Statua mutila dell'imperatore Federico II
Museo provinciale campano, Capua; fotografia: Deutsches Archäologisches Institut (DAI), Roma

In primo luogo occorre dunque cogliere esattamente quali siano i possibili modelli antichi cui si indirizzò (o verso cui fu fatta indirizzare) l'attenzione degli scultori attivi a Capua. Solo al confronto fra "modello" antico (per esemplativo che esso possa essere) e opera federiciana possono infatti emergere con chiarezza quelle "varianti" di cui si vuole comprendere l'ascendenza o, comunque, la contestualizzazione figurativa.

Per iniziare, si osserverà dunque che la statua di Federico II (fig. 1) copia modelli scultorei della Roma "imperiale," di cui esempi qui significativi possono essere le statue di togati, anch'esse mutile, nel giardino della Villa Massimo a Roma e nel museo provinciale stesso di Capua: se la prima, seduta (fig. 2), espone assai bene una simile monumentalità compositiva, la seconda, in piedi (fig. 3), evidenzia soprattutto il valore normativo assunto dal panneggio "classico." Se il modello, ovvero, i modelli classici possono avere dunque agito per la loro monumentalità e per al loro naturalezza d'insieme, essi tuttavia presentano divergenze che non ne permetterebbero mai di confonderli con la "copia" medievale. Queste divergenze si concretano in primissimo luogo nell'impostazione compositiva della figura seduta. La

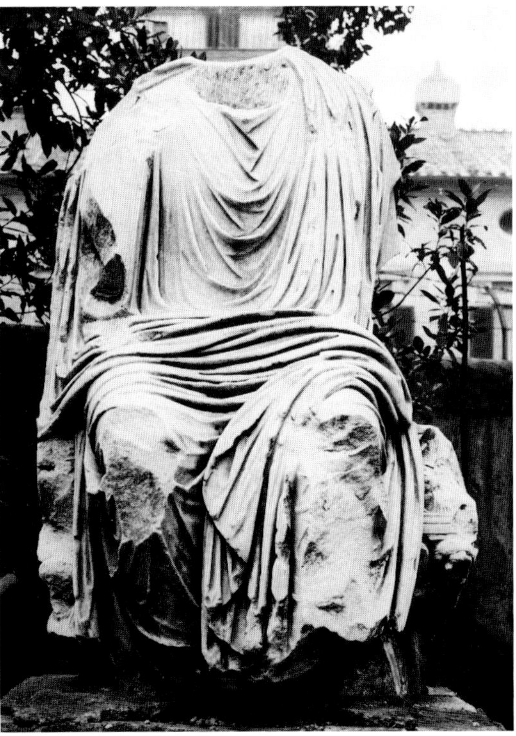

2. Statua mutila di togato
Accademia tedesca (Villa Massimo), Roma; fotografia: DAI, Roma

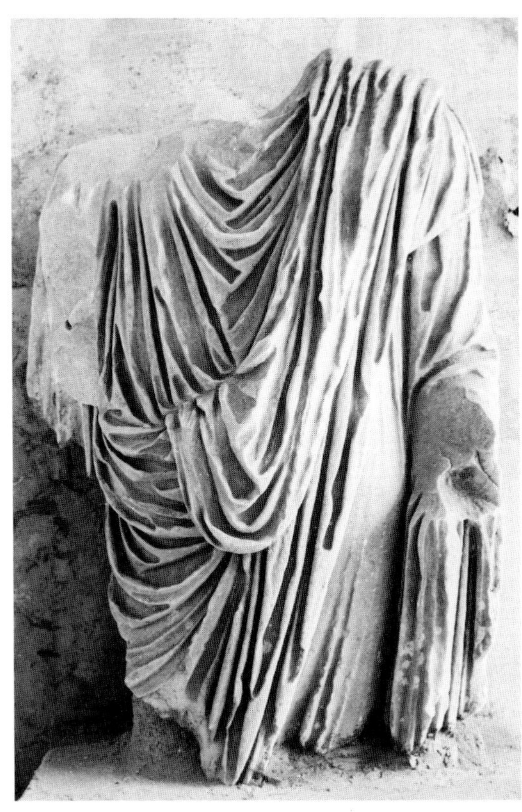

3. Statua mutila di togato
Museo provinciale campano, Capua; fotografia: DAI, Roma

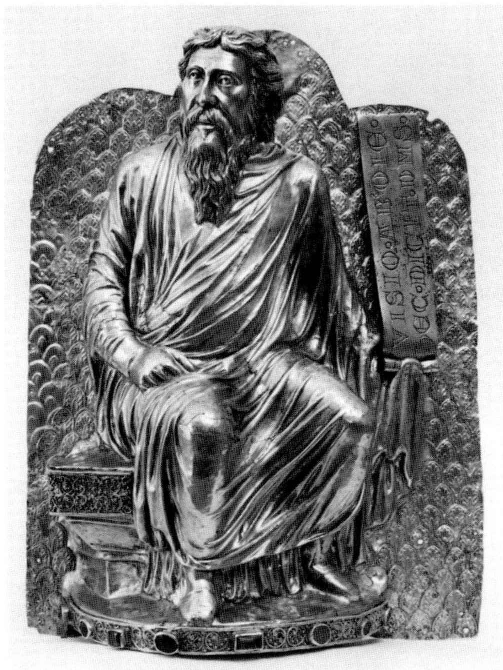

4. Reliquiario dei Tre Re Magi ("Dreikönigenschrein"), profeta Geremia (durante il restauro)
Duomo, Colonia (Köln); fotografia: Rheinisches Bildarchiv, Köln

gamba destra vi appare innaturalmente arcuata (come si vede dalla veduta laterale) ad assecondare una prospettiva dal basso, tutt'e due sono slargate all'altezza delle ginocchia e convergono sui piedi (o meglio, convergevano, secondo quanto è intuibile dal frammento ed è confermato dal disegno del Séroux d'Agincourt) in linea con la consuetudine rappresentativa medievale—attestata tanto nella monetazione quanto nella miniatura federiciane.[6] In secondo luogo non è ovviamente del tutto antica la maniera di drappeggiare le vesti, che tradisce, proprio al confronto dell'autentico brano "antico," una ben minore comprensione del rilievo "in profondità" e tendenze "medievali" di stilizzazione riconoscibili soprattutto nelle vedute laterali (fig. 6).

Per la statua capuana un riferimento gotico e francese venne formulato sia dal Poeschke che ne mise in stretto rapporto la concezione statuaria con quella espressa dal "maestro della Visitazione" di Reims, sia dallo Gnudi, il quale ne scrisse che "l'interpretazione del panneggio classico è sul piano di quella che s'incontra a Chartres (portale nord), a Parigi (frammenti dal portale centrale di Notre Dame nel museo di Cluny e nel museo Carnevalet), a Reims (portale occidentale destro) nei primi due decenni del secolo," sia infine—recentissimamente—dal Claussen, che l'ha collegata con le più moderne tendenze della plastica francese.[7] Che i confronti addotti dallo Gnudi siano i più adatti a spiegare la specifica assunzione di una "visione classica della realtà" che le si è detta propria, non saprei tuttavia sottoscriverlo senza qualche esitazione. Sia la statuaria di Reims, sia i frammenti dei musei parigini, sia pure il portale settentrionale di Chartres (che costituiscono i riferimenti cronologicamente più bassi—del primo decennio del Duecento—per lo studioso) mostrano una "fluidità" di panneggio che, nel quadro della cronologia stilistica del tempo, sta un gradino oltre la sua "articolata" caratterizzazione nella statua federiciana.[8] A differenziare quest'ultima dagli esempi francesi addotti interviene non solo una più esplicita e radicale adesione alla norma classica, ma anche un modo di reinterpretarla che già nell'impostazione compositiva si rivela non solo affine alle immagini federiciane sui sigilli e sulle monete, ma anche e più signifi-

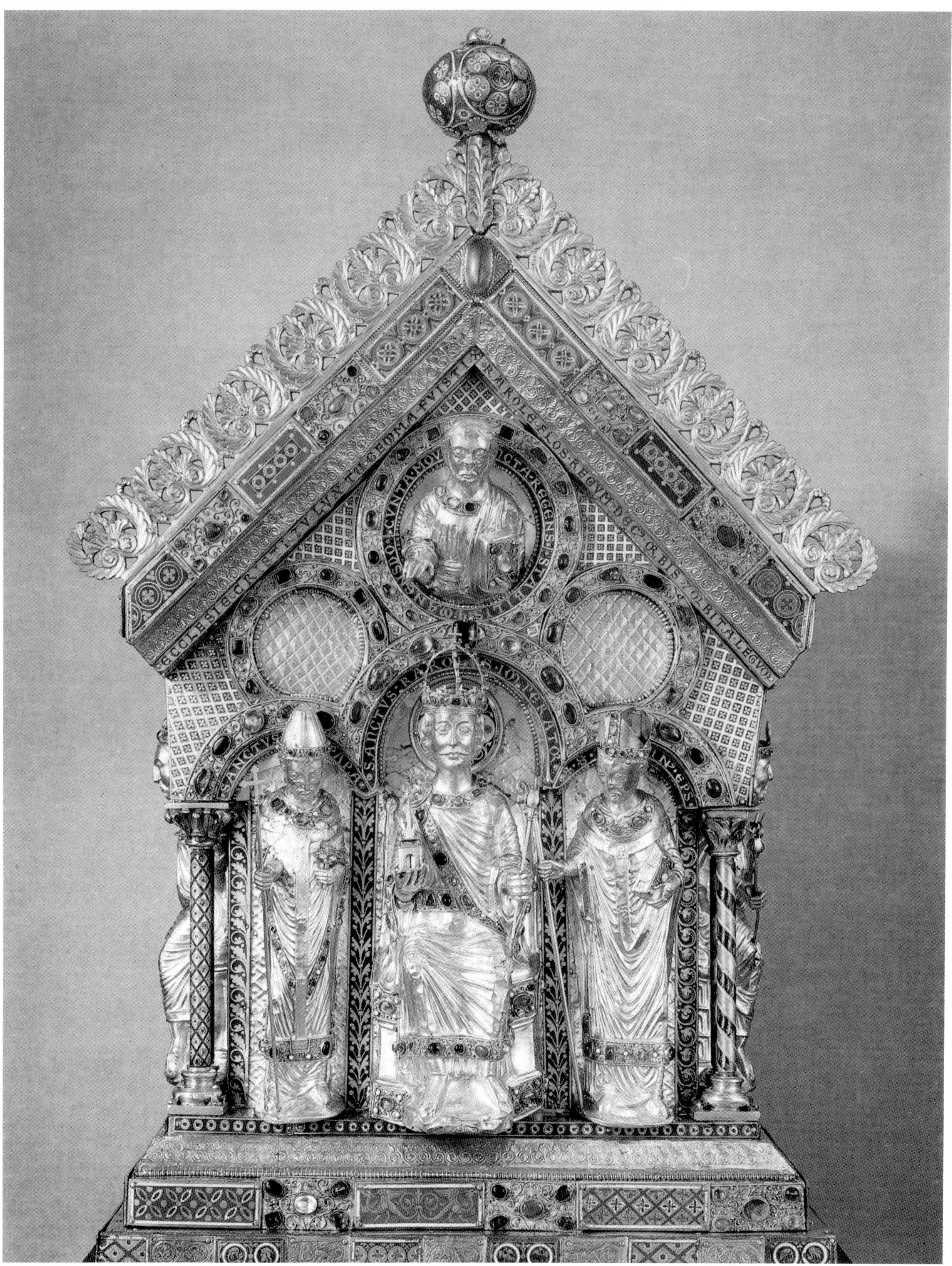

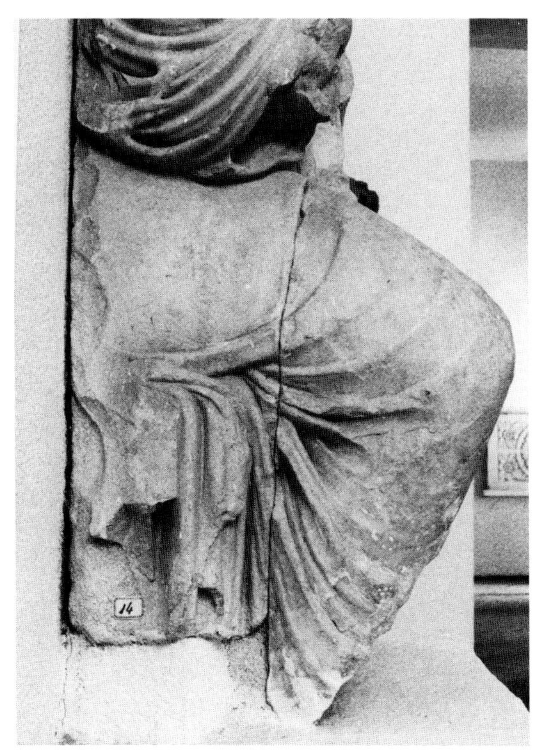

5. Reliquiario di Carlomagno ("Karlsschrein")
Duomo, Aquisgrana (Aachen); fotografia: Ann Münchow, Domkapitel, Aachen

6. Statua mutila dell'imperatore Federico II
Museo provinciale campano, Capua; fotografia: Valentino Pace

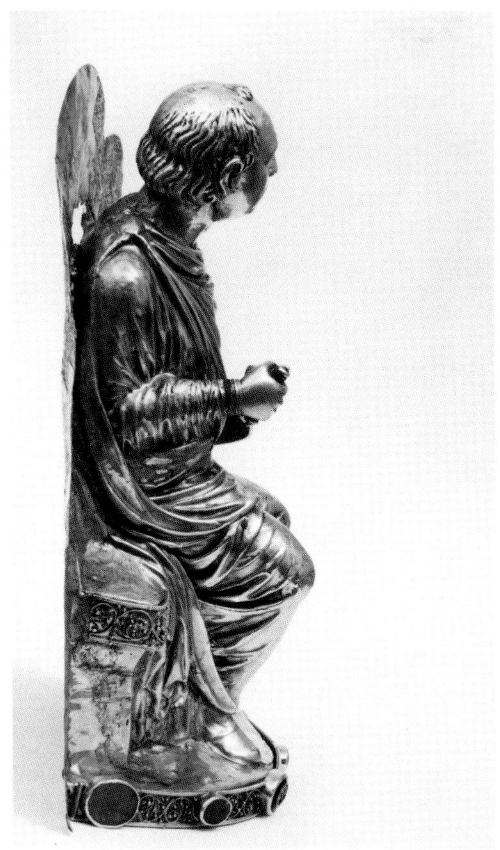

7. Reliquiario dei Tre Re Magi ("Dreikönigenschrein"), profeta Giona (durante il restauro)
Duomo, Colonia (Köln); fotografia: Rheinisches Bildarchiv, Köln

cativamente consonante con la "statuaria" (dirla "microstatuaria" parrebbe riduttivo) orafa sviluppata nelle terre dell'impero: è, a mio avviso, illuminante il confronto con la figura di Carlomagno stesso sul suo scrigno-reliquiario di Aquisgrana (fig. 5).[9] È di certo vero che differenze formali continuano a sussistere, ma l'indicazione della similitudine compositiva è preziosa nella misura in cui essa concretamente suggerisce da quale "area" di modelli Federico stesso possa essere stato suggestionato nel formulare e indirizzare i suoi "artisti" alla "visione classica della realtà" (per usare l'espressione dello Gnudi). È, soprattutto, di significativo interesse una duplice circostanza: che lo scrigno di Carlomagno sia stato concluso proprio in tempo per essere collocato nel duomo di Aquisgrana quando, nel 1215, Federico vi fu consacrato re di Germania; e che in esso sia stato sottolineato l'aspetto precorritore del programma capuano.[10]

Il rinvio allo scrigno di Carlomagno, *storicamente* concreto e *compositivamente* significativo, legittimamente autorizza a sondare la possibilità che il tramite *formale* per l'attivazione del "classicismo" federiciano sia stato svolto da oreficerie tedesche (o mosane). Quando, allora, si osservi ancora una volta la statua capuana dell'imperatore e, soprattutto, l'articolazione del suo panneggio (in particolare sulla sua destra) (figg. 1, 6) si scoprirà che essa, al di là dell'obbedienza al modello classico, è declinata proprio secondo quei canoni formali del "Muldenfaltenstil" che significativamente caratterizzano l'arte europea intorno al 1200 e che dalla produzione orafa di Nicolas de Verdun—in particolare da quel suo eccelso capolavoro che è lo scrigno dei re magi di Colonia—sono significativamente esemplati.[11] A titolo esemplificativo si valutino in proposito le possibilità di confronto della statua federiciana con le "statue" del profeta Geremia (fig. 4), o del profeta Giona (fig. 7).

Se così stanno le cose si può oltretutto rispondere concretamente a quella cruciale domanda che sempre, per correttezza metodologica, dovrebbe essere posta quanto ci si occupa della "trasmissione" e "ricezione" di uno "stile." Se, infatti, per il caso "capuano" non si sostiene l'inverosimile tesi che lo scultore sia stato egli stesso stato un francese (o, comunque, uno scultore proveniente da altre terre) deve allora pensarsi a quale canale di trasmissione possa aver reso possibile il fatto che uno scultore attivo a Capua e programmaticamente indirizzato a imitare l'arte antica ne abbia poi interpretato le forme secondo modi operativi del "gotico europeo."[12] Che poi a uno scultore campano (quale probabilmente egli fu) riuscisse di integrare così perfettamente il modello antico con quello medievale, non credo che debbano esserci ostacoli al ritenerlo possibile. Un caso analogo si era d'altronde già presentato tempo prima, a Salerno, per il cui duomo lo scultore del lettorino dei chierici, sul pulpito d'Ajello, aveva operato un'interpretazione antichizzante verosimilmente mediata anch'essa da modelli dell'oreficeria mosana.[13] Che, inoltre, fosse possibile operare formalmente in questa direzione mimetica dell'Antichità è ben evidenziato sia da altre parti dello stesso pulpito e dal vicino candelabro, sia dall'altro pulpito nel medesimo duomo salernitano.[14] È perfettamente vero che tra nessuno di quei pulpiti e la statua capuana c'è forma alcuna di passaggio, ma è ovvio che la forbice cronologica di più di cinquant'anni implichi diversità di situazioni, formali e mentali—di artista e di committente—delle quali non si può non tenere conto, così come non può non tenersi conto dei diversi requisiti imposti dalle specificità delle diverse situazioni.

Poiché nel caso della statua di Federico II il modello antico fu, per esigenza rappresentativa, un modello monumentale ciò comportò una più evidente adesione a quei modelli e un più spiccato risalto sul panorama della precedente produzione artistica, fino ad allora caratterizzata soprattutto da arredi liturgici di minore formato.

È nel tragitto dal progetto ideologico che le motiva e dalle scelte iconografiche che ne conseguono, fino ai modi esecutivi che le realizzano che si motiva la specificità della scelta espressiva capuana. Essa produce risultati diversi nella misura in cui diversi furono gli scultori e soprattutto diversi furono i loro modelli. Costante resta tuttavia il progetto estetico e ideologico. Così si spiega che ben diversa dalla statua dell'imperatore sia, come sempre osservato, l'immagine della monumentale testa della "Iustitia imperialis" (fig. 8) anch'essa peraltro non meno antichizzante.

Benché gravemente erosa dal tempo, anche

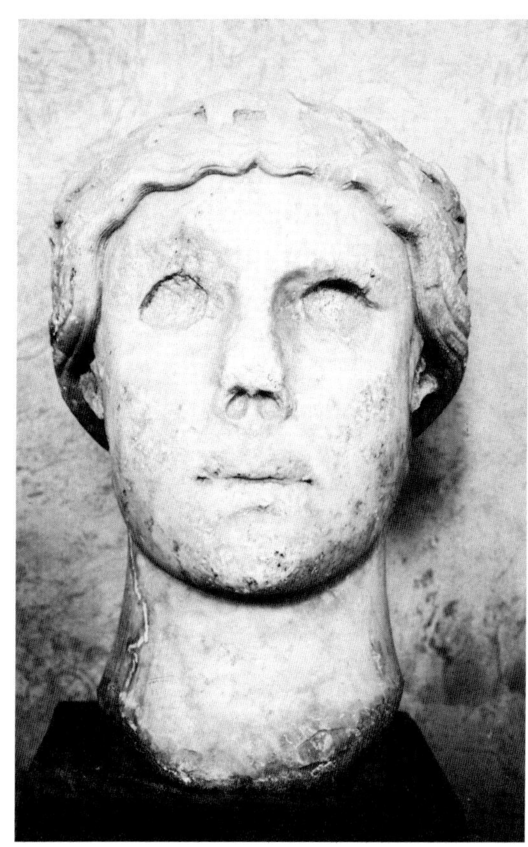

8. Testa della cosidetta "Iustitia imperialis"
Museo provinciale campano, Capua; fotografia: Soprintendenza ai Beni Artistici e Storici, Napoli

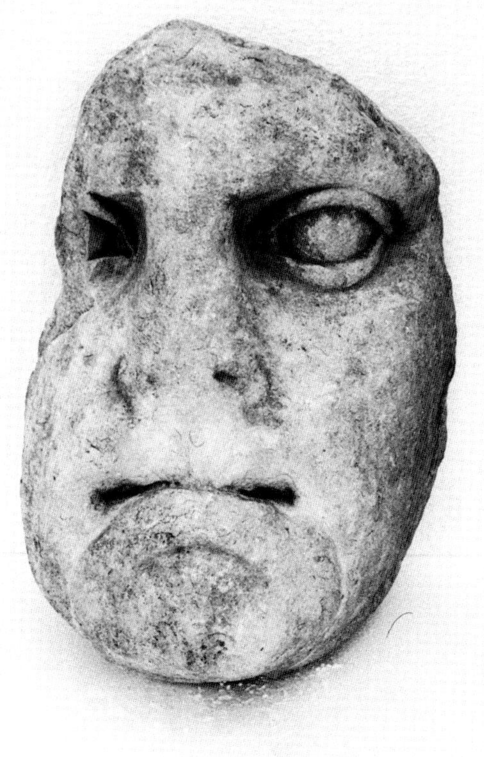

9. Testa frammentaria (dal Tempio adrianeo di "Venere e Roma")
Musei capitolini (depositi), Roma; fotografia: autore

di quest'opera può indirizzarsene l'ascendenza nella monumentale plastica romana di età imperiale, di cui possono essere qui usati come significative referenze una testa frammentaria di età adrianea rinvenuta nell'area capitolina (fig. 9) e altre simili protomi dal Tempio di Venere e Roma. Per la perduta immagine d'insieme può suggerirsi un modello sul tipo della statua di divinità o di personificazione femminile quale la famosa "Madama Letizia" romana.[15] Riconosciute le sue ascendenze antiche, ciò non toglie che, ancora una volta, possano coglierví varianti "moderne" o, comunque, indicative di un clima figurativo non più "antico." Così è per il sottile tralcio di vite che si dirama sulla sua capigliatura (nell'antichità pagana di esclusiva pertinenza dell'iconografia bacchica), così pure per la pettinatura innaturalmente bipartita nella stilizzazione sulla calotta cranica e nel fluido raccordo laterale che si conclude nel nodo sulla nuca.[16]

Le altre sculture di maggior prestigio del programma capuano sono quelle dei due cosiddetti "giudici." È a proposito di queste sculture che, da Ferdinando Bologna, è stata posta sul tappeto la questione "provenzale." Il loro scultore, cui spetterebbe anche la protome leonina (tanto da prendere il nome di "maestro del leone"), denuncerebbe "fondamenti romanico-provenzali," derivati dalla scultura "tarda di Elne, Arles-sur-Tech e Perpignano" con la cui chiesa di Saint Jean-le-vieux lo studioso ha prodotto uno specifico confronto. Ma tali confronti accertano soltanto un medesimo contesto classicista fra le diverse opere, senza comunque imporre di credere che tra loro sia stata in opera una qualsiasi relazione diretta, la cui esistenza non è oltretutto neppure necessariamente suggerita o avvalorata da altri fenomeni di cultura, all'incirca coevi.[17] Il giudizio sui busti capuani va necessariamente anch'esso contestualizzato alla loro collocazione. Eseguiti per essere inseriti entro clipei, essi hanno in primo luogo una forma non-antica. Ne deriva pure che essi "di profilo mancano" così come essi "mancano anche di prospetto" (come ha giustamente osservato il Bologna) senza che tuttavia debba necessariamente inferirsi una pregiudizievole caduta del loro tono classicista. Questi busti non dovevano essere visti di profilo e non pretendevano di caratterizzarsi con criteri ottici di antichizzante tridimensionalità. Se già la loro reciproca similitudine (di fisiognomia e di veste)—che per prima ne nega ogni valenza ritrattistica—sta a sottolinearne il valore di effigi simboliche, ciò che proprio deve sapersi apprezzare è la loro calibrata impostazione ottica e coerenza compositiva: ben ordinate le pieghe del manto si raccolgono nel nodo centrale e lasciano risaltare la testa, impiantata vigorosamente e spaziosamente sul busto. Ciascuna delle teste è caratterizzata dallo sguardo di occhi dalle pupille forate (per contenere una pasta oggi caduta), dalla barba fluente e trapanata, dalla calotta cranica solcata da una stilizzata rete di capelli—come nella scultura greca del V secolo, copiata ancora in età adrianea.[18] L'altra scultura che è stata assegnata allo stesso scultore—la protome leonina (fig. 10)—dimostra bene anch'essa con quanta attenzione i modelli antichi siano stati studiati, pur se di necessità fatti coesistere con modi formali "moderni." Per quanto infatti esplicitamente assertiva di una tendenza antichizzante per la stessa scelta d'immagine e per l'accurata resa del pelame a ciocche (come in leoni romani che poterono certamente essere visti e studiati)[19] è infatti ovvio che la specificità della sua destinazione a protome e l'inarcata monumentalità della fiera rispondono a criteri figurativi "non-antichi."

Altre mensole o protomi, ideologicamente del tutto "neutrali," mostrano comunque una significativa propensione a sviluppare un linguaggio diverso, *meno* vincolato alla norma "classica." È, per esempio il caso della splendida protome femminile—di cosiddetta "fisionomia graziosa" (fig. 15)—che introduce nell'arte federiciana quel precipuo carattere di equilibrio fra la ricezione di un modello classico e la sua interpretazione in termini di moderna sensibilità espressiva (il trattamento delle cavità orbitali, l'iride forata, eccetera) che si ritroverà anni dopo a Lagopesole (fig. 16). L'esito a cui essa perviene, cui perviene pure la bella mensola con testa virile dal doppio giro di capelli arricciolati, è tuttavia anche in questo caso assai difficilmente precisabile in termini formali, perché d'un lato non ha radici formali in Italia meridionale, d'altro lato non ha neppure cogenti assonanze con la scultura d'oltralpe (tali, cioè, da potersi assegnare a scultore "d'importazione" o potersene reperire i precisi modelli).[20] Compositivamente impensabile senza modelli che in questo caso sembrano peraltro essere stati indiscutibilmente francesi—anche se non deve di necessità pensarsi che agissero qui a Capua, negli anni trenta, per la prima volta—è invece il capitello binato a fogliame.[21]

In conclusione: così come avverrà a Castel del Monte, anche per Capua è giocoforza presupporre una già consolidata trama di condizioni operative (la perdita totale di un monumento come il palazzo imperiale di Foggia non può, a questo proposito, essere sufficientemente lamentata!) create dalla presenza di artisti (italomeridionali e non), di opere (antiche e moderne, di marmo o di metalli preziosi, monumentali e non), di materiale di lavoro (libri di disegno e simili) di cui, sconsolatamente, non resta più nulla se non l'*indiretta* testimonianza di queste sculture stesse.[22] Il programma figurativo voluto dal suo committente implicò consapevolmente connotazioni ideologiche "imperiali" e per tale ragione sviluppò consapevolmente un linguaggio formale strenuamente modellato sull'esempio dell'arte imperiale romana. Quella "ripresa" dell'antichità fu realizzata da scultori che si avvalsero dei modelli antichi disponibili, declinandoli figurativamente in un linguaggio che tuttavia non potè non essere "moderno" (ovvero "medievale") sia per la specificità della sua funzione e del suo contesto, sia pure per la disponibilità di altri modelli, d'oltralpe—opere o libri di disegni che fossero.

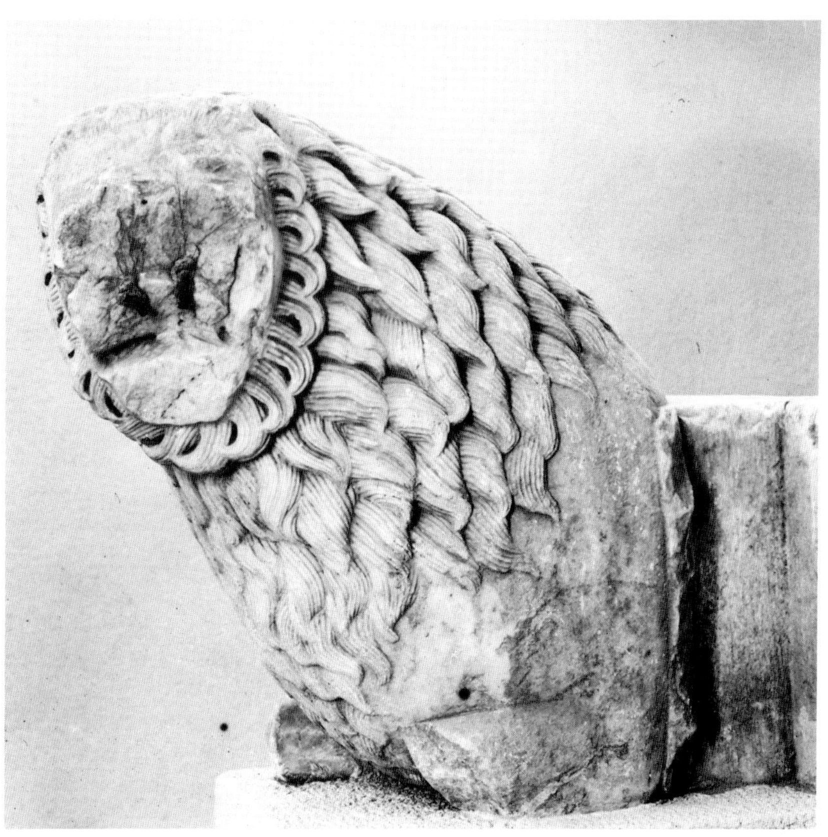

Nell'impresa immediatamente posteriore a Capua, quella di Castel del Monte, il quesito delle origini formali della sua scultura si ripresenta con lo stesso vigore, anche se esso cambia sostanzialmente di segno. Il "modello classico," dominante a Capua, vi perde infatti la sua normatività ideologica e, dunque, figurativa: da un castello di destinazione privata non è necessario trasmettere un messaggio di valenza sociale e il programma stabilito dall'imperatore ha scarso bisogno di modelli classici di supporto.[23] Ciò non toglie che, proprio sul portale d'ingresso, esso vi persista e sia affidato, oltre che all'impaginazione compositiva, alle due figure leonine di simbolica valenza, aggettanti sulle colonnine laterali (fig. 11). Pur essendo formalmente diverse dal loro omologo capuano,

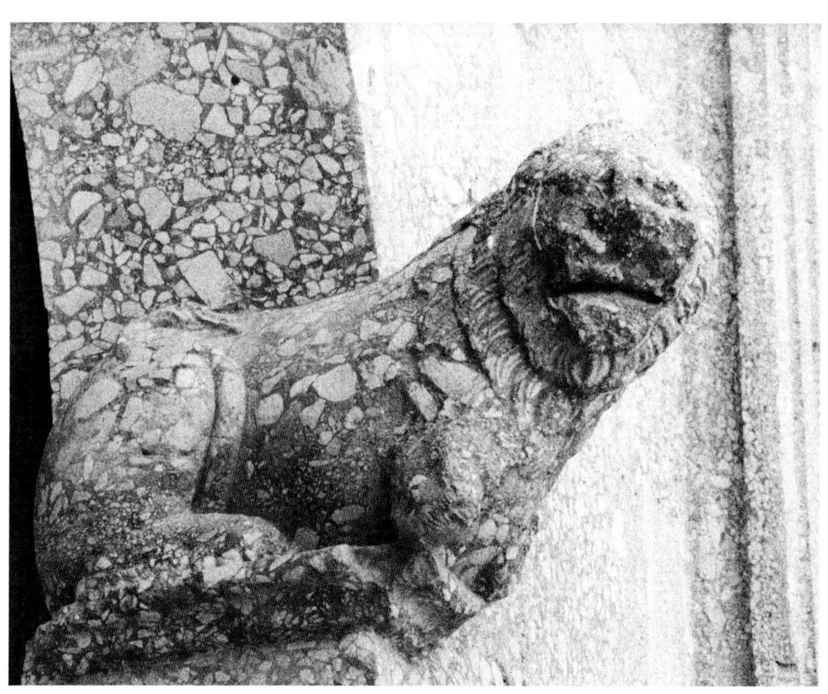

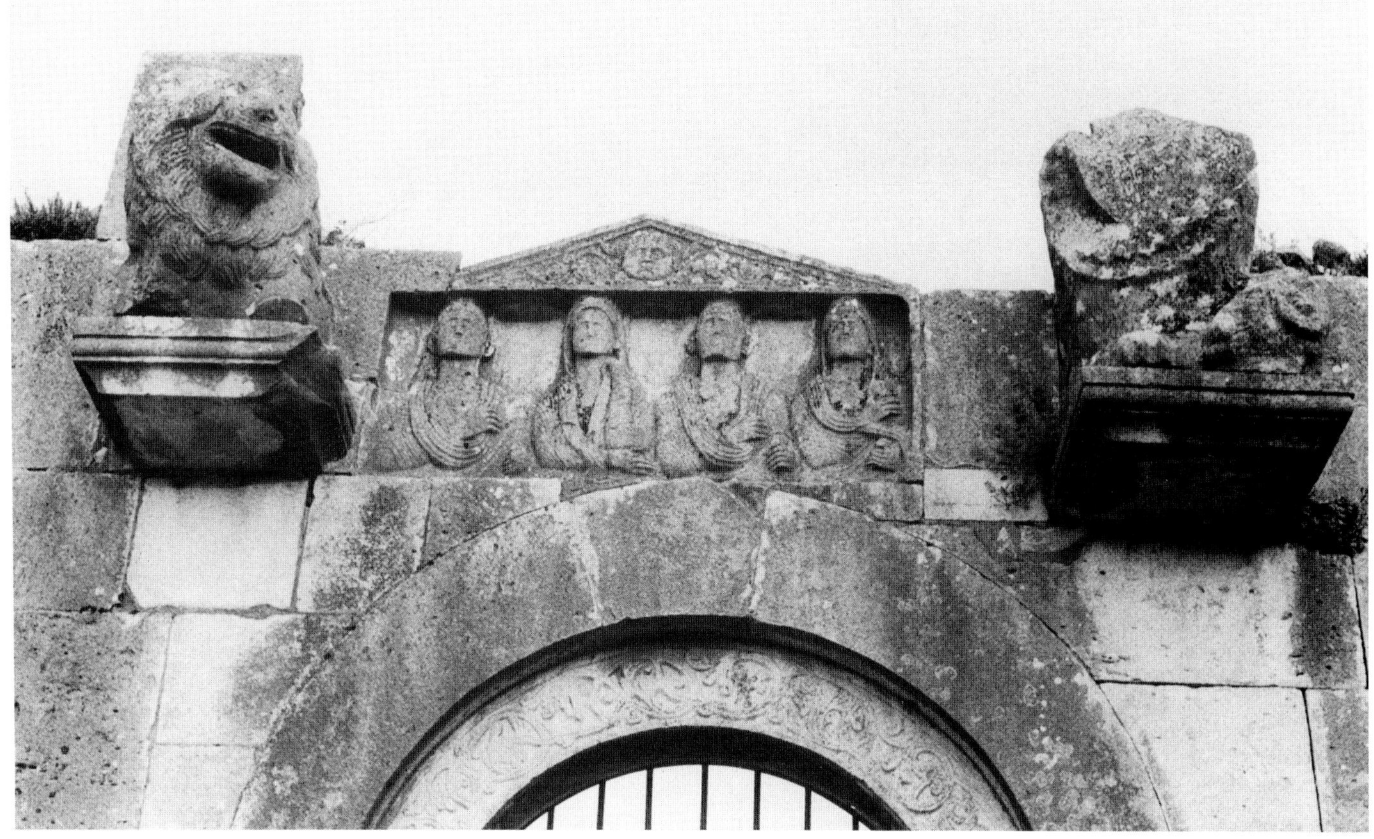

10. Protome leonina
Museo provinciale campano, Capua; fotografia: Soprintendenza ai Beni Artistici e Storici, Napoli

11. Castel del Monte, portale d'ingresso: leone
Fotografia: autore

12. Santissima Trinità, Venosa, portale d'ingresso al transetto settentrionale
Fotografia: autore

anch'esse sono modellate su prototipi antichi, nel contempo tenendo già presente, per collocazione, l'*uso* dell'antichità operato dalle fabbriche medievali, come—per fare solo un esempio—nella Trinità di Venosa (fig. 12).

A Castel del Monte la scultura figurativa occupa un ruolo sostanzialmente marginale e sono soprattutto gli stupefacenti capitelli, diversissimi fra loro, a esemplare l'altissimo livello qualitativo dei suoi scultori—quasi al pari di quello del suo straordinario architetto. Questi capitelli, e con essi le raffinate modanature architettoniche esprimono con eleganza innovative forme "gotiche" che non possono farsi rifluire totalmente nella cultura architettonica cistercense, delle cui maestranze è ben noto l'apporto ai cantieri federiciani, ma fanno presupporre la disponibilità di modelli francesi, in parte già individuati a Reims e alla Sainte-Chapelle, in parte ancora da individuare.[24]

Meno esplicita al riguardo è la scultura figurativa. Oltre che dai leoni d'ingresso e dai problematici frammenti inglobati sulla parete del cortile ottagonale, essa è rappresentata soltanto dai celebri "telamoni," dalle altrettanto celebri mensole e da un paio di chiavi di volta. Di essi il Poeschke, la Calò Mariani, la Romanini hanno scritto che la loro cultura figurativa s'inquadra in un contesto di ascendenze franco-tedesche, precisate con rinvii a Reims e Bamberg.[25]

Non nego che ci siano suggestive ragioni per suggerire questi raccordi, ma credo che un'impostazione metodologicamente corretta dell'analisi storico-artistica debba procedere oltre ed esplicitamente precisare non solo i limiti di un tale inquadramento—sempre indicati—ma anche i modi con cui esso si concretò. Ciò non soltanto per evitare che col richiamo a quelle carismatiche ascendenze si annulli l'intrinseca e distintiva specificità del monumento pugliese (e, essendo la questione valida per tutto il contesto figurativo "federiciano," degli altri monumenti italomeridionali nei quali si colgano analoghe premesse), ma anche perché il fenomeno sia storicizzato con la necessaria precisione e chiarezza. Un quesito del genere va dunque preliminarmente ramificato su linee differenziate: in primissimo luogo quella relativa ai "modelli" (modelli che, oltretutto, poterono combinarsi insieme); in secondo luogo, quella relativa all'esecuzione, senza poter ovviamente trascurare la specificità del contesto.

Per quanto attiene le chiavi di volta, quella di "testa fogliata" offre un caso esemplare. Indiscutibile la trama dei rapporti che sono stati segnalati con gli analoghi *motivi* espressi da Reims a Bamberg, la cui fama fu anche eternata dai disegni di Villard de Honnecourt.[26] Il tramite dei libri di modelli è dunque assolutamente plausibile e che a far circolare questi libri provvedessero artisti d'oltralpe o di Puglia—da lì di ritorno—è questione al limite qui secondaria perché non conduce ad accertare l'anagrafe artistica dello scultore stesso (cioè, della chiave di volta in questione).

Ben più difficile il caso dei celebri telamoni del settimo torrioncino e delle due mensole superstiti del terzo torrioncino. I telamoni sono sei uomini, nudi e a gambe divaricate, alcuni nell'esplicito atto di sostenere il peso sovrastante, altri apparentemente indifferenti alla fatica (fig. 13).[27] La loro apparizione è certamente suggestiva, sia perché il "tipo" di telamone non ha una folta tradizione nell'Italia meridionale, sia per la loro nudità. Se comunque l'idea di collocare scultura figurativa sotto mensole non era di per sè innovativa, appartenendo alla consolidata tradizione della scultura architettonica, essa qui lo divenne nel momento in cui per essa si scelsero a soggetto telamoni *nudi*, estranei alla specifica tradizione iconografica—fatto salvo qualche raro precedente.[28] Sia per questa specificità iconografica, sia ancor di più per la loro realizzazione plastica e per il loro ruolo di membrature architettoniche—ben evidenziato dalla Romanini[29]—i telamoni di Castel del Monte non appartengono tuttavia alla cultura figurativa francese, apparendo in verità piuttosto distanti dall'esempio di Reims—con cui sono stati specificamente confrontati. Se una relazione *formale* deve essere trovata, essa va semmai localizzata nell'area delle cattedrali padane, in particolare sui portali scolpiti da Niccolò o dalla sua bottega.[30] È tuttavia una relazione che chiarisce *solo* il preesistente impiego del motivo in una formulazione orientativamente simile (negli ovvi limiti di una distanza cronologica e stilistica di più generazioni, che ha peraltro il vantaggio di sottrarsi a ogni tentazione di far presupporre legami troppo diretti—come appunto si è supposto per Reims) ma che lascia inalterata la soluzione del problema in merito alla specifica, contestuale motivazione. Deciso infatti (da parte di chi?) l'impiego della forma telamone—che la si sia "vista" in Padania e/o la si sia ritrovata su libri di modelli—questa "forma" venne realizzata diversamente da quanto potè essere così conosciuto. In merito alla rara scelta iconografica (la nudità) fu verosimilmente proprio l'intelligenza del "progettista"—che capì il valore di articolazione spaziale delle sculture, ovvero la loro relazione con lo spazio architettonico—a motivarla. Queste sculture mostrano infatti una forma plastica che sa

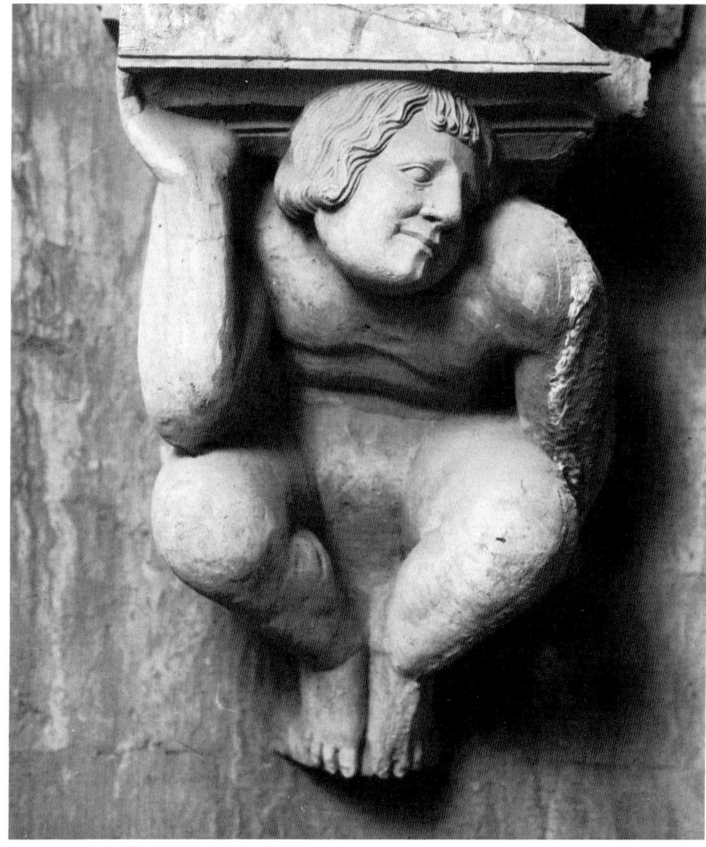

13. Castel del Monte, settima torretta, telamone
Fotografia: Istituto centrale per il catalogo e la documentazione Roma (ICCD)

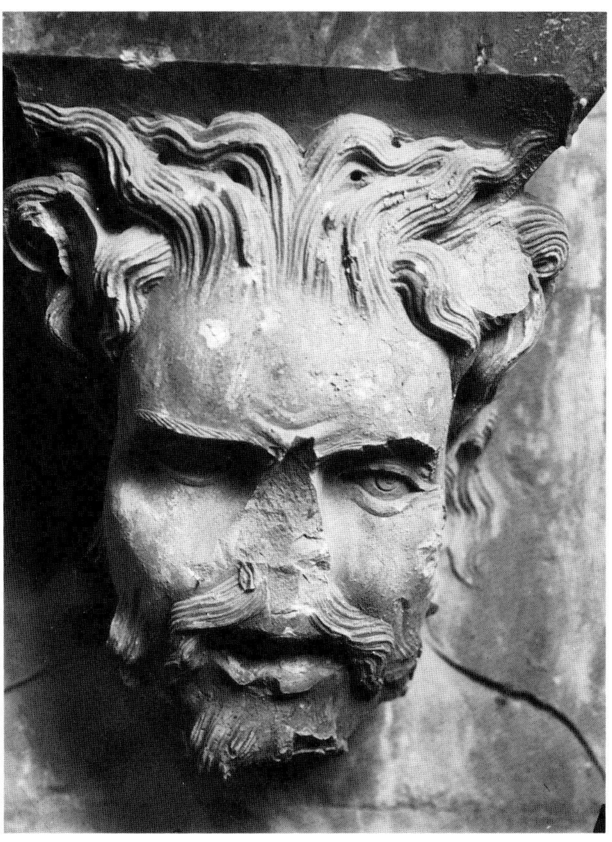

14. Castel del Monte, terza torretta, mensola con testa di fauno
Fotografia: ICCD, Roma

adeguarsi allo spazio architettonico, articolando le sue componenti figurative in consapevole rispondenza con le nervature sovrastanti (così le gambe *divaricate*) variando nel contempo le valenze d'immagine con espressioni differenziate e, soprattutto, con una sempre diversa gestualità (si osservino la diversa posizione delle braccia) che segna dinamicamente lo spazio.[31] Sembra cioè non azzardato pensare che la scelta delle figure *nude* sia avvenuta (ovvero: sia avvenuta *anche*) per consapevole intelligenza della loro possibile funzione di vere e proprie membrature architettoniche (a dimostrazione di ciò può valere il fatto che, per converso, esse non sarebbero potute essere tali se fossero state ammantate di vesti, come appunto i telamoni padani). Che, poi, queste figure nude siano state rese con così pronunciata volumetria—a palese contrasto con la suprema eleganza della *Bauplastik* francese—potè essere dovuto sia al loro intrinseco carattere "architettonico," sia pure alla propensione verso tali forme della stessa tradizione plastica pugliese.[32] Indipendentemente, infine, dalla ragione per la quale esse furono rappresentate nude resta da chiedersi perché in un paio di casi la loro nudità è anche sessualmente ben caratterizzata, mentre negli altri non lo è.[33]

Quando si pensi ai ben noti interessi per la verità della natura da parte dell'imperatore l'osservazione non può che dar adito a sorpresa e assume un preciso interesse. Si vorrebbe infatti sapere di più sul rapporto del monarca con l'ideazione e con l'esecuzione di *questo* programma, a maggior ragione quando si ricorda di quale carica ideologica e personale si è rivestita l'architettura del Castello stesso.[34] Troppo lontani dunque dai supposti modelli francesi, questi telamoni palesano cadenze "gotiche" di tipo soltanto estrinseco: si tratti dei segni della "moda" coeva—dalla cuffia alle pettinature—oppure di morfemi esecutivi ("motivi di stile") quali la coda dell'occhio siglata da sottili rughe.

Per le due teste-mensola il quesito impone una stessa trama metodologica, ma deve tenere nel giusto conto il diverso, altissimo, livello qualitativo raggiunto nel dettaglio *esecutivo* da una delle due mensole—quella "faunesca" (fig. 14). Se per i telamoni è infatti legittima la resistenza a pensarli eseguiti da uno scultore d'oltralpe e per l'altra mensola (quella femminile) la sua pertinenza italomeridionale è dimostrata dalle ulteriori tappe di lavoro del suo scultore—o del suo stretto seguito[35]—nel caso dello scultore della mensola faunesca si è di fronte a una personalità che non ha possibilità alcuna di confronto, in nessun'altra opera del suo tempo, "federiciana" o non. È uno scultore che rifinisce con estrema accuratezza ed eleganza le forme plastiche, quasi cesellandole, ottonendo risultati di patetismo espressivo analogo a quello della scultura romana di età antonina, di cui forse fu in grado di studiare opere (si osservi pure che egli è l'unico, a Castel del Monte, a rifinire gli occhi con l'iride). Come in Puglia, così a Reims non ha confronti. Pur se, tentati dalla suggestione della sua qualità, si indirizzi a ricercarne la provenienza dal cantiere di quella cattedrale o da altri limitrofi, la conclusione è negativa. Ad analoga conclusione negativa si è d'altronde costretti anche per altre personalità di primissimo piano della scultura "federiciana": per esempio, senza ritornare a caso di Capua, per lo scultore dell'eccelso "ritratto" nel museo di Berlino-Dahlem, esemplare testimonianza del livello qualitativo raggiunto dalla "promozione artistica" di Federico.

Quando allora si torni a sottolineare che Castel del Monte è quasi la tappa finale del percorso artistico della scultura federiciana, non dovrà più destare sorpresa che per alcune opere non possa farsi altro che constatarne la qualità e presupporne le radici genetiche in quell'ambiente, ricco di artisti e di modelli, di opere antiche e di opere moderne, che fu appunto la corte federiciana.

In questa prospettiva vanno anche contestualizzate le due splendide mensole di Lagopesole, di cui quella femminile (fig. 16) è stata suggestivamente confrontata, dalla Calò Mariani, con la Sinagoga di Strasburgo e, assai meno credibilmente, da altra studiosa, con teste della Galleria dei re di Giuda di Nôtre Dame.[36] La testa femminile è caratterizzata da tratti fisiognomici presenti con la medesima purezza di linee nel patrimonio classico italomeridionale—a confronto valga il rinvio ad alcune teste di età imperiale oggi conservate nel museo di Foggia.[37] Il coglierne pertanto assonanze con Strasburgo (quelle con Parigi è meglio lasciarle perdere) individua appunto la comune operatività di modelli classici, la cui "traduzione" nelle forme plastiche duecentesche assume peraltro, a ben guardare, flessioni formali leggermente differenti lì (a Strasburgo) e qui (a Lagopesole). Posteriore sia a Castel del Monte che a Capua, la scultura di Lagopesole potè senza dubbio avvalersi del patrimonio di esperienze artistiche ormai accumulatosi nella cerchia delle committenze federiciane. "In lontananza," dunque con le dovute varianti (non è la stessa "mano") la testa femminile di Lagopesole si allinea con alcune delle più belle "teste" dell'architettura capuana—la bella protome femminile (fig. 15) e la mensola con testa virile[38]—convincentemente inserendosi in uno dei solchi già tracciati dalla scultura federiciana.

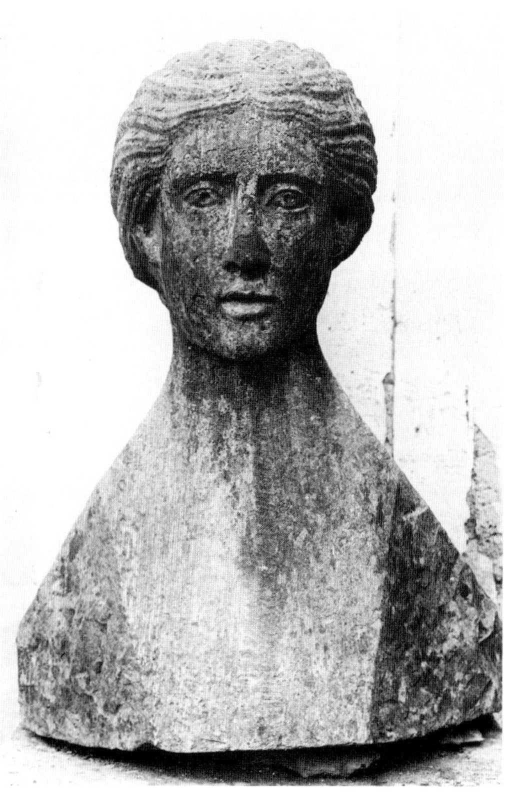

15. Antefissa con testa femminile
Museo provinciale campano, Capua; fotografia: Soprintendenza ai Beni Artistici e Storici, Napoli

Sia nel caso di Lagopesole, sia pure per gli altri cantieri federiciani si è supposto che l'operatività delle influenti forze figurative gotiche sia stata attivata dai viaggi dell'imperatore e dai suoi conseguenti apprezzamenti dei più recenti sviluppi artistici nelle terre da lui visitate, con il diretto apporto di artisti di lì importati.[39] Nel più restrittivo inquadramento che si è qui adottato per questo fenomeno l'ipotesi dei "viaggi" imperiali diviene di conseguenza largamente superflua e, comunque, inconclusiva. Le eventuali presenze di artisti d'oltralpe per l'esecuzione di committenze federiciane non devono infatti "spiegarsi" di necessità con i viaggi imperiali e con la geografia dei loro itinerari, soprattutto se si pensa che proprio le aree francesi da cui si vorrebbe far provenire questi artisti non furono—di regola—toccate da questi "viaggi."[40] Anche tenendo conto del documentato interesse di Feredico II per i fatti d'arte, mi sembra oltretutto non corrispondente al concreto corso degli eventi l'idea di un imperatore che approfittasse dei suoi spostamenti per volgerli in *grand tour* e dargli adito a reclutare maestri e maestranze per le sue committenze di là da venire nell'Italia meridionale. Indipendentemente dal preciso livello di "sviluppo stilistico" cui si attestano, o si vogliono fare attestare le opere

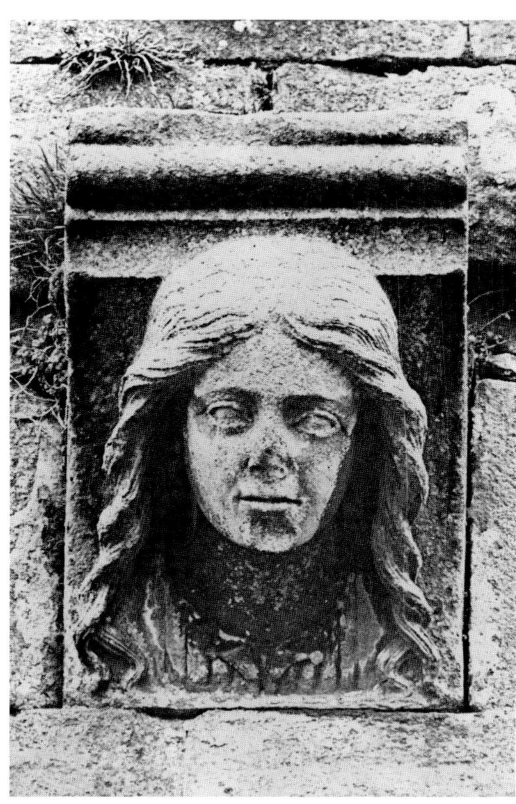

16. Castello di Lagopesole, mensola con testa femminile
Fotografia: DAI, Roma

"gotiche" federiciane, ciò che preliminarmente e soprattutto conta è il fatto, al limite troppo dimenticato, che l'imperatore ebbe tempo di formare e maturare il suo "gusto" già nei lunghi anni di soggiorno nelle sue terre durante il secondo decennio.[41] Al suo ritorno in Italia egli rimase consapevole della modernità raggiunta dalle arti figurative d'oltralpe. Che nella sua veste di imperatore-committente egli abbia potuto mantenere vivi i canali d'afflusso (per opere e per artisti) con le terre imperiali è un fatto che ha la plausibilità di un assioma e permette facilmente di evitare il ricorso alla meccanicistica tesi dei suoi "viaggi."

È il *palatium* di Foggia che avrebbe potuto offrirci la conoscenza su quel "primo" stadio di sviluppo dell'arte "federiciana" che non ci è stato trasmesso. Che il cornicione della cattedrale possa surrogarcelo resta dubbio: suggestivo che sia, il confronto con il minimo quoziente di scultura sull'archivolto non può infatti legittimamente farne desumere stessa data o stesso maestro, nè può autorizzarci a credere che nel perduto palazzo si sviluppassero forme plastiche analoghe a quelle del cornicione.[42] Non è questa la sede per discutere partitamente i quesiti, cronologici e formali, del cornicione foggiano, ma non può dunque eludersi la questione della sua eventuale "inerenza" all'"arte federiciana." Di certo può dirsi che esso, assai suggestivo per la violenta espressività delle sue immagini umane e ferine, per la sua spinosa vegetazione, è lontanissimo da quello che è documentatamente collegato altrove al patrocinio imperiale e riesce difficile pensare che simili forme si ritrovassero nel Palazzo.[43] Nella cattedrale di Foggia, come in quella di Troia e altrove (in primis, per il livello qualitativo, nella cattedrale di Trani), si sviluppano quelle forme del cosiddetto "terzo romanico pugliese" che furono motivate da altre scelte-estetiche e furono largamente indebitate ad altro contesto di modelli, tanto occidentali quanto orientali, di nuova o antica importazione.[44]

Non è questa dunque arte "federiciana." Non lo è per qualità formale e non lo è, verosimilmente, per committenza, dal momento che è assai improbabile che Federico II si sia occupato della cattedrale foggiana e, in particolare, delle scelte "decorative" ivi espresse. C'è d'altronde solo un caso per il quale è documentato il diretto interesse dell'imperatore per una fabbrica ecclesiale: ad Altamura, dove è peraltro significativo che *non* siano stati assunti modelli architettonici *moderni*, ma si sia sostanzialmente continuata la tradizione "barese," pur con qualche variante.[45] Può essere qui significativo ricordare il ben diverso uso "ideologico" delle forme achitettoniche ecclesiali da parte del sovrano che scalzò la dinastia sveva dall'Italia meridionale, Carlo d'Angiò: la chiesa di San Lorenzo maggiore a Napoli, con il suo coro "francese" ne dà la piena evidenza.[46] Ad Altamura anche la stessa scultura, in quelle pochissime parti dove è ancora duecentesca, non denota connotati formali assumibili in un contesto "federiciano."[47]

L'"indifferenza" di Federico, ovvero l'"irrelazionabilità" a scelte attuate dall'imperatore per quanto avveniva nell'ambito delle forme e delle immagini in contesti ecclesiali, coincide bene con quanto sappiamo del suo carattere "laico." Che, lui in vita, gli altri committenti non sempre—anzi, di rado—abbiano saputo adeguarsi al suo livello di scelte, è ben comprensibile. Due opposti casi possono comunque qui esporsi: quello del pulpito bitontino e quello dei capitelli troiani.

Quale ne sia il significato preciso—differentemente colto dallo Schaller e dal Paratore, dalla Neu-Kock e dal Thelen—è comunque convincimento comune a tutti gli studiosi che sul pulpito di Bitonto è rappresentato Federico II e che quel rilievo implica tematicamente una diretta valenza "federiciana," si tratti di rilievo storico o simbolico.[48] È altrettanto chiaro a tutti che il rilievo non si avvale di una qualità plastica che sia in qualche modo positivamente confrontabile con la scultura di committenza federiciana o che, comunque, raggiunga un livello qualitativo di rilievo, a confronto con quanto fatto nella pertinente area geocronologica. È vero che la scelta di un "regalo" denota il gusto di chi lo fa e non di chi lo riceve, ma rimane por sempre il fatto che un'opera tanto strettamente connessa con l'imperatore, di certo pensata perché egli la vedesse, mostra di non tenere affatto conto di quanto si realizzava al suo servizio.[49]

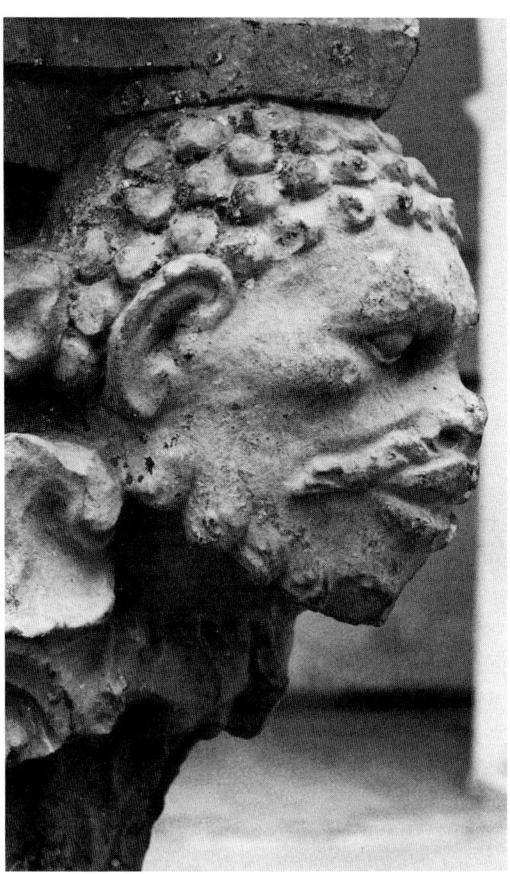

17. Capitello
Museo diocesano, Troia; fotografia: autore

Un caso opposto è quello dei celebri capitelli troiani (fig. 17) che, dopo essere stati resi noti dal Wentzel e dalla Ostoja, hanno immediatamente occupato un posto di rilievo a documentazione dei nessi francesi, per la precisione: chartrensi, della scultura "pugliese," ovvero "federiciana."[50] La referenza chartrense, ben indicata dal Wentzel—che pure altrettanto bene sottolineò le discordanze dal "gotico francese" della *forma* del capitello—e poi dallo Gnudi pare convincente, tanto più se per la data dei capitelli non vale l'*a quo* del 1229, postulato dal Wentzel, ma messo decisamente in dubbio dal Buschhausen (per il quale essi sono "kaum vor 1240 entstanden").[51] Non si sa quale fosse la loro originaria collocazione, così come non si sa nemmeno se essi siano stati originariamente destinati alla cattedrale troiana.[52] Se comunque si accetta che essi lo siano stati e che furono parte di un arredo ecclesiale, se si considera quanto si è qui sottolineato sull'"indifferenza" di Federico II alla sfera delle committenze di ambito ecclesiale, si dovrà allora conseguentemente evitare di applicare a questi capitelli quelle referenze "federiciane," che regolarmente li caratterizzano dal tempo della pubblicazione della Ostoja.[53] Qui, come altrove, occorre infatti, io credo, non lasciarsi prendere dalla suggestione di referenze *federiciane* per ogni aspetto moderno, dunque "gotico," della scultura italomeridionale di quel torno di tempo (a voler spingere al paradosso il "giusto" confronto chartrense, bisognerebbe convincersi di dover scorgere valenze federiciane a Chartres!). È invece apporto dello scultore dei capitelli troiani, della sua "sensibilità" artistica, l'aver promosso questa raffinata e variata rappresentazione di umanità nella sua opera, in conformità alle esigenze di cultura (non solo figurativa) del mondo cui apparteneva—così come è prova d'intelligenza artistica dello sconosciuto committente l'essersi servito dell'opera di questo scultore.

Non solo, inoltre, la coincidenza del committente con Federico II è lungi dall'essere possibile, ma anche l'eventuale presenza di uno scultore francese in Capitanata—se davvero francese egli fu e non soltanto "francesizzante"—non deve necessariamente spiegarsi con le scelte artistiche dell'imperatore.

Un tale asserto sarebbe rischioso se si credesse che esso voglia negare l'ormai consolidata opinione storiografica di un Federico II quale esponente decisivo del rinnovamento artistico italomeridionale. Ciò invece *non* è. Si vuole qui piuttosto negare il ruolo *unico* (ma non quello *preminente*) di Federico II quale mediatore o introduttore del "gotico" in Italia meridionale. Si vuole cioè sottolineare la presenza di altri attori (nel ruolo di committenti) sulla scena italomeridionale, anche se questi restino anonimi e siano meno prestigiosi. Il caso di Troia lo evidenzia al massimo livello, altri ve ne sono che inducono a postulare la loro esistenza. È, in primo luogo, il caso della cattedrale di Termoli, per l'esattezza del programma scultoreo della sua facciata, datato con diversità di pareri ai due estremi del trentennio iniziale del tredicesimo secolo.[54] Il quesito coinvolto da Termoli è quello usuale e già posto per analoghe "novità" di committenza federiciana: in qual misura e in quali modi fu coinvolta la diretta esperienza d'oltralpe e di *quale* oltralpe. È un quesito cui occorre cercare di rispondere con una risposta che ancora una volta differenzi, se necessario, l'aspetto ideativo-compositivo e quello esecutivo, per non cadere in insoddisfacenti genericità.

Ciò che sulla facciata della cattedrale di Termoli sorprende—e non ha mancato di sollecitare risposte alla sua presenza—è l'inusuale collocazione di due statue su mensole circolari, sporgenti dal retrostante parato murario, appena più in basso dell'imposta dell'archivolto sul portale centrale (fig. 18).[55] Per la loro disposizione esse non possono a rigore definirsi "statue-colonna" (come pure lo sono state) né, conseguentemente, possono farsi ascendere alla pur rarissima tradizione dei portali a statue-colonna sulla sponda adriatica dell'Italia meridionale.[56] Se la loro idea compositiva non deve farsi di necessità risalire a eventuali modelli dei grandi portali gotici francesi, nemmeno il tema iconografico delle figurette "calpestate" dai colonnari santi richiede una tale cogente ascendenza. È vero che esso è testimoniato largamente da monumenti francesi—con più significativa vicinanza a Saint-Denis, a Chartres e a Parigi (Saint-Germain-l'Auxerrois)—ma esso lo è anche in Germania (e, altrettanto significativamente, dalla statuaria lignea), cosicché può solo affermarsi che una tale idea compositiva fu verosimilmente trasmessa da un modello europeo.[57]

Di certo in Francia non si ritrova, né nel dodicesimo né nel tredicesimo secolo, un'opera che possa convincentemente accostarsi a Termoli (si tratti delle statue o degli altri brani scultorei) in termini di *diretta* trasmissione stilistica. È altresì certo che nulla fa trasparire, nelle statue in questione, la conoscenza degli sviluppi gotici "maturi"—da Chartres nord ad Amiens e oltre.[58] La grafica incisione delle pieghe sulla veste (in modo esplicito tra la cintura e il ginocchio) del perduto s. Sebastiano mostra, al proposito, la sostanziale incomprensione delle valenze naturalistiche della scultura francese, non diversamente da quanto palesa la rigidità formale delle sculture, di accertata vicinanza stilistica a queste di Termoli, dell'abbaziale di San Giovanni in Venere.[59]

La *collocazione* delle statue di Termoli lascia presupporre modelli la cui ascendenza non deve cogliersi sulle facciate delle grandi cattedrali francesi, ma, ancora una volta, insospettatamente, sulle facciate degli scrigni tedeschi: è lì, tanto nello scrigno colonese dei re magi quanto in quello di Carlomagno (per rimanere ai monumenti già chiamati in causa per Capua) che sulle "facciate" si collocano figure che si sporgono lateralmente al protagonista centrale, collocandosi per giunta su ripiani circolari non troppo diversamente ammorsati alla parete di fondo (fig. 5).

L'esperienza della scultura francese torna comunque a palesarsi in altre parti della facciata: per esempio in un paio di testine coronate femminili, collocate frontalmente fra le volute vegetali d'angolo di un capitello (fig. 19) (secondo una consuetudine compositiva italomeridionale), il cui modello d'immagine e la cui ascendenza di stile mi sembra infatti doversi fissare, tenuto ben presente il netto discrimine qualitativo, sugli esiti della grande scultura francese del secondo ventennio del secolo e, comunque, ad esso non anteriore.[60] Poiché anche in questo caso non di scultore francese si tratta (quanta diversità fra i nobilissimi volti femminili di Francia e

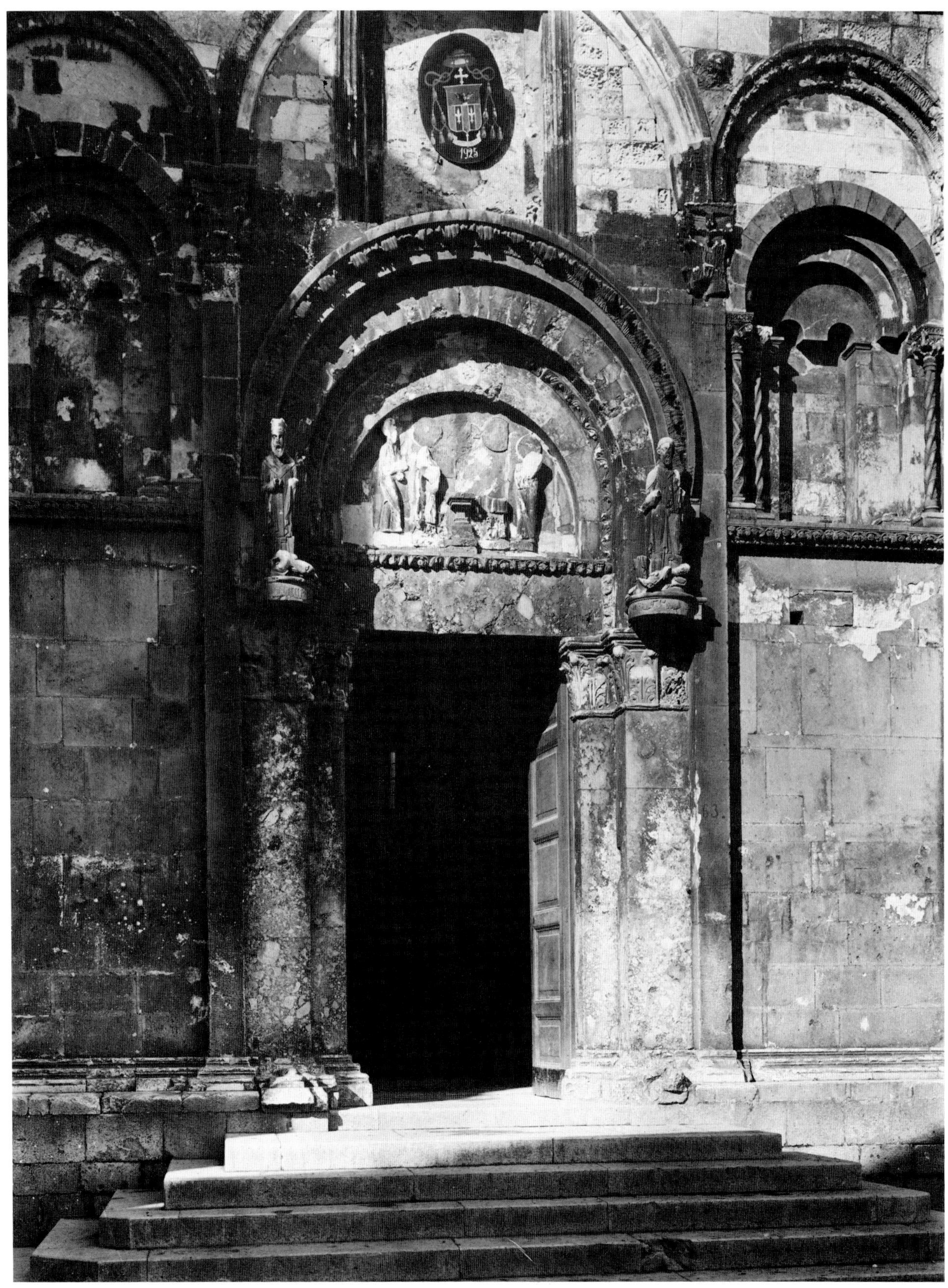

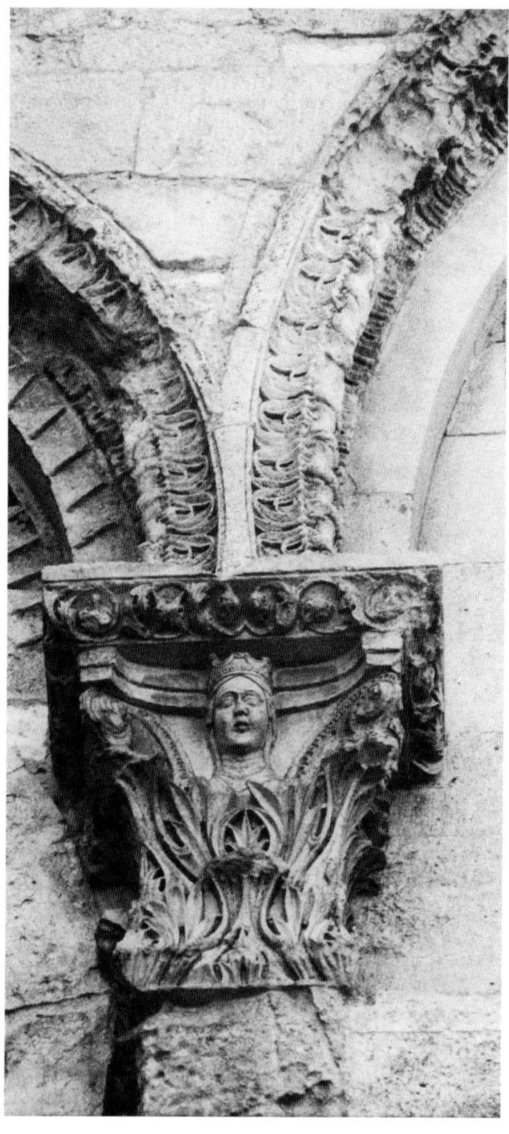

18. Duomo, Termoli, portale di facciata
Fotografia: ICCD, Roma

19. Duomo, Termoli, capitello sulla facciata
Fotografia: autore

quelli, un po' enfiati e dalle labbra carnose, di Termoli!) deve ancora una volta ipotizzarsi un canale di diffusione indiretto che, se la data lo permettesse, potrebbe implicare una formazione di questo scultore nel cantiere del maestro dei capitelli troiani, ovvero il suo tentato adeguamento a riformularne i modi di stile, da lui "sterilizzati" in una secca resa esecutiva.[61] Pur se espressa in questi termini indiretti la testimonianza di Termoli è dunque significativamente diramata per essere atta a esemplificarci un caso concreto di rinvio a perdute presenze gotiche e francesi (di scultori e di modelli) nel regno meridionale in età federiciana.

Tra i modelli non sarà oltretutto da sottovalutare, per altri casi, l'influente ruolo possibilmente svolto da altre, documentate importazioni: come quelle esemplativamente attestate da statue lignee ancora presenti in Italia meridionale.[62] La scultura di Termoli ci suggerisce peraltro anche la presenza di altre tendenze, che ne arricchiscono il quadro delle scelte artistiche. È in primo luogo il caso della sua scultura "decorativa," chiaramente indebitata a quella gerosolimitana e verosimilmente eseguita in larga parte—qui e altrove—da scultori provenienti d'oltremare.[63] Che scultori provenienti d'oltremare siano stati attivi anche per committenze *figurative* nei territori settentrionali della Puglia (in Capitanata) non è stato finora accertato, ma credo che ci sia un'opera che offre l'evidenza stilistica per poterlo regionevolmente supporre e per poter così integrare il quadro della cultura figurativa pugliese del tempo di un altro significativo apporto. Si tratta del gruppo della "Madonna col Bambino fra arcangeli" (fig. 20) sul portale settentrionale di quella cattedrale di Foggia, che proprio con quella di Termoli è stata già da tempo relazionata dalla letteratura storico-artistica.[64] Le sue figure mi sembrano infatti porsi sull'immediata linea di sviluppo dei celebri capitelli di Nazareth (fig. 21), cui l'accomunano la stilizzata qualità delle pieghe e la loro "tagliente" esecuzione in profondità, nonché la ricercata eleganza delle forme ornamentali, dagli orli perlinati alle bande del *loros* indossato dagli arcangeli (in origine verosimilmente adorne di paste colorate).[65] Di quest'opera la data potrebbe collocarsi intorno al 1200, se si ritengono convincenti le strette relazioni qui proposte con i capitelli di Nazareth—o se si aderisce alle argomentazioni del Buschhausen—oppure a qualche decennio più avanti, in piena età federiciana, se le si correla alla data di altre sculture foggiane.[66]

Foggia, Termoli, Troia—e altri ancora—furono tutti centri vitali di una cultura figurativa che, per committenza e per pluralità di espressioni artistiche, fu assai diramata e non può né deve farsi rifluire nel quadro dell'"arte federiciana," se non quando committenza e precisi nessi storici lo impongano. L'arte federiciana—la sua scultura, per

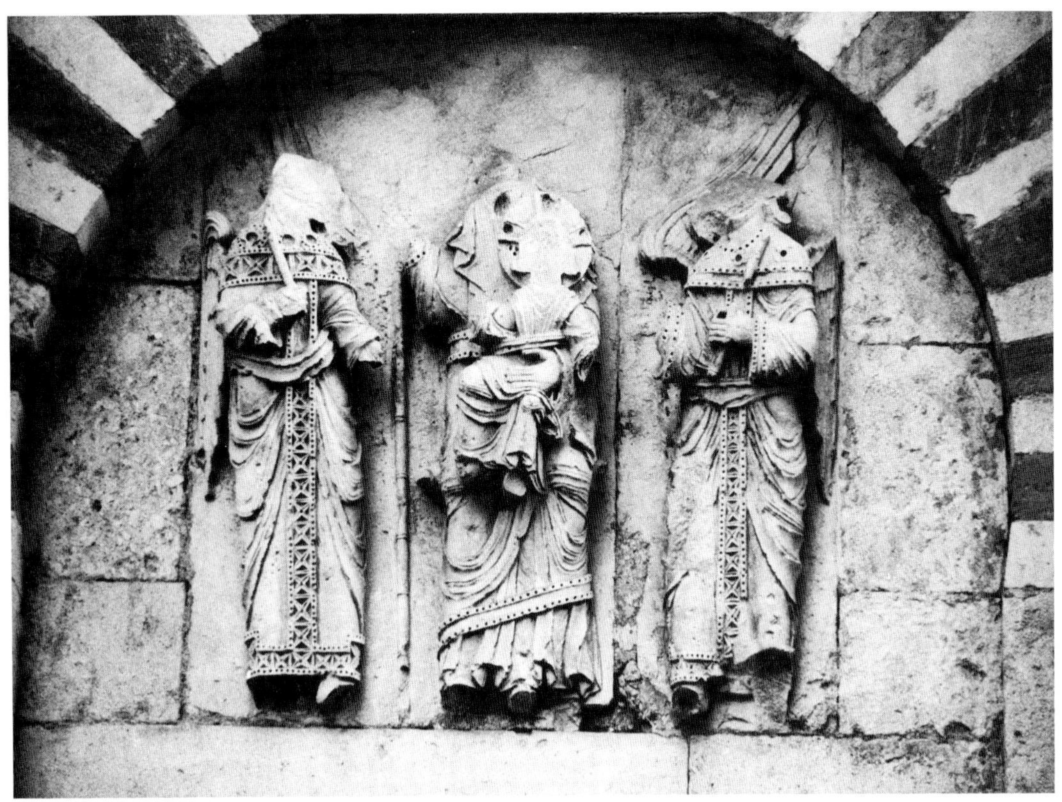

20. Duomo, Foggia, fianco nord, Madonna col Bambino fra due arcangeli
Fotografia: autore

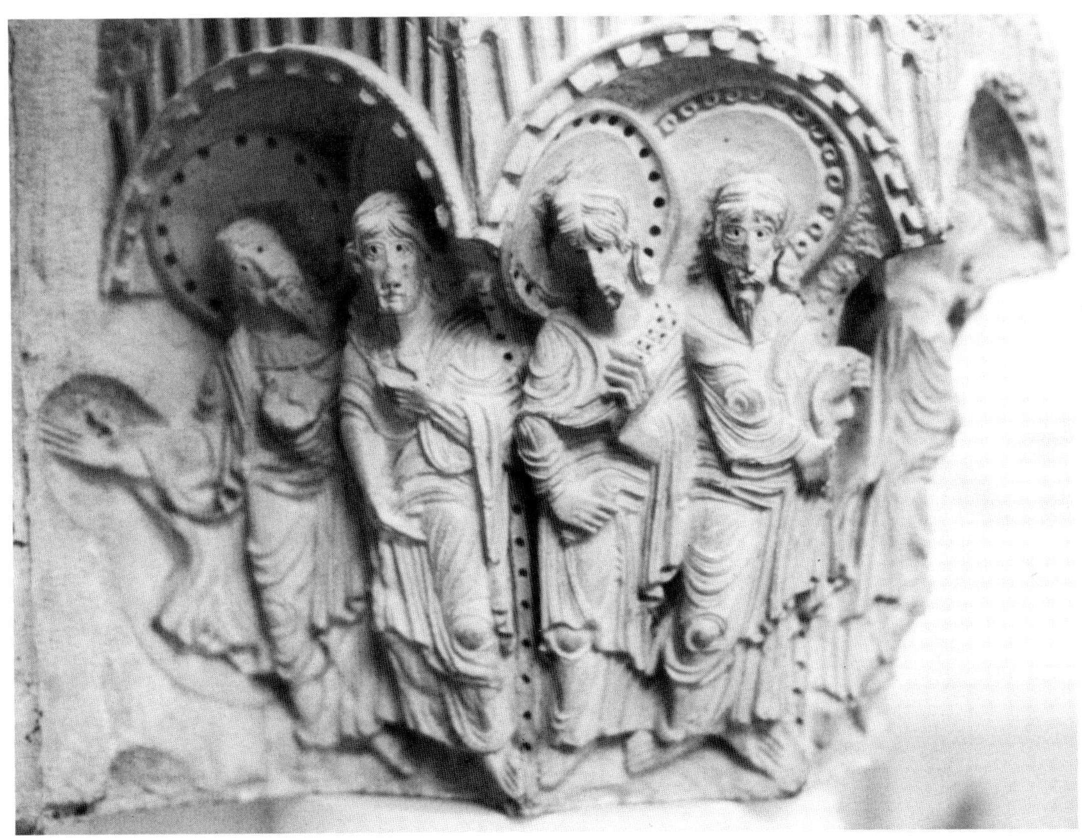

21. Basilica dell'Annunciazione, Nazareth, capitello
Fotografia: autore

l'ambito qui considerato—fu fenomeno intellettuale la cui consapevole stringenza di motivazioni e di scelte, ideologiche ed estetiche, ne è connotato peculiare e distintivo. Accuratamente distinguendosi la scultura "federiciana" dell'Italia meridionale dalla scultura dell'Italia meridionale "in età federiciana" non potrà che conseguirne una migliore storicizzazione dell'intero fenomeno.

NOTE

Il testo del presente articolo è conforme a quello letto durante il Colloquio di Washington solo nelle sue linee generali. Discussioni con colleghi hanno contribuito a precisare o a modificare le opinioni critiche espresse in quella sede. In modo particolare ricordo i vivaci e proficui scambi di idee avuti con Elizabeth B. Smith. Nello studio di opere discusse in questo saggio sono stato agevolato dalla disponibilità e cortesia di quanti sono preposti alla loro conservazione. Mi è grato di ricordare almeno Rolf Lauer, della *Domverwaltung* di Colonia, Herta Lepie, Direttrice della *Domschatzkammer* di Aquisgrana, e Charles T. Little, del Metropolitan Museum di New York.

Questo studio si è avvalso di contributi finanziari del CNR (Ricerca sulle "Presenze del Gotico europeo in Italia") e del Barbieri Center for Italian Studies, Trinity College, Hartford, Connecticut.

1. La letteratura sull'arte federiciana è immensa e non ha senso stare qui a riassumerla. Si segnalano qui quei testi che saranno più di frequente citati:

Ferdinando Bologna, *I pittori alla corte angioina di Napoli, 1266–1414 e un riesame dell'arte nell'età fridericiana* (Roma, 1969).

Maria Stella Calò Mariani, *L'arte del Duecento in Puglia* (Torino, 1984).

Federico II e l'arte del Duecento italiano, Atti della III Settimana di studi di storia dell'arte medievale dell'Università di Roma, 13–20 maggio 1978, a cura di Angiola M. Romanini, 2 voll. (Galatina, 1980) (= *Federico II*).

Cesare Gnudi, "Considerazioni sul gotico francese, l'arte imperiale e la formazione di Nicola Pisano," in *Federico II*, 1:1–17.

Gian Lorenzo Mellini, "Appunti per la scultura federiciana," *Comunità* 179 (1978), 235–336.

Joachim Poeschke, *Die Sieneser Domkanzel des Nicola Pisano. Ihre Bedeutung für die Bildung der Figur im "Stile nuovo" der Dante-Zeit* (Berlin e New York, 1973).

Joachim Poeschke, "Zum Einfluß der Gotik in Süditalien," *Jahrbuch der Berliner Museen* 22 (1980), 91–120.

Quando la stesura del presente testo era ormai completata sono venuti a mia conoscenza i seguenti tre saggi, dei quali ho perciò potuto dare conto solo con aggiuntive osservazioni nelle note:

Francesco Aceto, " 'Magistri' e cantieri nel 'Regnum Siciliae': l'Abruzzo e la cerchia federiciana," *Bollettino d'arte* 59 (1990), 15–96.

Ferdinando Bologna, " '*Cesaris imperio regni custodia fio*': la porta di Capua e la '*interpretatio imperialis*' del classicismo," in *Nel segno di Federico II. Unità politica e pluralità culturale del Mezzogiorno*, Atti del IV Convegno Internazionale di Studi della Fondazione Napoli Novantanove, Napoli 1988 (Napoli, 1989), 159–189.

Peter Cornelius Claussen, "Die Statue Friedrichs II. vom Brückentor in Capua (1234–1239)," *Festschrift für Hartmut Biermann*, a cura di Christoph Andreas, Maraike Bückling, e Roland Dorn (Weinheim, 1990).

2. Sulla porta capuana resta obbligatorio il rinvio alle due ben note monografie, di Cresswell Shearer, *The Renaissance of Architecture in Southern Italy: A Study of Frederick II of Hohenstaufen and the Capua Triumphator Archway and Towers* (Cambridge, 1935), e di Carl A. Willemsen, *Kaiser Friedrichs II. Triumphtor zu Capua. Ein Denkmal Hohenstaufischer Kunst in Süditalien* (Wiesbaden, 1953), anche se è ormai auspicabile che vengano sostituite da altra criticamente aggiornata sui tanti importanti contributi successivi, utilmente elencati da Michele Cordaro, "La porta di Capua," *Annuario dell'Istituto di Storia dell'Arte* (1974/1975–1975/1976) (Roma, 1977), 41–63. I più importanti studi sono quelli di Bologna 1969; Poeschke 1973, 67–72; Mellini 1978; Gnudi 1980; Bologna 1989; e Claussen 1990.

Un'appropriata contestualizzazione della plastica capuana ai fatti svevi è quella di Pierluigi Leone de Castris, *Arte di corte nella Napoli angioina* (Firenze, 1986). Ad essa, in quanto antefatto, non ha mancato di rivolgere la propria attenzione Maria Laura Testi Cristiani, *Nicola Pisano, architetto e scultore. Dalle origini al Pulpito del Battistero di Pisa* (Pisa, 1987). In un saggio altrove indirizzato, di Jens T. Wollesen, "A Pictorial *Speculum Principis*: The Image of Henry II in Cod. Bibl. Vat. Ottobonensis lat. 74, fol. 139v," *Word and Image* 5 (1989), 85–110, sono state svolte alcune importanti osservazioni sulle ascendenze d'immagine e ideologiche del monumento. Troppo tardi sono venuto a conoscenza del seguente testo, per poterlo reperire in tempo: Jill Meredith, "The Revival of the Augustan Age in the Court Art of Emperor Frederick II," in *Artistic Strategy and the Rhetoric of Power: Political Uses of Art from Antiquity to the Present*, a cura di David Castriota (Carbondale, Ill., 1986), 39–56, 190–192.

3. Tanto lapidaria quanto corretta è l'asserzione di Erwin Panofsky, *Renaissance and Renascences in Western Art* (Uppsala, 1960): "He (cioè Federico II) promoted the classical style as a matter of imperial policy rather than of 'aesthetic' preference" (citato dalla p. 66, edizione London, 1970). Ha svolto questa indicazione interpretativa il Bologna 1969, 29–34.

4. In modo particolare, Bologna 1969 (e 1989), Gnudi 1980, e Claussen 1990.

5. Per il concetto di stile "eterodiretto" si veda Ernst Kitzinger, *Byzantine Art in the Making* (Cambridge, Mass., 1977).

6. Per corrette osservazioni sul carattere "non-antico" della statua (e l'uso, ai fini della sua valutazione di stile, del disegno del d'Agincourt): Poeschke 1973, 69 e 1980, 100–106. Il Poeschke non ha naturalmente tralasciato di osservare che "römisch-antike Gewandstatuen der Sitzfigur vorbildlich gewesen sind" (1973, 69).

7. Poeschke 1973, 69 e 1980, 98–106; Gnudi 1980, 4 (e figg. 5–6); Claussen, 1990.

8. Per lo sviluppo della scultura gotica francese in questo giro d'anni sia sufficiente il rinvio al già classico volume di Willibald Sauerländer, *Gotische Skulptur in Frankreich, 1140–1270* (München, 1970).

9. Per lo scrigno di Aquisgrana: Ernst Günther Grimme, *Der Aachener Domschatz* (= *Aachener Kunstblätter* 42 [1972]) (Düsseldorf, 1972); *Karl der Grosse und sein Schrein in Aachen*, a cura di Hans Müllejans (Aachen e Mönchengladbach, 1988); *Der Karlsschrein im Aachener Dom*, Sonderheft der Zeitschrift *Die Waage* (Aachen, 1988). Sul suo recente restauro: Herta Lepie, "Die Konservierung des Aachener Karlsschreins ist abgeschlossen," *Kunstchronik* 43 (febbraio 1990), 50–55.

10. Per la disposizione delle immagini sulle sue testate lo scrigno di Carlomagno fu introdotto nella discussione capuana dal Mellini 1978, 305–306. "A un passo" dalla corretta comprensione del fondamentale ruolo (suo e dello scrigno di Colonia) di ascendente formale della statua capuana, è stato il Leone de Castris 1986, 128, nota 29. Per le valenze più propriamente ideologiche del suo programma esso è stato infine convincentemente inserito dal Wollesen 1989, 102–104, in una linea di "politica figurativa" che inizia col celebre Vaticanus Ottobonensis latinus 74 e a Capua si conclude.

11. Sullo scrigno colonese dei re Magi: *Der Schrein der Heiligen Drei Könige* (Köln, senza data); Peter Cornelius Claussen, "Zum Stil der Plastik am Dreikönigenschrein. Rezeptionen und Reflexionen," *Kölner Domblatt* 42 (1977), 7–42; Anton Legner, Albert e Irmgard Hirmer, *Deutsche Kunst der Romanik* (München, 1982), figg. 422–437. In generale, sullo "stile 1200": *The Year 1200, I, The Exhibition* [cat. mostra, Metropolitan Museum of Art], a cura di Konrad Hoffmann (New York, 1970); *The Year 1200: A Symposium* (New York, 1975), cui si aggiunga almeno: Peter Cornelius Claussen, "Antike und gotische Skulptur in Frankreich um 1200," *Wallraf-Richartz-Jahrbuch* 35 (1973), 83–108. Il ruolo e l'importanza di Nicolas de Verdun per la cultura figurativa italomeridionale nei suoi termini generali furono ben sottolineati dallo Gnudi 1980. Vi ha altresì esplicitamente accennato Antonio Giuliano, ". . . la luce de la gran Costanza," *Pact* 23 (1988), in corso di stampa. La possibilità di indicare almeno una perduta opera renana nel tesoro di Federico II è stata suggestivamente suggerita al Bologna 1969, 70, nota 132, dal passo della *Cronaca* di Salimbene sulla rotta di Vittoria.

Testimonianza di grande interesse per l'eventuale presenza di orafi nordici stessi in ambito "federiciano" è quella della Croce di Veroli nella quale Carlo Bertelli, in *Il Re dei Confessori. Dalla croce dei Cloisters alle croci italiane* (Milano, 1984), 107–119, ha significativamente rintracciato proprio l'operatività di modelli ascendenti allo scrigno di Colonia di Nicolas de Verdun. A un maestro orafo tedesco, il Dietrich von Boppard che le fonti ci dicono al servizio di Federico, questa Croce era stata in precedenza ipoteticamente attribuita da Angelo Lipinsky, "L'arte orafa napoletana sotto gli Angiò," in *Dante e l'Italia meridionale*, Atti del Congresso Nazionale di Studi Danteschi, Caserta e altrove, 10–16 ottobre 1965 (Firenze, 1966), 169–215 (pp. 184–185, nota 24), che è ritornato in più occasioni su questa attribuzione: "L'arte orafa alla corte di Federico II di Svevia," in *Dante e la cultura sveva*, Atti del Convegno, Melfi, 2–5 novembre 1969 (Firenze, 1970), 97–128 (106); "La stauroteca di

Velletri e l'orefice Dietrich da Boppard," *Bollettino di storia e d'arte del Lazio meridionale* 9 (1976–1977), 133. Una tale referenza è stata mantenuta dal Leone de Castris 1986, 126–127, nota 15. Per le menzioni dell'orefice nelle fonti: Jean L. A. Huillard-Bréholles, *Historia Diplomatica Friderici Secundi* . . . , 6 voll. (Paris, 1852–1861), 5, 2:1045–1046 e Johann F. Böhmer, *Regesta Imperii*, 5, 1–2, a cura di Johannes Ficker (Innsbruck, 1881–1882), 5, 1:554.

12. L'ipotesi che il Maestro della statua capuana sia stato a Reims e che lì abbia imparato il suo mestiere venne prudentemente avanzata dal Poeschke (1973, 69 e 1980, 98–106). La presenza di un maestro francese viene adesso sostenuta dal Claussen 1990 ("muß man annehmen, daß der fremde Anonymus nur für dieses Werk nach Capua gerufen wurde und nach der Fertigstellung sofort wieder zu anderen Aufgaben abgereist ist"; citato dalla p. 29). Per mio conto continuo tuttavia a crederla insostenibile, ancor più dopo i confronti proposti dal Claussen proprio perché essi mostrano, nel panneggio, i limiti *massimi* di somiglianza con la Francia (dove tridimensionalità e falcata plasticità, per esempio a Besançon, sono ben diverse da Capua). Devo comunque dare atto allo studioso tedesco che i suoi confronti "francesi" (Chartres e Amiens) sono invece estremamente convincenti per quanto attiene il *volto* dell'imperatore, realizzato—persino nella "copia" capuana—con stilemi esecutivi straordinariamente moderni. Non so quanto si possa essere oggi in grado di sciogliere "obiettivamente" la questione, ma devo almeno dire che *metodologicamente* quelle che io reputo le *differenze* esecutive fra il panneggio "imperiale" e i suoi presunti modelli francesi mi sembrano più decisive delle *affinità* di formule esecutive nei volti. Mi sembra cioè più verosimile il pensare che lo scultore attivo a Capua abbia mediato il modello stilistico del volto dell'imperatore da "esperienze" d'arte d'importazione. Per la circolazione di queste esperienze nell'Italia meridionale duecentesca un altro caso significativo è quello dei capitelli troiani (sui quali si veda oltre nel testo).

13. Valentino Pace, "Aspetti della scultura in Campania," in *Federico II*, 308–309, figg. 10–11.

14. Gnudi 1980, 6; Pace 1980, 302–306.

15. Il frammento, segnalatomi da Antonio Giuliano, è stato da lui pubblicato, senza commento, in *Villa Adriana* (testi di Antonio Giuliano e altri) (Milano, 1988), 37. Per comunicazione orale dello stesso Studioso (che volentieri ringrazio per la sua disponibilità a discutere con me questi e altri temi di ricezione medievale dal mondo classico) aggiungo quanto segue: di questo frammento, ritrovato nei grottoni dell'Aracoeli, è ipotizzabile la provenienza dal vicino Tempio di Venere e Roma per confronto con le protomi—altrettanto bene indicative del'area di modelli della testa capuana—sicuramente appartenenti a quel tempio (per le quali: Andrea Barattolo, "Afrodisia e Roma: nuove testimonianze per la storia della decorazione architettonica," *Mitteilungen des Deutschen Archäologischen Instituts. Römische Abteilung* 89 [1982], 133–151). Che un frammento del Tempio di Venere e Roma sia stato ritrovato nell'area capitolina fa pensare allo Studioso che esso vi possa essere stato riutilizzato proprio in età federiciana, quando—secondo quanto si deduce dalla documentazione grafica—una testa di spoglio venne utilizzata per la statua simbolica di "Iustitia" del *Tribunal* sul Campidoglio. Ne conseguirebbe un'ulteriore dimostrazione dell'uso ideologico delle scelte "antichizzanti" dell'imperatore: a Roma attuato con il ricorso a *spolia*, a Capua da una riformulazione dell'Antico per opera di scultori coevi.

16. Non trovo convincente, anche se a prima vista suggestivo (e, in via di principio, consonante con la mia convinzione dell'importante ruolo giuocato alle oreficerie) il confronto, fra la testa capuana e la testa reliquiario della Lambertuskirche di Düsseldorf, operato dal Mellini 1978, 310–311 e figg. 11–12, al fine di mostrare come "la crescita dello scultore di Capua dipendesse, più che dalla tarda plastica campana, e più che dall'influsso della scultura provenzale, soprattutto dalla relazione con l'oreficeria germanica."

17. Che, come osserva il Bologna 1969, 32 (e, ancora: 1989, 182) vi fossero intensi rapporti commerciali o anche politici fra Provenza e Campania e che fossero "provenzali i moventi di fondo della poesia che fiorì alla corte federiciana" non significa infatti di necessità che questi fatti creassero risvolti "artistici," ma soltanto che essi sono storicamente plausibili. L'evidenza visuale è tuttavia insufficiente a confermare un tale quadro di relazioni. Viene semmai da chiedersi, ove si pensi al caso della *moderna* lirica trobadorica, se sia lecito accostarle in un medesimo quadro culturale l'*arcaizzante* scultura "romanica" di Provenza! Esplicitamente o cautamente contrari all'ascendenza provenzale si sono dichiarati il Mellini 1978, 256 (n. 33) e la Testi Cristiani 1987, 16.

Nel vasto ventaglio di opinioni sul ruolo svolto dalla Provenza (che andrebbe inquadrato in una più ampia questione di metodo sulla diffusione dell'*Antikenrezeption* nell'arte medievale) non manca chi ha ipotizzato la presenza di uno scultore dell'Arelat alla corte di Federico II per eseguirvi la testa-ritratto di Lanuvio: Helmut Buschhausen, "Probleme der Bildniskunst am Hof Kaiser Friedrichs II.," in *Stauferzeit. Geschichte. Literatur. Kunst*, a cura di Rüdiger Krohn, Bernd Thum, e Peter Wapnewski (Stuttgart, 1978), 220–243 (239–240). L'esecuzione di questa testa è stata accreditata più convincentemente, a mio avviso, anche a botteghe cosmatesche romane: Peter Cornelius Claussen, "Scultura romana al tempo di Federico II," in *Federico II*, 1:325–338 (326–327).

18. Per riferimento esemplativo mi limito a citare a caso una testa di Hermes, da originale di Alkamenes, copiata in età adrianea, oggi conservata nel museo archeologico di Venezia (deposito dal museo Correr, n. 70). Il Poeschke 1973, 69–70, ha significativamente ipotizzato l'ascendenza del cosiddetto "Pier delle Vigne" dal tipo greco-arcaico dell'"Omero-Epimenide."

19. Sui leoni romani dell'Italia meridionale ha pubblicato una serie di articoli e ha in corso di stesura un volume, con il loro catalogo, Luigi Todisco. Si vedano per ora in particolare: "Leoni romani in Daunia," *Atti della Accademia Nazionale dei Lincei. Rendi-*

conti 41 (1986) (Roma, 1987), 165–182 e tavv. 1–8 fuori testo; "L'antico nel campanile normanno di Melfi," *Mélanges de l'École française de Rome* 99 (1987), 123–158; "Leoni funerari di *Luceria*," *Atti della Accademia Nazionale dei Lincei. Rendiconti* 42 (1987), (Roma, 1988), 145–155 e tavv. 1–6 fuori testo; "Il leone 'custos iusticie' di Bari," *Rivista dell'Istituto Nazionale d'Archeologia e Storia dell'Arte*, serie 3, 10 (1987) (Roma, 1988), 129–151. Leoni simili a quelli lucerini, melfitani, venosini e baresi esistettero senza dubbio anche a Capua. Da condividere dunque le osservazioni in merito della Testi Cristiani 1987, 16.

20. La protome femminile "con fisionomia graziosa" è assai ben riprodotta dal Willemsen 1953, alle figg. 73 e 80, oppure da Mellini 1978 (che usa questa aggettivazione) alla tav. 16. La protome maschile è quella riprodotta dal Willemsen 1953, alle figg. 83–84, dal Mellini 1978 alla successiva tav. 17.

Approfitto della presente nota per chiarire che sono stato purtroppo frainteso (e, per ironia della sorte, indebitamente lodato!) quando si è creduto che nel mio saggio sulla scultura campana di età federiciana (Pace 1980) abbia "in überzeugender Weise aufgezeigt" che a Capua predomini la tradizione campana (Claussen 1990, 38, nota 72). In realtà era mio intento mostrare che "La scultura 'regionale' ha . . . un posto assai marginale nel monumento sulle sponde del Volturno"! (ivi, 322). I soli confronti "campani" sono stati da me formulati per la protome leonina e, con ben diverso segno, per una seconda, rozza, protome virile.

21. Di questo capitello il Bologna 1969, 31 (e, ancora: 1989, 180) a commento alla tav. I.7, 85, ha scritto che esso "su di un impianto gotico, di tipo cistercense, tratta i baccelli e le foglie *con un gusto specificamente islamico*," che non mi riesce di cogliere e che non mi risulta sia stato colto da altri. Antonio Cadei, "Fossanova e Castel del Monte," in *Federico II*, 191–215 e figg. 1–29 fuori testo, ha giustamente osservato che "si sottrae ad ogni comparazione cistercense lo strano acanto a riccioli . . . che forma la decorazione esclusiva di un bel capitello fogliato della porta di Capua" (p. 213) poi riproposto a Castel del Monte e altrove. Joachim Poeschke 1980, 92–98, ha invece creduto di poter cogliere in capitelli del chiostro di Fossanova l'iniziale sviluppo del capitello capuano. Ho tuttavia l'impressione, benché non sia in grado di provarla con concreti riferimenti, che sia da ricercarsi in Francia l'origine (reinterpretata) della soluzione vegetale che avvolge il calato di sinistra del capitello capuano. Per confronti orientativi: Denise Jalabert, *La flore sculptée des monuments du Moyen Age en France* (Paris, 1965), tav. 59, B e E. A conclusioni sostanzialmente analoghe, pur se fondate su materiale comparativo desunto da sviluppi ornamentali su altre forme architettoniche (non su capitelli) è pervenuto Francesco Aceto 1990, 47 e figg. 33–36.

22. In merito agli artisti "d'importazione" sappiamo almeno della presenza di *orafi* tedeschi, fra i quali il Dietrich von Boppard cui si è qui accennato nella nota 11. Ivi anche un riferimento esemplativo a una possibile opera perduta. In merito all'"attività di Federico collezionista e antiquario" si leggano le pagine di Maria Stella Calò Mariani, "Federico II e le 'Artes Mechanicae'," in *Federico II*, 2:259–275, poi rifluite in Calò Mariani 1984, 89–91.

23. Sulla "funzione" dell'edificio: Giosuè Musca, "Castel del Monte, il reale e l'immaginario," *Castel del Monte* (Bari, 1981), 25–62.

24. La questione "francese" andrebbe naturalmente discussa partendo dalle più progredite risultanze critiche e filologiche sull'architettura stessa di Castel del Monte (e altrove), secondo un itinerario che dal volume di Camille Enlart, *Origines françaises de l'architecture gothique en Italie* (Paris, 1894), giunge fino ai giorni nostri con il contributo di Wolfgang Krönig per questo stesso convegno. La si deve necessariamente lasciare da parte, limitandocisi a implicarne la fondamentale rilevanza per l'analisi delle stesse forme plastiche. Che, comunque, modelli gotici francesi-*non cistercensi* abbiano svolto un importante ruolo nei capitelli di Castel del Monte venne indipendentemente indicato sia dal Poeschke 1973, 68, che dalla Calò Mariani (Maria Stella Calò Mariani, "Aspetti della scultura sveva in Puglia e in Lucania," *Archivio storico pugliese* 26 [1973], 441–474 [474]). Ad altre precisazioni contribuì ancora il Poeschke 1980, 117–118. Alla casistica si aggiunga anche il caso del capitello della sala superiore illustrato alla figura 26 nell'articolo del Cadei, da confrontare con quello della cattedrale di Soissons illustrato alla figura 5 di Poeschke 1980. Sui capitelli di Castel del Monte, dei quali sarebbero auspicabili una completa documentazione fotografica e uno studio sistematico, si veda per ora Cadei 1980 e Calò Mariani 1984, 121–127.

Il nesso Federico II-Cistercensi è stato più volte sottolineato in sede storiografica e trova il suo concreto appoggio documentario nel celebre passo della cronaca di Santa Maria della Ferraria. Sull'argomento resta fondamentale il pionieristico volume di Arthur Haseloff, *Die Bauten der Hohenstaufen in Unteritalien* (Leipzig, 1920) da integrare con una ricca bibliografia di cui i più recenti contributi sono quelli di Cadei 1980 e Calò Mariani 1984, 65–84, la quale ha meritoriamente introdotto alla discussione la chiesa cistercense di Santa Maria di Ripalta. Va comunque detto al proposito di questa bella chiesa e del suo corredo scultoreo che la chiave interpretativa federiciana nasce da una sostanziale petizione di principio che tende a far combaciare i due fenomeni ("federiciano" e "cistercense") sul presupposto dei buoni rapporti intercorsi fra imperatore e monaci e della presenza di componenti cistercensi a Castel del Monte. Nello specifico del fatto "artistico," e a una visione senza pregiudizi, dovrà tuttavia darsi il giusto rilievo alle differenze—qualitative, in primo luogo—fra il corredo scultoreo dei due edifici, esemplarmente mostrate dai *rozzissimi* peducci a forma umana sul braccio nord del transetto (troppo entusiasticamente commentati notandosene la "plastica essenziale e abbreviata") e dalla ben più *dura* esecuzione di larga parte dei capitelli. È d'altronde indubbio, come la stessa studiosa scrive, che "Non è noto se S. Maria di Ripalta sia stata oggetto immediato dell'interesse dell'imperatore."

25. Un primo generico accenno a dipendenze francesi per lo scultore dei telamoni ("uno scultore ben informato, se non francese egli stesso, di quel che s'era

fatto o si faceva nelle cattedrali di Francia [per esempio, a Reims, nel fianco occidentale della cattedrale]") fu formulato da Stefano Bottari, "Nicola Pisano e la cultura meridionale," *Arte antica e moderna* 5 (1959), 43–51 (45), oppure *Il contributo dell'archidiocesi di Capua alla vita religiosa e culturale del Meridione*, Atti del Convegno Nazionale di Studi Storici promosso dalla Società di Storia Patria di Terra di Lavoro, Capua e altrove 1966 (Roma, 1967), 65–72 (67). Precise osservazioni sulla dipendenza di Castel del Monte da Reims ha dedicato il Poeschke sin dal 1973, 70–72 e poi ancora—con estensione a Bamberg—nel 1980, 110–115. Sulla dipendenza della scultura di Castel del Monte da Reims e Bamberg ha poi particolarmente insistito (senza essere apparentemente a conoscenza del primo contributo del Poeschke) Angiola Maria Romanini nelle sue lezioni universitarie dell'anni 1977–1978 (delle quali, con il titolo *Federico II e l'arte del Duecento in Italia. Appunti dalle lezioni di Storia dell'arte medioevale a cura del dott. Alessandro Tomei* [Roma, 1978], furono divulgate "dispense" a stampa per uso degli studenti) e nel suo "Federico II e l'arte italiana del Duecento: Introduzione," in *Federico II*, v–ix. Un tale inquadramento del fenomeno federiciano in senso lato è stato espresso più volte dalla Calò Mariani, ad iniziare dal suo saggio d'esordio sull'argomento (Calò Mariani 1973, 441–474) fino alla sua "summa," cioè il volume sull'arte del Duecento in Puglia (Calò Mariani 1984).

26. La dipendenza da modelli reimsiani per la testa fogliata di Castel del Monte fu concisamente sottolineata dal Poeschke 1973, 71. In seguito: Romanini, in *Federico II*, viii e Calò Mariani 1984, 127–130. Sulle chiavi di volta del Castello è ritornata con alcuni cenni (non facilmente condivisibili sul piano metodologico) Angiola Maria Romanini, "I Cistercensi e la formazione di Arnolfo di Cambio," *Studi di storia dell'arte in memoria di Mario Rotili* (Napoli, 1984), 1:235–241 (237–238) e 2:tavv. 86–92.

27. Per la loro migliore documentazione fotografica: Poeschke 1980, figg. 27–32.

28. Una coppia di telamoni quasi completamente nudi è attestata in Puglia da un capitello "a stampella" (diversissimo dunque nell'insieme) oggi conservato nella Pinacoteca provinciale di Bari: Horst Schäfer-Schuchardt, *Die figürliche Steinplastik des 11.–13. Jahrhunderts in Apulien* (Bari, 1986), tavv. 206–207.

29. Romanini, *Lezioni*: "nei famosi ignudi l'architettura diventa esplicita nelle sue forme portanti . . . è questa una concezione antropocentrica del rapporto scultura-architettura del tutto estranea al mondo francese" (citato da p. 49).

30. A tutti note, queste opere sono state recentissimamente discusse in una specifica monografia: Christine Verzár Bornstein, *Portals and Politics in the Early Italian City-State: The Sculpture of Nicholaus in Context* (Parma, 1988). Per una rassegna fotografica può anche riuscire utile la consultazione dell'"Atlante iconografico," terzo volume di *Nicholaus e l'arte del suo tempo*, Atti del seminario tenutosi a Ferrara, Deputazione Provinciale Ferrarese di Storia Patria, 1981, a cura di Angiola M. Romanini (Ferrara, 1985).

31. Per quanto osservato dalla Romanini rinvio alla nota 29. Al rapporto fra sculture e ambiente architettonico ha dedicato belle espressioni di commento Maria Stella Calò Mariani: "La scultura in Puglia durante l'età sveva e proto-angioina," in Pina Belli D'Elia et al., *La Puglia fra Bisanzio e l'Occidente* (Milano, 1980), 254–316 (268), riutilizzate poi in Calò Mariani 1984, 127. Nutro tuttavia forti perplessità sulla effettiva rilevanza di quelle supposte valenze estetiche e psicologiche messe pure in risalto dalla studiosa, per esempio laddove scrive che nei telamoni "il trasmutare dell'espressione da un volto all'altro—sereno, intento, spaventato, triste, sorridente, irridente o grottesco—propone su altri registri, sempre sul filo tesissimo dell'indagine sul vero di natura, il processo di trasformazione continua della realtà, la mutevolezza stessa della vita."

32. Poeschke 1980, 112–115, che pure ha formulato il poco convincente rinvio a Reims, ha ben sottolineato che i telamoni sono "einheimische Werke." Anche il Mellini 1978, 319, aveva scritto che per il loro scultore "si tratta con ogni probabilità di un'altra presenza italiana." Riferendomi alla tradizione plastica pugliese penso a opere come la celebre sfinge del portale centrale di San Nicola (illustrata, per esempio, in Schäfer-Schuchardt 1986, tav. 104).

33. Non è dunque osservazione del tutto precisa lo scrivere che "gli attributi del sesso vengono mostrati senza veli," come si legge per esempio in Carl Arnold Willemsen e Dagmar Odenthal, *Puglia. Terra dei Normanni e degli Svevi* (Bari, 1966), 71.

34. Per il Musca 1981, 52–54, il programma della settima torre segnerebbe "la rivincita dei modi 'bassi' di rappresentazione . . . è la 'corda pazza' ed irriverente che prende il sopravvento e fa uno sberleffo, fa il solletico al gigante di pietra e al potere." Con divertita irriverenza il Musca ha anche scritto che i telamoni "mostrano una mimica che fa pensare, più che a uno sforzo teso a reggere le mensole, al soddisfacimento più o meno agevole di bisogni fisiologici"!

L'interpretazione del Musca può cogliere nel segno, dove ritrova nelle sculture quasi il corrispettivo delle *drôleries* ai margini delle pagine di un manoscritto miniato, ma non credo che ciò sia avvenuto senza il consenso del Committente ("il miope Federico," scrive invece il Musca, "ed anche chi ci vedeva bene, non poteva capire di che si trattasse dal piano di calpestio del vano scala, non poteva avvertire l'offesa recata alle paludate immagini di pietra volute dall'imperatore").

35. L'attività di questo "maestro" è stata sviluppata entro coordinate formali troppo generalizzate dal Mellini 1978, 318–321, che lo battezza "Maestro di Castel del Monte" e gli attribuisce in blocco telamoni e mensole. Al suo stretto seguito si collocano, come noto, le mensole sul cornicione meridionale della cattedrale di Ruvo, di cui manca tuttavia un'adeguata pubblicazione critica. Per ora valga il rinvio a Calò Mariani 1979, 282 (fig. alla p. 374) replicato in Calò Mariani 1984, 158–159 (fig. 225). Non mi interessa qui

entrare nel merito dell'identificazione dell'attività del suo "sosia" quale proposta dal Mellini a Pisa.

36. Calò Mariani 1973, 463 e 466. Marina Righetti Tosti-Croce, "La scultura del castello di Lagopesole," in *Federico II*, 237–252.

37. *Il museo di Foggia*, Quaderni del CSPCR di Foggia 8 (Foggia, 1986), schede 41, 53 e 54, con bibliografia.

38. La testa femminile è quella, qui già discussa precedentemente, riprodotta dal Mellini 1978, fig. 16. La testa maschile è quella riprodotta in Mellini 1979, fig. 17. L'affinità fra Lagopesole e Capua venne già sottolineata dallo Shearer 1935, 83 e 103. È stata ribadita dal Poeschke 1973, 70.

39. Calò Mariani 1973, 472 e Righetti Tosti-Croce 1980, 241.

40. Indipendentemente dalla *personale* soluzione che si voglia dare al problema, è infatti indubbio che sono soprattutto i centri delle grandi cattedrali francesi (Amiens, Reims, Chartres per Capua, Castel del Monte, Troia, secondo quanto discusso nel testo) quelli da cui *eventualmente* provennero artisti operosi (o "modelli" usati) per le committenze federiciane. Ciò è stato ben sottolineato dal Poeschke 1980, 92–93 (nota 8), così come in precedenza era stata giustamente sottolineata la ben diversa forza d'irradiazione dei modelli gotici francesi, rispetto a quelli tedeschi, dal Sauerländer 1969, 92.

Per quanto attiene l'arte delle terre imperiali, il caso degli scrigni tedeschi non contraddice l'assunto, perché rientra nel contesto delle decisive "esperienze estetiche" maturate da Federico nel suo pluriennale soggiorno tedesco del secondo decennio. Più difficile la questione sollevata dal cosiddetto "frammento Molajoli" della Pinacoteca provinciale di Bari, più volte collegato alla scultura gotica di Magonza: per esempio da Pina Belli D'Elia, "La mostra del gotico europeo e alcuni fatti di casa nostra," *Terra di Bari* 3.1 (1969), 5–14, (9–10), oppure da Mellini 1978, 318–319. Con tutta onestà confesso di non saper prendere posizione anche per via della sua estrema frammentarietà. Se comunque si dovesse adire all'opinione che esso è testimonianza dell'operatività di maestri d'oltralpe alla corte di Federico (ammesso, come verosimile, che per la corte di Federico esso sia stato eseguito), ciò non modificherebbe i termini del problema.

41. È assai significativo che, per esempio, moderne cadenze gotiche siano già state colte nel sigillo "tedesco" del 1215: Poeschke 1980, 101–102. Tangenzialmente, ma esplicitamente, hanno sottolineato l'importanza delle esperienze artistiche maturate durante il soggiorno tedesco del secondo decennio il Bologna 1969, 25 e il Leone de Castris 1986, 122.

42. Annamaria Lorusso, "Cattedrale di S. Maria Icona Vetere in Foggia. Il cornicione a mensole: proposte per una sua più precisa collocazione nel'ambito della scultura di epoca federiciana," in *Federico II*, 253–264. Pina Belli D'Elia, "Scultura pugliese di epoca sveva," in *Federico II*, 265–287. La monografia storico-artistica di base sulla chiesa foggiana è Ferdinand Jacobs, *Die Kathedrale S. Maria Icona Vetere in Foggia*, Diss., Hamburg, 1968. Tanto lo Jacobs, quanto la Lorusso hanno istituito uno stretto rapporto cronologico fra la data del 1223 dell'epigrafe e la fase della cattedrale cui spetta il cornicione. A mio avviso l'evidenza "stilistica" è troppo esigua (anche se non negativa) e la data del cornicione dovrebbe essere possibilmente guadagnata con confronti articolati su referenze formali più ampie. Tanto sulla cattedrale quanto sul palazzo: Aceto 1990, 28–38.

43. Oltretutto, tenuto pur presente quanto detto nella precedente nota, sarebbe importante il poter stabilire convincentemente la priorità di esecuzione delle due opere in questione. Ovvero: fu Federico II ad avvalersi delle maestranze già attive per la cattedrale, o viceversa? Ovviamente sarebbe importante il poter anche sapere—cosa che mai lo si potrà, a meno di inverosimili ritrovamenti documentari—chi sia stato il committente dei lavori della cattedrale. Lo Jacobs 1968, 179–212, è stato dell'avviso che fu Federico ad avvalersi del cantiere della cattedrale per il suo Palazzo—il chè implicherebbe che il cornicione *non* è "federiciano"!

44. Belli D'Elia, in *Federico II*, 276–277.

45. Renato Bonelli e Corrado Bozzoni, "Federico II e la cattedrale di Altamura," *Antichità viva* 21 (1982), n. 2–3, 5–20. Perfettamente d'accordo con gli Studiosi, quando scrivono che "gli autori del Duomo dimostrano di voler ignorare . . . la cultura e il gusto gotici," lo sono un po' meno nel ravvisare i decisivi modelli architettonici del duomo nelle "forme dell'architettura ottoniana e tardo-ottoniana" (per le citazioni: 15–16). La chiesa di Altamura attende comunque ancora uno studio esaustivo, che sciolga i problemi ben evidenziati dal saggio qui citato.

46. Jürgen Krüger, *S. Lorenzo Maggiore in Neapel*, Franziskanische Forschungen 31 (Werl/Westfalen, 1985). Valentino Pace, Recensione al volume di J. Krüger, *Bollettino d'arte* 52 (1988), 104–105.

47. La scultura della chiesa di Altamura è inscindibilmente connessa con l'architettura dell'edificio e, di conseguenza, con le sue fasi costruttive. Larghissima parte di essa sembra essere trecentesca, del tempo successivo al terremoto del 1316—così, per esempio, il fregio a testine e i capitelli del triforio, col fregio strettamente imparentati. Pertinente alla fase duecentesca dell'edificio (ma di epoca già post-federiciana) può essere un bel capitello di navata, con teste umane e immagini ferine in un contesto vegetale, nel quale, alla lontana, possono cogliersi ascendenze su motivi e forme delle mensole del salone di Lagopesole. Per una rassegna dei dati documentari e per la documentazione fotografica della scultura altamurana: Schäfer-Schuchardt 1986, vol. 1.1, 3–8 e 1.2, tavv. 1–21. Con le valutazioni cronologiche dello studioso, che assegna larga parte della scultura a data duecentesca, addirittura ante 1232 non posso essere d'accordo.

48. Hans Martin Schaller, *L'ambone della cattedrale di Bitonto e l'idea imperiale di Federico II* (Bari, 1970); Ettore Paratore, "L'ambone di Bitonto e la predica dell'abate Nicola di Bari," in *Federico II*, 1:227–235; Roswitha Neu-Kock, "Das Kanzelrelief in der Kathedrale von Bitonto," *Archiv für Kulturge-*

schichte 60 (1978), 253–267; Heinrich Thelen, "Ancora una volta per il rilievo del pulpito di Bitonto," in *Federico II*, 217–225.

49. È vero che, essendo la data di esecuzione del rilievo verosimilmente anteriore agli anni quaranta, esso non può, a rigore, confrontarsi con le opere "federiciane" posteriori—si tratti di Castel del Monte o di Lagopesole (sul problema dei capitelli di Troia si veda qui di seguito nel testo e alla nota successiva)—ma è anche vero che la scultura federiciana aveva già prodotto immagini "ufficiali" dell'imperatore, che in Puglia esse dovevano essere conosciute e che proprio dei loro modelli, o dei loro scultori, avrebbe dovuto avvalersi il rilievo bitontino. Se non lo fu, ciò può ben significare la loro "*indisponibilità*" per committenze estranee alla diretta volontà dell'imperatore.

50. Hans Wentzel, "Ein gotisches Kapitell in Troia," *Zeitschrift für Kunstgeschichte* 17 (1954), 185–188; Vera K. Ostoja, "To Represent What Is as It Is," *Metropolitan Museum of Art Bulletin* 23 (June 1965), 367–372. Che il capitello di New York sia un falso, come si tende a credere nel museo stesso (tanto che esso è conservato nei depositi) non mi pare plausibile. Contro l'ipotesi del falso si è anche espresso il Bologna 1989, 170 (alla nota 27).

51. Helmut Buschhausen, "Probleme," 1978, 220–243 (224–225 [nota 8] e 240); Gnudi 1980, 2–3. Troppo silenzioso sulle importanti indicazioni critiche di questi studiosi il paragrafo dedicato dall'Aceto 1990, 63–67, a questi capitelli. In linea di massima trovo plausibile la "referenza francese" dei capitelli, così come è stata soprattutto indicata dallo Gnudi. Mantengo tuttavia qualche riserva, almeno qui in nota, sulla piena e decisa attribuzione a uno "scultore" francese. Non tanto per motivi qualitativi—a ben guardare, ancora una volta, Chartres ha una qualità esecutiva più raffinata—perché potrebbe trattarsi di uno scultore francese semplicemente meno "dotato," quanto per più intrinseci motivi formali: il trattamento del fogliame mi appare difficilmente confrontabile con opere francesi, ancor meno "francese" mi pare l'incerta relazione compositiva fra il fogliame e le teste. Da ciò non è diminuito l'interesse dell'opera, pur sempre una straordinaria testimonianza di "referenza francese" nell'Italia meridionale del tempo.

52. Pina Belli D'Elia, in *Federico II*, 273, nota 18, è stata la prima studiosa, a mia conoscenza, ad aver ritenuto che i capitelli siano stati "inviati a Troia," perché la loro esecuzione manifesta una radicale diversità stilistica da quanto in opera nella cattedrale. Senza essere a conoscenza di questa opinione ha altresì proposto una loro originaria provenienza da Lucera, per via della loro iconografia, Paul H. D. Kaplan, "Black Africans in Hohenstaufen Iconography," *Gesta* 26 (1987), 29–36. Ma non è certo l'iconografia del "negro" a poter stabilirne la pertinenza federiciana—o, addirittura, lucerina—vista la sua diffusione altrove (Barletta, Termoli, eccetera). Al proposito, in generale: *L'image du noir dans l'art occidental* (Fribourg, 1979), con particolare riferimento all'Italia meridionale: 2, 1:108–120.

Per "stile" non può tuttavia affatto escludersi che questi capitelli siano stati eseguiti a Troia, anche perché essi non hanno altrove nessun addentellato "di mano" (o di bottega) con altre opere *in situ* o, comunque, note. La testa di negro fra le zampe del leone absidale di destra della stessa cattedrale (che confesso di aver potuto vedere con difficoltà dal basso e che mai è stata adeguatamente riprodotta) potrebbe forse esserne in qualche relazione. In merito alle presunte affinità con il busto di Barletta rinvio alla nota successiva.

53. Fu infatti la Ostoja che, diversamente dal Wentzel—il quale si era giustamente limitato a sottolineare la qualità "gotica" del capitello da lui ritrovato nella sagrestia del duomo di Troia—pose l'accento sul carattere "federiciano" (di "verismo psicologico") delle immagini umane rappresentate nel capitello di New York, da lei presentato, e in quello di Troia. Come in merito alla provenienza, così in merito alla funzione dei capitelli non può dirsi nulla di certo. Il Wentzel accennò a numerose possibilità, senza propendere per nessuna. Il Buschhausen, *Probleme*, 1978, 224–225, li riferì invece categoricamente a un ciborio.

Ad insinuare una più concreta valenza federiciana dei capitelli (al di là dello psicologismo sui loro caratteri di "verismo") ha concorso il contestualizzarli formalmente con altre opere collegate all'imperatore: in primis il busto di Barletta, addirittura attribuito al loro stesso scultore—ed identificato con Bartolomeo da Foggia—da Ferdinando Bologna 1969, 26–28. Ma il busto di Barletta è davvero duecentesco o, piuttosto (come pur sarei riluttante ad ammettere) quattrocentesco? Dopo l'accertamento dell'originarietà della sua famosa iscrizione (che, per essere già stata autorevolmente ritenuta "in capitale umanistica," era stata creduta posteriore alla scultura) sarebbe doveroso trarne le conseguenze ed esplicitamente smentire o il dato epigrafico o quello stilistico. Oltretutto non è da sottovalutare la posizione di chi, proprio sul versante dell'analisi formale, ha dubitato della data duecentesca dell'opera: Willibald Sauerländer, "L'Europe gothique, XIIe–XIVe siècles," *Revue de l'art* 3 (1969), 83–92 (92) e "L'époque des Hohenstaufen," *Revue de l'art* 39 (1978), 69–81 (70). A una data in età federiciana sembrerebbe ostare la pronunciata consapevolezza spaziale dell'opera—inarrivata persino oltralpe a quella data (per fare un esempio: il *Bamberger Reiter* è, al confronto, assai più rigido!)—così come legittima sospetti sulla tradizionale cronologia già il suo contrasto con la rigidità formale dell'arcaizzante panneggio. Vi si aggiunga il curioso modo di *acconciare* i capelli, non certo in sintonia con la moda testimoniata da manoscritti e da qualche scultura, né con quella classicheggiante di altre sculture imperiali, ma con curiose analogie con l'acconciatura della barba della figura umana dilaniata da due bestie su un angolo del cornicione di Foggia (la migliore illustrazione in Aceto 1990, fig. 24).

Per attente osservazioni sulle qualità formali del busto di Barletta: Buschhausen 1977, 241–243, del quale tuttavia non mi convincono le argomentazioni per cui si tratterebbe di un ritratto *post-mortem*, argomentazioni ribadite ancora nel suo "Die Rezeption der Antike und der Einbruch der französischen

Gotik in der unteritalienischen Plastik des 13. Jahrhunderts," *Studi di storia dell'arte in memoria di Mario Rotili* (Napoli, 1984), 201–209 e, più di recente in un altro scritto: Helmut Buschhausen e Johann Szilvassy, "Die Anwendung der forensischen Ähnlichkeitsdiagnose zur Identifizierung der antikisierenden Bildnisse Kaiser Friedrichs II.," *Ritratto ufficiale e ritratto privato*, Atti della II Conferenza internazionale sul ritratto romano, a cura di Nicola Bonacasa e Giovanni Rizzo, Roma 1984, Quaderni de "La ricerca scientifica" 116 (Roma, 1988), 197–217.

54. Sull'insieme dei problemi critici relativi a questa cattedrale, si veda Helmut Buschhausen, *Die süditalienische Bauplastik im Königreich Jerusalem* (Wien, 1978), 333–343 e Maria Stella Calò Mariani, *Due cattedrali del Molise. Termoli e Larino* (Roma, 1979). Contestualmente alla trattazione del Duecento pugliese la cattedrale di Termoli è anche oggetto di un paragrafo in Calò Mariani 1984, 37–45. Per qualche importante precisazione, anche in merito all'originarietà di collocazione delle sculture di facciata: Giuseppe Basile-M. Grazia Chilosi e Giovanna Martellotti, "La facciata della cattedrale di Termoli: un esempio di manutenzione programmata," *Materiali lapidei*, supplemento al n. 41 (1987) del *Bollettino d'arte*, 283–304.

55. Delle due statue originariamente collocate davanti al portale, quella di destra—identificata dubitativamente con s. Sebastiano—è oggi perduta, ma ne resta la preziosa documentazione fotografica di inizio secolo, pubblicata per la prima volta dalla Calò Mariani 1979, 35–37 e figg. 19a–b.

56. In area viciniore e storicamente collegabile a Termoli statue-colonna si ritrovano soltanto nel portale della chiesa abruzzese di San Clemente a Casauria, secondo un'idea compositiva che risale in ultima istanza alla Francia, eventualmente tramite la mediazione italosettentrionale. Più a Nord è ad Ancona che fu realizzato un portale a statue-colonna. Sulla chiesa abruzzese: Buschhausen, *Bauplastik*, 1978, 356–367 (ivi anche il richiamo ad Ancona) in attesa che ne venga pubblicata la monografia di Elizabeth B. Smith, della quale restano tuttora inedite le conferenze tenute su argomento casauriense a Princeton, New Jersey, nel dicembre 1987 e a Kalamazoo, Michigan, nel maggio 1989.

57. La derivazione dell'"*idea*" compositiva "*vom französischen Stufenportal*" è stata sottolineata dal Buschhausen, *Bauplastik*, 1978, 335–336. Lo è stata, ovviamente, anche da parte della Calò Mariani 1979, 43. Per gli esempi francesi qui riferiti: Sauerländer 1970, tavv. 49, 110–111 e 157.

Esemplativo per la presenza del tema nella statuaria lignea tedesca è il "S. Vito" di Münster: Géza Jaszai, *Werke des frühen und hohen Mittelalters*, Bildwerke des Westfälischen Landesmuseums für Kunst und Kulturgeschichte Münster 2 (Münster, 1989), 55 e 82 (n. 36), 66–67 (per le illustrazioni). Si tratta di una statua-reliquiario di 81 cm di altezza.

58. Calò Mariani 1984, 40, ha scritto che "il S. Sebastiano . . . nel nobile impianto e nel ritmo del panneggio dichiara una derivazione classica tradotta nei termini del gotico incipiente, *nella direzione, aggiugeremmo del Cristo di Amiens*." Nella sua monografia del 1979 la studiosa aveva invece più correttamente mantenuto una formulazione generica (senza il corsivo qui usato nella citazione) che non coinvolgeva Amiens (la cui plastica, oltretutto, è indicativa di un gotico non certo "incipiente"!). Si veda Calò Mariani 1979, 48. Del tutto fuori strada l'Aceto 1990, 48, che troppo ottimisticamente scrive che "le sculture di Termoli . . . hanno il fiato per reggere il confronto persino con le grandi statue allineate nello strombo dei portali [di Chartres sud]"!

59. La possibilità di modelli francesi del dodicesimo secolo (insieme con altri di altro segno) venne indicata per San Giovanni in Venere dal Buschhausen, *Bauplastik*, 1978, 353–354 ed è stata decisamente riassunta dall'Aceto 1990, 48 (figg. 46–47) con indicazione di altri monumenti, più recenti (e addirittura con un'assegnazione, a mio avviso assolutamente inverosimile, a scultore francese). Le relazioni fra San Giovanni in Venere e Termoli vennero già proposte dal Buschhausen 1978, 336–337, per la medesima "Einberechnung der Untersicht." Furono poi ribadite e specificate in relazione al modulo fisiognomico dalla Calò Mariani 1979, 48–49 e 1984, 40.

60. Le teste coronate femminili sono quelle sul capitello della quarta parasta, chiaramente riprodotte da Calò Mariani 1979, figg. 28a–b. Valgano i riferimenti ad analoghe teste coronate (in tutt'altro contesto figurativo) nei portali di Chartres, Parigi e Amiens: Sauerländer 1968, tavv. 92, 148, 168. La qualità, lo devo ribadire, è naturalmente ben altra.

61. Quest'ipotetica relazione di dipendenza dai capitelli di Troia è del tutto teorica e genericamente giustificata dalle assonanze, qui involgarite, con la scultura francese. Dovrà sempre sottolinearsi quanto è andato perduto. La datazione della scultura di Termoli è problema non facile, che la Calò Mariani ha affrontato con meritoria prudenza. Non saprei escludere, visto il divario di stili, che le sculture—statue, capitelli, rilievi—abbiano differenziate cronologie (L'Annunciazione, per esempio, che i restauri hanno mostrato di non essere originariamene pertinente alla facciata, ha uno stile tutto diverso da quello delle parti figurate dei capitelli, salvo il primo di sinistra). Poiché la questione cronologica è qui secondaria, nella misura in cui essa non investe la diretta attività di scultori "gotici" d'importazione, mi permetto di non approfondirla se non nei termini di cui qui di seguito nel testo.

62. Per l'ambito cronologico e stilistico in questione non ci sono riferimenti cogenti, ma a titolo esemplativo della verosimiglianza di queste importazioni—o della forte dipendenza formale da queste *perdute* importazioni—può almeno valere il riferimento alla statua lignea della Madonna col Bambino in trono, a Brindisi, che fu già contestualizzata al presente problema dal Wentzel 1954, 187 (e sulla quale si legga la successiva scheda (n. 14) in *Mostra dell'arte in Puglia dal Tardo antico al Rococo* [cat. mostra], a cura di Michele D'Elia (Bari, 1964), 15–16.

Per le linee generali della questione e taluni loro approfondimenti: Géza de Francovich, "Holzkruzifixe des 13. Jahrhunderts in Italien," *Mit-*

teilungen des kunsthistorischen Institutes in Florenz 5 (1938), 152–172; Géza de Francovich, *Scultura medievale in legno* (Roma, 1943); *Sculture lignee nella Campania* [cat. mostra], a cura di Ferdinando Bologna e Raffaello Causa (Napoli, 1950), 21–30. Nel Catalogo della *Mostra dell'arte in Puglia* sono schedate (ai numeri 11, 12 e 13) altre tre opere ben esemplative della vivace circolazione dei fatti plastici europei in quella regione. Ne *La Valle Siciliana o del Mavone*, Documenti dell'Abruzzo teramano 1.1) (Roma, 1983), 300–304, è discussa da Ferdinando Bologna una statua lignea di cui lo studioso mette in risalto (con un po' di ottimismo) la "fresca conoscenza dei fatti chartrensi" (p. 304).

63. La discussione sulla "direzione" dei nessi fra Terrasanta e costa adriatica nell'ambito della plastica monumentale è ampia ed articolata. Essendo qui inutile ripercorrerne le tappe in dettaglio, mi limito a indicare il più volte citato volume del Buschhausen 1979 e un mio articolo recensivo: Valentino Pace, "Sculpture italienne en Terre sainte ou sculpture des croisés en Italie? A propos d'un livre récent," *Cahiers de civilisation médiévale* 27 (1984), 251–257. Alla luce del possibile *a quo* del 1187 per la scultura di derivazione gerosolimitana (essendo quello il termine limite incontrovertibilmente stabilito da Zehava Jacoby, "The Tomb of Baldwin V, King of Jerusalem [1185–1186], and the Workshop of the Temple Area," *Gesta* 18.2 [1979], 3–14), mi chiedo se queste parti decorative di Termoli, tanto strettamente legate a Gerusalemme da far pensare a uno scultore gerosolimitano, non debbano datarsi al 1200 circa, in anticipo dunque sulle parti figurative—o almeno su parte di esse.

64. Sul portale settentrionale della cattedrale di Foggia: Jacobs 1968, 179–212; Buschhausen 1979, 312–313. Aceto 1990, 28, ne fa solo un generico accenno, con datazione (didascalia alla fig. 16) al terzo-quarto decennio del Duecento. A mio parere la lunetta della "Maestà" è di tutt'altra mano del rilievo con Cristo e angeli, col quale viene spesso a torto accomunata e di cui non deve dunque condividere la datazione.

65. Il confronto deve essere esperito con lo stile dei capitelli nel loro insieme e non può purtroppo avvalersi di simili esiti iconografici che ne facilitino la comprensione. Nonostante le differenze—nella scala di grandezze e d'impostazione, fra le figure *in movimento* di Nazareth e quelle *statiche* di Foggia—lo stile denota infatti, a mio avviso, basilari similitudini, soprattutto con il capitello di San Tommaso. Per l'inquadramento critico dei capitelli della Terrasanta rinvio a: Valentino Pace, "I capitelli di Nazareth e la scultura 'franca' del XII secolo a Gerusalemme," in *Scritti di storia dell'arte in onore di Roberto Salvini* (Firenze, 1984), 87–95. Non ha portato nuovi argomenti alla soluzione del loro problema formale il libro di Jaroslav Folda, *The Nazareth Capitals and the Crusader Shrine of the Annunciation* (University Park, PA-London, 1986).

66. Per le diverse opinioni cronologiche si veda la letteratura qui citata alla nota 64.

GARY M. RADKE
Syracuse University

The Palaces of Frederick II

Anyone who would attempt to discuss the palaces of Frederick II encounters numerous obstacles: paucity of extant remains, very few literary references, small amounts of comparative material, and the problematic term "palace" itself. For Frederick's contemporaries, the word *palatium* was fraught with ambiguity. It could, of course, refer to a rambling royal, papal, or imperial residence,[1] but the term *palatium* was just as frequently used like the modern Italian word *palazzo*, which is applied to most any multistoried, urban structure. Inventories and censuses frequently title the main building or hall of any castle a *palatium*, and even purely utilitarian structures, like the building housing three mills in a 1304 papal document, were termed the same.[2] Frederick himself sometimes used *palatium* interchangeably with *castrum*—which we think of as a fort, fortress, or castle—and also with *domus*, the word often applied to his hunting lodges and primary residences.[3] The handsome detailing and impressive luxury manifested in all his buildings—whether fortresses, hunting lodges, or palaces—served only to blur distinctions between what we usually view as separate building types.[4]

One road out of this dilemma might be to abandon the term *palace* altogether and see each of Frederick's buildings as uniquely serving complex, multiple functions, which in some ways they did. But in so doing I believe that we might also be in danger of losing a set of distinctions that *were* operable in the Middle Ages. No medieval writer has left us an unequivocal definition of what constituted a palace, but some writers did distinguish it from other types of structures. The chronicler of S. Giustina in Padua, for example, was very comfortable in dividing Frederick's buildings into two major categories: palaces and fortifications,[5] just as in 1242 Frederick used the two terms *domus* and *castrum* in his Repair Statute for distinguishing between primarily residential and primarily military structures.[6] The chronicler said that Frederick "had palaces built with incomparable fervor and of such beauty and proportions as though he was going to be able to live forever." Palaces, in other words, contributed to one's undying fame. The motivation for the erection of his fortifications was quite different. The chronicler tells us that Frederick "raised fortresses and towers on the tops of the mountains and in the cities as though he was afraid of being sieged by his enemies from one moment to the other." At least for the Paduan, then, palaces exhibited confidence; fortifications, fear. But the fear was two-edged, for castles powerfully intimidated his fearsome adversaries. As the chronicler concludes: "All this he made to demonstrate his power, by inciting fear and admiration, and thus impressing his name so profoundly in the memory of men that nothing would ever be able to cancel it out."

This is entirely consonant with an extremely rare and insightful passage on palaces by Theodoric's biographer, Cassiodorus.[7] He pointed out that there was a reciprocal relationship between a ruler and his palace. On the one hand, the ruler's power entitled him to a palace; on the other, the form and splendor of his palace confirmed and contributed to his status as a leader. Cassiodorus also insisted that a palace was a retreat, a place where the ruler could rest and relax, primarily in order to prepare himself for further public duty. Just as important, Cassiodorus continues, a palace was to have representational characteristics. Ambassadors, for example, would sense from outer aspects of the building the character of the ruler within. In turn, the ruler would delight in the palace's physical beauty and draw personal strength from it. A palace, then, served as both reward for and confirmation of power, as a retreat, source of strength, and a symbolic extension of the ruler himself.

In this context it does not seem quite so surprising that Frederick used both the terms *castrum* and *palatium* when writing to his overseer about construction at Castel Maniace in Siracusa.[8] The structure was obviously intended to serve as a major fortification and therefore the term *castrum* was appropriate, but Frederick clearly saw the structure in Siracusa—and all his major building projects for that matter—as reflections of himself and his imperial ideal.[9] He paid so much personal attention to its form because he understood that the classically detailed building would stand as a reflection of himself and his rule. In this and in insisting on what must have been a most comfortable and luxurious interior, Frederick was treating it, and his other major building projects, very much like a palace. This dual terminology made pragmatic sense insofar as Frederick continued to need to defend as well as rule his far-flung territory. He also must have known that contemporaries would have had little difficulty in viewing the structure in more than one way. For example, when Nicholas Iamsilla examined Manfred's motivation for rebuilding the *castrum* in Enna in Sicily, Iamsilla explicitly stated that "that city could not be ruled well without a *castrum*."[10] Iamsilla does not say "defended well" or "held well," expressions we would expect if the *castrum* were to be seen exclusively in military terms, but "ruled well," an expression that rings of administrative and governmental utility.

That said, does this mean that there were no structures that served *exclusively* as palaces, as those retreats, rewards, and symbolic extensions of the ruler that Cassiodorus describes, ones that did not combine a military aspect with a residential and representational one? Perhaps not. Frederick singled out Foggia as his imperial seat and referred to it with the obviously residential term *domus*, a term he also applied to his hunting lodges and retreats.[11] But his highly sympathetic chronicler Riccardo da San Germano used the obviously military term *castellum* to refer to Foggia,[12] and in the one surviving reference to Castel del Monte Frederick calls it a *castrum*.[13] All his buildings served multiple purposes. Still, one kind of function usually did predominate over the other. In applying the residential term *domus* to his retreats and the imperial seat at Foggia, Frederick shows that he did distinguish their primary function from that of his fortifications. Taken together, as the Paduan chronicler had done, they all gave witness to his imperial ideal, as Frederick clearly sensed when he ordered Lombard captives from the victory of Cortenuova to be shown Foggia and other imperial buildings in Capitanata.[14]

If we now turn to discuss specific buildings that may be understood as palaces of Frederick II—and one can argue for a good number of candidates, including the handsomely designed compound at Frederick's Saracen colony of Lucera and his finely outfitted hunting lodges—there is one that stands out from the rest: the compound in Foggia.[15] Centrally located amidst a ring of castles and mountains, it stood on the strategic crossroads between Frederick's Puglian ports to the east and Naples to the west. As luck would have it, only a part of a doorway and two inscriptions survive. At least the inscriptions are informative.[16] The longer of the two gives the date 1223 and explicitly states: "The Emperor Frederick ordered this to be built so that the city of Foggia might become the illustrious royal seat of the empire." In 1223, then, just two years after Frederick saw Puglia for the first time and as he was just bringing order to his Sicilian kingdom, he decided on a new geographic center for his empire, clearly recognizing that insular Sicily was too far south to serve as an effective center for realizing his imperial ambitions.

In spite of the extremely peripatetic life of Frederick II[17]—and of all medieval popes, kings, and emperors for that matter—Foggia quite clearly functioned as much as a capital as any city could. Frederick himself spent several months of most years there, frequently in winter.[18] His daughter was married there in 1239; Frederick spent the spring of 1240 there, holding a court day in April; and in 1241 his third wife, Isabella of England, died there in childbirth after an extensive period of residence. Frederick continued to refer to his own childhood capital of Palermo as "sedes regni nostro," but Foggia quickly became the focal point of his mainland kingdom. Surrounded by three main treasury centers at Melfi, Lucera, and Canosa, as well as by the famous ring of hunting lodges and their artificial lakes and tended gardens,[19] Frederick thus established a Puglian capital that recalled Palermo and its renowned suburban retreats even as it supplanted them.[20]

We are only certain of two architectural features of the palace at Foggia: the surviving entrance arch and a large courtyard that is mentioned in accounts of the 1273 wedding of the Angevin princess Beatrice.[21] Chroniclers are insistent that much of the interior boasted marble decorations—statues, pillars of verd-antique, multicolored floors, carved lions, and basins[22]—features that indeed seem plausible given Frederick's long residence at the Norman palace in Sicily. In 1240 Frederick ordered stone sculpture to be carried overland from Naples to Lucera, and two years later we hear of a male bronze statue and a cast of a cow for fountains in the same compound.[23] The richly colored and textured materials employed at Castel del Monte may also give us a hint of Foggia's splendors. But the specific configurations in which these kinds of materials appeared at Foggia and in what sequence they may have been arranged remain unknown.

A good number of Frederick's fortifications and hunting lodges were organized around courtyards and may at least provide a schema for imagining the lost palace. Fully centralized arrangements like Castel del Monte and Lucera do not appear in Frederick's surviving buildings until the 1240s, so the rectangular examples of Lagopesole and Gravina di Puglia may be informative.[24] At Gravina, which Frederick referred to as one of his "places of solace" and which, like Foggia, carried the designation *domus*, a description from 1309 speaks of a tower over the entrance with an upper story containing a chapel. To either side of the courtyard were service areas, while at the end of the court was a three-story residence whose uppermost story let out onto a great corbeled balcony overlooking the countryside. The same general configuration was followed by the Angevins when they built a new palace inside the fortifications of Lucera. But what did such a palace need to contain? What services might it have been required to accommodate?

We know that under Frederick "the administration of justice, the levying and collecting of taxes, the waging of war, the control of the fiscal system, the initiation of new laws and ordinances—all these were functions of the central government, the *curia regis*."[25] These functions were carried out through the offices of a well-developed bureaucracy that was increasingly centralized around the emperor himself. There were three main administrative units: the justiciary, the financial office or chamber, and the documents office or chancery. The grand master justiciar, his four high court judges, and their assistants regularly resided with the emperor, as did the officers of the chancery. Frederick's post-1242 Chancery Rules speak explicitly of a chancery building at least two stories high,[26] a *domus cancellarie* in which the notaries worked every day except Sunday and whose upper story and private areas were designated for the examination of petitions by the protonotary, who both headed the chancery and served as Frederick's personal secretary. Near the chancery were to be lodgings for counselors, the sealer of documents, notaries, judges, lawyers, and notaries of the court of justice.

Though much of the state treasury and archive were divided in the 1240s among Lucera, Canosa, and the emperor's frequent summer residence, Melfi, which also served as the seat of the exchequer court,[27] the chamberlain and his immediate staff needed to be accommodated wherever Frederick was in residence. Part of the treasury always traveled with him. In Frederick's siege city of Victoria, for example, looting Parmesans found gold, silver, precious stones, vases, vestments, decorations, splendid bed covers, and the emperor's ceremonial crown,[28] all of which would have been in the custody of the imperial chamber. The chamberlain was also head of the emperor's personal finance and management of the palace, delegating day-to-day management to the seneschal, who employed notaries and others to keep track of food, wine, bread, wax, and other kitchen expenses, as well as provisions for the emperor's wife and family. The cellarer and master cooks, their servants, and slaves were also obviously essential, as were the keepers of the menagerie that traveled with the imperial court and the court entertainers, who included the famous Saracen women who danced on top of rolling balls.[29] Space for the imperial marshall, his troops, their pages, and their horses would also have been highly desirable.

To be sure, not all these imperial retainers needed to be housed in permanent quarters. The Saracens of Lucera were renowned for their ability to make and raise the tents that were used during many of Frederick's travels,[30] and even the gerontocracy of the papal curia sometimes camped out in tents and wooden huts or borrowed quarters from other authorities.[31] Neither did imperial purveyors all reside in Foggia. The castellan of Salpi was entrusted with raising birds; horses were bred at Palazzo San Gervasio; Saracen girls were employed on looms at Lucera, Melfi, Canosa, and Messina; expert weapon makers and finishers, intarsists, carpenters, stone carvers, and furriers worked there as well.[32]

But at any place that might function as a palace, and surely at Foggia, the complex must have contained at least one major hall. Halls were primary distinguishing features of all medieval palaces.[33] It was here that kings, popes, and emperors held court, met ambassadors, and hosted splendid banquets. Halls were the most appropriate setting for the dispensing of justice. In them we need to imagine Frederick, as he has been described, enthroned and flanked by his logothete, sitting with a gigantic crown suspended over his head while his subjects approached him and prostrated themselves, as did all in attendance.[34]

In the case of a complex like Foggia, with its large courtyard, the hall was typically set across the far end of the court, opposite the entrance, as was also the case at Lagopesole. This insured that the main structure of the palace proper, the building containing the main reception halls and frequently the private rooms of the emperor and his family, was sited with its greatest and most impressive expanse highly visible to anyone approaching the façade. In German imperial palaces, as at both Goslar and Gelnhausen, for example, architectural emphasis was placed on the center of this long façade wall by means of a large window or impressive double-rise staircase. On the interior, the emperor's throne dominated the middle of the hall's long back wall and reinforced the lateral orientation of the space.[35]

The main halls of papal palaces, on the other hand, were not laterally but longitudinally oriented.[36] They were sometimes set so that their bulk, too, was highly visible, as at Viterbo, but thirteenth-century papal halls were not set in large courtyards and were all entered from or near their short ends. Impressive staircases frequently projected from their façades instead of clinging to them. Halls in Italian communal palaces and at Westminster and Windsor in England, for example, were oriented like papal ones, so the longitudinal type is not distinctly papal, but it *is* quite remarkably non-Germanic and nonimperial. After the Carolingian revival, halls in German imperial palaces were rarely oriented longitudinally. They were sometimes entered near their short ends, as was probably the case at Gelnhausen, but the major focus within them was on the middle of the broad back wall. The same would seem to have been true at the Norman palace in Palermo. Thus it is very possible that in this period of infamous conflicts between popes and emperors, the hall and palace complex at Foggia were just as distinct from papal halls and palaces as were the emperor's and the pope's convictions about the proper balance between sacred and secular authority in Italy.

What they may have had more in common was a concern for ample and impressive size.[37] Many papal halls verged on or exceeded thirty meters in length, as did the Norman hall at Palermo. Given the fact that the eleventh-century imperial palace at Goslar was of even greater size—nearly fifty meters long—as was Charlemagne's audience hall in Aachen, grand dimensions most likely prevailed at Foggia too.

Whether Frederick also erected a chapel in the palace complex is unknown. Sovereigns nearly always distinguished their official residences with impressive two-story chapels, as at Goslar or in Louis IX's famous Sainte Chapelle.[38] Chapels are the most commonly surviving elements of German imperial palaces, and Frederick grew up attending services in the splendid Palatine chapel in Palermo. Of course, Frederick was not much of a church builder—Charles of Anjou found it necessary to add chapels to most of Frederick's hunting lodges[39]—but Foggia was Frederick's capital, and when he founded the palace in 1223 he was still on relatively good terms with the papacy. Even after his second excommunication, Frederick founded the church of Saint Victor in his siege city of Victoria; so it is possible that, along with the ceremonial halls, apartments for himself and his family, administrative offices and lodgings, service facilities and storerooms, there was also a chapel.

By what financial mechanisms was Frederick able to indulge in such impressive amounts of construction? Thirteenth-century popes depended on local communes to build and finance their palaces outside Rome, but many of the funds necessary for Frederick's construction seem to have come from imperial coffers. In Viterbo, for example, Frederick entrusted his own agents to buy property for a provincial palace, in spite of the fact that local citizens might have been tapped as a ready source of financing.[40] They had already built a palace for his grandfather Barbarossa with private funds, and the commune later assumed the cost and responsibility for erecting a papal palace, so such arrangements were still a possibility in Frederick's time. In Catania the city did contribute 200 ounces of gold toward building the Castello Ursino, but this was forced construction, as must have been the repair of the *castrum* in Taranto, whose cost and supervision of construction were divided among the citizens of Taranto and other towns, the archbishopric, and individual nobles.[41]

Still, when it came to repair and maintenance of imperial property, including the palace in Foggia, the local citizenry was expected to take responsibility.[42] In Lucera, with its largely Saracen population, Frederick left no doubt about such duties; they extended to both the Christians and the Saracens of the town.[43] This practice was necessary because no centers save Foggia and Melfi saw Frederick for any extended period of time, and even his new capital, Foggia, and the ancient Apulian capital and site of his exchequer court, Melfi, could count on his personal presence for no more than several months a year. As any good medieval monarch, Frederick was always on the move.

Finally, I would like to consider briefly the structure that served as Frederick's palace at Lucera.[44] Like the palace at Foggia, it, too, is almost completely destroyed, but excavations and a few eighteenth-century drawings have allowed for some relatively secure reconstructions. Dominating Frederick's Saracen colony, the palace was a hybrid structure. Its base seems always to have consisted of a massive battered plinth that was frankly military in form and function, though the form we see now may date from Angevin times.[45] It was designed to be so impregnable that archaeologists have yet to determine where and how—or if—it was entered at that level. Above stood a multistoried palace with a central courtyard, probably square on the main level, octagonal on the upper story.

This is not the usual medieval palace. Though other royal, imperial, and papal palaces regularly had some defenses—there were towers, crenellations, and a secured entrance at Palermo, for example—palaces were distinguished from castles by their relative lack of fortification and their openly confident stance. This was usually made possible by situating the palace within a walled precinct or allowing the walls of the city in which it was located or the particular site to provide additional security. What is more, palaces were usually aggregate structures whose core buildings were laid out with room to grow; additions were expected and stretched out to an impressive extent. A form as self-contained and self-sufficient as the palace in Lucera flew in the face of this tradition. Whereas the organic growth of other palaces could easily accommodate changing and expanding state bureaucracy, often allowing chancery and chamber buildings to be linked into the complex from the very beginning, at Lucera Frederick's chancery building was a separate structure.[46] When Charles of Anjou took possession of Lucera, he felt compelled to erect an entirely new palace structure,[47] including a palatial residence for the king, a court dining hall, a contiguous structure for the office of the treasury, and another structure connected to that and divided into two parts for the kitchen and the dispensary, with yet other areas assigned to the king's cellarer and baker.

Frederick's palace was much more obviously a fortification. Indeed, in the 1242 Repair Statute that divided his buildings into residential and military categories, the structures at Lucera, both old and new, were termed fortifications.[48] Lucera was, after all, the site of an imperial mint and held part of the imperial treasury and archive. It was also a largely Saracen and therefore relatively volatile colony.[49] Though Frederick had great confidence in his Saracen warriors, he was certainly clear-sighted enough to realize that their loyalties could never be taken for granted. What he needed here, then, was a combination *castrum-palatium*, and that is what I believe he built. The self-contained form and massive battered plinth assured the security of the emperor and the treasury, even while the overall structure displayed so many features we have come to expect from our working definition of a palace: it was impressive and reflected the particular power and vision of Frederick. Ambassadors *could* sense from its exterior the character of the ruler within. Further, its rich decorations, including the marble and bronze statues mentioned earlier, must have made it a beautiful retreat and a place of solace for the emperor when he passed through this corner of his realm: not quite the harem that papal detractors claimed it to be, but certainly a luxurious residence.

Lucera demonstrates that, as in so many other fields, Frederick and his builders conceived strikingly novel and powerful solutions to complex problems. His palaces met many of the criteria that contemporaries expected of such structures—otherwise there would have been little sense in building them the way he did—and yet Frederick's palaces so expanded traditional expectations of this building type that they stood out from all others. And wasn't that the point after all? To give credit to the unique authority of the emperor and to set him apart, as well as above, all others was exactly what he desired.

NOTES

1. Jacques Gardelles, "Le palais dans l'Europe occidentale chrétienne du Xe au XIIe siècle," *Cahiers de civilisation médiévale* 19 (1976), 115–134 notes (115–116) that in Germany the term regularly referred to imperial building. The first recorded instance in papal documents dates from 813; see *Liber Pontificalis*, 2:134 and Karl Jordan, "Die Entstehung der römischen Kurie," *Zeitschrift der Savigny-Stiftung für Rechtsgeschichte, Kanonistische Abteilung* 28 (1939), 100–152, esp. 100–101, notes 2–5.

2. Augustin Theiner, *Codex Diplomaticus Dominii Temporalis S. Sedis* (Rome, 1861), *756–1334* (repr. Frankfurt am Main, 1964), 1:403.

3. Giuseppe Agnello, *L'architettura sveva in Sicilia* (Rome, 1935), 26, notes both terms in Frederick's references to Castel Maniace in Siracusa. The Angevins were similarly loose with their terminology. Note, for example, a document of 8 August 1271 "in palacio seu castro Orte," in Eduard Sthamer, *Capitinata* (*Capitanata*), vol. 1 of *Dokumente zur Geschichte der Kastellbauten Kaiser Friedrichs II. und Karls I. von Anjou* (Leipzig, 1912), 169.

4. Eugenio Dupré Theseider, "Federico II, ideatore di castelli e città," *Archivio storico pugliese* 26 (1973), 25–40, even claims that Frederick had no "vero palazzo reale" (28), but more often confusion has arisen from observations like those by Carl A. Willemsen, *I castelli di Federico II nell'Italia meridionale* (Naples, 1979), 53, noting how Frederick's castles approach palaces "proprio per i lussuosi, raffinati, e splendidi ornamenti."

5. Carl A. Willemsen and Dagmar Odenthal, *Puglia, terra dei Normanni e degli Svevi* (Bari, 1978), 55, give the text without fully exploring the implications for our topic.

6. *Acta Imperii inedita Saeculi XIII et XIV*, ed. Eduard Winkelmann, 2 vols. (Innsbruck, 1880–1885; repr. Aalen, 1964), 1:769–780.

7. Var. VII 5, 1, according to Wilhelm Ensslin, *Theoderich der Grosse* (Munich, 1947), 259.

8. See above, note 3.

9. See the thorough treatment of this ideal in Antonino de Stefano, *L'idea imperiale di Federico II* (Florence, 1927).

10. Quoted in Francesca Bocchi, "Castelli urbani e città nel regno di Sicilia all'epoca di Federico II," in *Federico II e l'arte del Duecento italiano*, ed. Angiola M. Romanini, 2 vols. (Galatina, 1980), 1:53–74, esp. 54.

11. Arthur Haseloff, *Die Bauten der Hohenstaufen in Unteritalien* (Leipzig, 1920), 1:94, records mention of 25 *domus* structures in Capitanata. More specifically, see Jean L. A. Huillard-Bréholles, ed., *Historia Diplomatica Friderici Secundi . . .*, 6 vols. (Paris, 1852–1861), 5:477, 627, 696, 813, 847, 853, 941, and 964.

12. Recorded in Haseloff 1920, 68.

13. Agnello 1935, 24–30, gives various references, including later Angevin ones.

14. Willemsen and Odenthal 1978, 63.

15. See especially Haseloff 1920, 65–184. More recent studies include Michele Bellucci, "Il palazzo imperiale di Foggia," *Archivio storico pugliese* 4 (1951), 121–136; Dankwart Leistikow, "La residenza dell'imperatore Federico II a Foggia," *La Capitanata* 14 (1976), 192–219; and Willemsen 1979, 17–19.

16. Sic Cesar fieri iussit opus istud
Proto Bartholomeus sic construxit illud
Anno ab Incarnatione MCCXXIII mense
Junii, undecima Indictione, regnante domino nostro
Frederico Imperatore Romanorum semper Augusto
Anno tertio, et Rege Siciliae anno vigesimosexto,
Hoc opus feliciter inceptum est,
Praephato Domino precipiente.

Hoc fieri iussit Fredericus Cesar ut urbs sit
Fogia regalis sedes inclita imperialis.

17. Haseloff 1920, 46–48, gives an exhaustive chronology of Frederick's stays in Capitanata. See also Gina Fasoli, "Castelli e strade nel 'Regnum Siciliae': L'itinerario di Federico II," in *Federico II e l'arte*, 1:27–52, esp. 46–49,]and the "Karte der Aufenthaltsorte Friedrichs II" in *Die Zeit der Staufer: Geschichte—Kunst—Kultur* [exh. cat., Württembergisches Landesmuseum], ed. Reiner Haussherr, 6 vols. (Stuttgart, 1977–1979), 4:map 9.

18. Frederick is recorded to have been in Foggia in February of 1221 and 1222, December through January 1222–1223, the end of April 1223, May through June and November through December 1225, September through December 1226, December 1227 through April 1228, August 1229, February through April 1230, May and November 1231, late September through November 1232, December 1234 through March 1235, March through May 1240, October and December 1241, January through April 1242, February 1243, October 1243 through March 1244, September 1246, November 1246 through January 1247, October 1249 through April 1250, and October through December 1250.

19. The most famous of these was S. Lorenzo in Pantano with its walled menagerie, lake, and bird hunting park. See Haseloff 1920, 79–85 and Willemsen 1979, 19, which also includes references to Frederick's great love for Apricena, especially at Christmas time (1226, 1230, and 1232, for example). Also popular were Gudiola, S. Gervasio, and Orta (Willemsen and Odenthal 1978, 63). For Orta see Don Ferrante, "Il palazzo di Federico II ad Orta in Capitanata," *Napoli Nobilissima* 10 (1901), 30, and Michele Cirillo, "Ancora del palazzo di Federico II ad Orta," *Napoli Nobilissima* 10 (1901), 75–77.

20. Angela Marino Guidoni, "Architettura, paesaggio e territorio dell'Italia meridionale nella cultura Federiciana," in *Federico II e l'arte*, 1:75–98 notes (84) that the villas in Palermo were admired by Arab visitors. Especially renowned were the villa at Altofonte, the artificial lake at Maredolce, and the hunting lodge at Favara. See Giulia Davì, "Il castello di Giuliana e il palazzo reale di Palermo," in *Federico II e l'arte*, 1:147–152, and, for plans and a freely interpreted reconstruction, Francesco Valenti, "Cronaca delle belle arti: Il palazzo reale di Palermo," *Bollettino*

d'arte 4 (1925), 512–528.

21. Haseloff 1920, 69.

22. Reported in Ernst Kantorowicz, *Frederick the Second, 1194–1250*, trans. Emily O. Lorimer (London, 1931), 323.

23. Texts in Sthamer 1912, 10 and Haseloff 1920, 107–108.

24. Discussion in Carl A. Willemsen, *Die Bauten der Hohenstaufen in Süditalien: Neue Grabungs- und Forschungsergebnisse* (Cologne and Opladen, 1968), 40–41. Willemsen and Odenthal 1978, 63, record an explicit description of Gravina from 1309.

25. Thomas Curtis Van Cleve, *The Emperor Frederick II of Hohenstaufen, Immutator Mundi* (Oxford, 1972), 256. Kantorowicz 1931, chap. 5, discusses the imperial bureaucracy at some length. See also Hans Martin Schaller, "Kanzlei und Hofkapelle Kaiser Friedrichs II.," *Annali dell'Istituto Storico Italo-germanico in Trento* 2 (1976), 75–116, and Huillard-Bréholles, 5:cxv–clviii.

26. *Acta Imperii*, 1:735–739.

27. General remarks on all three can be found in Haseloff 1920, 109. See also Willemsen 1979, 36–40.

28. Matthew Paris, *Historia Anglorum, Historia Minor*, ed. Sir Frederic Madden (London, 1869), 3:34 and the very detailed description in Salimbene de Adam, *Cronica*, ed. Ferdinando Bernini (Bari, 1942), 1:292. Salimbene examined and held the crown in the sacristy of Parma cathedral, where it was displayed.

29. For servants and slaves in general, see Haseloff 1920, 115–119, and Kantorowicz 1931, 310–313 and 323.

30. Fasoli 1980, 48, also suggests that Frederick may have had a double set of tents like the Byzantine emperors.

31. Pierre Toubert, *Les structures du Latium médiéval: Le Latium méridional et la Sabine du IXe siècle à la fin du XIIe siècle*, Bibliothèque des Écoles Françaises d'Athènes et de Rome 221 (Rome, 1973), 2:1051–1052 note 1, gives examples of huts and also notes that in the mid-thirteenth century Alexander IV once camped on the edge of the Lake of Subiaco. Giuseppe Ermini, *I parlamenti dello stato della chiesa dalle origini al periodo Albornoziano*, Biblioteca della *rivista di storia del diritto italiano* 5 (Rome, 1930), 46 note 94, documents meetings in churches, halls, loggias, bishop's palaces, and communal palaces.

32. For Salpi see Sthamer 1912, 172 and Haseloff 1920, 95. For yet other specialists, see Haseloff 1920, 111–114.

33. Eugène-Emmanuel Viollet-le-Duc, *Dictionnaire raisonné de l'architecture française du XIe au XVIe siècle* (Paris, n.d.), 7:1 and 14; Gardelles 1976, 118; and Pierre Héliot, "Nouvelles remarques sur les palais épiscopaux et princiers de l'époque romane en France," *Francia, Forschungen zur westeuropäischen Geschichte* 4 (1976), 193–212, esp. 208–209, all agree that this feature was practically obligatory. For an examination of this sort of structure in England see Hugh Braun, *An Introduction to English Mediaeval Architecture*, 2d ed. (London, 1968), 155–169.

34. See Kantorowicz 1931, 236.

35. See Fritz Arens, "Die staufischen Königspfalzen," in *Die Zeit der Staufer*, 3:129–142.

36. See the typological studies in my forthcoming book, *The Palazzo dei Papi in Viterbo: Profile of a Thirteenth-Century Papal Palace.*

37. R. Allen Brown, H. M. Colvin, and A. J. Taylor, *The History of the King's Works*, gen. ed. H. M. Colvin, *The Middle Ages* (London, 1963), 1:fig. 9, provide an excellent comparison of various halls.

38. Inge Hacker-Sück, "La Sainte-Chapelle de Paris et les chapelles palatines du Moyen Age en France," *Cahiers archéologiques* 13 (1962), 217–257, has made an admirable survey of this type.

39. Sthamer 1912, 5, gives the document showing that S. Lorenzo in Pantano lacked a chapel until 1269.

40. Cesare Pinzi, *Storia della città di Viterbo* (Rome, 1887), 1:373–374, note 1, records documents appropriating forty houses.

41. Agnello 1935, 400 for Catania and *Acta Imperii*, 1:774 for Taranto.

42. *Acta Imperii*, 1:772.

43. *Acta Imperii*, 1:771.

44. The most exhaustive study remains Haseloff 1920, 185–340; see also Willemsen 1968, 25–38.

45. Willemsen 1968, 25–38.

46. Petitions were to be collected and distributed "ante domum cancellarie" (*Acta Imperii*, 1:736).

47. Eduard Sthamer, *Apulien und Basilicata*, vol. 2 of *Dokumente zur Geschichte der Kastellbauten Kaiser Friedrichs II. und Karls I. von Anjou* (Leipzig, 1926), 102–107, gives the elaborate surviving accounts of 9 January 1280.

48. *Acta Imperii*, 1:771.

49. See David Abulafia's contribution, "Ethnic Variety and Its Implications," in this volume.

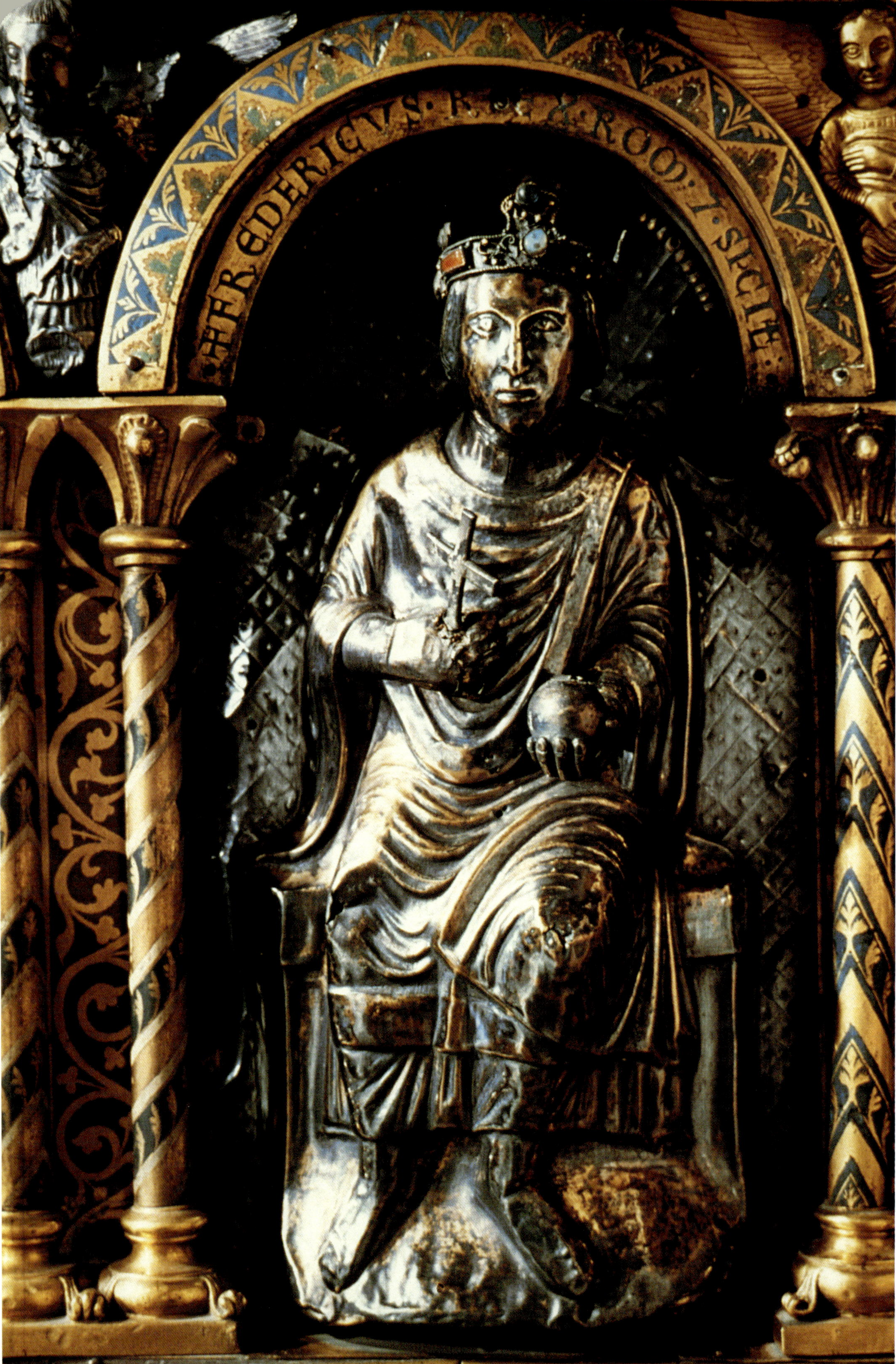

WILLIBALD SAUERLÄNDER
Zentralinstitut für Kunstgeschichte, Munich

Two Glances from the North: The Presence and Absence of Frederick II in the Art of the Empire; The Court Art of Frederick II and the opus francigenum

The reign of Frederick II from his election as king of Germany in 1215 until his death at Castel Fiorentino in 1250 corresponds to one of the most productive periods of medieval German art and architecture. From Trier in the west to Magdeburg in the east, early medieval cathedrals were rebuilt in modern forms. They were decorated with monumental statues which have been praised as the greatest achievements of the German or the Germanic genius surviving from the *Deutsche Kaiserzeit*, the imperial Middle Ages.[1] In addition to the bishops and the chapters of the cathedrals, the monastic orders, from the Augustinians and the Benedictines to the Cistercians and the Teutonic Order, were no less active as patrons. Castles were erected in great numbers, and construction in the growing cities was probably more extensive than ever since the days of the Romans.[2] But although German art historians since the thirties have often called this splendid production *imperial* and have labeled it with the untranslatable words *staufisch* or *spätstaufisch*, the most astonishing difference between the art of thirteenth-century Germany and Capetian France, Plantagenet England, or even the kingdom of Castile is the absence of a central monarchical power or, to put it bluntly, the absence of the emperor. There exists no Saint-Denis, no cathedral of Reims, no Sainte-Chapelle, or Westminster Abbey anywhere in thirteenth-century Germany. The bewildering diversity of art and architecture in the empire, which is much greater than in any other western European country, is one clear indication of growing political decentralization and the rapid deterioration of imperial power.[3] And yet a retrospective nostalgia, a desire to see the monumental presence of the emperor has been so fervent that art historians have tried hard to discover the absent Frederick in statues, images, and objects surviving from thirteenth-century Germany. They developed their own *Kyffhäusersage*.[4]

1. Aix-la-Chapelle, Minster, Frederick II, Shrine of Charlemagne, first half of thirteenth century
Photograph: Zentralinstitut für Kunstgeschichte, Munich

Strictly speaking there remain few monuments of German art from the first half of the thirteenth century that can surely or at least arguably be connected with the person or the intervention of Frederick II. The one case that cannot be doubted is the enthroned figure of the emperor on the shrine of Charlemagne at Aix-la-Chapelle (fig. 1). He appears as the last of sixteen rulers represented on the sides of this imperial reliquary. The inscription on the arch surrounding his head reads: "Fredericus Rex Rom(anorum) (et) Sici(l)iae."[5] The historical circumstances that explain the representation of Frederick II on the shrine of Charlemagne are rather pathetic. Charlemagne had been canonized, 29 December 1165, at the instigation of Frederick's grandfather, Emperor Frederick I Barbarossa.[6] The relics of the new saint were deposited in a wooden shrine, placed inside the chapel at Aix, "in locello ligneo in medio eiusdem basilice," as the *Continuatio Aquicinctina* reports.[7] The translation of Charlemagne to the present shrine with its ambitious iconographic program took place on 27 July 1215, the feast of Saint James the Great and the first anniversary of the battle at Bouvines. This translation was symbolically achieved by the then twenty-year-old Frederick II, who had been crowned king of Germany two days before.[8] In the annals of Reiner of Liège, the event is described as follows:

Feria secunda missa sollemniter celebrata, idem rex corpus beati Carlomanni, quod avus suus Fredericus imperator de terra levaverat, in sarcofagum nobilissimum, quod Aquenses fecerant, auro argento contextum reponi fecit, et accepto martello, depositoque pallio, cum artifice machinam ascendit, et videntibus cunctis cum magistro clavos infixos vasi firmiter clausit.[9]

The political significance of this solemn act and also of Frederick's representation as the last of the rulers on the shrine is evident. After his triumph over his unhappy rival, the Guelf Otto of Braunschweig, his peaceful entrance into the "capital and seat" of the kingship of Germany, Aix, and his coronation, Frederick became the legal successor of Saint Charlemagne and of the long series of rulers of the "Sacrum imperium" enthroned on Charlemagne's shrine. But there is also a deeper meaning to the iconography of Frederick's figure on the "sarcofagus nobilissimus." As is well known, Frederick had surprised his contemporaries at the moment of his coronation by taking the cross and announcing himself as a forthcoming crusader.[10] This announcement is reflected in his representation on the shrine by the cross that the king holds in his right hand.[11]

There remain for the art historian a number of delicate historical and, above all, chronological questions. A dendrochronological examination has shown that the oak used for the nucleus of the present shrine was cut at the earliest in 1182.[12] This confirms the earlier stylistic dating of the figures and the reliefs of the shrine to a period not before 1200.[13] The series of the rulers on the shrine, which is stylistically more or less of one issue, cannot have been complete in 1209. The predecessor of Frederick II in this gallery of emperors and kings, the already mentioned Otto of Braunschweig, shows an inscription that reads: "Otto IIII Romanor(um) I(m)perator."[14] Otto was crowned as Roman emperor by Pope Innocent III on 4 October 1209. Does this mean that the shrine of Charlemagne, which was initiated by the act of the Hohenstaufen Frederick I in 1165, was largely executed during the tenure of a ruler from the rival dynasty of the Guelfs?[15] Otto had been crowned king of Germany 9 June 1198 at Aix in open opposition to the elected candidate from the dynasty of the Hohenstaufen, Philip of Swabia.[16] Did Otto at this moment visually enter the succession of Saint Charlemagne by undertaking to complete a shrine begun by the Hohenstaufen Frederick I, who was the great foe of his father, Henry the Lion? In any case the shrine was still unfinished in summer 1215 at the time of the coronation of Frederick II. His image, stylistically similar to those of the other rulers, must have been added after June 1215. Of the eight narrative reliefs on the roof of the shrine, five celebrate Charlemagne as a crusader in Spain. About the ceremony that took place at Aix on 25 July 1215, David Abulafia writes: "Frederick was determined to show himself as the new Charlemagne. So after mass was ended, Frederick took the cross and vows, in the manner of a crusader."[17] Even if historians of style are reluctant to admit it, there is a good chance that the images celebrating Charlemagne as a crusader echo Frederick's vow to follow the example of Saint Charlemagne and to take the cross. This would date the reliefs on the roof of the shrine, or at least the majority of them, after Frederick's coronation. Be that as it may, the shrine was not complete by summer 1215. How much longer it took to be finished, we shall never precisely know. As Frederick is only called "Rex Romanorum et Siciliae," there is at least one secure *terminus ante quem*. Frederick was crowned as Roman emperor by Honorius III on 22 November 1220. After this date the inscription at Aix would have been different.

Thus Frederick II first appeared in German

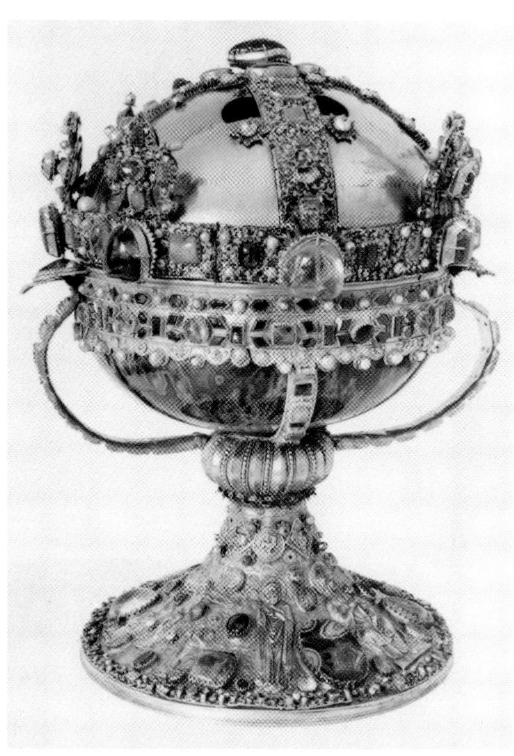

2. Reliquary, thirteenth century
Statens Historiska Museum, Stockholm; photograph: Antikvarisk-Topografiska Arkivet, Stockholm

art of the thirteenth century in dramatic circumstances. But how much like Frederick was this first "portrait"? Concerning facial expression, some historians have not hesitated to discover in these rather reticent features the emperor's famous *Schlangenblick*.[18] It is hard to follow such an all-too-confident suggestion. The best one can say is that Frederick appears as a fashionable young man of the early thirteenth century, without a beard—but so do two earlier rulers. His features may be called more youthful, and in this sense more modern, than those of most of his predecessors. Even such a statement is daring. Going further becomes mere wishful fantasy.

While a direct connection between Frederick II and the shrine of Charlemagne can be proved beyond doubt, my next example is based on a nostalgic identification of memorable historical circumstances with a glamorous object. The German Cistercian Caesarius of Heisterbach described in a well-known sermon Frederick's participation in the solemn translation of the relics of Saint Elizabeth, 1 May 1236.[19] Elizabeth was the daughter of King Andrew II of Hungary and the widow of Count Louis of Thuringia who had died in 1227 as a crusader following Frederick to the Holy Land. Elizabeth had died in the odor of sanctity in 1231. Her tomb soon became the center of a widespread pilgrimage, and in 1235 she was canonized by Pope Gregory IX.[20] Her translation on 1 May 1236 was a spectacular event, attracting princes, bishops, and an immense crowd of the faithful. The sources speak of no less than 1,200,000 people. Elizabeth was a royal saint, but as a child of the century of Saint Francis, she had turned with active charity toward the poor and the sick. Caesarius reports that Frederick himself carried her sarcophagus and that he put a golden crown with jewels on the head of the saint "who had been the daughter of a king." It was a homage of great symbolic moment: Elizabeth's royal crown on earth was transformed into the crown of heaven. From Edward the Confessor in England to Saint Louis in France, the twelfth and thirteenth centuries were the great period of royal saints.[21] Frederick's gesture must be seen in this fateful historical context. Other reports tell the same story in a different way. The chronicler Richard of Senones, who wrote somewhat later, also mentions Frederick's participation in the translation ceremony. However, he does not speak of a crown as the gift of the emperor. He states that Frederick gave his own golden cup, which was used as the precious receptacle for the head of Saint Elizabeth "who was said to have been his relative."[22] The church erected in her honor became Protestant in the days of the reform. Her shrine survived and is still shown at Marburg.[23] But the head-reliquary, with either Frederick's crown or cup, seems to have disappeared in the sixteenth century.

In 1919 Adolph Goldschmidt published a curious reliquary composed of a cup and a crown (fig. 2), which he had seen in the museum at Stockholm. Goldschmidt became interested in the piece because of its German origin. He proved, by a careful technical and stylistic analysis, that the mounting of the reliquary, its foot, and its crown had been made in Saxony between 1230 and 1240—just the right time for Frederick. But Goldschmidt left the questions of provenance and of the original function of the reliquary open and did not even mention a possible connection with Frederick's gift to Saint Elizabeth. He vaguely suggested that the piece might once have been part of the treasure of the so-called cathedral at Goslar and might have served as a head-reliquary of either Saint Nicholas or Saint Servatius.[24]

It was the new interest in medieval insignia, arising in the 1930s and culminating in Percy Ernst Schramm's monumental publication, *Herrschaftszeichen und Staatssymbolik*, which brought the Stockholm reliquary finally into direct connection with Frederick II and the ceremony of 1 May 1236.[25] Arpad Weixlgärtner, who published a detailed and careful study of the Stockholm piece in 1954, concluded rather emphatically: "In der ersten Hälfte des [13.] Jahrhunderts trieb der Stamm der Hohenstaufen in Friedrich II. sein eigenartigstes Reis. Es ist möglich, ja wahrscheinlich, daß mit ihm der Kronschmuck des Reliquiars zusammenhängt."[26] Moreover, it could be proven that the precious piece had been looted by the Swedish and stored at Würzburg in 1631.[27] Schramm then combined the reports of Caesarius of Heisterbach and Richard of Senones with the account of the looting of 1631 and the conjecture of Weixlgärtner in order to conclude that the Stockholm piece was the head-reliquary of Elizabeth with the cup and crown (or crowns) given by Frederick II in 1236.[28] It was an ingenious suggestion. The glamorous, even pompous, reliquary looted by the Swedish during the Thirty Years War, with its ancient bowl in an Ottonian (imperial?) mount, enriched by the remains of probably two (imperial?) crowns from the thirteenth century, would physically commemorate to this day the emperor's gift to the greatest royal saint of his reign. But not everyone seems to have been convinced by this hypothesis, and there are in fact good reasons to remain skeptical.[29] The foot of the Stockholm piece shows an elaborate iconographic program with a figure of the Virgin, scenes of the Crucifixion, and a Majestas Domini combined with a Deesis.[30] On the whole reliquary, however, there is neither an image nor the mention in an inscription of Saint Elizabeth. Thus the question must remain open whether the Stockholm piece is really the head-reliquary of Saint Elizabeth with the crown and cup given by Frederick. Frederick's magic for modern historians, archaeologists, and art historians is such that again and again, from Barletta to Stockholm, it has connected portraits and objects to his thrilling name.

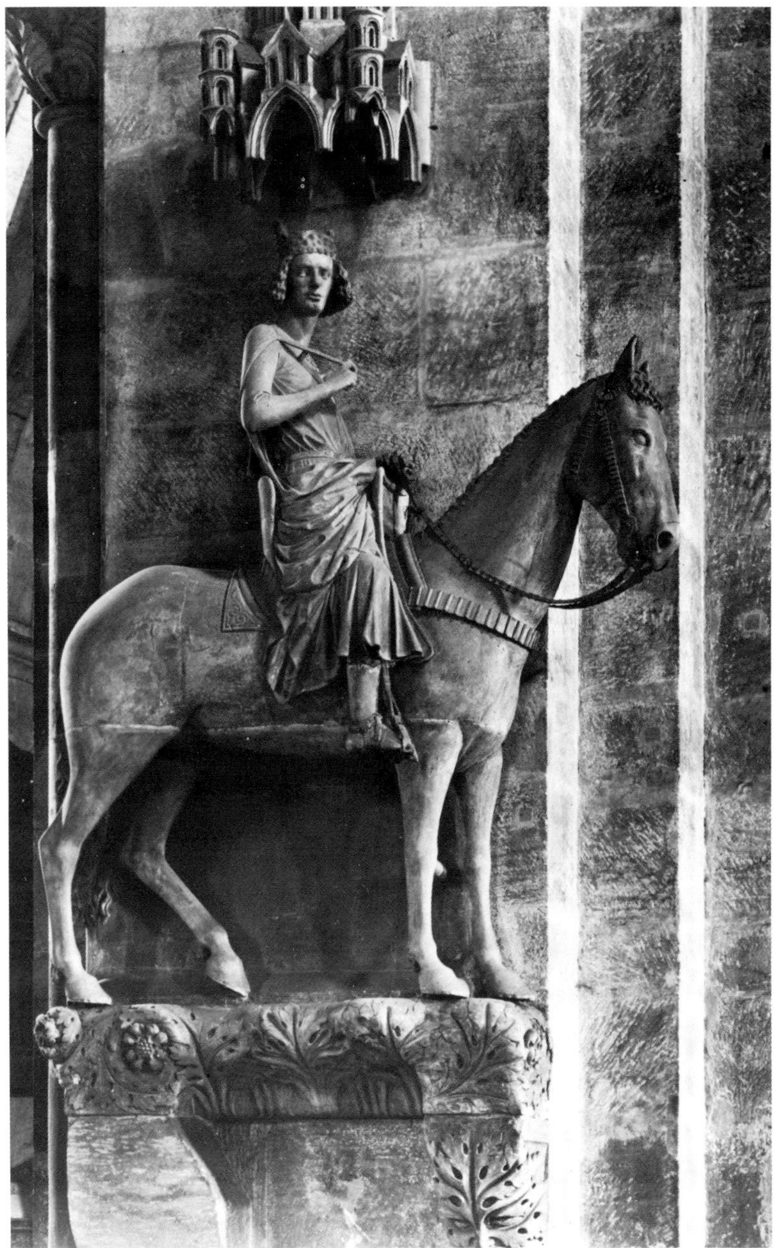

3. Bamberg cathedral, Rider, thirteenth century
Bildarchiv Foto Marburg

This seems particularly true of the two most ambitious "Kyffhäuser-dreams" connected with Frederick II in German art history: the statues in the interior of the cathedral of Saints Peter and George at Bamberg and on the "Alte Markt" in the town of

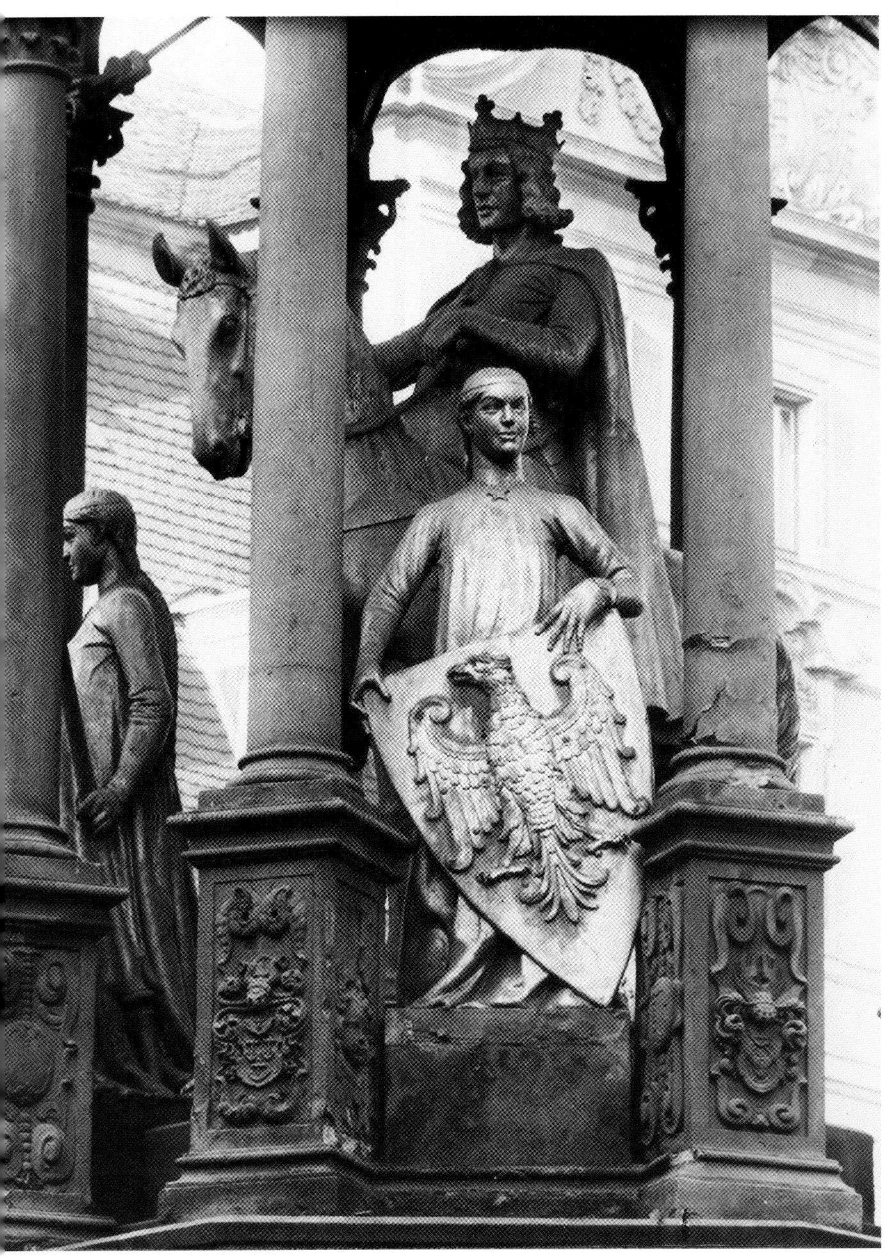

4. Magdeburg Rider, thirteenth century
Kulturhistorisches Museum, Magdeburg; photograph: Bildarchiv Foto Marburg

Magdeburg. The two cases should not be confounded. The rider at Bamberg (fig. 3) appears in an ecclesiastical context; the statue at Magdeburg is a public monument.

The figure at Bamberg remains for us strictly anonymous, and all we can say with certainty is that it represents a crowned ruler, either emperor or king. Since the sculpture stands inside a church, it should most likely commemorate a Christian monarch who was either canonized or at least venerated as a saint. There is no medieval document that identifies the statue. The rider is first mentioned in sources from the eighteenth century, where he is identified as Stephen of Hungary. King Stephen of Hungary, brother-in-law of Emperor Henry II, the founder of the see at Bamberg, had been canonized in 1083. Very early on he was venerated in the Franconian cathedral.[31] Stephen and eventually Henry II, who had been canonized in 1146 and was buried in the cathedral at Bamberg, remain in any rational analysis of the historical circumstances the most plausible candidates for the identification of the rider.[32] But the aura of Frederick II is such that as late as 1983 this beautiful and youthful king on horseback has been praised as a portrait or at least a *Kryptoporträt* by such an eminent historian as Gerhart Ladner.[33]

We come to much firmer ground if we turn now to the monument at Magdeburg (fig. 4). Here there is no doubt: the rider in the "Alte Markt"—in front of the town hall of Magdeburg—represents an emperor of the Holy Roman Empire.[34] After a long and controversial discussion, there seems to be general agreement that this monumental statue was erected by order of the archbishop as a symbol of the juridical privileges he held in the town. In the later local tradition, the monument has always been thought to be a statue commemorating Emperor Otto I, the founder of the archbishopric and the town of Magdeburg and the ruler who first made the archbishop his official representative as the justiciary in the city.[35] But again certain authors could not resist the temptation to identify the thirteenth-century statue not with the Ottonian but with the contemporary ruler, Frederick II, or at least to suggest the identification: "Doch ist es wahrscheinlich, daß sich in der Statue für die Menschen der Zeit gleichzeitig die Person des regierenden Herrschers, also Friedrichs II., spiegelt."[36] Naturally it is difficult to argue against such a vague and nostalgic suggestion. Still it remains highly improbable that the inhabitants of Magdeburg or even the sculptor of the statue had any idea what Frederick looked like.

However, the crux of the matter for Bamberg and Magdeburg lies elsewhere. Both statues, whomever they were intended to represent, reflect a "modern" image of the ruler, a new ideal that had its origin not in the empire but in Capetian France sometime between the end of the reign of Philip Augustus and the early years of the majority of Saint Louis. I adduce as a telling comparison the figure of Solomon (fig. 5) from the monumental stained glass window on the façade of the south transept of Chartres cathedral, which was donated by the royal house of France soon after the beginning of the regency of Blanche of Castile in 1227.[37] The similarities between the French window and the later German statues are not only and not even primarily a problem of so-called stylistic influence. It is the common ideal of a fashionable ruler—beautiful, young, with a particular type of hairstyle and stance—which is shared by the images at Chartres, Bamberg, and Magdeburg. After Bouvines, the models for royal iconography no longer came from Rome or Byzantium but from the court of the king of France. It is meaningless to look for the individual features or for the aura of Frederick II in the statues at Bamberg and Magdeburg. They reflect the new ideal of a Christian ruler which originated not in Germany or Italy but in Paris. So the first of our glances from the North has had a disappointing result. In the art of the empire one discovers more of the absence than the presence of Frederick II.

II

With our second glance focused on the court art of Frederick II and the *opus francigenum*, our perspective will be a very different one. It has always been correctly observed that the art and architecture of the southern kingdom of Frederick II cannot be fully accounted for within a regional South Italian context. Among the numerous proposals to explain the alienation of Frederick's architectural and artistic achievements from South Italian traditions—proposals that have suggested the influence of Islamic architecture or models from the Latin Kingdom of Jerusalem and that have underscored the impact of the Roman past—the possible connection with the rising Gothic art in the North, in the empire, and in Capetian France, has for a long time held a prominent place.[38] As far as Gothic motifs in Frederick's constructions in Sicily, Basilicata, and Apulia are concerned, there is already an old agreement among specialists that these motifs are best explained by the influence or the intervention of the South Italian houses of the Cistercians.[39] This is not a point I feel competent to discuss. In any case the Cistercians could hardly be the source of inspiration for one very characteristic aspect of Frederick's most prominent constructions: their sculpted figural

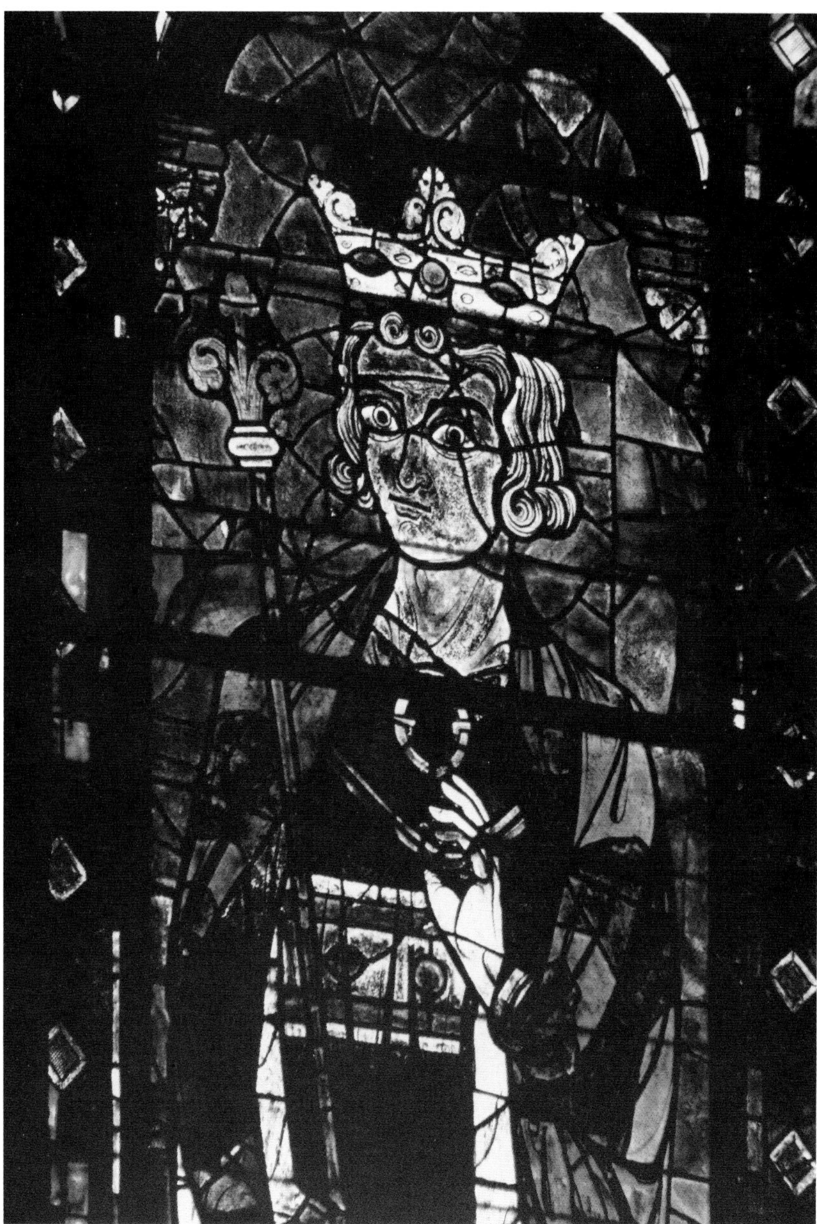

5. Chartres cathedral, northern transept, Solomon, stained glass window, thirteenth century
Photograph: Zentralinstitut für Kunstgeschichte, Munich

decoration. These statues, busts, and console figures demand a different explanation—either in terms of a continuity of a local Romanesque tradition of sculpture, an intentional return to classical models, or a direct influence from the great art centers of the North, in Germany or in France. The possibility of such a northern influence has been suggested more than once. As early as 1879 Cornel von Fabriczy introduced the sculpture on the choir screen at Bamberg as the source for the style of the fragments and busts from the Capua archway.[40] The art of an emperor from the house of Hohenstaufen should naturally have its roots only in Germany. A hundred years later Joachim Poeschke sought models for the same Capuan sculpture, as well as for the sculptural decoration of Castel del Monte, in the French coronation cathedral of Reims.[41] From this perspective, the art of Frederick II would be nothing more than a distant southern echo of the Gothic splendor of the kingdom of Saint Louis—just another example of the *opus francigenum*. With my second glance from the North I would like to discuss these two proposals.

Beginning with Capua, I want to touch on a more general problem before turning to the style of the sculptures and their origin. Modern art-historical scholarship from D. Salazaro to Carl Willemsen has called Frederick's construction at Capua a triumphator archway or even a triumphal arch.[42] I wonder if this classification is reasonable or if it is just another example of the enchanting influence that the magic of Frederick II has exercised even on architectural historians. If we follow the definition given in the *Oxford Classical Dictionary*, "triumphal arches were erected by the Romans to commemorate victories, and in honour of individual emperors." This clearcut definition certainly does not fit the gateway at Capua.[43] There exists no relationship between the erection of the gateway and a victory, and the figurative program of the arch would not justify the assertion that the monument was built in honor of an individual emperor such as Frederick. I am afraid that the classification of the gateway at Capua as a triumphal arch is still connected with an outdated vision of Frederick like the one formulated by Jakob Burckhardt in 1860 in the introduction to his famous book *Die Kultur der Renaissance in Italien*: "der erste moderne Mensch auf dem Thron."[44]

Regarding the archway, one source from the thirteenth century, Andrew of Hungary, says nothing of a triumphal monument but stresses instead a connection between the towers and the bridge over the Volturno: "Hic est pons, in cuius capite pater Manfridi Fredericus, cum quondam imperatorio statu gauderet, duas turres mire magnitudinis, fortitudinis et pulchritudinis, expensis in ea re aedificiis viginti milibus unciarum auri purissimi, construxit." To be sure, Andrew mentions immediately afterward the image of the emperor: "ibique suam imaginem in aeternam et immortalem memoriam sculpi fecit." This part of Andrew's description seems, at least to a certain degree, to justify the classification of the gateway as a triumphal arch. However, he then goes on to put the figure of the emperor in a context that has nothing to do with triumph, but is evidently juridical.

Extensis brachiis duobusque digitis, quasi os tumide comminacionis versiculos intonantem, quia etiam ibidem ad metum transeuntium ac eorum quibus recicantur, sunt consculpti:

Caesaris imperio regni concordia fio,
Quam miseros facio quos variare scio;
Intrent securi qui querunt vivere puri.
Infidus excludi timeat vel carcere trudi.[45]

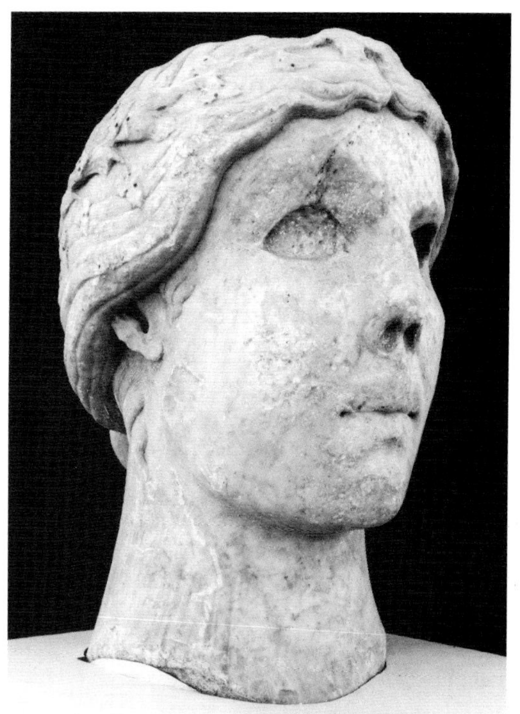

6. Concordia (?), thirteenth century
Museo Provinciale Campano, Capua

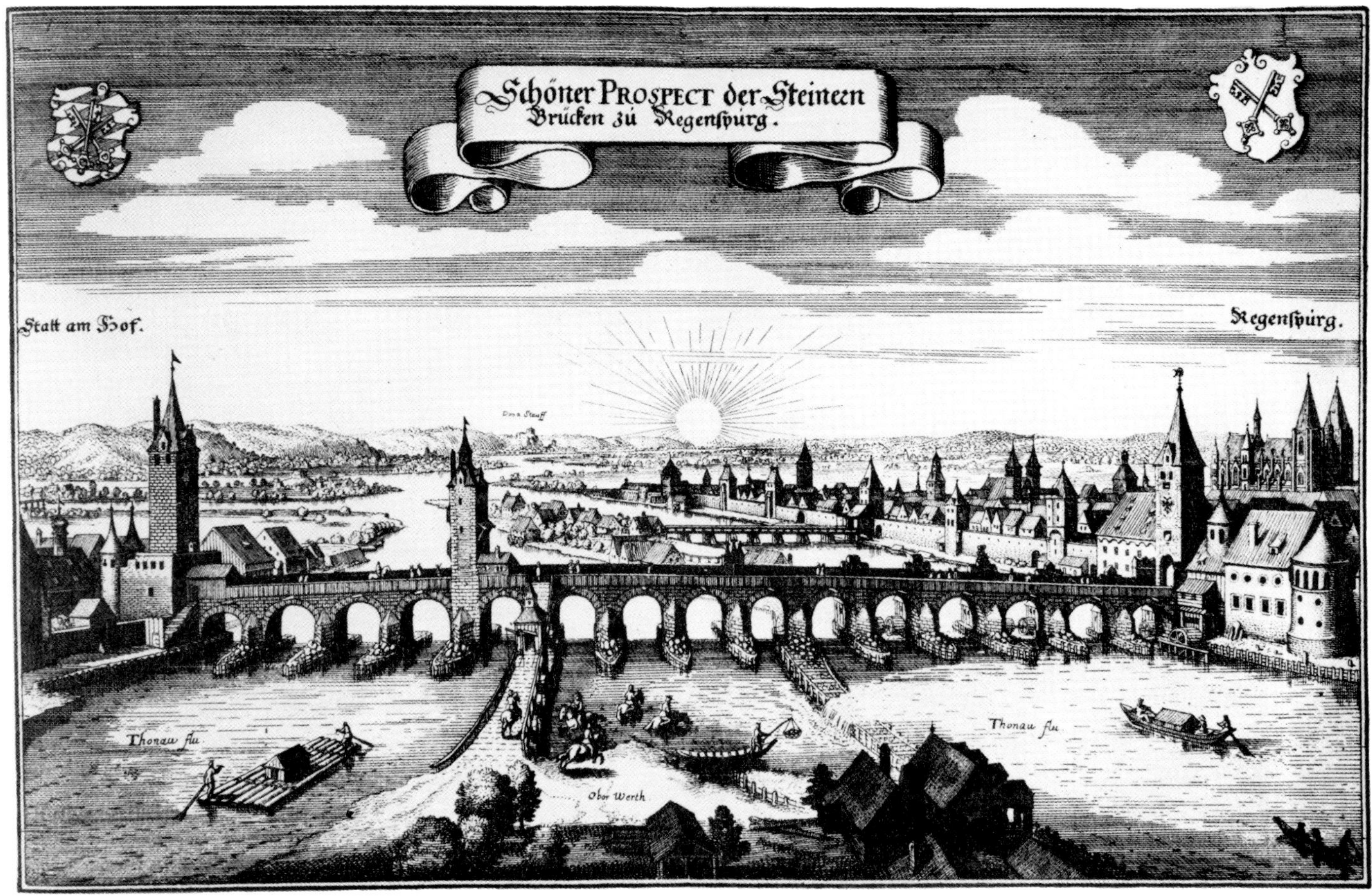

7. Bridge (Steinerne Brücke) at Regensburg, twelfth century; engraving by Matthäus Merian, c. 1640
Photograph: Zentralinstitut für Kunstgeschichte, Munich

The figurative program of the gateway is focused on the "Concordia Regni," the harmony in the empire. The famous female bust with a wreath of grape leaves (?) in her hair, which was meaningfully placed directly above the entrance of the gateway, does not represent justice—as has often been said—nor is it a personification of the city of Capua (fig. 6).[46] In light of the description by Andrew of Hungary, it must represent Concordia. The representation of the emperor—of Frederick—is related and subordinated to the dominant theme of "Concordia imperii." It does not express personal triumph. The juridical character of the program is strongly underlined by the inscription: security is granted to the pure, misery is announced to the disloyal, and prison awaits the faithless. When the gateway at Capua was erected, Frederick had already proclaimed the Constitutions of Melfi. As an art historian, I do not feel competent to discuss the possible links between the Constitutions and the program of the Capua gateway.[47] I would, however, like to draw attention to another potentially interesting connection. It is very surprising that the gateway at Capua seems never to have been studied in the context of the history of bridges. The connection between the medieval bridge, feudal lordship, and the exercise of justice is well known.[48] The gateway at Capua offers the most spectacular example of an iconography that visualizes the connection between the bridge, the feudal lord, and the justice exercised by him. However, it is not the only or even the earliest case of feudal bridge iconography.

The erection of statues of a country's ruler on bridges is well known from such post-medieval examples as the rider monuments

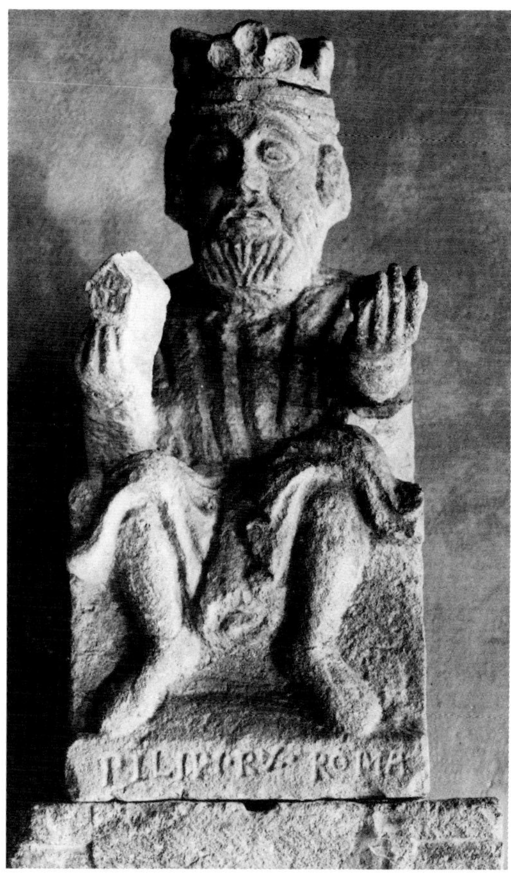

8. King Philip, early thirteenth century
Städtisches Museum, Regensburg; photograph: Presse-Bild-Poss

9. Judith Bridge, ruler and kneeling figure, twelfth century
Photograph: Zentralinstitut für Kunstgeschichte, Munich

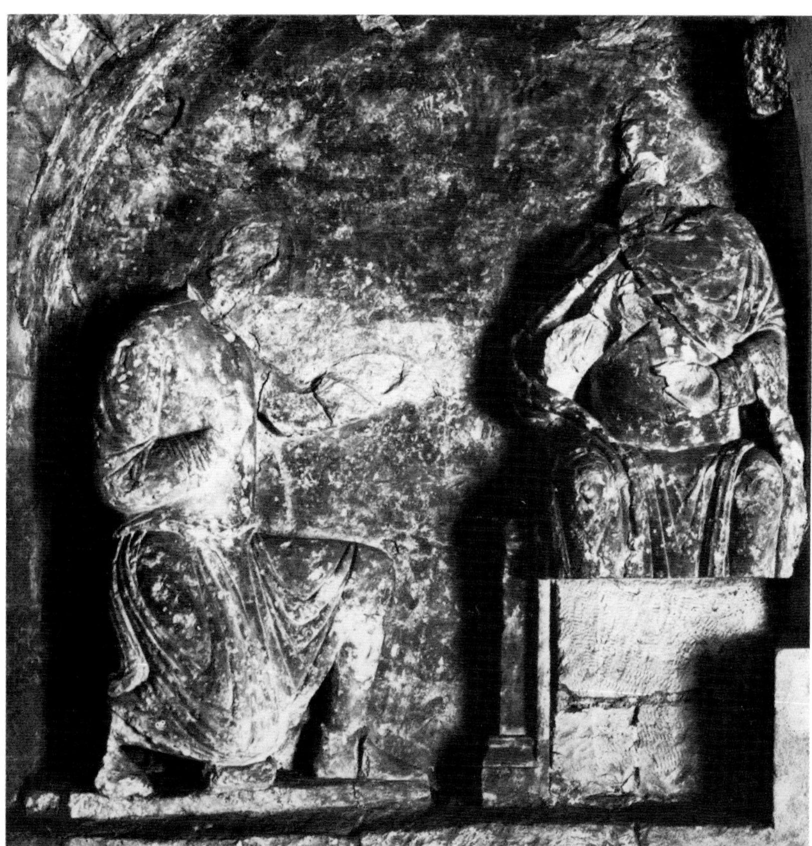

of Henry IV on the Pont Neuf at Paris and of the Great Elector on the Lange Brücke at Berlin. Less known are two examples from the twelfth and thirteenth centuries. The first is the so-called Steinerne Brücke, which crosses the Danube at Regensburg and was begun in 1135.[49] A pre-nineteenth-century view shows that the bridge carried three towers: one in the center and the other two on the north and south sides (fig. 7). These towers were decorated with a number of figures. Between them was a standing king with a bird.[50] On the central tower there appeared the figure of a seated king, who is identified by an inscription as PILIP RX ROM: Philippus Rex Romanorum (fig. 8). The ruler represented is Philip of Swabia, the youngest son of the emperor Barbarossa, who was king of Germany from 1198 until his murder at Bamberg in 1208. It has been suggested that the erection of this royal figure was connected with the granting of liberties to the city by Philip in 1207.[51] Be that as it may, the figure of Philip is an example of the iconic presence of a country's ruler on a bridge-gate several decades earlier than the gateway at Capua.

The next example comes from Prague. The famous Charles Bridge, which crosses the Moldava and connects the so-called Kleinseite with the Old City, dates from the time of Emperor Charles IV in the second half of the fourteenth century.[52] The Charles Bridge, however, had a twelfth-century predecessor, the so-called Judith Bridge, which seems to have been erected between 1158 and 1172 by order of Judith of Thuringia, the wife of King Vladislav I of Bohemia. Contemporary sources speak of a "Pragensis pontis opus imperiale" and claim that it was built in no more than three years. It may have been inspired by the slightly older Steinerne Brücke at Regensburg.[53] The tower at the end of the bridge on the so-called Kleinseite, where the royal castle was situated, was decorated with a relief that survives as a fragment (fig. 9). Judging from the style of the figures, there is no doubt that this relief dates from the time of the Judith Bridge. It shows two male figures, one enthroned and the other kneeling before him. There is general agreement that the figures represent a ruler and some kind of vassal paying homage to him. Since the figures are not nimbed, the

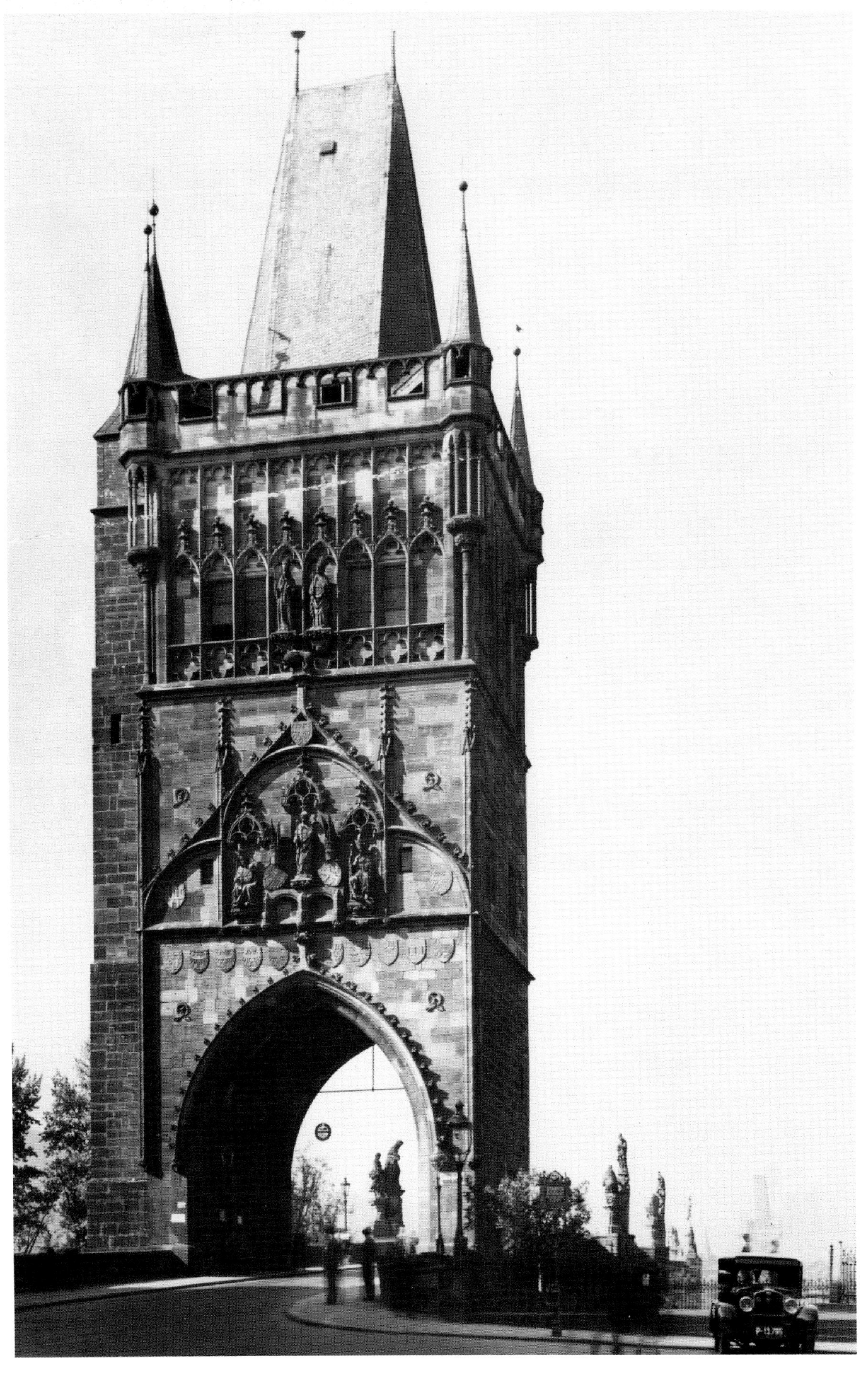

10. Altstädter Brückenturm, Prague, fourteenth century
Bildarchiv Foto Marburg

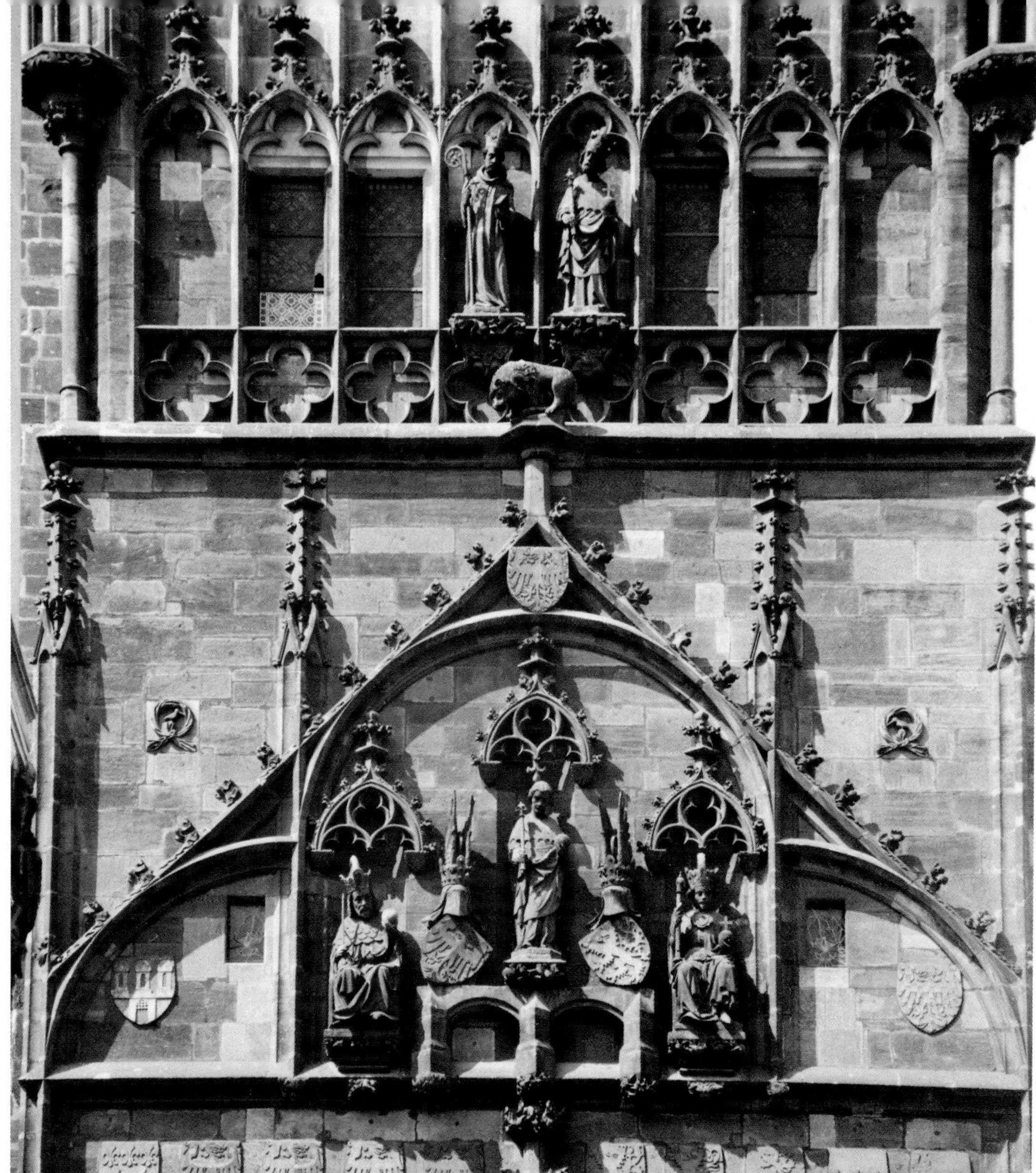

11. Altstädter Brückenturm, Prague, Saint Vitus, Charles IV, and Wenzel, fourteenth century
Photograph: Werner Neumeister

subject is probably a secular one, and thus another example of an image of a ruler on a bridge. One may doubt whether it will ever be possible to identify the two figures more precisely. Neither the identification of the relief as the promotion of Vladislav to the rank of king of Bohemia at Regensburg in 1158 nor the suggestion that the enthroned figure represents Vladislav, himself with the architect of the bridge kneeling before him, is anything more than a hypothesis.[54] The second proposal is most unlikely because the representation of an architect would make little sense in the context of feudal bridge iconography with its juridical character.

After the destruction of the Judith Bridge during a flood in the second quarter of the fourteenth century, Emperor Charles IV laid the foundation stone for a new bridge, the Charles Bridge, in 1357.[55] At the eastern end of the bridge, on the side of the Old City, stands the famous Altstädter Brückenturm (fig. 10). This tower was erected more than a century later than the gateway at Capua, but I would like to mention it as a last and particularly splendid example of feudal bridge iconography. On the outer side of the tower—the side facing the city—the iconographic program of the fourteenth century has been preserved, although with heavy nineteenth-century restorations (fig. 11). Immediately above the entrance to the bridge appears a group of three figures beneath a Gothic gable. In the center we see, not a personification as at Capua, but the patron of the cathedral, the city of Prague, and the kingdom of Bohemia—Saint Vitus. He is not only the protector of town and country but also the protector of the bridge, and thus is shown standing on an abbreviated image of the bridge itself. To his right is enthroned Emperor Charles IV. He is accompanied by the coat of arms of the empire. On the other side of the patron saint sits the emperor's son Wenzel, who became king of Germany and Bohemia after his father's death in 1378. He is shown with the coat of arms of Bohemia. The message of the program is clear: the bridge is under the celestial protection of the saint as it stands under the secular rule of the emperor and king.[56] But let me now end this digression on the iconography of bridges in the feudal age: it has had no other justification than to remind us of a context that should not be forgotten in studies of Frederick's gateway at the bridge at Capua.

Turning to matters of style at Capua, I must again begin with some general remarks. Concordia, the central personification of the Capua program, refers to a political ideal borrowed from the Romans. Correspondingly, the style chosen for the statues and busts on the gateway also tries to imitate Roman models. This basic ideological fact should be recalled in any discussion of the origin of the style of the Capua fragments. There remains then only one problem: what models were used by the craftsmen at Capua in the thirties of the thirteenth century in order to create statues and busts *all'antica*? In trying to answer this question, the historian of style is faced with the following dilemma. One can either turn directly to the Roman remains at Capua Vetere and elsewhere, or one can assume that the artists active at Capua had studied the contemporary ecclesiastical sculptures in Capetian France and in Germany, which show between 1190 and 1230 different variations of a pseudo-classical style.[57] In the last few decades, Cesare Gnudi and Joachim Poeschke have chosen this second way, comparing the torso of the emperor's statue at Capua with biblical figures from the cathedrals of Chartres, Paris, and Reims.[58] But in any reasonable historical perspective it remains rather difficult to imagine that

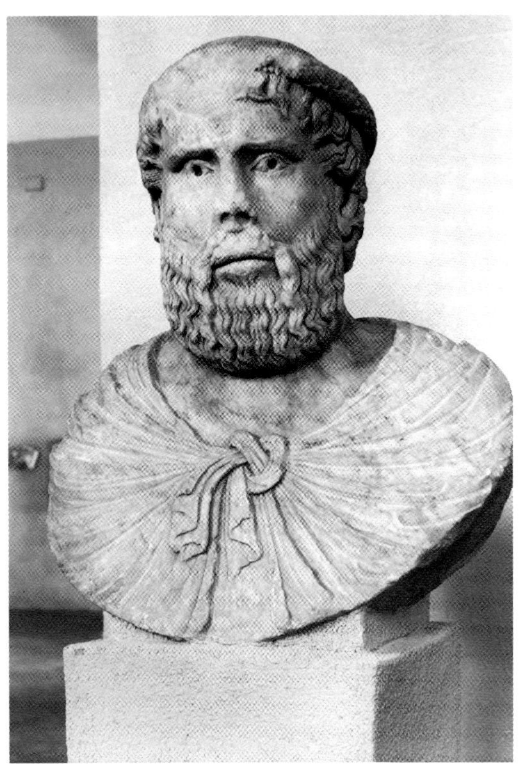

12. Male bust, thirteenth century
Museo Provinciale Campano, Capua; photograph: Bildarchiv Foto Marburg

Frederick called craftsmen from a cathedral in the France of Saint Louis to decorate his thoroughly secular gateway at Capua or that these craftsmen left the French cathedrals in order to go to work in southern Italy. It makes much more sense historically to assume that we see here the results of an intentional choice of Roman models in order to render Caesar's program in Caesar's language.

The two male busts, which once decorated the two medallions flanking the central personification of Concordia and which have been erroneously but characteristically identified as portraits of Piero della Vigna and Taddeo da Suessa, are a case in point (fig 12). As independent portrait busts in a secular context, the two pieces seem to be nearly unique from the period between late antiquity and the Quattrocento. The one exception that comes to mind is the little bust in gilded bronze, which shows Frederick's grandfather Barbarossa.[59] This bust is evidently the testimony of an intentional imperial *renovatio* at the court of the twelfth-century emperor. The cathedrals in France and

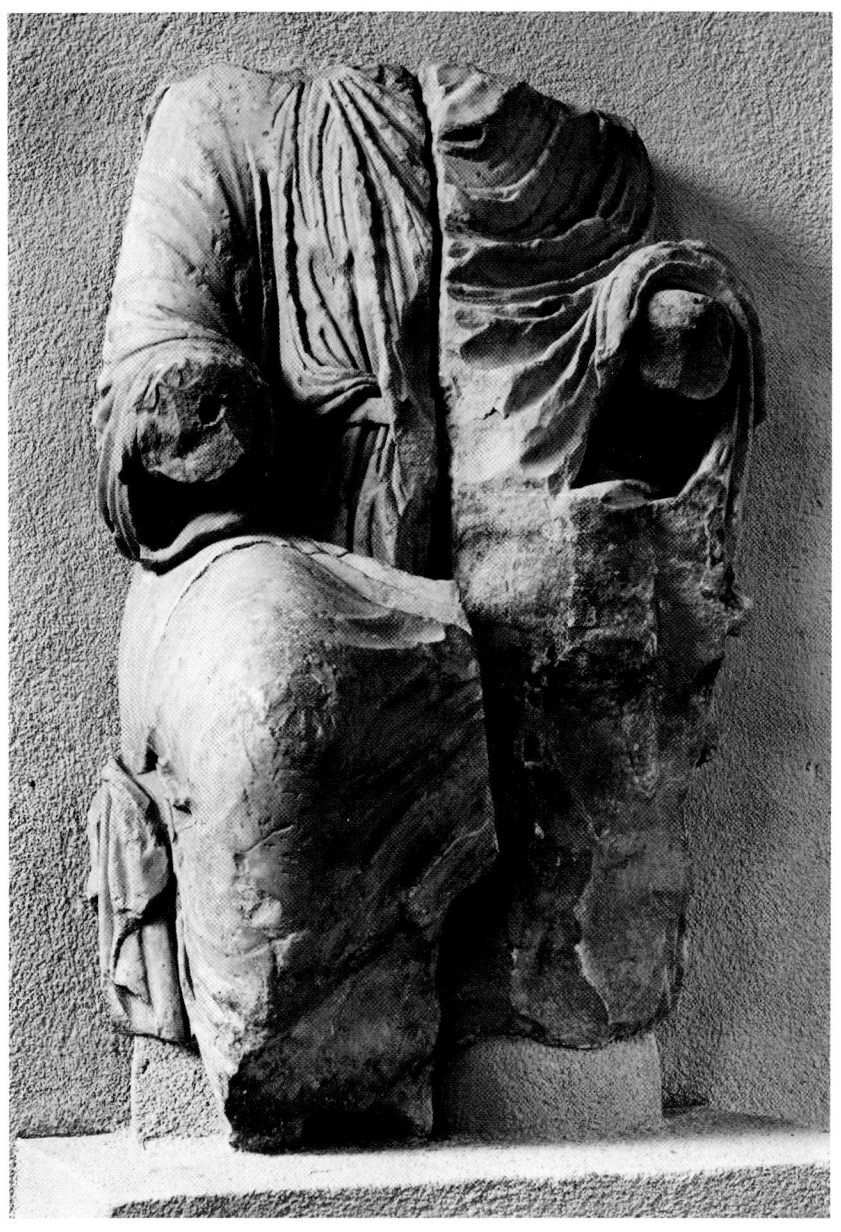

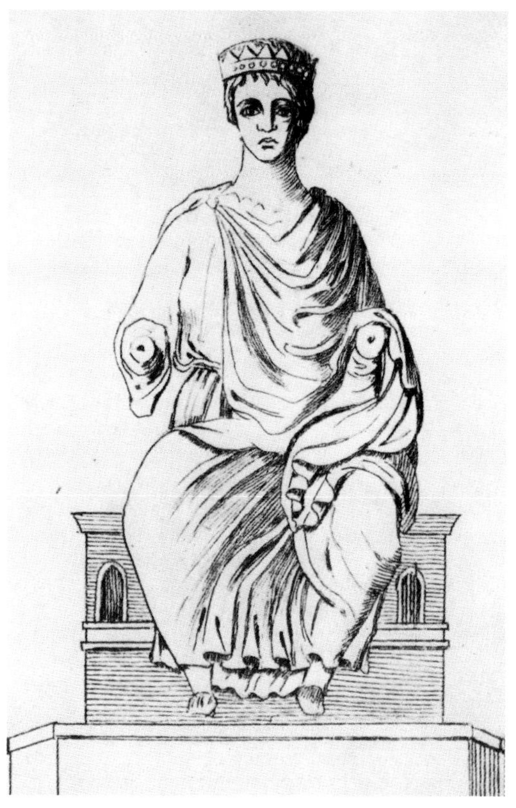

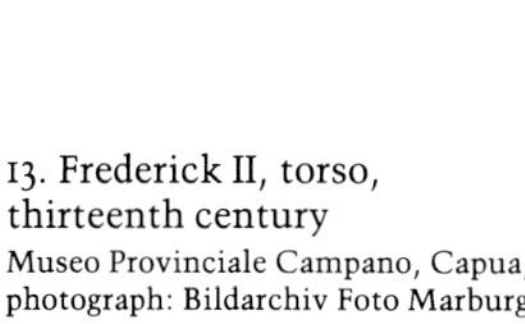

13. Frederick II, torso, thirteenth century
Museo Provinciale Campano, Capua; photograph: Bildarchiv Foto Marburg

14. Frederick II at the gateway at Capua
After Séroux d'Agincourt 1823, pl. 27, no. 4

Germany kept many reliquary busts in their treasures. The secular portrait bust in stone, however, seems to have been totally unknown to the North in the thirteenth century. The Capua busts can be explained only as documents of an intentional revival of a lost and condemned Roman "habit" in the circle of Frederick II. It is not at all surprising that they remain rather clumsy pieces of sculpture. Their style is thoroughly linear, almost like drawing. Such a style may be convenient for the sculpting of reliefs on late Romanesque pulpits and portals. But it remains totally at odds with the fully rounded busts, the execution of which was imposed on the medieval craftsman by an unusual program of imperial revival. There is a telling contradiction here between ideological ends and stylistic means.

It was the torso of the statue of the emperor that Gnudi and Poeschke used for their comparisons with either Chartres and Paris or Reims (fig. 13). Judgments in this case are particularly difficult. In the early nineteenth century, Séroux d'Agincourt published a view of the statue when it was still nearly complete (fig. 14).[60] What survives today is a heavily damaged torso and the plaster cast of the head, which naturally precludes any judgment as to the state of conservation of the lost orginal.[61] D'Agincourt's view of the statue is sufficiently precise to demonstrate iconographically that it did not follow a Roman model. The figure was shown seated on a kind of medieval bench or throne, wearing a crown, a girdle, and a sort of chlamys. It corresponds to the representations of Frederick on the second and third seals which he used after his imperial coronation in 1220.[62] It is a specific kind of ruler's statue for which I know no precise parallel from the first half of the thirteenth century in France.[63] If the iconographic type of the Frederick statue is medieval and not Roman, one may call its drapery style "pseudo-classical." This style is much less linear than that of the two male busts. But does it then have to come from the sculpture *all'antica* at Chartres, Paris, or Reims, as has often been supposed? Could it not also have occurred that the carvers of Frederick at Capua and the craftsmen of the cathedrals of France borrowed their common pseudo-classical drapery quite independently from one another and from similar Roman models? In summary, I would suggest that the imitation of Roman forms on the sculpture from the Capua gateway was dictated by the imperial ideology of the program. It was Caesar's language borrowed from ancient Rome and not from the Church.

The gateway at Capua, which was finished in 1239, could not be called a Gothic building. Castel del Monte, which was begun no earlier than 1240, is most decidedly Gothic, however, Gothic with a unique character.[64] The importance of the Cistercian houses in southern Italy for the transmission of Gothic architectural know-how to the shops working for the emperor at places such as Castel Maniace, Castel Ursino, and Castel del Monte has often been stressed.[65] But the architecture of Castel del Monte, with its unique blend of classical and Gothic motifs and its sophisticated use of colored stones and marbles, gives an impression of imperial splendor and courtly luxury that is a far cry from the austerity of any Cistercian building. With the disappearance of all the great royal constructions in France and England from the reign of Saint Louis and Henry III, northern architecture of the thirteenth century is known exclusively as ecclesiastical architecture. Castel del Monte is one of the rare examples of Gothic secular architecture of the highest level of quality which has come down to us relatively well preserved. If more of the secular architecture of the period had survived, perhaps the superb elegance and

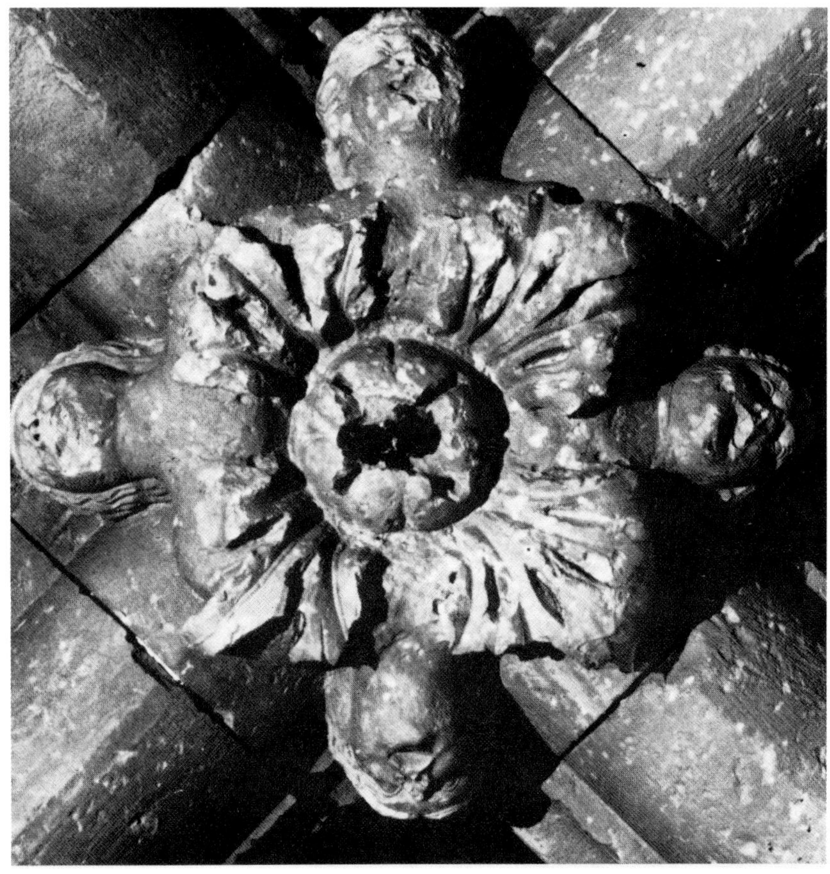

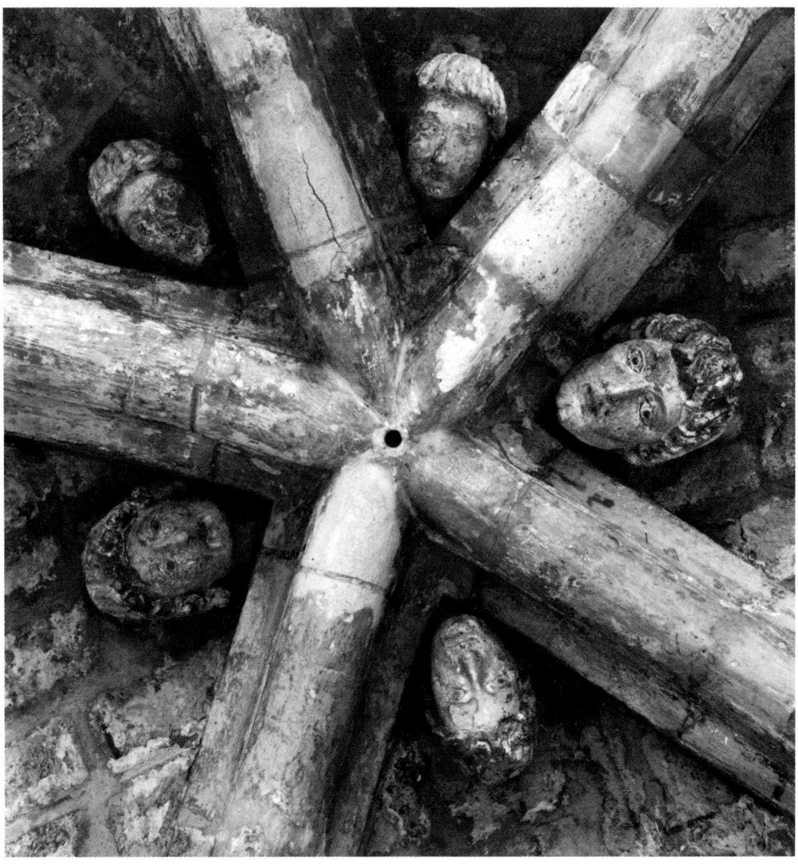

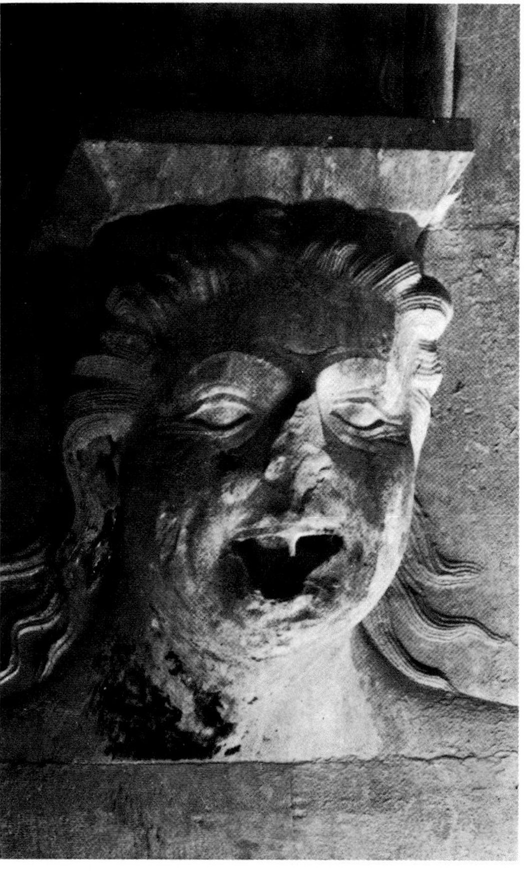

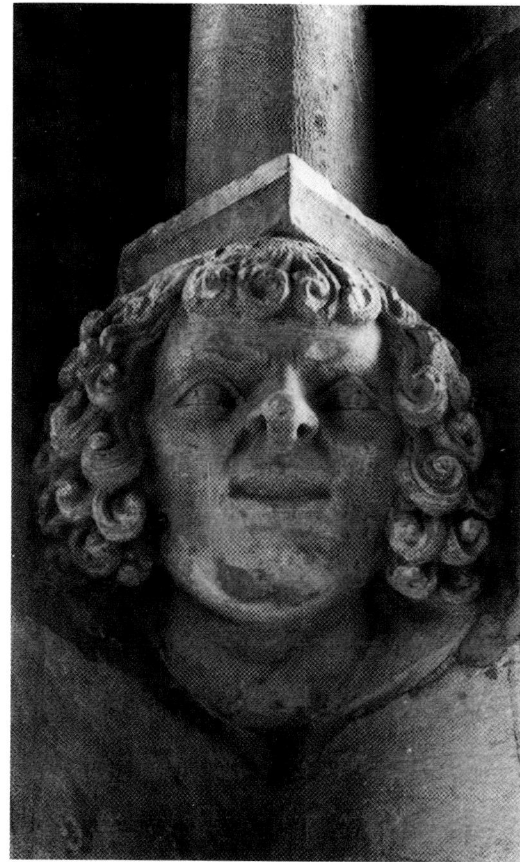

15. Castel del Monte, keystone with flower and heads, thirteenth century
Photograph: Zentralinstitut für Kunstgeschichte, Munich

16. Noyon cathedral, gallery of the choir, keystone with heads, twelfth century
Bildarchiv Foto Marburg

17. Castel del Monte, tower 3, console head, thirteenth century
Photograph: Zentralinstitut für Kunstgeschichte, Munich

18. Reims cathedral, tower of the transept, console head, thirteenth century
Bildarchiv Foto Marburg

flawlessness of Castel del Monte might seem less unique and also less close to Cistercian models.

The art historian is particularly impressed by the surprisingly modern use of decorative sculpture in the interior of Castel del Monte. Much of the surviving sculpture in the castle is connected with the most clearly Gothic aspect of the construction, the rib-vaults. The sculptures are either keystones, console heads, or atlantes supporting the ribs. Keystones with a flower and heads between the ribs, such as we find in room 7 of the upper floor at Castel del Monte (fig. 15), were frequent in northern France since the twelfth century. I need mention only the famous examples in the galleries of the choir of the cathedral at Noyon (fig. 16).[66] Console heads beneath ribs, as found at Castel del Monte on the vaults over the staircase of tower 3 (fig. 17), also occur often in French Gothic buildings, for example, in the transept towers of Reims cathedral (fig. 18). Atlantes supporting ribs, as on the vault over the staircase of tower 7 (fig. 19), have their counterparts in the North. One example comes from the chapel of Saint John in the cathedral of Strasbourg (fig. 20). Nothing similar seems to exist in Italy, so the French origin or, to put it more cautiously, the French inspiration of this kind of decorative sculpture in connection with rib-vaults can hardly be doubted. However, the employment of console heads and atlantes beneath ribs and the decoration of keystones with heads was so widespread in northern France, in Burgundy and Alsatia, and also in England that it would be pointless to claim a specific source for its sudden appearance at Castel del Monte toward the middle of the thirteenth century. Moreover, one should be aware that the same kind of keystones, console heads, and atlantes as we find in churches must once have existed in secular buildings as well and may have been

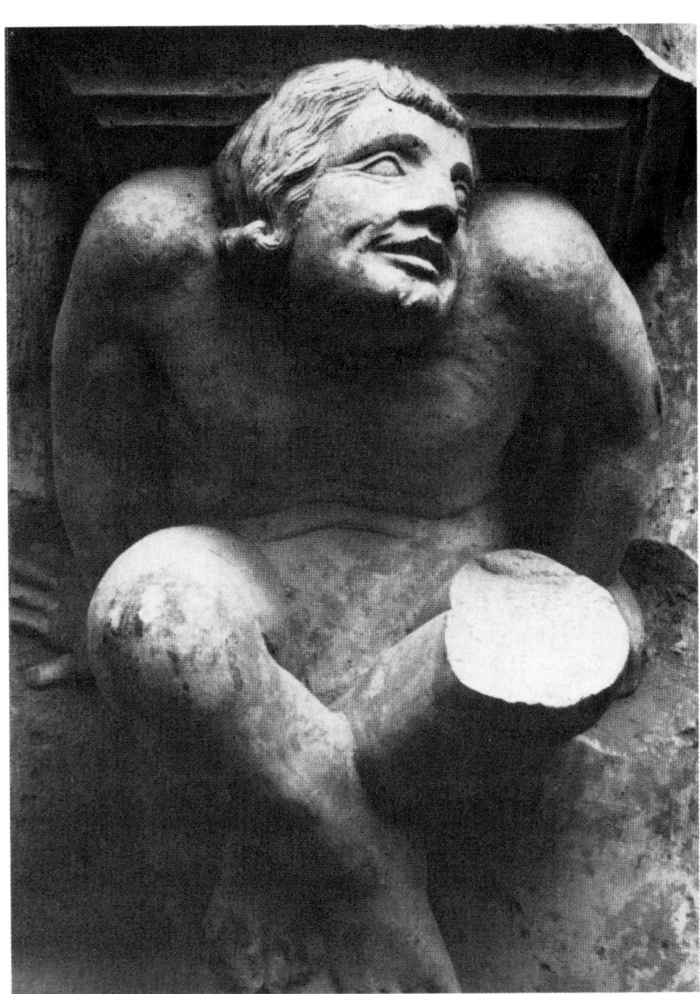

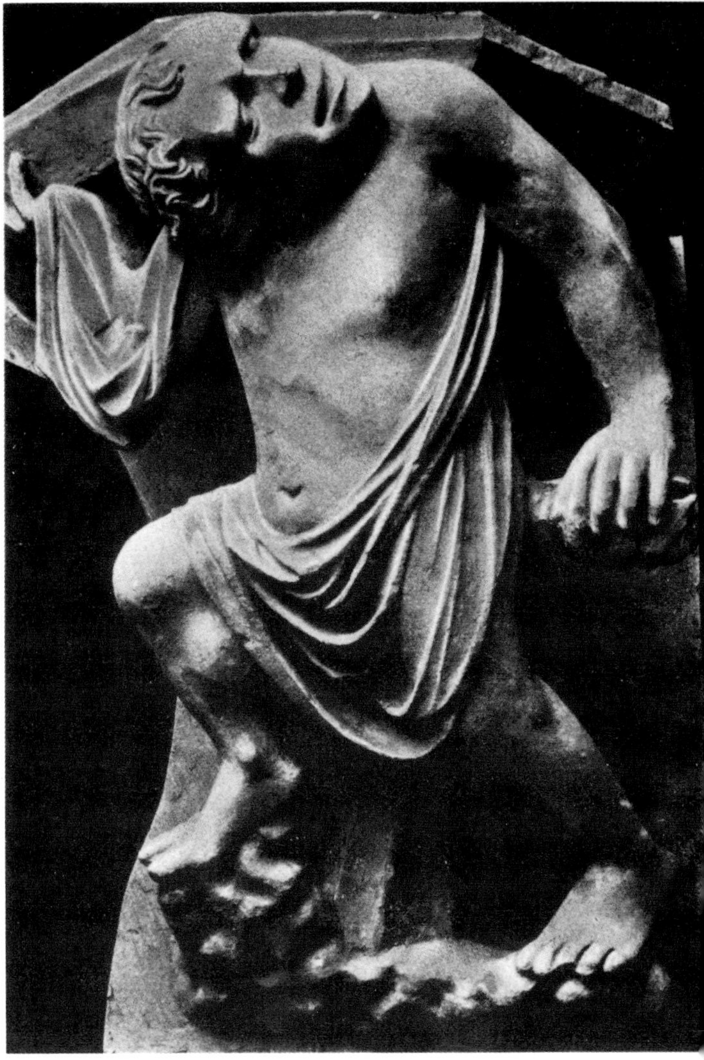

19. Castel del Monte, tower 7, atlas figure, thirteenth century

20. Strasbourg cathedral, Chapel of Saint John, atlas figure, thirteenth century
Photograph: Zentralinstitut für Kunstgeschichte, Munich

transmitted to Castel del Monte from some lost northern castle or palace as from a cathedral or from an abbey church.[67]

If the setting of the consoles and atlantes at Castel del Monte is inspired by northern models, this inspiration does not imply that the style of the sculpture in the Apulian castle is also of northern origin. All the surviving sculpture at Castel del Monte, including the torso of the rider in the courtyard and the so-called Molajoli head, seems stylistically homogeneous and was probably made by one small workshop, possibly even by a single artist.[68] Moreover, I see no connection between the figures at Castel del Monte and the earlier fragments from the gateway at Capua. The most striking difference between Capua and Castel del Monte is the change in the attitude toward antiquity. At Capua the impact of Roman models is evident; at Castel del Monte it has become of secondary importance. This difference may be explained in part by external circumstances. The Roman style at Capua represented the conscious choice of a monumental language for the statues and busts of an official imperial gateway. The surviving sculpture at Castel del Monte is decorative and could be handled with a much greater freedom and even with a certain wittiness. But it is undeniable that the sculptures at Castel del Monte are also more modern than those at Capua. The heads

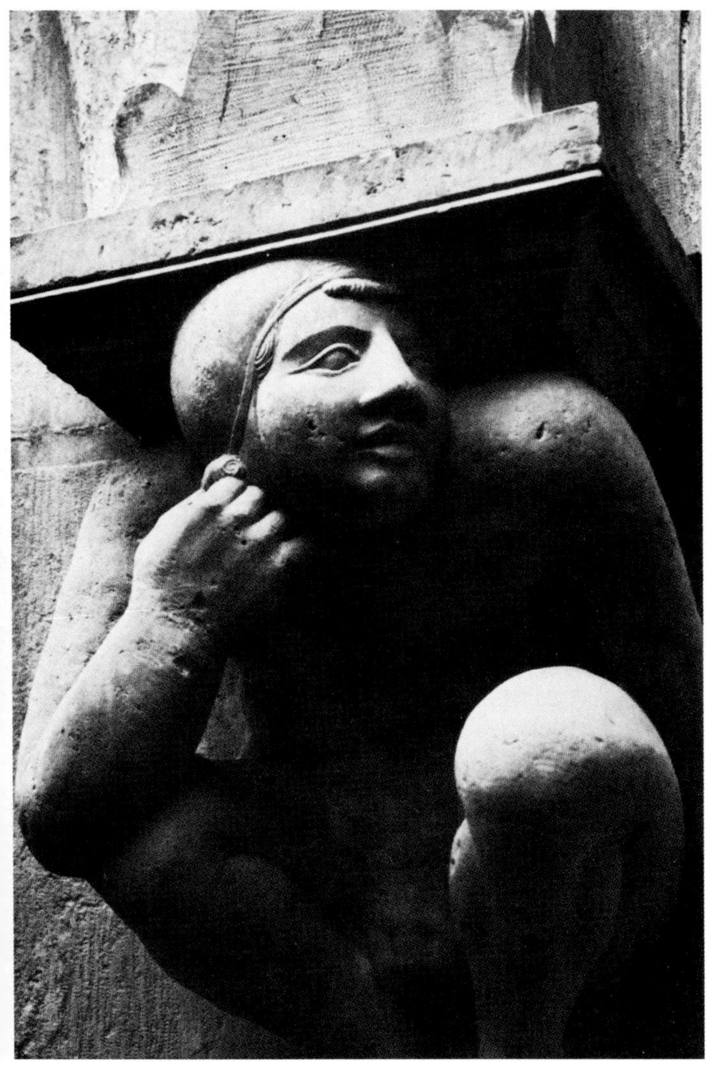

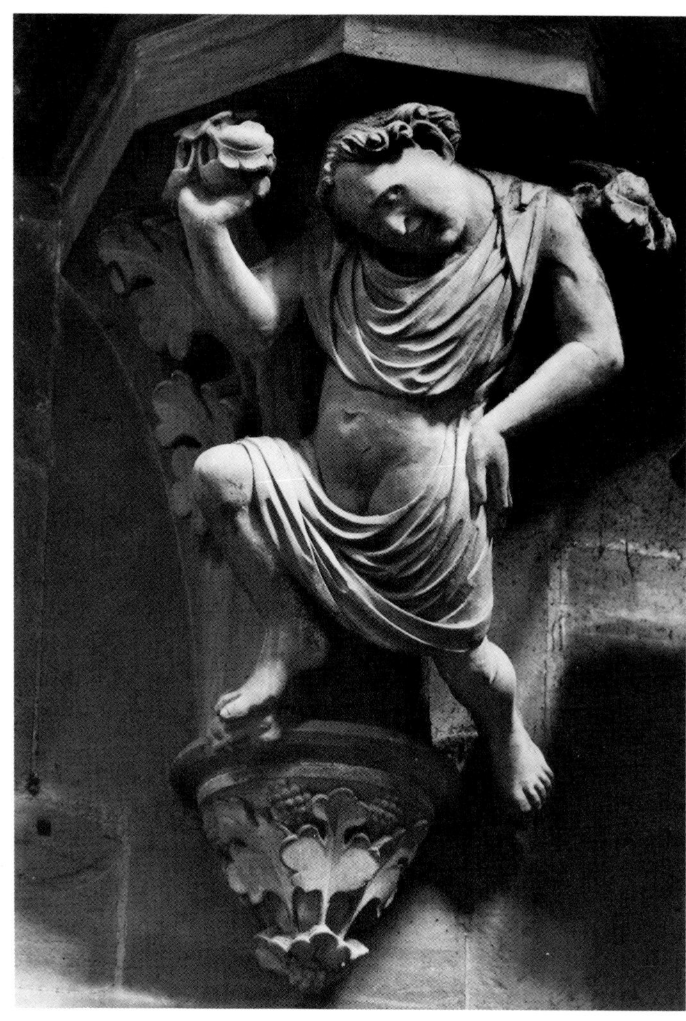

21. Castel del Monte, tower 7, atlas figure, thirteenth century
Photograph: Zentralinstitut für Kunstgeschichte, Munich

22. Strasbourg cathedral, south transept, atlas figure, thirteenth century
Bildarchiv Foto Marburg

and atlantes in the towers of the castle show a robust naturalism, a physical energy, and a physiognomic expressiveness that is a parallel to the modernity of the mid-thirteenth-century art in the French and English courts and in some smaller centers of the empire.[69] Not at Capua but in front of the atlantes of tower 7 at Castel del Monte is one reminded of Frederick's famous sentence: "Intentio vera nostra est manifestare . . . ea, que sunt sicut sunt."[70]

Having said this, I must also add that all detailed comparisons between the sculpture from Castel del Monte and possible models in France, England, or Germany remain for me surprisingly elusive. Poeschke's comparison between the funny, naked atlantes in Castel del Monte (fig. 21) and the heavily clothed and twisted atlantes on the choir of the cathedral at Reims can at best be called counterproductive.[71] Even if we turn to one of the rare northern atlantes, which are at least semi-nude, the contrast remains striking. The atlas figure in the transept of the cathedral at Strasbourg is shown in profile and in movement (fig. 22). Compared to such northern examples, the atlantes at Castel del Monte—short, muscular figures that really give the impression that they are supporting with athletic strength the heavy weight of the vaults over their necks—look surprisingly natural and amusing. In a certain way they are closer to the famous "telamoni" of the Italian Romanesque church portals than to any northern atlas figure. On the other hand, their nudity and the variations of their attitudes and expressions have a nearly pagan freedom—even their private parts are shown with unrestrained openness. Gothic art in the North also discovered the beauty of plants and watched the natural expression of laughing or screaming faces. But nowhere in the North do we meet the same frankness in the representation of nudity and of nearly sportsmanlike "bodybuilding." The atlantes at Castel del Monte are secular sculpture in the full sense of the word—joyous, witty, and amusing. They belong to the court and are certainly not borrowed from the cathedral.

NOTES

1. See Wilhelm Pinder, *Die Kunst der deutschen Kaiserzeit* (Leipzig, 1937).

2. For the castles see Hans-Martin Maurer, "Burgen," in *Die Zeit der Staufer: Geschichte—Kunst—Kultur* [exh. cat., Württembergisches Landesmuseum] (Stuttgart, 1977), 3:119–128, and Walter Hotz, *Pfalzen und Burgen der Stauferzeit* (Darmstadt, 1981) with bibliography. For the towns see Cord Meckseper, "Städtebau," in *Die Zeit der Staufer*, 3:75–86, and Cord Meckseper, *Kleine Kunstgeschichte der deutschen Stadt im Mittelalter* (Darmstadt, 1982).

3. See Willibald Sauerländer, *Das Jahrhundert der großen Kathedralen* (Munich, 1990), 330–334.

4. The *Kyffhäusersage* or *Kaisersage* is the curious belief that Emperor Frederick II never died but is sleeping in a Thuringian mountain and will one day return to restore the German empire. See Franz Kampers, *Die deutsche Kaiseridee in Prophetie und Sage* (Munich, 1896). Ernst Kantorowicz, "Zu den Rechtsgrundlagen der Kaisersage," *Deutsches Archiv für Erforschung des Mittelalters* 13 (1957), 115–150.

5. For the inscription on the shrine of Charlemagne, see *Die Kunstdenkmäler der Rheinprovinz. Stadt Aachen, I: Das Münster* (Düsseldorf, 1916), 210.

6. For the canonization of Charlemagne, see Odilo Engels, "Des Reiches heiliger Gründer: Die Kanonisation Karls des Großen und ihre Beweggründe," in Hans Müllejans, ed., *Karl der Große und sein Schrein* (Mönchengladbach, 1980), 37–46.

7. Otto Lehmann-Brockhaus, *Schriftquellen zur Kunstgeschichte des 11. und 12. Jahrhunderts für Deutschland, Lothringen und Italien* (Berlin, 1938), no. 13.

8. See David Abulafia, *Frederick II: A Medieval Emperor* (London, 1988), 120.

9. *Reineri Annales*, Monumenta Germaniae Historica, Scriptores, XIV, 673.

10. Abulafia 1988, 121.

11. For this observation see Renate Kroos, *Der Schrein des heiligen Servatius in Maastricht* (Munich, 1985), 124.

12. See Herta Lepie, "Die Geschichte der Sicherung und Konservierung des Karlsschreins," in Müllejans 1980, 149.

13. The fundamental stylistic study of the shrine remains Hermann Schnitzler, *Die Goldschmiedeplastik der Aachener Schreinswerkstatt* (Düren, 1934).

14. See *Die Kunstdenkmäler.*

15. See Kroos 1985, 123, note 428. She cites a charter of Otto for the chapter at Aix, dating from July 1198, in which the king declares that he follows "predecessoris itaque nostri Friderici Romanorum imperatoris exemplo." Kroos asks with good reason if Otto did not in a similar way push the work on the shrine of Charlemagne following the example of his predecessor Frederick?

16. See the chapter "Die Doppelwahl von 1198," in Herbert Grundmann, *Wahlkönigtum, Territorialpolitik und Ostbewegung im 13. und 14. Jahrhundert* (Munich, 1973), 17–20.

17. Abulafia 1988, 121.

18. "Bekanntlich trägt der Schrein Karls des Großen in Aachen als letzte Herrscherfigur die Silberstatuette Kaiser Friedrichs II., deren Augen, wie die keines anderen Bildes, den 'Schlangenblick' dieses einzigartigen Mannes wiedergeben"; Klaus J. Heinisch, *Kaiser Friedrich II. in Briefen und Berichten seiner Zeit* (Darmstadt, 1968), 36.

19. See the excellent article by Helmut Beumann, "Friedrich II. und die heilige Elisabeth: Zum Besuch des Kaisers in Marburg am 1. Mai 1236," in *Sankt Elisabeth: Fürstin, Dienerin, Heilige* [exh. cat., Landgrafenschloß and Elisabethkirche, Marburg] (Sigmaringen, 1981), 151–166.

20. For Elizabeth see *Sankt Elisabeth.* Fundamental remains Albert Huyskens, *Quellenstudien zur Geschichte der hl. Elisabeth, Landgräfin von Thüringen* (Marburg, 1908). For a brief treatment, see Matthias Werner in *Lexikon des Mittelalters,* 3:1838–1841, with extensive bibliography.

21. See my forthcoming article, "Royal Images from Saint-Denis to Reims," to be published in the *Annales.*

22. See Beumann 1981, 153–154.

23. Erika Dinkler-von Schubert, *Der Schrein der hl. Elisabeth zu Marburg* (Marburg, 1964).

24. Adolph Goldschmidt, "Ein mittelalterliches Reliquiar des Stockholmer Museums," *Jahrbuch der Preussischen Kunstsammlungen* 40 (1919), 1–16.

25. Percy Ernst Schramm, *Herrschaftszeichen und Staatssymbolik,* 3 vols. (Stuttgart, 1954–1956).

26. Arpad Weixlgärtner, *Das Reliquiar mit der Krone im Staatlichen Historischen Museum zu Stockholm,* 2 vols. (Stockholm, 1954), 1:100.

27. Olle Källström, "Das Reliquiar in Stockholm mit den von Friedrich II. gestifteten Kronen und seinem Becher, A. Der kunstgeschichtliche Befund und die Schicksale des Reliquiars seit 1631," in Percy Ernst Schramm, *Kaiser Friedrichs II. Herrschaftszeichen* (Göttingen, 1955), 27–32; Bengt Thordeman, "Det Stora Stockholms-Relikvariet i ny Belysning," *Fornvännen* 50 (1955), 227–244.

28. Schramm 1955, Schramm 1954–1956, 3:886–887. A useful summary of the state of research on the Stockholm reliquary is given by Aron Andersson, in *Sankt Elisabeth,* 513–517.

29. Abulafia 1988, 247, refers to Schramm's results without a question mark. Florentine Mütherich, in *Denkmale der deutschen Könige und Kaiser,* ed. Percy Ernst Schramm and Florentine Mütherich, 2 vols. (Munich, 1981), 1:206, is clearly skeptical: "über die frühere Geschichte, die Herkunft und Zusammenfügung der Krone sind bisher nur Vermutungen möglich." Beumann 1981, 154, is cautious and writes only: "in der Tat das Kopfreliquiar Elisabeths gewesen sein könnte."

30. See the illustrations in Weixlgärtner 1954, 2:pls. 57–61.

31. For the arguments in favor of the identification of the rider as Stephen of Hungary, see Renate Kroos, "Liturgische Quellen zum Bamberger Dom," *Zeitschrift für Kunstgeschichte* 39 (1976), 105–146, esp. 142–146.

32. For a brief discussion of the different opinions on the identification of the rider, see Willibald Sauerländer, in *Die Zeit der Staufer,* 1:315–317. A new paper on the identification of the Bamberg Rider is announced by Jörg Traeger.

33. Gerhart Ladner, "Die Anfänge des Kryptoporträts," in *Von Angesicht zu Angesicht: Porträtstudien. Michael Stettler zum 70. Geburtstag* (Bern, 1983), 78–97. Ladner compares the head of the statue at Bamberg with a sixteenth-century engraving by Aliprando Capriolo, suggesting that the Bamberg sculptor and the Italian engraver both used the statue from the gateway at Capua as their model. The identification of the rider with Frederick II had been proposed earlier. See Otto von Simson, "The Bamberg Rider," *Review of Religion* 4 (1940), 257–281, and Wilhelm Reinhold Valentiner, *The Bamberg Rider* (Los Angeles, 1956).

34. For this monument in general, see Dietrich Schubert, *Von Halberstadt nach Meißen* (Cologne, 1974), 287–292.

35. The most substantial discussion of the problems connected with the statue at Magdeburg is found in Berent Schwineköper, "Zur Deutung der Magdeburger Reitersäule," in *Festschrift Percy Ernst Schramm,* 2 vols. (Wiesbaden, 1964), 1:117–142.

36. Berent Schwineköper, "Motivationen und Vorbilder für die Errichtung der Magdeburger Reitersäule: Ein Beitrag zur Geschichte des Reiterbildes im hohen Mittelalter," in *Institutionen, Kultur und Gesellschaft im Mittelalter: Festschrift für Josef Fleckenstein* (Sigmaringen, 1984), 343–392, esp. 391. See also Valentiner 1956 and Virginia Roehrig-Kaufmann, "Magdeburg Rider Group: State of Research and Preliminary Suggestions for Further Work," in *Der Magdeburger Dom,* ed. Ernst Ullmann (Leipzig, 1989), 205–209.

37. For this window see Yves Delaporte, *Les vitraux de la cathédrale de Chartres,* 4 vols. (Chartres, 1926), 1:493–499.

38. See, for instance, the chapter "Castel del Monte—Frédéric II et l'architecture française," in Émile Bertaux, *L'art dans l'Italie méridionale, I: De la fin de l'Empire romain à la conquête de Charles d'Anjou* (Paris, 1903), 719–752.

39. See, for instance, Antonio Cadei, "Fossanova e Castel del Monte," in *Federico II e l'arte del Duecento italiano,* Atti della III settimana di Studi di Storia dell'Arte medievale dell'Università di Roma, ed. Angiola M. Romanini, 2 vols. (Galatina, 1980), 1:191–215. See also Carla Ghisalberti, "I legami culturali e stilistici tra la scultura architettonica federiciana dell'Italia meridionale e il mondo cistercense," in this volume.

40. Cornel von Fabriczy, "Zur Kunstgeschichte der Hohenstaufenzeit," *Zeitschrift für Bildende Kunst* 14 (1879), 180–189, 214–222, 236–243.

41. Joachim Poeschke, "Zum Einfluß der Gotik in Süditalien," *Jahrbuch der Berliner Museen* 22 (1980), 91–120.

42. D. Salazaro, *L'arco di trionfo con le torri de Federigo II a Capua* (Caserta, 1877); Cresswell Shearer, *The Renaissance of Architecture in Southern Italy: A Study of Frederick II of Hohenstaufen and the Capua Triumphator Archway and Towers* (Cambridge, 1935); Carl Arnold Willemsen, *Kaiser Friedrichs II. Triumphtor zu Capua* (Wiesbaden, 1953).

43. *The Oxford Classical Dictionary* (Oxford, 1961), 926.

44. Jakob Burckhardt, *Die Kultur der Renaissance in Italien* (repr. Stuttgart, 1940), 5.

45. Cited in Shearer 1935, 16, note 3.

46. Following Willemsen 1953, 44, the identification of the female bust as "La fedeltà di Capua" occurs first in Scipione Sannelli, *Annali della Città di Capua* (manuscript in the Biblioteca Comunale at Capua). For the identification of the bust as a "Justitia Imperialis" or "Justitia Caesaris," see Willemsen 1953, 65. Peter Herde has drawn my attention to a review of Willemsen's book by Friedrich Baethgen, in *Deutsches Archiv zur Erforschung des Mittelalters* 11 (1954–1955), 623–624. Baethgen showed that Willemsen gave the inscription not after Andrew of Hungary but in a later wording from the *Gesta Romanorum*, where one reads "Caesaris imperio regni custodia Fio." This later wording may have partially suggested the identification of the bust as imperial justice.

47. An article by Beat Brenk, "Antikenverständnis und weltliches Rechtsdenken im Skulpturenprogramm Friedrichs II. in Capua," is announced in *Musagetes, Festschrift Prinz.*

48. See, for instance, Jean Mesqui, *Le pont en France avant le temps des ingénieurs* (Paris, 1986), 13–18, on "Seigneurie et seigneuries du pont," and Erich Maschke, "Brücke," in *Lexikon des Mittelalters*, 2:724–730.

49. For the Steinerne Brücke, see Felix Mader in *Die Kunstdenkmäler von Bayern, Oberpfalz XXII, Stadt Regensburg* (Munich, 1933), 3:236–242, with earlier bibliography, and Helmut-Eberhard Paulus, "Die Steinerne Brücke in Regensburg," *Jahrbuch der Bayerischen Denkmalpflege* 40 (1986), 143–168.

50. The king with the bird has been identified as Saint Oswald, Emperor Otto IV, or Henry the Fowler. See Mader 1933, 239–240. None of these identifications is entirely convincing. Recently Paulus 1986 opted for an identification of the statue with Frederick II. This proposal is also open to contradiction. The statue at Regensburg would be nearly the only representation of Frederick II that shows the emperor with a beard.

51. See Willibald Sauerländer in *Bayern—Kunst und Kultur* [exh. cat., Stadtmuseum, Munich] (Munich, 1972), 323.

52. Rudolf Chadraba, *Die Karlsbrücke* (Prague, 1974).

53. See Erich Bachmann, ed., *Romanik in Böhmen* (Munich, 1977), 119–120, for the history and construction of the Judith Bridge.

54. For these suggestions see Bachmann 1977, 120, and Jiři Mašin in Bachmann 1977, 182. Paulus 1986, 146–147, mentions a third hypothesis: Vladislav endows his son Frederick with the crown of Bohemia.

55. See Chadraba 1974, 11.

56. For this program see Chadraba 1974. It is, however, difficult to follow all the details of Chadraba's farfetched interpretation of the iconography of the Altstädter Brückenturm.

57. See Sauerländer 1990, 92–107: "Monumentale Skulptur all'antica."

58. See Poeschke 1980, and Cesare Gnudi, "Considerazioni sul gotico francese, l'arte imperiale e la formazione di Nicola Pisano," in *Federico II e l'arte*, 1:1–17.

59. For this bust see Hermann Fillitz in *Die Zeit der Staufer*, 1:393–394.

60. Séroux d'Agincourt, *Histoire de l'art par les monuments: Sculpture*, IVe partie (Paris, 1823), pl. XXVII, 4.

61. For the plaster cast of the head, see Willemsen 1953, 37–43.

62. See Carl A. Willemsen, *Die Bildnisse der Staufer* (Göppingen, 1977), figs. 53–54.

63. The closest parallel would be the statue of Dagobert in the cloister at Saint-Denis, which seems, however, to date not earlier than 1250. See Willibald Sauerländer, *Gotische Skulptur in Frankreich 1140–1270* (Munich, 1970), 172.

64. The bibliography on Castel del Monte until 1978 is discussed by Wolfgang Krönig, "Castel del Monte—Frédéric II et l'architecture française," in *L'art dans l'Italie méridionale. Aggiornamento dell'opera di Émile Bertaux sotto la direzione di Adriano Prandi*, 5 vols. (Rome, 1978), 5:929–951.

65. See Cadei 1980, Krönig 1978, and Michele Cordaro, "Il problema delle origini dell'architettura federiciana," in *Federico II e l'arte*, 1:121–138.

66. Charles Seymour, Jr., "Têtes gothiques de la cathédrale de Noyon," *Gazette des Beaux Arts* (1937), 137–142. For further examples see Robert Branner, "Keystones and Kings," *Gazette des Beaux Arts* (1961), 65–82, and Ludwig Schreiner, *Die frühgotische Plastik Südwestfrankreichs* (Cologne and Graz, 1963), pls. LXXI–LXXII.

67. A rare example of a beautiful console head coming from a royal palace—the palace at Clarendon—is found in the Salisbury and South Wiltshire Museum; see Sauerländer 1990, 299, pl. 277.

68. All the sculptures from Castel del Monte are reproduced in Carl A. Willemsen, *Castel del Monte* (Frankfurt, 1982). An Italian edition with the same illustrations appeared in Bari in 1984. For the Molajoli head, see Bruno Molajoli, "Una scultura di Castel del Monte," *Bollettino d'arte* 28 (1934–1935), 120–125.

69. See Sauerländer 1990, 142–151: "Der Elefant im Tower und das Lächeln von Reims."

70. See *Friderici Romanorum imperatoris secundi, De arte venandi cum avibus*, ed. Carl A. Willemsen, 2 vols. (Leipzig, 1942), 1:2.

71. See Poeschke 1980, 110–115, figs. 27–33. The coif on the head of a caryatid at Castel del Monte (Poeschke, fig. 30), which seems specifically French to Poeschke, was known in Italy since the twelfth century. See, for instance, an illustration of the *Relatio Translationis Sancti Geminiani* in the Archivio Capitolare at Modena, reproduced in Geza de Francovich, *Benedetto Antelami* (Milan, 1952), pl. 290, and other examples, pls. 180, 189, 190, 314, 322.

POSTSCRIPT

After this paper went to press, the article by Beat Brenk, "Antikenverständnis und weltliches Rechtsdenken im Skulpturenprogramm Friedrichs II," here announced as forthcoming in note 47, appeared in *Musagetes, Festschrift Wolfram Prinz*, ed. Ronald G. Kecks (Berlin, 1991), 93–103. Brenk's conclusions come very close to the arguments proposed in this paper. He is more detailed in tracing ancient models for the busts on the gateway. He sees the program as a juridical one without, however, referring to the *concordia imperii*. Whether the emperor interfered as closely in the erection of the gateway and in the style of its sculpture as Brenk assumes remains a question of surmise. A second paper which also appeared too late to be included in the notes of this article must be mentioned: Peter Cornelius Claussen, "Die Statue Friedrichs II. vom Brückentor in Capua (1234–1239). Der Befund, die Quellen, und eine Zeichnung aus dem Nachlass von Séroux d' Agincourt," in *Festschrift für Hartmut Biermann*, ed. Christoph Andreas and others (Weinheim, 1990), 19–39. It presents interesting new material and information on the statue of the emperor. I do not share the author's opinion on the northern sources of this statue.

being an island with a Muslim majority into one in which, by 1240, Islam had to all intents ceased to exist.[24] One was the emigration of leading Muslims, who resettled in North Africa and Spain; the Muslim religious authorities disapproved of Muslims living under Christian rule, for they were well aware of the restrictions this would place on free practice of Islam; and, more important, they identified the practice of Islam with the exercise of real political authority. The conquest of Sicily and the Holy Land, and the Spanish *reconquista*, resulted for the first time in large numbers of Muslims falling under Christian authority; and both religions found it hard to adjust to the new reality. A second reason for the decline of Sicilian Islam was extermination. There certainly were pogroms, and Frederick II's tough repression of the last Muslims in Sicily was not a novelty.[25] A third reason was conversion, not so much by Latin missionaries as by a slow process of osmosis that brought Muslim peasants into the local Greek churches; this is demonstrated by the gradual transformation in personal names from those of Islam to those of Greek Orthodoxy.[26] An élite of administrators, often non-Sicilian Muslims like Philip of Mahdiyyah, accepted Christianity; and some, like Philip, were probably not sincere converts.[27] At Messina the civil servant Abd al-Massih told ibn Jubayr: "You can boldly display your faith in Islam. . . . But we must conceal our faith, and, fearful of our lives, must adhere to the worship of God and the discharge of our religious duties in secret."[28] It is true that ibn Hammud, an unconverted Muslim, held a government office; this reflected his exceptional standing in the Muslim community, and yet he still suffered expropriation and persecution.[29] For the other Muslims in government, Palermo was well worth a mass. By Frederick II's reign, Muslims played no part in the royal administration, though Uberto Fallamonaco, *secretus* of western Sicily, appears to have been of Muslim descent. The writing skills of Arabic speakers were still required at the start of the thirteenth century; by the late Middle Ages they had to be supplied as special services by Arabic-speaking Jews or by inhabitants of the Sicilian-Hafsid condominium of Pantelleria.[30]

In other words, by the time Frederick came of age, Sicily no longer stood beyond the Latin Christian frontier; that frontier now lay at Pantelleria and Tunis. A massive immigration of "Lombardi," settlers from northwestern Italy, Campania, and elsewhere, had helped fill some of the gaps left by the disappearance of Muslim cultivators. The decline of the Muslim population did, however, lead to a collapse in specialized agriculture based on Arab technology: the sugar industry, for instance, went into a crisis.[31] The island became even more of a center for grain production, though just when the North Africans were desperate for additional food supplies. The loss of Sicily's Muslims did not therefore lead to a break in contact with North Africa; in a sense it even enhanced that contact, at a commercial level, in the form of massive grain shipments.[32]

Since the 1190s the Muslims were in revolt; the harsh economic régime to which many were subject, and the sudden imposition of the overlordship of the archbishops of Monreale around 1180, created a violent reaction. Old autonomies were stripped away by William II; but on his death the royal government also became greatly enfeebled, and German warlords, Genoese pirates, and others seized what they could in Sicily.[33] The Muslims, too, looked for a radical solution: the recreation of a Muslim state in the mountains of western Sicily. A Sicilian *intifada* broke out, consisting of rebels hopeful of support from Africa and determined to shake off what they saw as foreign rule. The rebels even minted their own coins in defiance of the royal minting laws; they were not mere guerrillas but had actual charge of mountainous territory in western Sicily.[34]

Frederick II's reassertion of royal power in the 1220s involved the merciless destruction of the Muslim rebellion. In 1222 Frederick launched an attack on Iato, where ibn Abbad (or Benaveth), the leader of the rebels, was based. An eight-week siege was sufficient to bring about the surrender of the Saracens. In a famous episode, ibn Abbad was taken to Frederick's pavilion, a prisoner; he prostrated himself before Frederick and begged pardon, but Frederick in his fury struck ibn Abbad with his spur and tore his body open. Soon after, ibn Abbad was publicly hanged at Palermo.[35]

At first sight, Frederick's solution to the problem of the Muslim rebellion has no obvious parallels elsewhere in Western Europe. He created a Saracen colony at Lucera in Apulia, at the other edge of the Sicilian kingdom; he expelled the Christian population of Lucera, even including the bishop, and turned Lucera into a garrison town. There is no evidence that it ever became an important center of Islamic culture, though it is certainly true that Frederick often resided at his castle there and enjoyed the company of his belly dancers and Muslim musicians (who were not, or not all, Lucerans; some were certainly black slaves).[36] The castle at Lucera was a composite structure consisting of a royal palace built on top of a massive glacis; clearly, Frederick felt the need to defend the palace from potentially restive Lucerans.[37] The discovery of Chinese celadon ware in the British excavations at Lucera castle is some indication of the contacts Frederick, or an immediate successor, enjoyed with the East, though even then the pottery probably reached the Sicilian court via Egypt; it is not evidence of the quality of life in the town of Lucera.[38] Although many of the Lucera Saracens were certainly soldiers, some remained active as pastoralists and others were lured back to the soil by promises of plow teams. In the imperial register of 1239–1240, Frederick is found offering one thousand cattle to the Lucera Muslims, with the aim, he says, of binding the Saracens to the soil "as was the case in the time of King William."[39] Frederick sought to create an economically viable community in an area that, like Sicily, was not already very densely settled; but he also sought to isolate the Lucera Muslims from the Islamic world. Thus he permitted them freedom from commercial tolls in the whole of southern Italy (from the *plateaticum, jus dohane, passagium*), but not in Sicily; and he instructed his officials to ensure that Saracen shepherds did not cross to Sicily.[40] The island was to be empty of Muslims; in fact, this was far from easy to ensure, since Muslim rebels held out in the hills, few in number but still a source of trouble as late as the 1240s.

Some outlying territories, too, notably Malta, retained a high proportion of Muslims even though an attempt was made to deport rebel Christians, from Celano in the Abruzzi, into their midst.[41] Forced deportation thus was a tool not merely in the management of Muslims but also in that of Christians. This again was a phenomenon of the frontier: as in Spain, mass population movements, for security, or to increase agricultural productivity, had long been a fact of life. Frederick's deportations from Sicily bear comparison with the expulsion of the Muslims from newly conquered Cordoba, Seville, and other Andalusian towns by the Castilian king in the 1230s and 1240s (though new Muslim settlement was, interestingly, permitted in Cordoba later on). There, too, expulsion of one group was matched by settlement by another. Contemporaries, at the papal curia most notably, viewed Castilian policy with surprise.[42] It is notable that in the Castilian case the Moors were expelled out of Christian Andalusia, toward Muslim Granada or North Africa; in the Sicilian, they were condemned to "internal" exile. Only in 1287, with the Catalan conquest of Minorca, was virtually an entire Muslim population not merely expelled but enslaved.[43] Frederick's policy at Lucera is much less radical—original insofar as it was applied to non-Christians, but traditional insofar as it was a standard Mediterranean solution, known in southern Italy at least since Byzantine times, to the problem of how to deal with a disaffected population. Frederick's actions recall the Byzantine practice of deporting large populations from one side of the empire to another; in the tenth and early eleventh centuries, this policy had brought Armenians and even Bulgars to Apulia. Occasional voluntary mass movements of north Italians and Provençaux into Sicily and southern Italy in this period may also have stimulated ideas about less than voluntary transfers within the *regno*.[44]

It is a moot point whether Lucera was intended to remain a lone beacon of Islam in Italy. Lucera was a long way from the Muslim world, about as far away from Africa as anywhere in the *regno*. The Muslims of Lucera, unlike those of Sicily, could not expect to maintain close religious contact with Tunisia, let alone to receive military aid against Frederick, as had happened during difficult phases of the Sicilian revolt. Isolated in Apulia—"in media christianorum planitie"—the Luceran Muslims would surely experience the same assimilation into the surrounding Latin society that so many Sicilian Muslims had experienced in the twelfth century. Many already understood Italian. Moreover, there is some evidence of conversion campaigns. In 1233 Gregory IX solicited Frederick's help in ensuring that the Dominicans be allowed to preach Christianity to the Lucerans.[45] Frederick insisted that he, too, was keen to convert all the Saracens in Lucera and that many had already converted. James Powell suggests that the pope was worried that the Lucerans spoke the same language as their Christian neighbors and that they might therefore infect them with Islam.[46] This is perhaps one element, assuming that *intelligunt* really does mean "they speak" as well as "they understand"; but more important was the feeling that this self-contained group of Muslims was ripe for conversion, at a moment when Gregory IX, Ramon de Penyafort, and others were beginning to plan still more ambitious preaching campaigns against Jews and Muslims, based on the close study of Arabic and Hebrew in special language academies set up for training missionaries.[47] The prospect of an easy kill against Islam in Apulia must have seemed too good to miss, especially since just now Frederick and the papacy were on reasonably good terms.

A second letter of Frederick II indicates that his concern for the Christianization of Lucera was still alive in 1236. Now we find him insisting that one-third of the population had decided to turn Christian already, and rebutting accusations that he has been neglectful of the need to convert them. Interestingly, he claims credit not merely for deporting the Saracens from the Sicilian mountains to Apulia, which he obviously saw as a positive achievement for Christianity; he also claims credit for Christianizing western Sicily by strengthening Christian settlement there and by removing the Muslim menace from the island. Lucera has to be seen as a two-pronged policy, both arms of which are intended to benefit the Christians.[48] As Powell says, the letter of 1236, "which has been cited to show that Frederick had little interest in the conversion of the Luceran Muslims actually demonstrates the opposite."[49]

The problem of the loss of the agricultural skills of the Islamic world after the disappearance of Islam from Sicily also had to be faced. Frederick sought to attract North African settlers to Sicily, turning not to the Muslims but to the Jews. This again was not unheard of: in Seville, Majorca, and elsewhere contemporary Spanish kings actually encouraged them to settle, bringing in Jews from northern Spain, southern France, and North Africa.[50] It is not unlikely that Frederick was consciously imitating Spanish practice. The imperial register of 1239–1240 lays out Frederick's plans to bring Jewish settlers, possibly from the island of Jerba, who would know how to plant and tend date palms and who could introduce to Sicily indigo, henna, and "other various seeds which grow in North Africa and yet are not now seen to grow in Sicily."[51] This remark seems to confirm the evidence from the Monreale estates that agricultural skills brought to Sicily by the Arabs had declined seriously since about 1200.[52] Half of the Jews' produce was to be paid to the crown, and, like other Jews, the settlers were to be treated as "serfs of the chamber"; they were liable to the poll-tax, of Muslim origin, and to taxes on wine and what appears to be kosher slaughter. The *secretus* of Palermo, Uberto Fallamonaco, was worried that too many settlers might come; he placed severe limits, insisting, for instance, that the palm grove was to be leased to them for only five or ten years. No doubt he hoped that local imitators who had learned the appropriate technology could then take over.[53] The North African Jews were specially conceded the right to have their own synagogue, no doubt because their customs differed from those of Sicily, but it was preferably to be an old disused one, a symbol (perhaps) of the desuetude of the "Old Law."[54] Even the repair of old synagogues had met with disapproval in the Roman law codes, but the wish to ensure that they do not build one afresh certainly fits into the spirit of traditional Roman and papal legislation concerning the Jews. Toleration did not mean encouragement.

III

Frederick's legislation in Sicily contains important clues to his outlook toward Jews and Saracens. Interestingly, he sometimes couples the two, insisting twice in the Constitutions of Melfi of 1231 that both are too severely persecuted at the moment: in other words, some disabilities can be imposed, but this must not extend so far that they are denied access to proper exercise of justice. "We do not," he says, "desire them to be persecuted simply because they are Jews or Saracens."[55] He even exempts the Jews from a general prohibition on the charging of interest, since Christian laws against usury do not apply to Jews;[56] in fact, his decree mirrors that of the Fourth Lateran Council.[57] On the other hand, earlier legislation of 1221 demanded that Jews wear a distinguishing costume, again in line with the decrees of the Fourth Lateran Council. Similar restrictions were placed on prostitutes, for both groups consisted of outsiders who could not really belong to a Christian society and yet were entitled to protection by Christian rulers.[58]

Frederick's approach to the Jews of Germany provides important parallels. Accusations from Fulda that Jews had crucified Christian children to pour scorn on the Passion led Frederick to investigate the charge with a thoroughness that is generally assumed to reveal his skepticism about the whole notion. He saw clearly that such a charge, already known from other areas of Europe, would affect the status of all Jews in Christendom and would unleash great violence against the Jews far beyond Fulda. He summoned a tribunal which failed to agree on the matter, and Frederick himself then took direct charge.[59] He wrote to Christian rulers elsewhere in Europe asking that Jewish converts to Christianity be sent to Germany; their knowledge of Jewish law and practice would surely settle the matter once and for all, while their new commitment to Christianity would mean that they would not automatically defend Judaism. The converts demonstrated that Jewish law did not permit human sacrifice, and Frederick then accepted that the charges were a fabrication: "We can surely assume that for those to whom even the blood of permitted animals is forbidden, the desire for human blood cannot exist, as a result of the horror of the matter, the prohibition of nature, and the common bond of the human species in which they also join Christians."[60] The reference to the common bond of the human species was not a mere throwaway line, at a time when Christians were denigrating Jews and other non-Christians as less than human, or incompletely human, because of their obstinate refusal to heed the reasonable arguments of those who sought to convert them. It is interesting, too, to find that one of the sources upon which Frederick's judgment depended was the Talmud. It was described in neutral terms as a book of Jewish "decrees," and it is thus clear that at this stage growing suspicion of the Talmud, in France and at the papal curia, had not significantly influenced Frederick II.

In July 1236 Frederick issued a privilege in favor of the Jews, describing the accusations against the Jews and their refutation, forbidding others from repeating the libel, and stating that the Jews were under the special supervision of the emperor, as *servi camere nostre*.[61] They were thus in general exempt from interference by other great lords, while the emperor could hope to enjoy revenues from their economic activities. The state of "chamber serfdom," as it is often, perhaps wrongly, translated, was a privileged condition of dependence as well as a sign of the subservience of Jews to Christian authority.[62] Such dependence was certainly in Frederick's mind, too, for in a privilege to Vienna of 1237 he insisted that Jews should not hold office in the city government since imperial authority has imposed perpetual servitude upon the Jews as punishment for their crime: "cum imperialis auctoritas a priscis temporibus ad perpetrati Iudaici sceleris ultionem eisdem Iudeis indixerit perpetuam servitutem."[63] However, the terms *servus* and *Knecht* did not have entirely negative connotations in the Hohenstaufen period.[64] The state of *Kammerknechtschaft* was in certain respects analogous to the state of immediacy in which imperial cities and, later on, the Swiss stood; it was a guarantee of relative safety in the much-fragmented political world of medieval Germany. Frederick II's privilege was soon paralleled by grants from German princes, notably that awarded by Frederick II von Babenberg in Austria in 1244; the duke's desire to guarantee the physical safety of the Jews in his principality is emphasized again and again.[65] The parallels can be extended further if we look at the copious documentation from Spain in the same period, again guaranteeing the physical and economic well-being of the Jews.[66]

On the other hand, Frederick did not mention the Jews in his more widely ranging Landpeace of Mainz in 1235. The separation of the Jews from other beneficiaries of the emperor's grace in Germany has excited comment, not least since a major concern of the document was the prevention of private warfare within Germany; the consequent assumption is that the lack of reference to the Jews made them more vulnerable.[67] However, it is likely (as Dietmar Willoweit has suggested) that the Mainzer Landfriede was intended to be binding on all who inhabited Germany, Jew or Christian, male or female, lord or peasant. The Landpeace had little explicit to say to merchants, peasants, and women, so that Jews were not the only apparent omission.[68]

The papacy joined in the condemnation of the ritual murder charge.[69] Once again, we find that Frederick's position is in many respects close to that of the papal curia; the great distance is that between papal thinking and the emerging popular image of the Jew as the vengeful and bloody enemy of all Christians. On the other hand, as has been seen, the papacy was becoming deeply hostile to the Talmud. Innocent IV's brief repetition of Frederick's refutation shows that even a decade after the Fulda libel there were constant accusations against Jews of child murder.

IV

Frederick's contact with Jews and Muslims did, of course, exist on other levels. He was capable of expressing himself in Arabic, and his respect for Islam puzzled the Muslims he met in Jerusalem during his remarkable crusade.[70] As a young man he had been exceptionally enthusiastic about going on crusade, and an interest in the fate of the Holy City remained with him throughout his life.[71] But as king of Sicily his involvement in the politics of the Muslim world naturally took on a more complex character; commercial ties to Egypt and Tunisia, and political ambitions in Jerba and Tunis inherited from the Normans, meant that he had a deeper understanding of the Arab world than other crusaders—an understanding that paid off triumphantly when he negotiated the surrender of most of Jerusalem, Nazareth, and Bethlehem to the kingdom of Jerusalem.[72] His ability to play Middle Eastern politics does not, of course, qualify him for the role attributed to him by Gregory IX and, above all, Innocent IV as a secret ally of Islam.[73]

It is worth adding that the reconquest of Jerusalem by Frederick II's deft diplomacy resulted not in Jewish settlement but in the expulsion of the city's Jews. It is possible that Frederick himself was not involved in the decision, which was little more than a reenactment of twelfth-century practice. After a few years the emperor's representative permitted a single Jewish dyer to live within the walls of Jerusalem, so as to provide aid to Jewish pilgrims who came by day to pray at the Western Wall.[74] The many Muslims of al-Quds were also obliged to leave the Old City, but the Temple Mount remained in Muslim hands. Such a solution to the problem of the ownership of Jerusalem naturally satisfied no one.

V

The other main area of contact he had with Jews and Muslims lay in the intellectual sphere. It is doubtful whether any Muslim scholars spent more than the briefest time at his court, and then only on embassies from Egypt and elsewhere.[75] In this respect Roger II's court provides a far better example of Christian patronage of Arab learning (including that of native Arabs).[76] In fact, much the same qualification applies to Jewish scholars too; his meetings with Judah ha-Cohen and other Spanish Jews were rare, and the native Sicilian Jews played no identifiable role in the translation work which did go ahead. The translators appear to have been organized by Michael Scot, Frederick's astrologer, and were drawn from a common background: they were mostly members of the ibn Tibbon family, Provençal Jews of Spanish origin, or their close associates.[77] Jacob Anatoli, brother-in-law of Moses ibn Tibbon, translated Ptolemy's *Almagest* and works by Averroes; but to imagine him frequenting the imperial court on easy terms is to stretch the evidence too far.[78] The Jewish scholars who worked for Frederick were thus products of Spanish and southern French Hebrew learning; they were not torchbearers of south Italian Jewish scholarship.

It is likely, too, that the famous questions about the nature of the universe sent to Muslim scholars by Frederick II were as much part of a diplomatic initiative in the 1240s toward the Almohad rulers of Morocco as they were an act of philosophical inquiry.[79] The replies from the philosopher ibn Sab'in of Ceuta were somewhat scornful of the knowledge Frederick had displayed; nonetheless it is certainly striking that a medieval emperor should have entered into correspondence with Muslim scholars as far afield as Ceuta and the Yemen, without any apparent intention of converting them to Christianity.

It is also clear that Frederick's *De arte venandi cum avibus* was influenced by Arab zoological learning and hunting treatises. Michael Scot's successor, Master Theodore, translated Moamyn's *De scientia venandi per aves*, and Frederick spent the six-month siege of Faenza in 1240–1241 checking Theodore's draft. The illuminations of the beautiful Vatican manuscript of part of the hunting book of Frederick II perhaps show the influence of Arabic models. But the ultimate source of Frederick's method lay with Aristotle, whose *De animalibus* he knew well. His taste for the natural sciences is part of a tradition going back to Roger II, but it must be stressed that the physical universe in which he believed was most emphatically a Christian one. The questions he posed to Michael Scot reveal a wish to obtain a literal description of where God sits and what his angels and saints continually do before him. It is a complete, integrated universe in which Heaven and Hell are geographically defined spaces.[80]

VI

Nearly everything we know about Frederick's religious outlook suggests that he saw himself as a Christian. His view of the crusades was far from unconventional; he associated with Cistercians and Franciscans; he insisted in his law code on his appointment by God to rule over mankind. He, or more likely his advisers, flirted with radical movements critical of the wealth of the Church; but, though Frederick's attitude to the papacy was much complicated by his violent quarrels with Gregory IX and Innocent IV, he did not believe that the papacy and the empire were necessarily opposed. It is thus hardly surprising that his treatment of Jews and Muslims was guided by traditional papal practice and recommendations; even the creation of Saracen Lucera was less original than is generally assumed. His approach to unbelievers was conservative rather than (as sometimes assumed) lax or sympathetic; it was fully in line with his overall policy of restoring the rights of his predecessors as kings of Sicily and as Christian Roman emperors.

NOTES

1. William C. Jordan, *The French Monarchy and the Jews* (Philadelphia, 1989), 147–150, emphasizes Louis IX's deeply felt hostility to Judaism.

2. For a fuller assessment of Frederick's aims, see David Abulafia, *Frederick II: A Medieval Emperor*, 2d ed. (New York, 1992).

3. My understanding of this subject owes much to Anna Sapir Abulafia and to the studies she is undertaking for her forthcoming book on *The Jews and the Twelfth-Century Renaissance*.

4. Saint Bernard in Patrologia Latina 182, Ep. 567, col. 567c; compare Rabbi Ephraim of Bonn, "Sefer Zekhirah," trans. Shlomo Eidelberg, *The Jews and the Crusaders: The Hebrew Chronicles of the First and Second Crusades* (Madison, Wis., 1977), 122: "whosoever touches a Jew to take his life, is like one who harms Jesus himself"; however, the view of Gillian R. Evans, *The Mind of St. Bernard of Clairvaux* (Oxford, 1983), 32, is rather exaggerated.

5. Robert Chazan, *Daggers of Faith: Thirteenth-Century Christian Missionizing and Jewish Response* (Berkeley and Los Angeles, 1989), 23–24; Evans 1983, 226–227.

6. Augustus Jessopp and Montague R. James, *The Life and Miracles of St. William of Norwich* (Cambridge, 1896).

7. The same question, in a modern guise, is sometimes said to affect the refusal of the Vatican to recognize Israel as a sovereign state.

8. Edward A. Synan, *The Popes and the Jews in the Middle Ages* (New York, 1965), appendix 7, title 68, 233, 235.

9. Frederic W. Maitland, "The Deacon and the Jewess," in Frederic W. Maitland, *Roman Canon Law in the Church of England* (London, 1898), 158–179; the church council that dealt with this matter also reaffirmed the decisions of the Fourth Lateran Council on the role of the Jews in a Christian society.

10. There is a conundrum here: Jewish law also encouraged social separation, especially at meal times, and the wearing of beards by men. But it appears that around 1200 Jews wore similar clothes to Christians and that their identity was not immediately obvious. In works of art of the thirteenth century, Jews were occasionally distinguished by their features (notably, by giving them large noses), but this was far from universal and may not even represent reality: Bernard Blumenkranz, *Le juif médiéval au miroir de l'art chrétien* (Paris, 1966), 24–25, 28, 32. The use of grotesque noses by artists may simply be an attempt to make Jews look ugly. For a bizarre discussion of noses, see the eccentric book of Arthur Koestler, *The Thirteenth Tribe* (London, 1976), 168–170.

11. Jeremy Cohen, *The Friars and the Jews: The Evolution of Medieval Anti-Judaism* (Ithaca, N.Y., 1982), 42.

12. Chazan 1989, 33–34. Hyam Maccoby, *Judaism on Trial: Jewish-Christian Disputations in the Middle Ages* (Rutherford, N.J., 1982), 19–38, contains a translation of the 1240 debate; the editor's introduction is, however, flawed.

13. James Muldoon, *Popes, Lawyers and Infidels: The Church and the Non-Christian World, 1250–1550* (Philadelphia, 1979), 10–11, though the discussion can be taken rather further.

14. Cohen 1982, 52–60; Bernard Septimus, *Hispano-Jewish Culture in Transition: The Career and Controversies of Ramah* (Cambridge, Mass., 1982); Bernard Septimus, "Piety and Power in Thirteenth-Century Catalonia," in *Studies in Medieval Jewish History and Literature*, ed. Isadore Twersky (Cambridge, Mass., 1979), 197–230.

15. See Cohen 1982 and Chazan 1989, the latter of which makes better sense. Maccoby 1982, 97–150, translates the Hebrew and Latin reports of the 1263 debate. The *Decretum* of Gratian also encouraged disputations between Christians and other unbelievers in the hope that by reason they would be drawn to Christianity: Muldoon 1979, 4, referring to *Corpus Iuris Canonici*, ed. Emil Friedberg, 2 vols. (Leipzig, 1879–1881), vol. 1, *Decretum*, C.23 q.4 c.17.

16. Cohen 1982, 80–84, 109–110.

17. Richard W. Southern, *Western Views of Islam in the Middle Ages* (Cambridge, Mass., 1962), 32–37.

18. Muldoon 1979, 6–14.

19. David Romano, *Judíos al servicio de Pedro el Grande de Aragón (1276–1285)* (Barcelona, 1983) shows that the Aragonese court became more hostile to the Jewish officials during the thirteenth century; James I was more benign than his son Peter the Great, who was under great pressure from the nobles during the War of the Sicilian Vespers.

20. Romuald of Salerno, *Chronicon*, ed. Carlo A. Garufi, Rerum Italicarum Scriptores, ser. 2, 7:1:236.

21. Jews who became Christians could find themselves in financial difficulty because they were cut off from their previous business associates; those involved in moneylending might be in special difficulty. See Jordan 1989, 149–150.

22. *The Travels of ibn Jubayr*, trans. Ronald J. C. Broadhurst (London, 1952), 359.

23. Ibn Jubayr, 360.

24. For a fuller discussion, see David Abulafia, "The End of Muslim Sicily," in *Muslims under Latin Rule, 1100–1300*, ed. James M. Powell (Princeton, 1990).

25. Hugo Falcandus, *La Historia o Liber de Regno Sicilie e la Epistola ad Petrum Panormitane Ecclesie Thesaurarium*, ed. Giovanni B. Siragusa, Fonti per la storia d'Italia (Rome, 1897), 73, reveals the bloodthirsty approach of the king's kinsman Roger Sclavus to the Muslims in the mid-twelfth century.

26. A detailed account of this process by Jeremy Johns is in press; the outlines of his approach can be seen in his article "The Monreale Survey: Indigenes and Invaders in Medieval West Sicily," in *Papers in Italian Archaeology 4: The Cambridge Conference*, part 4,

Classical and Medieval Archaeology, ed. Caroline Malone and Simon Stoddart, British Archaeological Reports, International series 246 (Oxford, 1985), 215–221.

27. Ibn Jubayr reports that some Latin women at the royal palace in Messina actually converted secretly to Islam: ibn Jubayr, 341. However, ibn Jubayr himself admits that there were many strange stories circulating about the court of William II.

28. Ibn Jubayr, 342.

29. Ibn Jubayr, 358–360; also Hugo Falcandus, 119. For information about his business activities, see David Abulafia, *The Two Italies: Economic Relations between the Norman Kingdom of Sicily and the Northern Communes* (Cambridge, 1977), 247–249.

30. Henri Bresc, "Pantelleria entre l'Islam et la Chrétienté," *Cahiers de Tunisie* 19 (1971), 105–127; Henri Bresc, *Un monde méditerranéen: Économie et société en Sicile, 1300–1450*, 2 vols. (Rome and Palermo, 1986), 2:582–584; also compare 2:622–623. Malta also remained as an island of Arabic in the Sicilian kingdom. This may reflect the longer survival of Islam there than in other parts of the kingdom and a greater continuity in population (even after conversion to Christianity) than in many areas of Sicily proper. Maltese Arabic was the language of the peasantry, but the late medieval nobility, partly of non-Maltese origin, spoke a form of Italian.

31. Henri Bercher, Annie Courteaux, and Jean Mouton, "Une abbaye latine dans la société musulmane: Monreale au XIIe siècle," *Annales: Économies, sociétés, civilisations* 34 (1979), 525–547.

32. Tunis became a Sicilian protectorate, probably not for the first time, and acquired a vast, though generally transient, Christian population: Robert Brunschvig, *La Berbérie orientale sous les Hafsides des origines à la fin du XVe siècle*, 2 vols. (Paris, 1940–1947), 2:431–472. The literature on Frederick II's grain exports to Africa includes James M. Powell, "Medieval Monarchy and Trade: The Economic Policy of Frederick II in the Kingdom of Sicily," *Studi medievali*, ser. 3, 3 (1962), 420–524, and Erich Maschke, "Die Wirtschaftspolitik Kaiser Friedrichs II. im Königreich Sizilien," *Vierteljahrschrift für Sozial- und Wirtschaftsgeschichte* 53 (1966), 289–328, reprinted in *Stupor Mundi: Zur Geschichte Friedrichs II. von Hohenstaufen*, ed. Gunther Wolf, 2d ed. (Darmstadt, 1982), 349–394; Abulafia 1988, 331–332.

33. David Abulafia, "Henry Count of Malta and His Mediterranean Activities, 1203–1230," in *Medieval Malta: Studies on Malta before the Knights*, ed. Anthony Luttrell (London, 1975), 104–125, reprinted in David Abulafia, *Italy, Sicily and the Mediterranean, 1100–1400* (London, 1987), no. 3.

34. Franco D'Angelo, "La monetazione di Muḥammad ibn ᶜAbbād emiro ribelle a Federico II di Sicilia," *Studi Magrebini* 7 (1975), 149–153; see also Jeremy Johns, "Monte Guastanella: Un insediamento musulmano nell'Agrigentino," *Sicilia archeologica* 16:33–51. See now Ferdinando Maurici, *L'Emirato sulle montagne: Note per una storia della resistenza musulmana in Sicilia nell'età di Federico II di Svevia* (Palermo, 1987).

35. Abulafia 1988, 144–145.

36. Abulafia 1988, 146–148.

37. See the contribution by Gary M. Radke, "The Palaces of Frederick II," in this volume.

38. David B. Whitehouse, "Ceramici e vetri medioevali provenienti dal Castello di Lucera," *Bollettino d'arte* 51 (1966), 171–178.

39. *Constitutiones regum regni utriusque Siciliae, mandante Friderico II Imperatore per Petrum de Vinea Capuanum Praetorio Praefectum, et Cancellarium . . . et Fragmentum quod superest Regesti eiusdem Imperatoris Ann. 1239 & 1240*, ed. C. Carcani (Naples, 1786), 307; Abulafia 1988, 334–335.

40. *Acta Imperii inedita saeculi XIII et XIV*, ed. Eduard Winkelmann, 2 vols. (Innsbruck, 1880–1885; repr. Aalen, 1964), 1:763; and Carcani 1786, 295.

41. For the Maltese population, see the document in *Acta Imperii*, 1:938; Anthony Luttrell, "Approaches to Medieval Malta," in *Medieval Malta*, 1–70, esp. 36–40; David Abulafia, "The State and Economic Life in the Kingdom of Sicily under Frederick II," in *Frederick II: Theory and Practice of Government*, paper distributed at the Centro E. Majorana, Erice, Sicily, 18–24 September 1989 (Italian edition in press, Palermo); Abulafia 1990. Celano is mentioned in *Ryccardi de sancto Germano notarii Chronica*, ed. Carlo A. Garufi, Rerum Italicarum Scriptores, ser. 2, 7:2:112–113, in only one version of the text.

42. Felipe Fernández-Armesto, *Before Columbus: Exploration and Colonization from the Mediterranean to the Atlantic, 1229–1492* (Philadelphia, 1987), 51–60; Muldoon 1979, 111–119. Both cite Oldradus de Ponte, *Consilia* (Venice, 1571), 126–127: the despoliation of the Moors was "openly contrary to the precepts of charity."

43. Fernández-Armesto 1987, 36; Elena Lourie, "La colonización cristiana de Menorca durante el reinado de Alfonso III 'El Liberal,' Rey de Aragón," *Analecta sacra Tarraconensia* 53–54 (1980–1981), 135–186; Ramón Roselló Vaquer, *Aportació a la història medieval de Menorca: El sigle XIII* (Ciutadella, 1980); Micaela Mata, *Conquests and Reconquests of Menorca* (Barcelona, 1984), 9–62. In a paper at the 13th Congress of the History of the Crown of Aragon, Palma de Mallorca, September 1987, Henri Bresc argued that the events of 1287 were a novelty, marking a new attitude to the Muslims among Christian Mediterranean rulers.

44. Vera von Falkenhausen, *Untersuchungen über die byzantinische Herrschaft in Süditalien vom 9. bis ins 11. Jahrhundert* (Wiesbaden, 1967), 23–24, which tends, however, to suggest that settlement rights in Byzantine Apulia were as often a favor as a punishment.

45. Jean L. A. Huillard-Bréholles, ed., *Historia Diplomatica Friderici Secundi . . .*, 6 vols. (Paris, 1852–1861), 4:452.

46. James M. Powell, "The Papacy and the Muslim Frontier," in *Muslims under Latin Rule* (hereafter Powell 1990).

47. Cohen 1982, 107.

48. Huillard-Bréholles, 4:831.

49. Powell 1990.

50. Fernández-Armesto 1987, 23, 66–67.

51. Carcani 1786, 290–291.

52. Bercher and others 1979.

53. Abulafia 1988, 336.

54. Carcani 1786, 290–291.

55. Constitutions of Melfi (1231), title 18 (21), in Carcani 1786.

56. Constitutions of Melfi (1231), title 6 (9), in Carcani 1786.

57. Synan 1965, appendix 7, pp. 232, 234, title 67, *De usuris Judaeorum*, speaking of "si de cetero quocumque praetextu Judaei a Christianis graves et immoderatas usuras extorserint."

58. *Ryccardi de sancto Germano notarii Chronica*, 96–97; Abulafia 1988, 143–144.

59. Monumenta Germaniae Historica, *Leges*, sectio IV, 2:274–275; here Frederick explains the course of events.

60. Translation from Robert Chazan, *Church, State and Jew in the Middle Ages* (New York, 1980), 125–126, by kind permission of Professor Chazan.

61. Monumenta Germaniae Historica, *Leges*, sectio IV, 2:274–275.

62. There is now some agreement that the important work of Guido Kisch, *The Jews in Medieval Germany*, 2d ed. (New York, 1970), 142–153, exaggerated the novelty of "chamber serfdom" and misunderstood some aspects of its meaning. See Dietmar Willoweit, "Vom Königsschutz zur Kammerknechtschaft. Anmerkungen zum Rechtsstatus der Juden im Hochmittelalter," in *Geschichte und Kultur des Judentums: Eine Vorlesungsreihe an der Julius-Maximilians-Universität Würzburg*, ed. Karlheinz Müller and Klaus Wittstadt (Würzburg, 1988), 71–89, esp. 80–86.

63. Cited by Willoweit 1988, 82, and Kisch 1970, 149, from Friedrich Keutgen, *Urkunden zur städtischen Verfassungsgeschichte* (Berlin, 1901) 211, §165.

64. Willoweit 1988, 84: "Der Begriff *servus*, Knecht, hat in der Stauferzeit noch keinen eindeutig negativen Gehalt."

65. Text (in English) in Chazan 1980, 84–88.

66. Chazan 1980, 69–75, for examples of 1115, 1149, 1170, 1239.

67. Abulafia 1988, 245.

68. Willoweit 1988, 81, 86.

69. Élie Berger, *Les registres d'Innocent IV*, 4 vols. (Paris, 1884–1921), 1:§2815, §2838, §3077, all of 1247; 2:ccxvii–ccxx.

70. For the reactions of the Muslims in the Middle East, see for instance the collection of texts translated by Francesco Gabrieli, *Arab Historians of the Crusades* (Berkeley and Los Angeles, 1969), 267–275.

71. Abulafia 1988, 120–122.

72. Abulafia 1988, 183.

73. The main account of Frederick's Eastern policy is the Polish study (with a German summary) of Jerzy Hauzinski, *Polityka orientalna Fryderyka II Hohenstaufa*, Uniwersytetu Adama Mickiewicza w Poznaniu Serie historica (Poznan, 1978).

74. Joshua Prawer, *The History of the Jews in the Latin Kingdom of Jerusalem* (Oxford, 1988), 90–91; Mustafa A. Hiyari, "Crusader Jerusalem, 1099–1187," *Jerusalem in History*, ed. K. J. Asali (Brooklyn, N.Y., 1989), 170.

75. Charles H. Haskins, *Studies in the History of Mediaeval Science* (Cambridge, Mass., 1927), 252–253, a point that Haskins clearly finds embarrassing to his general argument.

76. For the overall picture, see Abulafia 1988, 251–270; see also 48–52 on the Norman comparison.

77. Colette Sirat, *A History of Jewish Philosophy in the Middle Ages* (Cambridge, 1985), 212–232. On Scot, see Lynn Thorndike, *Michael Scot* (London, 1965).

78. Haskins 1927, 251–252, again exaggerates the closeness of contact with Frederick II.

79. Haskins 1927, 264; Abulafia 1988, 258, 263.

80. Abulafia 1988, 258–259, 262.

Novitiorum studia variarum [illegible] cupientium apud dictatorie facultatis. Incipit Summa dictaminis
circa stilum quem Romana servat curia debent assidua meditatione versari. cui ille magister [illegible]
sit eruditio rudium sit doctrina scolarium bonorum illuminato [illegible]
dictator. Congrua quidem amplectens et ita collaudamus obscuramus propria et exquisita
requirentes. Indecentia respuit obscura contempnit detestatur impropria et rudia inspe-
dit. Hec igitur inordinate cuilibet epistole sunt diligenti attendenda, ut dictamen decora compositione perfulgens inducat quod scribitur ex corde prodire scribentis et per hec fa-
cilius ad dandum effectum verbis recipientis animus inducatur. Cum autem epistola dicatur
ab epi quod est supra et stolon quod est missio quasi supermissio, talis ordo in ipsa mittenda dignoscitur requiri ut quod salutationis titulo
mandat ponatur immediate prohemium sicut facti qualitas exiget, ac tandem narratio negotii, conclusio subsequatur.
Et quia dictamen nichil aliud est quam congruus cuiuslibet rei tractatus ad rem ipsam convenienter applicatus, videndum est
quid debeat personis congruitate suarum. [illegible] congrua [illegible] personarum et qualitatibus negotiorum
respectus. Nam alloquendi sunt principes, reges ceterique magistros secundum suam precellentiam dignitatum. Verba vero
minoribus considerata sui status conditione scribuntur. Ut si papa Imperatori, Regi vel principi scribat, decet
oratorie uti nominibus que congruant altitudini talium. Papa illos est karissimos in Christo filios in titulo salutationis
appellat. In narratione vero imperiale vel Regia celsitudine serenitate excellentia vel magnificentia
rogat attente et hortatur. Sed [illegible] omnibus cuiuscumque dignitatis conditionis existant, et illud scilicet salutem
et apostolicam benedictionem. Et est ad omnes fideles papa salutatio generalis. Excommunicatis autem scribit spiritum consilii sanioris.
Paganis vero deum diligere et timere. Patriarchas insuper archiepiscopos et episcopos vocat [illegible] reliquos
omnes dilectos filios nominando. Eodem autem [illegible] scribendo Imperatori vel Regi vocat eos in narratione
karissimos in Christo filios nostros in salutatione tacet. [illegible] in patriarchis Episcopis et Card. [illegible]
et diaconos Card. [illegible] filios nostros appellet in processu narrationis. [illegible] Imperator et Reges et cetere persone [illegible]
devotos et humiles si papa scripserint dicunt Sanctissimo in Christo patri et domino .. dei gratia sacrosancte Romane ecclesie summo
Pontifici .. Imperator vel Rex reverentiam filialem et pedum oscula beatorum. Alie inferiores [illegible]
libitum ad [illegible] se salutant. Illud autem observandum est [illegible] omnibus de suis [illegible]
[illegible] dignitate positis se premittunt. [illegible] Card. [illegible] et episcopis in salutatione preferuntur
[illegible] papa scribit imperatori vel regi rogat [illegible]
illos [illegible] sed apostolicam procedendum. [illegible]
Ceterum in [illegible] litteris [illegible] congruit [illegible] modestie [illegible] benignitatis et
iustitie [illegible]. Nec convenit [illegible] dictatio [illegible]
[illegible]
[illegible]
[illegible] laudandus. [illegible]

PETER HERDE
Universität Würzburg

Literary Activities of the Imperial and Papal Chanceries during the Struggle between Frederick II and the Papacy

Among the cultural activities of the court of Frederick II, the chancery, that is, the group of notaries and other stylists that drafted and engrossed his diplomas, mandates, and letters, played an important role.[1] The same is true of the papal chancery with its sophisticated organization of notaries, *abbreviatores*, scribes, and other officials as part of the Roman curia.[2] The highlights of their literary production are not to be found among the hundreds of routine documents that emanated from both chanceries in the more or less traditional, and often stereotypical, forms that were recorded in the formularies frequently used by officials as a help for drafting documents.[3] Rather we find numerous examples of exceptional stylistic elegance among the letters, circulars, and memoranda that accompanied the struggle between the emperor and the popes, especially Gregory IX and Innocent IV, justifying the actions of both the imperial and papal sides and propagating their ideas. Their literary qualities are the result of the *Ars dictaminis*, the art of letter writing, a learned discipline that originated in Italy around 1100. It then spread to France after about the middle of the twelfth century, whence it traveled to England, Germany, and Norman Sicily (which had close contacts with the Angevin Empire), and finally returned to Italy around 1200, where Bologna and Capua became prominent centers.[4]

There were several stylistic levels of the *Ars dictaminis*; we are especially interested here in the highest, the "supreme style" (*stilus supremus*), which is characterized by rhetorical figures including rhythmical prose, cursus (that is, the system of rhythmical clausulae at the end of the sentences or parts of sentences, or *cola*), tropes, and topics (*topoi*).[5] The *Ars dictaminis* had already influenced the papal chancery around 1100.[6] It was in French cathedral schools such as Chartres and Orléans and in northern Italy in the second half of the twelfth century that the *stilus supremus* developed its "baroque" characteristics: a difficult syntax, artificial grammatical constructions, an overload of embellishing adjectives, extravagant word combinations, bizarre wordplays, alliterations and assonances, frequent use of climax, antithesis, and parallelism, and excessive quotations from the Vulgate, from Roman and canon law, from a limited number of classical Latin authors such as Virgil, Ovid and Pseudo-Ovid, Horace, and Martial, and also from contemporary Latin authors.[7]

All of these phenomena, most probably with the University of Bologna serving as intermediary,[8] were taken over by the Capuan school of the *Ars dictaminis* and from there by the papal and imperial chanceries of the thirteenth century. Its first representa-

For Hans Martin Schaller, 7 September 1993

Fr. di gra. Roman. Imperat. semp. aug. Jerusal. et Sicil. Rex. Venerab. Salzeburg. archiepo. et universis suffraganeis ei. dilectis principibus suis gratiam. ...

[illegible]

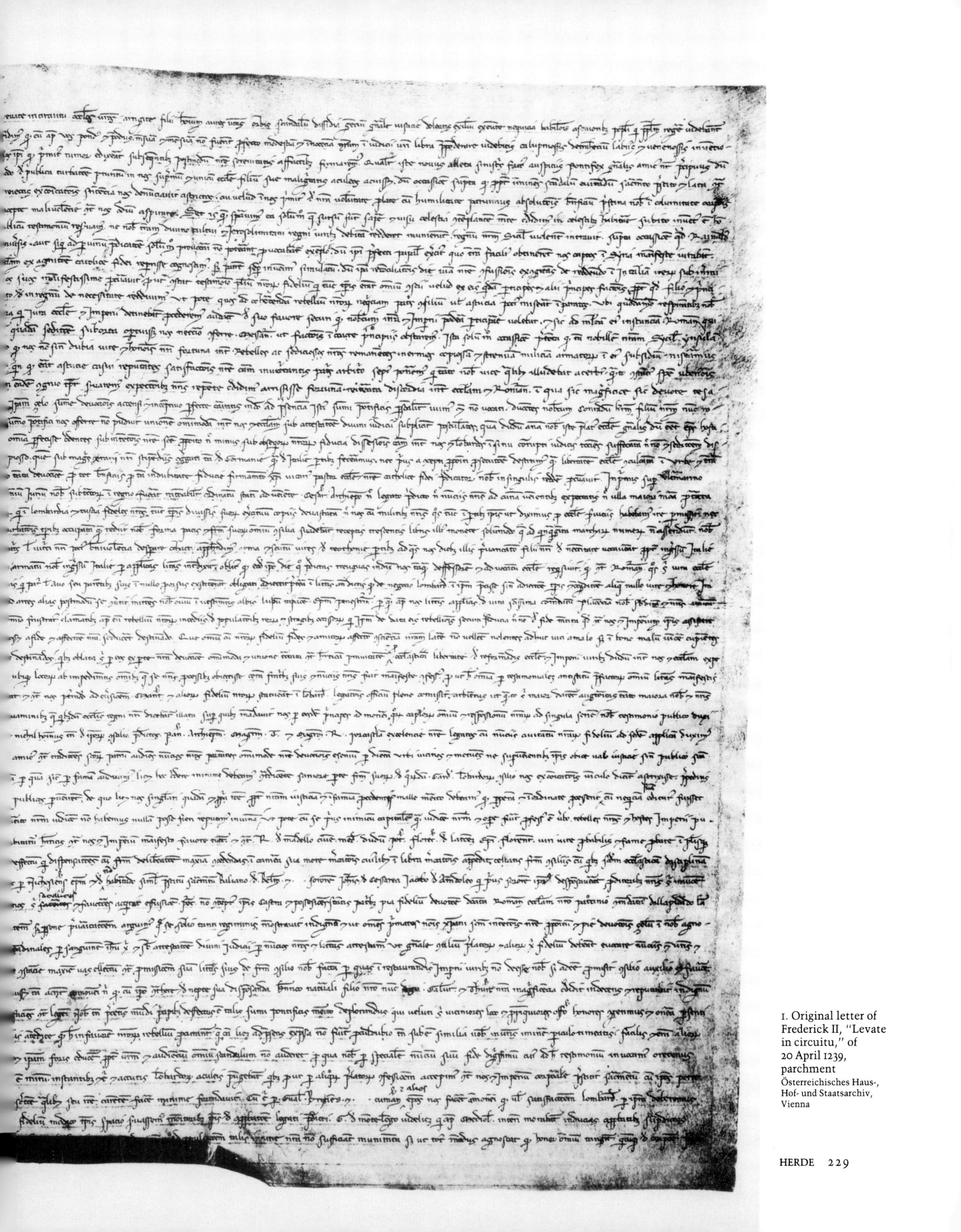

1. Original letter of Frederick II, "Levate in circuitu," of 20 April 1239, parchment
Österreichisches Haus-, Hof- und Staatsarchiv, Vienna

tives were Archbishop Rainald of Capua, Cardinal Thomas of Capua, and Petrus de Vinea or Piero della Vigna. Rainald, who is the author of numerous letters preserved in a collection from Capua and surroundings,[9] served as protonotary in Frederick's chancery in 1218.[10] Together with a group of notaries and other officials from Campania,[11] he brought a "high style" culture to the royal chancery. Palermo, where Frederick spent his youth, had no rhetorical tradition. Thus the few letters and encyclicals from the beginning of Frederick's reign clearly show Capuan influence.[12] Rainald was also subdeacon and chaplain of Innocent III and one of the pope's advisers.[13] Thus there were close connections between the papal and imperial chanceries which later survived the fierce struggle between empire and papacy. Thomas of Capua was the most influential stylist in the papal chancery under Honorius III and at the beginning of the pontificate of Gregory IX. He is the author of an *Ars dictandi*, a manual for the training of papal scribes and notaries.[14] The *Summa dictaminis*, the earliest of the large curial letter collections, has been transmitted under his name. It consists of more than six hundred letters extant in about eighty manuscripts.[15]

The best known of the great stylists from Capua, however, is Piero della Vigna.[16] Born in Capua shortly before 1200, the son of a judge, he probably studied at Bologna where he might have become acquainted with the rich north Italian tradition of the *Ars dictaminis* of Buoncompagno, Guido Faba, and others.[17] He became a member of the imperial court sometime between 1220 and 1224 and served the emperor in several offices (*magne imperialis curie iudex* from 1224; *imperialis aule protonotarius et regni Sicilie logotheta*, first mentioned in 1243, in which function, from about 1239/1240 on, he headed the chancery, the office of the chancellor being vacant since 1221) until his imprisonment and suicide in 1249, which was prompted mainly by his involvement in cases of corruption for personal enrichment and also possibly by treason.[18] Piero della Vigna does not seem to have been occupied with routine chancery matters. He obviously was one of the emperor's most important diplomats and later a kind of "prime minister" and drafted many of the emperor's private letters, propaganda manifestoes, circular letters, and very important diplomas, such as the privilege granted to the University of Naples at its foundation in 1224.[19] However, we do not know to what extent he offered his pen to the emperor. Comparison of style in order to attribute diplomas and letters to specific *dictatores* is a reputable diplomatic method and can successfully be used for standard material until the end of the twelfth century and even later.

This method, however, is hardly applicable to letters and manifestoes written in a highly rhetorical style and drafted by authors with an intimate knowledge of Latin and a high degree of stylistic versatility. In these cases we can rarely distinguish between the products of the teacher and his pupils. Thomas of Capua can hardly have written all of the more than 600 letters contained in the collection transmitted under his name, nor can Piero della Vigna be the author of the approximately 550 letters contained in the different recensions of the collection ascribed to him in the rubrics of many of the roughly eighty manuscript copies.[20] Certainly a great number of these letters must have been drafted by Thomas and Piero, but others might have been the work of their collaborators or pupils, such as Nicolaus de Rocca, Salvus de Baro, or Terrisius de Atina, in the imperial chancery. There are hardly any convincing criteria to distinguish between the products of the master and his companions.

It is even more difficult to decide to what extent Frederick II himself contributed to the formulation of the letters emanating from the chancery under his name (fig. 1). Whereas Ernst Kantorowicz was convinced that Piero della Vigna, "as Logothetes, 'one who places words', . . . was, both in writing and speaking, the mouthpiece of imperial thought and act, the creator of the imperial diction and the majestic utterance,"[21] Charles Homer Haskins was more skeptical: "How far he was himself affected by the baroque Latin of the South it is impossible to say, for the pompous language of his legislation doubtless owes less to the Emperor than to his jurists and secretaries, nor can we safely seek his personal touch in what the Pope (Gregory IX) called the 'dictatoris facunditas' of the correspondence which emanated from his chancery."[22] Haskins further pointed out that in the only work safely attributable to the emperor, *De arte venandi cum avibus*, his book on falconry, "the treatment is matter-of-fact, the style simple and unadorned," which, however, does not "suffice to prove that he may not have indulged in fine writing on other occasions."[23] Friedrich Baethgen rightly, it seems, asserted that the propaganda and rhetoric of the encyclical letters about the messiah-emperor were, to a great extent, the product of his surroundings and hardly showed "the innermost nerve of his ruler consciousness," and "the concrete contents of his imperial conceptions proved to be relatively limited, his actual political behavior was much more cautious, more flexible, much more aiming at compromises than one would expect after such pompous declamations."[24]

But there are still problems that have gone largely unnoticed by scholars. With very few exceptions, the texts of these propagandistic and rhetorical letters are extant only in letter collections and in formularies. There were hardly any copies made by the recipients, and very few originals of such letters have survived.[25] It cannot be doubted that many of these letters were sent to the recipients, or circulated if there was no specific addressee. As they did not confer permanent rights and were thus of little legal importance, it is understandable that their recipients did not copy them and destroyed the originals after some time. On the other hand, since only fragments of the registers of the imperial chancery have survived, we are unable to check which letters were actually sent out by the chancery. The same is true of propagandistic papal letters. Although the papal registers, starting with Innocent III, have survived,[26] it has long been known that many very important letters emanating from the papal chancery were not registered.[27] Thus it is necessary to consider the origins and transmission of these letters.

After drafting the texts, the imperial and papal notaries or other stylists retained the minutes and probably collected them in files. Frequently they revised and redrafted such letters, which therefore have come down to us in several versions. We often do not know which of these versions was actually engrossed and sent out as an original letter. Furthermore, some of these letters might not have been approved by the emperor or the pope and thus may never have left the chancery. Further still, since drafting such letters was considered to be a literary activity, many notaries invented fictitious letters as a sort of stylistic exercise, and in many cases, especially if they correctly dealt with, or alluded to, actual events, it is almost impossible for us to distinguish between real and fictitious letters.

It has been convincingly shown that many of the great stylists of the imperial and papal chanceries, under whose names the large letter collections have been transmitted, were either members of the same family or had close professional contacts and that they exchanged or handed down the files of their stylistic masterpieces to succeeding generations.[28] This is true of Thomas of Capua, Piero della Vigna, Marino Filomarino (of Eboli), vice-chancellor under Innocent IV under whose name a large letter collection exists in numerous manuscripts,[29] as well as Nicolaus de Rocca,[30] Henry of Isernia,[31] Richard of Pofi (fig. 2),[32] Berard Caraccioli of Naples,[33] Jordan Pironti of Terracina,[34] and Peter of Prece.[35] The first recensions of many of these collections were obviously codified from the numerous files of minutes and copies during the long vacancy of the Holy See after the death of Clement IV, which lasted for almost three years from November 1268 to September 1271.[36] At this time the notaries of the papal chancery, whose work was discontinued after the death of a pope, were unoccupied and had ample time to indulge in literary activities. It is highly probable that it was Piero's most important pupil, Nicolaus de Rocca, who brought his master's material to the curia when he entered the papal service after 1266 and compiled, between 1268 and 1271, the first recension, adding his own material and that of other stylists.[37] Later recensions were compiled under Boniface VIII in 1295 and 1303, at the University of Paris around 1300, and under John XXII in 1317–1318.[38]

There is nothing strange about the fact that this famous collection containing numerous antipapal letters of Frederick II should have been codified at the papal curia, since these texts had long lost their political importance. They were considered mainly as examples of excellent literary style and could be used as a source of inspiration for drafting other letters. The aesthetic and intellectual value of such letters by now far exceeded their political contents.[39] Many of these collections were later rearranged and reedited and thus have come down to us in several recensions. Some have a more or less systematic arrangement according to the contents of the letters; others lack any order and were clearly copied in a rather haphazard fashion, but often contain more correct texts.[40] Editorial work on these collections is extremely difficult. One has to collate virtually hundreds of letters in numerous manuscripts to find out something about their textual history, and even after such time-consuming work it is often difficult to decide which recension is the oldest, which arrangement one should follow in a modern edition, and which of the different versions of an individual letter is the genuine one.

Many historians who have written on Frederick II and the contemporary popes have hardly realized these problems and have indiscriminately used such letters as they found them, printed in more or less unsatisfactory editions, and asking no questions about their authenticity. Considering the enormous difficulties of the textual tradition, it is understandable that none of the thirteenth-century collections has so far been critically edited, although work on some of them has been going on for several decades. Certainly as early as the sixteenth century, lawyers and scholars became interested, for political and religious motives, in the antipapal letters of the Piero della Vigna collection. A first edition was published in 1529 in Alsatia,[41] followed by Simon Schard's Basel edition of 1566, which was reprinted and enlarged by Johann Rudolf Iselin also at Basel in 1740.[42] Other partial editions also appeared that were based on only one or two manuscripts that the editors happened to know of. The collections of papal letters have never been published as a whole. Modern editors such as Jean-Louis-Alphonse Huillard-Bréholles,[43] Johann Friedrich Böhmer,[44] Julius Ficker,[45] Eduard Winkelmann,[46] and Ludwig Weiland[47] were interested in the individual letters, and although especially Winkelmann and Weiland were well aware of the fact that many of the letters have come down in different versions, none of them actually embarked on a study of their textual history in the context of the collections. They often published a mixture of different versions.

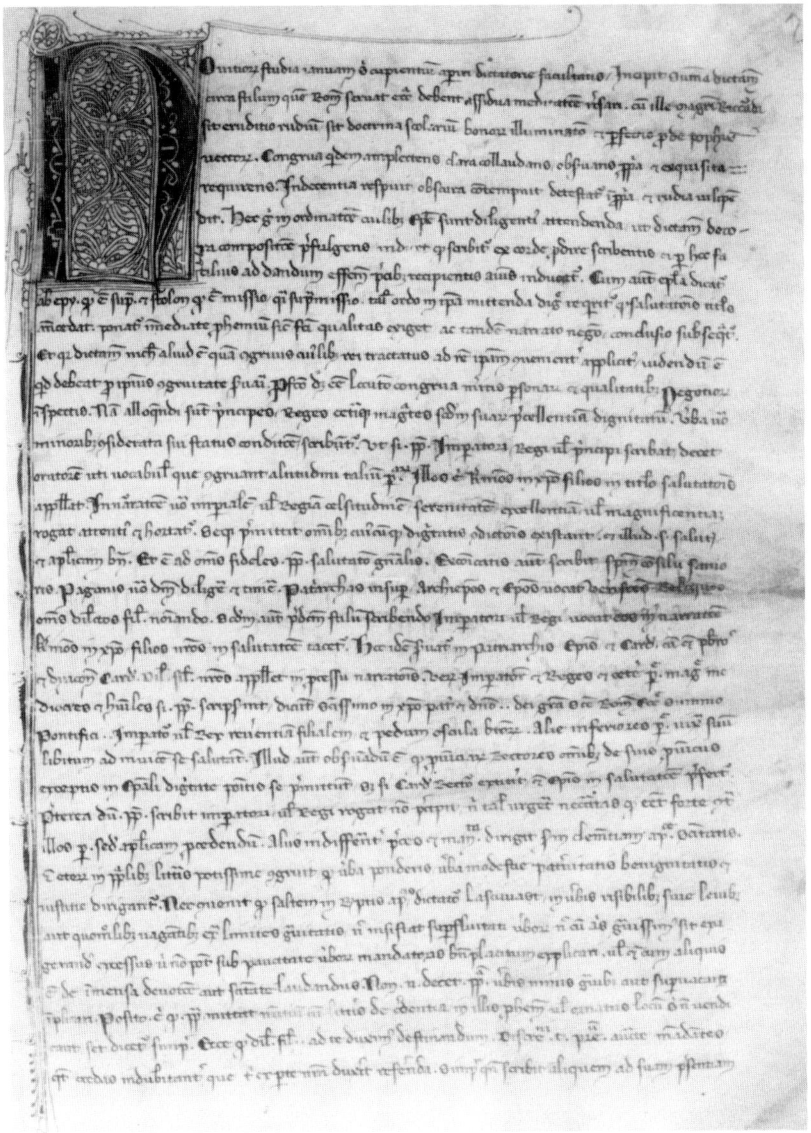

2. Letter collection of Richard of Pofi, thirteenth–fourteenth century, parchment
Stadtbibliothek, Bern (166)

Let me demonstrate some of the problems thus far described. The only collection that has survived in its original form is the letter and memorial book that Albert Behaim, an extremist partisan of Gregory IX and Innocent IV in Bavaria,[48] started at the papal curia at Lyons in the summer of 1246 (fig. 3).[49] It was written on paper mostly by clerics of his following and is today the oldest paper manuscript preserved in a German library

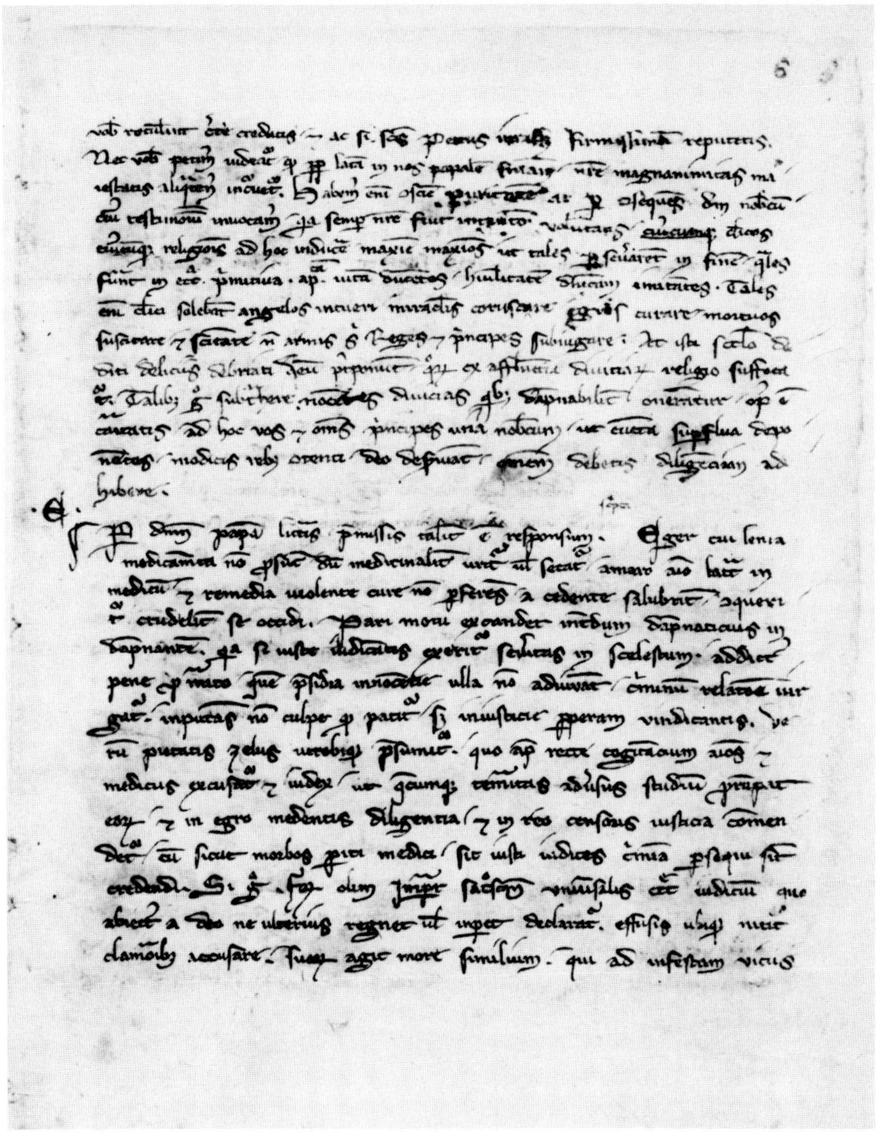

3. Letter and memorial book of Albert Behaim, original manuscript, c. 1246, paper
Bayerische Staatsbibliothek, Munich (lat. 2574b)

(Munich, Staatsbibliothek, lat. 2574b), although the paper was not produced in Germany. The book contains miscellaneous material; besides letters, there are large excerpts from literary works, business notes, and many other things. It begins with copies of some of the most important encyclical letters of Frederick II, Gregory IX, and Innocent IV from the final stage of the struggle between emperor and pope after 1239. There is no chronological order: no. 1 is "Etsi cause nostre" of 31 July 1245;[50] no. 2, "Illos felices," which lacks a date in all textual witnesses but must be from the end of 1245 or the beginning of 1246.[51] The copies contain numerous errors. Both letters are certainly authentic. Letter no. 3 is the purported answer by Innocent IV, "Eger cui lenia," also lacking a date, but before September–October 1245.[52] With a few exceptions, among them the brilliant historian of the medieval papacy Johannes Haller,[53] scholars have used this letter as one of the most important sources of Innocent IV's conceptions about the relationship between spiritual and temporal powers.[54] But as I have shown elsewhere in detail,[55] there is not the slightest evidence that the letter, preserved in a shorter and two enlarged versions, is authentic or had ever been sent out by the papal chancery. Obviously it was a pamphlet drafted by one of the chaplains of Cardinal Rainer of Viterbo, who is the author of some of the most vicious manifestoes directed against the emperor.[56] The draft was copied in several letter collections, redrafted and enlarged, and attributed to Innocent IV. Most of the copies of imperial and papal letters and manifestoes in Albert's collection are erroneous. In one case Albert's copy is the only transmission, and the text is so hopelessly corrupt that all efforts to emend it have been unsuccessful.[57] Most of the polemics on both the imperial and the papal side were strongly influenced by eschatological speculations[58] based on Joachim of Fiore[59] and strengthened by the invasion of the Mongols, the tribes, so it seemed, of Gog and Magog that had broken Alexander's gate[60] and were now heralding the coming of Antichrist and the end of time. Frederick, in some of the papal encyclicals, was identified with the Antichrist or his forerunner, an accusation that was reciprocated by the imperial side.[61] This explains why Albert had a copy of a basic text of eastern and western eschatological speculation in his manuscript: Pseudo-Methodius, a text ascribed to Bishop Methodius of Patara (died c. 311) but originally written in Syriac shortly after the middle of the seventh century as a reaction to the Arab invasions. The text is a prophecy about the return of the Byzantine emperor at the end of time. A Greek version of this treatise was translated into Latin, probably early in the eighth century in Provence, and thus became a standard text of western eschatology.[62] It is based on Oriental sources such as the Syriac Cave of

Treasures.[63] The transmission of the Latin version, extant in about two hundred manuscripts, in post-Carolingian times has never been studied in detail.[64] The text of Albert's copy is so corrupt that it is hardly comprehensible. Almost all of the Oriental names were misunderstood by the copyists. Obviously at this time (as so often nowadays) the incomprehensibility of a text was confused with profundity of thought.

The ideas expressed in the propagandistic manifestoes of both sides have been studied in great detail.[65] I may therefore limit myself to outlining some of the main subjects of this war of propaganda. There is Frederick's appeal to the monarchical idea and the idea of the brotherhood of all kings during his campaign in Lombardy in 1237–1238 and later.[66] There are his addresses to the city of Rome, which he tried to win over to his side in 1236 and 1238 by recalling the splendor of the ancient city and the glory of the Caesars whose successor he purported to be.[67] The second excommunication of the emperor by Gregory IX in March 1239 brought about an onslaught of rhetoric and propaganda on both sides. Piero della Vigna's *stilus supremus* first climaxed in Frederick's manifesto of 20 April 1239: "Levate in circuitu oculos vestros" (Isaiah 49:18; 60:4) (a letter of which an original has been preserved). Beginning with quotations from the Old Testament, it defended the emperor's position by distinguishing between the sacred institution of the papacy and individual unworthy popes, by trying to play off the college of cardinals and the other European monarchs against the pope, and by emphasizing the right of the temporal power to repulse unjustified papal demands in cases of emergency.[68] Gregory IX reacted by issuing his first apocalyptic manifesto on 1 July 1239, "Ascendit de mari bestia," defaming, by a combination of quotations from the Apocalypse and the Old Testament and vicious accusations, Frederick as Antichrist.[69] Obviously, after the death of Cardinal Thomas of Capua in 1239, who had tried to reconcile emperor and pope,[70] hardliners such as Cardinal Rainer of Viterbo had gotten the upper hand at the curia. Rainer and his chaplains were masters of the *stilus supremus* described above. They created the apocalyptic and eschatological atmosphere of their manifestoes by excessive use of the Vulgate, especially the Old Testament, and by interweaving sometimes hundreds of quotations from the Apocalypse, Psalms, Proverbs, the Book of Daniel, the Prophets and others. They did not have to refer to the contemporary eschatological treatises by Joachim of Fiore and his followers.

Extreme examples of this style are the circulars that were spread shortly before the Council of Lyons in 1245 to influence the participants at the council: "Aspidis ova"[71] and "Iuxta vaticinium Isaie" of July 1245,[72] both, of course, copied in Albert Behaim's collection.[73] These and similar pamphlets of the imperial side[74] were not issued as papal or imperial letters but anonymously, and were distributed as single unsealed sheets of parchment or in letter collections, originally as loose quires.[75] The rebuttals by Frederick and his partisans were of the same stylistic level, drawing mainly on the Vulgate.[76] The emperor, his stylists, and the chancery made no effort to imitate classical, Ciceronian style or to draw inspiration from Roman authors. Classical quotations in both the imperial and papal manifestoes are rare and limited to standard passages that were commonly used.[77] Their style therefore always remained within the limits of the contemporary *Ars dictaminis*. There were no humanistic or classical trends here comparable to those in the art of the imperial court.[78] After the death of Gregory IX, under Innocent IV (1243–1254), papal letters began to reflect the sober legal mind of the new pope, the greatest canon lawyer of the Middle Ages, and of his new vice-chancellor, Marino Filomarino (of Eboli). Although the bombastic style of Rainer's *dictatores* that had been quite consistent with Gregory IX's mentality did not disappear immediately, it was eventually replaced by a more logical and legal argumentation.[79]

To sum up briefly, the importance of imperial and papal letters as a source of the literary activities at Frederick II's court and the papal curia has become evident, although numerous problems of the textual history of these letters and of the collections in which they are transmitted remain unsolved. Taking this into account and also considering the rhetorical tradition of which they are part, one should be cautious when using them to reconstruct imperial and papal ideologies and political reality. When Ernst Kantorowicz took most of this material at face value, depicting Frederick as "Messiah-Emperor," he gave rise to a long controversy,[80] the result of which Friedrich Baethgen summarized in his warning quoted above: Frederick's political behavior was much more realistic, flexible, and cautious than might be expected after reading such pompous declamations. The same is certainly true of Gregory IX and Innocent IV. Yet these letters, together with other sources, bear witness to a high standard of literary culture that was of considerable influence during the rest of the century, even if it was not a forerunner of the future civilization of the Renaissance.

NOTES

1. The basic work, though somewhat out of date, is still Harry Bresslau, *Handbuch der Urkundenlehre für Deutschland und Italien*, 2d ed. (Leipzig, 1912; repr. Berlin, 1958) 1:512–583. The best modern work on Frederick II's chancery is Hans Martin Schaller, "Die Kanzlei Kaiser Friedrichs II.: Ihr Personal und ihr Sprachstil," *Archiv für Diplomatik* 3 (1957), 207–286 and 4 (1958), 264–327. Most recently see Hans Martin Schaller, "Kanzlei und Kultur zur Zeit Friedrichs II. und Manfreds," in *Cancelleria e cultura nel Medio Evo. Comunicazioni presentate nelle giornate di studio della commissione, Stoccarda, 29–30 agosto 1985*, 16 Congresso Internazionale di Scienze Storiche, Commission Internationale de Diplomatique (Vatican City, 1990), 119–127. On Frederick's diplomas see especially Paul Zinsmaier, "Die Reichskanzlei unter Friedrich II.," in *Probleme um Friedrich II.*, ed. Josef Fleckenstein, Vorträge und Forschungen 16 (Sigmaringen, 1974), 135–166. The entire source material was expertly collected in *Die Regesten des Kaiserreichs unter Philipp, Otto IV., Friedrich II., Heinrich (VII.), Conrad IV., Heinrich Raspe, Wilhelm und Richard*, nach der Neubearbeitung und dem Nachlass Johann Friedrich Böhmers neu herausgegeben und ergänzt von Julius Ficker und Eduard Winkelmann, 3 vols. (*Regesta imperii*, V, 1–3; Innsbruck, 1881–1901; repr. Hildesheim, 1971); vol. 4, *Nachträge und Ergänzungen*, bearbeitet von Paul Zinsmaier (*Regesta imperii*, V, 4; Cologne and Vienna, 1983) (hereafter cited as BFW plus number).

2. Bresslau 1912, 269–352; Peter Herde, *Beiträge zum päpstlichen Kanzlei- und Urkundenwesen im dreizehnten Jahrhundert*, 2d ed. (Kallmünz, 1967); Gerd Friedrich Nüske, "Untersuchungen über das Personal der päpstlichen Kanzlei 1254–1301," *Archiv für Diplomatik* 20 (1974), 39–240 and 21 (1975), 249–431. There are no comprehensive up-to-date regesta for papal letters and privileges, but August Potthast, *Regesta pontificum Romanorum inde ab a. post Christum natum MCXCVIII ad a. MCCCIV*, 2 vols. (Berlin, 1874–1875; repr. Graz, 1957), is still useful, especially in connection with the more recent *Initienverzeichnis zu August Potthast, Regesta pontificum Romanorum (1198–1304)*, mit einer Vorbemerkung von Hans Martin Schaller, Monumenta Germaniae Historia Hilfsmittel 2 (Munich, 1978). The more important papal source material from Innocent III to Clement IV is also listed in BFW nos. 5621–9971.

3. On formularies of the imperial and papal chanceries, see Harry Bresslau, *Handbuch der Urkundenlehre für Deutschland und Italien*, 2d ed. (Berlin and Leipzig, 1931), 2:225–280; formularies of the papal chancery: Peter Herde, "Papal Formularies for Letters of Justice (13th–16th Centuries): Their Development and Significance for Medieval Canon Law," in *Proceedings of the Second International Congress of Medieval Canon Law* (Vatican City, 1965), 321–345; Peter Herde, *Audientia litterarum contradictarum: Untersuchungen über die päpstlichen Justizbriefe und die päpstliche Delegationsgerichtsbarkeit vom 13. bis zum Beginn des 16. Jahrhunderts* (Tübingen, 1970), 1:12–19; Peter Herde, "Formularies," in *The*

New Catholic Encyclopedia (1967), 5:1027–1028; Peter Herde, "Formel, -sammlungen, -bücher," *Lexikon des Mittelalters* (Munich and Zurich, 1987), 4:646–648. The basic research for the chancery of Frederick II was done by Gerhart Ladner, "Formularbehelfe in der Kanzlei Kaiser Friedrichs II. und die 'Briefe des Petrus de Vinea,'" *Mitteilungen des österreichischen Instituts für Geschichtsforschung* 12 (1933), 92–195.

4. See Bresslau 1931, 2:247–264; Charles Homer Haskins, *Studies in Mediaeval Culture* (Oxford, 1929), 170–192; Hans Martin Schaller, "Ars dictaminis," *Lexikon des Mittelalters* (Munich and Zurich, 1980), 1:1034–1039 (an up-to-date survey); Schaller 1958, 266–289; James J. Murphy, *Rhetoric in the Middle Ages: A History of Rhetorical Theory from Saint Augustine to the Renaissance* (Berkeley, Calif., 1974), 194–268.

5. Schaller 1958, 269–272.

6. Schaller 1958, 272–273.

7. Eduard Norden, *Die antike Kunstprosa vom VI. Jahrhundert v. Chr. bis in die Zeit der Renaissance*, 5th ed. (Stuttgart, 1958), 2:711–731; Hans Niese, "Zur Geschichte des geistigen Lebens am Hofe Kaiser Friedrichs II.," *Historische Zeitschrift* (hereafter *HZ*) 108 (1912), 473–540, esp. 516–533; Antonino de Stefano, *La cultura alle corte di Federico II imperatore* (Palermo, 1938), 167–215; Schaller 1958, 274–275.

8. Niese 1912, 518.

9. Karl Hampe, "Über eine Ausgabe der Capuaner Briefsammlung des Cod. lat. 11867 der Pariser Nationalbibliothek," *Sitzungsberichte der Heidelberger Akademie der Wissenschaften*, philosophisch-historische Klasse (hereafter *Sitzungsberichte*) (1910), 8. Abh., 7–16. See also Karl Hampe, "Mitteilungen aus der Capuaner Briefsammlung I, II," *Sitzungsberichte* (1910), 13. Abh., 3–44; see Schaller 1957, 224; Schaller 1958, 284.

10. Schaller 1957, 221.

11. Schaller 1957, 229–230, 238.

12. Schaller 1958, 284.

13. Hampe 1910, 8. Abh., 15; Schaller 1957, 224.

14. Emmy Heller, "Die 'Ars dictandi' des Thomas von Capua: Kritisch erläuterte Edition," *Sitzungsberichte* (1928–1929), 4. Abh., 3–60.

15. Hans Martin Schaller, "Studien zur Briefsammlung des Kardinals Thomas von Capua," *Deutsches Archiv für Erforschung des Mittelalters* 21 (1965), 371–518.

16. Among the numerous studies on Piero della Vigna, some of the older works are still useful: Giuseppe De Blasiis, *Della vita e delle opere di Pietro della Vigna* (Naples, 1860), and especially Jean-Louis-Alphonse Huillard-Bréholles, *Vie et correspondance de Pierre de la Vigne, ministre de l'empereur Frédéric II* (Paris, 1865; repr. Aalen, 1966). For bibliographical references see Emilio Bigi, "Piero della Vigna," *Enciclopedia Dantesca* (Rome, 1973), 4:511–516, and the basic synthesis by Hans Martin Schaller, "Della Vigna, Pietro," in *Dizionario biografico degli Italiani* (Rome, 1989), 37:776–784.

17. Schaller 1957, 242–244.

18. Fedor Schneider, "Nachlese in Toscana," *Quellen und Forschungen aus italienischen Archiven und Bibliotheken* 22 (1930), 57–86; Ernst Kantorowicz, *Kaiser Friedrich der Zweite* (Berlin, 1928), 1:608–611; Ergänzungsband (Berlin, 1931), 245; Friedrich Baethgen, "Dante und Petrus de Vinea," *Sitzungsberichte der Bayerischen Akademie der Wissenschaften*, philosophisch-historische Klasse (Munich, 1955), Heft 3, 3–49; Schaller 1989, 780–781.

19. Niese 1912, 526, note 4; Schaller 1957, 242–243.

20. Ladner 1933, 146–195; Hans Martin Schaller, "Zur Entstehung der sogenannten Briefsammlung des Petrus de Vinea," *Deutsches Archiv für Erforschung des Mittelalters* 12 (1956), 114–159; Hans Martin Schaller, "L'epistolario di Pier delle Vigne," in *Politica e cultura nell'Italia di Federico II*, ed. Sergio Gensini, Centro di studi sulla civiltà del tardo Medio Evo San Miniato, Collana di Studi e Ricerche 1 (Pisa, 1986), 95–111.

21. The quotation is from the English translation by Emily O. Lorimer of Ernst Kantorowicz, *The Emperor Frederick the Second, 1194–1250* (London, 1931; repr. New York, 1957), 299. See Kantorowicz 1928, 275 and the modification 276, Eng. trans. 300–301: "How much in these letters is Piero della Vigna, and how much Frederick, will never be known."

22. Haskins 1929, 127.

23. Haskins 1929, 127.

24. Friedrich Baethgen, "Kaiser Friedrich II. 1194–1250," in *Die großen Deutschen. Deutsche Biographie*, ed. Hermann Heimpel, Theodor Heuss, and Benno Reiffenberg (Berlin, Frankfurt, and Vienna, 1960), 1:154–170, here 164. See also Eduard Sthamer, "Eigenes Diktat des Herrschers in Briefen der sizilischen Kanzlei des 13. Jahrhunderts," in *Festschrift Alexander Cartellieri . . .* (Weimar, 1927), 141–158, esp. 148–153.

25. One of the few examples that have been preserved as an original is the famous letter, addressed to the Archbishop of Salzburg, of 20 April 1239, "Levate in circuitu," BFW no. 2431, ed. Monumenta Germaniae Historica, *Constitutiones et acta publica*, ed. Ludewicus Weiland (Hannover, 1896), 2:290–299, no. 215. See my figure 1.

26. For the editions, most of them by the École Française de Rome, see Leo Santifaller, *Neuere Editionen mittelalterlicher Königs- und Papsturkunden: Eine Übersicht*, Österreichische Akademie der Wissenschaften, Mitteilungen der Wiener Diplomata-Abteilung der Monumenta Germaniae Historica 6 (Vienna, 1958), 40–43.

27. Herde 1967, 241–242 (with bibliographical references).

28. Schaller 1965, 371–394. However, some of the conclusions remain hypothetical because of the scantiness of the sources.

29. *Die Formularsammlung des Marinus von Eboli*, untersucht und bearbeitet von Fritz Schillmann, vol. 1: Entstehung und Inhalt (Rome, 1929), has indexed

the collection (the second volume has never been published). His conclusions that Marinus was the author, or editor, of the collection have, however, been corrected by Carl Erdmann, "Zur Entstehung der Formelsammlung des Marinus von Eboli," *Quellen und Forschungen aus italienischen Archiven und Bibliotheken* (hereafter *Quellen und Forschungen*) 21 (1929–1930), 176–208. Erdmann has convincingly shown that the first recension of the collection was edited after 1268 when Marinus had left the papal curia. The wrong ascription of the collection to Marinus is due to the fact that it includes two treatises on papal letters written by him; see Peter Herde, "Marinus von Eboli: 'Super revocatoriis' and 'De confirmationibus.'" Zwei Abhandlungen des Vizekanzlers Innocenz' IV. über das päpstliche Urkundenwesen, *Quellen und Forschungen* 42–43 (1963), 119–264, also separately, Tübingen, 1964.

30. Haskins 1929, 133–135; Karl Pivec, "Der Diktator Nicolaus von Rocca: Zur Geschichte der Sprachschule von Capua," in *Amann-Festgabe*, pt. 1, Innsbrucker Beiträge zur Kulturwissenschaft 1 (Innsbruck, 1953), 135–152; Schaller 1957, 275–276, no. 55; Schaller 1965, 386–387.

31. Karl Hampe, *Beiträge zur Geschichte der letzten Staufer: Ungedruckte Briefe aus der Sammlung des Magisters Heinrich von Isernia* (Leipzig, 1910).

32. Ernst Batzer, *Zur Kenntnis der Formularsammlung des Richard von Pofi* (Heidelberg, 1910); Karl Hampe, "Ungedruckte Briefe zur Geschichte König Richards von Cornwall aus der Sammlung Richards von Pofi," *Neues Archiv der Gesellschaft für ältere deutsche Geschichtskunde* 30 (1905), 673–690. I am preparing a critical edition of this text extant in forty-seven manuscripts. The collection seems to have originated during the vacancy of the Holy See from 1268 to 1271. See Bresslau 1931, 265–267. See my figure 2.

33. F(erdinand) Kaltenbrunner, "Römische Studien. I. Die Briefsammlung des Berardus de Neapoli," *Mitteilungen des Instituts für österreichische Geschichtsforschung* 7 (1886), 21–118, 555–635 (with an index of the letters contained in this collection). This collection is of later date starting with Urban IV, the last papal letters being those of Honorius IV with ever later additions. See Bresslau 1931, 267–268. Dietrich Lohrmann, "Berard von Neapel, ein päpstlicher Notar und Vertrauter Karls von Anjou," in *Adel und Kirche: Festschrift für Gerd Tellenbach* (Freiburg, 1968), 477–498; and Dietrich Lohrmann, "Caracciolo, Berardo," in *Dizionario biografico degli Italiani* (Rome, 1976), 15:313–317.

34. Paolo Sambin, *Un certame dettatorio tra due notai pontifici (1260): Lettere inedite di Giordano da Terracina e di Giovanni da Capua*, Note e discussioni erudite 5 (Rome, 1955).

35. Eugen Müller, *Peter von Prezza, ein Publizist der Zeit des Interregnums* (Heidelberg, 1913); Rudolf M. Kloos, "Petrus de Prece und Konradin," *Quellen und Forschungen* 34 (1954), 88–108; Rudolf M. Kloos, "Ein Brief des Petrus de Prece zum Tode Friedrichs II.," *Deutsches Archiv für Erforschung des Mittelalters* 13 (1957), 151–170, repr. in *Stupor Mundi: Zur Geschichte Friedrichs II. von Hohenstaufen*, ed. Gunther Wolf (Darmstadt, 1966), 525–549.

36. Schaller 1956, 147–148; Schaller 1965, 412–416. See above, notes 29 and 32.

37. Schaller 1956, 146–151; Schaller 1986, 103–111.

38. Schaller 1986, 106–107.

39. Schaller 1986, 108.

40. Schaller 1956, 151–159; Schaller 1965, 404–412.

41. *Querimonia Friderici Imp. [. . .] A [. . .] Petro de Vineis [. . .] Anno MCCXXX conscripta* per Johannem Secerium (Hagenau, 1529).

42. *Epistolarum Petri de Vineis, cancellarii quondam Friderici II imperatoris [. . .] libri VI*, ed. Simon Schard (Basel, n.d., but 1566). An anonymous new edition was *Petri de Vineis, cancellarii quondam Friderici II. imp. Rom. epistolarum libri VI [. . .] post cl. v. Simonis Schardic JC. editionem anni MDLXVI denuo cum Haganoensi exemplari collatum [. . .]* per Germanum Philalethen (Ambergae, 1609). The editor (Philalethes is a pseudonym) had, according to the title, compared Schard's text with that of the 1529 Hagenau edition. *Petri de Vineis [. . .] epistolarum [. . .] libri VI [. . .]* curavit Joh. Rudolphus Iselius (Basel, 1740); reprinted with a valuable introduction by Hans Martin Schaller, 2 vols. (Hildesheim, 1991).

43. *Historia Diplomatica Friderici Secundi sive constitutiones, privilegia, mandata, instrumenta quae supersunt istius imperatoris et filiorum ejus. Accedunt epistolae paparum et documenta varia*, ed. Jean-Louis-Alphonse Huillard-Bréholles, 6 vols. in 11 (Paris, 1852–1861), with Preface and Introduction. This edition does not meet modern critical standards, but for many texts it is still the only edition.

44. Johann Friedrich Böhmer, *Acta imperii selecta: Urkunden deutscher Könige und Kaiser 928–1398, mit einem Anhang von Reichssachen* (Innsbruck, 1870; repr. Aalen, 1967), 233–315.

45. Julius Ficker, *Forschungen zur Reichs- und Rechtsgeschichte Italiens* (Innsbruck, 1874), 4:305–464.

46. Eduard Winkelmann, *Acta imperii inedita saeculi XIII et XIV: Urkunden und Briefe zur Geschichte des Kaiserreichs und des Königreichs Sizilien*, 2 vols. (Innsbruck, 1880–1885; repr. Aalen, 1964), 1:96–788; 2:6–76, 680–724.

47. See above, note 25.

48. The most detailed study on Albert is still Georg Ratzinger, *Forschungen zur bayerischen Geschichte* (Kempten, 1898), 1–321, 628–640. See Winfried Stelzer, "Albert Böheim," in *Die deutsche Literatur des Mittelalters*, Verfasserlexikon 1 (Berlin and New York, 1978), 116–119; Peter Herde, "Albert Behaim," in *Lexikon des Mittelalters* (Munich and Zurich, 1980), 1:288.

49. A bad edition of parts of the letter book was published by Constantin Höfler, *Albert von Beham und Regesten Pabst Innocenz IV.* (Stuttgart, 1847), 55–220. A new edition of the entire collection by Thomas Frenz and myself will soon go to press. See my figure 3.

50. Fols. 3r–4v; Höfler 1847, 81–85; BFW 3495, see also 3499.

51. Fols. 5r–6r; Höfler 1847, 79–81; BFW 3541.

52. Fols. 6r–9v; Höfler 1847, 86–91; BFW 7584.

53. Johannes Haller, "Die Formen der deutsch-römischen Kaiserkrönung," *Quellen und Forschungen* 33 (1944), 84; reprinted in Johannes Haller, *Abhandlungen zur Geschichte des Mittelalters* (Stuttgart, 1944), 280–334, esp. 317–318. More recently, Joannes A. Cantini, "De autonomia judicis saecularis et de Romani pontificis plenitudine potestatis in temporalibus secundum Innocentium IV," *Salesianum* 23 (1961), 407–480, has convincingly argued that there are basic contradictions between Innocent IV's conceptions about the relationship between spiritual and temporal powers as laid down in his Apparatus on the decretals and the pertinent ideas expressed in "Eger cui lenia," the authenticity of which, according to Cantini, is therefore doubtful. His arguments were, however, largely rejected by Brian Tierney, "The Continuity of Papal Political Theory in the Thirteenth Century: Some Methodological Considerations," *Mediaeval Studies* 27 (1965), 232–245, and Dolcini (see below, note 55).

54. See Cantini 1961, 411–412, and Herde 1967 (below, note 55), 471, note 14.

55. Peter Herde, "Ein Pamphlet der päpstlichen Kurie gegen Kaiser Friedrich II. von 1245/46 ('Eger cui lenia')," *Deutsches Archiv für Erforschung des Mittelalters* 23 (1967), 468–538. Carlo Dolcini, " 'Eger cui lenia' (1245/46): Innocenzo IV, Tolomeo da Lucca, Guglielmo d'Ockham," *Rivista di storia della Chiesa in Italia 29* (1975), 127–148, reprinted in Carlo Dolcini, *Crisi di poteri e politologia in crisi: Da Sinibaldo Fieschi a Guglielmo d'Ockham* (Bologna, 1988), 119–146, in trying to "save" the authenticity of the letter, completely misses the main points of my argument. Apart from the controversial and often futile efforts to point out analogies or differences between "Eger cui lenia" and Innocent IV's Apparatus (the first one being a propagandistic pamphlet, the last one a scholarly work), the undeniable parallels in the wording of Rainer of Viterbo's pamphlet "Iuxta vaticinium Isaie" and "Eger cui lenia" suggest authorship by one of Rainer's chaplains present at Lyons in 1245–1246 (I have also pointed out differences, 501–506). But this fact is in no way "decisivo" (Dolcini 1975, 137) in my argument and does not exclude that the minute could have become an official paper letter. But Dolcini does not even mention the problems that derive from the fact that the text of the letter has only been preserved in letter collections, in three very different versions all without address and date (see my edition, 511–538), that it has not been included in the papal registers (which are fairly comprehensive for the pontificate of Innocent IV), and that not a single copy by a recipient is known. Tolomeo of Lucca and later authors used the letter as they found it in manuscripts of letter collections where it was ascribed to Innocent IV. That they repeated this attribution is certainly not a proof that "Eger cui lenia" is an authentic letter of Innocent IV. Dolcini's arguments therefore go largely astray. James Muldoon, "Extra ecclesiam non est imperium: The Canonists and the Legitimacy of Secular Power," *Studia Gratiana* 9 (1966), 575, without knowing my article, in taking Cantini's arguments into account, already arrived at a possible solution: "Again, the letter, although not written by Innocent himself, could have been composed by someone conversant with his thought and who intended it as an explication of Innocent's position."

56. Elisabeth von Westenholz, *Kardinal Rainer von Viterbo* (Heidelberg, 1912), especially 108–132. See Herde 1967, 494.

57. Innocent IV, 2 April 1246, "Cum in te," fol. 10r; Höfler 1847, 92–93; BFW 7604.

58. Friedrich Graefe, *Die Publizistik in der letzten Epoche Kaiser Friedrichs II: Ein Beitrag zur Geschichte der Jahre 1239–1250* (Heidelberg, 1909), 17–270; Kantorowicz 1928, 550–558; Kantorowicz 1931, 227–232 (sources and literature); Otto Vehse, *Die amtliche Propaganda in der Staatskunst Kaiser Friedrichs II.* (Munich, 1929), 68–190; Hans Martin Schaller, "Das letzte Rundschreiben Gregors IX. gegen Friedrich II.," in *Festschrift Percy Ernst Schramm zu seinem siebzigsten Geburtstag von Schülern und Freunden zugeeignet* (Wiesbaden, 1964), 1:311–314; Hans Martin Schaller, "Endzeit-Erwartung und Antichrist-Vorstellungen in der Politik des 13. Jahrhunderts," in *Festschrift für Hermann Heimpel zum 70. Geburtstag am 19. September 1971* (Göttingen, 1972), 2:924–947.

59. Marjorie Reeves, *The Influence of Prophecy in the Later Middle Ages: A Study in Joachimism* (Oxford, 1969), 309–310, 312; Schaller 1972, 938–939.

60. Andrew Runni Anderson, *Alexander's Gate, Gog and Magog, and the Inclosed Nations* (Cambridge, Mass., 1932); Gian Andri Bezzola, *Die Mongolen in abendländischer Sicht, 1220–1270: Ein Beitrag zur Frage der Völkerbegegnungen* (Bern and Munich, 1974).

61. Graefe 1909, 44, 121, 124, 127, 145, 175–176, 222, 258, 261. See Kantorowicz (above, note 58); Schaller 1972, 935–940.

62. The Latin text was edited from Carolingian manuscripts by Ernst Sackur, *Sibyllinische Texte und Forschungen* (Halle, 1898), 1–96; the Greek text by Anastasios Lolos, *Die Apokalypse des Ps.-Methodios*, Beiträge zur klassischen Philologie 83 (Meisenheim am Glan, 1976); Anastasios Lolos, *Die dritte und vierte Redaktion des Ps.-Methodios*, Beiträge zur klassischen Philologie 94 (Meisenheim am Glan, 1978). But see Thomas Frenz, "Textkritische Untersuchungen zu 'Pseudo-Methodios': Das Verhältnis der griechischen zur ältesten lateinischen Fassung," *Byzantinische Zeitschrift* 80 (1987), 50–58. The original Syriac text was edited by Paul J. Alexander, *The Byzantine Apocalyptic Tradition*, ed. Dorothy deF. Abrahamse (Berkeley, Calif., 1985), 13–51.

63. Ernest A. Wallis Budge, *The Book of the Cave of Treasures* (London, 1927).

64. Otto Prinz, "Eine frühe abendländische Aktualisierung der lateinischen Übersetzung des Pseudo-Methodios," *Deutsches Archiv für Erforschung des Mittelalters* 41 (1985), 1–23; Otto

Prinz, "Bemerkungen zum Wortschatz der lateinischen Übersetzungen des Pseudo-Methodios," in *Variorum Munera Florum: Latinität als prägende Kraft mittelalterlicher Kultur. Festschrift für Hans F. Haefele*, ed. Adolf Reinle, Ludwig Schmugge, and Peter Stolz (Sigmaringen, 1985), 17–22.

65. See above, note 58.

66. Graefe 1909, 7, 47–50, 185, 225–229; Wolfram von den Steinen, *Das Kaisertum Friedrichs des Zweiten nach den Anschauungen seiner Staatsbriefe* (Berlin and Leipzig, 1922), 46–61; Franz Dölger, "Die 'Familie der Könige' im Mittelalter," in Franz Dölger, *Byzanz und die europäische Staatenwelt* (Darmstadt, 1976), 34–69; Kantorowicz 1928, 513–523; Kantorowicz 1931, 218–223; Vehse 1929, 80–81, 124.

67. Vehse 1929, 59–60; von den Steinen 1922, 24–27; Kantorowicz 1928, 402–416; Kantorowicz 1931, 176–184.

68. See above, note 25. Graefe 1909, 17–29; Kantorowicz 1928, 416–417, 458, 463; Kantorowicz 1931, 184, 200, 208. On the concept of "necessitas," see Gaines Post, *Studies in Medieval Legal Thought: Public Law and the State, 1100–1322* (Princeton, 1964), 241–309.

69. BFW 7245; Graefe 1909, 29–40; Kantorowicz 1928, 454–456; Kantorowicz 1931, 199.

70. Schaller 1965, 390–392.

71. BFW 7548; Graefe 1909, 99–119, 157–163.

72. BFW 7550; Graefe 1909, 128–157, see also 119–128 ("Confusa est mater," BFW 7549).

73. Fols. 27r–31v; fols. 32r–34v; Höfler 1847, 61–73, 73–79; BFW 7550, 7548. See Karl Hampe, "Über die Flugschriften zum Lyoner Konzil von 1245," *Historische Vierteljahrschrift* 11 (1908), 297–313; von Westenholz 1912, 108–132; Kantorowicz 1928, 543–546; Kantorowicz 1931, 227; Schaller 1972, 938–939.

74. BFW 2434, 2454, 11308; see Graefe 1909, 43–47, 51–62, 68–84, 236–268; Kantorowicz 1928, 453–454, 550–558; Kantorowicz 1931, 199, 228–231; Vehse 1929, 75–78. A good selection was published by Hans Martin Schaller, *Politische Propaganda Kaiser Friedrichs II. und seiner Gegner* (Germering bei München, 1965).

75. See Schaller 1965, 402.

76. Vehse 1929, 156–157. So far the most complete identification of quotations is in Graefe 1909.

77. Vehse 1929, 157–159. For details see Graefe 1909.

78. Kantorowicz 1928, 276, Eng. trans. 300; he states: "Piero della Vigna is the last creative writer of living Latin. It was a living language that spoke with pomp and pride and smooth-flowing magnificence from his obscure periods. Its comprehensiveness and joy in style bore within them the seeds of classic humanistic Latin." This opinion can hardly be justified as there is no connection between the "baroque" style of the thirteenth century *Ars dictaminis* and the revival of Ciceronian Latin by the later humanists; see the pertinent remarks by Paul Oskar Kristeller, *Studies in Renaissance Thought and Letters* (Rome, 1956; repr. 1969), 564.

79. Schillman 1929, 25; Vehse 1929, 110, 175; Herde 1967, 494–499; Schaller 1972, 938.

80. See Albert Brackmann, "Kaiser Friedrich II. in 'mythischer Schau,'" *HZ* 140 (1929), 534–549, and the ensuing controversy: Ernst Kantorowicz, " 'Mythenschau': Eine Erwiderung," *HZ* 141 (1930), 457–471, and Albert Brackmann, "Nachwort," *HZ* 141 (1930), 472–478. For a very detailed but less severe criticism, see Karl Hampe, "Das neueste Lebensbild Kaiser Friedrichs II.," *HZ* 146 (1932), 441–475 (with some substantial remarks on Frederick's relationship to the "baroque" Latin of his chancery, 446–448); also Friedrich Baethgen's review in *Deutsche Literaturzeitung* 51 (1930), 75–85. These and many more articles on Frederick II have been conveniently collected in *Stupor Mundi* (above, note 35) and a second edition of the same title (Darmstadt, 1982) with additional articles. On the debate about Kantorowicz's book, see also Eckhart Grünewald, *Ernst Kantorowicz and Stefan George* (Wiesbaden, 1982), 86–101, and Hermann Jakobs, "Die Mediävistik bis zum Ende der Weimarer Republik," in *Geschichte in Heidelberg*, ed. Jürgen Miethke (Berlin, 1992), 59–65; also the controversial chapter in Norman F. Cantor, *Inventing the Middle Ages: The Lives, Works, and Ideas of the Great Medievalists of the Twentieth Century* (New York, 1991), 79–117. The most recent monographs on Frederick II are much more sober than that of Kantorowicz; see Thomas Curtis Van Cleve, *The Emperor Frederick II of Hohenstaufen: Immutator Mundi* (Oxford, 1972); David Abulafia, *Frederick II: A Medieval Emperor* (London, 1988); and now especially Wolfgang Stürner, *Friedrich II. Teil 1: Die Königsherrschaft in Sizilien und Deutschland 1194–1220.* Gestalten des Mittelalters und der Renaissance, ed. Peter Herde, vol. 2 (Darmstadt, 1992), of which part 2 will deal with the questions discussed here.

PIERO MORPURGO
Vicenza, Italy

Philosophia naturalis *at the Court of Frederick II: From the Theological Method to the* ratio secundum physicam *in Michael Scot's* De Anima

Throughout his life Michael Scot never lost the enthusiasm he experienced during his sojourn in Toledo when it is thought he translated the *Libri Naturales* of Aristotle.[1] Michael Scot's influence would reach far and wide. His works—the *Liber Introductorius, Liber Particularis, Liber Phisionomiae,* and the *Commentary on the Movements of the Sphere by Sacrobosco*—would be quoted by Vincent of Beauvais.[2] Michael Scot's *De Anima* would be the main source of chapters on the subject in *De Proprietatibus Rerum* by Bartholomaeus Anglicus.[3] Even Dante, in his description of the spots of the moon and in the *Questio de Aqua et Terra,* would make use of the works of Michael Scot.[4]

The basis for his reputation among medieval philosophers should be sought in several areas: in the continuous interchange between theological and scientific sources in Michael Scot's writings;[5] in his endeavor to reconcile the biblical idea of Nature and the new science; in his idea of a Nature with its own laws and rules, a Nature in which his contemporaries were no longer constrained to search merely for allegorical paths to God;[6] in a glorification of astronomy and astrology as new paths leading to God;[7] and in his compounding of the new philosophical thought with the mass of ancient beliefs on demons and medieval magic.[8]

The idea of a Nature alive, full of its own potencies, and ruled by the same stars that he saw above his head, fascinated Michael Scot. Yet the fascination was mixed with fear. He remained a Franciscan closely in touch with the popes and the Roman curia.[9]

He was as awed by the idea of the angels of the Apocalypse as he was by the sidereal powers.[10] This tension is expressed in his writings for his emperor, Frederick II, and it can still be sensed by the modern reader—sensed, perhaps, with some surprise, at least if we approach Michael's writings with the idea that such tensions, between natural science and religious belief, were simply the result of a thirteenth-century renewal.[11] Many of the trends characteristic of thirteenth-century philosophy can be traced to the prohibition, in 1210, of the study of Aristotle's *Libri Naturales.* The enthusiasm of some contemporaries—Alexander Nequam and Robert Grosseteste—was cooled by this prohibition.[12] Michael Scot, too, was aware of it. But his passion for books was such that, rather than turn away from them, he chose to be a member of the imperial court, the court philosopher of the Hammer of the World, the Antichrist: the Puer Apuliae, Frederick II. To see Michael Scot's choice as representing a farewell to his faith in the Church is to misjudge him. His dialogues, which almost certainly reflect talks he had with the emperor, display him as exhorting the emperor to be a good Catholic. These dialogues, in fact, do not demonstrate an abandonment of religion by Michael Scot, but rather a distinctly religious element in the court culture of the emperor.

This aspect of Frederick II's intellectual milieu differs from that suggested by papal letters from the years when Gregory IX was beginning to threaten Frederick. Gregory doubtless had reason to present a one-sided picture. He wished to prevent the promulgation by Frederick II of those laws contained in the *Liber Augustalis*, which the pope saw as threatening the freedom of the Church. By the very act of their promulgation, Frederick II, as the pope saw it, was a persecutor of the Church: "necessario sequitur ut dicaris Ecclesiae persecutor."[13] But from the imperial court itself we obtain rather a different picture. Michael Scot's *Liber Introductorius*, a work directly addressed to the emperor, breathes an air of quiet reason, as it discusses, one by one, against a background of normal, pious belief, the main themes of the scientific renaissance. It is as if, in Frederick's court, the Catholic faith walked hand in hand with the astronomers' natural science.

Let me offer some examples. In the *Sermo suasionis in bono*,[14] the philosopher says amicably to his emperor that each of us is better than all other creatures, better than angels and planets, in fact, "post Deum solo homo." Therefore man has the right to understand everything in Nature. Not only are all the properties of trees, flowers, fruits, stones, and stars at his disposal, even the angels, the moon, the sun, and the four elements should be regarded as his servants. Thus mankind, to realize its power, has only to pursue research into Nature and make use of the results of experiments.

In another dialogue Frederick II emphasizes the beauty of all the sciences, including the practical, saying: "I praise the mechanical arts and I want to glorify their craftsman, just as I have done for the authors of books, for both of them are useful and necessary."[15] There is no doubt that the emperor welcomed all these practical experts into his court and addressed many questions to them.

The questions suggested by Frederick II were forwarded to various scientists of the Mediterranean world. In sending them the emperor was following the suggestion of Michael Scot. In fact, in the *Liber Phisionomiae* there is a series of such counsels to the emperor. We read, for instance:

My Emperor . . . you should search into different books and mainly into the scientific ones. . . . Once you have done all your duties, once you are freed from calls to fight, you should look for the nourishment of your soul. . . . Thus you should ask the doctors of all the branches of science in order to get various opinions, and it would be better that all these scientists should have the occasion to meet you so that you can hold discussions with them. . . . In so doing you will keep a high level of science in your kingdom, so that your kingship will last for many years and your offspring will not inherit a neglected desert. . . . Nevertheless, you must not fall into any vice and you should be a friend of God.[16]

In a passage like this we find clearly reflected that idea of inquiry, scientific as well as administrative, that Frederick espoused in attempting to rule his kingdom in accordance with the principles of reason.

Ratio accompanied by *auctoritas*, and fortified by the strength of the ruler, were the guiding principles of Frederick II. He believed that he must rule as a *missus Domini*, a messenger from heaven. The rationality thus enthroned was the same that should be sought in Nature, even if this implied at times a denial of the authority of Aristotle, as when the emperor was preparing his masterpiece, the *De arte venandi cum avibus*.

The foundations of this interpretation of Nature met with some hostility even in the Swabian court. In fact, even the master of the University of Naples, Terrisio d'Atina,[17] explained that Nature does not possess its own autonomy: "Discite quod natura sui iuris non est." This statement also echoes Alan of Lille, who says that Nature is merely the Vicar of God, *Dei auctoris vicaria*, and only a minister of the Lord, *Dei magistri humili discipula*.[18] It should also be added that Terrisio d'Atina refused to admit the autonomous power of the stars: "Discite quod per se nihil sydera possunt." Therefore we may wonder whether the entire philosophical milieu of Frederick's court was so innovative or so fascinated by the sciences of the stars.

What remains hidden from our view is the history of the education of the emperor as a child; however, the subject should still be considered, even if the sources are not very generous. If we wish to catch something of the *curriculum studiorum* of the emperor, we should also regard Michael Scot's works as one of the main sources for understanding Frederick's own thought—a philosophical kind of thought that seems not so innovative, at least during his collaboration with Michael Scot.

Once again it should be stressed that Michael Scot was either conservative or very cautious in his lectures to the emperor. First of all, Michael wrote that it is impossible to assert the eternity of the World.[19] With these words, we dispel the myth of his being a leader of the Averroistic sect. In the *Liber Introductorius* we may recognize, instead of many elements of renewal, an enormous number of theological quotations: from Isidore of Seville, Bede, Augustine, Bernard of Clairvaux, William of Saint Thierry, Alcher of Clairvaux, and so on. Michael Scot uses all these sources with the aim of building one of the first encyclopedias of natural sciences. Later, Vincent of Beauvais, in the tracks of Michael, will offer, in his *Mirror of Nature*, a much better product to Parisian students.[20] This peculiar series of quotations from ancient sources, and not from the new material offered by the Latin Aristotle and the modern Arabic and Hebrew scientists, evokes John of Salisbury. In fact, in his *Metalogicon*, the philosopher says that anyone wishing to study the soul must leave aside Plato and Aristotle and make use of the works of the ancient church fathers, and this approach was the one adopted by Michael Scot.[21]

Furthermore, it is striking that no passages from the Latin Aristotle were used by the famous translator. In the *De Anima* there are four interpolations with the name of Philosophus, and only once do we read that any rational being "omnia scire desiderat naturaliter," which is a quotation from the *Metaphysics*.[22] Thus, after having explored the sources of Michael Scot's works, we may say that his *ratio secundum physicam* should be linked with the theories of Nature of the Salernitan School. Nevertheless, despite the Aristotelian influence of the physicians from Salerno, Michael Scot shows much more the traces of Platonic, Hippocratic, and Galenic thought than of the Aristotelian view of Nature.

In this case, three hypotheses should be considered:

(1) that the *Liber Introductorius* was written before the translations of the Aristotelian works concerned;

(2) that Roger Bacon[23] and Albert the Great[24] were right in saying that Michael Scot did not know any foreign languages, any more than he knew the physical sciences (we must recall that Roger Bacon said that the Aristotelian works began their diffusion in the Occident around 1230);

(3) that according to the idea of one of Scot's first biographers, J. Wood Brown, Michael Scot was Frederick's tutor during his minority.

Among these hypotheses the last is the most fascinating. Unfortunately we have no evidence to support it, nor is any information provided on this topic in the imperial register or even in the works of Scot himself. Thus the only reliable source is the *Liber Introductorius* and the other parts of his trilogy, the *Liber Particularis* and the *Liber Phisionomiae*.

The scheme followed by Michael Scot in preparing this trilogy is the same used by the enigmatic philosopher of the twelfth century, Honorius Augustodunensis, in his *Elucidarium*, namely, four main divisions on angels, man, Nature, and the Lord, with some references to Ambrose's *Commentary on Genesis*.[25]

Nevertheless, Michael Scot's aim was rather different from that of Augustodunensis and from that of the commentary written by Robert Grosseteste on the *Hexaemeron* as well, for the *Liber Introductorius* is a kind of justification, based on theological sources, of both astrology and astronomy.[26]

Scot's method is very close to that of the masters of the so-called medical School of Salerno. Bartholomew of Salerno declared in his commentary on the *Isagoge Iohannitii:* in theology, from various tiny signs, we can reach a certain knowledge of our Creator; and in a similar manner, in *physica*, from the science of elements and from the analysis of their mixture, we can understand the causes of birth and of death, *generatio* and *corruptio*.[27] Michael Scot added that everything that occurs on this Earth by Nature happens only "per viam corrumptionis et divisionis"; in fact, the act of Creation occurred only once and that was enough.[28] Thereafter

Nature had her freedom in the same way as a "semen in pomo reclusum."

Another analogy with the Salernitan masters is that represented by Michael Scot's philosophical method. This approach is also based on division, according to which each part of matter should be divided into its components. Thus Scot, in applying the *methodus divisivus* in the *Liber Introductorius*, says that there is a main distinction between the macrocosmos and the microcosmos, followed by other divisions: the *natura naturans*, that is, God and the *natura naturata*, or the elements and their power in the generation of Nature.[29] Here it appears that the elements are the roots of earthly Nature.[30] These elements, better called the *elementata*, that is, the elements derived from the four pure and celestial elements, are given the power to control that continuous creation which takes place on the Earth.[31] Michael Scot compares the Creator to a baker, who, once he has been provided with flour and yeast and has the necessary dough, will be able to make as many loaves as he likes, "ut est pasta fermentata de qua extrahuntur multi panes." In a similar manner, Nature has been granted her own autonomy in the matter of generation.

In the middle of this universe are the angels as celestial officers (*offitiales celi*), the moon, the winds, the stars, and the planets. Each of these has the duty of providing enough signs to rational man to show the way to Heaven. Among the various circles of the sky, the soul, once it has become free of the flesh, will recognize its similarity to God and the angels. In this freedom the soul will have knowledge of everything and will be able to see any event happening in the World.

It should also be added that some souls have a likeness to demons, and wizards are able to make use of these wicked souls to achieve their wishes, or merely to enjoy themselves. In fulfilling the purposes and commands of magicians, these perverted souls will destroy houses, castles, and bridges. They will kidnap good souls and shake them into the winds. Therefore Michael Scot says that anyone who deals with magic will try to ruin the faith: "magica ars destruit religionem."[32] He adds that the gift of prophecy is the only permissible kind of divination.

The idea of a *ratio secundum physicam* dismisses magical arts. Yet we frequently encounter in Michael Scot's works a measure of contradiction on this point. In the middle of the *prohemium* of the *Liber Introductorius*, for instance, Nature suddenly ceases to be ruled by the *commixtiones elementorum*. Instead we are confronted with a great crowd of spirits, fighting each other to gain control of human minds.

On a religious plane, nevertheless, Nature has lost her autonomy. Each creature must now feel the presence of the Lord and the approaching End of the World. "Tota natura corporis amministratur per angelos," that is, our bodies are ruled by the angels and it often happens that souls have been dragged into boiling water because "angeli Dei vindictas faciunt quandoque, propter Deum, causa peccatorum que nimio committuntur ut probatur in Apocalypsi."[33]

A slow shift appears in Michael Scot's thought as we read the fourth part of his *Liber*, devoted to a study of the soul, a description of the soul as the engine of the heart. This idea clears the way for the exaltation of the rationality of the human mind. For the soul and science are one and the same according to Michael Scot. It is the duty of *ratio* to rule the body in an absolute freedom. *Ratio* is never affected by movements of the stars: "nec subiecta est ministerio stellarum." Here we have, in fact, a statement of the total freedom of the intellect: "intellectus autem percipit formas rerum universales . . . ipse simplex est et incorruptibilis, ac operatur suam proprietatem sine instrumento corporeo et ipse solus in nobis divinus est et non humanus."[34] It is therefore only corrupted souls who will fall into the hands of the Antichrist when the time comes.

Once the fear of the End of the World has disappeared, Michael Scot explains to us that only mankind can understand Nature, and this gift (here Michael Scot follows Saint Augustine) is due to the power of "intelligentia, ratio et memoria."[35] These represent the potent means that mankind has at its disposal for understanding everything. Michael Scot further asserts that the creative act of God is very close to our human way of thinking, "unde cogitare in homine est quoddam creare."[36]

The activity of the sun and that of the

intellect resemble each other, for as the sunbeam does not affect the glass in passing through it, so *ratio* can inspect everything without the risk of doing it damage.[37] In Michael Scot's thought the scientist is not allowed to inquire into those things that belong to God, for the scientist's task is confined to the description of the elements. Research into the first principles of God should be left to the captiousness of philosophers, and so should the unsolved question of the birth of the elements.[38] The field of the scientist is limited to the order of Nature, and he must not become involved in superstitious complications. The physician thus will make every effort to heal his patient but will avoid magical practice.[39]

Yet we meet contradiction here too. Michael Scot, against his previous claim, adds that the physician, once he senses real agony in his patient, should call a wizard to give a measure of relief even if this practice has been prohibited by philosophers and the clergy.[40]

In Michael Scot, *ratio secundum physicam* deals only with Nature and not with miracles. Any event that could be defined *contra naturam* should be left to theology. Michael Scot states that in Nature we must study only what rules birth, growth, and death. Everything in Nature is ruled by the elements, so, for example, once the four qualities of the elements have been intermixed in the human embryo, the soul appears. The sense of hearing relies on movements of air. In the same way the organs of sight draw on the power of fire.

Thus the idea of the alteration of bodies, the principle of the mutation of the balance of the four elements, is outlined as the reason for an illness; therefore a disease is not *contra naturam*. Against the course of Nature there is only the intervention of God by "miracula, id est omnia que sunt contra naturam sive que per naturam non posse fieri."[41] According to Nature, human status implies the presence of a rational soul. No one can strip the human body of *ratio*, for this can never happen *per naturam*. The human soul, *ratio*, and *scientia* are the same thing, and they have freedom in studying the world of Nature.

Above all, Michael's emphasis is on a *ratio* that is not affected by the action of the stars, for the planets ruled by the angels have in their power only human flesh, not the soul. It is the task of Nature to teach, to control what happens in this sublunar world. The task of mankind is to know how Nature works.

This knowledge of Nature will depend on man's taking four main steps. These are based on:

(1) the five senses, which give us the idea of what we need for our life and what should be avoided;

(2) the imagination, which will give us an idea of what will happen in the near future;

(3) the intellect, which represents the power of choice between different options, mainly "inter bonum et malum." This last field is made accessible to the intellect because the *ratio*, in perceiving Nature and *sensibilia*, has opened the way to the *insensibilia*;

(4) the memory, which possesses the virtue by which we can postulate the idea of God, as well as the existence of Hell, despite the fact that we have never seen them.[42]

By these means the soul will understand the principles of generation.[43] By these powers *ratio* will comprehend how a natural eclipse occurs, an eclipse different from the prodigious eclipse that took place *contra naturam* during the crucifixion of Christ. The primary elements and the derived elements, *elementa et elementata*, will be once again the main fulcrum of generation. Their mixture is the mirror of what was happening in the macrocosmos at the moment the World was created: their birth happened in the same way and at the same time. Thus angels, stars, and elements have a mutual relationship.

It is now possible, as Michael Scot states in the final part of the *De Anima*, to understand growth and decay in Nature because among the soul, the *artes*, and all the sciences there is a marvelous likeness. The likeness arises from the fact that the foundations of *gramatica, dialectica, rhetorica, aritmetica, geometria, musica*, and *astronomia* are all joined in the soul. It is in the soul that the roots of all these sciences are thereforc to be found. Even the idea of number, and of every spoken word and of any geometrical figure, all are rooted in the human soul.[44]

This resemblance between Nature and soul could be easily comprehended if we looked to the stillness of the stars above our heads. The human soul expresses the same unchanging principles as the planets. Because stars and souls look alike, astronomy is the only science which, when it has described the movements of the stars, offers us an idea of what happens inside the various celestial spheres. Astronomy can establish all these links, and then, by deduction from the movements of the stars, man can understand the movements of earthly bodies.[45]

The *ratio secundum physicam* used by Michael Scot in his analysis of the human mind is in the theological mainstream of his century. As a scientist, he offers us a justification of his inquiries into the world of Nature: that these researches have led the human being onto the tracks of his Creator. This statement cannot fail to remind us of the thought of Maimonides. The Hebrew philosopher wrote about the vanity of astrological beliefs on one hand, and on the other, in *The Guide of the Perplexed*, admitted that philosophers and astronomers could provide us with a good representation of the motions of the planets, without, in doing so, telling how they truly are. In other words, he posited an astronomic theory which he did not allow to affect the deity.[46]

From this point of view, Michael Scot, with his exaltation of the role of the astronomers, is very close in some respects to the Maimonidean position. We know that *The Guide of the Perplexed* was a text that circulated within the Swabian court.[47] We also know that Michael Scot discussed these topics with the Hebrew translator Anatoli.[48] Scot was firmer and less skeptical in defending the *creatio ex nichilo*, and doing so on the neo-Platonic ground of the *De processione mundi* of Dominicus Gundissalinus.[49]

Michael Scot concludes in *De Anima* that the souls of kings and emperors will reside in Heaven just behind the souls of philosophers.[50] He had strong hopes that he would glimpse Heaven, and perhaps he did. But Dante, for his part, placed Michael Scot in Hell, condemning him to walk backward because of his arrogance in trying to see too far.[51]

NOTES

1. The main dates for Michael Scot are as follows: c. 1210, he arrived in Toledo; 1215, he attended the Fourth Lateran Council and discussed with Pope Innocent III the controversy regarding the primacy of the archbishop of Toledo; 1217, in Toledo, he translated the works of al-Bitruji; 1220, in Bologna as a physician, he met Frederick II while presumably translating the *De Animalibus* of Aristotle; 1224, Pope Honorius III offered him the archbishopric of Cashel in Ireland (he refused); 1227, Pope Gregory IX renewed the offer of an archbishopric (Canterbury); after 1228, he wrote his *Liber Introductorius*; 1229, Leonardo Pisano sent the first draft of his *Liber Abaci* to Michael Scot for his suggestions; 1232, translation of the *Abbrevatio Avicennae* attributed to Michael Scot; 1235, presumed death of Michael Scot according to the poet Henry of Avranches; 1252–1253, a *magister* Michael Scot was active as chancellor of John and Matilda of Chartres.

See John Wood Brown, *The Life and Legend of Michael Scot* (Edinburgh, 1897); Charles Homer Haskins, "Michael Scot," in Haskins, *Studies in the History of Mediaeval Science* (Cambridge, Mass., 1927; repr. 1960), 272–298; Lynn Thorndike, *Michael Scot* (London, 1965); Piero Morpurgo, "Il concetto di natura in Michele Scoto," *Clio—Rivista trimestrale di studi storici* 21 (1985), 1–17; and José Gil, *La escuela de traductores de Toledo y sus colaboradores Judios* (Toledo, 1985).

2. Lynn Thorndike, "Manuscripts of Michael Scot's 'Liber Introductorius,'" in *Didascaliae: Studies in Honor of Anselm M. Albareda* (New York, 1961), 425–447. Lynn Thorndike, *The Sphere of Sacrobosco and Its Commentators* (Chicago, 1949).

3. Raymond James Long, *Bartholomaeus Anglicus, On the Properties of Soul and Body* (Toronto, 1979); the editor did not know that this book was based on Michael Scot's work.

4. Piero Morpurgo, "Michele Scoto e Dante: Una continuità di modelli culturali?" in *Filosofia, scienza e astrologia nel '300 europeo*, ed. Graziella Federici Vescovini and Francesco Barocelli (Padua, 1992), 79–94.

5. Piero Morpurgo, "Fonti di Michele Scoto," *Rendiconti dell'Accademia Nazionale dei Lincei* 38 (1983), 59–71.

6. Tullio Gregory, "Forme di conoscenza e ideali di sapere nella cultura medievale," *Giornale critico della filosofia italiana* 67 (Jan.–Apr. 1988), 1–62.

7. *Liber Introductorius*, San Lorenzo del El Escorial, MS. f. III 8 (= MS. E), fol. 52va: "anima est substantia simplex, invisibilis, incorporea, immortalis etc., est similis Deo . . . est similis soli Deo quia una est in quolibet corpore . . . est similis arti astronomie in eo quod scit veraciter indagare celestia et cursus corporum superiorum, toto tempore et multis modis."

8. *Liber Introductorius*, MS. E, fol. 42rb: "Qui sunt tormentatores animarum? Responsio: demones et non angeli Dei. Quare non angeli Dei? Quia proprium angelorum est bene facere incessantere, sicut

demonum male facere . . . Quid est infernus? Respondeo: locus penarum et tormentorum sine misericordia."

9. Juan Rivera Recio, "Personajes hispanos asistentes en 1215 al IV Concilio de Letrán," *Hispania Sacra* 4 (1951), 335–338; Raoul Manselli, "La corte di Federico II e Michele Scoto," in *L'averroismo in Italia*, Atti dei Convegni Lincei (Rome, 1979), 63–80.

10. *Liber Introductorius*, Oxford, Bodleian Library, MS. Bodley 266 (= MS. B), fol. 144vb:

"Septem sunt divisiones firmamenti . . . in ipso autem sunt quedam hospitia angelorum et sunt plena sapientia, et ibi septem sunt sedes parate et super illas sedes sunt hospitia multarum mansionum et in qualibet mansione est spiritus pervigilis . . . isti angeli habent multas legiones ceterorum angelorum qui serviunt senatoribus septem sciendo quod quilibet senatorum habent discretum numerum legionum sub se que ad singula que sibi rationaliter invocentur celeriter currunt. [fol. 13va] . . . mali spiritus sunt predones Dei, moventur enim tales angeli de suis hospitiis, precepto Dei vel Eius permissione, licencia et habita a bonis angeḷis propter vindictam."

11. *Renaissance and Renewal in the Twelfth Century*, ed. Robert L. Benson and Giles Constable (Cambridge, Mass., 1982).

12. Richard Hunt, *The Schools and the Cloister: The Life and Writings of Alexander Nequam (1157–1217)* (Oxford, 1984), 68, note 10; Richard Southern, *Robert Grosseteste: The Growth of an English Mind in Medieval Europe* (Oxford, 1986), 141–181.

13. Antonio Marongiù, "Politica e diritto nella legislazione di Federico II," in *Il "Liber Augustalis" di Federico II di Svevia nella storiografia*, ed. Anna Laura Trombetti Budriesi (Bologna, 1987), 65–85.

14. Piero Morpurgo, "Il 'sermo suasionis in bono' di Michele Scoto a Federico II," *Rendiconti dell'Accademia Nazionale dei Lincei* 38 (1983), 287–300.

15. Piero Morpurgo, "Federico II e la fine dei tempi nella profezia del cod. escorialense f. III 8," *Pluteus* 1 (1983), 135–167.

16. *Liber Phisionomiae*, Oxford, Bodleian Library, MS. Canon. Misc. 555 (= MS. O), fol. 59rb:

". . . est utile tibi (Frederick II) inquirere diversos doctores et magistros propter diversas scientias eo quod diversi diversa sentiunt scientiarum. . . . Unde ex meo consilio doctores magistris et homines ingeniosos nam curialiter invitetis apud vos et sepe loquamini cum multis, verba vestra coram eis sapienter et domestice comoventes. Putate in diversis propter diversa et facite sibi questiones quando erunt vobiscum et dicta eorum servate ut in posterum vobis et alteri valeant iuvare. . . . Manutene studium scientiarum in tuo regno et fac fieri sepe disputationes ante conspectum tuum ut tuus animus glorietur et tuum ingenium in melius reformetur.

Tuum studium sit velle regnare diu et hoc erit si te dederis virtutibus vicia evitando, et de tali moralitate alibi tibi dicemus, si Deus voluerit. Sed hic dicemus quod des cor tuum cognitioni boni intellectus secundum mensuram discretionis, sit amicus Dei, fide spe et opere perfecte."

17. Francesco Torraca, "Maestro Terrisio di Atina," *Archivio storico per le province napoletane* 37 (1911), 231–242.

18. Gillian R. Evans, *Alan of Lille: The Frontiers of Theology in the Later Twelfth Century* (Cambridge, 1983), 27–49.

19. *Liber Introductorius*, MS. B, fol. 1vb: "dicunt multi quod mundus sit ab eterno, cum investigantes motum predicti circuli non reperiant suum finaliter intellectum, et quod mundus non sit eternus patet aperte quia creatura non est a se facta."

20. Vincentius Bellovacensis, *Bibliotheca Mundi seu Speculi Maioris Vincentii Burgundi Praesulis Bellovacensis Ordinis Praedicatorum. Tomus Secundus Speculum Doctrinale* (repr. Graz, 1965), Lib. I, c. 1: "Quid sit Philosophia iuxta Michaelem Scotum."

21. John of Salisbury, *Metalogicon*, ed. C. C. J. Webb (Oxford, 1929), Lib. IV.3.167.

22. *Liber Introductorius*, MS. E, fol. 34vb: "Rationalis enim creatura desiderat omnia scire naturaliter (Aristotle, *Metaphysica* 980a21), sicut angelus, demon, et anima hominis tantum."

23. Roger Bacon, *Opus tertium*, in Rerum Britannicarum Medii Aevi Scriptores, ed. J. S. Brewer (London, 1859), 15:91.

24. Albertus Magnus, *Metereorum*, 3 *tract.* IV, 26: "Michael Scotus qui in rei veritate nescivit naturas nec bene intellexit libros Aristotelis"; *Opera omnia Beati Alberti Magni* (Paris, 1890), 4:697.

25. Honorius Augustodunensis, *L'Elucidarium et les lucidaires: Contribution, par l'histoire d'un texte, à l'histoire des croyances religieuses en France au moyen age*, ed. Y. Lefevre (Paris, 1954). The *Prohemium* of the *Liber Introductorius* has identical questions and the same kind of answers; therefore we may argue that Michael Scot was reading (*legere*) the book and discussing (*disputare*) its contents in the presence of his emperor. Ambrosius, *Hexaemeron*, ed. Carl Schenkl (Vienna, 1897), Corpus Scriptorum Ecclesiasticorum Latinorum 32.1.

26. Robert Grosseteste, *Hexaemeron*, ed. Richard Dales and Servus Gieben (London, 1982), Auctores Britannici Medii Aevi 6; Piero Morpurgo, "Note in margine a un poemetto astrologico presente nei codici del *Liber Particularis* di Michele Scoto," *Pluteus* 2 (1984), 1–14.

27. *Commentum in Isagogem Iohannitii*, Oxford, Bodleian Library, MS. C.C.C. 293 B, fol. 85vb: "In theologia namque ductu rationis a corporeis subiectis, sensu perceptibilibus, ad incorporeas et insensibiles complectio procedit, sicut philosophi ex creaturarum dispositione, motu, ordine, aliquam sibi noticiam comparande, ex effectu scilicit causam conicientes. . . . In phisica vero, ex formis rerum sensibilibus et manifestis ad insensibiles formas et occultas ratio procedit."

28. *Liber Introductorius*, MS. E, fol. 32rb: "Dicimus etiam quod non est aliquid in hoc volubili ac trans-

mirabili mundo quod naturaliter nascatur et producat germen nisi per viam corrumptionis et divisionis."

29. *Liber Introductorius*, MS. B, fol. 2rb: "Nam natura naturans est natura divina, et natura naturata est essentia quattor elementorum opere quorum est motus admirabilis, eo quod motu ipsorum, id est coniunctione, diversa generantur et concipiuntur."

30. *Liber Introductorius*, MS. E, fol. 44va: "multa sunt que non sunt elemencta nec ex elemenctis facta, de quibus habemus cognitionem, ut de sole etc. . . . omnia naturalia aut sunt elemencta aut ex elemenctis facta seu composita evidenter, et ratio commixtionis elementorum erit in quolibet elemenctato."

31. *Liber Particularis*, MS. O, fol. 15vb: "Item notandum est quod omne elemenctum, quanto plus approximat firmamento in altum, cessans a centro terre, tanto plus est purius et clarius."

32. *Liber Introductorius*, MS. B, fol. 22rb: "et est sciendum quod ars magica in phylosophia non reperitur nec recipitur eo quod est magistra omnis iniquitatis et malicie . . . magica quidem ars destruit religionem divine legis, et cultura demoni persuadet, morum corrumpcionem ingerit, et ad omne scelus mentes sequancium impellit, unde eos cecat et infatuat."

33. *Liber Introductorius*, MS. B, fols. 16–17.

34. *Liber Introductorius*, MS. E, fol. 37vb.

35. *Liber Introductorius*, MS. E, fol. 34vb; fol. 36ra: "Natura est esse earum que cum sint quocumque modo per intellectum capi possunt."

36. *Liber Introductorius*, MS. E, fol. 40va.

37. *Liber Introductorius*, MS. E, fol. 40vb:

"Et sicut radius solis penetrat vitreum absque corruptione vitri, sic anima rationalis intrat loca et videt singula tam longinqua quam propinqua. . . . Et sicut sol totum mundum illuminat, licet plus unum locum quam alium, ratione vicinitate ipsius, sic omnis anima est manifestior in uno loco corporis sui quam in alio. Unde sicut sol in medio celi relucet plusquam in terra, sic anima rationalis plus illuminat in medio corporis ut in pectore et in capite quam in alia parte et ibi plus suam vim operatur."

38. *Liber Particularis*, MS. O, fol. 37rb:

"De origine elementorum. . . . Unde sciendum est quod elemenctum est essencia simplex nominata, corpus continens admixturam cuiuslibet alteri elemencti. . . . Deus enim, solus, omnipotens et creator ex nichilo, ante principium creaturarum, sic particulatarum creando fecit unum ens quod yle appellatur. . . . Et de hac yle multi diversa dixerunt. . . . Nos vero dicimus quod non est sensus hominis diffinire yle nisi per sententia cavilosa, ut patet per diffinitiones philosophorum."

39. Piero Morpurgo, ed., "Il capitolo *de informacione medicorum* del *Liber Introductorius* di Michele Scoto," *Clio—Rivista trimestrale di studi storici* 20 (1984), 651–661.

40. *Liber Introductorius*, MS. B, fol. 174rb:

"Tali enim infirmitati alicuius non potest rationaliter subveniri per viam physice, sed subveniendum est per consimilem scientiam illius qua homo patitur et est male impeditus. Tunc debet medicus ei dare consilium sapienter ut inquirantur divine et incantatrices, quamvis videatur inhonestum et nephas in studium aput ceteros sapientes et religiosos; causa est ut magis amet videre sanitatem infirmi quam penas continuabiles nimie gravitatis quibus posset cadere in disperationem sui."

41. *Liber Introductorius*, MS. B, fol. 12vb.

42. *Liber Introductorius*, MS. E, fol. 40ra: "Timemus infernum solo intellectu anime, nec oculi nostri viderunt eum, nec nostra caro probavit penas."

43. *Liber Introductorius*, MS. B, fol. 8rb.

44. *Liber Introductorius*, MS. E, fols. 52vb–55vb.

45. *Liber Introductorius*, MS. B, fol. 21rb: "est igitur astronomia mobilis magnitudinis disciplina et cursus planetarum et contemplativa, ad rerum noticiam id est ad cognitionem complessionis rerum et ad situm mundi naturalem."

46. Moises ben Maimon, *De la Guia dels Perplexos i altres escrits—Edició a cura d'Eduard Feliu* (Barcelona, 1986).

47. Ernst Kantorowicz, *Federico II imperatore* (Berlin, 1931; Italian trans. Milan, 1976), 374.

48. Giuseppe Sermoneta, "Federico II e il pensiero ebraico nell'Italia del suo tempo," in *Federico II e l'arte del Duecento italiano*, ed. Angiola Maria Romanini, 2 vols. (Galatina, 1980), 2:183–197.

49. Dominicus Gundissalinus, *De processione mundi*, ed. G. Bülow (Münster, 1925).

50. *Liber Introductorius*, MS. E, fol. 49rb:

Et nota differentiam animarum salvancium . . . unde quidam recipiuntur in ordine Seraphym ut boni heremite atque sancti religiosi qui plus permanserunt in contemplacione Dei quam in studio philosophie. Alie recipiuntur in ordine Cherubim, ut phylosophi et religiosi qui studuerunt peritia scire phylosophiam. Alie recipiuntur in ordine Thronorum ut Sancti, Pape, Imperatores Reges. [fol. 50vb] Quare dicendum est quod qui perfecte in Deo delectatur, opere dominationis carnis pretermissa inquisitione phylosophie iam incepit trascendere ordinem Seraphym ad placendum Deum, sic omnis astronomus bene se habens iam trascendere incipit ordinem Cherubym etc.; unde credibile est quod astronomus, ratione scientie, plus Deo vicinat.

51. Dante Alighieri, *Divina Commedia*, Inferno XX, 115–117.

MASSIMO OLDONI
Università degli Studi di Salerno

La promozione della scienza: L'Università di Napoli

Ogni momento della storia dell'uomo ha i suoi inquinamenti, reali o metaforici. E l'uomo respira sempre l'aria che si merita. Federico II non ama le metafore, ma gli piacciono le immagini che si riferiscono alla tavola e all'alimentazione; non ama l'ozio o i facili divertimenti, ma cerca l'esercizio di ludi aristocratici e intellettuali; non è un tipo che ride facilmente, ma predilige l'allegria cólta dei giovani studenti che fanno la spesa al mercato come semplici cittadini; e, soprattutto, Federico II ama l'aria pura, l'ama talmente che decide di dedicare all'aria un *titulus*, il 48, delle *Costitutiones Regni Siciliae*, emanate nel 1231.

Salubritatem aeris divino iudicio reservatam studio provisionis nostre in quantum possumus disponimus conservare; mandantes ut nulli amodo liceat in aquis cuiuslibet civitatis vel castri vicinis, quantum milliare ad minus protenditur, linum vel canapum ad macerandum ponere, ne ex eo, prout pro certo didicimus, aeris dispositio corrumpatur. Quod si fecerit, linum ipsum immissum et canapum amittat, et curie applicentur. Sepulturas etiam mortuorum quas urne non continent profundas quantum mensura dimidie canne protenditur, esse iubemus. Si quis contra fecerit, unum augustalem curie nostre componat. Cadavera etiam et sordes, que fetorem faciunt per eos quorum fuerint coria extra terram ad quartam partem milliaris vel in mari aut flumine proiici debere mandamus. Si quis autem contra hec fecerit, pro canibus aut magnis animalibus que maiora sunt canibus unum augustalem, pro minoribus vero dimidium curie nostre componat.

La salubrità dell'aria è un dono di Dio e a noi spetta conservarla dando disposizioni precise: si eviti di mettere a macerare all'aperto il lino o la canapa. I corpi dei defunti siano sepolti ben in profondo, quant'è lunga la metà d'una canna; se non basta, ci sono i mari e i fiumi che tutto portano via. L'aria, dunque, è un bene prezioso, come la salute, e chi si dedica a curare il prossimo deve fare studi rigorosi: praticare la logica per tre anni almeno; studiare medicina per cinque anni ed avere esperienze dirette di chirurgia; dopo, il futuro medico dovrà sostenere un impegnativo esame secondo le norme dettate dalla Curia e, infine, potrà accedere alla licenza di "medico." Questo medico visiterà i malati almeno due volte al giorno e, se l'infermo lo richiede, una volta di notte; non dev'essere troppo esoso nel chiedere danaro, non deve fare imbrogli mettendosi d'accordo con i farmacisti che confezionano le medicine, e non deve avere uno studio fisso dove ricevere i clienti più ricchi stabilendo la quantità del compenso ancor prima della visita. Occorre che chi prepara i farmaci lo faccia a spese proprie, secondo le norme dettate dalla legge di Federico, e questi farmaci non potranno essere custoditi più a lungo d'un anno. È necessario che tutti i medici conoscano bene le opere di Ippocrate e di Galeno e chi esercita la pratica della chirurgia deve provare di saperla eseguire offrendo periodicamente un saggio delle proprie capacità di fronte a un collegio di medici che valuterà le conoscenze di anatomia dimostrate dal candidato.

Detto questo nel *titulus* 46 del terzo libro delle *Costitutiones*, Federico aveva già fermato la sua attenzione sul grave *dispendium et irrecuperabile damnum* che possono derivare *ex imperitia medicorum*, al punto che nessuno deve presumere di definirsi "medico" se prima non lo ha dimostrato in presenza del collegio degli archiatri di Salerno, avendo da quelli un attestato scritto da esibire all'imperatore in persona o ad un suo rappresentante. Chi non rispetta questa norma merita un anno di carcere e subisce la confisca dei beni.

Quando Federico II emana queste disposizioni sono ormai passati sette anni dall'Atto di Fondazione dell'Università di Napoli, eppure nello straordinario favore che la critica riserva all'eccezionale stagione storica a culturale riassunta da questo grande protagonista del sapere medievale rimangono alcune zone da chiarire, alcuni tratti oscuri. Le ricerche del Monti, dello Hampe, del grande Haskins, di De Stefano, e del fondamentale editore Huillard-Bréholles hanno già spiegato molto; eppure molto ancora resta da fare, oppure è necessario—come credo—riproporci in modo nuovo problemi forse antichi, forse ancora insoluti. L'edizione dei testi, per esempio, si affianca ad un essenziale sforzo di concettualizzazione, di problematizzazione sui tanti dati eruditi di cui disponiamo.

Sappiamo che l'importanza data nel Regno ai giudici e alle Corti di giustizia provoca l'esigenza d'uno studio approfondito del diritto; è stato detto che da tale esigenza nasce lo *Studium* di Napoli come fucina di formazione dei quadri giuridico-amministrativi dello stato federiciano, con il medesimo sforzo organizzativo che già nell'alto Medioevo aveva caratterizzati il programma scolastico carolingio di Alcuino. Ma poi quando Niccolò Jamsilla ci presenta il *De arte venandi cum avibus* colpisce che la *perspicacitas ingenii* dell'autore, tutta attenta *circa scientiam naturalem, patet in quantum ipse imperator studiosus fuerit philosophiae:* per i medici occorre la *logica*, per gli uccelli e la natura serve la *philosophia.* Non è un caso: un particolarissimo scienziato filosofo del secolo decimo aveva già definito la filosofia come *comprehensio veritatis divinarum et humanarum rerum*, suddividendo la filosofia in pratica e teoretica, e la teoretica in *phisica naturalis, mathematica intellegibilis, theologia intellectualis.* Nella celebre disputa sulla filosofia che Gerberto d'Aurillac ha con Otrico di Magdeburgo nel 981/982 a Ravenna, di fronte ad Ottone III, sono gettate le basi per un'analisi sul concetto di scienza e di filosofia che tutto il Medioevo seguente eredita, vista la diffusione che le fonti, da Richero di Reims in poi, hanno dato al dibattito. In questo senso è certo che il progetto scientifico di Federico II viene da lontano, si salda alla tradizione più rigorosa del sapere medievale e utilizza precedenti dottrine teorico-sperimentali della cultura greco-latina, araba ed ebraica che passa per il tramite di Gerberto d'Aurillac, Costantino Africano, Adalarco di Bath e, nel tempo di Federico, per il personaggio angolare di Michele Scoto fino a compiersi nelle figure di Arnaldo di Villanova e di Ruggero Bacone. Ma prima, per Federico, ci sono le necessità intellettuali e organizzative della Curia e, nel programma del suo sviluppo, c'è l'occasione di affiancare a città di collaudata tradizione culturale, come Salerno, realtà nuove da fondare, com'è il caso di Napoli.

L'*acquisitio scientiae* è un bisogno dell'uomo perché, come ha detto Aristotele, *omnes homines naturaliter scire desiderant* e, come aggiunge Federico nella sua *Encyclica, sine scientia mortalium vita non regitur liberaliter.*

L'*Encyclica* è del 1232: indirizzata ai *magistri in philosophia docentes*, accompagna *quosdam libros sermoniales et mathematicos*, opere in greco e in arabo di Aristotele e altri filosofi, ed ora tradotti, per volontà dell'imperatore, in lingua latina. Questa *Encyclica* è un programma, un manifesto mentale di grande rilievo, eppure è stato talvolta trascurato dalla critica. Nonostante la *turba negociorum* e la *ratio civilis* che impongono a Federico una partecipazione quotidiana molto attiva, egli non trascura di dedicarsi *in exercitationis lectione* e non ammette di restare nell'ozio mentale. Federico dice che i suoi armadi sono stracolmi di libri scritti in tutte le lingue e custodisce con affetto speciale i libri di filosofia e di matematica. La cultura latina non può perdere questo patrimonio necessario al prestigio e alla crescita della scienza, la quale, tenendo a freno la lussuria e neutralizzando i pericoli della cieca ignoranza, impedisce che le energie si disperdano e che, da qui, diventi fiacco lo stesso vigore della giustizia. La committenza intellettuale di Federico trova nell'*Encyclica* la sua formulazione teorica più compiuta: "Voi, famosi alunni della filosofia, voi uomini dotti che sapientemente traete dalle cisterne antiche acque novelle, voi che sapete propinare alle labbra degli assetati sorgenti melliflue di scienza, dovete trasmettere alla comune utilità dei giovani questi testi essenziali alla rifondazione della conoscenza." L'intero passo ha il tono d'un autentico programma d'espansione della cultura:

Considerantes verumtamen quorum conspectibus, quorumque iudiciis operis cepti primitie possent decentius deputari: ecce vobis potissime, velut philosophie preclaris alumnis, de quorum pectoribus promptuaria plena fluunt, libros aliquos quos curiosum studium translatorum et lingua iam potuit fidelis instruere, consulte providimus presentandos vel destinandos. Vos igitur viri docti, qui de cisternis veteribus aquas novas prudenter educitis, qui fluenta melliflua sitientibus labiis propinatis, libros ipsos tanquam exennium amici Cesaris gratanter accipite, et ipsos antiquis philosophorum operibus, qui vocis vestre ministeriis reviviscunt, quorumque nutritis famam, dum dogmata sternitis sapienter ut expedit, aggregantes, eos in auditorio vestro, in quo gratia virtutum fructificat, erroris rubigo consumitur, et latentis scripture varietas aperitur, tum mittentis favore commoniti, tum clari transmissi operis meritis persuasi, ad communem utilitatem studentium et evidentis fame noste preconium publicetis.

Due anni più tardi, Federico comunica a tutti gli studenti presso l'Università di Bologna che ormai lo Studio di Napoli è pronto ad ospitarli e possono *sub securitate et protectione* trasferirsi colà, nella calende di settembre.

L'aria da tutelare, le sorgenti del sapere, l'acqua cui attingere: per Federico lo studio è cibo e i giovani sono un'ipoteca sul futuro. Per questo, dopo l'*Encyclica*, la sua lettera d'invito a Napoli è punteggiata di *topoi* già collaudati nell'Atto di Fondazione. Napoli è *civitas uberrima*, un luogo ricco di *salubritas aeris* dove *doctores theologi, professores utriusque iuris, magistri artium liberalium* sono convocati *ad instituendum et fovendum professionum et scientiarum gymnasia* per ricreare quella *opulentia pacis* e *universitas rerum scolarium* tipiche di ogni città del sapere. Questa è l'ideologia di Federico, la sua proposta *in progress* che, se attuata, gli consentirà di sconfiggere i limiti stessi della biografia, secondo quanto gli auspica Michele Scoto: "Veramente io credo che, se mai uomo in questo mondo potesse sottrarsi alla morte in virtù del suo sapere, tu saresti coluiche prima d'ogni altro dovresti sfuggire alla morte": *O bone imperator, per memetipsum oppinor vehementer quod si unquam fuisset homo in hoc mundo qui per suam doctrinam evasisset mortem, tu es ille qui inter ceteros debuisset evadere.* Nella ricostruzione di questo progetto è fortissimo il dato globalmente umanistico: filosofia, matematica, medicina; latinità, grecità e culture altre concorrono ad una fisionomia aperta dell'universo federiciano che ha nelle quattro stesure dell'Atto del 1224 la sua data d'origine. Ma quale rapporto passa fra la cultura della Magna Curia e il manifesto programmatico dello *Studium* di Napoli? Cosa vale di più per Federico: la cultura della Corte o la scienza prefigurata nel futuro attraverso i piani di studio previsti per gli studenti? Prima di tentare di dare una risposta a queste domande è opportuno cercare di capire bene cosa c'è scritto nelle quattro stesure del 1224, e che cosa di nuovo sia aggiunto nelle altre quattro stesure dell'Atto di riforma, del 1239.

Il regno di Sicilia è ricco e fecondo di frutti, e gli abitanti del Regno non devono essere privati di questi frutti della dottrina, non devono essere costretti a mendicare *aliena suffragia*: trovino invece all'interno dei confini del Regno *paratam mensam propinationis* perché la *nativa fertilitas* della mente ispira *alta consilia*. L'esempio degli antichi è grande: la *clara prioritas* serve da modello, la scoperta che in passato *in regno studia floruisse*, non solo per i figli del sud ma anche per gli stranieri, convincono Federico II a voler ancora respirare la *suavitas odoris* del sapere e rinnovare questa *gratam temperiem antiquorum* secondo la volontà di costituire lo *Studium* di Napoli. La stessa volontà di ripetere—anzi, di far rivivere—l'antico rafforza il peso politico del documento: Napoli, *antiqua mater et domus studii*, toccata dalla *puritate fidei* e dall'*amenitate situs*, Napoli *paranympha scientiae et hospitalaria singularium facultatum*, Napoli che si mostra *gratiosa* verso docenti e discenti. In questo *salubre convivium* sono invitati *hilariter magistros et scholares* e, come nel passato sia a Napoli che a Salerno tutti accorrevano per studiare et *gaudere sunt soliti*, così oggi, nella Napoli di Federico, deve rivivere quel clima: l'internazionalismo di queste proposizioni e della volontà imperiale è rivolto, nella struttura di *epistola*, al Capitanato di Sicilia, a Pietro d'Isernia, a tutti i dotti del tempo, al Giustizierato della Terra di Lavoro.

Il testo delle quattro stesure dell'Atto è molto simile nella scelta dei vocaboli, prodotto di un'attenta e ben esperta cancelleria; variano soltanto le omissioni e i risalti dati. Costanti riferimenti ad immagini di abbondanza (*ubertas victualium, mensa propinationis, fecunditas fertilitatis cibus scientiae*), eguali sono anche i rimandi al modello degli antichi. Nella terza stesura dell'Atto, quella indirizzata *archiepiscopis, episcopis et aliis ecclesiarum prelatis, marchionibus, comitibus, baronibus, iusticiariis, camerariis, comestabulis, baiulis, iudicibus et universis per regnum Siciliae constitutis* Federico è più esplicito: i *famelici et ieiuni doctrinarum* potranno soddisfare la loro *aviditas* senza *mendicare in alienis regionibus* i princìpi del sapere. *Hilares et prompti satis ad professiones*, gli studenti educati nel dolce clima e nella bellezza di Napoli saranno in grado di preparare un'età ancora più bella. A Napoli, peraltro, è facile arrivare: per terra o per mare c'è posto per tutti, il luogo è sicuro e chi si sentirà stanco e affaticato per un'esistenza condotta fra i rischi e le incertezze, troverà a Napoli motivi nuovi per scoprire che il sapere libera da ogni privazione, da tutte le angustie e i disagi.

Credo sia molto interessante accostare i testi di questa quadruplice stesura.

I

Sollicitudo continua curas nostras exagitat, qualiter regnum nostrum Sicilie, naturaliter rerum victualium ubertate fecundum, prudentum virorum copia nostris temporibus artificialiter decoremus; ut fideles nostri regnicole scientiarum fructus, quos indesinenter esuriunt, per aliena mendicare suffragia non coacti, paratam in regno sibi mensam propinationis inveniant: et quos ingeniorum nativa fertilitas ad consilia reddit alta conspicuos, literarum scientia faciat eruditos. Ad quod licet progenitorum nostrorum nos clara prioritas invitet exemplis, dum eorum temporibus sic diversarum scientiarum in regno studia floruisse comperimus, ut non solum ad incolas filios, sed ad extraneos etiam extendisse probetur suavitatem odoris; nos tamen super hoc tanto libentius sine cuiusquam inductione concurrimus quanto per hoc utilius honori nostro consulere credimus, et exaltationem omnimodam regni nostri omni qua possumus diligentia procuramus. Volentes itaque super hoc antiquorum gratam renovare temperiem, et regni nostri fastigia tripudialibus novitatis nostre principiis augmentare, universale studium in civitate nostra Neapolis, consulta nuper deliberatione, providimus reformandum: ut civitas ipsa antiqua mater et domus studii, sicut puritate fidei et situs amenitate prefulget, sic renovata quasi paranympha scientie et singularium hospitalaria facultatum, docentibus et addiscentibus se prebeat gratiosam. Ad hoc igitur tam salubre convivium magistros quoslibet et scholares hilariter invitamus; fidelitati tue mandantes quatenus presens beneplacitum nostrum per iurisdictionem tuam solemniter studeas publicare, firmam singulis fiduciam oblaturus quod immunitates et libertates omnes, quibus olim tam in Neapolitano quam in Salernitano studio uti et gaudere sunt soliti, faciemus universis et singulis illuc ire volentibus inviolabiliter observari.

II

Noster instanter, quem in subditorum semper emolumenta dirigimus, sollicitatur affectus, qualiter regni nostri Sicilie preclara possessio, sicut rerum ubertate victualium ad dispositionem divini numinis natura profluente tripudiat, sic ad nostre provisionis edictum virorum perfectione scientium, fortuna favente, valeat fecundari. Ad quos etsi progenitorum nostrorum nos memoranda prioritas invitet exemplis, dum diversarum scientiarum doctores dudum in regno comperimus et multos artium liberalium munimentis provectos ad ardua, quos innata ruditas honoris et glorie reddidisset indignos, sic nos super his et priorum tempora reviviscere volumus ut que per intervalla quantalibet quassata videntur, iam passa desidiam sub iuventutis nostre primordiis similiter iuvenescant: ac dum fideles nostri regnicole paratam sibi mensam propinationis inspexerint, non solum supervacuum sibi reputent aliena proinde flagitare suffragia, sed gloriosum existiment extraneos alios ad gratitudinis huiusmodi participium evocare. Cumque civitatem Neapolitanam, antiquam utique matrem et domum studii, tam marine vicinitatis habilitas quam terrene fertilitatis fecunditas reddant utiliter tanto negocio congruentem, generale studium in civitate ipsa mandavimus reformari, ut quam localis amenitas plenitudine rerum gratificat, docentibus et addiscentibus undique collecta commoditas efficiat gratiosam.

III

Fredericus Dei gratia Romanorum imperator et semper augustus, Jerusalem et Sicilie rex, archiepiscopis, episcopis et aliis ecclesiarum prelatis, marchionibus, comitibus, baronibus, iusticiariis, camerariis, comestabulis, baiulis, iudicibus et universis per regnum Sicilie constitutis, fidelibus suis, presentes litteras inspecturis gratiam suam et bonam voluntatem. Deo propitio, per quem vivimus et regnamus, cui omnes actus nostros offerimus, cui omne quod agimus imputamus, in regnum nostrum desideramus multos prudenter et providos fieri per scientiarum haustum et seminarium doctrinarum: qui facti discreti per studium et per observationem iusti Deo serviant, cui serviunt omnia, et nobis placeant per cultum iusticie, cuius preceptis omnes precipimus obedire. Disponimus autem apud Neapolim, amenissimam civitatem, doceri artes cuiuscunque professionis et vigere studia: ut ieiuni et famelici doctrinarum in ipso regno inveniant unde ipsorum aviditati satisfiat, neque compellantur ad investigandas scientias peregrinas nationes expetere, nec in alienis regionibus mendicare. Bonum autem hoc rei nostre publice profuturum intendimus, cum subiectorum commoda speciali quadam affectionis gratia providemus, quos sicut convenit eruditos pulcherrima poterit spes fovere, et bona plurima promptis animis expectare; cum sterilis esse non possit accessio, quam nobilitas sequitur. Cum tribunalia preparantur, sequuntur lucra divitiarum, favor et gratia comparantur. Insuper studiosos viros ad servitia nostra, non sine meritis et laudibus, convocamus, secure illis qui discreti fuerunt per instantiam studii, iuris et iusticie regimina committentes. Hilares igitur et prompti satis ad professiones quas scholares desiderant animentur, quibus ad inhabitandum eum locum concedimus, ubi rerum copia, ubi ample domus et spatiose satis, et ubi mores civium sunt benigni; ubi etiam necessaria vite hominum per terras et maritimas facile transvehuntur, quibus per nos ipsos utilitates querimus, conditiones disponimus, magistros investigamus, bona promittimus, et eis quos dignos viderimus donaria conferemus. Illos siquidem in conspectu parentum suorum ponimus, a multis laboribus liberamus, a longis itineribus et quasi peregrinis absolvimus: illos tutos facimus ab insidiis predatorum; et qui spoliabantur fortunis suis et rebus, longa terrarum spacia peragrantes, scholas suas levioribus sumptibus et brevioribus cursibus a liberalitate nostra se gaudeant assecutos. De numero autem doctorum, quos ibi duximus destinandos, mittimus magistrum R. de Benevento iudicem et magistrum Petrum de Ysernia, fideles nostros, civilis scientie professores, viros magne scientie, note virtutis et fidelis experientie, quam nostre semper exhibuerunt et exhibent maiestati, de quibus, sicut de aliquibus regni nostri fidelibus, fiduciam gerimus pleniorem.

Volumus igitur et mandamus vobis omnibus qui provincias regitis, quique administrationibus presidetis ut hec omnia passim et publice proponatis, et iniungatis sub pena personarum et rerum ut nullus scholaris legendi causa exire audeat extra regnum, nec infra regnum aliquis addiscere audeat alibi vel docere: et qui de regno sunt extra regnum in scholis, sub pena predicta eorum parentibus iniungatis ut usque ad festum Sancti Michaelis nunc proximo revertantur. Conditiones autem quas scholaribus concedimus erunt iste: in primis, quod in civitate predicta doctores et magistri erunt in qualibet facultate. Scholares autem, undecunque venerint, secure veniant morando, stando et redeundo, tam in personis quam in rebus nullam sentientes in aliquo lesionem. Hospitium quod melius in civitate fuerit scholaribus locabitur, pro duarum unciarum auri annua pensione, nec ultra extimatio eius ascendet. Infra predictam autem summam et usque ad illam, omnia hospitia extimatione duorum civium et duorum scholarium locabuntur. Mutuum fiet scholaribus ab illis qui ad hoc fuerint ordinati, secundum quod eis necesse fuerit, datis libris in pignore et precario restitutis, receptis a scholaribus fideiussoribus pro eisdem. Scholaris vero qui mutuum recipiet, iurabit quod de terra aliquatenus non recedet, donec precaria restituet, vel mutuum ab eo fuerit exsolutum, vel alias satisfactum fuerit creditori. Predicta autem precaria a creditoribus non revocabuntur, quam diu scholares voluerint in studio permanere. Item omnes scholares in civilibus sub eisdem doctoribus et magistris debeant conveniri. Omnes igitur amodo, qui studere voluerint in aliqua facultate, vadant Neapolim ad studendum, et nullus ausus sit pro scholis extra regnum exire, vel infra regnum in aliis scholis addiscere vel docere: et qui sunt de regno extra regnum in scholis, usque ad festum Sancti Michaelis proximum venturum sine mora dispendio revertantur. De frumento autem, vino, carnibus, piscibus, et aliis que ad victum pertinent, modum nullum statuimus, cum in his omnibus abundet provincia.

IV

Etsi ad perfectionem studii generalis, quod nuper in civitate Neapoli providimus reformandum, particularia studia ubique per regnum mandaverimus interdici, nostre tamen intentionis non fuit sic loca quelibet depauperare doctoribus, ut artis saltem grammatice rudimenta noviciis, velut lactantis matris ubera famelicis infantibus, precidantur: sed ad illos tantum extendi volumus nostre serenitatis edictum, qui auditoribus suis, ruditate deposita, in facultatibus aliis ingenia potiora petentibus, cibos iam possint scientie solidos ministrare. Propter quod fidelitati tue precipiendo mandamus, quatenus magistris quibuslibet, qui per terram iurisditionis tue pueros in artis grammatice primitiis edocent, nullam occasione predicta molestiam inferas, sed particularia eorum studia regere sine impedimento quolibet patiaris.

Roffredo di Benevento e Pietro d'Isernia hanno carta bianca nell'essere i punti di riferimento di questa nuova costruzione intellettuale. Gli studenti, poi, troveranno condizioni di vita ottimali: docenti per ogni tipo di studio; la possibilità di risiedere, andare e venire in tutta sicurezza personale. Saranno alloggiati meglio che a casa loro, con uno stipendio di due once d'oro all'anno; saranno loro dati in prestito libri con l'obbligo della frequenza alle lezioni e con l'obbligo di non studiare al di fuori di questa città, dove la facilità di trovare pane, vino, carne, pesce e tutto quanto può rendere ricca la tavola darà modo agli studenti di sentirsi a casa loro anche quando andranno a fare la spesa al mercato. Così i *famelici infantes* del mondo universitario di Federico si prepareranno ad essere i protagonisti della nuova gestione amministrativa e scientifica dello stato. *Cum tribunalia preparantur, sequuntur lucra divitiarum*: questo è il teorema da dimostrare e qui agisce la riforma degli studi di Federico; e questo è il mondo in cui egli crede. Il *cibus* della *scientia* è *solidus*, non soffre i capricci della politica e gli *studia particularia* consentono di affrontare *sine impedimento* qualsiasi imprevisto. Eppure, forse, Federico insegue un sogno.

La limpidezza di tali affermazioni ideologiche, redatte nel lucidissimo latino di Pier della Vigna—che, però, non è certo il "massimo stilista latino del Medioevo" (Kantorowicz)—confina con l'utopia e appartiene tutta al disegno intellettuale dell'imperatore. La Napoli del 1224 è certo una creatura di Federico, ma sullo sfondo di questa identità c'è sempre un persistente riferimento al modello degli antichi. Federico sa che, nell'alto e centrale Medioevo, Napoli e Salerno hanno avuto un ruolo determinante per la cultura nel Mediterraneo. Napoli come frontiera di latinità e grecità, testimoniata attraverso le scuole dei traduttori funzionanti fino nella costa d'Amalfi; Salerno, tanto vicina e protagonista di questa identica realtà, arricchita dal primato d'essere la più antica Scuola Medica d'Europa, dalla fine dell'ottavo secolo, e dove nel secolo decimoprimo le due personalità di Alfano I e di Costantino Africano rendono possibile uno sviluppo internazionalista della cultura salernitana in cui agiscono, accanto alla tradizione cassinese, recuperi arabi e indoeuropei la cui portata è ancora da studiare, specialmente nelle sue fasi più "alte" situabili, negli anni che vanno dalla fine del secolo decimo ai primi quindici anni del decimosecondo. In questo senso la Napoli di Federico II è il punto d'arrivo d'una evoluzione intellettuale cominciata molti decenni prima, ancor prima della venuta dei Normanni in Italia, accanto ai primi scambi di presenze che avvengono nel mondo cassinese. Già altrove ho studiato questo fenomeno e non voglio qui ripetermi, ma non è un caso che Arnaldo di Villanova, attivo a Napoli nei primi dieci anni del Trecento e insegnante presso lo *Studium*, abbia il ruolo di sistematore della lunga eredità dei *Regimina sanitatis* che, da Salerno, passano dentro la cultura scientifica federiciana e si fissano nella grande opera critico-esegetica del sapiente spagnolo. Fra le due estremità di Salerno e di Arnaldo da Villanova sta la stagione federiciana, con le sue ascendenze e i suoi esiti, entrata in contatto con questi saperi, anzi movimentandoli, suggerendo ad essi caratteri essenziali.

L'apertura dello *Studium* di Napoli data al 29 settembre 1224, giorno della festa di San Michele; si tratta d'uno *studium*, perché il termine *universitas* indica una collettività, un gruppo di individui organizzati in un quadro sociale preciso, e nei testi federiciani il concetto di *universitas* denota questa collettività eterogenea di docenti/discenti che, insieme, vivano un fatto intellettuale comune; non quindi un'università nel senso della struttura, ma un'università definita come totalità d'intenti. Nell'idea federiciana, pur rispettando lo schema "città d'abitanti = città di studenti," si vuole anche rafforzare la vocazione scientifica di una istituzione in linea con gli interéssi dell'imperatore così cólto e così esperto di trattatistica-greco-araba e di testi medico-naturalistici. La critica ha ampiamente dimostrato come questa Napoli diventi un centro promotore d'iniziative autonome e ricettore di correnti culturali esterne, e come proprio a medici di corte sia affidata la custodia della biblioteca regia che negli stessi anni vede avviata la sua formazione.

Percorsi sperimentali e dottrinali, quindi, che dal Mezzogiorno mediterraneo cassinese latino raggiungono un Mezzogiorno mediterraneo non più solo cassinese, ma greco, ebraico ed arabo, proprio come i quattro mitici fondatotori dell'*hyppocratica civitas* salernitana. Michele Scoto muore nel 1235 e nello stesso anno muore anche quel Nicola-Nettario, del Monastero di Casole, la cui importanza—come ha dimostrato il Berschin—non è minore di quella del maestro del *Liber Introductorius*. Il rapporto latinità/grecità che passa nell'opera di questi due intellettuali, attivi in piena età federiciana, arricchisce di forti direzioni interdisciplinari e internazionali il progetto universitario di Federico operante su Napoli. Certo Federico II/Michele Scoto è l'altro complesso binomio che può affiancarsi al più noto Federico II/Pier della Vigna; entrambi rapporti intensi e drammatici, il primo connotato da un discepolato dell'imperatore verso il filosofo risolutore di quesiti essenziali—come ha illustrato Haskins con grande autorità—il secondo intrecciatosi alla quotidianità della vita politica e, quindi, più esposto alle dispari vicende del Regno.

Intanto, a distanza di quindici anni dal manifesto ideologico scolastico del 1224, Federico ci consegna altre quattro stesure di lettera par la rifondazione dello *Studium generale* di Napoli: indirizzate, nel 1239, ai docenti e ai discenti; ad Andrea di Cicala, giustiziere incaricato di provvedere alla sicurezza ed alle comodità degli studenti; a Bartolomeo Pignatelli, chiamato per il riordino dello Studio ad insegnare e commentare le *Decretali* dello stesso Federico; infine, la lettera è indirizzata al clero, ai baroni, ai giudici, ai baiuli, ai militi *et universo populo Neapolis*. Eppure fra 1224 e 1239 la storia dello *Studium* non è uniforme, né così toccata dal favore che Federico aveva sperato. Nel 1229 registriamo la prima chiusura dello Studio allorché le truppe pontificie occupano il Regno. Nel 1234 un tentativo di nuova apertura dello *Studium* con quell'invito agli studenti bolognesi dove si disegna l'immagine della città culla di benessere ambientale e intellettuale:

Fridericus, Dei gratia Romanorum imperator semper augustus, Ierusalem et Sicilie rex, universis scolaribus Bononie commorantibus, dilectis suis, gratiam suam et bonam voluntatem. Imperii Romani solio dispensante Domino presidentes, etsi ad publica mundi negotia ex commisso nobis onerum et honorum officio debita sollicitudine teneamur, inter universales tamen reipublice curas quibus imperialis sedes vehementius occupatur, non dedignamur ad specialia commoda singulorum nostre mentis aciem inclinare, ut qui milites nostros arma scire volumus et non leges, velimus viros scientiarum et cuiuslibet professionis amicos, quorum eloquentia nostrum decorat imperium, nichilominus in ipsis nostro tam opere quam sermone proficere ac virtutis acquisite meritis et consilio militare, cum non minus scientia quam qualitate virorum imperii ac regnorum moderamina disponantur. Statutum ergo olim studium aput Neapolim civitatem uberrimam et locum in regno nostro salubritate aeris in quibuslibet oportunitatibus preelectum, cordi nobis est in integrum reformare. Cuius reformationi non dubitetis nos efficacem operam adhibere, cum in instanti per litteras nostras et nuncios doctores theologos ac utriusque iuris professores ac magistros quarumlibet artium liberalium ad instituendum et fovendum quarumlibet professionum et scientiarum in eadem civitate gymnasia convocemus, libertatibus et immunitatibus universis necnon consuetudinibus scolaribus approbatis iuxta priorem concessionem indultam tam doctoribus quam docendis per documenta publica confirmandis. Itaque cuiuslibet professionis doctores in civitate predicta confidimus in kalendas proximi venturi mensis septembris sine dilatione qualibet convenire ut apto tempore ferventioris studii regimen prosequantur. Cum igitur plerique vestrum ex predicti loci experientia non ignorent quanta singulis ibidem studentibus oportunitas famuletur quantave pacis opulentia et rerum copia universitas scolarium consuevit habundare, et subprobatur doctoribus et facundis spes leta proficiendi, quemlibet animamus et universitatem vestram ad idem studium invitamus; prudentie vestre mandantes quatinus confidenter et unanimiter ad predictam civitatem sub securitate et protectione nostri culminis vos conferre curetis prevenientes tempore iam studio quam studentibus oportuno. Gratiam enim nostram favorabilem et benignam adventus inveniet singulorum, et promptiorem curam vestris profectibus impendemus. Cives insuper exercitio studii precedentis vestris quodammodo assuefactos moribus et conformes ad commoditates vestras benevolos habebitis et attentos; et sic dante Deo nichil in studio vobis deerit ad profectum, nec inquietari poterit vestra tranquillitas favoris nostri robore premunita.

E da ultimo, nel 1239, il 14 novembre, *ad supplicationem magistrorum et scholarium Neapolis*, l'effettiva riapertura, interdetta però ai ribelli di Milano, Brescia, Piacenza, Alessandria, Bologna, Ravenna e Treviso:

Fredericus magistris et scolaribus Neapolis. Conceptum dudum serenitatis nostre propositum circa Neapolitani studii debitum incrementum oblivisci non patitur votum nostrum, quin ipsum tamquam manuum nostrarum structuram memorabilem posteris et generaliter omnibus fructuosam prosecutione laudabili prosequamur et firmamento stabili quolibet eventu firmemus, ex quo non tantum subiectorum nostrorum propenso consilio profectum multifarie vidimus procurari dum in regno nostro liberalium artium vigerent studia, quam fame et posteritati nostre dignius fore consultum. Et ut exuberante gratia ad omne firmamentum ipsius excellentia nostra evidenter ostenderet, non solum in urbe nostra Neapolis tam amoenissima et formosa, cui terra et mare deserviunt, ipsius sedem locavimus et cultum indiximus generalem, quam etiam magnis immunitatibus decorare magistros et omnem cetum scolarium nostra munificentia non ommisit. Cumque nuper nos in Italia circa depopulationes nostrorum rebellium magnifice moraremur in castris, nuncios vestros magistrum G. de Antiochia et T. de Cremona fideles nostros ad nostram presentiam destinatos benigne recepimus et petitiones vestras in sinu clementie nostre clementer admisimus; et inter tot occupationum genera quibus nostra munificentia trahebatur, non inspecta presentis temporis qualitate, tamquam studii et virtutum quarumlibet zelatores, ad ordinationem et cultum Neapolitani studii direximus aciem mentis nostre, et quantum honori nostro, qualitati temporis et indempnitati vestre vidimus ad presens posse consulere, libenter in petitionibus vestris duximus annuendum. Statuimus igitur et presenti iussione decernimus ut omnibus fidelibus nostris regnicolis regnorum nostrorum Ierusalem et Sicilie ad nominatum studium licitus sit accessus et mora. Ultramontanos etiam infra presentem gratiam nostram volumus contineri, ut eis liceat predictas scholas appetere et ibidem studendo morari. Italicos etiam infra presens mandatum de terris que nobis et imperio famulantur volumus comprehendi; Mediolanensibus, Brixiensibus, Placentinis, Alexandrinis, Bononiensibus, Faventinis, Ravennatibus ac Trevesinis nostris et imperii rebellibus exceptis omnino, quibus omnem nostre maiestatis gratiam denegamus. Ad Tuscos autem, Marchesanos, omnes de ducatu Spoleti et etiam Campaninos presentem immunitatis nostre gratiam extendi decernimus, volentes studiorum Neapolis limina visitare, de terris illis scilicet que H. karissimo filio nostro regi Turrium et Gallure misso de latere nostro generaliter legato in Italiam fideliter adheserunt, aliis qui restiterunt eidem et pape subsunt dominio et quoquomodo sequuntur eumdem factorem schismatis et erroris presenti gratia denegata. Vos igitur sic presentem munificentie nostre gratiam ad maiestatis nostre personam, honorem et fidelitatem nostram respectum habentes debitum, animo fideli recipite. Civibus etiam Neapolis fidelibus nostris decentius et modestius solito convivatis, ut et vobis cedat ad commodum et profectum voti quod geritis, et nos tam de fide vestra erga nostram excellentiam, quam etiam de processu ac incremento studii per effectum operis et exhibitionem devotionis et fidei merito gaudeamus.

Nel 1240 la facoltà di Teologia è sconvolta a causa dell'espulsione dal Regno dei Frati Minori e dei Domenicani. Nel 1252 Corrado IV, volendo far rivivere i fasti scientifici di Salerno, sposta lo *Studium* nell'antica capitale del Principato longobardo; e soltanto con Manfredi, fra 1258 e 1259, lo *Studium* torna a funzionare. Dunque una storia accidentata, i cui segni restano nel tono di quell'Atto di tentata rifondazione, del 1239, caratterizzato, per contrasto di vocaboli, dallo stile stesso dell'*Epistola*. In una situazione politica incerta, in un malessere sociale diffuso, Federico fa appello ad un *firmamentum stabile* del tutto inesistente; usa di preferenza il verbo *firmare* e *decorare*; cerca una *benignitas* che non c'è nell'aria assai poco respirabile, adesso, degli eventi storici maturati nelle ribellioni dell'Italia settentrionale. Quell'utopia d'internazionalismo ricercata per lo *Studium* sembra smentita nei fatti, smentita proprio con questa esclusione delle province del nord. L'*hilariter* diventa un *libenter* e la città, sempre *amoenissima et formosa*, risente della vicinanza delle *depopulationes nostrorum rebellium*. I *fideles regnicoli* sono affiancati da un *papa factor schismatis et erroris*. La oggettiva complessità del momento si fa ancora più difficile se pensiamo che quell'Andrea di Cicala, chiamato a provvedere alla qualità della vita degli studenti, diventa sette anni più tardi uno dei protagonisti della Congiura di Grosseto, ordita insieme a Guglielmo di Sanseverino, Giacomo di Morra, Pandolfo di Fasanella e Tibaldo Francesco. I tempi cambiano: i *fideles* di ieri sono diventati i traditori di oggi. Ieri Federico mandava una lettera ai dottori e agli studenti di Bologna perché si adoperassero a far copiare nei loro codici quelle leggi e disposizioni emanate nel giorno dell'incoronazione:

Fridericus Romanorum imperator et semper augustus, universis sacrarum legum doctoribus et scolaribus Bononie commorantibus salutem et gratiam suam. Ad honorem omnipotentis Dei et Ecclesie sancte sue, in die quo de manu sacratissimi patris nostri H. summi pontificis suscepimus imperii diadema, edidimus quasdam leges quas presenti pagina fecimus adnotari, per imperialia vobis scripta mandantes quatenus eas faciatis in vestris scribi codicibus et de cetero legatis solempniter tamquam perpetuis temporibus valituras.

Oggi quei dotti e quei discepoli sono esclusi dal nuovo programma. Sono forse i primi segni della fine del sogno di Federico?

Il progetto Napoli conosce, nella lunga stagione della Corte, momenti pari e momenti dispari: non è un'affermazione sicura di continuità, perché Napoli, così vicina a Roma, così peninsulare e tanto presente nelle cose d'Italia, questa Napoli non è Palermo, e quello che riesce là, oltre lo Stretto, dentro la Magna Curia, può non essere egualmente proponibile altrove. Ma Napoli non è Palermo: troppo differenti le condizioni d'esercizio della cultura nei due centri federiciani. Napoli è il progetto, Palermo è la sede del potere. In questo dissidio il meraviglioso fiore di Federico comincia a marcire. Saba Malaspina, uno dei massimi critici dell'azione dello *stupor mundi*, uno dei recensori più acuti di questo *vir inquisitor et sapientiae amator*, come lo definisce Manfredi, Saba Malaspina non ha dubbi: nel progressivo blocco dei meccanismi politici e istituzionali dell'azione federiciana va letto anche l'avvicinarsi di una più generale crisi del Regno. Saba scrive così:

Sed auditu mirabile! Iste Caesar, qui fuerat in orbe monarcha, et per universa mundi climata coeperat venerari, credens fortassis suam per artis experientiam mathematicae coaequare naturam, qui mores ante lapsum erroris cum magnis aequaret, studuit rerum opiniones sollecita curiositate perquirere, ac profunde coelestia perscrutari; sicque dum subtili indagatione naturalia vestigabat, astrologos et nigromanticos adeo venerabatur et aruspices, quod eorum divinationibus et auspiciis Friderici velocissima cogitatio ad similitudinem venti motu celeri denuo vagabatur.

Credendo di poter eguagliare la natura di Dio soltanto con la sua *ars mathematica*, arte della conoscenza, indagando i segreti della natura e onorando astrologi e negromanti, Federico *lapsus est in laquem improvisum*, cadde nel laccio improvviso in cui ogni creatura è destinata a restare impigliata. D'altro canto già nell'*Encyclica* Federico aveva teorizzato che senza il sapere la vita non conosce libertà: gli armadi e i libri sono la scorta d'una ricchezza tutta intellettuale che, al suo eccesso, ha un laicismo senza umiltà. Ma il messaggio culturale di quel passo dell'*Encyclica* convince ancor oggi per la grandezza e la genialità della visione:

Dum librorum ergo volumina, quorum multifarie multisque modis distincta chirographa nostrarum armaria divitiarum locupletant, sedula meditatione revolvimus, et accurata contemplatione pensamus, compilationes varie ab Aristotele aliisque philosophis, sub grecis arabicisque vocabulis antiquitus edite in sermonialibus et mathematicis disciplinis, nostris aliquando sensibus occurrerunt; quas adhuc originalium dictionum ordinatione consertas, et vetustarum vestium, quas eis etas prima concesserat, operimento contectas, vel hominis defectus aut operis ad latine lingue noticiam non perduxit. Volentes igitur ut veneranda tantorum operum simul authoritas apud nos, non absque multorum commodis communibus, vocis organo traductione innotescat, ea per viros electos et in utriusque lingue prolatione peritos instanter iussimus, verborum fideliter servata virginitate, transferri.

Ma il mondo, dopo Federico, non ripete più la stessa parabola di sapienze. Non saprei dire, infatti, se Federico sia più grande se inteso come punto d'arrivo del Medioevo oppure come inizio d'una età nuova. Forse in lui si sommano entrambe le funzioni, anche se sembra più difficile portare a compimento un Medioevo già tutto in espansione, piuttosto che preannunciare il secondo Duecento dove ancora tante cose sono destinate a maturare e quasi sempre nel segno tracciato da Federico. Una conclusione possibile è questa: la *Magna Curia* sembra una realtà più stabile e irripetibile di quanto non sia stato lo *Studium* di Napoli che, con Angioini e Aragonesi, conosce altre fasi alterne di splendore.

La leggenda negativa che nasce intorno alle figure di Federico e di Michele Scoto—così come il De Stefano l'ha precisamente ripercorsa per dati essenziali—non riguarda mai la corte di Palermo dove almeno due generazioni di sapienti d'ogni provenienza si sono riconosciute anche nel risolvere raffinati ludi intellettuali del tipo di quelli che lo stesso Federico propone al suo filosofo sapiente, Michele Scoto, nell'*epistola* che tanto ha interessato lo Haskins, riportata nel *Liber Particularis*. La verità resta nel fatto che la Corte fabbrica i quesiti federiciani, apre le porte a matematici arabi e a Leonardo Fibonacci, inaugura conoscenze nuove di astronomia e astrologia che, sull'esempio di Enrico Aristippo ed Eugenio l'Emiro, portano a nuova gloria l'*Almagesto* tolemaico e le sapienze dei maghi; poi, l'igiene, le acque termali e la cura del corpo sembrano far rivivere le pratiche salernitane. Accanto alla diffusione dell'Aristotele commentato da Averroè e delle opere di Avicenna, di Al-Farabi, di Maimonide e di Alpetragio sembra rimanere poco spazio per le crisi d'identità, anche perché, intanto, il *De arte venandi*, i poeti, gli epistolografi e i giuristi fanno completo il quadro di questo universo enciclopedico che ruota attorno all'enciclopedismo di Federico.

Ma Napoli è altra cosa: l'impianto dello *Studium* richiede una struttura funzionale ad uno scopo, che non subisca attacchi dall'esterno; e non bastano i ventuno docenti di diritto, né Terrisio d'Atina, Gualtiero d'Ascoli, Maestro Martino, Nicola di Rocca. Il manifesto scientifico che leggiamo nel Proemio del *De arte venandi cum avibus* ha, nei suoi fondamenti, la calma d'una lunga ricerca troppo lontana dalla prontezza che l'avvio dello Studio di Napoli richiedeva: "Ho differito per circa trent'anni la redazione di quest'opera perché non mi sentivo preparato a sufficienza. Ho cercato con diligenza tutto ciò che sarebbe stato utile trattare nel libro . . .": *cum sollicitudine et studio* Federico prepara il *De arte venandi*, pur travolto nei difficili e intricati affari del governo del suo regno:

Nos tamen, licet proposuissemus ex multo tempore ante componere presens opus, distulimus fere per triginta annos propositum in scripto redigere, quoniam non putabamus nos sufficere, nec legeramus unquam aliquem precessisse, qui huius libri materiam complete tractasset, particule vero aliquot ab aliquibus per solum usum scite erant et inartificialiter tradite. Ideo multis temporibus cum sollicitudine et studio diligenti inquisivimus ea, que huius artis erant, exercitantes nos mente et opere in eadem, ut tandem sufficeremus redigere in librum, quicquid nostra experientia aut aliorum didicerat, quos, quia erant experti circa praticam huius artis, non sine magnis dispendiis ad nos vocavimus de longinquo vocatosque undecumque nobiscum habuimus, deflorando quicquid melius noverant eorumque dicta et facta memorie commendando.

È scritto così nel Proemio del *De arte venandi*: vi affiora una quieta *experientia* ben diversa dall'urgente programma di restaurazione dei quadri scolastici che regola gli Atti di Napoli. In realtà esiste una sostanziale lontananza fra il clima della *Magna Curia* e l'aria non più pura dello *Studium*: la prima è una realtà costante ed espansiva, la seconda è un'organizzazione di grandi risultati spesso intermittenti, vittima delle situazioni politiche e dei mutamenti di consenso. La testimonianza di Salimbene, in tal senso, è molto eloquente:

. . . Cum imperatore Friderico secundo, qui multa mala fecit Ecclesie Dei, que eum nutrivit et coronavit . . . et postea contra Ecclesiam levavit calcaneum, eam multipliciter affligendo . . . Dominus imperator Fridericus misit elefantem in Lombardiam cum pluribus dromedariis et camelis et cum multis leopardis et cum multis gerfalcis et asturibus. Et transierunt per Parmam, ut vidi oculis meis.

Un re degno della tradizione di Alessandro e di quell'*Historia*, un re che provocò ribellioni dovunque e fu scomunicato mentre un'eclissi calava sul mondo:

Item in historia Alexandri filii Philippi regis Macedonie legitur quod ipse rex Alexander habuit in exercitu suo centum elefantos . . . Excommunicatus est Fridericus imperator a papa Gregorio nono. . . . Facta est solis eclipsis, in qua sol orribiliter et terribiliter obscuratus fuit; et stelle apparuerunt, ut vidi oculis meis ego frater Salimbene de Parma.

Salimbene, come Saba Malaspina, collabora al mito negativo di Federico mentre Napoli con il suo *Studium*, aperto-chiuso-riaperto, sembra riuscire a fabbricare, nonostante tutto, un eguale mito positivo.

Perché nonostante tutto, la forza di quegli Atti di fondazione e rifondazione rimane intatta: nei tempi lunghi si dimostra davvero come l'avvio d'una nuova età che Manfredi riesce a ripetere almeno in parte. L'aria di Napoli non è più quella voluta dal sogno di Federico: l'amenità, la bellezza della città sono quasi scomparse; eppure vi si studiano ancor oggi quelle lingue indoeuropee e orientali che Federico sentiva come un patrimonio di cui la latinità occidentale doveva impadronirsi. La scienza del diritto vi è ancora esercitata secondo l'aulica tradizione. La promozione di quella scienza forse non è bastata al compimento del programma di Federico e i medici salernitani non riuscirono a guarirlo dalla dissenteria. Né la sua *ars*, erede diretta della *mathesis* medievale, riesce ad evitargli la fine. Eppure con la scomparsa di Federico inizia, forse, la lezione della sua eredità; in questa potremo trovare nuovi elementi del suo genio che ha avuto una qualità su cui il Medioevo si può dichiarare chiuso: il primato della sperimentazione scientifica, il prevalere della logica sulla teologia; e il malessere esistenziale e dottrinale di Michele Scoto ne resta una prova. Nell'età di Federico II la cultura, pur toccando vertici irripetuti, denuncia già tutta la drammaticità e lo smarrimento del ricambi o intellettuale per un Medioevo ormai giunto, nel culmine, alla sua fine.

BIBLIOGRAFIA

Testi

Federico di Svevia. *De arte venandi cum avibus*, edizione Carl A. Willemsen, 2 voll. Leipzig, 1942.

Historia Diplomatica Friderici Secundi, edizione Jean L. A. Huillard-Bréholles, 6 voll. Paris, 1852–1861.

Pier della Vigna. *Vie et correspondance de Pierre de la Vigne*, edizione Jean L. A. Huillard-Bréholles. Paris, 1865.

Saba Malaspina. *Rerum Siculorum Historia*. In Ludovico Antonio Muratori, Rerum Italicarum Scriptores, vol. 8; poi in G. Del Re, *Cronisti e scrittori sincroni napoletani* (Napoli, 1868), 2:205–408.

Salimbene de Adam. *Cronica*, edizione G. Scalia, 2 voll. Bari, 1966.

Studi

Da questi studi è possibile risalire a bibliografie più specializzate sui singoli argomenti.

Abulafia, David. *Frederick II: A Medieval Emperor*. London, 1988; *Federico II. Un imperatore medievale*. Torino, 1990.

Cattaneo, G. *Lo specchio del mondo. Federico II di Svevia*. Milano, 1974.

Cilento, N. *Civiltà napoletana del Medioevo nei secoli VI–XIII*. Napoli, 1969.

De Stefano, Antonino. *La cultura alla corte di Federico II imperatore*. Palermo, 1938.

Haskins, Charles Homer. *Studies in the History of Medieval Science*, 2° ed. Cambridge, Mass., 1927.

Kantorowicz, Ernst. *Federico II imperatore*. Milano, 1976 (edizione originale Berlin, 1928); *Frederick the Second*. London, 1931.

Monti, G. M. *Per la storia dell'Università di Napoli*. Napoli, 1924.

Oldoni, Massimo. "La *Hyppocratica Civitas* e le relazioni culturali fra Napoli, Salerno e il Mediterraneo." In *Luoghi e metodi di insegnamento nell'Italia medievale (secc. XII–XIV)*. Galatina, 1989.

Oldoni, Massimo. *La cultura latina*. In *Storia e civiltà della Campania*, vol. 2, *Il Medioevo*, a cura di G. Pugliese Carratelli, 295–400, in particolare il capitolo 4, "La tradizione scientifica," 344–376. Napoli, 1992.

JAMES M. POWELL
Syracuse University

Economy and Society in the Kingdom of Sicily under Frederick II: Recent Perspectives

On 29 February 1240, Frederick II wrote Angelus Frisarus, master of the ports in Sicily "this side of the River Salsa," an oft-cited letter ordering him to buy grain on behalf of the royal fisc and to transport it to Tunis or other North African ports where there was a shortage. Until the royal fleet was loaded and had sailed, merchants, among whom the Genoese were the most prominent, should not be permitted to carry Sicilian grain for sale in North Africa. Scholars have frequently cited this letter to support the argument that Frederick was deeply involved in the exporting of grain in competition with the Pisans, Genoese, and others.[1] His action has been taken to demonstrate his commitment to an economic policy that favored the interests of his Sicilian subjects against those of foreign merchants. But his intentions were much more circumscribed. Frederick wanted to make a killing, but he did not wish unduly to upset his relations with the sea powers. He instructed Angelus to "permit the ships of the merchants which are already loaded and have paid duty to sail." In fact, this *mandatum* was aimed at ensuring the income of the royal treasury.[2] Frederick's subjects were the losers.

Additionally, Frederick's establishment of new ports on the Adriatic coast in 1239, which has generally been viewed as encouraging agricultural exports from Apulia by merchants and ships from the kingdom, was something less than that.[3] By his treaty of 1232, Frederick had put the Venetians in a very favorable position for trade with the kingdom; with mounting political tensions during the latter part of the decade, he wished to exert pressure on Venice to woo her from her alliance with the Lombards and the papacy. The creation of new ports was aimed directly at Venetian interests in Apulia, but was not intended to end Venetian domination of the Adriatic trade in the kingdom. Above all, he did not wish to alienate the Venetians further. Frederick told Johannes Cioffus, his master chamberlain in the area, to allow royal subjects to carry animals and victuals to Venice for sale, but "cautiously, lest it seem that that would be permitted to everyone and should come to the notice of the Venetians."[4] Neither in the case of the Sicilian grain sale nor in the opening of new ports in favor of the *Pugliese* did Frederick II turn his back on those powerful north Italian merchants who had already played a critical role in the economic life of the kingdom under his Norman predecessors. The use of these examples and others of a similar nature to support the argument that Frederick pursued economic policies aimed at promoting the internal development of the kingdom of Sicily stems from an older effort to portray him as an early mercantilist. This view was founded on a conception of economic modernization that paralleled the

Burckhardtian idea of the state as a work of art. The study of medieval economies during the past half century has swept that older image away, but left us with a picture of Frederick's economic achievements that remains imperfect because it fails to take into full consideration important research on the kingdom of Sicily carried out during the last quarter century.

This research reflects major revisions of medieval economic history that have shaped discussions during the past fifty years. The dominant view, whose major exponent was the late Cambridge historian Michael Postan, posited a demographic upsurge beginning in the tenth century as the underlying factor in the expansion of the medieval agrarian economy and the prosperity of the twelfth and early thirteenth centuries. Thereafter, however, Europe was moving toward a Malthusian catastrophe. On the continent, Philippe Wolff had also begun to pay more attention to demography, as did Robert Lopez in the United States.[5] The influential *Annales* school in France produced a number of economic historians with strong interests in demography, though it is probably fair to say that the towering influence of Postan in England gave a particularly English stamp to the numerous studies of the rural economy produced by his students and others. Of course, there have been dissenters and critics. While strongly committed to the importance of demography in history, the American medievalist David Herlihy has raised questions about Postan's Malthusian arguments.[6] From another perspective, Robert Brenner has attacked the demographic model for ignoring class conflict and political power.[7] While others have become concerned about the neglect of politics, few would join in Brenner's total critique. Once thrust onto the stage, demography has proven a powerful tool for interpreting economic change.

But the demographic approach cannot supply the entire explanation of medieval European economic expansion. There is also an institutional and political case to be made. In this area, there is greater need for the integration of political and cultural factors, recognizing the importance of that diversity that sprang from tensions within the structure of Western European society. Beginning in the eleventh century, under the aegis of those who desired to free the Church and its institutions from domination by the lay aristocracy, there was an increasingly intense competition over the ownership of lands, rights, and jurisdictions that fueled massive disputes among those who held claims to them. Bishops, abbots, nobles, townsmen, and kings litigated and fought over the patchwork of rights that were the foundation of their economic present and future. The eleventh-century religious reform cast doubt on much of the traditional order, nowhere with greater impact than on the titles to property held by every sector of society above the lowest. The reform movement motivated bishops and other churchmen to seek the restoration of rights and properties that had been alienated. But the struggle was not merely between the clergy and the laity; rather, the ruling groups within both the hierarchy and the laity divided along lines of local loyalties and conflicting property interests without clear distinctions of status. Economic class did play a role in these conflicts, but it was generally subsidiary to other kinds of social organization.[8] To understand Frederick II within the framework of the medieval economy, it is essential to place him not only against the background of the changing demographic conditions of his period, but also to demonstrate how concerns over order and rights reflected both his political and economic interests.

Recent studies of the economic and social development of the kingdom of Sicily have underlined the critical nature of the changes that occurred in the twelfth and thirteenth centuries. Both David Abulafia and Henri Bresc have focused on the twelfth century as a period of fundamental transformation.[9] In "Medieval Monarchy and Trade," I stressed the beginnings, during the thirteenth century, of a pattern of commercial dependence on the northern Italian communes and of a process of agrarian transformation leading to the growth of great estates.[10] But the age of Frederick II deserves more detailed studies. The most important research to date on the economy of the *regno*, that in David Abulafia's *Two Italies*, in Mario del Treppo's *Amalfi medioevale*, and, most recently, in Henri Bresc's *Un monde méditérranéen: Économie et société en Sicile*, deals, the first two, with the twelfth century, and the latter, with the fourteenth and fifteenth centuries.[11] Aside from Erich Maschke's 1966 essay in the *Vierteljahrschrift für Sozial- und Wirtschaftsgeschichte* and brief studies by David Abulafia, Francesco M. de Robertis, and Salvatore Tramontana, the thirteenth century has received only passing attention.[12]

Nevertheless, research into the earlier and the later periods has already suggested substantial modifications of the picture of the thirteenth century advanced by an earlier generation of scholars. Their view stressed the riches of the *regno*, the flourishing state of its agriculture, its commercial precocity under Muslims, Byzantines, and the independent cities of southern Italy as well as the growth of industry in these same hands. The present view is less optimistic. Mario del Treppo's *Amalfi medioevale* has demonstrated internal agricultural and industrial growth, but within a framework limited by the resources of the region, an Amalfi "senza mercanti." He finds no Amalfitan merchant class competing for hegemony in the eastern Mediterranean in the early twelfth century. Del Treppo's Amalfitans resemble very much their counterparts in other parts of Italy, every bit as aggressive in their investments as were Tuscan entrepreneurs. The limited records provide interesting evidence of a "high farming" mentality. In 1194 a proprietor of a vacant piece of land granted it out on a lease, *ad pastinandam*, that is, for the planting of a vineyard, but he instructed the farmer, "If the vineyard does not yield a profit, you may make there an orchard and olive trees."[13] Del Treppo's study of investments in mills demonstrates how capital flowed toward potentially rewarding investments throughout our period. He argues, however, that certain types of commercial development were constrained by the absence of a populous and agriculturally rich hinterland. Amalfi, in his view, enjoyed success within the framework of its resources. The narrow focus of Del Treppo's study clearly forbids certain types of generalizations. It points the way for other much needed regional studies, however, and demonstrates their feasibility. One of the most promising areas, given the abundance of documentation, would certainly be the *Terra di Bari*. At the same time, continued research on Amalfi's commercial significance by scholars like Armando Citarella and Bruno Figliuolo suggests that more remains to be done in that area as well.[14] While we cannot provide an adequate demographic description of Amalfi, there is evidence of continued economic growth into the thirteenth century.[15] Moreover, the emigration of "Latins" from this region to Sicily under the Normans as well as under Frederick II indicates that there was quite likely growth in population. On the Apulian side of the mainland, however, Eugenio Dupré Theseider has found evidence of efforts to settle peasants on the royal domain, at Altamura, that suggests a competition for dependents.[16] However, his evidence, which also shows that Frederick was seriously concerned with exploiting his estates effectively, is too limited to support conclusions about demographic trends.

Abulafia has generally been pessimistic about the economic policies of the Normans and of Frederick II.[17] Focusing more on commerce than on agriculture, he has stressed the development of economic ties of dependence between the North and the South. On the other hand, Henri Bresc deals much more with the internal social and economic development of the island of Sicily. While his major focus is on the fourteenth century, he treats briefly of the earlier period. His major theme is the depopulation of the island through the flight and expulsion of the Muslim population and the failure of immigration from the mainland to recoup these losses. The eventual emergence of the *latifundia* is closely related to this fundamental demographic factor. Sicily remained underpopulated. Sicilian farmers were every bit as committed to the quest for agrarian profits as their counterparts in England, but here, in the long run, production for a specialized market that channeled the economy into the grain and olive trade confirmed its status as a satellite of the north Italian cities with their vigorous growth and increasing prosperity.[18]

Failure marked the attempts of the South to develop industry and trade or to break out of the limits of commercial agriculture. The absence of any strong demographic engine to move the train forward was the most important negative in the development of the Sicilian economy. Although Bresc does not hesitate to praise and blame specific measures taken by Frederick II, the main direction of the Sicilian economy was only partially influenced by the presence or absence of specific economic policies or, indeed, of other deliberate human actions. Bresc's main exception was the pressure to flee put on the Muslim population by the immigrants and the crown. However, it would be a serious mistake to argue that Bresc's neglect of political factors invalidates his demographic argument. On the contrary, the directions pointed out in his work must be pursued further. We can never expect to understand the problems of the medieval and early modern Sicilian economy without a better comprehension of those areas that Bresc has explored in his pioneering study.

At the same time, however, we must pay attention to those policies that, at critical moments, influenced the course of historical development. It is no condemnation of Frederick II to argue that he was not a man ahead of his time in economic terms. On the other hand, in common with most medieval rulers, he shared a view that his prosperity was largely tied up with that of his subjects and that the promotion of their good was beneficial to his own. His views were very much shaped by the dominant threads of his own time, threads that were tied into the conflicts over rights and jurisdictions that permeated every level of early thirteenth-century society. As Philip de Novare, himself a great legal authority on the kingdoms of Cyprus and Jerusalem and author of a history of the wars of Frederick against the Ibelins in Syria and Cyprus, recognized, it was Frederick's intense commitment to the securing of his rights as he saw them that led to his conflict with John d'Ibelin.[19] Frederick's defense of his claims as an underlying motivation of his policies has not received sufficient attention from scholars.

The importance of this theme reaches back to the troubled childhood of Frederick, when he was forced to barter away royal rights in exchange for tenuous political support. But the psychological impact of childhood insecurity need not be exaggerated. No period of medieval history prior to the thirteenth century witnessed a more intense competition over rights, jurisdictions, and properties than was reflected in the booming litigation in the courts and the violence in town and countryside. The problem was especially exacerbated in northern Italy, where the rise of communes reflected the need for parties to defend the interests of one group against another. The development of legal machinery represented a necessary effort to establish order but also led to the imposition of "solutions" by one group on another. Frederick's laws of 1220, especially that on the resignation of privileges, expressed his own intention of enforcing his rights in the kingdom of Sicily against nobility, churches, monasteries, towns, and foreigners.[20] The lengthy negotiations to secure these ends, illustrated in the manner in which he used the clause "salvo mandato et ordinatione nostra" to protect his interests, were very likely a prelude to the baronial rebellion against him in the 1220s. The theme of royal rights was also important in the negotiations leading up to Frederick's marriage to the heiress of Jerusalem and in his approach to rule in the Latin kingdom. It dominates the Constitutions of Melfi of 1231, the fundamental law of the kingdom for more than five hundred years. Finally, it furnishes the most coherent explanation for his conflict with the communes in northern Italy and with the papacy. The struggle over rights produced abstract defenses but was grounded in genuine interests that were perceived as essential to preserving the order of society. Economic interests combined with a commitment to right order to divide medieval society into complex political groups.

To separate economic policies aimed at betterment of the whole society from fiscal policies directed to the needs of the state, as some have tried to do, is not merely anachronistic; it also distorts the fundamental meaning of Frederick's reign. Only if we understand that Frederick was a medieval king can we appreciate the way in which he both cherished and exploited the kingdom of Sicily. It was his kingdom in a very personal sense. He could extract from it what he needed to fight his wars, but he could also protect its interests against the depredations of others. Frederick was moved chiefly by the needs and advantages of the moment. Only in moments of reflection, or when the awe of his own majesty raised up his eyes from the minute details of medieval government, could he achieve some vision of a better society. In that he was also a product of his age, an age in which lawyers, theologians, physicians, and others with a modicum of education turned their minds and hearts toward peace, order, and the dream of justice. This spirit, too, animates the Constitutions of Melfi. This dimension of Frederick has provided inspiration for those present-minded historians who delight in a past that is like their own age.

Recent research on economy and society in the kingdom of Sicily enables us, for the first time, to make some tentative comparisons between the *regno* and the rest of Europe. From the eleventh to the thirteenth centuries, the kingdom of Sicily shared in the prosperity and growth of Western and Central Europe as a whole, though underpopulation slowed its rate of development. From the thirteenth through the fifteenth centuries, the region was affected by recurrent crises, which left the economy more and more victim to external market forces. It also experienced the fourteenth-century depression, but it seems to have had strong internal tendencies toward depression well before the plagues and economic crises of the fourteenth century. The question we must raise is whether these developments were inevitable; were there alternatives?

The conventional economic wisdom of the twelfth and thirteenth centuries recognized the problem of underpopulation and attempted to remedy it through immigration. The efficient distribution of labor in both town and countryside forms one of the basic themes of economic development during the demographic expansion of the twelfth and thirteenth centuries. In the kingdom of Sicily, colonists were enticed not merely from the mainland, especially from Calabria and the area around Salerno, but also from Tuscany. Tuscans came to play a prominent role in Messina in this period. Royal encouragement of colonization was not limited to the island of Sicily. We have already noted that Frederick II developed at least two agrarian settlements on the mainland, one at Altamura.[21] Such internal development was characteristic of great lords in many parts of Europe and was equally pursued by bishoprics, monasteries, and communes. It is quite easy to find other examples in which Frederick encouraged the economic development of his domain. He wrote the justiciar of the *Terra di Bari* in early July 1238 to express his concern about the neglect of agricultural development. In the course of the letter, Frederick laid partial blame for the poor harvests on the "laziness and negligence" of the peasants ("desidiam et negligenciam hominum").[22] Erich Maschke has emphasized Frederick's effort to change the mentality of the South Italian peasantry, which lay at the root of the economic problem.[23] Frederick's solution, on the other hand, to compel farmers to expand production by increasing the number of oxen and encouraging their natural increase, seems closely related to his effort to promote more efficient distribution of labor in order to prevent loss to the "tocius reipublice regni nostri, specialiter nostrum."[24] He was concerned about losses both to his subjects and the fisc. There is no need to stress these concerns for agrarian profits. There is a greater need to show that developments in the *regno* followed the general lines that we find in other parts of Europe.

As has often been noted, Frederick sometimes took measures to benefit the fisc at the expense of his subjects. The export of grain in 1239 and 1240 furnishes an example. Genoese and other merchants were buying on the open market for export to North Africa. Frederick used royal authority to buy grain and to sell it ahead of the merchants and to their loss. But the loss was not that of foreign merchants alone. He used his own fleet. He purchased grain through his officials rather than native merchants. He took advantage of the shortage in North Africa to benefit the royal treasury rather than to favor the interests of native over foreign merchants.[25] There is little need to multiply examples of this kind. The pressure of war, Frederick's continuing need for cash to pay his creditors, and his measures to increase his income have all been amply documented. Not so adequately noted is the fact that these actions are entirely consistent with and, indeed, spring from the same mentality as Frederick's "high farming." Behind that mentality lay the intense competition to secure and exploit one's rights as effectively as possible. To illustrate the value set on this ideal in southern Italy in the thirteenth century, we need only see the esteem in which contemporaries held Abbot Balsam of Cava, who was assiduous in securing the rights of his monastery from Frederick in the 1220s and who prepared a register listing its properties.[26] Still, Frederick II held him in the highest regard and supported his efforts. He was celebrated in the history of the monastery as one of its greatest abbots. As soon as we recognize that competition over concrete rights, as well as such factors as population growth, were important in moving the medieval economy, we begin to understand the reasons for Frederick's involvement in economic matters and the rationale behind his "economic policies." Abulafia is quite correct in writing that "medieval rulers attempted to manage the economy of their realms in order to maximize their income, not in order to achieve economic growth *per se*."[27] Defense of rights was a wellspring of economic policy.

We can now return to the examples with which we began this paper. The letters to Angelus Frisarus and to the master chamberlain establishing new ports show that Frederick was well aware of the economic and political consequences of his actions. He acted for temporary advantage and hoped to avoid the worst results by concealing what he was doing or by allowing his competitors to share the benefits to a limited degree. His exercise of economic power was largely conceived for fiscal and political purposes. It was not part of a long-range commitment to encourage local merchants, who were cut out in favor of the fisc in the sale of grain to North Africa and were treated as minor figures in the establishment of new ports. Although it is arguable that some of Frederick's measures, particularly the promotion of immigration, were in the long-term interest of the economy of the kingdom, the impressive studies by Bresc do not suggest that this was so. In fact, Bresc demonstrates that none of the commercial or industrial initiatives of Frederick II bore significant fruit over the long term.[28]

Frederick's decade-long war with the papacy and the northern Italian communes from 1239 to 1250 was an important factor in the temporary ruin of the economy of the *regno*. Costs for mercenaries and fortifications, and the need to keep large armies in the field, drained the kingdom of cash, a large part of which was spent in the north. Virtually all of the evidence about the implementation of Frederick's economic policies comes from these war years, reflecting enormous fiscal pressures. As Abulafia has attested, the most valuable evidence, that contained in the surviving portion of Frederick's register from 1239 to 1240, must be read against the background of the political crisis that erupted at just this time.[29] That crisis colors the meaning of these documents so that it becomes impossible to read their economic meaning separately from their fiscal and political purposes. But even at the height of crisis, when desperation marked his policies, Frederick sacrificed his fiscal needs to his vision of his imperial role.

Excommunicated and deposed at the Council of Lyons in 1245, he found himself faced with an extremely delicate situation. King Louis IX of France began preparations for a crusade. In July 1249 Frederick responded to Louis' request to assist his brother Alphonse with victuals and war horses for his journey to the East.[30] It was a time of severe shortage in the kingdom of Sicily, but Frederick wanted to demonstrate to Louis the strength of his own commitment to the crusade: "we prefer that we and our subjects should lack food rather than that you and your loyal subjects and other nobles of your kingdom should suffer need in the pursuit of such a useful and holy cause, if our generosity can supply your and their needs." Frederick assured Louis that he would give Alphonse 1,000 salmas of grain and fifty war horses and allow him to purchase whatever else he needed for himself and his contingent. Frederick, whose ties with the French monarchy were always strong, demonstrated that he was still the crusader of twenty years earlier. He was a medieval ruler, generous to an old ally despite the fact that his treasury was empty and his cupboard nearly bare.[31]

The task of examining the economic initiatives of Frederick II against the background of economic and social life in the kingdom of Sicily has received only a brief treatment in this paper. I have tried to suggest some directions for future research, both in terms of local studies of economic development and of the motivating forces behind medieval economic planning. I have also tried to indicate the extent to which recent research has made possible some reinterpretation of the policies of Frederick II. Suffice it to say, the

Burckhardtian view of Frederick II, which took on heroic dimensions in Ernst Kantorowicz's biography, has shrunk dramatically in light of those studies that emphasize the decisive role of demographic factors in the economic development of Sicily and, to some degree, of the whole *regno*. Kantorowicz' Frederick was indeed "the wonder of the world" and the epigone of modernization. Such a model is virtually impossible to conceive of within the framework of recent historiography. But have we gone too far? Have we neglected too much those measures that might have altered the course of economic development of the *regno* had they been successful? Were the wars and taxes of Frederick II decisive in shaping the economic future of the South and of Sicily?

It is not enough that we repeat old answers to these questions. The reshaping of the history of the social and economic development of the *regno* precludes such a step. Too much research still needs to be done before our answers can be more than tentative. But allow me at least to suggest some possible answers. On one level, in common with many of his contemporaries, Frederick interacted with the changing economic environment of his kingdom. His approaches to these problems are not, for the most part, strikingly different from those undertaken by other lords interested in increasing their incomes. On another level, the pressures of warfare and his attendant needs drove him to innovate in fiscal areas in ways that served as an example to the Angevins and other rulers. There is in his fiscalism an understanding, albeit not fully developed, of the economic significance of taxation. If this had a positive aspect that contributed to better management of the state, it had its negative side in the burden placed on the kingdom of Sicily. For if, as Antonio Marongiù has suggested, the *regno* was the "model State of the Middle Ages," it was a model that suffered much in the experiment.[32] Finally, I would suggest that Frederick's wars must be read as an effort to force a solution to that crisis which first emerged from the reform movement of the eleventh century. His reign is indeed the moment of decision. The economic implications of his possible victory have never been explored, but it seems certain that it would have made the road to state centralization much smoother. The struggle over rights, if not ended, would at least have been directed toward one solution. Control of resources might well have fallen into even fewer hands and at a much more rapid rate. Frederick's defeat, while it brought less than a total shift in policy under the Angevin and Aragonese rulers of the South, promoted the disordered and untidy world of Italian and German politics and extended the reasons for economic conflict into the next century. But it also hastened the dénouement that saw foreign dominance of the economic life of the *regno* under the Angevins furnish one pillar to the fortunes of the great northern patrons of Renaissance art. Nor should we forget that King Robert of Naples used his share of the profits toward a similar end.[33]

NOTES

The author wishes to thank the Institute for Advanced Study, Princeton, and his colleagues in residence during 1989–1990 for their support. Special thanks to James Muldoon for reading the manuscript and to the members of the Delaware Valley Medieval Conference for their helpful comments.

1. Erich Maschke, "Die Wirtschaftspolitik Kaiser Friedrichs II. im Königreich Sizilien," *Vierteljahrschrift für Sozial- und Wirtschaftsgeschichte* 53 (1966), 289–328, esp. 303–306.

2. Jean L. A. Huillard-Bréholles, ed., *Historia Diplomatica Friderici Secundi . . .*, 6 vols. in 12 with preface and introduction (Paris, 1852–1861), 5:793.

3. Maschke 1966, 302.

4. *Constitutiones Regum Regni utriusque Siciliae mandante Friderico II Imperatore . . . cum Graeca earundem Versione e regione Latini Textus adposita, quibus nunc primum accedunt Assisiae Regum Regni Siciliae et Fragmentum quod superest Regesti eiusdem Imperatoris, Ann. 1239 & 1240*, ed. C. Carcani (Naples, 1786), 233; known as the Carcani edition.

5. For further discussion of recent trends in economic history, see James M. Powell, "Crisis and Culture in Renaissance Europe," *Medievalia et Humanistica* 12 (1984), 201–224; Ian Blanchard, "Review of Periodical Literature in Economic and Social History, 1986: Medieval," *Economic History Review* 41 (1988), 122–128; and Robert Brenner, "Agrarian Class Structure and Economic Development in Pre-industrial Europe," *Past and Present* 70 (1976), 30–75. See also Ronald Witt, "The Landlord and the Economic Revival of the Middle Ages in Northern Europe, 1000–1250," *American Historical Review* 76 (1971), 965–988, and John Edwards, "'Development' and 'Underdevelopment' in the Western Mediterranean: The Case of Córdoba in the Late Fifteenth and Early Sixteenth Centuries," *Mediterranean History Review* 2 (1987), 3–45.

6. David Herlihy, *Medieval and Renaissance Pistoia* (New Haven, Conn., 1967), 112–116.

7. Brenner 1976, 30–37.

8. A good study of these conflicts is found in Duane Osheim, *An Italian Lordship: The Bishopric of Lucca in the Late Middle Ages* (Berkeley, Calif., 1977), 58–85; see also my *Anatomy of a Crusade, 1213–1221* (Philadelphia, 1986), 67–88, which discusses the effects of such rivalries on crusade recruitment in the early thirteenth century. See David Herlihy, "Church Property on the European Continent, 701–1200," *Speculum* 36 (1961), 81–105, and Gregorio Penco, *Storia della chiesa in Italia* (Milan, 1977), 353–357. Other recent examples may be found in James R. Banker, *Death in the Community: Memorialization and Confraternities in an Italian Commune in the Late Middle Ages* (Athens, Ga., 1988), 18–21, and Chris J. Wickham, *The Mountains and the City: The Tuscan Appennines in the Early Middle Ages* (Oxford, 1988), 320–335.

9. David Abulafia, *The Two Italies: Economic Relations between the Norman Kingdom of Sicily and the Northern Communes* (Cambridge, 1977); Henri Bresc, *Un monde méditerranéen: Économie et société en Sicile, 1300–1450*, 2 vols. (Rome and Palermo, 1986), 1:13–16.

10. James M. Powell, "Medieval Monarchy and Trade: The Economic Policy of Frederick II in the Kingdom of Sicily (A Survey)," *Studi Medievali*, ser. 3, 3 (1962), 420–524, esp. 487–488.

11. See above, note 9; see also Mario del Treppo and Alfonso Leone, *Amalfi medioevale* (Naples, 1977).

12. See above, note 1 and Francesco M. de Robertis, "La politica economica di Federico II di Svevia," in *Atti delle seconde giornate federiciane*, Oria, 16–17 ottobre, 1971, Società di Storia Patria per la Puglia, Convegni 4 (Bari, 1974); Salvatore Tramontana, "L'età di Federico II," in *Storia d'Italia*, ed. G. Galasso, 23 vols. (Turin, 1979–1984), 3:659–768. For recent views, see David Abulafia, *Frederick II: A Medieval Emperor* (London and New York, 1988), 214–225, and his forthcoming essay, "The State and Economic Life in the Kingdom of Sicily under Frederick II," to be published with the *Acta* of the conference on Frederick II and the Mediterranean World, held in Erice, 18–24 September 1989.

13. Del Treppo 1977, 34.

14. Armando Citarella, *Il commercio di Amalfi nell'alto medioevo* (Salerno, 1977) and Bruno Figliuolo, "Amalfi e il Levante nel medioevo," in *I Comuni Italiani nel Regno Crociato di Gerusalemme*, ed. Gabriella Airaldi and Benjamin Z. Kedar (Genoa, 1986), 573–664.

15. Del Treppo 1977, 168–169.

16. Eugenio Dupré Theseider, "Federico II, ideatore di castelli e città," in *Atti delle seconde giornate federiciane* (Bari, 1974), 65–80, esp. 69–75.

17. Abulafia 1988, 214–225.

18. Bresc 1986, 1:7–21.

19. Philip de Novare, *The Wars of Frederick II against the Ibelins in Syria and Cyprus* (New York, 1936), 63–64; also Raoul Manselli, "Federico II e la cultura policentrica del suo tempo," in *Federico II e l'arte del Duecento italiano*, ed. Angiola M. Romanini, 2 vols. (Galatina, 1980), 2:301–309, esp. 303.

20. James M. Powell, "Frederick II and the Church in the Kingdom of Sicily, 1220–1224," *Church History* 30 (1961), 28–34.

21. Dupré Theseider 1974, 69–75.

22. *Acta Imperii inedita saeculi XIII et XIV*, ed. Eduard Winkelmann, 2 vols. (Innsbruck, 1880–1885; repr. Aalen, 1964), 1:633.

23. Maschke 1966, 301.

24. *Acta imperii*, 1:633.

25. Huillard-Bréholles, 5:792–793.

26. Paul Guillaume, *Essai historique sur l'abbaye de Cava* (Cava dei Tirreni, 1877), 144–147, and Mario Rotili, "La miniatura nello 'Scriptorium' della Badia

di Cava nel Duecento," in *Federico II e l'arte*, 2:113–125, esp. 115–116.

27. Abulafia 1988, 214.

28. Bresc 1986, 1:16–18; Maurice Aymard, "Production, commerce et consommation des draps de laine du XIIe au XVIIe siècle," *Revue historique* 246 (1971), 5–12, esp. 9–10.

29. Abulafia 1988, 325–327.

30. Huillard-Bréholles, 6:748–750.

31. Huillard-Bréholles, 6:634–635. Frederick wrote that he did not have sufficient money to pursue his siege of Parma.

32. Antonio Marongiù, "A Model State in the Middle Ages: The Norman and Swabian Kingdom of Sicily," *Comparative Studies in Society and History* 6 (1964), 307–320.

33. David Abulafia, "Southern Italy and the Florentine Economy, 1265–1370," *The Economic History Review*, ser. 2, 33 (1981), 377–388.

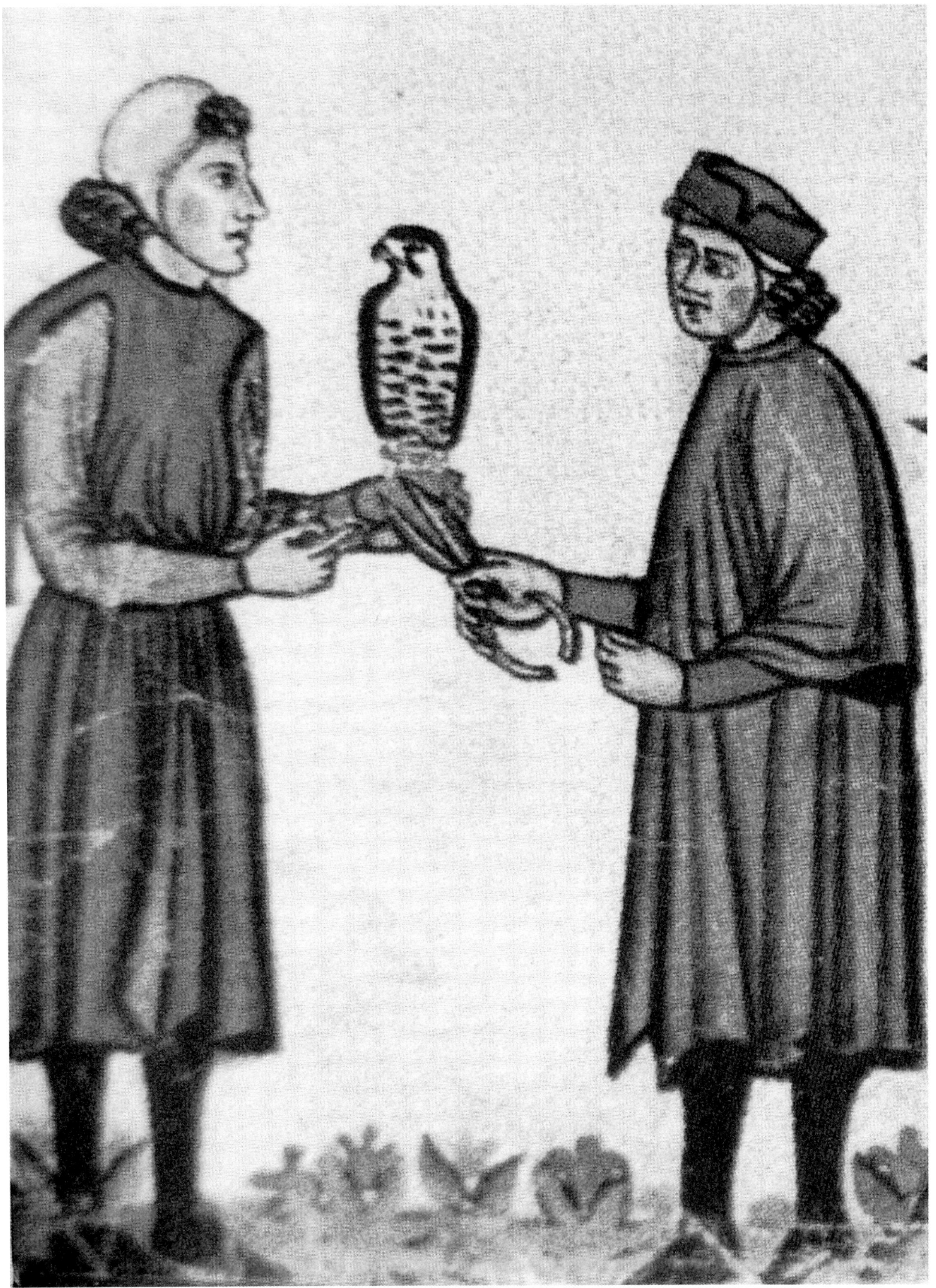

ANTONIO THIERY
Radiotelevisione Italiana, Rome

Federico II e la conoscenza scientifica

Arte e conoscenza

Qual'è stato e qual'è il ruolo dell'immagine e dell'esperienza visiva nella formazione e nel trasferimento delle conoscenze? L'immagine può soltanto decorare, illustrare, descrivere, edificare, raccontare, documentare, confermare quello che già conosciamo, copiare la realtà? Deve essere spiegata per essere compresa? Può tutt'al più, come avviene davanti ad un'opera d'arte o al cinema, produrre sensazioni, emozioni, godimento estetico? O può anche, attraverso l'evocazione, attivare processi conoscitivi? Gli studi di quest'ultimo secolo sull'antropologia e la psicologia hanno messo sufficientemente in evidenza come il pensiero visivo (attraverso i simboli, l'analogia e la percezione) porti a costruire un vero e proprio sistema di comunicazione presso quei popoli e quelle civiltà che non sono state condizionate dal sillogismo concettuale della dialettica. Il pensiero visivo, però, non vive solo in antitesi al pensiero concettuale, può vivere in un sistema, in cui l'occhio della mente e l'occhio della ragione si integrino in modo inscindibile. Anche molte nostre culture occidentali apparentemente solo concettuali, sono fortemente percettive. Non negherò pertanto il ruolo dei documenti scritti (concettuali) nel ricostruire la vicenda politica di Federico II. Esaminerò piuttosto i documenti visivi (percettivi), fondamentali per ricostruire la vicenda culturale. L'alto medioevo ha un ruolo centrale dello studio degli strumenti, specialmente di quelli visivi, della conoscenza e rappresenta, in proposito, un laboratorio straordinario. Ma anche il Duecento, quando si determinano i presupposti della moderna organizzazione scientifica, può offrire risultati di grande interesse. Alastair C. Crombie, in un'opera che mi appare sempre più importante, perché a mano a mano che si vanno colmando le molte lacune (conosce poco Federico II, pochissimo il mondo arabo e musulmano, niente quello africano e vicino-orientale), appare, nella sua struttura, sempre più valida e convincente, fissando alcuni elementi conoscitivi ormai sufficientemente certi.

La scienza dimostrativa e sperimentale del Duecento

Nel Duecento nasce una scienza dimostrativa e sperimentale. Il metodo dell'osservazione, dell'esperimento, dell'uso di strumenti matematici si estende a tutto il dominio delle scienze naturali. L'algebra è sempre più usata per risolvere problemi geometrici. Lo studio della luce si sviluppa in modo determinante fino a provocare la nascita di una ricerca sistemica sull'ottica. La luce diventa uno degli elementi maggiormente studiati perché, legata al platonismo agostiniano, consente di sviluppare il concetto di grazia e di illuminazione interiore, ma è anche, al tempo stesso, qualcosa di concreto, di manipolabile che può essere sottoposto a trattamento matematico. Studi nuovi nascono sulle forze della natura che fino ad allora erano state conosciute, vissute, percettivamente (ad esempio il magnetismo) e sulla teologia occidentale (fondata sempre più sulla illimitata dignità e responsabilità di ogni individuo).

Prende corpo, attraverso Francesco d'Assisi ed il suo ordine, l'aspetto sacrale delle attività scientifiche dell'uomo, recuperando la tradizione palestinese e del cristianesimo primitivo secondo la quale l'ignoranza è il peggiore dei peccati e la conoscenza, non solo strumento, ma struttura di salvezza. È nel graduale svincolamento dell'algebra dalla geometria (merito di Fibonacci e del fondamentale contributo del mondo arabo e musulmano alla conoscenza) che si determina non solo un'avanzamento della tecnologia e della scienza, ma un radicale cambiamento della visione del mondo.

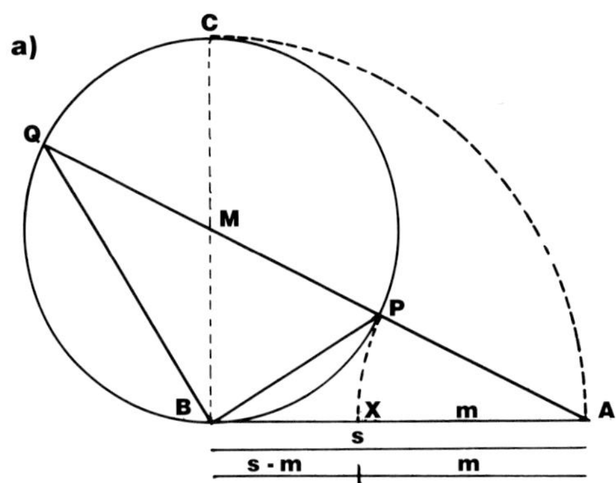

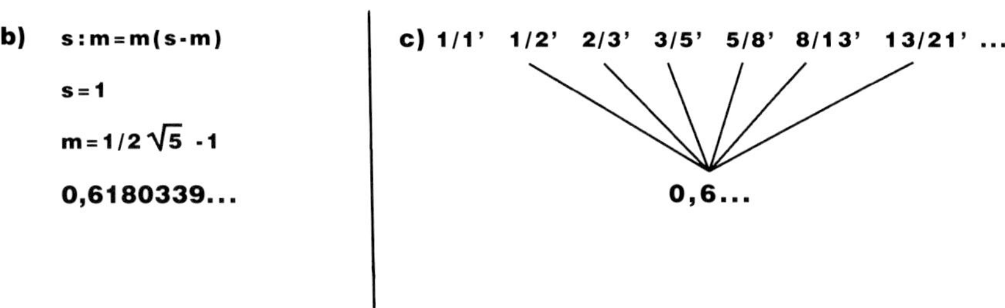

1. Dalla sezione aurea, ai rapporti conoscitivi della sequenza di Fibonacci
Disegno: autore

Dalla sezione aurea alla sequenza di Fibonacci

Non ripeterò osservazioni già fatte in altre occasioni, ma ricorderò il passaggio che si verifica nel 13° dalla sezione aurea dei Greci (i rapporti sono espressi in chiave geometrica e concettuale), alla dimostrazione algebrica di un numero irrazionale, che sviluppa poi la famosa sequenza di Fibonacci (fig. 1).

La proporzione euclidea della divisione del segmento in media ed estrema ragione (la media proporzionale tra l'intero segmento e la parte residua) si può così scrivere utilizzando la matematica simbolica: s:m = m:(s−m). Poiché quando quattro grandezze sono in proporzione lo sono anche i numeri che le misurano, se prendiamo come unità di misura s = 1 e detta *x* la misura del segmento *m*, si ha

$1:x = x:(1-x)$, da cui $x^2 + x - 1 = 0$;

per la formula fondamentale delle equazioni di 2° grado: $ax^2 + bx + c = 0$

$$x = \frac{-b -/+ \sqrt{b^2 - 4ac}}{2a}$$

$$x = \frac{-1 +/- \sqrt{1+4}}{2}$$

dovendo essere *x* positivo, avremo:

$$x = \frac{-1+\sqrt{5}}{2}\text{, cioè } \tfrac{1}{2}\sqrt{5}-1.$$

Si ha un numero irrazionale (0,6180339 . . .), che consente di individuare, nello sviluppo di una frazione continua la sequenza di Fibonacci: 1 1 2 3 5 8 13 21 34, e così via, fino all'infinito. Ogni numero è la somma dei due che lo precedono. Ogni numero ha un analogo rapporto (il numero irrazionale 0,6 . . . non più inteso come sezione aurea, ma come rapporto che consente la conoscenza) con il numero che lo segue. Una sequenza alla quale Fibonacci aveva pensato studiando la nascita dei conigli, e che ritroveremo puntualmente nello sviluppo evolutivo di piante ed animali.

La frazione ½ $\sqrt{5}$ −1 ed il numero irrazionale 0,6 . . . . . non sono più la media proporzionale tra l'intero segmento e la parte residua, tra l'intera altezza dell'uomo e le sue membra, tra l'altezza e la largezza di un edificio, ma lo strumento di conoscenza dell'organizzazione della natura. Lo sviluppo algebrico della dimostrazione geometrica non è una semplice esercitazione fine a stessa (ancora oggi nelle scuole italiane la sequenza di Fibonacci, quando viene presentata, viene proposta agli studenti come una curiosità ed un gioco), ma costituisce il passaggio dal concetto della divina armonia, alla straordinaria intuizione che la natura si sviluppa secondo forme organizzate, strutturate, misurabili, descrivibili, conoscibili attraverso la matematica e l'algebra.

La visione sistemica della natura e della conoscenza

Il classicismo della divinità dei numeri e della dimostrazione dei teoremi geometrici è superato da un nuovo rapporto con la concretezza delle cose. Così come è superato il concetto deterministico che la natura crea da se stessa.

La sezione aurea dei Greci esprime l'armonia, il sublime, il bello. La sequenza di Fibonacci riassume la visione di sistema che è alla base della organizzazione e della conoscenza della natura e del creato di Francesco d'Assisi. Dall'arte come rappresentazione, all'arte come conoscenza. La visione sistemica è l'elemento determinante nella nascita della conoscenza moderna, e il fondamento dei contemporanei studi sull'ecologia e sull'ambiente. Non sarà mai sottolineato a sufficienza che la scoperta scientifica più radicale del Duecento consiste proprio nella individuazione della sistemica unitarietà del creato (o del cosmo), attraverso la organizzazione delle complementari differenze, tutte ugualmente necessarie e interdipendenti. La conoscenza non si risolve nel raggiungimento di fini o di mete, ma nella individuazione di punti di partenza sempre nuovi.

Il *Cantico delle creature* di Francesco d'Assisi ed il *De arte venandi cum avibus* di Federico II rappresentano i due terminali di una conoscenza nuova dell'uomo e della natura e delle sue manifestazioni cosali. Nasce una ricerca continua di conoscenza, che si risolve in Francesco in una sempre rinnovata laude al Signore ed in Federico II in sempre nuove curiosità e sperimentazioni. L'uomo, con Francesco, non è più il re del creato. Non è più il solo a portare significazione dell'Altissimo. Le cose, gli animali, come dimostra Federico II nel suo *Trattato di ornitologia*, vanno studiate nelle loro essenze, nel rapporto con la natura vista nella sua globalità, nella sua organizzazione, nel suo sistema. È quì che si definisce quella mentalità scientifica di Federico II, che Gabriele Pepe nel 1937 e Antonino de Stefano nel 1938 misero bene in evidenza.

Non mancano gli studiosi, come August Nietzsche, che riconoscono a Federico II grande originalità, ma negano ogni modernità. L'imperatore svevo, infatti, farebbe derivare i movimenti degli uccelli dalla forma di una parte del corpo. Indirizzo scientifico, questo, più vecchio di quello che determinerà il secolo successivo, spiegando, invece, il movimento come una tendenza improntata alla aspirazione verso la perfezione. Ma un'errore del genere non serve certo a modificare il complesso di acquisizioni sul sistema della conoscenza. Agli inizi del nostro secolo il grande matematico positivista Poincaré si pone il problema se uno scienziato che esamina al microscopio un rinoceronte conosca quel tipo di animale. Conclude in modo negativo. Solo i dogmatisti ingenui credono di poter conoscere le cose. Il lavoro dello scienziato è indirizzato a far conoscere l'unica cosa conoscibile, cioè il rapporto tra le cose. E Federico II, come aveva ben notato il Pepe, per il suo abito mentale di osservatore e di matematico cercava un metodo di conoscenza e, conseguentemente la razionalità nelle leggi della natura e nell'organizzazione dello stato. Non certo una razionalità dialettica, come vedremo fra poco.

A testimoniare il programma politico di Federico II, sintetizzato dalla simbolica e distrutta porta di Capua, c'è, tra l'altro, un goffo disegno attribuito a Fra Giocondo. È questa un'opera sfavorevolmente giudicata dagli storici dell'arte, da quelli che George Duby definirebbe gli storici positivisti accaniti nel verificare l'attendibilità dei piccoli fatti. Attraverso le sue esitazioni, le sue omissioni, il suo semplificare il disegno alla ricerca dell'essenziale comunicativo, per mezzo dei suoi stessi errori, Fra Giocondo rivela l'immagine del mondo e dello Stato di Federico II. Bisogna tener conto di un pensiero che non si preoccupa di classificare logicamente i fatti e di descriverli, ma di procedere per associazioni di simboli, costruendo la conoscenza attraverso la percezione visiva ed i rimandi analogici al sistema strutturale dell'organizzazione della natura. Con queste premesse, ritroveremo nel goffo disegno di Fra Giocondo il sistema riassuntivo, reso esplicito, dalla sequenza di Fibonacci.

Le proporzioni delle sculture sono modificate sulla base dell'importanza dei personaggi raffigurati. La testa di Capua domina la scena in ordine di dimensioni, e perciò di valore (un procedimento analogo, tipico delle culture simboliche, lo ritroveremo anche nel pulpito di Bitonto). Poi viene il sovrano. I dati sensoriali sono stati selezionati. Gli stimoli e le risposte non arrivano isolati, ma nella configurazione dei segni. La porta di Capua non serve a descrivere la visione dello stato che ha l'imperatore, ma avvia un itinerario conoscitivo, che attivando, attraverso il visivo, tutte le facoltà psichiche, emotive e sensoriali, porta ad assumere in sé la *Justitia Caesaris* (fig. 2).

La modernità scientifica di Federico II

La modernità di Federico II non va dunque misurata sulle teorie relative al movimento degli uccelli, ma nella ricerca della totalità e unitarietà della conoscenza. Marie Dominique Chenu, in un libretto del 1927 (*La teologia come scienza nel XIII secolo*) rileva come, per la teologia, si assista nel Duecento ad un passaggio progressivo dalla dialettica (cioè da tecniche di elaborazione verbale e concettuale) ad una filosofia dello spirito, che, al di là delle formulazioni razionali, comporta una conoscenza del mondo e dell'uomo. La riscoperta, attraverso le traduzioni mediate dall'arabo, dell'Aristotele metafisico, psicologo, moralista (e non solo dialettico) porta, soprattutto a Toledo (che diventa un centro di irradiazione), alla nascita di studi naturalistici e medico-filosofici che mostrano un certo sdegno per i dialettici di Parigi.

La Spagna e Toledo sono il terminale della strada attraverso la quale giunge in Europa la cultura orientale ed araba. Alessandro Bausani ha mostrato con chiarezza che in Europa si diffondono solo quegli elementi musulmani, ad esempio nelle matematiche e nelle scienze, che sono stati assorbiti dalla cultura spagnola. Il grande matematico al-Bīrūnī, che sarà ignorato dalla Spagna, rimarrà ignoto fino all'Ottocento alla cultura europea. Non si può certo considerare una novità assoluta per il Duecento la mediazione del mondo arabo ed il passaggio, in Europa, dal ragionamento per pensiero, fondato su tecniche di elaborazione verbale e concettuale, al pensiero percettivo fatto di evocazione e di associazioni analogiche e simboliche. Nell'esame dell'alto medioevo, ed in particolare dei documenti visivi delle culture cosiddette barbariche, in Francia, in Irlanda, in Germania, nella Penisola Iberica, nella stessa Italia, emergono elementi sempre più convincenti per riconoscere ambienti

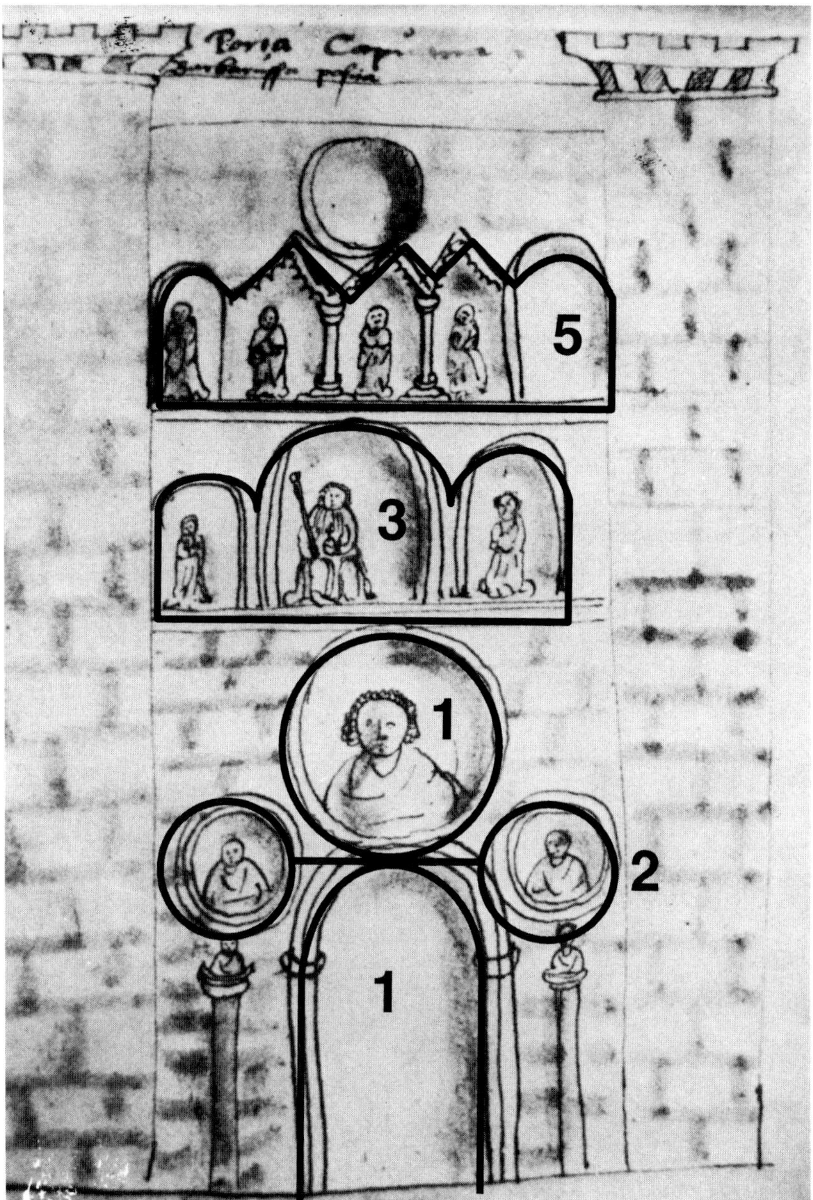

2. La Porta di Capua nel disegno di Fra Giocondo e la sequenza di Fibonacci
Da Ernst Kantorowicz, *Federico II imperatore* (Milano, 1976), tav. 3; elaborazione: autore

culturali estranei alla tradizione classica, ellenistica e romana. Ambienti culturali che rimandano spesso all'antichità più remota, al mondo siro-mesopotamico, alla tradizione del cristianesimo primitivo non ancora ellenizzato e romanizzato, all'Africa settentrionale.

Speculazione filosofica e civiltà cosale

Alla speculazione filosofica si contrappone una civiltà cosale: l'uomo (fatto di terra) si confronta con le cose della terra; conosce manipolando, trasformando ed utilizzando le cose, non seguendo la concettualizzazione del pensiero sillogistico e mitico, ma creando mimicamente, ripetendo cioè i gesti primordiali dell'uomo, degli antenati o i grandi gesti creatori della divinità. Questa cultura percettiva e cosale (che si esprime stentatamente o non si esprime affatto nella parola scritta e nel libro) è sovrastata e spesso cancellata, nella organizzazione statale o ecclesiastica dalla cultura dominante di tipo concettuale e sintattico. Trova, invece, grande espressione nel vivere quotidiano e religioso (dal momento che fa appello alla conoscenza individuale) ed accompagna secoli che definiamo *bui* perché non li capiamo.

Nel Duecento esplode e trova elementi di diffusione negli ordini monastici (soprattutto in quello francescano) e nelle strutture organizzatorie del sapere, promosse, attraverso la corte e le università laiche, da Federico II. Legato ad una cultura simbolica e percettiva è la *Leggenda dei tre compari*, l'unica fonte certa del lungo travaglio mentale e spirituale che porta alla conversione di Francesco d'Assisi. La *Leggenda dei tre compari*, normalmente giudicata un banale scritto, perché lontana dai canoni della composizione classica, è invece un documento di incredibile interesse storico.

I libri o le cose?

Sono molti a mettere in evidenza come la natura e l'uomo, nel 1200, agli spiriti che lavorano sulla teologia si rivelano essenzialmente tramite le opere di Aristotele, e, quindi, attraverso gli antichi libri e non mediante lo spettacolo diretto, lento, inconsapevole, ma vivificante della natura e dell'uomo. Ma non va dimenticato l'iter della traduzione di questi libri. Normalmente dal greco al siriaco (che ha soppiantato il greco nell'area soggetta all'ellenismo); dal siriaco all'arabo; dall'arabo al volgare; dal volgare al latino. E non si tratta solo di traduzioni linguistiche, ma di trasposizione di testi portatori di una cultura, in scritti intellegibili a culture profondamente diverse. I testi, i libri, nota Chenu, e non le cose furono alla base dell'insegnamento e della cultura. Debolezza questa di ogni rinascita. Ma se questo è vero negli spiriti che si dedicavano alla teologia, è pur vero che nascono centri di elaborazione delle conoscenze, anche ecclesiastici, con differenziazioni profonde.

C'è indubbiamente un elemento unificante della cultura del Duecento: il passaggio dalla dialettica ad una teoria della scienza ben definita che postulava metodi di indagine e di interpretazione. Si supera, quindi, una forma di conoscenza razionale, il cui metodo consiste essenzialmente in definizioni, in ragionamenti, in dimostrazioni, nel raggiungimento di verità definitive ed indeformabili, di dogmi.

Si avvia, piuttosto, il sistema del pensiero scientifico che dominerà le scienze europee fino al Settecento. Ma è un dominio sotterraneo, fortemente osteggiato, come testimoniano le prescrizioni dei quattro Concili Lateranensi, dalla Chiesa di Roma o come testimoniano gli scritti di Innocenzo III (sì proprio lui che accettò l'ordine Francescano e che, come tutore di Federico fanciullo, ne cercò in ogni modo il condizionamento).

Si supera la speculazione filosofica; e la conoscenza, che non è mai definitiva, si realizza rendendo sempre più intellegibile, attraverso l'osservazione e l'esperimento, con la matematica, il mondo della natura. E la conoscenza non è esoterica, riservata a pochi. Si realizza, soprattutto per merito del pensiero islamico, quella che Alessandro Bausani, con felicissimo termine, definisce la democratizzazione della scienza. Invano cercheremo, infatti, in queste epoche una cultura colta ed una cultura popolare. Troveremo differenziazioni profonde tra classi dominate e potere politico ed economico.

L'unità della conoscenza

Nel Duecento l'unità fondamentale dei metodi della conoscenza si basa su quattro elementi:

(1) nello sviluppo del concetto di sistema e di interazione;
(2) nel passaggio dalla dialettica stilizzata e dalle elaborazioni verbali e concettuali, alla conoscenza manipolativa della natura e dell'uomo;
(3) nella estensione dei metodi di osservazione, di sperimentazione e di misurazione matematici a tutto il dominio delle scienze;
(4) nel riconoscimento che ogni gesto dell'uomo, e, quindi, tutto l'universo dei linguaggi porta a esperienze conoscitive che non sono concluse in se stesse, ma che sono il punto di partenza per conoscenze sempre nuove.

Se c'è, però, unità nei fini, c'è una forte differenza nei modi e negli strumenti operativi. Nascono alcune tendenze che sono pienamente vitali ancora oggi. San Francesco pone le cose della natura, del creato, al centro del mondo in uno spirito sistemico di solidarietà. Per Grossatesta (1168–1253) l'universo è nato da un punto di luce. Le leggi dell'ottica, quindi, sono il fondamento della realtà fisica e la visione è l'elemento primo della conoscenza. Un altro francescano, Ruggero Bacone (i cui scritti fondamentali vanno datati tra il 1266 ed il 1268), si pone il problema di una riedificazione del sapere, che sia al tempo stesso riedificazione della chiesa e della società civile, attraverso la inestricabile connessione di tutte le scienze. Se è vero che "solum in mathematici est demonstratio vera et potens" è anche vero che "sine experientia nihil sufficienter sciri potest." E l'esperienza può solo confermare (e confermare sul terreno psicologico) verità già acquisite. Non potrà mai produrne alcuna. Non è un principio di certificazione e di verifica.

Gli studi più recenti e più attenti vanno mostrando sempre più la cultura orientale di Francesco; il ruolo fondamentale di una cultura palestinese (di cui non troviamo però traccia nei libri dell'epoca) nella sua formazione scientifica e religiosa. Lo stesso rifiuto del possesso, del dominio e dell'accumulo appare in rapporto strettissimo con i contemporanei pensatori della Siria musulmana. Il rifiuto della ricerca della bellezza nelle sacre scritture non è un radicale rigorismo, ma un riferimento chiaro a quella cultura percettiva ed analogica che modella la *Leggenda dei tre compari*, l'unico testo, come ho ricordato, che spieghi, non certo con i termini della dialettica, la conversione e la formazione culturale di Francesco. I viaggi in Terra Santa e nella Penisola Iberica non mirano certo alla conversione degli infedeli, ma al confronto con le proprie radici culturali.

La conoscenza della natura e dell'uomo troverà in Tommaso D'Aquino (così condizionato dai quei centri di studio promossi da Federico II) l'avvio di una cultura teologica (ormai indipendente dalla filosofia) che non si risolve in un esercizio dialettico, ma prende forma, attraverso una elaborazione sistemica dei dati rivelati, in un corpus scientifico, in una *Summa theologica*. La teologia cattolica, nell'epoca moderna, deve larga parte del suo sviluppo alla conoscenza scientifica elaborata da Tommaso.

Il terzo polo è rappresentato da Federico II che fissa la sua continuità nelle scuole e nelle università laiche, e che appare uno scienziato interessato non a problemi occasionali, ma a scelte metodologiche. Se Chenu ha rilevato negli spiriti teologici un collegamento stretto con Aristotele, Federico II mostra come lo stesso Aristotele non sia più un punto di riferimento immutabile e ripeterà con convinzione: Aristotele discorda dal vero. "Non sic se habet." Non è verisimile ciò che scrive Aristotele. L'imperatore svevo trova nell'osservazione, nella percezione visiva, in stretto collegamento con la cultura francescana, lo strumento chiave della conoscenza. Questo della percezione visiva che avvia la conoscenza è uno dei temi chiave che dovremo studiare con molta forza e con molto coraggio nei prossimi anni. Indicazioni precise emergono dallo stesso Federico II e più ancora da Ruggero Bacone: tra tutti i sensi solamente la vista conduce alla differenziazione, al sapere, e infine alla saggezza. Certo anche la vista della parola scritta nel libro, ma soprattutto la vista interiore, dell'occhio della mente, la percezione.

È difficile trovare documenti scritti del XII secolo e del Duecento che consentano di capire fino in fondo una tematica così complessa, per noi occidentali. Ma la parola scritta, come ricorda il grande arabista Michele Amari, conserva solo qualche documento del potere. Dovremo necessariamente convenire che i libri conservano solo qualche testimonianza del Duecento. La scrittura, infatti, è un promemoria usato prevalentemente per trasferire le conoscenze acquisite attraverso il pensiero concettuale.

Non va dimenticata la lunga tradizione esoterica, fin dalla più remota antichità, che siamo soliti definire il *mysterium absconditum*, legato ad ogni religione, anche a quella cristiana, e ad ogni forma di conoscenza. I misteri, gli elementi fondanti di una fede o di una cultura, vengono rivelati oralmente, gestualmente, visivamente attraverso percorsi iniziatici mentali e fisici. La nascita nel Duecento delle società segrete e dei Cavalieri teutonici ed il loro stretto collegamento con Federico II, conferma, se ce ne fosse bisogno, che molta parte della conoscenza è tramandata secondo percorsi iniziatici. Lo stesso contrasto di Cielo d'Alcamo, fondamentale per riconoscere la cultura non solo letteraria del Duecento, era tramandato oralmente.

Scrittura ed immagine: globalità dei linguaggi e multimedialità

Uno studio sempre più attento, in chiave visiva e non storico artistica, del Medioevo, tende a rilevare una profonda frattura tra scrittura ed immagine, al punto che si può sicuramente dire che, in molte regioni europee, quanto viene acquisito attraverso il pensiero percettivo, attraverso le associazioni simboliche ed analogiche, viene riproposto e tramandato essenzialmente attraverso linguaggi audiovisivi difficili da capirsi da chi, come noi, si è formato su una cultura sintattica e classificatoria. La grande diffusione dei *media* del mondo moderno, della televisione che penetra ormai nella totalità delle case, a differenza del libro, la grande recrudescenza dell'analfabetismo, soprattutto di quello di ritorno, che colpisce persone spesso con un elevato grado di alfabetismo di partenza (che sapevano cioè leggere e scrivere molto bene e spesso in più lingue) concentra l'attenzione sulla cosiddetta multimedialità.

L'uomo, da quando è sulla terra, ha comunicato con una globalità di linguaggi molto diversi, ma integrati: il gesto, la linea, il colore, i rumori, il suono, la parola parlata e scritta. Questa globalità dei linguaggi (un vero e proprio sistema comunicativo, che trova il suo elemento qualificante nella complementarietà delle diversità) è sempre stata percepita attraverso i sensi ed essenzialmente attraverso l'udito e la visione ed è stata tramandata attraverso un insieme articolato, organico e non omogeneo di strumenti che vanno dal libro, alla parola parlata, alla memoria (sollecitata da un insieme di tecniche), alle opere visive. Se oggi disponiamo di registratori elettronici del suono e dell'immagine, dobbiamo anche convenire che, in altre epoche, culture e civiltà, esistevano altri "registratori": la memoria, la pittura, la scultura, il disegno, l'architettura conservavano e trasmettevano quelle che Michele Amari chiama con termine globalizzante le testimonianze dell'ingegno. Quelli visivi appaiono sempre più come strumenti comunicativi completi che consentono, meglio del libro, una piena comunicazione e che diventano strumenti per la formazione delle conoscenze. Io credo che uno degli errori fondamentali che spesso commettiamo è quello di ricercare nei testi scritti testimonianze del visivo di epoche, come il Duecento, che evidenziano come si comprenda solo ciò che si vede.

È forte la tentazione di spiegare il visivo con la parola scritta e, spesso, anche i più esperti nel campo della massmediologia moderna, come Umberto Eco, sostengono che l'immagine per essere compresa deve essere spiegata: la percezione, cioè, dovrebbe essere spiegata con i concetti. Al contrario la psicologia moderna riconosce chiaramente come le conoscenze su cui si basa la percezione solo in parte si sovrappongono alla comprensione concettuale; così percezione e concetti possono non andare d'accordo. Vengono evidenziati alcuni parametri di riferimento che ci consentono di leggere fino in fondo il ruolo del Duecento e di Federico II nella formazione e nel trasferimento delle conoscenze e dell'uso sistemico, autenticamente integrato, correttamente multimediale, dei media della comunicazione, almeno in quell'epoca. Ogni strumento parla un suo linguaggio. Il libro trasmette la parola scritta; la cosiddetta opera d'arte trasmette il complesso dei linguaggi audiovisivi. Federico II aveva ben sperimentato la interdipendenza degli elementi nel sistema dei linguaggi comunicativi quando aveva osservato che i falchi, con gli occhi cuciti perdono non solo la vista, ma anche l'olfatto.

I parametri di riferimento ai quali ho fatto cenno sono i seguenti:

(1) le percezioni sono rappresentazioni simboliche del mondo, e, quindi, non sono figure. Al concetto di arte come rappresentazione va sostituita, almeno per molte epoche e civiltà, l'esperienza conoscitiva dell'immagine;
(2) le interazioni simboliche obbediscono a regole non fisiche e queste regole sono efficaci, anche se del tutto diverse dalle leggi fisiche. Sono certo più difficili da studiarsi. Al razionale letto come insieme di definizioni, di ragionamenti, di dimostrazioni dialettiche (che sfociano spesso, come nella grande arte greca o del rinascimento italiano, nel sensazionale, nello spettacolare e nel trionfalistico) si contrappone l'emozione, l'evocazione, la partecipazione mistica, l'esperienza concreta e fantastica;
(3) i simboli liberano l'immaginazione e la percezione dalle limitazioni della fisica. Al realismo del mito si contrappone, dunque, lo psicologismo del simbolo. L'allegoria e la triade sillogismo/deduzione/concetto trovano nell'analisi, nella cultura grafica e sintattica e nell'arte come rappresentazione la loro struttura espressiva. Di contro il visionario immaginifico trova nella sintesi, nel simbolo, nella parabola, nella linea, nel colore, nelle cose della natura naturale e della natura costruita dall' uomo, i propri media espressivi;
(4) le conoscenze immagazzinate nel passato (archetipico o scandito dall'eredità genetica: due valutazioni in netta contrapposizione) e quelle acquisite con l'apprendimento sociale ed individuale, sono fondamentali per la percezione. Quanto è stato appreso in passato (anche attraverso esperienze emotive, fantastiche e legate al visionario immaginifico) crea delle analogie per affrontare il presente e predire il futuro, per avviare forme di conoscenza che saranno sempre punto nuovo di partenza.

Si conosce, cioè, non solo per deduzione e per concetto, per classificazione, ma anche per stimolazioni simboliche e per analogia. Le due forme di conoscenza, profondamente diverse, non sono in antitesi; possono (anzi dovrebbero) coesistere in una stessa cultura o civiltà, in uno stesso contesto sociale, in uno stesso individuo.

Quelli che leggono spiegazioni concettuali non capiscono

Queste osservazioni, che derivano dalla scienza e dalla sperimentazione moderna e dall'esame dei nuovi media e delle nuove tecnologie telematiche, trovano nel libro delle visioni di Angela da Foligno indicazioni delle più chiare. Nel processo conoscitivo c'è sempre una voce, c'è la scrittura (ma, con un ruolo marginale. È detto infatti che quelli che la leggono non capiscono), c'è la visione. Una visione tutta conoscitiva non di qualcosa di reale, di oggetti, o di scene, o di idee concettuali o platoniche, o di qualcosa di rappresentato. Ma la visione della luce che fa conoscere, che diventa essa stessa atto di conoscenza. Vedendo con gli occhi, si attiva la vista interiore.

Una delle intuizioni più profonde di Federico II, in piena armonia con la cultura del tempo, è proprio questa: la visione crea impressioni profonde; produce convinzioni durature; attiva in-formazioni (forma dentro in modo durevole) e conoscenze. L'oggetto visivo è un medium comunicativo. Ho già ricordato, in anni passati, la porta di Capua. Nella visione delle torri e della facciata e nel passaggio fisico attraverso la porta, si realizza un cambiamento emotivo, evocativo, esistenziale di stato individuale, sociale e politico. Ricorderò ora brevemente le altre opere visive legate direttamente alla progettazione di Federico II.

Non c'è dubbio che queste opere possano essere lette anche come oggetti artistici. Ma se il Duecento segna, anche in campo religioso, il passaggio dalla teologia dialettica, scritturistica e comparativa, alla teologia simbolica, credo che alle soglie del 2000 si possa superare la filologia comparativa, per leggere queste opere come strumenti comunicativi, integrati in un sistema multimediale, mirati a formare ed a trasmettere le conoscenze. Non che la critica testuale sia inutile o impedisca di fare scienza. L'esempio più tipico viene da Ruggero Bacone, grande innovatore, ma al tempo stesso legato ad una teologia testuale e, perciò, secondo una bella immagine di Chenu, come sempre in ritardo.

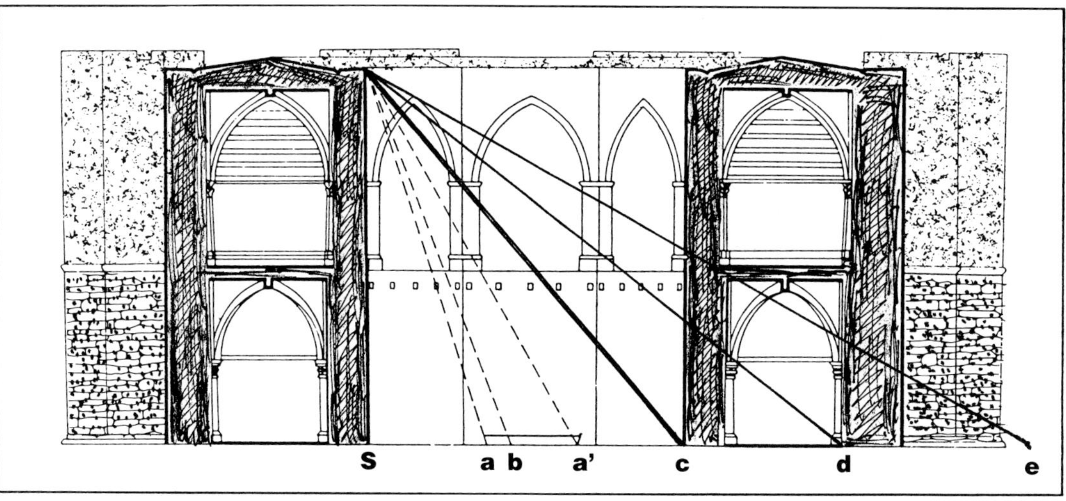

3. Le ombre proiettate dalla parete Sud nel corso dell'anno: (*a–a'*) le ombre di giugno e ottobre delimitavano la vasca; (*b*) le ombre di luglio delimitavano il sedile nella vasca; (*c*) l'ombra a mezzogiorno negli equinozi; (*d*) l'ombra teorica a mezzogiorno dell'ingresso del Sole nei Pesci e nello Scorpione; (*e*) l'ombra teorica a mezzogiorno dell'ingresso del Sole nell'Acquario e nel Sagittario
Da Aldo Tavolaro, "Una stella sulla Murgia," in *Castel del Monte* (Bari, 1981), fig. 3; elaborazione: autore

Castel del Monte

Castel del Monte costituisce certamente, al di là dei suoi valori metasegnici ed artistici sui quali a lungo si discute (dal momento che rappresenta un'opera di straordinaria bellezza), un documento visivo complesso della cultura e delle acquisizioni scientifiche del Duecento. È al tempo stesso un laboratorio astronomico; un laboratorio di ricerca e sperimentazione scientifica, un percorso conoscitivo, una visione immaginifica. Sugli aspetti astronomici, Aldo Tavolaro ha scritto pagine di estremo interesse, che ho in passato sottovalutato, pur avendole pienamente condivise.

Le proporzioni del castello, come mostra la sovrapposizione di uno schema di Vitruvio per la costruzione degli orologi solari, sono determinate dal sole, il cui ingresso, nei vari segni zodiacali, è scandito da elementi architettonici fondamentali (fig. 3). Ad esempio, le pareti interne del cortile proiettano un'ombra che coincide con la lunghezza del cortile a mezzogiorno, nei giorni degli equinozi, quando il sole entra nei segni dell'ariete e della bilancia. A mezzogiorno del 21 febbraio e del 21 ottobre, quando il sole entra nei segni dei pesci e dello scorpione, l'ombra, in questo caso teorica (ma apprezzabile con il visionario immaginifico) coincide con il perimetro maggiore delle sale.

Le intenzioni del progettista non lasciano dubbi, dal momento che si potrebbero citare ancora decine di esempi. La forma non regolare del cortile richiama, attraverso le misure ed i numeri delle aperture angolari, l'asse di inclinazione e, perciò, il variare delle stagioni. La divina proporzione, la sezione aurea risulta sistematicamente nelle misure dell'edificio nel rapporto di 0,6, ma è presente, nella ripetizione della sequenza di Fibonacci attraverso elementi strutturali e funzionali dell'edificio. L'orientamento concorre a definire Castel del Monte non soltanto un calendario astronomico, ma una sperimentazione compiuta di misurazione matematica delle conoscenze astronomiche dell'epoca. Non siamo di fronte ad una esercitazione antiquaria e ripetitiva, basata sulle curiosità. La configurazione del calendario astronomico, come avevo già rilevato, era possibile empiricamente sulla base delle conoscenze già acquisite nel IX e nel X secolo.

Ora credo di dover aggiungere che le conoscenze empiriche, in questo caso, anche dopo l'incontro intellettuale e fisico tra Federico II e Fibonacci, sono rivisitate alla luce della convinzione che la matematica rappresenta l'unica *demonstratio vera et potens*. Castel del Monte, anche negli aspetti che mi erano sembrati ovvi, come quelli legati all'astronomia, conferma il passaggio da una scienza empirica ad un sistema scientifico. Un'altro degli aspetti fondamentali del Duecento è proprio questo: la cultura classica è padroneggiata in modo esemplare. Ma non si tratta di un recupero antiquario o imitativo. Fa parte del bagaglio conoscitivo essenziale per andare avanti, per proporre soluzioni spesso radicalmente nuove. Non viene buttato via nulla. Se ne ricerca la conferma o il superamento attraverso i metodi scientifici nuovi ed in particolare traducendo la geometria in algebra, dimostrando, come in un laboratorio scientifico, *cum parvis numeris*, con i numeri piccoli, come ricorda Fibonacci, quanto era stato dimostrato in altro modo.

Castel del Monte, bisogna ricordarlo, risponde, fin nei più minuti dettagli, alle conoscenze sulla trasformazione delle figure piane e dei solidi ed alle conoscenze matematiche che penetrano e descrivono quei processi. L'edificio, dunque, riproduce scientificamente le leggi della simmetria matematica (da non confondersi con quella araldica), che è essenzialmente conoscenza della natura e dell'uomo; leggi che erano usate empiricamente fin dalla più remota antichità. L'uso della matematica, il graduale svincolamento dell'algebra dalla geometria, il perfezionamento della trigonometria, il gusto arabo della precisione: tutto quanto, cioè, rappresenta l'innovazione scientifica del Duecento, è sperimentato in Castel del Monte. I due elementi archetipici del quadrato (che rappresenta la complessità e sistematicità dell'esperienza conoscitiva dell'uomo sulla terra e l'accesso alle verità supreme, sparse nei quattro angoli del mondo e aperte solo agli iniziati) e del cerchio (che simboleggia non solo la perfezione spirituale, ma la sfera della libertà cosmica, la totalità sintetizzatrice), si confondono.

Gli assi di simmetria hanno otto punti in comune (un numero altamente simbolico nelle strutture della conoscenza). L'ottagono che ne deriva è la quadratura del cerchio, la sintesi delle sintesi, il tutto, la conoscenza globale, è il mandala che le culture antiche, centro asiatiche, ma anche altomedievali hanno sempre inseguito. La sperimentazione di Castel del Monte consente la penetrazione fisica e mentale, attraverso la matematica, nel mandala riassuntivo di ogni esperienza umana (fig. 4).

C'è un centro (il centro, non certo geografico, del mondo) raffigurato a Castel del Monte da una vasca ottagonale piena d'acqua che genera la vita. Otto sono gli elementi vitali (dove quadrato e cerchio si confondono) che generano, partoriscono la vita nuova nelle torri, riproponendo ancora nel quadrato e nel cerchio che genera l'ottagono elementi generativi sempre rinnovati. Una creazione sempre nuova e che non ha fine

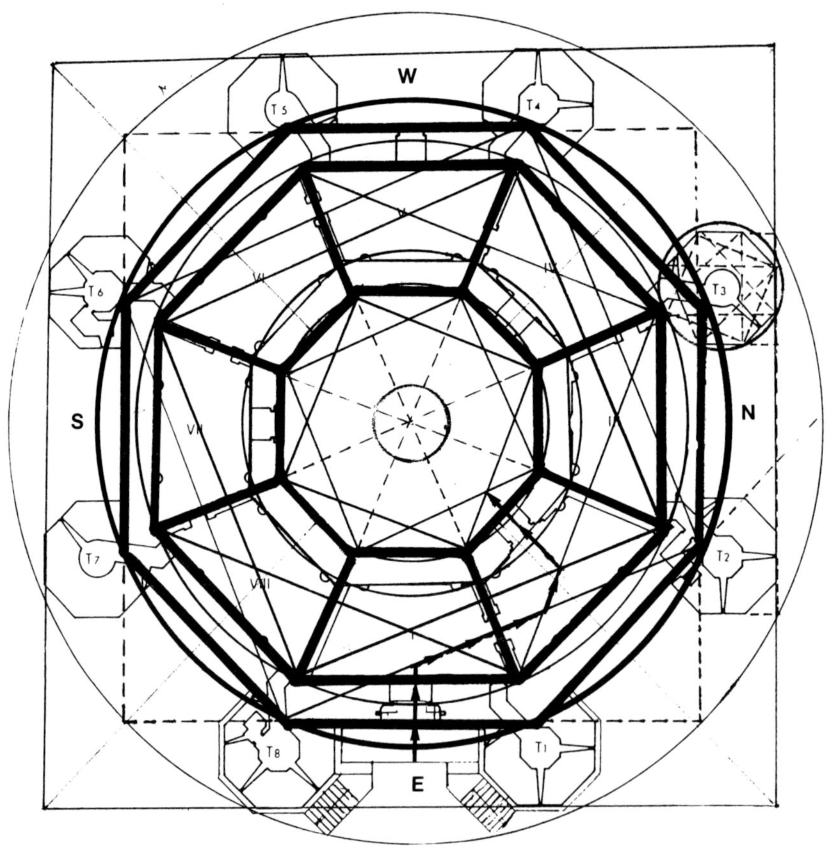

4. Cerchio e quadrato si confondono, con un processo generativo senza fine
Disegno: autore

come la conoscenza che si evolve, genera sempre, a *flos*, nuove *quaestiones*, che vengono proposte anche attraverso la pietra, le variazioni di luminosità ed il colore. Troppo facilmente dimentichiamo che gran parte dell'edificio era coperto dalla simbolica breccia corallina.

In questa rilettura matematica delle leggi generative della natura c'è a parer mio la chiave del sapere scientifico di Federico II; la riaffermazione, in chiave sperimentale e matematica della rinnovabilità delle leggi della natura, del processo generativo continuo, della straordinaria capacità della natura di organizzarsi dinamicamente secondo evidenti parametri sistemici e secondo forme geometriche, sempre misurabili attraverso le incognite dell'algebra.

Il percorso conoscitivo, ovviamente, punta al centro, dove si rompe la distanza tra cielo e terra e dove la creatura diventa creatore cono-

7. La visione immaginifica rompe le barriere della fisica
Disegno: autore

8. Una reta di triangolazioni, misurabili algebricamente, individua percorsi mentali e visivi per la conoscenza
Disegno: autore

provvedimenti amministrativi concreti. In particolare Federico II favorì la conservazione ed il miglioramento delle razze, la cura delle malattie, l'allevamento.

Il *De arte venandi cum avibus* è composto di due trattati (di Ornitologia e di Falconeria), il primo propedeutico al secondo. La critica moderna è unanime a sottolineare che si tratta di un'opera centrata sulla sperimentazione e sull'osservazione, e l'osservazione è molto accurata.

Dal momento che l'opera è stata composta nel Duecento, nell'epoca in cui sono molti a credere che si comprende ciò che si vede (e la metodologia dell'osservazione ne è la prova evidente), le immagini che accompagnano il testo non hanno né carattere decorativo, né illustrativo, ma sono approfondimenti, espressioni sintetiche, stimoli visivi che favoriscono il trasferimento e l'apprendimento del frutto delle osservazioni. Viene elaborato un modello di manuale che è tutt'oggi alla base degli studi delle università di medicina e di scienze naturali in tutto il mondo. Malgrado la grande diffusione della fotografia e dell'immagine elettronica, persino sui grandi settimanali si continua a proporre la scienza, la natura e gli animali attraverso disegni colorati sintetici, riassuntivi ed evocativi. Questo ruolo evocativo dell'immagine è chiaro in ogni pagina. A puro titolo di esempio ricorderò il folio 7 recto relativo ai modi ed ai tempi di abbandono dell'acqua da parte degli uccelli acquatici per procurarsi il cibo, o il folio 7 verso, relativo all'ordine in cui gli uccelli partono per recarsi al pascolo e del loro ritorno ai rifugi palustri o acquatici. Nei disegni del folio 8 è riassunta visivamente la posizione assunta dagli uccelli quando dormono, quando non dormono e quando sono in acqua. Nel folio 9 ecco le abitudini alimentari di alcune specie di uccelli. Nel folio 11 verso e 12 c'è il modo di procurarsi il cibo da parte degli uccelli anfibi. Ed i falchi ed i falconieri al lavoro si vedono bene nel folio 62 verso, con una descrizione visiva e manualistica dei nodi o nel folio 64, ed ancora nel folio 76 (figg. 9–10).

La formazione scientifica di Federico II

Come e dove formò Federico II il suo amore per un metodo scientifico così innovativo? Il ruolo degli uomini di corte è evidente. I saggi

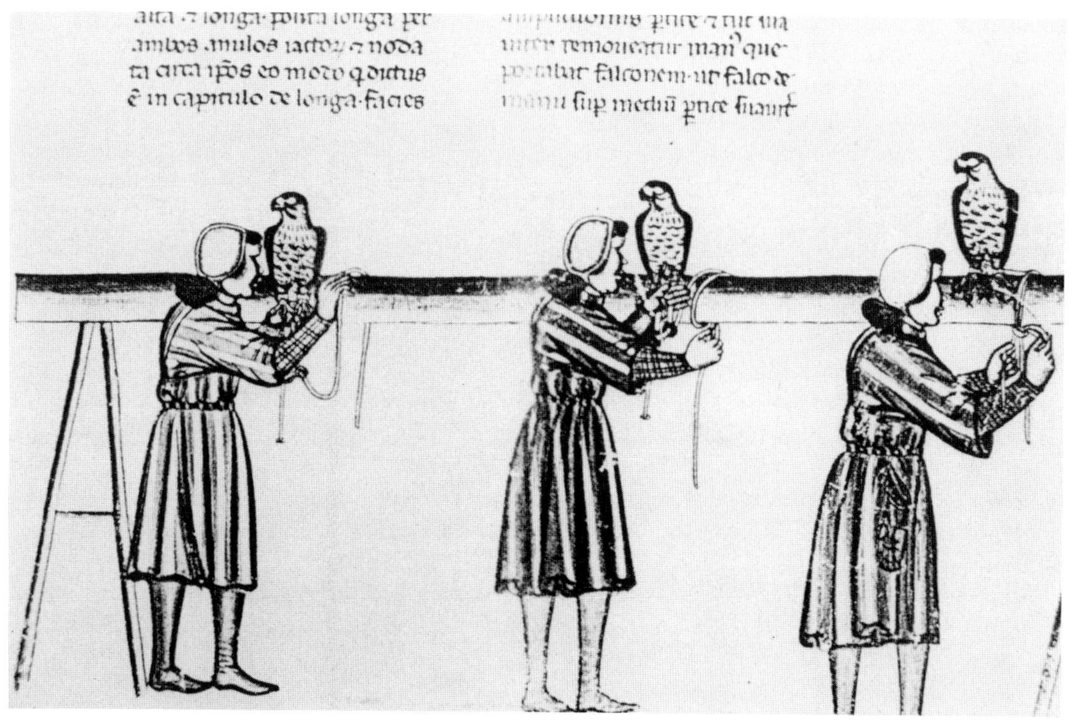

9. Federico II, *De arte venandi cum avibus*: falchi, falconieri e nodi, MS. Palatinus latinus 1071, folio 76r, prima metà del Duecento
Da *Das Falkenbuch Kaiser Friedrichs II., nach der Prachthandschrift in der Vatikanischen Bibliothek, Codex Ms. Pal. Lat. 1071* (Dortmund, 1980)

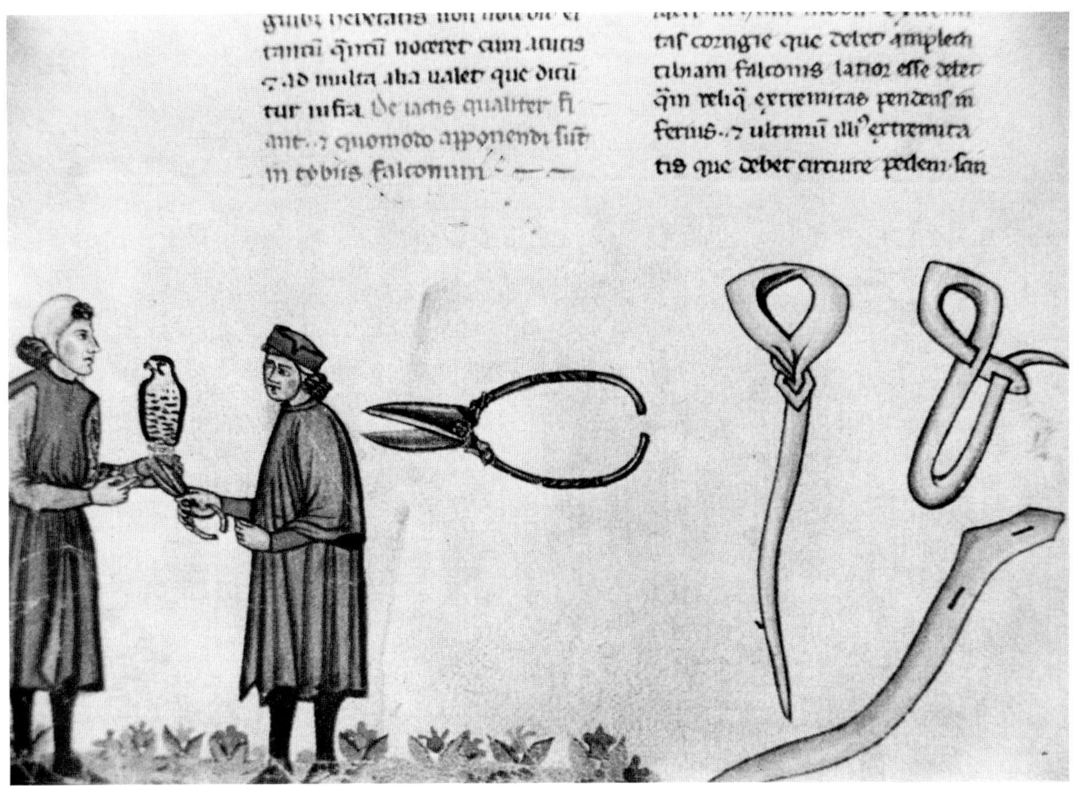

10. Federico II, *De arte venandi cum avibus*: falchi, falconieri e nodi, MS. Pal. lat. 1071, folio 62v, prima metà del Duecento
Da *Das Falkenbuch Kaiser Friedrichs II.*

di Francesco Gabrieli (profondo conoscitore del mondo islamico) e di Giorgio Nebbia (chimico e attento ricercatore dei rapporti merceologici tra Oriente ed Occidente nel medioevo) hanno mostrato con cura le acquisizioni scientifiche della itinerante corte sveva. Perché non va certo dimenticato il frenetico viaggiare di Federico II e della sua corte, che risiedette a Palermo per tempi assai limitati e frammentati. Ma gli uomini sapienti che lo circondarono non sono sufficienti a mostrare in che modo si è avviato un processo destinato a sconvolgere il sistema scientifico.

I suggerimenti e le indicazioni per trovare risposte a queste domande vengono proprio da Federico II e dalla lettera già citata: "Ante suscepta regiminis onera, a juventute (la conoscenza) quesivimus, formam ejus indesinenter amavimus et in odore unguentorum suorum semper aspiravimus indefesse."

Gli oneri del governo furono assunti con la maggiore età il 26 dicembre 1208. Già l'anno successivo, nel 1209, Federico andrà sposo a Costanza d'Aragona e comincerà la lotta politica per la conquista del titolo imperiale, acquisito, sotto gli auspici di Innocenzo III, da Ottone di Brunswich. La grande immersione nella conoscenza dura, dunque, fino al compimento del quattordicesimo anno. È lo stesso Federico II a spiegare che cosa avvenne "post regni nostri curas assumptas." Non sopporta certo di passare senza impegni il poco tempo lasciato libero dagli impegni del regno e della famiglia. Questo tempo lo spende "totum in lectionis exercitatione (in letture), ut anime clarius vigeat instrumentum in acquisitione scientie, sine qua mortalium vita non regitur liberaliter."

La conoscenza, dunque, libera, rende conveniente la vita. La lettura è fondamentale per l'acquisizione delle conoscenze, ma viene utilizzata essenzialmente dopo l'assunzione degli impegni di governo, quando non è più possibile un'immersione totale. La maggiore età del dicembre 1208 rappresenta, per esplicita dichiarazione di Federico II, un termine *ante e post quem* per riconoscere la formazione della mentalità scientifica, l'iniziazione alla formidabile logica ed alia visione dell'unità e dell'universalità del sapere umano, dell'imperatore svevo.

La formazione di Federico bambino

Di Federico bambino conosciamo l'essenziale, ma abbiamo pochissime notizie. Nasce a Jesi il 26 dicembre 1194. Vive a Foligno i sui primi tre anni di vita, fino alla morte del padre Arrigo VI, quando è richiamato a Palermo ed eletto re di Sicilia. Nel 1198 muore la madre e i *famigliari* designati da Costanza nel testamento furono arcivescovi e vescovi latini.

Tra il 1194 ed il 1197 Federico è dunque a Foligno, affidato a Corrado di Urslingen, duca di Spoleto e governatore di Assisi. Sono quegli gli anni in cui Francesco ha assistito al battesimo di Federico a San Ruffino (1195) e in cui diventa maggiorenne e gaudente, avviando il lungo processo della conversione, che trova nell'adesione ad una cultura non certamente classica, ma orientale e percettiva, il punto di riferimento primario. Lo psicologismo del simbolo si contrappone all'astrazione delle tendenze metafisiche e vive la realtà attraverso il gesto oculare (la visione), corporeo e globale, laringo-boccale (la parola). L'Umbria ha vissuto già nel III/IV secolo l'avvento di monaci siriaci che si sistemano nelle lauree eremitiche della Val Nerina. Questi movimenti trovano in Benedetto (non sappiamo quanto singolo e reale monaco o quanto simbolo riassuntivo di un movimento monacale) ed in Gregorio Magno (il cui orientalismo appare sempre più evidente) le espressioni organizzatorie. Sarà proprio Gregorio, nei *Moralia in Job*, nel catechismo fondamentale per tutto il medioevo, a dire che abita in Occidente chi ama le cose caduche ed in Oriente chi guarda alle cose supreme.

Abbiamo per il resto notizie molto vaghe su che cosa capita in Umbria nel medioevo. Certo è che nasce e si diffonde il ruolo dell'abbazia di san'Eutizio, nella Val Nerina, il cui ruolo culturale ed economico, completamente dimenticato, non sarà secondario rispetto a Montecassino. E si tratta certo di un punto di riferimento di monaci orientali. Se crediamo alla moderna psicologia, i primi tre anni di vita sono fondamentali nella conoscenza. Le esperienze emozionali, tattili, visive, relazionali, comportamentali allora condotte informano tutta l'esistenza di un uomo. È certo singolare l'analogia, nella visione del mondo, della natura e della conoscenza tra Francesco e Federico, collegati dalle leggende dell'epoca (tra l'altro Francesco nel 1198 prende parte, proprio contro Corrado di Urslingen, alla battaglia di Assisi), ma soprattutto dall'aver vissuto il primo gli anni iniziali della conversione, il secondo gli anni iniziali della vita nello stesso ambiente culturale e naturale. Ebbero non solo in Innocenzo III ed in Onorio III punti di riferimento comune, ma anche in Corrado di Urslingen.

Per ricostruire la formazione di Federico, è certo fondamentale poter conoscere meglio Foligno, l'Umbria, l'orientalismo che condiziona Francesco e che non può essere limitato alla supposta derivazione da una famiglia ebrea, essendo evidente, ad esempio, nella lenta conversione, un percorso iniziatico del tutto analogo all'esperienza giudaico-cristiana. Al tempo stesso è evidente, come ho già ricordato, una visione della natura, della richezza, dell'accumulo facilmente riscontrabile nei cosiddetti santi musulmani del XII secolo.

Nel 1197 Federico come si è detto è a Palermo, dal 1198 ha tutori e maestri latini, in una città nella quale esistevano, come riconosce quel geniale studioso che fu Ugo Monneret de Villard, due grandi tradizioni e due grandi culture: la bizantina e la musulmana. La tradizione latina, di contro, era quasi inesistente dal punto di vista culturale.

Federico II vive, dunque, la sua formazione in una grande città islamica (200 o 300 mila abitanti) che ha fama di essere, insieme a Cordoba, la più bella del mondo, con maestosi edifici, con industrie fiorenti (marcate da una sempre crescente innovazione tecnologica), con grande lusso e ricchezza.

Mentre Innocenzo III, nel 1205, esorta maestri e studenti di Parigi a recarsi in Grecia ed a resuscitare gli studi letterari nella terra di origine, Federico, orfano, abbandonato, in una situazione di estrema povertà, vive in una città, con trecento moschee, piena di *paràdeisos*, i grandi giardini della terra, ricchi di acqua che dà la vita e la conoscenza. L'architettura civile e religiosa di Palermo era dichiaratamente legata alla cultura araba d'Africa e di Spagna. La città non apparteneva culturalmente et etnicamente all'Occidente che nasceva, abitata, com'era, in prevalenza da arabi, africani e berberi. Federico vive anche nel ricordo del grande nonno Ruggero, profondo conoscitore di astronomia, di filosofia, di scienze occulte, di matematica, che aveva sempre guardato all'Africa come alla terra promessa per costruire non un impero commerciale, ma un dominio marittimo centrato sul Mediterraneo e sul possesso delle colte sponde africane.

Federico ascolta nel porto e nei mercati quanti, in ogni lingua ed appartenenti ad ogni cultura, hanno qualcosa da raccontare. Apprende quanto la ricerca del senso della realtà fisica delle cose utilizzate porta a sperimentare e ad acquisire nuove conoscenze.

Al di là degli insegnamenti dei suoi maestri latini e del cardinal Savelli (il futuro Onorio III) Federico è evidentemente anche sommerso da informazioni visive. Non deve andar lontano, basta che giri nel palazzo del Cassaro o nei giardini dei castelli dei re normanni, che, come ben riconosce George Marçais, portano il marchio assai bene riconoscibile dello stile degli edifici africani. Se a Foligno non è riconoscibile nulla degli anni in cui Federico vi soggiornò bambino, a Palermo esistono alcuni edifici visti, vissuti da Federico e che, a mio parere, ebbero un ruolo fondamentale nella formazione della mentalità scientifica del futuro imperatore. L'esempio più rilevante è rappresentato dalla Cappella Palatina, proprio nel palazzo reale, dove Federico viveva. Qui, come in una grande mediateca (in una teca non solo dei libri, ma delle immagini, dei suoni e dei gesti) si confrontano e si contrappongono due grandi civiltà: quella allegorica, narrativa, classificatoria del mondo bizantino e della cultura concettuale e quella sintetica, analogica, simbolica del mondo vicino orientale, spagnolo ed africano e della cultura percettiva (fig. II).

Nel soffitto una serie di mandala, di elementi ottagonali, indicano con grande chiarezza all'uomo le strade della conoscenza, secondo modelli largamente sviluppati in Egitto, nella Berberia orientale ed in Spagna.

I frequenti riferimenti all'Africa, già rilevati sotto il profilo stilistico da Georges Marçais e approfonditi da Guiseppe Bellafiore, sul piano culturale spingono a guardare al grande africano che plasma larga parte della cultura medievale. Mi riferiscono a Sant'Agostino, che nelle *Confessioni* ci offre chiare indicazioni sulla sua formazione. Narra delle difficoltà ad imparare il greco (anche un altro grande uomo del medioevo, Gregorio Magno, pur abitando per quattro anni a Costantinopoli si trova in difficoltà psicologica ad imparare il greco!). E conferma che non imparò a scuola ("non a docentibus, sed a loquentibus, in quorum et ego auribus partoriebam quidquid sentiebam"), ma nel

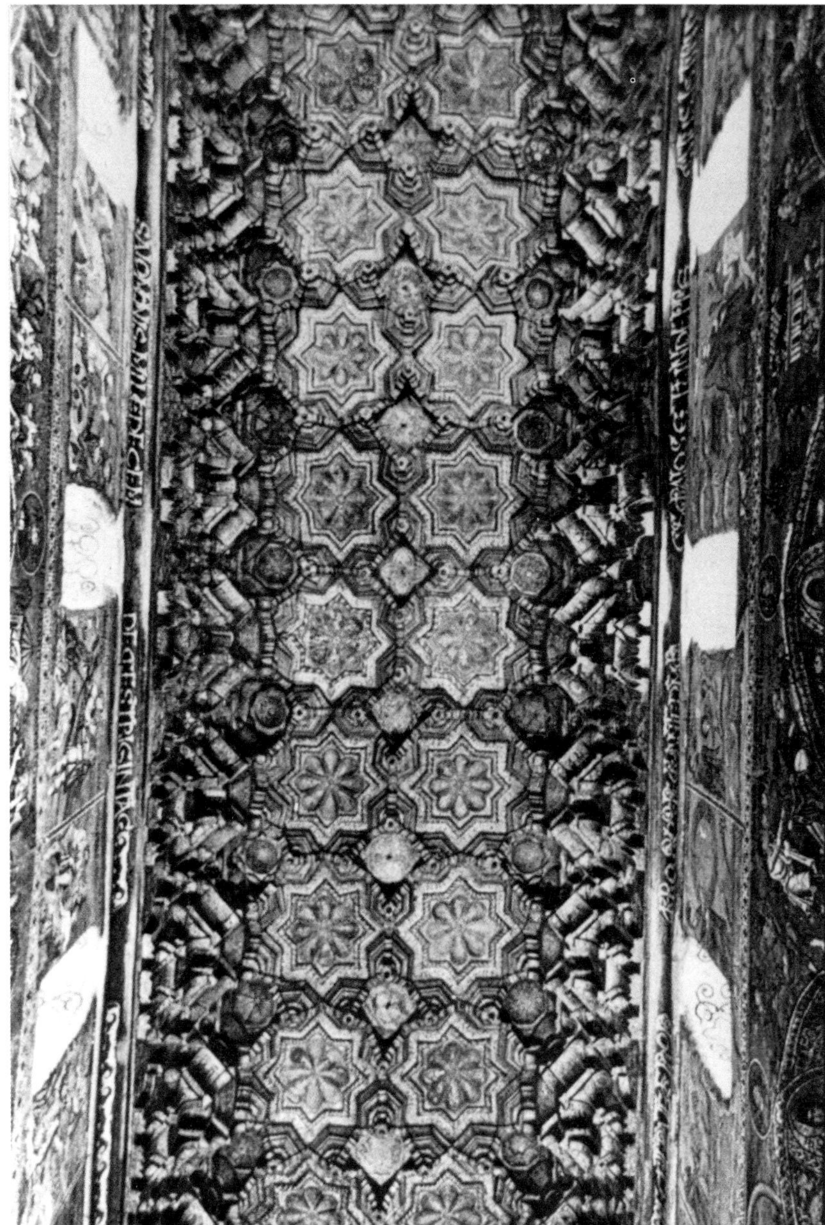

II. Palermo, Cappella Palatina, il soffitto: mandala ottagonali e stalattiti, del Duecento
Fotografia: SOC.AR.CO., Palermo

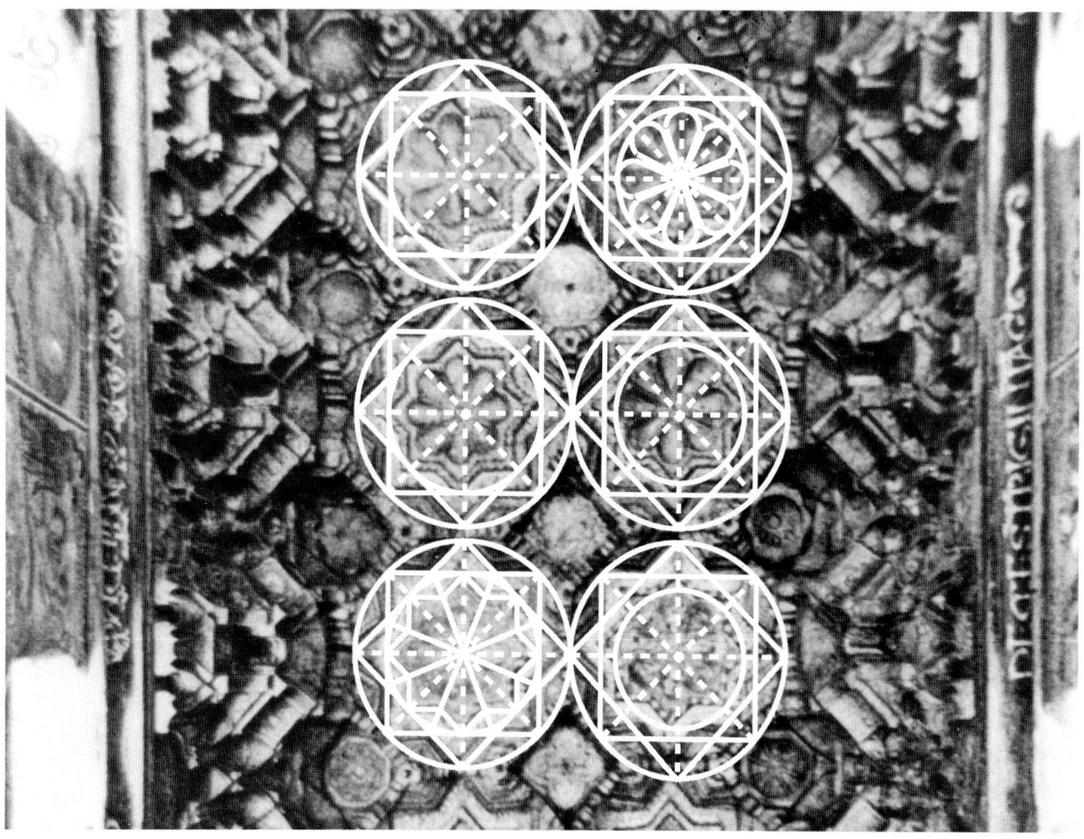

12. Palermo, Cappella Palatina, il soffitto, del Duecento
Fotografia: SOC.AR.CO., Palermo

contatto quotidiano con chi possedeva un sapere esistenziale e nelle cui orecchie partoriva i suoi sentimenti. Al di fuori delle regole della grammatica e della retorica c'è la libera curiosità: "hinc satis elucet maiorem habere vim ad discenda ista liberam curiositatem, quam meticulosam necessitatem." Da questa e non dalla pedante costrizione viene la forma per imparare. E la libera curiosità porta Federico II bambino a concentrarsi su quel ripetuto motivo ottagonale che porta alla conoscenza. Un motivo che è già pienamente sviluppato, ad esempio, nella moschea di Cordoba e che nell'intera Spagna altomedievale, in Africa, in India è segno della conoscenza suprema.

Questi elementi, che anche il Marçais, cadendo nell'errore della nostra epoca, definisce decorazioni, sono invece strumenti conoscitivi, che evocano direttamente la conoscenza. Bisognerà studiare fino in fondo come funziona la percezione visiva. Credo che lavorando a lungo, in *équipe*, tra matematici, fisici, naturalisti, storici dell'arte e della cultura, smontando queste immagini con il concorso del grafic computer (una protesi per ritrovare in piccola parte le capacità atrofizzate della nostra mente), simulando i percorsi conoscitivi della mente, sarà possibile riconoscere in modo plausibile quali meccanismi si mettono in moto e quali conoscenze questi mandala trasmettono.

Mi sembra comunque evidente che da questo soffitto Federico II deriva la visione della conoscenza organizzata come sistema, che si trasforma e si evolve secondo regole matematiche (fig. 12). Fondamentale mi appare anche la presenza delle stalattiti, così presenti in tutta la cultura islamica, ogni qual volta si determina un percorso iniziatico che porta alla conoscenza suprema. Anche in ambiente cristiano la stalattite (ad esempio, nella spagnola chiesa di San Juán de la Peña, in un santuario mozarabico, tappa fondamentale nella via dei pellegrinaggi verso Santiago de Compostela) diventa elemento determinante nel rapporto tra fedele e Dio.

Nel mondo arabo le stalattiti sono organizzate matematicamente, ed appaiono in percorsi iniziatici, come a Palermo, nella Zisa, dove, attraverso alcune nicchie, la grande fontana, i motivi simbolici, troviamo non solo modelli espressivi presenti in tutta l'Africa, ma soprattutto un modello conoscitivo. E non mi fermerò a ricordare l'intreccio tra quadrato e cerchio in molti edifici laici e cristiani di Palermo nell'età di Federico II: San Cataldo, la piccola Cuba, San Giovanni degli Eremiti.

Il visivo, la grande percezione, dunque, dovrà essere studiata non solo in chiave estetica. Ed un ruolo significativo, insieme, e non solo per la Palermo del Duecento, dovrà assumere lo studio delle illusioni ottiche (che Richard Gregory chiama le più curiose tra le percezioni), le percezioni extra-sensoriali (quelle che si verificano senza l'attività degli organi di senso fisiologicamente accertati), i cosiddetti fenomeni occulti. Ci può essere percezione senza segnali fisici, attraverso legami non materiali afferenti al cervello, ma anche in totale assenza di cervello.

Non c'è dubbio che nel XII secolo e nel Duecento le pratiche che definiamo magiche (basti pensare all'alchimia) hanno consentito di fare scoperte indubbiamente importanti e durevoli. Un esempio chiaro è quello dell'origine della bussola magnetica, che entra stabilmente in Europa nel 1195, un anno dopo la nascita di Federico. La storia inizia in Cina, con una tavola per la divinazione. Gli indovini scoprirono che la magnetite puntava sempre verso sud: avevano così un apparecchio magico che funzionava. Trasformando la magnetite in ago oscillante sull'acqua, si ebbe la bussola da marinaio che diventava attendibile e usciva dall'ambito dell'occulto ed entrava nel mondo della scienza e della tecnologia, anche se l'attrazione magnetica restava, e in verità resta, misteriosa.

Se la nostra scienza mostra una forte preferenza per le osservazioni facilmente ripetibili, Federico II nel suo *De arte venandi cum avibus*, ma anche a Castel del Monte, a Capua, a Bitonto, mostra una preferenza per le osservazioni che diano messaggi sull'organizzazione e sul funzionamento della natura. C'è soprattutto la convinzione che la natura ci dà dei segni come messaggi da leggere. Se questa visione è giudicata oggi lontana dalla scienza, la moderna psicologia mostra tutti i limiti di una classificazione logica dei fatti. Il concetto di simboli dotati di potere, infatti, è stato sempre centrale nelle interpretazioni della mente. Ed è difficile descrivere adeguatamente i poteri di parole e musica, i processi percettivi del visivo (ma anche della migliore amica della scienza, la matematica), con i concetti normalmente accettati dalla scienza. Il *Puer Apuliae* appare sempre più figlio dell'Umbria e di Palermo. Studiare quei movimenti orientali che determinano la cultura visiva e percettiva di queste due regioni d'Italia rimane la scommessa dei prossimi anni.

Sarà fondamentale porre a confronto (per evidenziarne, al di là delle apparenti similitudini, le profondissime differenze) la concettuale Cappella Palatina di Aquisgrana (dove Federico II passò un'intera notte in compagnia con le ossa di Carlo Magno), con il mandalico cortile di Castel del Monte. Collegamenti semantici (e non stilistici) sarà invece possibile trovare tra Castel del Monte (progettato da Federico II al ritorno da Gerusalemme) e la Cupola della Roccia, che manifesta i suoi simbolismi di centro del mondo, di scrigno, di ascesa verso la conoscenza (in questo caso religiosa) che libera. Ma fondamentale sarà anche ricostruire a tutto tondo, come un insieme sistemico, la vicenda culturale e politica di Federico, legato, in un modo o nell'altro, a tutti quei personaggi reali del XII secolo e del Duecento, che la nostra scuola occidentale ha reso protagonisti di favole e di leggende, dando un significato del tutto negativo al visionario.

Questo breve scritto, realizzato sullo stimolo di Alberto Weismuller, deriva direttamente dall'approfondimento di due miei precedenti articoli, ai quali misi mano su sollecitazione di Angiola Maria Romanini prima e di Giosuè Musca poi. Non avrei mai pensato, infatti, di lasciare il mio laboratorio dell'Alto Medioevo non italiano, per studiare fatti italiani del Duecento, nel quale, a dire il vero, attraverso Francesco d'Assisi, Federico II e Tommaso d'Aquino, ho trovato occasioni straordinarie per dar sfogo alle mie fantasie storiche.

BIBLIOGRAFIA

Molti di noi passano la vita a scrivere sempre lo stesso articolo, ed ovviamente rimando a quei due scritti precedenti per le indicazioni bibliografiche e per i necessari approfondimenti. Si veda pertanto: Antonio Thiery, "Federico II e le scienze. Problemi di metodo per la lettura dell'arte federiciana," in *Federico II e l'arte del Duecento italiano*. Atti della III settimana di studi di storia dell'arte medievale dell'Università di Roma, 15–20 maggio 1978, a cura di Angiola M. Romanini, 2 voll. (Galatina, 1980), 277–299; Antonio Thiery, "Semantica sociale, messagio e simbolo," in *Potere, società e popolo nell'età sveva*, 1983 (Bari, 1984), 191–247.

Mi limito a dare alcune indicazioni bibliografiche essenziali sull'ultima parte di questo articolo: da dove Federico II derivò la sua formazione scientifica?

Amari, Michele. *Biblioteca arabo-sicula*. Leipzig, 1855–1857; Torino, 1880–1881.

Amari, Michele. *Storia dei musulmani di Sicilia*, 3 voll. in 4. Firenze, 1854–1872.

Gli Arabi in Italia, cultura, contatti e tradizione, a cura di Francesco Gabrieli e Umberto Scerrato. Milano, 1979.

Atti del Convegno di Studi su Federico II. Jesi, 1976.

Atti del Convegno Internazionale di Studi Federiciani, 1950. Palermo, 1952.

Bausani, Alessandro. "Il contribuito scientifico." In *Gli Arabi in Italia, cultura, contatti e tradizione* (Milano, 1979), 629–660. (Va ricordato che il Bausani, oltre che grande islamista, era un buon matematico.)

Bellafiore, Giuseppe. *Dall'Islam alla maniera, profilo dell'architettura siciliana dal IX al XII secolo*. Palermo, 1975.

Bellafiore, Giuseppe. *La Cattedrale di Palermo*. Palermo, 1976.

Bellafiore, Giuseppe. *La Zisa di Palermo*. Palermo, 1978.

Castel del Monte. Bari, 1981.

Chenu, Marie Dominique. *La théologie comme science au XIII siècle*. Paris, 1927, edizione rivista 1957; *La teologia come scienze nel XIII secolo*. Milano, 1971, 1985.

Crombie, Alastair Cameron. *Augustine to Galileo*. London, 1952; *Da S. Agostino a Galileo*. Milano, 1970.

De Stefano, Antonino. *La cultura alla corte di Federico II imperatore*. Palermo, 1938.

De Stefano, Antonino. *La cultura in Sicilia nel periodo normanno*. Palermo, 1938.

De Stefano, Antonino. *Federico II e le correnti spirituali del suo tempo*. Roma, 1922.

Gabrieli, Francesco. "Federico II e la cultura musulmana." In *Atti del Convegno Internazionale di Studi Federiciani* (Palermo, 1952), 435–447.

Gregorio Magno. *Moralia in Job 1, 31*: "Quisquis vero superna desiderant, quia in Oriente habitet, demonstrat." In J.-P. Migne, Patrologia Latina, vol. 75, col. 576. (Il fondamentale libro di Gregorio Magno, è bene ricordarlo, rappresenta l'abecedario del medioevo.)

Gregory, Richard. *Eye and Brain: The Psychology of Seeing*. London, 1966.

Gregory, Richard. *Odd Perception*. London, 1986.

Grundmann, Heinrich. "Federico II e Gioachino da Fiore." In *Atti del Convegno Internazionale di Studi Federiciani* (Palermo, 1952), 83–90.

Huillard-Bréholles, Jean L. A. *Historia Diplomatica Friderici Secundi*, 6 voll. Paris, 1852–1861.

Levi della Vida, Giorgio. "Il mondo islamico al tempo di Federico II." In *Atti del Convegno Internazionale di Studi Federiciani* (Palermo, 1952), 149–160.

Loria, Gino. *Storia della matematica*. Torino, 1929. (Su Fibonacci si veda vol. 1:379–410.)

Marçais, Georges. *L'art musulman*. Paris, 1962.

Marçais, Georges. *Manuel d'art musulman*. Paris, 1926–1927.

Mieli, Aldo. *La science arabe et son rôle dans l'évolution scientifique mondiale*, 2° ed. Leiden, 1966.

Monneret de Villard, Ugo. *Le pitture musulmane a soffitto della Cappella Palatina di Palermo*. Roma, 1950.

Musca, Giosuè. "Castel del Monte: il reale e l'immaginario." In *Castel del Monte* (Bari, 1981), 23–62.

Nebbia, Giorgio. "Federico II e lo sviluppo delle scienze ai suoi tempi." In *Atti delle giornate federiciane* (Bari, 1968), 67–74.

Nietzsche, August. "Federico II e gli scienziati del suo tempo." In *Atti del Convegno di Studi su Federico II* (Jesi, 1976), 107–127.

Pagliaro, Antonino. "Carattere e tradizione del contrasto di Cielo d'Alcamo." In *Atti del Convegno Internazionale di Studi Federiciani* (Palermo, 1952), 407–425. (Si veda p. 417: il testo era tramandato oralmente.)

Pepe, Gabriele. *Lo stato ghibellino di Federico II*, 2° ed. Bari, 1951; 1 ed., *La tirannide di Federico II*, 1937.

Pierantoni, Ruggero. *L'occhio e l'idea. Fisiologia e storia della visione*. Torino, 1982.

Pierantoni, Ruggero. *Forma Fluens*. Torino, 1986.

Potere, società e popolo nell'età sveva (1983). Bari, 1985.

Sarton, Georges. *Introduction to the History of Science*, 3 voll. in 4. Baltimore, 1927–1948.

Scerrato, Umberto. "Arte islamica in Italia." In *Gli Arabi in Italia, cultura, contatti e tradizione* (Milano, 1979), 275–571.

Società, potere e popolo nell'età di Ruggero II. Bari, 1979.

Tavolaro, Aldo. "Una stella sulla Murgia." In *Castel del Monte* (Bari, 1981), 73–98.

Thiery, Antonio. "La cultura icononica irlandese: problemi di metodo per la conoscenza dell'alto medioevo italiano." In *Atti del Convegno Internazionale di Studi di Storia dell'Arte del Medioevo e del Rinascimento nel Centenario della Nascita di Mario Salmi* (1989). Firenze, 1993.

Contributors

David Abulafia is reader in Mediterranean history at the University of Cambridge and has been a fellow of Gonville and Caius College, Cambridge, since 1974. His books include *The Two Italies* and *Frederick II*, both of which have also appeared in Italian. He has published several dozen articles in British, American, Italian, and Israeli journals and essay collections on the economic, social, and political history of the Mediterranean, including studies of the Jews and Muslims in the medieval kingdoms of Sicily, Naples, and Majorca.

Rebecca W. Corrie holds the Ph.D. from Harvard University. She is associate professor and chair of the fine arts department at Bates College. Among other awards, she has received a Fulbright-Hays grant, a Whiting fellowship, and a fellowship from the National Endowment for the Humanities. She has published several articles on thirteenth-century Italian painting and given numerous papers in the United States and abroad. She is working on a book on the Conradin Bible.

Carla Ghisalberti is an associate of the Cattedra di Storia dell'arte medievale of the University of Rome "La Sapienza" and a member of the editorial staff of the Enciclopedia dell'arte medievale of the Istituto dell'Enciclopedia Italiana. Her main area of research is the architectural decoration of Cistercian abbeys, the subject of her doctoral thesis of 1990. Her published work is contained in the catalogues *Les batisseurs des cathédrales gothiques* (1989), *I Longobardi* (1990), *Bernardo di Chiaravalle* (1990), and *Italian Renaissance Architecture from Brunelleschi to Michelangelo* (1993).

Peter Herde studied history, medieval Latin, and English and German literature at the universities of Heidelberg and Munich from 1953 to 1958, completing his Ph.D. in medieval history at the University of Munich in 1958. He was professor of medieval and modern history and director of the Historical Institute, University of Frankfurt, from 1968 to 1976, and has held the same position at the University of Würzburg since 1976. He has also been a visiting professor of history at the University of Washington and the University of Chicago as well as a visiting fellow at the Institute for Advanced Study, Princeton, and at Dumbarton Oaks, Washington. He is the author of studies of the medieval Holy Roman Empire and the papacy, in addition to having an interest in medieval and modern Bavarian history and the history of World War II.

Virginia Roehrig Kaufmann was an Ailsa Mellon Bruce senior fellow at the Center for Advanced Study in the Visual Arts at the National Gallery of Art in Washington (1992–1993). She was previously a fellow at the

Herzog August Bibliothek in Wolfenbüttel (Germany) and at the Kunsthistorisches Institut of the Free University in Berlin, where she was supported by a grant from the Gerda Henkel Foundation. She has published extensively on medieval metalwork and illuminated manuscripts as well as on sculpture.

Wolfgang Krönig studied history, art history, and archaeology in Munich, Vienna, and Berlin. He completed his thesis in 1932. From 1933 to 1934 he was a fellow and assistant at the Bibliotheca Hertziana, Rome. He received his doctorate in Cologne in 1938 and became professor of art history there in 1947. His focus of research was Flemish painting and medieval architecture, especially of central and southern Italy. Among his many publications are *Zur Baukunst der Hohenstaufen in Unteritalien, Castel del Monte* (1937), "Castel del Monte, der Bau Friedrichs II." (*Kunstchronik*, 1956), *Staufische Baukunst in Unteritalien* (1950); *Cefalu,der sizilische Normannen-Dom* (1963), *Monreale und die normannische Architektur in Sizilien* (1966), *Il castello di Caronia* (1977), and *Bildhandbuch der Kunstdenkmäler Siziliens* (1986). In recognition of his efforts to improve cultural relations between Italy and Germany, he received the Comturkreuz of the Order of Merit of the Italian Republic in 1977; an honorary doctorate from the University of Rome in 1980; and the Premio Selinon of Sicily in 1980.

At the time of his death in 1992, Wolfgang Krönig was working on a monograph about landscape painter Philipp Hackert.

Jill Meredith, associate curator of the Duke University Museum of Art, coauthored the catalogue of its medieval art collection. She received the Ph.D. from Yale University in 1980 and has taught at Duke, Columbia, and Yale universities and Hamilton College. Her research areas include thirteenth-century Italian art and new attributions for works in the Brummer collection of medieval art at Duke University based on the neutron activation analysis of limestone samples from French Romanesque and Gothic sculpture.

Piero Morpurgo holds a research doctorate in medieval history and teaches history and Italian literature in Vicenza. He is preparing the edition of Michael Scot's *De Anima* for the series *Pluteus—Testi* and has written on Dante, medieval prophecy, historiography, Norman and Swabian institutions, medieval medicine and science, and Hebrew philosophy. He is the author of many biographies for the Istituto dell'Enciclopedia Italiana and for the Dizionario Biografico della Storia della Letteratura Italiana Einaudi, and of two monographs: *Filosofia della natura nella Schola salernitana del secolo XII* and *L'idea di natura nell'Italia normanno-sveva.*

Massimo Oldoni is professor of medieval Latin literature and head of the department of philology and medieval history at the University of Salerno. He is a member of *Studi Medievali*, Spoleto, and editorial director of *Nuovo Medioevo*, Naples. He has written extensively on medieval literature, especially Merovingian, Longobardic, Saxon, and Norman; his recent studies concern fantasy literature and oral culture in the Middle Ages. He recently published *La cultura latina in Campania (secc. V–XIII)* and *Il Medioevo latino in Italia.* He has also written texts and programs for RAI—Radiotelevisione Italiana; he has published two books of poetry, and in 1986 was awarded the Prize for Italian Culture.

Giulia Orofino received her degree in the history of art at the University of Florence. Her research focuses mainly on the history of miniatures in southern Italy. She has published essays and articles on scientific and secular miniatures of the Norman-Swabian and Angevin eras. She is editing the corpus of miniatures of the high Middle Ages at Montecassino and teaches at the University of Cassino.

Valentino Pace has taught history of art at the universities of Heidelberg, Bonn, and Munich, and at Johns Hopkins and Princeton universities. He has served as a foreign adviser of the International Center for Medieval Art. Now a member of the Dipartimento di Studi sulle Società e le Culture del Medioevo at the University of Rome "La Sapienza," he teaches early Christian and medieval art history at Trinity College (Rome). His publications focus on Roman, South Italian, and Mediterranean art of the Middle Ages. His most recent book concerns the art of South Italy (Darmstadt, 1993).

James M. Powell is professor of medieval history at Syracuse University. In 1989–1990 he was a visiting member of the Institute for Advanced Study, Princeton. His book, *Anatomy of a Crusade, 1213–1221,* won the John Gilmary Shea Prize of the American Catholic Historical Association in 1987. His most recent work is *Albertanus of Brescia: The Pursuit of Happiness in the Early Thirteenth Century.*

Gary M. Radke is associate professor of fine arts and director of the university honors program at Syracuse University. His research and publications have focused on thirteenth-century papal palaces and late fifteenth-century Florentine sculpture. He is currently at work on a project that reexamines Renaissance art across all of Italy.

Willibald Sauerländer is the author of numerous studies of medieval art, architecture, and sculpture, as well as of art and intellectual history of the early modern period. Among these is the forthcoming Andrew W. Mellon Lectures, "Changing Faces: Art and Physiognomy, a History of Representing the Passions." For almost two decades he was director of the Zentralinstitut für Kunstgeschichte, Munich, and several times has been visiting professor at the Institute of Fine Arts, New York University, and many other American and European universities.

Antonio Thiery, an executive of RAI (Italian state television), is a medievalist and cultural historian who studies the role of visual communication and symbolic thought on vocational training and the transfer of knowledge. He specializes in the study of the Mozarabs, who lived in the Iberian peninsula during the eighth to eleventh centuries, and in the study of semantic communications between medieval Europe, North Africa, and the "East."

William Tronzo is visiting associate professor in the history of art at Duke University. He received his doctorate from Harvard University, and has been a fellow at the American Academy in Rome, the Institute for Advanced Study in Princeton, the Bibliotheca Hertziana, and the Center for Advanced Study in the Visual Arts, National Gallery of Art. His publications include books on late antique wall painting and court art of the twelfth-century Mediterranean world, as well as studies on the liturgical arts, icons and church decoration, and medieval aesthetics.